39.95
80€

D0582222

Science Fiction Master Index of Names

For Wade and Dorthe,
who maintained a
treasured friendship
across years and miles

Science Fiction Master Index of Names

Compiled by
KEITH L. JUSTICE

McFarland & Company, Inc., Publishers
Jefferson, North Carolina, and London

ACKNOWLEDGMENTS

Many people are direct or indirect contributors to a book, either by virtue of the things they do or the things they teach. The staffs of the Union Public Library, the Meridian Junior College—L.O. Todd Library, the Meridian Public Library and the Mississippi State University—and Mitchell Memorial Library helped by providing books and assistance, and J. Grant Thiessen at Pandora's Books supplied a number of volumes I was unable to obtain anywhere else.

But those who deserve the most thanks are Virginia, Beverly, and Christopher, who have put up with the book for nearly two years; they have detoured around it when it was a 60,000-card file spread out across the living room floor; they have eaten their meals on the portion of the dining room table not occupied by the book in various stages of its metamorphosis; and they patiently submitted to the inconveniences caused by a project that has taken nearly twice as long as was originally planned.

To them must go any praise for what the book is, and to me any blame for what it is not.

Library of Congress Cataloguing-in-Publication Data

Justice, Keith L.
Science fiction master index of names.

1. Science fiction—Indexes. I. Title.
Z5917.S36J87 1986 [PN3433.8] 016.8093'876 85-42533

ISBN 0-89950-183-4 (acid-free natural paper)

Printed in the United States of America

McFarland   Box 611   Jefferson NC 28640

3857608

TABLE OF CONTENTS

Acknowledgments   iv

Preface   vi

Introduction   1

Using the Index   3

Works Indexed (Listing by code)   9

Master Index of Names   13

Works Indexed (Listing by author/editor)   381

Works Indexed (Listing by title)   387

PREFACE

This project grew from a rudimentary list I was keeping several years ago. While in graduate school I elected to do my thesis on Robert Silverberg and so was sometimes given permission to do supplementary shorter papers on Silverberg in preparation for the thesis.

One such paper was a 40-page bibliography for the research methods course required of every first-year graduate student. It was during the preparation of this first Silverberg bibliography that I began to find out just how difficult it can be to do serious research on SF authors.

I knew exactly what type of reference work I needed, but of course it did not exist. Over a period of two years I coped as best I could with inadequate indexes and interlibrary loan. I spent an alarmingly disproportionate percentage of my meager part-time teacher's salary on new books which would not be in the libraries for months, and I funneled vast numbers of coins into photocopying machines.

Ironically, I never wrote the thesis. I switched departments for reasons that matter little now, stayed in graduate school for another year, and took my degree in another field. But I never forgot how frustrating it was to attempt serious scholarly research in the SF field with its near-total lack of indexing access to secondary materials.

If this index saves just one teacher, critic, researcher, bibliographer, or student a small fraction of the time I lost when I had need of such a book and it did not exist, then the fickle and unpredictable gods who hold whimsical sway over the dark dominions of literary research will smile briefly on us both.

INTRODUCTION

Science fiction has been a legitimate area of literary concern for a relatively short period of time. Actual acceptance of science fiction criticism as a useful and necessary tool for exploring literature can be dated from the 1960s, though full and unquestioned acceptance of SF may not be accomplished in the twentieth century.

But in spite of the controversy over the relative merits of genre fiction as a division of the mainstream literary structure, SF continues to receive more and more attention. An SF author who began his writing apprenticeship in the 1950s by producing two SF books per year might have scratched out a meager living from the unyielding soil of genre paperback publishing. SF books today routinely receive record advances, film rights to SF properties are sold for astronomical sums, and SF and fantasy titles that appear on best-seller lists are no longer strangers in strange lands.

Such is the commercial expansion of SF in the past three decades.

If SF had been accepted and studied and criticized for the past century, there would be standard reference materials in plenty and little apparent need for a master index. However, there are as yet very few "standard" SF reference volumes. Beyond the Contento anthology/collection index and the Hall book review index, few SF reference books can be considered universally accepted and likely to be found in any library with even a rudimentary collection of secondary materials on SF.

And, of course, there is the regrettable circumstance of many seminal reference works for the SF field being out of print and difficult to obtain even under the best of conditions.

This shortage of standard and readily accessible materials creates a serious problem for the researcher. Compiling annotated bibliographies, for example, becomes extremely difficult when the compiler has no way to know what books to buy, find, beg, borrow, and consult. Many SF reference volumes are obscure small press items or privately printed books now long out of print and nearly impossible to find. And even when books are known to exist somewhere, there is the problem of access to

1

them. The books must be purchased, often at great expense, or borrowed, often with great difficulty.

Thus the need for a master index to reduce initial research time from weeks or months to minutes.

This index will serve a variety of purposes. It can be used as a general index to find what books contain information about a specific person; it can be used to check if a writer, critic, or other person is represented or mentioned in a particular reference or nonfiction book; and it provides indexing for many books which do not have integral indexes and which are not indexed in any other way.

In addition, this master index can be useful to those who use the inter-library loan system. The index will indicate by the presence (or absence) of a name whether any of the titles indexed must be borrowed to obtain information. If a book can be located but is not available for borrowing through inter-library loan, the appropriate page numbers are included in this volume so photocopies of the necessary pages can be ordered.

A century hence, when the chaff has been separated and the full range of standard SF references determined, perhaps a master index will have little utility. But until then, it is hoped that this volume may provide a means for the student, critic, researcher, teacher, scholar or bibliographer to plan his first steps on the long journey of research through the diverse and sometimes obscure volumes which make up the bulk of the SF reference field.

USING THE INDEX

The index is arranged in the simplest form that could be devised. The two major objectives of this project were to present the greatest amount of information possible in a form that avoids as much pedantry as possible.

The supplemental material includes three basic listings of the works indexed: a listing by the codes selected to represent the works, a listing by title, and a listing by author or editor. The listings by code and by author or editor give titles only, while the listing by title presents full bibliographic information.

The main body of the index is arranged alphabetically by last name. Those names which are listed or mentioned in a work in a non-standard form are alphabetized by the portion of the name most recognizable or applicable as a name. When a reference was made by last name only in one of the works indexed, and subsequent research could not discover the full name of the person referred to, the last name is indexed without the given name.

The compiler of this index is not an expert on alphabetizing in the multitude of languages represented by the names herein, so in most cases the rule of "last separate and distinct word" was applied (see examples below).

Titles, if given in the works indexed, were retained but were placed in parenthesis. Titles such as Mr., Ms., Miss and Mrs. were not retained unless they proved useful for identification purposes. A list of examples may best illustrate how titles and non-standard name forms were indexed:

Name as it might appear in an indexed work	Name as it would be indexed in this volume
Baron Michel Foucault	Foucault, (Baron) Michel
Pope John I	John I, (Pope)
Princess Anne	Anne, (Princess)
Mr. Smith	Smith, (Mr.)
Mr. John Smith	Smith, John
Dr. John Smith	Smith, (Dr.) John

3

Professor John Smith	Smith, (Prof.) John
Mrs. Ann Smith	Smith, Ann
Mrs. A. L. Smith	Smith, (Mrs.) A. L.
Pliny the Elder	Pliny (the Elder)
Lester del Rey	Del Rey, Lester
Gerry de la Ree	De La Ree, Gerry
King Arthur	Arthur, (King)
Aaron Smith-Jones	Smith-Jones, Aaron
Baron Ludwig von Holz	Von Holz, (Baron) Ludwig
Captain James Jones	Jones, (Capt.) James

Biblical names (Job, Adam, Eve, Cain, Abel, and so on) were indexed, as were mytho-historical figures who actually existed in some form (King Arthur, Johnny Appleseed) and religious figures (God, Christ, Satan). Greek and Roman gods, as well as other deities and mythological figures, were omitted from the index.

Every effort was made to exclude the names of fictional characters from this work. In professionally done reference indexes, real persons are alphabetized by their last names and fictional characters by their first names but many SF reference indexes do not incorporate this useful device. Many of the works indexed herein have critical or descriptive passages that include discussions of characters to be found in fantasy or science fiction novels, so it is possible some of the names appear here by mistake. Weeding out the Conans and the Valentine Michael Smiths was relatively easy, but for any characters whose names may have been inadvertently included the compiler apologizes in advance.

References to major schools of political, religious, philosophical, or psychological thought which are described by making adjectives from the name of the originator or other major proponent (Marxist, Calvinistic, Platonic, Freudian, Jungian, etc.) were indexed under the appropriate name. This allows the tracing of references to various ideologies and disciplines through the SF nonfiction canon.

When birth and/or death dates were given in an indexed work, the dates were retained and are included as an additional point of identification.

Names have been "regularized" to avoid unnecessary multiple listings and cross references. When names were spelled differently in different works, a consensus was reached by selecting the spelling or form of the name that seemed to be the most popular or most widely recognized. Each separate word of each name has been capitalized because of limitations inherent in the computer equipment which was scheduled to be used to help sort the index. Apologies to Lester del Rey, andrew offutt, e. e. cummings, and others for this necessary simplification, but all names are rendered as if spelled with capitals (Del Rey, Offutt, De La Ree, Cummings, etc.).

Names, especially those of authors, are listed in some reference books under the "true" name and in others under pen names or name variations. Entries in this index refer to the name under which the information actually appears in the indexed work (except for names with disparate spellings which have been arbitrarily reconciled with the single most widely recognized spelling). Appropriate cross references are indicated. This volume is not intended to be a thorough index of pseudonyms, but because of the necessary cross referencing it does provide a good working list of house names and pseudonyms used by many authors. However, cross indexing is not provided for every possible name variation. For example, if a researcher is seeking information about Bob Olsen, it is assumed that when he or she finds there is no listing for a "Bob" Olsen the next logical step will be to check under Robert Olsen. Name variations which are not readily apparent are cross referenced.

Each work indexed for this volume was assigned a three-character code designation. AOW, for example, is the designation for Anatomy of Wonder and BYS for Billion Year Spree. Under each name entry the codes are listed along with appropriate page numbers. Only one periodical is indexed, that one being the first ten volumes of Extrapolation. A code listed as BYS 103 means the person listed is mentioned in some context on page 103 of Billion Year Spree. A code listed as EXT 7/1 22 indicates the reference is Extrapolation, volume 7, number 1, page 22.

All critical material written about an author is "double indexed" by critic and subject. Thus a ten-page essay on Ursula Le Guin that appears in a book of SF criticism will be referenced under Le Guin and under the name of the critic. An author is not indexed for complete books written about him or her, i.e. there are no page number references for Heinlein for a book such as Heinlein in Dimension.

Pseudonyms were indexed when they referred to individuals in some form. Thus the pseudonyms "Two Wags," "A Lady and a Gent," or "Two Women of the West" would be indexed while indeterminate group pseudonyms such as "The Members of the Board" or "A Group of Concerned Citizens" would not.

When initials were used as a reference in one of the works indexed, the initials were treated as a pseudonym; "H.S.," for example, would be indexed under H.S. rather than S., H.

Because of the number of page references in this volume, a name mentioned on two or more consecutive pages is listed the same as if the given number of pages were all devoted to a dis-

cussion of that one person. A listing such as MIH 12-5 for the
writer John Smith would mean either that Smith was discussed
in More Issues at Hand at length on the pages 12 through 15 or
that he is at least mentioned on all four pages. This was done
to consolidate some of the lengthier page references, and in any
case the title of the work is usually sufficient to indicate the
thoroughness of the treatment of the author in question. In a
book such as Billion Year Spree or Pilgrims Through Space and
Time, authors are generally mentioned in very brief passing
references; works such as the Reginald, Tuck, or Nicholls SF
encyclopedias, and collections of critical essays, normally
treat authors at much greater length.

When author or reference names included words such as
"de, " "de la, " "von, " or "van der, " the additional words were
considered to be part of the last name. Rules with too many ex-
ceptions usually are self-defeating, so the pattern was used
without exception. Thus Guy de Maupassant and L. Sprague de
Camp are alphabetized under "De Maupassant" and "De Camp. "

On occasion, a birth or death date— but not both—was available for a deceased reference. A year date followed by a dash
indicates a reference who is still living or for whom a death
date was not available. A date preceded by a dash indicates a
reference for whom a death date is known but not a birth date.
A date followed by a question mark is a "best guess" published
in one of the indexed volumes but apparently not authenticated.
A question mark following a birth or death date means only the
year date immediately preceding the question mark is not authenticated. If both dates are in question, both will have question
marks.

Names such as McCoy or McClain are indexed as if the "Mc"
prefix were spelled "Mac. " Names which include the abbrevia-
tion "St. " are alphabetized as if spelled out completely.

Only one exception was made to the general alphabetizing pattern. According to the framework set up for alphabetical arrange-
ment in this volume, saints should have been listed by their
first names followed by the saint designation in parenthesis. For
example, St. Augustine should have been indexed as "Augustine,
(St.), " but instead is listed in the index as "St. Augustine. "
Saints were indexed in this fashion to make it possible for a researcher to find out quickly and easily which saints have been
mentioned or discussed in SF reference materials.

The code listing of works indexed in this volume includes
three indicators which may be of some value to the researcher.
Books which are mass market paperbacks are identified by the
word "paper" in brackets. Hardcover and trade paperback books
are generally printed from the same plates (when the book is
issued in both forms by the same publisher), so pagination, and,

therefore, the page references in this index, will be the same
for books that are issued in both forms more or less simultane-
ously (e. g. the books in the Writers of the 21st Century series).
Mass market paperbound books are normally set in a completely different type with completely different pagination when a
hardcover/trade paperback reference or nonfiction book is issued
in mass market form (for example, the hardcover and mass market paperback editions of Pohl's memoirs, The Way the Future
Was). The [paper] indicator will clarify which books are hardcover and/or trade paper and which are mass market paperback.

The second indicator is an asterisk, used to designate those
books which have no integral index and for which this master index represents the only index access currently available. The
third is the double asterisk, which indicates those few volumes
whose contents were only partially indexed. Partial indexing
was done in select cases when certain books (e. g. The Robot
Book or Yesterday's Tomorrows) seemed to be of interest to SF
research because of historical material taken from SF writers
and their fiction, but when the majority of the figures mentioned
in the books did not seem likely to be researched in an SF context.

Two or three of the works indexed do not have pagination. A
code reference in brackets, such as [FJT], means the name reference is to be found in the unpaginated work for which FJT is
the identifying code.

Whenever there was a discrepancy between the facts as pre-
sented by two different reference books, and no method could be
discovered for authenticating the information by using other
sources, the information arbitrarily deemed accurate was the
material from the more authoritative source. As an example,
the name Peter Phillips is listed in Who Goes There as a house
pseudonym and in the Nicholls encyclopedia as the name of a
British journalist and writer born in 1921 who wrote a number of
SF stories; some of the same story titles are attributed to the
house name in the one book and to the fiction-writing journalist
in the other. The Nicholls compilation must be considered the
more authoritative source, so Phillips is listed as an identified
writer rather than a house name.

In cases where similar names were to be found in separate
sources but the information given in each source was not enough
to establish that all the similar names were in fact the same person, the names were listed separately.

The 132 reference and nonfiction books selected for indexing
in this volume represent a diverse range of material. A special
effort was made to include a number of the newest and most com-
prehensive critical materials, such as the two Magill surveys, as
well as more obscure material such as The Shudder Pulps and
The Weird Tales Story. This was done in an effort to provide

index access as thorough and wide-ranging as possible for SF and related genres.

The operative word is "related." Every reader, writer, and critic of SF is familiar with the phenomenon of weird, fantasy and supernatural fiction being lumped almost indiscriminately with SF. No one has ever quite logically explained the relationship, but many of the most popular SF authors (especially those who entered the field during one of the celebrated and variously identified Golden Ages) wrote material for the "other" magazines that were "related" to SF. It is to be hoped that this intentional inclusion of some of the more offbeat or obscure secondary materials will give broader index access to reference and critical materials across the entire SF spectrum.

WORKS INDEXED
(Listing by code)

Also see pages 381-394

AAL Aliens and Linguists (Meyers)
ACC Arthur C. Clarke (Olander & Greenberg)
ACE Arthur C. Clarke (Rabkin)
AC2 Arthur C. Clarke, 2nd edition (Rabkin)
ALW Alternate Worlds (Gunn)
AOW Anatomy of Wonder (Barron)
ASF Asimov on Science Fiction*
ATA Against Time's Arrow: The High Crusade of Poul
     Anderson (Miesel)*
BAA British and American Utopian Literature 1516-1975
     (Sargent)
BFP Science Fiction and Fantasy Authors—A Bibliography
     of First Printings of Their Fiction (Currey)
BRS A Basic Reference Shelf for Science Fiction Teachers
     (Tymn)
BYS Billion Year Spree (Aldiss)
CAT Science Fiction—Its Criticism and Teaching (Parrin-
     der)
CEN Critical Encounters (Riley)
COT The Creation of Tomorrow: Fifty Years of Magazine
     Science Fiction (Carter)
CSC The Craft of Science Fiction (Bretnor)
CSF The Checklist of Science Fiction and Supernatural
     Fiction (Bleiler)
CUA The Clockwork Universe of Anthony Burgess
     (Mathews)*
CWD Conan's World and Robert E. Howard (Schweitzer)*
CWN Colin Wilson: The Outsider and Beyond (Bendau)*
CYR The Classic Years of Robert A. Heinlein (Slusser)*
DMK Dream Makers (Platt) [paper]
DTS Drug Themes in Science Fiction (Silverberg)
EFP Environmental Fiction for Pedagogic Purposes
     (Rabiega)
ES1 Encyclopedia of Science Fiction and Fantasy Vol. 1
     (Tuck)

9

ES2   Encyclopedia of Science Fiction and Fantasy Vol. 2
       (Tuck)
ETN   Engines of the Night: Science Fiction in the Eighties
       (Malzberg)*
EXT   Extrapolation (Clareson)*
FAN   The Future as Nightmare (Hillegas)
FBK   The Fantasy Book (Rottensteiner)
FFC   Fantasy for Children—An Annotated Checklist (Lynn)
FFR   Fantasfeer (Spaink, Gorremans, Gaasbeek)**
FHT   Frank Herbert (Miller)
FJT   The Fiction of James Tiptree, Jr. (Dozois)*
FLR   Fritz Leiber (Frane)
FLT   Fantasy Literature (Apter)
FL1-FL5 Survey of Modern Fantasy Literature Vols. 1-5
       (Magill)
FRN   The Frankenstein Catalog (Glut)**
FSU   The Farthest Shores of Ursula K. Le Guin (Slusser)*
FTF   Faces of the Future (Ash)
FUT   Futuropolis (Sheckley)*
HEN   Harlan Ellison: Unrepentant Harlequin (Slusser)*
HFI   The Science Fiction and Heroic Fantasy Author Index
       (Wells)
HID   Heinlein in Dimension (Panshin)
HWK   Heinlein's Works (Searles)
IAC   Index to Science Fiction Anthologies and Collections
       (Contento)
IAH   The Issue at Hand (Atheling/Blish)
IMS   The Immortal Storm—A History of Science Fiction
       Fandom (Moskowitz)
INT   Intersections: The Elements of Fiction in Science Fiction
       (Wymer, et al)
ISW   In Search of Wonder (Knight)
JGB   Earth is the Alien Planet: J. G. Ballard's Four-Dimension-
       al Nightmare (Pringle)*
JHN   Joe Haldeman (Gordon)
JVN   Jack Vance (Underwood and Miller)
KAU   The Known and the Unknown: The Iconography of Science
       Fiction (Wolfe)
KVT   Kurt Vonnegut: The Gospel from Outer Space (Mayo)*
KWS   Keep Watching the Skies (Warren)**
LEX   Lexikon der Science Fiction Literatur 1 (Alpers, Fuchs,
       Hahn, Jeschke)
LTN   Language of the Night (Le Guin and Wood)*
MFW   Many Futures, Many Worlds (Clareson)
MIH   More Issues at Hand (Atheling/Blish)
MSF   Metamorphoses of Science Fiction (Suvin)
MSM   Modern Science Fiction—Its Meaning and Its Future

(Bretnor)
NDA Science Fiction and the New Dark Age (Berger)
NWO New Worlds for Old: The Apocalyptic Imagination,
      Science Fiction, and American Literature (Ketterer)
OMN Omni's Screen Flights/Screen Fantasies (Peary)**
OSR SF: The Other Side of Realism (Clareson)
OWB Of Worlds Beyond (Eshbach)
PJF Philip Jose Farmer (Brizzi)
POE The Pattern of Expectation (Clarke)
PST Pilgrims Through Space and Time (Bailey)
RAH Robert A. Heinlein (Olander and Greenberg)
RBY Ray Bradbury (Olander and Greenberg)
RFA A Requiem for Astounding (Rogers)
RGS A Reader's Guide to Science Fiction (Searles, Last,
      Meacham and Franklin) [paper]
RHN Robert A. Heinlein: America as Science Fiction
      (Franklin)
RSG Robert Silverberg (Clareson)
RZY Roger Zelazny (Yoke)
SFA The Science Fiction of Isaac Asimov (Patrouch) [paper]
SFB The Science Fiction Book: An Illustrated History
      (Rottensteiner)*
SFD SF in Dimension (Panshin)
SFE The Science Fiction Encyclopedia (Nicholls)
SFH Science Fiction: History, Science, Vision (Scholes
      and Rabkin)
SFN The Science Fiction Novel (Davenport)
SFS Science Fiction Story Index 1950-1968 (Siemon)
SFW Science Fiction Writers (Bleiler)
SF1 Science Fiction and Fantasy Literature Vol. 1: Indexes
      to the Literature (Reginald)
SF2 Science Fiction and Fantasy Literature Vol. 2: Contem-
      porary Science Fiction Authors II (Reginald)
SHL Robert A. Heinlein: Stranger in His Own Land (Slusser)*
SIH Science Fiction—An Illustrated History (Lundwall)
SIN Science Fiction—An Introduction (Allen)
SL1-SL5 Survey of Science Fiction Literature (Magill)
SOI Shadows of Imagination (Hillegas)
SOT Seekers of Tomorrow (Moskowitz)
SRB The Science Fiction Reference Book (Tymn)
STF Structural Fabulation (Scholes)
STH Strange Horizons (Moskowitz)
SV1 Science Fiction Voices 1 (Schweitzer)
SV2-SV3 Science Fiction Voices 2 & 3 (Elliot)
TBC The Bradbury Chronicles (Slusser)*
TDI The Delani Intersection (Slusser)*
TFC The Fantastic: A Structural Approach to a Literary

Genre (Todorov)

THM   The Haunted Man: The Strange Genius of David Lindsay (Wilson)*

TJB   A Clash of Symbols: The Triumph of James Blish (Stableford)

TPS   Turning Points: Essays on the Art of Science Fiction (Knight)

TRB   The Robot Book (Malone)**

TSF   Teaching Science Fiction (Williamson)

TSO   The Space Odysseys of Arthur C. Clarke (Slusser)*

TSP   The Shudder Pulps (Jones)

UFS   Urban Futures—Science Fiction and the City (White)

UKL   Ursula K. Le Guin (Olander and Greenberg)

VES   Visual Encyclopedia of Science Fiction (Ash)

VF1   Voices for the Future (Clareson)

VF2   Voices for the Future 2 (Clareson)

VFS   The View from Serendip (Clarke)

VMW   Vonnegut's Major Works (Holland)

WAA   Science Fiction: What It's All About (Lundwall) [paper]

WBW   Worlds Beyond the World: The Fantastic Vision of William Morris (Mathews)*

WFS   The Way the Future Was (Pohl)*

WGT   Who Goes There: A Bibliographic Dictionary (Rock)

WIF   The Science Fiction Handbook—The Writing of Imaginative Fiction (de Camp)

WSF   The World of Science Fiction: The History of a Subculture (del Rey)

WTS   The Weird Tales Story (Weinberg)*

YTS   Yesterday's Tomorrows (Corn and Horrigan)**

A

A. E. pseud. of George William Russell. CSF 1 FAN 145
A. F. S. pseud. of Anita Silvani CSF 1
A. K. H. pseud. of Alice K. Hopkins. CSF 1
Aalders, W. J. BAA 167
Aandahl, Vance (1944-) EXT 8/1 16 IAC 28 SFE 15 SFS 2
Aarne, Antti. EXT 1/2 38
Aaron, Daniel. BAA 167
Aarons, Edward Sidney (1916-75) SF1 3
Abbot, Anthony. CSF 1
Abbot, Charles T. SRB 9
Abbot, Daisy. WFS 10
Abbot, Griffith. WFS 10
Abbot, Henry pseud. of Edward Stratemeyer. STH 162
Abbot, Pudna. WFS 88
Abbott, Bud (1895-1974) INT 39
Abbott, Edwin A. (1838-1926) AOW 51, 93 BYS 106 ES1 1 EXT 3/1 29 EXT 10/1 10-1 FFR 1 FL2 561-5 FTF 41 IAC 28 MSF 29, 167 NWO 39, 204-5, 234 RHN 44 SFE 15 SF1 3 SL2 792-6 SRB 250 WAA 76 WGT 1 see also A. Square
Abbott, Gordon. IAC 28
Abdullah, Achmed (1881-1945) AOW 98 CSF 1 ES1 1 SF1 3
Abe, Kobo (1924-) AOW 126 FBK 150 FFR 1 HFI 1 LEX 156 SFB 142 SFE 15 SF1 3 SL3 1040-4 VES 261
Abel. IAH 125 TDI 57 WBW 32
Abel, Richard Cox. SFE 15 SF1 3

Abell, Kathleen. FFC 45
Abellan, Jose Luis. BAA 167
Abendsen, Hawthorne. NWO 243-9
Abensour, M. BAA 280
Abernathy, Carlton. IMS 11
Abernathy, Robert (1924-) COT 103, 105, 132, 135, 254 ES1 1 FFR 1 IAC 28 IAH 106 ISW 122, 126 SFE 15 SFS 2 SOT 431 VES 167
Abernethy, Francis E. SRB 496
Ableman, Paul V. (1927-) IAC 28 SFE 15 SF1 3 SF2 789
About, Edmond (1828-85) CSF 1 EXT 5/1 14 POE 86 PST 31, 247, 249 SFE 15 SF1 3 SL3 1340-3
Abraham. WBW 7-8, 11
Abraham. ETN 24
Abrahams, Doris Caroline. see Caryl Brahms
Abrahamsen, Christine (1916-) SF2 869 WGT 1 see also Cristabel
Abramov, Alexander (1900-) IAC 28 SFE 15 SF1 3 SF2 789
Abramov, Sergei (1944-) IAC 28 SFE 15 SF1 3 SF2 789
Abrams, John W. RFA 155
Abrams, M. H. NWO 10
Abramson, Arnie. WFS 303
Abramson, Arnold E. STH 45
Abramson, Ben. IAH 52
Abrash, Merritt. BAA 197
Abrashkin, Raymond (1911-1960) AOW 333 SF1 3-4
Abrojal, Tulis. CSF 1 SF1 4
Achorn, Kendall L. CSF 1

Ackerman, Forrest J (1916-)
ALW 8,176 AOW 394,403 ASF
28-9, 243 COT 18,106,184,300
ES1 1-2 ETN 12,128 EXT 7/2
45 FFR 1 FRN 17,34-5,56-8,
73-5, 83, 95,101,103-4,118,166,
222-3, 231-3, 401, 443, 447 IAC
28-9 IMS 13,15-6,19-20,22-3,
32, 47, 53-4, 66, 68, 73, 75, 77, 94-
5, 97-9,122-3,137-9,145-6,161,
182,199,213-4, 222,225-6,228,
236,239,241,244 ISW 24-5
KAU 21,198 KWS ix-x, 4,111,
128,241 LEX 156 PJF 59 SFE
16 SFS 2 SF1 4 SF2 789-90
SIH 168,190 SOT 3,107,307,312
SRB 89,98,112,118 STH 243,
266 WAA 179,245 WFS 94,301
WGT 1 WIF 17,135,138 WSF
75, 77
Ackerman, Philip G. IMS 9
Ackerman, Wendayne. SIH 168,
190 WGT 1
Ackermann, Elfriede Maria.
BAA 280
Ackerson, Duane. IAC 29
Acton, Frances. CSF 2
Acton, John Dalberg. SFN 110
Acton, (Lord). CSC 111
Acworth, Andrew. BAA 55
Adair, Hazel pseud. of Hazel
Iris Addis. SF1 4
A'Dair, Jeanne. SF1 4
Adam. ASF 141 CYR 28 EXT
7/1 24 HEN 50,59 IAH 62 IMS
1 INT 102,114 JGB 17,21 KVT
51 NWO 3,23-4,139 SFB 53
SFE 16-7 VFS 129
Adam, Helen. IAC 29
Adam, Robert James (1924-) see
Paul MacTyre
Adam, Ruth Augusta (1907-) CSF
2 SF1 4 SF2 790
Adam, Verney. VES 322
Adamov, Grigory B. LEX 157
MSF 264-5
Adams, Adrienne. FFC 12,51,
55,57, 75, 83-4,103,119
Adams, Arthur Henry (1872-1936)
SF1 4
Adams, Brooks. RAH 21-2
Adams, Clara. EXT 10/1 21
Adams, Ephraim Douglass. BAA
197-8

Adams, Eustace Lane (1891-)
SF1 4
Adams, Francis Alexandre (1874-)
SF1 4
Adams, Fred C., Jr. SF1 4
Adams, Frederick B., Jr. BAA
167
Adams, Frederick Upham (1859-
1921) BAA 56 CSF 2 EXT 1/1
5 SF1 5
Adams, Hazard (1926-) SF1 5
Adams, Harriet S. SFE 17
Adams, Henry Cadwallader (1817-
1899) AOW 40 FAN 32 NWO
207-8 SF1 5
Adams, J. WGT 1
see also Skelton Kuppord
Adams, J. Donald. EXT 1/2 29
Adams, Jack pseud. of Alcanoan
O. Grigsby. CSF 2 SF1 5
Adams, John. ES1 2 HFI 1 SFE
17 SF1 5
Adams, John (1735-1826) COT
242
Adams, Louis J. A. IAC 29
SFS 2
Adams, Percy G. BAA 167
Adams, Pete. IAC 29
Adams, Richard (1920-) AOW 93,
118 FBK 112 FFC 1 FL3 1268-
70,1387-91 FL5 2079-83 HFI 1
LTN 265 SF1 5 SF2 789 SRB
25,250
Adams, Richard Locke. MSF 142
Adams, Robert M. EXT 9/1 16
HFI 1
Adams, Robert P. BAA 167
Adams, Robert P. BAA 198
Adams, Robert Pardee. BAA 280
Adams, Samuel Hopkins (1871-
1958) AOW 78 CSF 2,207 EXT
1/1 5,20 EXT 7/1 20,27 SFE
17 SF1 5
Adams, W.S. ES1 2
Adams, Walter Marsham (1838-)
SF1 334
Adams, William Wheen Scovell.
SF1 5
Adamski, George (1891-) ES1 2
VFS 177
Adamson, Jack H. BAA 167
Adcock, Arthur St. John. CSF 2
Addams, Charles Samuel (1912-)
ES1 2

Addeo, Edmond G. HFI 60 SFE
17 SF1 5
Adderley, James Granville (1861-
1942) CSF 2 NWO 71,101
SF1 5
Addington, Sarah (1891-1940)
SF1 581
Addis, Eric Eldrington. WGT 1
Addis, Hazel Iris (1900-) ES1 2
WGT 1 see also Hazel Adair
Addison, Hugh pseud. of Harry
Collinson Owen. CSF 2 SF1 5
Addobati, Michael. IAC 29
Adeler, Max pseud. of Charles
Heber Clark. CSF 2 SF1 5
Adelphos. CSF 2 SF1 5
Aderca, Felix (1891-1962) SIH 94
SL4 1613-6
Adhemar, Joseph Alphonse. EXT
1/1 2
Adkins, Nelson F. BAA 198
Adkins, P. H. SF1 5
Adkinson, Robert K. SF1 5
Adlard, Mark (1932-) BAA 152-3,
161 BYS 304 HFI 1 IAC 29
LEX 157 RGS 4-5 SFE 17 SF1
5 SF2 791 SFW 93,100 SIH 94
VES 168
Adleman, Robert H. (1919-) SF1 5
Adler. CWN 54
Adler, Alfred. MSM 238
Adler, Allen A. (1916-) ES1 2
HFI 1 ISW 101-3 SFE 17 SF1 6
Adler, Georg. BAA 167,198
Adler, Jack. WFS 146
Adler, Max. BAA 198
Adler, Mortimer J. EXT 6/1 9
VFS 252
Alderberth, Roland (1923-) ES1 2
Adolph, Anna. BAA 60 CSF 2
Adorno, Theodor W. BAA 198
MSF 82
Adrian, (Prof.) A. D. MSM 263
Adriani, Maurilio. BAA 167,198
Adriel, Jeanne. SF1 6
Adye, (Maj. Gen. Sir) John (1857-
1930) CSF 2 SF1 6
Aermont, Paul. BAA 30
Aeschylus. MFW 5 MSF 87
Aesop. ASF 191 CAT 68 MSF
215,279 MSM 14 VFS 43
Afford, Malcolm R. SOT 107
Agee, James. IAC 29

Agel, Jerome. IAC 122 AOW 337
SF1 6 VFS 270
Aggeler, Geoffrey. BAA 198
Aghill, Gordon pseud. of Randall
Garrett, Robert Silverberg.
SFE 19
Agle, Nan. FFC 128
Agnew, Ewan. CSF 2
Agnew, Jack. IMS 70-2,95,135,
143,156,162,186,200,222,233
STH 115 WIF 131
Agnew, Spiro. ETN 104 RHN 198
Agostini. EXT 8/1 23
Agricola. BAA 72 SF1 6
Agrippa, Cornelius. EXT 6/2 28
Ahasuerus. SIH 25
Ahern, Michael. IAC 29
Ahmed, Rollo. ES1 2
Ahonen, Erkki. SIH 93
Aichinger, Helga. FFC 11
Aichinger, Ilse (1921-) ES1 3
SF1 6
Aickman, Robert Fordyce (1914-
1981) ES1 3 FL3 1412-6 IAC
29 SFS 2 SF1 6 SF2 791
Aiken, Anna Laetitia (1743-1825)
SF1 7
Aiken, Charles. SF1 7
Aiken, Conrad P. EXT 6/1 20
EXT 7/2 37 FBK 67 IAC 29
SFS 2
Aiken, Howard. MFW 190
Aiken, Joan Delano (1924-) FFC
16,24,45,138,153 SF1 6,581
SF2 791 WGT 1
Aiken, John. BAA 280
Aiken, John K. (1913-) BAA 150
HFI 1 SF1 6-7 SF2 791-2
Aikin, Anna L. CSF 2
Aikin, Charles. BAA 53 CSF 2
Aikin, John (1747-1822) CSF 2
SF1 7
Aimard, Gustave. CSF 2
Ainger, Canon Alfred. BAA 198
Ainsworth, Ruth Gallard (1908-)
FFC 17,28 SF1 7 SF2 792
Ainsworth, William Harrison
(1805-1882) CSF 2-3 ES1 3
POE 68-9 SF1 7
Ainsworthy, Roy. SF1 7
Aisenstein, Alan J. IMS 54-5
Aitken, Robert (1872-) WGT 1
Akeley, Henry. WTS 84

Akers, Alan Burt pseud. of Henry Kenneth Bulmer. AAL 113-4 HFI 1-2 IAC 29 RGS 5, 206 SFE 19 WSF 282

Akin, William E. BAA 167

Akinari, Ueda. FBK 150

Akino, Fuku. FFC 14, 35, 147

Akira pseud. of Erica Maria Moore. SF1 7

Akutagawa, Ryunosoke (1892-1927) CSF 3 FBK 150 FL3 1304-6 SFB 142 SF1 7

Alan, A. J. pseud. of Leslie H. Lambert. CSF 3 ES1 3

Alban, Anthony pseud. of Anthony Allert Thompson. ES1 3 HFI 2 NDA 28 SFE 19 SF1 7

Albano, Michael W. CSF 3 SF1 7

Albee, George Sumner. IAC 29

Albert, Edward. CSF 3

Albert, Marvin H. SF1 7

Albertson, Garrett Vinton. BAA 1 SF1 7

Albin, Michel. FHT 67

Albrecht, Howard. SF1 7

Albrecht, Lillie. FFC 82

Albright, Donn. RBY 239

Alcock, (Sir) John. FTF 71

Aldani, Lino (1926-) IAC 29 LEX 157-8 SL4 1739-41 WAA 235

Alden, Henry Mills (1836-1919) SF1 7

Alden, Raymond. FFC 17

Alden, William L. CSF 3

Aldiss, Brian W. (1925-) ACC 244 ACE 38 AC2 36 ALW 7, 30, 144, 176, 212, 235 AOW 80, 126-9, 291-2, 294-5, 337-8 ASF 19 BAA 125, 130, 135, 140, 145, 161, 167, 241 BFP 1-8 BRS 6 CAT 18-9, 24-7 COT 5, 74, 268, 278, 299 CSC 74 CYR 9, 59 DMK 269-80 DTS 7, 35, 40 EFP 18 ES1 3-5 ETN 21, 56, 65, 105 -6, 128, 160 EXT 5/1 3 EXT 6/2 22 EXT 8/1 16 EXT 9/2 63 FBK 154 FFR 1-3 FHT 66 [FJT] FL1 404-9 FL2 951-4 FRN 17, 28, 245, 445 FTF 60, 94, 194 [FUT] HFI 2 HWK 6 IAC 29-32, 127 IAH 128, 135-6 ISW 127, 243-4 JGB 4, 14, 20, 61 KAU 6, 29, 61, 66-7, 72, 95, 105, 121, 126, 156, 166, 177, 179, 228 LEX 158-60 LTN 12, 250 MFW 20, 24 MIH 7, 11-2, 15-6, 18-9, 40, 80, 98-100, 105, 107, 125, 128-30, 135, 138-46 MSF 242 NWO vi, ix, 125-6, 139, 204, 235, 255-60 OSR 116-29, 354 POE 289 RAH 222, 257 RBY 102 RGS 5-6 SFA 7, 134-6 SFB 7, 100 SFD 17, 31, 34-5, 54-6, 63, 76, 83, 85-9, 241, 245-6, 295, 318, 320 SFE 19, 21 SFH 38, 41, 50, 55, 63, 75, 83, 88, 90-2, 97, 99, 237 SFS 2-3, 55 SFW 3-9, 25-30, 108, 251-8 SF1 8-9 SF2 792-3 SIH 12, 56-7, 199 SL1 125-9, 443-8 SL2 840-4, 926-31, 936-9 SL3 1235-7 SL4 1764-7 SOT 245 SRB 14, 17, 70, 75, 118, 127, 251, 329, 333, 337, 342, 357, 496 STF 63 TPS 73-95 TSF 58, 237, 244, 248 VES 73, 82, 88, 100, 115, 143, 154, 164, 167-8, 175, 179, 207, 214, 231, 237, 242, 256, 258, 261-2, 303, 310, 330 WAA 3, 127, 130, 139, 169, 175, 244 WFS 299-301, 305-6 WGT 2 WSF 15, 176, 255, 387 see also C. C. Shackleton

Aldiss, Margaret C. (1933-) SF1 9 SF2 793

Aldrich, Thomas Bailey (1836-1907) AOW 34, 51 CSF 3 ES1 5-6 EXT 1/1 5

Aldridge, Alexandra. BAA 198

Aldridge, John. CWN 29

Aldrin, Edwin "Buzz" FTF 26 JGB 33-4 VFS 78

Alejandro pseud. of Alejandro Canedo. RFA 141, 148, 155, 157, 166, 181, 200, 204 WSF 110

Alexa (pseud.) SF1 9

Alexander (the Great). CUA 36 CWD 53 [FUT] RFA 145 SFB 30-1

Alexander, David (1907-) ES1 6 IAC 32

Alexander, Evelyn. CSF 3

Alexander, Holmes Moss (1906-) SF1 9 SF2 793

Alexander, James. IAC 32

Alexander, James Bradun (1831-) BAA 73-4 CSF 3 SF1 9

Alexander, Lloyd C. (1924-) AOW 308 ES1 6 FFC 17, 41, 45, 111, 159, 173, 184 FL1 256-61 FL2 571-4 IAC 32 SF1 9 SF2 793-4

Alexander, Robert. CSF 3 SFE 21 SF1 9
Alexander, Robert William (1905-) CSF 3 WGT 2 see also Joan Butler
Alexander, Sigmund Bowman. CSF 3 ES1 6 SF1 9
Alexander, Thea. HFI 2
Alexander, W. SFS 3 IAC 32
Alfred, Hans. VES 182
Alfred, Joe. VES 207
Alfven, Hannes (1908-) SF2 953 WGT 2 see also Olof Johannesson
Algatchie. CSF 3
Algeo, John. FL2 698-700 FL3 1375-7 FL4 1840-7 FL5 2203-5
Alger, Horatio (1834-1899) [FJT] RHN 21,151 STH 162-3,165
Alger, Leclaire Gowans (1898-) ES1 6 WGT 2
Alger, Martin. SRB 97
Alger, William Rounseville. CSF 3
Ali, Muhammed. CWN 24 RHN 158 VFS 216
Alier, I. M. pseud. of Hugo Gernsback. SFD 23
Aliki. FFC 83
Alington, Adrian Richard. BAA 110
Allan, Angus P. SF1 9
Allan, James D. AAL 157-8
Allan, John. ALW 55 FBK 35-7
Allan, Mabel Esther (1915-) FFC 159,170 SF1 10
Allan, Mea (1909-) SF1 10 SF2 794
Alland, William. SRB 58
Allen, Alfred. CSF 3
Allen, Arthur Bruce (1903-) CSF 3 SF1 10
Allen, Barbara Jo. SF1 10
Allen, Charles Grant Blairfindie (1848-99) BAA 35 CSF 4 ES1 6-7 EXT 7/1 13,17 SFE 24-5 SF1 10 WGT 2-3
Allen, Charles R. SF1 10
Allen, David. SF1 10 VES 331
Allen, Dexter. ES1 6
Allen, Dick pseud. of Richard Stanley Allen. ALW 30,179 EXT 9/2 25 IAC 32-3 SF1 10 SF2 794-5 SRB 496

Allen, Edward. IAC 33
Allen, Edward Heron. ES1 6
Allen, F. M. pseud. of Edmund Downey. CSF 3-4
Allen, Grant. ALW 85 IAC 33 PST 90-1, 226, 236, 248, 298, 311 SFS 3
Allen, Harold W. G. SF1 10
Allen, Henry Francis. BAA 36, 44 SF1 10 WGT 3 see also Pruning Knife
Allen, Henry M. CSF 104
Allen, Henry Ware. BAA 104-5
Allen, Henry Wilson (1912-) ES1 7 HFI 2 SFE 25 SF1 10 WGT 3
Allen, Herbert F. BAA 198
Allen, Irwin (1916-) SFE 25 SOT 246 WSF 313
Allen, Johannes (1916-) SF1 10 SF2 795
Allen, Judson. AAL 194, 204 BAA 198
Allen, Judy. FFC 1, 59, 173 SF1 10
Allen, L. David (1940-) pseud. of Louis David Allen. ACC 57, 244 AOW 363-4 FHT 66 KAU 138, 140 RAH 258 SFE 25 SFH 237 SFW 267-76, 467-73 SRB 463 WSF 284, 382
Allen, Lori. IAC 32-3 SF1 10
Allen, Louis David (1940-) SF1 10 SF2 795 see also L. David Allen
Allen, Luman. CSF 4
Allen, Marijane. IAC 33
Allen, Marion Campbell (1914-) ES1 7 SF1 10 SF2 795
Allen, Marjorie. FFC 151
Allen, P. R. BAA 198
Allen, Paul C. FLR 60, 62
Allen, Richard Stanley (1939-) see Dick Allen
Allen, Robert pseud. of Allen Robert Dodd. CSF 4 SF1 11
Allen, Steve. IAC 33 ISW 122 SFN 89 SFS 3
Allen, Thomas B. ES1 7
Allen, Virginia French. IAC 33 SF1 11
Allen, Walter. FTF 50 KAU 6
Allen, Ward. BAA 198-9
Allen, Willis Boyd. CSF 4
Allen, Woody. KVT 22-3 SFH

Allen, Woody (cont.)
142 TRB 64, 66, 112-3
Allende, Salvador. MSF 75
Allfrey, Katherine. FFC 181
Allighan, Garry (1898-) AOW 129
BAA 135 ES1 7 SFE 25 SF1 11
Allingham, Cedric (1922-) ES1 7
Allingham, Margery Louise (1904-
1966) ES1 7 EXT 8/1 5 IAC 33
SFE 25 SF1 11 SF2 795
Allinson, A. A. BAA 167 SF1 11
Allinson, Clyde pseud. of William
Knoles. SF1 11
Allison, Leonard (1933-) SF1 11
Allison, Ruth see Allison Rice
Allman, James. CSF 4 SF1 11
Allonby, Edith. CSF 4 SF1 11
Allott, Kenneth (-1973) ALW 75
AOW 338 BAA 106 EXT 2/1
5, 7-8 EXT 3/2 36, 40 FAN 11
SF1 11
Allport, Arthur pseud. of Ray-
mond Z. Gallun. IAC 33
Allsop, Kenneth. CWN 4, 25-6, 53
Allum, Tom. AOW 308 ES1 7
SF1 11
Allyn, Henry. CSF 4
Alper, Gerald Arthur. HFI 3
IAC 33 SFE 25 SF1 11
Alpers, Hans Joachim (1943-)
LEX 161-2
Alpert, Hollis. IAC 33 SFS 3
Alsop, Stewart. WAA 243
Alter, Robert Edmond (1925-65)
HFI 3 SF1 11 SF2 796 WGT 3
Alterman, Peter S. IAC 33
UKL 64-76
Alterton, Margaret. NWO 61
Althaus, Friedrich. BAA 167
Altheim, Franz. BAA 167
Altizer, Thomas J. J. NWO 28
Altman, David. WFS 163-5
Altman, Robert. CSC 263
Altov, Henrich (1926-) AOW 297
IAC 33 SFB 122 SL5 2117-21
Altshuler, Harry. IAC 33
WGT 3
Alvarez, A. EXT 6/1 20
Alvarez, John pseud. of Lester
del Rey. RFA 120
Alvarez, Luis. ACE 12, 21, 23
AC2 10, 19, 21 VFS 243
Alvim-Correa. VES 101
Amber, Gracie pseud. of Gerda
Koontz. SF1 12

Ambler, Eric (1909-) CSF 4
SF1 12
Ambrosius, Merlin. WTS 51
Ambrus, Glenys. FFC 5
Ambrus, Victor. FFC 5, 27, 45-
6, 194
Amelio, Ralph J. (1939-) BRS 10
SF1 12 SF2 796 SRB 463
Amersin, Ferdinand. BAA 168
Amery, Carl (1922-) LEX 162-3
Amery, Jean. BAA 199
Amery, Leopold Stennett (1873-
1955) CSF 4 SF1 12
Ames, Delano L. (1906-) CSF 4
SF1 12
Ames, Eleanor Maria (1831-1908)
WGT 4 see also Eleanor Kirk
Ames, Joseph Bushnell (1878-
1928) CSF 4 SF1 12
Ames, Russell Abbot. BAA 168
Amis, Kingsley (1922-) AAL 123
ALW 30-1, 99, 239 AOW 240,
285, 338 BAA 168, 241 BYS
256-7, 282, 284, 311, 320 CAT
xv, 26, 71-2, 105 COT 134-5
CWN 25 ES1 7-8 ETN 174
EXT 2/1 20-1 EXT 4/2 28, 33
EXT 5/1 4, 17-8 EXT 5/2 29-
30 EXT 6/1 2 EXT 6/2 22
EXT 7/1 1, 15 EXT 7/2 40
EXT 9/1 19 EXT 10/2 80, 86
FAN 7-9, 134, 152, 164 FBK 152
FFR 4 FL2 661-5 FRN 17, 75
FTF 12-3 HFI 3 HID 192 IAC
33 IAH 135 ISW 7-8, 173 JGB
4 KAU 94 MFW 169 MIH 15-6,
29-35, 58, 70, 104, 126 NDA x
NWO 16-7, 24, 100 RBY 213
SFB 8 SFD 63 SFE 29-30 SFH
50, 237 SFS 3 SFW 403, 476-7,
528 SF1 12 SF2 796 SIH 12
SL1 43-7 SOI xvi, 150, 153 SOT
2 SRB 70, 236, 335, 497 TPS
100-16 TSF 244-5 VES 116,
330 WAA 124, 243, 245 WGT 4
WSF 359-60
Ammons, A. R. IAC 33
Amon, Santiago. BAA 199
Amos. EXT 8/1 23
Amosov, Nikolai M. (1913-) AOW
129 HFI 3 LEX 163-4 SFE 30
SF1 12 SRB 350 VES 261
Amoss, Berthe. FFC 160
Amper, Drax. SF1 12
Amsbury, Clifton. IMS 8-9

Amundson, Grace. IAC 33
Ananda. VFS 120
Anastasio, Dina. FFC 28
Anckarsvard, Karin. FFC 90
Anderegg, Michael A. BAA 199
Anders, William. ALW 232 SFB
72 VFS 105,198-9
Andersen, Hans Christian. FFC
1-2,12,17-8,24,53,103 FLT 96
LTN 59,61-2,65 MSF 183 POE
69 RAH 93 SRB 21 WAA 74
WIF 40
Anderson, Adrienne Wynne Bar-
ton. SF1 12 SF2 796
Anderson, Andrew A. CSF 4
SF1 12
Anderson, Andy (1932-) SF1 12
Anderson, Arthur James. CSF 4
Anderson, Carl D. FTF 10
Anderson, Chester (1932-) AOW
129 DTS 7-8,35 ES1 8 HFI 3
SFD 68 SFE 30 SF1 12
Anderson, Colin. BAA 150 HFI
3 NDA 74,76-7 SFE 30-1 SF1
12 UFS 2
Anderson, Imbert Enrique (1910-)
SF1 14
Anderson, Jack. IAC 33
Anderson, Jo see Stella Benson
Anderson, Karen Kruse (1932-)
ES1 8 IAC 33 SFS 4 SF1 581
SOT 323 WFS 291,301
Anderson, Kathleen. FFC 30
Anderson, Lindsay. CWN 25
ETN 132-3
Anderson, Margaret. FFC 160
Anderson, Mary. FFC 112 SF1
12
Anderson, Mildred. FFC 53
Anderson, Olof W. AOW 45,51
CSF 4 SFE 31 SF1 12
Anderson, Poul (1926-) AAL 7,
13,18,70,95-7,109-10,112-3,
119,141-3 ALW 161,216,218,
227 AOW 118,130-3,285,288,
291-2,294,296,300,309 ASF
43,147,222 BAA 120-1,125,
130,133,138,143,156,199 BFP
9-15 BYS 96,257,261,285-6,
295,303 COT 70-2,112-3,140-1,
162,193,227,230,251,272-3,
285,297,302 CSC 36,42,55,65,
95,111,170,173 EFP 5 ES1 8-
10 ETN 47,68,100,163 EXT
4/2 31 EXT 5/1 3,21-2 FFR

5-6 FL1 173-7 FL2 1021-8
FL3 1160-3,1417-9 FL4 1913-
7 HFI 3-5 HID 2,122,131,141-
2,180 IAC 33-6 IAH 80-4,121,
123,141-2,145,149 ISW 95,129,
135-6,196 JVN 131-2,162,218-
9,223-4 KAU 32,104,204 LEX
164-7 LTN 36-7,121-2 MFW
30-1,34-5,39,41,43,46,48,73-
4,200,207-8 MIH 44,57,72,90-
1,132 MSM 132,180 NWO 254-
5 OMN 13 RFA 133,143-4,146,
148,155,158,164,174,191,194-
5,201-4,207-10,212-3 RGS 6-
9,207 SFB 12,100 SFD 16-7,
19-20,33,75-6,85,131,241,250-
1,258-9,261-2,266-9,272,295,
297,312-3 SFE 31-2 SFH 115
SFS 4-6,40-1 SFW 259-65,345-
7 SF1 13 SF2 797-8 SIH 170
SL1 242-6 SL2 977-80 SL5
2236-40,2264-8,2411-5 SOT
416-7 SRB 5,16,114,251,331,
341,349,374 STH 86-7,157 SV2
41-50 TJB 5,25,46 TPS 205-14
TSF 58,234 VES 74-6,81-3,87,
92,104,112,116,118,123,147,
182,194,197,229,269 WFS 204,
291-2 WGT 4-5 WIF 114,194
WSF 110,148,172,184-7,206,
387 see also Winston P. Sanders
Anderson, Sherwood. IAH 18
TBC 8,54-5 WIF 151
Anderson, Stella Benson (1892-
1933) WGT 5
Anderson, Susan Janice. [FJT]
IAC 36,167 LTN 131,259
Anderson, William Charles (1920-)
AOW 307 ES1 10-1 HFI 5 SFE
32 SF1 14 SF2 798-9 VFS 105
WGT 5
Andersson, Vic. IAC 36
Anderton, Elizabeth Anne. BAA
280
Andom, R. pseud. of Alfred Wal-
ter Barrett. CSF 5 SF1 14
Andre, Lee pseud. of L. R. Andrus.
SF1 14
Andreae, Johann Valentin. BYS
66 CSF 5 EXT 8/1 23 FAN 4
PST 25,230 SFH 173
Andreae, Percy. CSF 5
Andreas, Peter. ES1 11
Andree. EXT 1/1 20
Andreota, Paul (1917-) SF1 14

Andres, Stefan. POE 259
Andress, Ursula. FBK 100
Andrevon, Jean-Pierre. IAC 36
SFB 139 SFE 32-3
Andrew, J. O. BAA 46
Andrew, Stephen pseud. of Frank
George Layton. CSF 5
Andrew, William. IAC 36 SFS 6
Andrews, Carolyn S. EXT 6/1
2-21
Andrews, Cecily Isobel (1892-)
SF2 1122 see also Rebecca
West
Andrews, Charles M. ES1 11
Andrews, Claire (1940-) SF1 14
Andrews, Elton V. pseud. of
Frederik Pohl. IMS 169-70
Andrews, Frank Emerson (1902-)
ES1 11 FFC 153 SF1 14 SF2
799
Andrews, James Sydney (1934-)
FFC 170 SF1 14 SF2 799
Andrews, John W. SL4 1963-6
Andrews, Keith (1930-) SF1 14
Andrews, Lewis M. BAA 160
SF1 14
Andrews, William S. BAA 27
Andreyev, Leonid N. (1871-1919)
CSF 5 IAC 36 SF1 14 WTS 28
Andrezel, Pierre pseud. of Karen
Blixen. CSF 5
Andrus, L. R. see Lee Andre
Anet, Claude pseud. of Jean
Schopfer. AOW 52 CSF 5 SFE
34 SF1 14
Anex, Guy. SF1 14
Anfilov, Gleb. IAC 36
Angell, Roger. MSM 115-6
Angelo. CSF 5 ES1 11 SF1 14
Angelucci, Orfeo M. ES1 11
SF1 15
Angenot, Marc. CAT 32, 46-7,
112-4 MSF 147,163,206
Anger, Fred. IMS 41
Anglin, Norman. CSF 5
Angoff, Charles (1902-) CSF 5
ES1 11 SF1 15 SF2 799 WGT 5
Angus, John. CSF 5 SF1 15
Anker, Larsen Johannes (1874-
1957) SF1 15
Anski, S. STH 120
Anmar, Frank pseud. of William
F. Nolan. IAC 36 SFS 6
Annan, David.' SF1 15
Anne (of Austria). SFN 107

Annesley, Maude. CSF 5 SF1 15
Annett, Cora. FFC 112,128
Annixter, Paul. FFC 112,129
Anonym, Mon. SF1 15
Ansky, S. pseud. of Solomon
Rappoport. CSF 9
Ansle, Dorothy Phoebe see
Laura Conway
Anson, (Captain) pseud of
Charles Vernon. CSF 9 SF1 15
Anson, August. BAA 107 CSF 9
SF1 15
Anstey, F. pseud. of Thomas
Anstey Guthrie. CSF 9 FBK
116 FL2 760-7 SFE 35 SFW
180 SF1 15 VES 209
Antheil, George (1900-59) SF1 15
Anthony, (Mother). EXT 10/1 21
Anthony, Barbara (1932-) see
Antonia Barber
Anthony, John pseud. of John
Ciardi. CSF 9 IAC 37 SFS 6
Anthony, K. NWO 124
Anthony, Kaye. CSF 9
Anthony, Piers pseud. of Piers
Anthony Dillingham Jacob. ALW
212 AOW 133-4, 399 COT 74,
84, 162, 196-7 EFP 18 FFR 6-7
FL2 695-7 FL5 2185-91 HFI 5
IAC 37 LEX 167-8 NDA 107
NWO 187, 253 RGS 9-10, 207-8
SFD 35 SFE 36-7 SF1 15-6
SF2 800 SL1 354-7 SL3 1308-
11 SL4 1596-1602 SRB 264
VES 84, 180, 280 WSF 233
Anthony, R. WTS 27
Anton, J. L. SOT 71
Anton, Ludwig (1872-) ES1 17
SFE 39
Antoni, A. EXT 2/1 6
Antonick, Robert J. (1939-) SF2
955-6 see also Nick Kamin
Antoniorrobles pseud. of Antonio
Robles Soler. HFI 5 SF1 16
Antrobus, Rosie. IAC 37
Anvic, Frank pseud. of Jory
Sherman. SF1 16
Anvil, Christopher pseud. of
Harry C. Crosby, Jr. ALW
212 BAA 137 ETN 65,68 FFR
7 HFI 5-6 IAC 37 LEX 168
MIH 87 RFA 206,208,211 RGS
10 SFE 39-40 SFS 6 SF1 16
WSF 183
Apel, Johann. CSF 9

Apollinaire, Guillaume pseud. of
Wilhelm Apollinaris Kostrowit-
zky (1880-1918) ES1 17 FL2
728-9 MSF 161 STH 38
Apostolides, Alex. ETN 127 IAC
37 ISW 131 RFA 202-3 SFE 40
SFS 6,32 STH 246
Appel, Benjamin (1907-77) ALW
30,65 BAA 133 ES1 17 EXT
2/2 28 FFC 47 HFI 6 SFE 40
SF1 16 SF2 799
Appel, H.M. TSP 15,62
Apple, A. E. SF1 16
Appleman, Mark Jerome (1917-)
SF1 16 SF2 800
Appleseed, Johnny. RBY 66, 77,
124 TBC 57 TSO 47
Appleton, Jane Sophia. BAA 24
MSF 177
Appleton, Lawrence pseud. of
H. P. Lovecraft. EXT 3/1 15-6
Appleton, Victor (house name)
ES1 17-8 EXT 1/1 5 EXT 5/1
4 EXT 7/1 26 PST 98 SFE 40
SF1 16-7,581 SL5 2298-302
VES 322 WIF 69 WSF 19 see
also Howard Garis, Edward
Stratemeyer
Appleton, Victor, II (house name)
AOW 303,309 FFR 7 SF1 17-8
Appuhamy. VFS 14-8,23-6
Apuleius, Lucius. FBK 12,44
MSM 127 SFB 29,101 WIF 28,
81
Aqbar. MSF 38
Aquinas, (St.) Thomas see St.
Thomas Aquinas
Aquino, John. SRB 463
Arago, Dominique Francois.
POE 59,66
Aratovsky, Y. IAC 37
Aratus. ALW 43 BAA 15 CSF 9
POE 149 PST 22 SF1 18
Arawiyah, Al pseud. of Horatio
Nelson Crellin. CSF 3 SF1 18
Arbib, Richard. VES 117
Arbur, Rosemarie. SL1 488-92
SL4 1799-804 SL5 2201-6
Arbuthnot, John (1667-1735)
SF1 18
Arbuthnot, May Hill. AOW 307
Arch, E. L. pseud. of Rachel
Ruth Cosgrove Payes. HFI 6
SFE 40 SF1 18-9
Archambault, Alberic A. (1887-

1950) CSF 9 SF1 19
Archer, Denis. CWD 46
Archer, Dirce. EXT 5/1 4
Archer, Ethel. CSF 9
Archer, Lee (house name) SFE
40 WGT 5 see also Harlan
Ellison
Archer, Rexton. TSP 131
Archibald, Joe. TSP 29,89
Archimedes. MSM 256 VFS 189
WAA 33
Ardan, Michael. ALW 66,69
Arden, Clive pseud. of Lily Clive
Nutt. SF1 19
Ardies, Tom (1931-) SF1 19
SF2 801
Ardizzone, Edward. FCC 3,25,
27, 73-4,132,137,187
Ardrey, Robert (1908-) ACE 39-
40 AC2 37-8 BAA 112 CSC
110 CSF 9 ES1 18 RAH 30
SFE 40 SF1 19 SF2 801
Arelsky, N. MSF 261
Arendt, Hannah. EXT 9/2 59
NDA 86-8,99 POE 303
Ari. VFS 22-3
Ariosto, Ludovico. ALW 42
FBK 123 FTF 18 HFI 6 MIH
71 PST 16 SFB 70 SOI 43
WAA 77 WIF 34 WSF 13,292
Ariss, Bruce Wallace, Jr. (1911-)
ES1 18 HFI 6 IAC 37 SFE 41
SF1 19 SF2 801
Aristophanes. AOW 12-4, 80
BYS 58 EXT 8/1 23 MSF 55,
87, 94, 99 RAH 229 SFB 13
SFD 37 VES 224 WIF 28,184
Aristotle. ACC 140 CUA 19,21,
23,33,36-8 CWN 43 ETN 99
EXT 5/1 18 INT 14 ISW 55
MFW 263 MIH 48 MSF 18,48,
82, 242 PJF 20-1,37 SFA 114
SFB 9 SFD 38,45 SFH 117,121
SFN 12 TJB 19 VFS 189 WBW
5 WSF 317
Ariza, Pedro Alarcon Y (1833-91)
SF1 7
Arkin, Alan. FFC 2,112 IAC 37
SFS 6
Arkwright, Richard. MSF 194
Arkwright, William (1857-1925)
CSF 9 SF1 19
Arlen, Michael (1895-1956) BAA
99 CSF 10 ES1 18 FL2 605-6

Arlen, Michael (cont.)
SFE 41 SFN 39 SF1 19 WGT 5
Arlt, Gustave O. EXT 2/2 32
Armand, Emile. BAA 199
Armitage, (Dr.) WTS 44
Armitage, Eileen. FFC 84
Armour, Donald. CSF 10 SF1 19
Armour, Frances J. CSF 10
SF1 19
Armour, John F. BAA 68 CSF 10
Armour, Margaret pseud. of
Margaret MacDougall. CSF 10
ES1 18 SF1 19
Armour, R. Coutts. WGT 5
Arms, George. BAA 199
Armstrong, Anthony pseud. of
George Anthony Armstrong
Willis. CSF 10 SFE 41 SF1 19
Armstrong, Charles Wicksteed
(1871-) BAA 46, 105 CSF 10
WGT 5
Armstrong, Martin Donisthorpe
(1882-1974) CSF 10 ES1 18-9
SF1 19
Armstrong, Neil. ALW 232 COT
52-5 FTF 26, 38 VFS 11-2, 78,
152, 163
Armstrong, Terence Ian Fytton
(1912-1970) CSF 10 SF1 19
WGT 5 see also John Gawsworth
Armstrong, Willimina (1866-) see
Zamin Ki Dost
Armytage, W(alter) H(enry)
G(reen) (1915-) AOW 338 BAA
168, 199 ES1 19 EXT 7/1 1-17
EXT 7/2 29 EXT 8/1 1 EXT
9/1 1 EXT 9/2 24, 33-60 EXT
10/1 48-9 EXT 10/2 50 SFE 41
VES 330
Arnason, Eleanor. BAA 159
IAC 37
Arndt, Hans-Joachim. BAA 199
Arndt, Ursula. FFC 136
Arne, Aaron pseud. of Alf A. Jor-
genson. ES1 19 SF1 20
Arneson, D. J. SF1 20
Arnette, Robert (house name) SFE
41-2 WGT 5-6 see also Roger
P. Graham, Robert Silverberg
Arno, Enrico. FFC 3, 12
Arnold, Andrew W. CSF 10
Arnold, Charles. IAC 37
Arnold, Douglas. IAC 37
Arnold, (Sir) Edwin Lester (1857-
1935) BYS 139-41, 169 CSF 10

ES1 19 FL5 2156-8 HFI 6 SFE
42 SF1 20 SL3 1209-12 STH
198-9 VES 80, 148 WAA 101, 243
Arnold, Frank Edward (1914-)
CSF 10 ES1 19 IAC 37 SFE 42
SF1 20
Arnold, H. F. WTS 27
Arnold, Herb. RHN 150
Arnold, Jack (1916-) IAC 37 KAU
187, 189, 198, 201 SFE 42 SRB
58
Arnold, (Mrs.) John Oliver.
CSF 10
Arnold, Kenneth. ES1 19 VES
339 WFS 265 WIF 93
Arnold, Matthew (1822-88) ACC
173 CAT 135 EXT 9/1 20 IAH
82 MIH 122 POE 171 TSO 34
WBW 55
Arnold, Ralph Crispian Marshall
(1906-70) SF1 20
Arnold, Samuel James. CSF 10
Arnold-Foster, Hugh. POE 183
Arnothy, Christine (1930-) SF1 20
Arnoux, Alexandre Paul (1884-
1973) CSF 11 SF1 20
Arnquist, James Dennis. BAA
280
Aronin, Ben (1904-) CSF 11
SF1 20
Aronstam, Noah Ephraim (1872-
1957) SF1 20
Arouet, Francois Marie (1694-
1778) WGT 6 see also
Voltaire
Arozin. BAA 85
Arquette, Lois Duncan (1934-)
SF2 884 see also Lois Duncan
Arr, Stephen. IAC 37 see also
Stephen A. Rynas
Arrhenius, Svante. BYS 165 COT
65 IAC 37 ISW 74 RFA 56 SFH
158 WTS 43
Arrighi, Mel (1933-) SF1 20 SF2
801
Arrow, William (house name)
SFE 42 WGT 6 see also Don
Pfeil, William Rotsler
Artaud, Antonin. CWN 49
Arthur, (King). ASF 35, 142, 192
ATA 22 CUA 55 WBW 11, 47
WIF 33-4
Arthur, Robert pseud. of Robert
Arthur Feder. ES1 19 IAC 38
SFS 6 SF1 20

Arthur, Ruth Mabel (1905-) FFC
28,160,170 SF1 20, 581 SF2
801
Arthur, Timothy S. CSF 11
Arthur, Wallace. SF1 20
Arthur, William. SF1 21
Artmann, H. C. FBK 74,144
Artzybasheff, Boris (1899-) ES1
20 FBK 119
Arundel, Honor. FFC 129
Arvonen, Helen see Margaret
Worth
Asbell, Bernard (1923-) SF2 993
see also Nicholas Max
Asbjornsson. LTN 25
Asbury, Herbert (1891-1963) CSF
11 ES1 20 EXT 3/1 19 SF1 21
Ascher, Eugene. CSF 11 ES1 20
SF1 21
Ascoli, Georges. BAA 199
Aseyev, Nikolai N. MSF 253
Ash, Alan. ES1 20 SFE 43
SF1 21
Ash, Brian (1936-) AOW 339
BAA 168 RAH 258 SFE 43
SRB 63, 70 TSF 245, 249 VES
330-1 WSF 282-3
Ash, Fenton pseud. of Frank
Atkins. CSF 11 STH 168
Ash, Lee. RBY 240
Ash, Paul pseud. of Pauline
Ashwell. IAC 38 SFS 7
Ashbee, Charles Robert (1863-
1942) BAA 76 EXT 9/2 46 SF1
21 WGT 6
Ashbury, Nellie. STH 92
Ashby, Richard. HFI 6 IAC 38
SFS 7 SF1 21 STH 227
Ashby, Rubie Constance (1899-)
CSF 11 SF1 21 WGT 6
Ashby, William Ross (1903-)
ES1 20
Ashe, Geoffrey Thomas (1923-)
BAA 199 SF1 21
Ashe, Tamsin. IAC 38
Ashkenazy, Irwin. WGT 6 WTS
41 see also G. Garnet
Ashley, Arthur Ernest (1906-)
SF2 1112 see also Francis
Vivian
Ashley, Fred pseud. of Frank
Atkins. CSF 11
Ashley, Michael Raymond (1948-)
AOW 368 FL1 217-21, 468-71
FL2 757-9, 817-21 FL3 1441-

51 FL5 2532-8 IAC 38 SFE 43
SF1 21 SRB 63, 74 TSF 245
Ashley-Brown, William (1887-
1970) SF1 21
Ashton, Francis Leslie (1904-)
CSF 11 ES1 20 SFE 43-4 SF1
21 VES 140 WIF 51
Ashton, Helen Rosaline (1891-
1958) CSF 11 SF1 21
Ashton, Marvin. SF1 21
Ashton, Rosabel H. SF1 21
Ashton, Stephen. ES1 20 SF1 21
Ashton, Winifred (1888-1965)
WGT 6 see also Clemence Dane
Ashton-Gwatkin, Frank Trelawny
Arthur (1889-) WGT 6 see also
John Paris
Ashwell, Pauline. HID 104 ISW
127 RFA 209 WGT 6 see also
Paul Ash
Asimov, Isaac (1920-) AAL 20,
23,37, 45-6, 70, 72-3, 78, 93, 140
ALW 7-9,13,31, 34, 36, 46-8,
107, 117-8, 136, 155, 157, 160,
162-3, 166-9, 171, 179, 184-5, 213-
5, 218, 225, 227, 239 AOW 89,
134-6, 285-6, 292-4, 296, 298-9,
303, 309-10, 345, 351, 353, 362,
398 BAA xix, 118-9, 123, 125,
130, 150, 161, 199 BFP 16-21
BYS 227-9, 236, 249, 269, 279,
285-6, 302 CAT 88, 97, 100-1,
108, 122, 137, 139 CEN 1-22
COT 7, 19, 22, 25, 47-8, 57, 62,
77, 79-80, 105, 163, 166, 180, 186,
188, 205-6, 222, 246, 250, 261-2,
269, 278, 284, 292-5, 298 CSC
12, 30, 42, 60-1, 65-6, 74, 84, 93,
102, 125, 128-9, 169-70, 172-3,
197, 200, 227, 240 DMK 1-7
EFP 9-10, 12, 18-9 ES1 20-3
ETN 12, 14, 16-7, 21, 23, 31, 33-
4, 45, 58-9, 64, 68, 71, 159-60,
163, 177 EXT 3/1 26-7 EXT
5/1 3, 6 EXT 7/2 40, 42 EXT
8/1 4, 6 EXT 9/2 63 EXT 10/1
1-2 EXT 10/2 64-5, 69-115
FAN 154, 189 FBK 124 FFR 7-
13 FHT 43, 50, 58 FTF 15, 67,
84, 86, 90, 120-4, 151-2, 155-7,
170, 172-3, 176-8, 191-2 HFI 6-
7 HID 6, 21, 31, 103-4, 122 HWK
48 IAC 38-42 IAH 28-9, 45, 106-
7, 133, 142 IMS 159, 183, 210, 213,
244 INT 8-10, 14, 17, 21, 26, 52-

Asimov, Isaac (cont.)
3, 70-1, 79, 89, 91-3, 96-9 ISW
vi, 90-4, 120, 122-3, 126, 129, 192,
221, 249 KAU 9, 24-6, 33, 64, 88-
9, 94, 102, 105, 125, 129, 153, 157-
64, 175-6, 178, 181, 221 KWS
269, 363 LEX 168-71 LTN 252,
254, 258 MFW ix, 2, 4-6, 9-10,
16-7, 33-5, 37-8, 40-1, 44, 46, 82-
3, 86, 104, 140, 147-8, 160, 170,
190, 208-9, 219, 225, 234-5, 245-
6, 249-50, 290-1 MIH 23, 36, 49,
99-100, 106, 110 MSF 13, 23, 29,
82, 120, 136, 242, 279 MSM 15,
32, 81, 83, 132, 157- 96, 303-4
NDA ix, 31, 36-8, 111, 114-5, 130,
188, 205, 212, 215-6 NWO 47, 76,
102, 183, 253, 255 OMN 50-5,
162, 261 OWB 95, 97 POE 277
RAH 31, 231 RBY 24, 36-7, 83-
4, 104-5, 187 RFA 68-9, 81, 83,
90, 92, 95, 97, 100, 104-8, 112, 118,
131, 134, 137, 144, 155, 158, 166-7,
170-4, 176, 184, 194, 199, 202-3,
205-8, 213 RGS 11-2, 208 RHN
15, 206 SFB 10-1, 60, 62, 78-9,
100 SFD 4, 32, 55, 57, 64, 73, 83,
97, 208-11, 213, 232, 235-6, 239,
242-4, 250, 256, 266, 291, 296, 304,
307-8, 310-3, 318 SFE 44-5 SFH
40-1, 51, 58-63, 65, 69, 84, 92, 113,
115-6, 132, 136, 148-50, 157, 181-
2, 188, 216, 240, 243 SFN 28, 39,
47, 83, 110, 116 SFS 7-10 SFW
267-76, 330, 394 SF1 22-3 SF2
802 SIH 139, 141, 179, 184, 190
SIN 9, 31-9, 128, 158 SL1 318-21
SL2 819-31, 909-14, 995-99 SL3
1476-9 SOI 154 SOT 6, 20, 62,
82, 121, 157, 159-60, 193, 199, 218,
249-66, 275, 278, 315, 320, 330-1,
412 SRB 3, 7, 13, 77, 112, 311, 315,
320, 322-3, 327, 331, 354-5, 497
STF 79 STH 45, 67, 154-5, 157,
159 TDI 8 TJB 4, 17, 24-6, 31,
46, 48 TPS 29-61, 273-6 TRB
54, 60, 62-4 TSF 26-32, 55, 129-
30, 228, 231, 234, 237-8, 248-9
VES 72, 75, 81, 83, 87, 93, 95-6,
110-1, 122, 125, 129, 143, 149-50,
156, 159, 161, 167-9, 174, 176, 180-
1, 183-4, 189, 230, 256-8, 302-3,
307, 314-5, 328, 330 VFS 151-7,
159, 201, 211, 259 VF1 88-103,
267-8 WAA 51-2, 56, 121, 131-2,
217, 242 WFS 17, 71-3, 78, 88-9,
97, 117-8, 124, 127, 129, 161, 178,
181, 200, 202, 223, 230, 241, 284-
5, 300 WGT 6-7 WIF 60, 90, 95,
145, 149, 154, 156, 160, 184, 194,
237, 272 WSF 4, 95, 100-1, 103-
4, 107, 109, 112-3, 116, 125, 135,
137-8, 148, 151-2, 173, 175, 183,
203, 218, 224, 238, 240-2, 251,
324, 331, 338, 386-9 WTS 48
YTS 23, 76 see also Paul French
Asimov, Janet. ASF 213-4, 292-
3 see also Janet Jeppson
Askew, Alice. CSF 11
Askew, Claude. CSF 11
Askham, Francis pseud. of Julia
E. Greenwood. CSF 11 SF1 23
Aspeto, M. CSF 11 SF1 23
Asprin, Robert Lynn. HFI 7
LEX 171
Asquith, (Lady) Cynthia (1887-
1960) CSF 11-2 ES1 23-4 FBK
78 IAC 42 SF1 23
Asquith, Milton. IMS 186
Assollant, Jean Baptiste Alfred
(1827-86) SF1 23
Astaire, Fred. WFS 55, 131
Astarita. VES 197
Asterley, Hugh Cecil. SF1 23
Astle, Richard. FL2 998-1003
SL2 739-43 SL3 1357-61 SL5
2402-6
Aston, Benjamin Gwilliam. CSF
12 SF1 24
Astor, John Jacob (1864-1912)
AOW 52 BAA 50 BYS 142 CSF
12 EXT 1/1 5 FTF 43 MSF 203
POE 152-3 PST 69-70, 192, 221,
232, 244, 256, 264-5, 267-8, 273,
275-6, 280, 283, 291 SFE 46 SF1
24 SL3 1098-101 SOT 237 STH
4, 227 VES 69, 225 WAA 39
WIF 54 YTS 6
Astor, William Waldorf (1848-
1919) ES1 24 SF1 24
Astrop, John. FFC 141
Asturias, Miguel Angel (1899-
1974) AOW 118 ES1 24 SF1 24
SF2 802
Athanas, William Verne (1918-62)
WGT 7
Athanasius (of Alexandria) MSF 45
Athanassiades, Nikos (1904-)
SF1 24
Atheling, William. MIH 8

Atheling, William, Jr. pseud. of
James Blish. ALW 184 EXT
8/1 7 HID 192 ISW 154,192
MIH 6-8, 21, 28, 31, 39, 116, 121
NWO 134 RAH 258 SFH 237
TJB 52 VES 330 WAA 245
Atherton, Gertrude Franklin Horn
(1857-1948) CSF 12 ES1 24 IAC
42 SFE 49 SF1 24 SOT 305
Atherton, John. IAC 42 SFS 10
Atherton, Mary. CSF 12
Athey, Henry. BAA 58 CSF 12
SF1 24
Atholl, Justin. SF1 24
Atkey, Bertram. CSF 12 IAC
42 SF1 24 SIH 110
Atkey, Philip (1908-) WGT 7
Atkins, Frank. CSF 12 WGT 7
see also Fenton Ash, Fred
Ashley, Frank Aubrey
Atkins, John Alfred (1916-) AOW
136 ES1 24 EXT 9/2 53 FAN
113 SFE 49 SF1 24 SF2 802
Atkinson, Allen. FFC 172
Atkinson, Geoffroy. BAA xx, 168
Atkinson, Leslie. FFC 172
Atkinson, Percy. STH 75-6
Atlas, Charles. KVT 30 RHN
54, 129
Attanasio, A. A. AAL 63-4 IAC
42
Attebery, Brian. FL3 1196-208
FL5 2206-13
Atterley, Joseph pseud. of George
Tucker. ALW 55, 95 AOW 18
CSF 12 EXT 5/1 4 MSM 210-1
SFE 50 SF1 24 STH 52
Attila (the Hun). INT 62 MSF 256
Atwater, Florence. FFC 139
Atwater, Richard. FFC 139
Atwood, Margaret. MFW 125
Aubin, Etienne. SF1 24
Aubrey, Frank pseud. of Frank
Atkins. ALW 85 CSF 12 SFE
50, 52 SF1 24-5 STH 168 VES
140
Aubrey, Rollo Lennox Smeaton.
SIH 158-9
Auctor, Ignotus pseud? of W. Dorr
Legg. SF1 25
Aucuy, M. BAA 199
Auden, Renee. SF1 25
Auden, W. H. BAA 109 EXT 9/2
47-8 EXT 10/1 21, 27, 31, 33, 44
FBK 98 FLT 49 IAC 42 ISW

273 KAU 89 MFW 281, 287-8
NWO 15-6, 92, 253 SOI 80 TDI
8 THM 39
Auden, Wystan. POE 262-3
Audoin, Ch. BAA 200
Audubon, John James. ISW 267
Auerbach, Arnold M. IAC 42
SFS 10
August, Lee. HFI 7
August, Leo pseud. of Don Segall.
SF1 25
Augustine (of Hippo). MSF 21, 93
Augustinus. BAA 58, 60 SF1 25
Augustus, (Emperor). CUA 6
Aumbry, Alan. IAC 42
Aurangzeb, (Mogul Emperor)
(1618-1707) VFS 31
Aurelianus, Ambrosius. WIF 33
Austen, Jane (1775-1817) CAT 112
COT 181 EXT 9/2 29 EXT 10/2
106-8 FBK 19 FLT 12 FL3
1127-31 LTN 182 SFD 43, 66
SFH 16 THM 7
Austin, Alex. SF1 25
Austin, Benjamin Fish (1850-
1932) SF1 25
Austin, Erwin. FFC 20
Austin, Frederick Britten (1885-
1941) AOW 46, 96, 98 CSF 12
ES1 24 SFE 52 SF1 25
Austin, H. BAA 200
Austin, J. L. AAL 223
Austin, Jane Goodwin (1831-94)
SF1 25
Austin, John Osborne. CSF 12
Austin, Mary Hunter (1868-1934)
SF1 25 WGT 7 see also Gor-
don Stairs
Austin, Phyllis. CSF 12
Austin, William (1778-1841) CSF
12 SF1 25
Ausubel, Herman. BAA 200
Authwise, Eugene. BAA 30
Autolycus pseud. of Paul J.
Searles. IMS 191
Autran, Charles. BAA 168
Autrey, Gene. MSM 67
Auzias-Turenne, Raymond (1861-)
SF1 27
Avallone, Michael Angelo, Jr.
(1924-) ES1 25 FRN 57 SFE
54 SF1 27 SF2 802 WGT 8
see also Troy Conway
Aveling, Edward. WBW 21
Avenel, Anthony. ES1 25

Averill, Esther. FFC 82,112
Avery, Gillian. FFC 79
Avery, James. IMS 199-200,
202,204,210,247
Avi. FFC 139
Avice, Claude Pierre (1925-)
see Pierre Barbet
Avineri, Shlomo. BAA 200
Axelrod, George (1922-) ES1 25
Axhausen, Gunther. BAA 168
Aycock, Roger Dee (1914-) BAA
123 ES1 25 see also Roger Dee
Ayer, A.J. BAA 200
Ayer, Jacqueline. FFC 14
Ayer, James. BAA 221
Ayers, Clarence E. COT 26
Ayers, Stuart. IMS 33

Aylesworth, John B. (1938-) ES1
25 HFI 7 SFE 55 SF1 27 SF2
803
Aylesworth, Thomas Gibbons
(1927-) SF1 28 SF2 803
Ayme, Marcel Andre (1902-67)
ES1 25 FFC 12 HFI 7 IAC 42
SFE 55 SF1 28
Ayraud, Pierre (1908-) see
Thomas Narcejac
Ayre, Thornton pseud. of John
Russell Fearn. COT 73 VES
95
Ayrton, Michael (1921-75) ES1
25 SF1 28 SF2 803
Ayscough, John pseud. of Francis
B. Bickerstaffe-Drew. CSF 12

B

B.B. pseud. of James Denys
Watkins-Pitchford. SF1 28
Babbage, Charles. FTF 113
MFW 194
Babbitt, Natalie. FFC 2-3,46,
86,139
Babcock, Dwight Vincent (1909-)
ES1 26
Babcock, Elisabeth. FFC 153
Babcock, George. BAA 86 CSF
13 SF1 28
Babcock, William Henry (1849-
1922) BAA 168 CSF 13 SF1 28
Babel, Isaac. WAA 71
Babelon, Jean. BAA 200
Baber, Asa (1936-) IAC 42 SF1
28 SF2 803
Babeuf, Francois Noel. EXT
10/2 75 MSF 118-9
Babits, Mihaly (1883-1941) BYS
189 FBK 16 FL3 1121-3 SFE
55 SL2 708-11
Bacas, Paul Edmond. BAA 123

Bach, Johann Sebastian (1685-
1750) CUA 38-9 ETN 12 LTN
29,127,189 MIH 122 TDI 10
WFS 65
Bach, Marcus. BAA 200
Bach, Peggie. FFC 167
Bach, Richard David (1936-) FL2
808-10 SF1 28 SF2 803
Bachelard, Gaston. KAU 55,59
Bachelder, John. BAA 41 SF1
28 WGT 8 see also Former
Resident of the Hub
Bacheller, Addison Irving (1859-
1950) CSF 13 SF1 28
Bachelor, George C. CSF 13
SF1 28
Bachmann, Hans. EXT 2/1 5
Bachnow, Wladlen (1924-) LEX
172
Backus, W. Elwyn. WTS 32,34
Backvis, Claude. BAA 200
Bacon, Edgar Mayhew. IAC 42
Bacon, (Sir) Francis (1561-1626)

Bacon, (Sir) Francis (cont.)
ACE 27 AC2 25 ALW 32, 43, 45
AOW 19, 344 BAA 3 BYS 66
CAT 78 CSF 13 EXT 3/1 4, 30
EXT 4/2 18, 26 EXT 6/2 33, 35,
37 EXT 8/1 23 EXT 9/2 28
EXT 10/2 76 FAN 9, 15, 66, 68
FTF 19, 99 IAC 42 INT 49
KAU 28 MFW 5, 265, 268 MSF
23, 45, 65, 96, 100-2, 104, 108-10,
115, 129, 194, 197, 259 MSM 127-
8 NWO 114 POE 5, 23, 81 PST
24-6, 227, 237, 239, 261, 270, 272,
293, 302, 319 SFE 55-6 SFH
173, 218 SFN 92 SFS 10 SIH
65, 79 STF 39 STH 1 VES 124-
5, 160 VFS 173 WAA 53 WIF
35, 39, 49, 56, 227
Bacon, Gretrude. IAC 42
Bacon, Jonathan. SRB 281
Bacon, Joseph Dodge Daskam
(1876-1961) SF1 28
Bacon, Leonard. STH 8-9
Bacon, Martha Sherman (1917-)
FFC 3, 79, 170 SF1 28
Bacon, Peggy (1895-) FFC 29, 59,
92, 119 SF1 28
Bacon, Roger (1214?-1294?)
DTS 12 EXT 7/1 7 FTF 17-8,
100 POE 3 TJB 53, 57
Bacon, Walter. SF1 28
Baczko, Bronislaw. BAA 200
Bade, William Lemoine (1928-)
ES1 26 IAC 42 SFE 56 SFS 10
Baden, Frances Henshaw. CSF
183
Badger, Joseph Edward, Jr.
(1848-1909) CSF 13 SF1 28
Baen, James P. (1943-) ALW
220 IAC 42 LTN 248 SFE 56
WSF 280
Baer, Austin R. RFA 202
Baerlein, Anthony. CSF 13 SF1
29
Baerlein, Henry Philip Bernard
(1875-) ES1 26
Bagby, Stephen. W TS 24-5
Bagg, D. B. EXT 6/1 20
Bagley, John. CSF 13 SF1 29
Bagley, Simon. IAC 43
Bagnall, R. D. (1945-) SFE 56
Bagnall-Stubbs, James. SF1 29
Bahl, Franklin (house name)
WGT 8 see also Roger P. Graham
Bahnson, Agnew Hunter, Jr. (1915-

1964?) AOW 136 ES1 26 HFI 8
SFE 56 SF1 29
Bahr, Hans-Dieter. BAA 200
Bahr, Robert pseud. of Sam
Moskowitz. IMS 189
Bailey, Albert Edward (1871-1951)
SF1 581
Bailey, Andrew Jackson (1840-
1927) SF1 29
Bailey, Anthony. EXT 10/1 22
Bailey, Carolyn. FFC 80, 129
Bailey, Charles Waldo, II (1929-)
ES1 26 SFE 56 SF1 29 SF2 804
Bailey, Hilary (1936-) BAA 140
BYS 298, 305 IAC 43, 192 SFE
56 SF1 29 VES 123
Bailey, j(ames) O(sler) (1903-)
AAL 106, 143 ALW 7, 30, 68, 70,
75-6 AOW 79, 339 BAA 168, 200,
280 BRS 6 ES1 26 EXT 1/2 24
EXT 2/1 17-9 EXT 3/1 22 EXT
5/1 5, 16a EXT 7/1 1, 26-7 EXT
7/2 48 EXT 8/2 31-2, 58 EXT
9/1 2 EXT 9/2 28, 62 EXT 10/2
70 FAN 7 FRN 17 IMS 33 MFW
183 MSM xiv, 199, 217 NWO 17,
70-1 SFE 56 SFH 237 SFN 40,
48 SFW 16, 78 SF1 29 SF2 804
SRB 70, 497 TSF 245 VES 330
WIF 226 WSF 263
Bailey, Mike. LTN 268
Bailey, Paul Dayton (1906-) CSF
13 ES1 26 SFE 56 SF1 29
SF2 804
Bailey, Thomas pseud. of Edward
Bellamy Partridge. CSF 13
SF1 29
Bailey, William C. IAC 43
Baillie-Saunders, Margaret Elsie
(1873-1949) SF1 29
Bain, Francis William (1863-1940)
CSF 13 ES1 26 SF1 29
Bain, Willard. ES1 26
Bainbridge, Oliver. SF1 29
Baines, Cuthbert Edward. SF1
29
Bains, Louis. IMS 137
Bair, Patrick. BAA 118 ES1 26
MSM 74 see also David Gurney
Baird, Edward. WSF 296
Baird, Edwin (1886-1957) FBK 83
WIF 76 WTS 3-4, 14, 19, 21-3,
25, 27-8, 56-7
Baird, John Cranmer (1869-1922)
CSF 13 SF1 29

28

Baird, Theodore. MSF 224
Baker, Arthur Ponsford. SF1 29
Baker, Betty pseud. of Betty Lou
Baker Venturo (1928-) ES1 26
FFC 3, 46, 112 SF1 30
Baker, D. Petersen. SF1 30
Baker, Denys Val (1917-) ES1 26
SF1 30 SF2 804
Baker, Dorothy. IAC 43
Baker, Elizabeth. FFC 129
Baker, Emerson. SF1 30
Baker, Ernest A. BAA 200 EXT
4/2 17
Baker, Edgar Frank (1908-) CSF
13 ES1 26-7 SF1 30
Baker, George Augustus (1849-
1906) CSF 13 ES1 27 SF1 30
see also P. T. Olemy
Baker, George Philip (1879-1951)
SF1 30
Baker, Gordon. SF1 30
Baker, J. Wayne. BAA 200
Baker, James H. BAA 200
Baker, Jules. IAC 43
Baker, Margaret Joyce (1918-)
FFC 72, 82, 129 SF1 30
Baker, Nina Brown (1888-1957)
SF1 581
Baker, Olaf. FFC 72
Baker, Rachel Maddux (1912-)
WGT 8
Baker, Robert Allen (1921-) ES1
27
Baker, (Robert) Michael (Graham)
(1938-) FFC 95 SF1 30 SF2 804
Baker, Russell Wayne (1925-)
IAC 43 SFS 10 SF2 805 SF1 30
Baker, Scott (1947-) LEX 172
Baker, W. Howard. SF1 30
see also Peter Saxon
Baker, W. R. IAC 43
Baker, William Elliott Smith.
BAA 34 CSF 13
Bakhmetyev, Vladimir M. MSF
251
Bakhnov, Vladlen. IAC 43 SFS
10
Bakhtin, Mikhail. MSF 54, 56, 79
Bakunin, Michael. UKL 80, 117
Balch, Frank. CSF 14
Balch, William S. BAA 33
Balchin, Nigel (1908-70) BYS 256
ES1 27 EXT 8/1 5 HFI 8 IAC
43 SFE 56 SF1 30 WGT 8
Bald, R. C. FAN 186

Baldassarri, Mariano. BAA 200
Balderston, John L. CSF 14
SOT 152
Baldick, R. BYS 54, 110
Baldini, Massimo. BAA 168, 200
Baldissera, Alberta. BAA 200-1
Baldry, H. C. BAA 168, 201
Baldwin, (Mrs.) Alfred (1845-
1925) CSF 14 ES1 27 SF1 30
Baldwin, Bee. ES1 27 SFE 56
SF1 30
Baldwin, Edward C. BAA 201
Baldwin, F. Lee. EXT 3/1 22
IMS 94
Baldwin, James. EXT 10/2 106-
8 NWO 4
Baldwin, Michael. FFC 192
Baldwin, Oliver Ridsdale (1899-)
WGT 8 see also Martin Hussing-
tree
Balfour, Arthur. FAN 78
Balfour, Frederic Henry. CSF
14 WGT 8
Balfour, Margaret Melville. CSF
14 WGT 8
Balint, Emery (1892-) ES1 27
SF1 30
Balke, Betty T. IAC 43 STH 20-1
Ball, Brian Neville (1932-) ES1
27 HFI 8 IAC 43 LEX 172
SFE 57 SF1 31 SF2 805 WGT 9
Ball, Clifford. SOT 326
Ball, Frank Norman. BAA 135
SF1 31
Ball, Frank P. BAA 88 CSF 14
Ball, John Dudley, Jr. (1911-)
ES1 27 MSF 94 SFE 57 SF1
31 SF2 805 WBW 18-22, 25,
27, 31
Ball, Kurt Herwarth (1903-) LEX
172-3
Ball, Patricia Sylvia (1936-) SF2
1085
Ball, (Sir) Robert. EXT 5/2 41
IAC 43
Ball, W. W. R. IAC 43
Ballantine, Betty. ALW 186
WFS 197-8 WSF 247-8, 283,
301-2
Ballantine, Ian. ALW 186 ES1
28 WFS 196-9, 201, 229-30, 247
WSF 205-6, 225, 283, 301-2
Ballantine, Richard. WFS 198
Ballantyne, Robert Michael (1825-
1894) FAN 167 SF1 31 STH 184

Ballard, Guy Warren. WIF 50
Ballard, J(ames) G(raham) (1930-)
AAL 57 ALW 212,235-6 AOW
39,136-9,285,289,293-4,299
BAA 134-5,161 BFP 22-4 BYS
188,247,286,294-5,298-301,
303,317 CAT 17-8,104,137
CSC 55,74,173-4,227 DMK 215-
225 EFP 13 ES1 28 ETN 2,21,
32,55,65,105-7,139 EXT 7/2
47 EXT 8/1 16,18 EXT 10/1
47 EXT 10/2 115 FAN 153 FFR
14-6 FL4 2002-4 FTF 87,162-3
[FUT] HFI 8 IAC 43-5 INT 15,
22,26-7,51,69-70,80-1,91,103-
4,110 ISW 126 KAU 93,104,
127,146,184,189 LEX 173-5
MFW 24,251,290 MIH 5,105,
126-8 MSF 67,242 NDA 160,
212 NWO ix,76,135,147,187,
235,241,255 OSR 116-129,199-
203 POE 294 RHN 87,161 RGS
12-4 SFB 130-1 SFD 89,233,
295 SFE 57-8 SFS 10-1 SF1
31 SF2 806 SFW 220,277-82
SIH 54,56-7,95,118 SL1 453-6
SL2 629-38 SL3 1274-7 SL4
1994-8 SL5 2478-81 SRB 343
TSF 58-9 VES 131-3,152-3,165,
170,215,220,237,240-1,256,258,
261-2,302,310 VF2 82-105,200-
1 WAA 62-3,69,232,242 WFS
301 WSF 243,254-5,387
Ballinger, William Sanborn (1912-)
SF1 31 SF2 806 WGT 9
Ballou, Arthur W. (1915-) AOW
310 ES1 29 SF1 31 SF2 806
Ballou, William Hosea (1857-1937)
CSF 14 SF1 31
Balmer, Edwin (1883-1959) ALW
145 AOW 52,98-9 CSF 14 EFP
7 ES1 29 EXT 1/1 5 EXT 3/1
28 IAC 45 KAU 127,146-7 KWS
59 MSM 56-7,221 NWO 34,137-
9 PST 125-7,192,196,210,214,
229,241,246,253,259,264,275
SFB 19,128 SFE 58 SFS 11 SF1
31-2 SL5 2463-8 SOT 40,123,
206 SRB 11,297 STH 98,123-6,
132-3,138 VES 82,107,131 WIF
91 WSF 87,309,385
Balmer, Katherine. STH 124
Balmer, Thomas. STH 124
Balogh, Barnard. CSF 14 SF1 32
Balsdon, John Percy Vyvian Dacre

(1901-77) BAA 105 CSF 14 SFE
58 SF1 32 SF2 806
Baltadonis, John V. IMS 70-2, 79,
84, 95, 103, 105-7, 110, 115-7, 122-
3, 127, 136, 143, 147, 153-7, 162,
186, 200, 213, 222, 226, 232-6, 241,
250 WFS 58
Balter, Elsie. WGT 9 see also
Arthur Cooke
Balzac, Honore De
see De Balzac, Honore
Bamber, George Everett (1932-)
EFP 19 HFI 8 IAC 45 SFE 58
SFS 11 SF1 32 SF2 806
Bamber, Wallace R. STH 142-3
Bamburg, Lilian. CSF 14
Bamman, Henry A. (1918-) SF1
32 SF2 807
Bancroft, George. POE 82-3
Bancroft, R.W. VFS 56
Banda. VFS 21-2
Bandaranaike, (Mrs.) VFS 123
Baner, Skulda V. FFC 82
Bangs, John Kendrick (1862-1922)
CSF 14-5 ES1 29 FL2 752-6
IAC 45 PJF 56 SFE 58 SF1 32-
3 SOT 71 WGT 9 see also Two
Wags
Bangsund, John. LTN 16, 223
SF1 33
Banim, John (1798-1842) BAA 19
CSF 15 SF1 33 WGT 9
Banim, Michael (1796-1874) WGT
9
Banis, Victor. SF1 33
Banister, Manly Miles (1914-)
ES1 29 HFI 8 IAC 45 LEX 176
SFE 58 SFS 11 SF1 33 SF2 807
Bankoff, George Alexis (1903-)
see George Borodin
Banks, Lynne Reid. FFC 46
Banks, Raymond E. (1918?-)
ALW 212,219 ES1 29-30 IAC
45 SFE 58 SFS 11
Banks, Richard. FFC 12
Bannerman, (Sir) Alexander (1871-
1934) SF1 33
Bannett, Ivor. CSF 15 SF1 33
Banning, Margaret Culkin. BAA
201
Bannon, Barbara A. LTN 270
Bannon, Mark. SF1 33
Banta, R. E. WTS 80
Barag, G. SOI 161
Barbara pseud. of Mabel O. Wright

Barbara (cont.)
CSF 15
Barbeau, Clayton C. SF1 33
Barber, Antonia pseud. of Barbara
Anthony. FFC 160 SF1 33
Barber, Dorothy Elizabeth Klein.
EXT 10/1 22-3, 34, 37
Barber, Dulan Friar (1940-) SF1
33 SF2 807
Barber, Elsie Oakes. BAA 118
Barber, Margaret Fairless (1869-
1901) ES1 30 WGT 9
Barber, Otto. BAA 280
Barberis, Pierre. BAA 201
Barbet, Pierre pseud. of Claude
Pierre Avice. AOW 139 FFR 16
HFI 9 IAC 45 LEX 176 SFE 59
SF1 33 SF2 807
Barbor, Herbert Reginald. BAA
87 CSF 15 SF1 34
Barbould, (Mrs.) EXT 5/1 20
Barbour, Douglas. SFW 329-36
SL2 583-6, 681-6 SL4 1560-5
SL5 2482-7 TDI 8 UKL 100, 153,
173, 244-5
Barbour, Ian. KAU 5
Barbour, John. HEN 13-4, 23
Barbusse, Henri (1874-1935) CWN
30 SFE 59 SF1 34
Barclay, Alan pseud. of George
B. Tait. IAC 45 SFE 59 SFS
11 SF1 34
Barclay, Florence Louisa Charles-
worth (1862-1921) CSF 15 SF1
34 WGT 9 see also Oliver San-
dys
Barclay, Gabriel (house name)
SFE 59 WGT 9-10 see also
C. M. Kornbluth
Manly Wade Wellman
Barclay, Marguerite F. see
Helene Barczynka
Barczynka, Helene pseud. of
Marguerite F. Barclay. CSF 15
Bard, Stanley. VFS 117
Bardens, Dennis. ES1 30
Barfield, A(rthur) Owen (1898-)
AOW 396 ES1 30 EXT 10/1 39
SFE 59 SOI 7-9, 31, 71 WGT 10
Barfield, Rodney. BAA 201
Barfoot, John. IAC 45
Bargone, (Frederick) Charles
(1876-1957) WGT 10 see also
Claude Farrere
Barham, Richard Harris (1788-

1845) CSF 15 WGT 10
Baring, Maurice (1874-1945) CSF
15 ES1 30 IAC 45 SF1 34
Baring-Gould, Sabine (1834-1924)
BAA 168 CSF 15 ES1 30 SF1
34
Baring-Gould, William S. EXT
1/2 29
Barion, Hans. BAA 201
Barjavel, Rene (1911-) AOW 139
ES1 30 FFR 16 HFI 9 LEX
177 SFB 139-40 SFE 59 SF1
34 SL5 2389-91
Barker, Albert W. (1900-) SF1
34 SF2 807
Barker, Arthur W. BAA 92 SF1
34 SRB 6
Barker, Carol. FFC 86
Barker, Elsa (1869-1954) SF1 34
Barker, Eric. CSF 15
Barker, Granville pseud. of Har-
ley G. Granville-Barker. CSF
15
Barker, Gray. ES1 30
Barker, Leonard Noel (1882-)
WGT 10 see also L. Noel
Barker, Nugent. SF1 34
Barker, Shirley Francis (1911-
1965) ES1 30 SF1 34 SF2 807
Barker, Thomas W. HFI 9
Barkun, Michael. BAA 168 CSC
100
Barlow. ETN 63
Barlow, George. BAA 201
Barlow, J. Swindells. SF1 34
Barlow, James Henry Stanley
(1921-) BAA 130 ES1 30 SFE
59 SF1 34 SF2 808
Barlow, James William (1826-
1913) BAA 44 CSF 15 SF1 34
WGT 10
Barlow, Joel. MSF 139 POE 36-7
Barlow, Robert H. EXT 3/1 7, 9,
22 IMS 20, 93, 133-4, 178 SOT
308
Barmeyer, Eike. BAA 168
Barnaby, Hugo pseud. of Ernest
H. Fitzpatrick. CSF 15
Barnard, Marjorie Faith (1897-)
BAA 117 SF1 34 WGT 10 see
also M. Barnard Eldershaw
Barner, Marian F. EXT 3/1 21
Barnes, Arthur Kelvin (1911-69)
AOW 139 COT 189 DTS 18 ES1.
31 FFR 16-7 HFI 9 IAC 45

Barnes, Arthur Kelvin (cont.)
IMS 29,138 LEX 178 SFE 59
SF1 35 SF2 808 SOT 111,327,
357 VES 95,147 WGT 10 WIF
157,229 see also Kelvin Kent
Barnes, James (1866-1936) AOW
37 CSF 16 EXT 1/1 5 SF1 35
Barnes, Joshua. BAA 7 CSF 16
Barnes, M. J. E. AAL 3,78,169
Barnes, Myra Edwards (1933-)
SFE 59
Barnes, S. B. BAA 201
Barnes, Willis (1843-) SF1 35
Barnett, Ada. CSF 16 SF1 35
Barnett, (Rev.) Canon Samuel
August. BAA 51
Barney, B. H. SOT 106
Barney, John Stewart (1868-1925)
AOW 37,52 CSF 16 EXT 1/1
5 EXT 7/1 23 SFE 60 SF1 35
Barney, Maginel. FFC 96
Barney, Natalie Clifford (1878?-
1972) SF1 35
Barnhouse, Perl T. BAA 120
ES1 31 ISW 210-3 SF1 35
Barnum, P. T. MSF 197 SFN
109
Baron, Lawrence. BAA 201
Baron, Walter. CSF 16
Baronian, Jean-Baptiste. FBK
145
Baronte, Gerve. CSF 16
Barr, Alan. BAA 201
Barr, Densil Neve pseud. of
Douglas Norton Buttrey. BAA
125 ES1 31 SFE 60 SF1 35
Barr, Donald (1921-) EXT 10/1
22 HFI 9 SFE 60 SF1 35 SF2
808
Barr, George (1938-) FRN 107,
166 SFE 60 SRB 126 VES 186,
208,234,291
Barr, James Angus Evan Abbot
(1862-1923) CSF 16 SF1 35
Barr, Martin W. CSF 16
Barr, Robert (1850-1912) ALW
82 AOW 52 CSF 16 ES1 31
IAC 45 SFE 60 SF1 35 STH 35,
73-4 VES 149 WGT 10
Barr, Stephen. IAC 45 SFS 11
Barr, Tyrone C. ES1 31 HFI 9
SFE 60 SF1 35
Barrault, Jean Louis. WAA 90
Barren, Charles MacKinnon (1913-)
SFE 60 SF1 35 SF2 808

Barrenechea, Ana Maria. EXT
9/1 17
Barrett, Alfred Walter (1869-)
WGT 10 see also R. Andom
Barrett, Charles Lee (1909-) ES1
31
Barrett, Eaton Stannard (1786-
1820) SF1 35
Barrett, Ethel. SF1 35
Barrett, Frank (1848-1926) CSF
16 SF1 35
Barrett, Geoffrey John (1928-)
SFE 60 SF1 35-6 SF2 808
Barrett, Laurence I. (1935-) SF1
36 SF2 808-9
Barrett, Mike. FLR 62
Barrett, Neal, Jr. FFR 17 HFI
9 IAC 45 SFE 60 SF1 36 SFS
11
Barrett, William Edmund (1900-)
CSF 16 ES1 31 EXT 6/1 18
HFI 9 SFE 60 SF1 36 SF2 809
Barrie, (Sir) James Matthew
(1860-1937) ALW 89,91 CSF 16
ES1 31 FBK 114 FFC 173-4
FL1 358-9 FL3 1230-3 SF1 36
Barringer, Daniel Moreau (1900-)
ES1 31 SF1 36
Barringer, Leslie (1895-1968)
FL3 1099-104 HFI 9 SF1 36
Barrington, Michael pseud. of
Barrington J. Bayley, Michael
Moorcock. CSF 16 SFE 60
Barron, Arthur S. EXT 1/2 29
Barron, Donald Gabriel (1922-)
ES1 31 SFE 60 SF1 36
Barron, Neil (1934-) AOW ix-
xiii,xv-xxi,337-91 BAA 168,
201 FHT 66 FL5 2517-38 PJF
40,73 RHN 196 SFE 60 SL3
1424-8 SL5 2366-9 SRB 64
TSF 242-58 WSF 381
Barron, William. WTS 20
Barroso, Magdaleno Girao. BAA
201
Barrow, Percy. CSF 16
Barrows, Marjorie. IAC 45
Barrows, P. S. see Cepre
Sarbrow
Barrows, Ruth Marjorie Wescott.
ES1 31-2 SF1 36 SF2 809
Barry, Iris (1895-) CSF 16 SF1
36
Barry, Richard Hayes (1881-)
CSF 16 SF1 36

Barry, William. BAA 201
Barry, William Francis (1849-1930) CSF 17 POE 219-20 SF1 36
Barrymore, Lionel. SFB 49
Barshofsky, Philip. IAC 45
Barsky, Arthur. SF1 36
Barstow, Emmuska Orcay (1865-1947) WGT 10
Bartel, Philip Jacques. DTS 15 IMS 34, 84
Bartelt, Robert. FFC 193
Barter, Alan Frank (1933-) ES1 32 IAC 45-6 SF1 36 SF2 809
Barth, Barry. LTN 269
Barth, John (1928-) ALW 31, 238 AOW 140, 351 BAA 141-2 BYS 257 CAT 17 ES1 32 ETN 12 FBK 153 FL1 236-41 FL2 616-8 HFI 9 IAC 46 KVT 28 NWO 9, 36 SFD 4 SFE 60-1 SF1 36-7 SF2 809-10 SL2 873-7 SOI xiii STF 8, 69
Barth, Melissa E. FL1 347-9 FL2 690-4 FL3 1169-72, 1423-7
Barthell, Robert. KAU 9 TSF 219-27
Barthelme, Donald (1931-) BYS 257 ES1 32 ETN 12, 99, 141 EXT 8/1 17 FBK 153 FL1 347-9 FL3 1423-7 IAC 46 RSG 77 SFD 4 SFE 61 SFS 11
Barthes, Roland. BAA 201 CAT 54 JGB 6-7 KAU 55 MSF 18, 43, 50-1, 54, 61, 147 STF 4 TDI 3-5, 9
Bartholomew, Cecilia. MSM 92, 105
Bartier, Pierre. SFB 110
Bartle, L. E. WGT 10
Bartlett pseud. of Lewis A. Ricci. CSF 17
Bartlett, Frederick O. CSF 17
Bartlett, John (1820-1905) ASF 119
Bartlett, Alice Elinor Bowen (1848-1920) WGT 10-1
Bartlett, Frederick Orin (1876-1945) SF1 37
Bartlett, Landell. ES1 32 CSF 17 SF1 37
Bartlett, Maurice. FFC 133
Bartlett, Vernon Oldfield (1894-) BAA 102 CSF 17 SF1 37 SF2 810

Barton, Catherine Josephine (1857-) CSF 17 SF1 37
Barton, Eustace Robert (1854-) WGT 11 see also Robert Eustace
Barton, Ralph. IAC 46
Barton, Samuel. AOW 37, 52 CSF 17 EXT 1/1 5 EXT 7/1 27 SFE 61 SF1 37
Barton, William Renald, III (1950-) HFI 10 SFE 61 SF1 37 SF2 810
Bartsch, Gunter. BAA 201
Baruch, Hugo Cyril K. (1907-) BAA 112 ES1 32 WGT 11
Barzevi, A. H. BAA 96-7 CSF 17 SF1 37
Barzman, Ben. ES1 32 HFI 10 SFE 61 SF1 37
Barzun, Jacques. EXT 6/1 20
Basch, Joan Patricia. IAC 46 SFS 11
Basevi, (Col.) Charles Edward. CSF 17
Bashford, Henry Howarth (1880-1961) CSF 17 ES1 32
Basil, Otto (1901-) LEX 178-9 SF1 37 SF2 811
Bass, T. J. pseud. of Thomas J. Bassler. AOW 140 BAA 152, 161 CSC 77, 83-6 HFI 10 IAC 46 LEX 179 RGS 14-5 SFE 61 SF1 37 SL2 940-4 VES 220
Bassett, Edward Barnard. BAA 28 WGT 11
Bassler, Thomas Joseph (1932-) BFP 25 SF2 811 WGT 11 see also T. J. Bass
Bastard, George. EXT 2/1 8
Bastide, Roger. BAA 202
Bastos, Augusto Roa. FBK 134
Bataille, Georges. TFC 159-60
Bataller, Ferrandiz Jose. EXT 6/1 14
Batchelor, John M. BAA 38, 163 SF1 37
Bateman, Robert Moyes Carruthers (1922-73) BAA 138 BYS 295 ES1 32 HFI 10 SFE 61 SF1 37 SF2 811 STH 66
Bates, Arlo (1850-1918) CSF 17 ES1 32-3 SF1 37
Bates, Chris. LTN 238
Bates, Emily Katharine. CSF 17
Bates, H. W. EXT 6/2 34-5
Bates, Harry (1900-) ALW 129,

Bates, Harry (cont.)
141, 219 AOW 293 BFP 26 COT
14, 147 ES1 33 ETN 12 EXT
7/2 39 IAC 46 IMS 8 KAU 155
KWS 25-6 LEX 179-80 MSM 31
RFA vii-xxii, 4, 9-10, 12, 14, 18,
22, 30, 32, 36, 64, 83, 93, 153, 182-
4 SFB 82 SFD 25-7, 29, 320
SFE 61 SFS 11 SOT 16, 93, 206
SRB 12 STH 266 VES 148, 178
WGT 11 WSF 53-4, 56-7, 67, 75,
98, 217, 309, 383 WTS 132 see
also Anthony Gilmore, H. G.
'Winter
Bates, Herbert Ernest (1905-74)
CSF 17 ES1 33 SF1 37 WGT 11
Bates, Ralph (1899-) ES1 33
Bates, Russell L. IAC 46
Bates, William H. IAH 66 SFB
89
Batherman, Muriel. FFC 63
Bathrick, David. BAA 202
Bathurst, Benjamin. RFA 163
Batista, Fulgencio. RHN 65
Batkin, Leonid M. BAA 202
Bato, Joseph. FFC 3, 185
Batt, Leon. SF1 37
Batteau, Dwight W. (1916-) AAL
66 ES1 33 IAC 46 SFS 11
Battegazzore, Antonio M. BAA
202
Baudelaire, Charles Pierre (1821-
67) ASF 165 BYS 43, 93 EXT
6/1 6 EXT 7/2 33 FBK 37, 74
HEN 12, 51 MSF 168 MSM 103
SHL 60 THM 8 WFS 32 WIF 45
Baudet, Henri. BAA 169
Baudin, Henri. BAA 169
Bauer, Gerald M. IAC 46
Bauer, Hermann. BAA 169
Bauer, Ludwig. CSF 17
Bauer, Wolfgang. BAA 169 ES1
33
Baugh. 2/1 17
Baughman, Grace A. SF1 38
Baum, L(yman) Frank (1856-1919)
AOW 304, 310 COT 205 CSF 17
ES1 33 FBK 113-5 FFC 102, 174
FFR 17 FL3 1196-1208 IAC 46
ISW 43 PJF 12, 16, 63 RAH 167
SFD 208 SFE 62 SFN 40 SFW
59, 130, 132 SF1 38 SOT 191, 394
SRB 23 TRB 105 WGT 11 WIF
149
Baum, Thomas. FFC 139 HFI 10

IAC 46 SF1 38
Bauman, Carolyn Busey. SF1 38
Baumann, Zygmunt. BAA 169
Baumer, Franz. BAA 169
Baumgardt, Doris. IMS 245 WFS
78-9, 92-3, 96-7, 108, 118-22, 124,
127-8, 131-2, 135, 144-4, 207 see
also Leslie Perri
Baumgardt, Lois. IMS 245
Baumgartl, Isidor (1860-) SF1 38
Baumgartner, Robert. FFC 133
Baumhauer, H. FFC 105
Baumhofer, Walter M. TSP 22
Bax, Martin (1933-) SFE 62
Baxter, Caroline. FFC 101
Baxter, Charles. IAC 46
Baxter, Garrett. BAA 95-6, 98
Baxter, George Owen pseud. of
Frederick Faust. TSP 132
Baxter, Gregory pseud. of Eric
De Banzie, John Ressich. CSF
17
Baxter, John Martin (1939-) ALW
187, 191 AOW 339 BRS 11 ES1
33-4 HFI 10, 183 IAC 46 KAU
198 MFW 100 SFE 62 SFS 11
SF1 38 SF2 811 WGT 11-2
Baxter, Maria. ES1 34
Baxter, Richard. BAA 5
Baxter, Sylvester. BAA 202
Bayldon, Arthur Albert. ES1 34
Bayle, (Monsieur) pseud. of
Simon Tyssot De Patot. SF1 38
Bayley, Barrington J. (1937-)
AAL 59 BFP 27 FFR 17 HFI
10 IAC 46 RGS 15 SFE 62 SF1
38 SF2 812 SL3 1126-9 VES
178 WGT 12 see also Michael
Barrington, P. F. Woods
Bayley, G. W. WTS 22
Bayley, Victor. BAA 105
Bayliss, Alfred Edward MacDuff
(1892-1961) IAC 46 SF1 38 ES1
34
Bayliss, John Clifford (1919-) ES1
34 IAC 46 SF1 38 SF2 812
Bayliss, Marguerite Farlee (1895-)
CSF 17 SF1 39
Bayly, Ada Ellen (1857-1903) see
Edna Lyall
Bayne, Charles Joseph (1870-)
BAA 62 CSF 17 SF1 39
Baynes, Pauline. FBK 126 FFC
71, 89, 177
Bazhov, Pavel Petrovich (1879-

Bazhov, Pavel P. (cont.)
1950) SF1 39
Beach, Charles A. pseud. of
Mayne Reid. CSF 17 SF1 39
Beach, Rex. STH 126
Beachcomber. VFS 267
Beachcroft, Nina. FFC 185
SF1 39
Beadle, Irwin. ALW 74, 78-9
Beagle, Peter S(oyer) (1939-)
ALW 212 ASF 328, 330 BFP 28
CSC 34 ES1 34 EXT 10/1 22
FFR 17 FL2 526-34 HFI 10
IAC 46 SFD 318 SFE 62 SF1
39 SF2 812 SRB 252
Beal, John Robinson (1906-)
SF1 39
Beale, Charles Willing (1845-
1932) AOW 52 CSF 17 EXT 1/1
6 EXT 5/1 4 SFE 62 SF1 39
Beals, Carleton (1893-) CSF 17
SF1 39 SF2 812
Beaman, Emeric Hulme. CSF 18
Beamish, Annie O'Meara De Vic
(1883-) SF2 see also Noel De
Vic Beamish
Beamish, Noel De Vic pseud. of
Annie O'Meara De Vic Beamish.
SF1 39
Bean, Normal pseud. of Edgar
Rice Burroughs. ALW 108
SFB 46
Bean, Norman pseud. of Edgar
Rice Burroughs. SFB 46 WIF
65
Beane, Sawney. TSP 196
Bear, Greg (1951-) IAC 46 LEX
180-1 VES 153
Beard, Charles A. BAA 101
Beard, Daniel Carter (1850-1941)
BAA 46 SF1 39 SOT 236-7
Beard, Henry N. SF1 39
Beard, James H. IAC 46 SOT
179, 236 WGT 12 see also
Philip James
Beard, John Relly (1800-76) CSF
18 SF1 39
Beard, Wolcott Le Clear. CSF 18
Beardsley, Aubrey Vincent (1872-
98) ES1 34 EXT 6/2 32 FBK 70
SF1 39
Bearne, Colin Gerald (1939-) SF1
39 SF2 813
Beatie, Bruce A. EXT 10/1 22,
34

Beaton, George pseud. of Edward
Fitz-Gerald Brenan. SF1 39
Beaton-Jones, Cynon. FFC 153
Beattie, Eunice. CWN 56
Beattie, George B. STH 142
Beatty, Jerome, Jr. (1918-) AOW
306, 310 ES1 34 SF1 39-40 SF2
813
Beatty, John (1828-1914) CSF 18
EXT 1/1 6 SF1 40
Beatty, Rose Mabel (1879-1932)
CSF 18 SF1 40
Beauchamp, Gorman. AAL 200
BAA 202
Beauclerk, Helen De Vere (1892-
1969) CSF 18 SF1 40
Beaujohn, Paul pseud. of Beatrice
Lamberton Warde. CSF 18 SF1
40
Beaumont, Charles pseud. of
Charles Nutt. ALW 212 BYS
261, 279 COT 169 ETN 98 EXT
8/1 6 FBK 154 FFR 17 HFI 10
IAC 46-7 ISW 129-30, 221 KWS
97-8 LEX 180 MFW 246 SFE
63 SFS 12, 90 SFW 471 SF1 40
SOT 300
Beaumont, Donna Brooks see
John G. Claxton
Beaumont, Edgar. WGT 12
Beaumont, Jack. IMS 97
Bebbington, William George.
ES1 34
Bechdolt, Jack pseud. of John
Ernest Bechdolt. CSF 18 SFE
63 SF1 40
Bechdolt, John Ernest (1884-1954)
ES1 34 HFI 10 WGT 12 see
also Jack Bechdolt
Becher, Don. SF1 40
Bechhofer, C. E. CSF 18
Bechtel, Louise S. EXT 10/1 23
Beck, Calvin Thomas (1930-) ES1
34 SF1 40
Beck, Christopher pseud. of
Thomas C. Bridges. CSF 18
Beck, Claire P. IMS 46, 63-5, 94,
105-6, 110-1, 133-4, 178-80
Beck, Clyde F. IMS 46, 65, 178
VES 326-7
Beck, Evelyn Torton. BAA 202
Beck, J. H. BAA 202
Beck, Louisa Adams (-1931) CSF
18 ES1 34-5 SF1 40 WGT 12
see also L. Moresby

Beck, Robert E. SF1 40
Beck, William S. CAT 133
Becke, Louis (1855-1913) ES1 35
Becker, Carl. BAA 169 EXT
1/2 25 EXT 2/2 33 MFW 290
Becker, George J. BAA 202
Becker, Kurt (1915-) ES1 35 SF1
41
Becker, Mary Kay. SF1 41
Becker, Stephen. IAC 47 SFS 12
Beckett, Samuel. AOW 358 BYS
9,257,319 CUA 3-4 CWN 10,36
FBK 134 IAC 47 NWO 9
Beckford, William (1760-1844)
ALW 45 BYS 16-7,29,108 CSF
18 ES1 35 FBK 20-2,24,83
FL4 2023-8 HFI 10 MIH 11,79
PST 27 SF1 41 SIH 16 TFC 77
WAA 82 WIF 41
Beckman, Charles, Jr. IAC 47
Beckman, Kaj. FFC 11
Beckmann, Johannes. BAA 202
Becquer, Gustavo Adolpho (1836-
70) FBK 16,141
Beddoes, Thomas Henry Willough-
by. CSF 18
Bede, Venerable. COT 93 EXT
6/2 26
Bedford, Sybille. SFW 101-2
Bedford-Jones, Henry (1887-1949)
IAC 47 SFE 63 SF1 41 TSP 85,
145 WGT 12 WTS 44
Beebe, Maurice. NWO 63
Beecher, Edward N. CSF 18
Beecher, Jonathan. BAA 203
Beeching, Jack. ES1 35 HFI 11
SFE 64 SF1 41 SF2 813
Beecroft, John. FFC 129
Beeding, Francis pseud. of John
Leslie Palmer, Hilary A. Saun-
ders. CSF 19
Beeger, Lina. BAA 203
Beeks, Graydon. FFC 139
Beemish, Cragg. SF1 41
Beer, Gillian. CAT 51,62,89
Beer, Lionel. IAC 47
Beer, Patricia. IAC 47
Beer, Richard Cameron (1894?-
1959) SF1 41
Beer, Stafford. MFW 219
Beer, Wilhelm. FTF 21
Beerbohm, (Sir) (Henry) Max(imil-
ian) (1872-1956) CSF 19 ES1 35
FL1 423-4 FL3 1378-9 FL5
2217-9 IAC 47-8 SF1 41

Beery, Wallace. WIF 56
Beesley, Dorothy Gladys Smith
(1896-) WGT 12
Beetem, Doris. IAC 48
Beethoven, Ludwig Von see Von
Beethoven, Ludwig
Begbie, (Edward) Harold (1871-
1929) CSF 19 SFE 64 SF1 41
WGT 12
Begbie, Jean. CSF 19
Begley, Walter. BAA 203
Begouen, Max Henri. CSF 19
SFE 64 SF1 41
Behan, Brendan. VFS 117
Beheim-Schwarzbach, Martin.
CSF 19
Behl, C. F. W. BAA 203
Behn, (Mrs.) Aphra. BAA 8
Behn, Harry (1898-1973) FFC 129
SF1 41 SF2 814
Behrens, William W., III. IAC
48 INT 48
Behrman, S. N. SFN 96
Beiderbecke, Bix. EXT 7/2 37
Beith, John Hay (1876-1952) WGT
12 see also Ian Hay
Beja, Morris. ACC 123,143 EXT
10/2 67-8 OSR 263-5,354
Belarski, Rudolph. TSP 30
Belasco, David (1853-1931) CSF
19 SF1 41 WGT 12-3
Belaval, Emilio S. IAC 48
Belayev, Alexander (1884-1942)
ES1 35 IAC 48 LEX 181 MSF
260,263 SFE 65 SFS 12 SF1
42 SOT 431
Belcher, C. Davis. IAC 48
Belfont, Ronald. CSF 19
Belfour, Hugo John (1802-27)
WGT 13 see also St. John Dorset
Belgion, Montgomery. EXT 8/2 56
Beliard, Octave. EXT 2/1 8
Beling, Mabel Ashe. ES1 35-6
Belisarius. SFA 113-5
Belkin, Norman. IAC 48
Bell, Alexander Graham. ALW
63,81 MSF 194 VFS 106,241,
245,249-50,254
Bell, Corydon. FFC 74
Bell, Daniel. BAA 203 POE 314
VFS 187
Bell, Emerson. STH 163 see also
Gilbert Patten, Burt L. Stan-
dish

Bell, Eric Temple (1883-1960)
ALW 141 BFP 29-30 COT 291
ES1 36 EXT 3/1 28 EXT 5/1 3
EXT 7/2 38 IAC 48 IMS 138,159
MIH 22 OWB 21-2 RFA 32 SFB
135 SFN 47 SFS 12 SRB 295,
304 VES 137 WGT 13 WIF 85,
187 see also John Taine
Bell, Florence E. CSF 19
Bell, George W. BAA 67 CSF 19
SF1 42 WIF 112
Bell, Harry. SRB 127
Bell, Henry Hesketh. CSF 19
Bell, John J. CSF 19
Bell, John Keble (1875-1928) WGT
13 see also Keble Howard
Bell, Neal. HFI 11 SF1 42
Bell, Neil pseud. of Stephen
Southwold. CSF 19 SFE 64
SF1 42
Bell, Norman Edward (1899-) ES1
36 FFC 153 SF1 42 SF2 814
Bell, Paul W. SF1 42
Bell, Robert. CSF 19 ES1 36
SF1 42
Bell, S. G. BAA 203
Bell, Thornton. HFI 11
Bell, William Dixon. CSF 19
SF1 42
Bellairs, John (1938-) FFC 29,185
FL1 508-10 SF1 42 SF2 814 SRB
252
Bellamy, Charles J. BAA 35,39
Bellamy, Edward (1850-98) ALW
33,60-2,95 AOW 34,52-3,344,
348 ASF 143 BAA xviii-xix,38-
9,56,58,203 BYS 66,87 CAT
10,78,138 COT 259 CSC 131
CSF 19-20 ES1 36-7 EXT 1/1 6
EXT 2/2 32-3 EXT 5/1 4,16
EXT 5/2 31 EXT 6/2 40 EXT
7/1 20,27 EXT 7/2 48 EXT 8/2
37 EXT 9/1 4,18 EXT 9/2 31,
33 EXT 10/2 74,86,99 FAN 4,
10,26,33-4,41,59,66,76,175
FFR 18 FTF 42,65,70,100-2
HFI 11 HID 125 IAC 48 INT 49
MFW 121-2,287 MIH 26,102
MSF 54,76,87,120,144,165,169,
171-80,182-4,188-94,198-201,
203,218,220,247,251,267,279
MSM 143,166 NDA 17,199 NWO
vi,12,20,96-7,102-18,126 OSR
282-88 OWB 16 POE 22,126,
153,161-4 PST 49,56,59-60,71,

73,82,93,95,107,198,213,225-6,
236,247-8,276,281,291,293-5,
298,303,319 RHN 12 SFE 64-5
SFN 12 SFS 12 SF1 42 SIH 60,
74,76-7,79,170 SL3 1246-50
SRB 10-1 STH 1 VES 124,126,
148,160,255,260 WAA 20,149
WBW 31,33 WIF 39,57,173,242
WSF 342 YTS 4-6,9,11-2,30,
36,51,62-3
Bellamy, Francis Rufus (1886-
1972) ES1 37 HFI 11 ISW 96-7
SFE 65 SF1 42
Bellamy, Hans Schindler (1901-)
ES1 37 EXT 7/1 16 NWO 7
Bellem, Robert Leslie. TSP 144
Beller, William Stern (1919-)
ES1 37
Bellessort, Andre. EXT 2/1 9
Belli, Angela. MFW 63
Bellin, Edward J. (house name)
WGT 13 see also Henry Kuttner
Belling, Rudolph. IAC 48
Bellini, Tina see Salambo Forest
Belloc, Joseph Hilaire (1870-1953)
BAA 93 CSF 20 EXT 8/2 49
SFE 65 SF1 43 TSP 66
Belloni, Antonio. WAA 235
Belot, Adolphe. CSF 20
Belove, Benjamin (1880-) CSF 20
SF1 43
Bellow, Saul (1915-) ETN 98 NWO
3,29 SFB 10 SFE 65 STF 22
STH 45 VFS 187
Bellows. WBW 30
Bellsmith, Henry Wentworth. BAA
56
Bemlemans, Ludwig. FFC 82
IAC 48
Ben-Ami, Gad. BAA 201
Benary-Isbert, Margot (1889-)
FFC 3 SF1 43
Benchley, Nathaniel Goddard
(1915-) FFC 3,60,113 SF1 581
Bendau, Clifford P. SL2 543-7,
940-4 SL5 2079-84,2463-8
Bendemann, Oswald. BAA 280
Bender, John. TSP 160
Bendick, Jeanne. FFC 35,107
Bendiner, Robert. COT 201
Bendix, Hans (1898-) SF1 43
Benedict, Myrle. IAC 48 SFS 12
Benedict, Ruth. EXT 7/2 37 RAH
161-2

Benedict, Steve (1899-) IAH 35
VES 133 WGT 13
Benedict, Stewart Hurd (1924-)
ES1 37 SF1 43
Benedikt, Michael. IAC 48
Benefield, John Barry (1883-)
CSF 20 ES1 37 SF1 43
Benello, C. George. BAA 156
Benet, Laura (1884-) ES1 37 SF1
43 SF2 814
Benet, Robert Ames. STH 57-8
Benet, Stephen Vincent (1898-1943)
ALW 38 COT 232-3, 235, 241, 245-
6, 248, 252, 291 CSF 20 ES1 37-8
EXT 5/1 4 EXT 7/2 37 EXT 8/1
5 FAN 168 FFR 18 FL3 1428-
32 IAC 48 IMS 2 INT 54, 97
ISW 35, 110 MFW 22, 36 MSM
33 SFE 66 SFN 40 SFS 12 SF1
43 SOT 205 STH 84 VES 167
WSF 129
Benford, Greg(ory) (1941-) AAL
126-7 ALW 212 AOW 140, 289
ASF 151-2 BFP 31 CAT 134
COT 27, 285 CSC 68 DMK 251-
9 ETN 10, 35, 43, 121-2 FFR 18
HFI 11 IAC 48 LEX 181-2 MFW
286 RGS 15-6 SFE 66-7 SF1
43 SF2 814 SL2 1004-7 SL3
1026-30 SRB 371, 497 SV3 44-
52 VES 82-3
Benford, James. DTS 42 IAC 48
Benham, Charles. CSF 20 SF1
43
Benites, Manuel. CWD 35
Benjamin, Harold R. W. see J.
Abner Peddiwell, Raymond
Wayne
Benjamin, Judy-Lynn. WFS 290
see also Judy-Lynn Del Rey
Benjamin, Lewis Saul (1874-1932)
ES1 38 WGT 13
Benjamin, Marcus. EXT 5/2 41
Benjamin, Park. EXT 7/1 27
SRB 10
Bennet, Robert Ames (1870-1954)
BAA 64 CSF 20 EXT 1/1 6 MFW
120, 127, 131-3 SF1 43 see also
Lee Robinet
Bennett. WTS 93
Bennett, Alfred Gordon (1901-62)
CSF 20 ES1 38 SFE 67 SF1 43
Bennett, Anna Elizabeth. FFC
185

Bennett, Arnold. ALW 144 CAT
75 EXT 8/2 55 FAN 12 LTN
118 SIH 43 STF 6 STH 182, 206
Bennett, Arthur (1862-1931) BAA
46, 62 POE 151 SF1 44
Bennett, Carl. LTN 238
Bennett, Charles A. BAA 203
SOT 246
Bennett, Diana. BAA 150 SF1 44
Bennett, Donald C. BAA 203
Bennett, Enoch Arnold (1867-1931)
CSF 20 STH 196 SF1 44
Bennett, Floyd. WFS 11, 30
Bennett, G. J. IAC 48
Bennett, Geoffrey Martin (1909-)
ES1 38 SF2 1067 WGT 13
Bennett, George. ES1 38
Bennett, Gertrude Barrows (1884-
1939?) ALW 114 BAA 82-3 BFP
32 ES1 38 WGT 13 see also
Frances Stevens
Bennett, H. STH 196
Bennett, James Clark (1866? -
1942) SF1 44
Bennett, Jeff. SF1 44
Bennett, John (1865-1956) ES1 38
SF1 44
Bennett, Keith. COT 65 IAC 48
SFS 12
Bennett, Kemys Deverell (1919-)
ES1 38-9 IAC 48 SFS 12 SF1 44
Bennett, Margot M. (1912-) AOW
140 ES1 39 HFI 11 ISW 250-3
SFE 67 SF1 44 SF2 814
Bennett, Richard M. BAA 109
CSF 99 FFC 18, 36, 100 SF1 44
Bennett, Robert. HFI 11
Bennett, William Edward (1898-)
ES1 39 WGT 13
Benoit, Pierre (1886-1962) CSF
20 ES1 39 FL1 69-70 HFI 11
MSF 261 SF1 44 VES 140 WIF
51
Benrekassa, Georges. BAA 203
Bensell, E. B. FFC 181
Bensen, Donald Roynold (1927-)
ES1 39 IAC 48 SFE 67 SF1 44
SF2 815 SRB 373 WSF 206, 248
Bensen, Greg. COT 70
Benson, Allan Ingvald. WGT 13
Benson, Arthur Christopher
(1862-1925) BAA 78 CSF 20
ES1 39 SFE 67 SF1 44
Benson, Edward Frederick (1867-
1940) CSF 20-1 ES1 39-40 FBK

Benson, Edward F. (cont.)
63 FL3 1433-5 IAC 48 SFE 67
SF1 44 SOT 73,368 WIF 71
Benson, Edwin (house name) WGT
13 see also Richard Shaver
Benson, Hugh. IAH 57-8,60
Benson, Robert Hugh (1871-1914)
BAA 70 CSF 21 ES1 40 EXT
2/2 28 EXT 9/2 38 FAN 145
PST 93-4,198,248,268,276,292
SFE 67 SF1 45 STH 3-4 VES
128
Benson, Stella (1892-1933) CSF
21 ES1 40 IAC 48 SF1 45
Benson, Theodora (1906-) ES1 40
Bentham. EXT 8/1 21
Bentley, John (1908-) ES1 40 HFI
11 SF1 45
Bentley, Joseph Goldridge. EXT
6/1 12
Bentley, Norman K. CSF 21
SF1 45
Bentley, Wilder. BAA xx,169
Bentlif, Syd. ES1 40 SF1 45
Benveniste, Asa. IAC 48
Benwell, Gwen. ES1 40
Beraud, Henri. CSF 21
Berckmann, Evelyn Domenica
(1900-) ES1 40 SF1 45 SF2 815
WGT 13
Bercovitch, Sacvan. NWO 35
Berdanier, Paul F. SFS 12
Berdyaev, Nicholas. FAN 83
POE 235 SFB 92
Berenberg, David P. BAA 203
Berens, Lewis H. BAA 56
Beres, Louis Rene. BAA 169
Beresford, Elizabeth. ES1 40
FFC 60,129,170 SF1 45
Beresford, J(ohn) D(avys) (1873-
1947) ALW 144 AOW 53 BAA
79,110,112,169 CSF 21 ES1
40-1 EXT 8/2 56 EXT 9/2 44
HFI 11 IAC 48 LEX 182 RFA
81 SFB 89 SFE 67-8 SF1 45
SIH 183-4 SL2 945-9 SL4
1780-3 SOT 214 SRB 11,15
STH 36-8,74 VES 261 WSF 20-
1,386
Beresford, Leslie. BAA 86 CSF
21-2 SFE 68 SF1 45 WGT 13-4
see also Pan
Beresford, Marcus see Marc
Brandel
Berg, Alban. WFS 105

Berg, Bjorn. FFC 22
Berg, Joan. FFC 55
Bergamini, David. HFI 11
Bergaust, Erik R. (1925-) ES1 41
Berge, Francois. EXT 2/1 9
Bergengren, Ralph. FFC 95
Berger, Albert I. BAA 203 COT
213-4,298,301 SL1 265-71,493-
6 SL2 533-8,548-53 SL3 1062-
7 SL5 2127-31
Berger, David. TSP 22
Berger, Hans. AAL 111
Berger, Harold L. (1923-) BAA
169,280 RAH 258 SFE 68 SRB
68 TSF 245
Berger, Harry, Jr. BAA 203
MSF 52
Berger, Michael. IAC 48
Berger, Peter. KAU 85
Berger, Thomas Louis (1924-)
BAA 156 FL1 57-60 HFI 11
IAC 48 SFE 68 SF1 45 SF2 815
Berger, Yves (1936-) ES1 41 SFE
68
Bergerac, Cyrano De see De Ber-
gerac, Cyrano
Bergeron, Richard. IAH 1 MIH
7
Bergey, Earle K. (-1952) ES1 41
ISW 284 SFE 68 SRB 43 VES
149,187,194,289,291 WAA 146
WSF 120
Berggren, Elfred. SIH 139
Bergier, Jacques. NWO 11 SFB
120
Bergin, Paul A. HFI 183 SF1 45
Bergler, Edmund. IAH 145 MIH
144
Berglund, Edward P. FBK 81
SF1 45 SRB 67
Bergman, Ingmar. CSC 264
Bergman, Ingrid. WAA 90
Bergmann, Franz. CSF 22
Bergmann, Gustav. CSC 109,118,
182
Bergner, Yosl. FBK 128
Bergonzi, Bernard (1929-) AOW
339 BAA 169 BYS 115 COT 9,
297 EXT 8/2 31,37-9,41,55-6,
60-2 EXT 9/1 22 FAN 17,34,
37 KAU 94 MSF 222-3 NWO
95,134 OSR 204-15,354 SFB
10 SF1 46 SF2 815-6 SRB 83
Bergquist, N.O. ES1 41

Bergson, Henri. ACC 102 MSF 81

Bergstresser, Marta. IAC 48

Bergues, Helene. BAA 203

Berington, Simon (1680-1755) BAA 11 CSF 22 SF1 46 WGT 14

Berk, Howard (1926-) HFI 11 SFE 68 SF1 46

Berlin, Isaiah. JVN 222

Berlinger, Rudolph. BAA 203

Berman, Barbara L. FL1 308-13 FL2 791-3 FL4 1821-5, 1834-9, 1969-71

Berman, Lucy. SF1 46

Berman, Ruth. IAC 49 SF1 46

Bermann, Richard Arnold (1883-1939) see Arnold Hollriegel

Bermel, Albert. IAC 49 SFS 12

Bermont, Hubert Ingram (1924-) SF1 46 SF2 816

Bern, Donald. COT 153 IAC 49

Berna, Paul (1913-) AOW 310 ES1 41 SF1 46

Bernal, A.W. IMS 8 VES 147 WTS 39

Berkeley, Bishop. FLT 111-2, 128

Berkeley, Edmund Callis. SF1 46

Berkeley, Elizabeth. EXT 3/1 3

Berkeley, George (1685-1753) CYR 15 UKL 64, 71

Berkeley, Reginald Cheyne (1890-1935) CSF 22 SF1 46

Berkey, John. SRB 40

Berkman, Alexander. UKL 224

Berle, Alf K. SFW 179 SOT 154

Berlin, Irving. SFN 93

Bernal, J.D. ACE 18-9 AC2 16-7 BAA 169 CAT 82-3, 98-9, 101 FTF 118 VFS 189, 221, 262

Bernanos, Georges (1888-1948) CSF 22 ES1 41 SF1 581

Bernanos, Michel (1924-1964) FL3 1179-82 HFI 11 KAU 188 SF1 46

Bernard, Christine Ruth (1926-) ES1 41 SF1 46 SF2 816

Bernard, Edward. BAA 138

Bernard, Joel. SF1 46

Bernard, John. BAA 86 CSF 22

Bernard, Kenneth. IAC 49

Bernard, L.L. BAA 204

Bernard, Rafe. ES1 41-2 SFE 68 SF1 46-7

Bernard, Raymond. ES1 42

Bernardi, Walter. BAA 169

Berneri, Marie Louise (1918-1949) BAA 169 ES1 42 EXT 5/1 5 FAN 184 MSF 41, 60

Berners, Gerald H. CSF 22

Berners, (Lord) pseud. of Gerald Hugh Tyrwhitt-Wilson. SF1 47

Bernott, Joan. IAC 49

Bernstein. VFS 73

Bernstein, Eduard. BAA 169

Bernstein, Jeremy. ACE 75 AC2 74

Bernstein, Morey (1920?-) ES1 42 ISW 215-6

Bernstein, Samuel. BAA 204

Bernstein, Zena. FFC 123, 134

Berriault, Gina (1926-) SF1 47

Berridge, Jesse. SF1 47

Berrigan, J.R. BAA 204

Berrill, Norman John (1903-) ES1 42

Berry, Adrian. KAU 33

Berry, Bryan (1930-55) BAA 120 ES1 42 EXT 6/2 51 LEX 182-3 SF1 47 SFE 68-9 VES 315 WGT 14

Berry, Charles W. ES1 42

Berry, D(ouglas) Bruce. EXT 5/1 9 SF1 47

Berry, James R. AOW 311 HFI 11 SF1 47

Berry, John. SRB 114

Berry, John Edgar (1915-) IAC 49 SFS 12 SF1 47

Berryman, John. IAC 49 RFA 66 SFS 13

Berson, Harold. FFC 73-4, 90, 128

Bert, Charles. IMS 71

Bertagnoni, Marialisa. BAA 204

Berthet, Elie Bertrand (1818-91) CSF 22 SF1 47

Berthoud, Samuel Henri. POE 88

Bertignono, Giovanni (1904-63) see Jack Bertin

Bertin, Eddy C. (1944-) FFR 19-21 IAC 49 LEX 183-4 WGT 14

Bertin, Jack pseud. of Giovanni Bertignono. SF1 47 SF2 816

Bertin, John. ES1 43 HFI 12

Berton, Pierre (1920-) FFC 181 SF1 47 SF2 816

Berwick, Edward. BAA 41
Besant, (Sir) Walter (1836-1901)
   BAA 33 CSF 22 ES1 43 EXT
   7/1 10 FL3 1311-2 SFE 69
   SF1 47
Bess, Donovan. WFS 146
Bessand-Massenet, Pierre (1899-)
   ES1 43 SF1 47
Bessemer, Henry (1813-98) EXT
   9/2 29
Bessiere, Richard. WGT 14 see
   also F. Richard-Bessiere
Best, Harry. SF1 47
Best, (Oswald) Herbert (1894-)
   AOW 141 CSF 22 ES1 43 FFC
   129 PST 132-3, 187, 197, 233,
   235, 254-5, 259, 288, 308, 313
   SFE 69 SF1 47 SF2 816 SRB
   300
Bester, Alfred (1913-) AAL 28-9,
   30, 58, 213 ALW 54, 136, 160,
   215-6, 219 AOW 141, 285, 288-9,
   292, 295, 299 ASF 149 BAA 204
   BFP 33-4 BYS 247-8, 265, 279,
   281 COT 101, 104, 131, 134, 161,
   276 CSC 33, 81, 84, 182, 193, 228
   CWD 9 DMK 93-102 ES1 43
   ETN 30, 36, 40, 42, 47-8, 56, 98,
   101, 130, 141-2, 161 EXT 3/1 26
   EXT 5/1 3 EXT 6/2 51 EXT
   8/1 6-7 EXT 10/2 65 FFR 23-
   4 [FJT] HFI 12 HID 179 IAC
   49-50 IAH 15, 41, 113 INT 8
   ISW 4-6, 84, 234-6, 250 KAU 27,
   184, 216-7 LEX 184-5 MFW 11,
   229-30, 281, 290-1 MIH 21, 28-
   9, 48 MSM 32, 298 NDA 104
   NWO 108, 125 PJF 12, 73 RAH
   258 RFA 64, 72, 94, 96, 100, 106,
   213 RGS 16-8 RHN 16, 212
   SFD 56, 291, 306, 313 SFE 69
   SFN 10, 77-96, 114, 117 SFS 13
   SFW 283-90, 396 SF1 48 SF2
   816-7 SIN 39-47 SL2 529-32
   SL5 2163-72 SOT 112, 193, 218,
   244, 259, 395, 406, 420-2 SRB
   112, 318, 324, 364, 369 STH 45,
   158-9 SV1 18-25 TBJ 5 TDI
   31 TPS 259-66 TSF 55, 234-5
   VES 150, 189, 207, 234, 238-9,
   326, 328 WAA 117, 131 WFS
   194, 227, 301 WGT 14 WIF 91
   WSF 174, 183, 211, 215, 387
Best-Maugard, Adolfo. FFC 130
Besterman, Catherine. FFC 130

Beston, Henry. FFC 130
Bethancourt, T. Ernesto. FFC
   60, 160 HFI 12
Bethurum, Truman (1898-) ES1
   43
Betiero, Thomas Jasper. CSF
   22 SF1 48
Bettauer, Hugo (1872-1925) CSF
   22 SF1 48 STH 43-4
Bettelheim, Bruno. SRB 31 UKL
   22
Bettina. FFC 77
Beuf, Carlo Maria Luigi (1893-)
   ES1 43 SF1 48
Beuttler, Edward Ivan Oakley see
   Ivan Butler
Bevan, Alistair pseud. of Keith
   Roberts. IAC 50 SFS 13
Bevan, C. Elnith. CSF 22 SF1
   48
Beverley, Barrington. CSF 22
   SF1 48
Bevington, David M. BAA 204
Bevington, Louisa Sarah. BAA
   40-1
Bevis. VFS 18
Bevis, H(erbert) U(rlin) (1902-)
   HFI 12 SF1 48 SF2 817
Beyer, William Gray. ES1 43
   HFI 12 SFE 70 SF1 48
Beyle, Henri see Stendhal
Beymer, William Gilmore (1881-)
   CSF 22 SF1 48
Beynon, John pseud. of John
   Wyndham Parkes Lucas Beynon
   Harris. CSF 22 IAC 50 VES
   71, 139 SFS 13 STH 51
Bhattacharya. LTN 113
Biagi, L. D. CSF 22 SF1 49
Bialkowski, Stanislaus (1897-)
   LEX 185
Biamonti, Francesco. SF1 49
Bianchi, Ed. IAC 50
Bianchi, Ruggero. BAA 204
Bianco, Margery Williams. FFC
   80, 82, 130
Bianco, Pamela. FFC 80, 83-4
Bickerstaffe-Drew, Francis
   Browning (1858-1928) WGT 14
   see also John Ayscough
Bickman, Martin. UKL 245
Bicknell, Treld. LTN 253
Bidez, Joseph. BAA 169
Bidney, David. MSF 35
Bidston, Lester. CSF 23

Bidwell, Benson (1835-) CSF 23
SF1 49
Biegel, Paul. FFC 46
Biemiller, Carl Ludwig, Jr.
(1912-) AOW 305, 311 ES1 43-4
SF1 49 SF2 817
Bien, Herman Milton (1831-95)
CSF 23 SF1 49
Bier, Jesse (1925-) ES1 44
Bierbower, Austin (1844-1913)
AOW 53 CSF 23 EXT 1/1 6
NWO 162 PST 77, 88, 197, 256
SFE 71 SF1 49
Bierce. HEN 21
Bierce, Ambrose (1842-1914?)
ALW 33, 59, 87 AOW 34, 54, 344
BYS 53 COT 291 CSF 23 ES1
44-5 EXT 1/1 6 EXT 3/1 29
EXT 5/1 16a EXT 7/2 48 FLR
15 FBK 30, 53, 72, 80 FFR 24
FL3 1436-40 HFI 12 HID 28
HWK 15 IAC 50 ISW 78 MFW
85, 195, 208 MSF 203-4 NWO
8, 20, 36, 160-1, 254 PST 62, 72,
266, 283, 318 RAH 145 RHN 48
SFB 51, 57 SFE 71 SFS 13 SF1
49 SL1 283-7 SOT 367 SRB 11
TFC 47 VES 173, 181 WGT 14
WIF 73, 77 WSF 129 WTS 39,
48, 130
Bierman, Judah. AAL 204 BAA
204 UKL 245
Biese, Y. M. BAA 169
Biesterfeld, Wolfgang. BAA 169
Bigelow, Charles. LTN 269
Bigelow, Clement. OWB 84
Bigg, Henry Robert Heather.
BAA 44
Biggle, Lloyd, Jr. (1923-) ALW
212, 219 AOW 142, 294, 397
BAA 131, 136, 143, 153 BFP 35-
6 ES1 45 FFR 24-5 HFI 12-3
IAC 50 LEX 186-7 RGS 18-9,
208 SFE 71 SFS 13 SF1 49-50
SF2 817 SIN 159 VES 157, 170,
179, 231 WFS 278
Biggs, John, Jr. (1895-) SF1 50
Biggs, Lancelot. WTS 44
Bigley, Cantell A. pseud. of
George Washington Peck. SF1
50
Bignola, Robert. WAA 88
Bignon, Jean Paul (1662-1743)
CSF 23 WGT 14 see also Mr.
De Sandisson

Bikkers, Alex V. W. EXT 7/1
6-7
Bikle, George Brown, Jr. BAA
204, 280
Bileck, Marvin. FFC 100, 105
Bilenkin, Dmitri (1933-) IAC 50
LEX 187 SL4 1934-8
Biles, Jack I. BAA xx
Bilibin, I. FFC 50
Bilker, Audrey L. IAC 50
Bilker, Harvey L. IAC 50
Bill, Alfred Hoyt (1879-1964) CSF
23 SF1 50
Bill, Edward Lyman. CSF 23
Billings, Edith S. see Maris
Herrington Billings.
Billings, Maris Herrington pseud.
of Edith S. Billings. CSF 23
SF1 50
Billy (the Kid) see Billy Bonney
Binder, Eando pseud. of
Earl Binder
Otto Binder
AOW 142-3 COT 99, 129, 168-
70 DTS 20 EXT 2/1 3 FFR 25
FRN 29, 40, 42, 47-9, 261, 306-7
HFI 13 IAC 51 IMS 16, 20, 34,
45, 75, 93, 147, 182, 186, 197, 213,
221, 231 ISW 132-3 KAU 121
LEX 187-8 PST 158-9, 225, 284
RFA 41, 46, 51, 63, 91 RGS 19
SFE 71-2 SFS 13-4 SFW 267
SOT 107-8, 110, 116-7, 121 STH
154, 219 VES 130, 133, 172, 175,
178, 180, 185, 316-7 WSF 116
WTS 39, 86 YTS 75
Binder, Earl Andrew (1904-1965)
ALW 141 ES1 45 IMS 34 SF1
50 WGT 14-5 WTS 39, 86 see
also
Eando Binder
John Coleridge
Binder, Jack. ES1 45 IMS 34
RFA 62-3 VES 287 WTS 86
Binder, Otto Oscar (1911-74)
ALW 141 BFP 37-8 ES1 45-6
FRN 29, 33-5, 47-9, 261, 306-7,
325, 338, 407-8, 431 IMS 34, 84
ISW 161 SF1 50 SF2 817-8
SL1 22-7 WGT 15 WIF 88, 136
WTS 39, 54, 86 see also
Eando Binder
John Coleridge
Binder-Strassfurt, Eberhart.
FFC 182

Bing, Jon (1944-) IAC 51 SFE 72 SL3 1114-7 WAA 234
Bings, Henry (1922-64) LEX 188-9
Bingenheimer, Heinz (1923-64) BAA 170 ES1 46 EXT 5/1 5
Bingfield, William. SF1 50
Bingham, Carson pseud. of Bruce Bingham Cassiday. SF1 51
Bingham, Roger. SF1 51
Binkley, Ric. VES 195, 315
Binkowski, Richard. EXT 10/1 18
Binks, Robert. FFC 95
Binns, Archie. FFC 73
Binns, Jack (1884-1959) SF1 51
Binns, Ottwell. CSF 23 SF1 51
Binswanger, Ludwig. CWN 54
Birch, Albert G. CSF 23 ES1 46 IAC 51 WTS 4, 20, 120
Birch, John. ETN 67 LTN 151 MIH 57 WFS 85
Birchby, Sidney L. STH 150
Bird, Arthur. BAA 60 SF1 51
Bird, Christopher. IAC 51
Bird, Robert Montgomery (1806-54) EXT 4/1 3-5, 8-9, 11
Bird, William Henry Fleming (1896-1971) SF1 51 SF2 818 see also Lee Elliot, Rand Le Page, Paul Lorraine, Kris Luna
Birdwell, Russell. SF1 51
Bireley, Richard. IAC 51
Birkenhead, (Earl of) POE 240-3
Birkhead, Edith. SF1 51
Birkin, (Sir) Charles Lloyd (1907-) CSF 23 ES1 46-7 IAC 51 SF1 51 SF2 818 WGT 15
Birkmaier, Elizabeth G. CSF 23 EXT 1/1 7 SF1 51
Birley, Julia. IAC 51
Birmingham, Lloyd. VES 159
Birnie, Mary Simpson. SF1 51
Birnstingl, Edgar (1898-1915) CSF 23 SF1 51
Biron, (Sir) Henry Chartres (1863-1940) WGT 15 see also Hyder Ragged
Birren, Faber (1900-) SF2 968 see also Gregor Lang
Bisbee, Eugene Shade. CSF 23 SF1 52 SRB 6
Bischoff, David. HFI 13 IAC 51
Bisellius. EXT 8/1 20

Bisenieks, Dainis. EXT 10/1 23, 34-5
Bishop, Claire Huchet. EXT 2/1 9
Bishop, Donald H. BAA 204
Bishop, Farnham (1886-1930) CSF 23 SF1 52
Bishop, Gerald Vernon (1949-) IAC 51 SF1 52 SF2 818
Bishop, H. G. IAC 51
Bishop, Michael (1945-) AAL 78-9 AOW 143 BFP 39 COT 269 FFR 25 [FJT] HFI 13 IAC 51 LEX 189-90 RGS 19-20 SFD 224-7, 229 SFE 74 SFW 398 SRB 376
Bishop, Morchard pseud. of Oliver Stonor. BAA 204 CSF 23 SF1 52
Bishop, Morris (1893-1973) IAC 51 SF1 52 SF2 819
Bishop, William Henry (1847-1928) BAA 53 CSF 23-4 ES1 47 SF1 52
Bishop, Zealia Brown-Reed. ES1 47 EXT 3/1 3, 6 IAC 51 SF1 52 WGT 15 WTS 32
Bisinger, Josef. BAA 170
Bisland, Elizabeth. STH 195-6
Biss, Gerald. CSF 24 SF1 52
Bisserov, George. SF1 52
Bissot, Douglas. FFC 118
Bittner, Jim. LTN 18, 238-9
Bitzius, Albert (1797-1854) see Jeremias Gotthelf
Bixby, (Drexel) Jerome (Lewis) (1923-) ALW 212 AOW 134, 143, 297 ES1 47 FFR 25 FRN 255 HFI 13 IAC 51 KAU 48 LEX 190 RSG 81 SFD 311 SFE 74 SFS 14 SF1 52 SF2 819 SOT 401 VES 179, 208, 318 WGT 15 see also Alger Rome
Bjorklund, Lorence. FFC 155
Black, Angus. SF1 52
Black, Branton. TSP 131
Black, D. M. IAC 51-2
Black, Dorothy Delius (1899-) ES1 47 SF1 52
Black, F. J. BAA 204
Black, Frank Burne. SF1 52
Black, James Macdougall (1879-1949) SF1 52

Black, Ladbroke Lionel (1877-1940) CSF 24 SFE 74 SF1 52
Black, Max. EXT 6/1 20
Black, Pansy E. CSF 24 SF1 52
Black, William (1841-98) CSF 24 ES1 47 SF1 53
Blackburn, John Fenwick (1923-) AOW 143 BYS 295 ES1 47 SFE 74 SF1 53 SF2 819
Blackden, Paul. SF1 53
Blackie, J. IAC 52
Blackie, John. EXT 9/2 59
Blackledge, Katharine Treat (1866?-1924?) CSF 24 SF1 53
Blackmon, Robert C. pseud. of Roger Howard Norton. TSP 103
Blackmun, Kathryn. EXT 10/1 23, 34
Blackmur, Richard P. EXT 9/2 39 MIH 21
Blackstock, Charity pseud. of Ursula Torday. SF1 53
Blackstone, Valerius D. pseud. of J. A. Galpin. SF1 53
Blackwelder, Eliot. EXT 5/2 40
Blackwood, Algernon (1869-1951) CSF 24-5 ES1 47-9 EXT 5/1 4 FBK 55, 69-70, 78, 80 FLR 15 FL1 217-21, 468-71 FL2 757-9, 817-21 FL3 1441-51 IAC 52 ISW 221 SFE 76 SF1 53-4 SOT 309, 367 WIF 73 WTS 17, 47, 123
Blade, Alexander (house name) SFE 76 WGT 15-6 WIF 120 see also Howard Browne, Randall Garrett, Roger P. Graham, Edmond Hamilton, Heinrich Hauser, Herb Livingston, Louis H. Sampliner, Richard S. Shaver, Robert Silverberg, Don Wilcox, Leroy Yerxa
Blade, William. WSF 116
Blaikley, Editha L. CSF 25
Blaiklock, Russel. IMS 29
Blain, William. SF1 54
Blaine, John pseud. of Harold Leland Goodwin. SF1 54
Blair, Andrew. BAA 30 POE 139 SF1 54 WGT 16
Blair, Andrew James Fraser (1872-1935) CSF 25 WGT 16 see also Hamish Blair
Blair, Eric Arthur (1903-50) ASF 275-6 BAA 113, 117 ES1 49 SFN 69 WGT 16 see also George Orwell

Blair, H. A. EXT 10/1 23
Blair, Hamish pseud. of Andrew James Fraser Blair. CSF 25 SFE 76 SF1 54
Blair, Peter Hunter. SF1 55
Blaisdell, Elinore Rosenburg (1904-) CSF 25 ES1 49 EXT 3/1 19 SF1 55
Blaisdell, Mary Frances. FFC 130
Blake, Alan pseud. of Omar Gwinn. TSP 134
Blake, E. Michael. IAC 52
Blake, Justin pseud. of John Griffith Bowen.
Blake, Kevin. SF1 55
Blake, Nicholas pseud. of Cecil Day Lewis. SF1 55
Blake, Quentin. FFC 91, 132, 138, 145
Blake, Robert. WTS 40
Blake, Stacey. CSF 25 SF1 55
Blake, Thomas A. ES1 49 SFE 76 SF1 55
Blake, William (1757-1827) ACC 209 ALW 52 CUA 17, 20, 24, 26 CWN 7, 13, 30, 42-3, 50 EXT 7/1 16 EXT 10/2 65 FSU 40 HEN 4, 38 JGB 16-7 KAU 27 MSF 74, 113, 115, 117-9, 121-5, 134-5, 144, 183-4, 197, 229 NWO ix, 10, 16, 26-8, 43, 55, 107, 167, 239 PJF 32, 34-5, 39, 64 RBY 169, 177, 206-7 RZY 24, 28 SOI 93, 95 SOT 235 TBC 43 THM 3-4, 20, 26, 36, 39 UKL 65, 70, 73-5, 136 VMW 36 WAA 86 WBW 4 WTS 25
Blakeborough, Richard (-1918) ES1 49
Blakely, Douglas. IMS 112
Blakemore, Felix John. BAA 92 CSF 25 SF1 55
Blamires, Harry (1916-) ES1 49 SF1 55 SF2 820
Blanchard, Calvin. BAA 27-8
Blanchard, Charles Elton (1868-) BAA 98 SF1 55
Blanchard, Henry Percy (1862-1939) BAA 74 CSF 25 SF1 55
Blanchet, Leon. BAA 170
Bland, Charles Ashwold. SF1 55
Bland, Edith Nesbit (1858-1924) WGT 16 see also Edith Nesbit
Bland, Frederick. IAC 52

Bland, Thomas Augustus (1830-)
SF1 55
Blane, John. CSF 25
Blankenship, William D. HFI 13
Blassingame, Lurton. TSP 51
Blassingame, Wyatt (1909-) TSP
15, 18, 22, 28, 41, 46, 50-1, 54, 58,
97-9, 102, 144, 156, 164, 215, 223-
6 WGT 16 see also William
Rainey
Blatchford, Robert (1851-1943)
BAA 70 CSF 25 ES1 50 SF1
55
Blatt, Lee. IMS 186
Blatty, William Peter (1928-)
ALW 186 AOW 225 FBK 7, 10
FFR 25 FL1 501-3 KWS 91
SF1 55 SF2 820
Blaustein, Albert Paul (1921-)
ES1 50 SF2 875 WGT 16 see
also Allen De Graeff
Blavatsky, Helene P. (1831-91)
ACC 56 CSF 25 ES1 50 EXT
1/1 3, 14 EXT 9/2 62 ISW 25
MSF 202 SF1 55 WIF 48, 66, 78
Blaydes, R. O. SF1 55
Blayre, Christopher pseud. of
Edward Heron-Allen. CSF 25-6
SFE 76 VES 220
Bleackeley, Horace William (1868-
1931) BAA 83 CSF 26 SF1 56
Blech, Aimee pseud. of Lionel
Dalsace. SF1 56
Blegvad, Erik. FFC 55, 67, 69,
81, 89, 104, 113, 142, 183
Bleich, David. BAA 204, 280
Bleiler, E(verett) F(ranklin)
(1920-) ALW 175, 184 AOW 286-
7, 359 BAA 170 BRS 3 ES1 50-
1 EXT 4/1 1 EXT 5/1 5, 9 EXT
7/2 46 EXT 8/2 57 EXT 9/2 31
FAN 145 FBK 60 IAC 52 MSM
36, 96, 101, 265 RHN 10 SFE 76-
7 SFN 47 SFS 14 SFW 11-8,
31-7, 53-71, 83-9, 91, 151-9, 573-
82 SF1 56 SRB 64, 320 VES 313,
331 WAA 245 WIF 175, 203 WSF
200
Bleriot, Louis. FTF 40
Bleunard, Albert (1852-) CSF 26
SF1 56
Bleunard, Andre. POE 111
Bleymehl, Jakob. BAA 170
Bliesener, Erich. BAA 280
Blinn, Edith. SF1 56

Blish, James (1921-75) AAL 19,
22, 30, 40-1, 43, 71, 77, 116 ACC
149, 158, 171 AC2 27-8 ACE 29-
30 ALW 7, 60, 136, 156, 160, 164,
184, 187, 218 AOW 83, 118, 144-
6, 286-7, 290, 292, 294, 311, 339-
40 ASF 151 ATA 3-4, 6, 53 BAA
126, 128, 132, 137, 143, 148, 170,
204 BFP 40-4 BYS 56, 205, 237,
242-3, 251-3, 273, 281, 310 CAT
xvi, 18-9, 81 COT 19, 86-7, 158-
9, 222, 297 CSC 33, 65, 291 EFP
10, 13, 19 ES1 51-3 ETN 33, 45,
100, 146 EXT 3/1 26 EXT 4/2
31 EXT 5/1 3 EXT 6/2 51 EXT
7/1 1 EXT 8/1 13 EXT 10/2 55
FAN 154 FBK 154 FFR 26-7
FL1 122-8 FRN 15-6 FTF 67,
78, 149, 152-3, 173-4, 178, 185-7,
189, 191 [FUT] HFI 13-4 HID
48, 92, 101, 122, 160, 192 IAC 52-
4 IAH 18, 50, 54-64, 85, 87 IMS
47, 55, 64-7, 70, 73, 79, 83, 86-7,
104, 113, 141, 184 INT 27-8, 122
ISW xii, 4, 26, 135, 150-7, 241, 265-
6, 268-74 JGB 34 JVN 25 KAU
32, 59, 72, 78, 83-4, 93, 104, 109,
121-4, 129, 184, 208-14, 216 LEX
190-3 LTN 12, 134, 251 MFW
11, 86, 101, 104, 170, 228, 232 MIH
17, 27, 34, 37-8, 41, 43-4, 53, 88-9
MSF 22, 68, 143, 279 MSM 79
NDA 130-2, 156-8, 188, 212, 215
NWO 35, 48, 89, 102, 149, 253, 255
OSR 166-70, 354 POE 301 RAH
222 RFA 188-9, 195, 198, 200,
202-4, 206-7 RGS 20-1, 209 RSG
11 SFA 131 SFB 12, 21, 100, 137,
152 SFD 27, 63, 73-4, 76, 94, 128,
291, 308, 314 SFE 77-8 SFN 76
SFS 14-5 SFW 289, 291-6, 308,
394, 401 SF1 56-7 SF2 820 SIN
154 SL1 233-7, 303-7, 358-62,
497-501 SL2 569-73 SL4 1888-
91 SOT 76, 97, 247, 367, 386, 412-
3 SRB 114, 252, 317, 323, 325, 328,
330, 351, 356 STH 14-5, 17-8, 20,
48 TPS 144-62 TSF 55, 231, 235
UFS 2 VES 75-7, 81, 83, 87, 136,
168-9, 187, 190, 202, 209, 226-7,
232, 235, 249, 259, 261, 309, 329-
30, 335, 342 WAA 117 WGT 16-
7 WIF 91, 146, 152 WFS 17, 58,
126-7, 135, 161, 187, 202, 228, 273-
4 WSF 74, 77, 125, 138, 168, 172,

Blish, James (cont.)
175, 200, 215, 222, 225, 314, 340.
372, 387 see also William Athe-
ling, Jr. , Donald Laverty, John
MacDougal, Arthur Merlyn
Blish, Judith. VES 235
Blish, Virginia. ISW 266, 270
Blishen, Edward (1920-) LTN 33,
265 SF1 57 SF2 820
Bliss, Arthur. WFS 57
Bliss, Douglas Percy (1900-) ES1
53 CSF 26 SF1 57
Bliss, Edgar Janes. SF1 57
Blissett, Nellie K. SF1 57
Blissett, William. EXT 10/1 23
SOI 102
Blitzer, Charles. BAA 170
Blixen, Karen (1885-1962) ES1 53
SF2 879 WGT 17 see also
Pierre Andrezel
Bloch. CWN 39
Bloch, Alan. IAC 54 SFS 15
Bloch, Bertram. SF1 57
Bloch, Chayim (1881-) CSF 26
FBK 57-8 SFB 53 SF1 57
Bloch, Ernst. BAA 170, 205 CAT
73, 77 MSF 7, 12, 39, 42, 52, 54,
57-8, 61-2, 64, 81-2, 84, 98, 148,
192
Bloch, Ivan. POE 186-7
Bloch, Lawrence. IAC 57
Bloch, Marie. FFC 83
Bloch, Regina Miriam. SF1 57
Bloch, Robert (1917-) ALW 143,
160, 184, 194 AOW 94, 146, 403
BAA 132, 145, 205 BFP 45-8
BYS 48, 177, 303 CAT 71 COT
276 CSF 26 ES1 53-4 EXT 3/1
9-10 FBK 78, 81, 85, 154 FFR
27 FL3 1452-6 FRN 29-30, 36,
42, 73-4, 77, 95, 103-4 HFI 14
HID 179 IAC 54-7, 60 IMS 22-3,
25-6, 75, 77, 93, 110, 189 ISW 4-7
LEX 193-4 MIH 28-30, 36 NDA
159 NWO 262 OMN 4-5, 85-9,
224-32 SFB 58 SFD 19 SFE 78
SFN 11, 13, 97-121 SFS 15 SF1
58 SF2 820-1 SOT 4, 6, 108, 266,
290, 296, 321, 323-4, 335-51 SRB
100, 125 STH 45, 116, 121, 152,
249, 254 VES 88, 153, 177, 274,
328 WFS 301 WGT 17 WIF 78,
80, 120, 135 WSF 74, 78, 116, 215,
300 WTS 29, 39-41, 43-6, 48-9,
54-6, 59, 92, 123-4, 126, 128-32
see also Wilson Kane

Bloch-Laine, Francoise. BAA 205
Block, Lawrence. SFS 15
Blodgett, Eleanor Dickinson. BAA
205
Blodgett, Mabel Fuller (1869-1959)
CSF 26 MFW 126 SF1 58
Blok, Alexander A. MSF 251, 256
Blondel, Roger (1895-) see B. R.
Bruss
Bloom, C. IMS 97
Bloom, Harold. FLT 152 NWO
28 WAA 85
Bloom, Ursula Harvey (1896?-)
SF1 58 SF2 821
Bloom, William (1948-) SF1 58
Bloomer, C. Hamilton. IMS 46,
63-8, 78, 113, 123-4
Bloomer, James Moses (1841-)
CSF 26 SF1 58
Bloomfield, Howard. SOT 52
Bloomfield, Leonard. AAL 14
Bloomfield, Paul (1898-) BAA
170, 205 SF1 58
Blore, Trevor. SF1 58
Blot, Thomas pseud. of William
Simpson. AOW 54 CSF 26
EXT 1/1 7 SFE 78 SF1 58
Blotner, J. L. BAA 205
Blow, Ernest J. ES1 54 SFE 78
SF1 58
Blow, Marya Mannes (1904-)
WGT 17
Blower, Elizabeth (1763-) CSF 26
WGT 17
Bluck, R. S. BAA 205
Blue, Peter. SF1 58
Blue Wolf pseud. of Robert Scott.
CSF 26 SF1 58
Bluebeard. WTS 21
Bluemantle, Bridget pseud. of
Elizabeth Thomas. CSF 26
Bluher, Rudolf. BAA 170
Bluhm, William T. BAA 205
Blum, Edgar C. CSF 26 SF1 58
Blum, Irving D. BAA 205, 280
Blum, Ralph (1932-) AOW 146
HFI 14 NDA 105-6 SFE 79 SF1
58 SRB 351
Blumgarten, James. HFI 15
Blundell, Peter pseud. of Frank
Nestle Butterworth. SF1 58
Blunt, Wilfrid Jasper Walter
(1901-) SF1 59 SF2 821
Blyth, Harry (1852-98) WGT 17
Blyth, James (1864-1933) BAA

Blyth, James (cont.)
70 CSF 26,153 SF1 59 STH
34-5
Boaden, James (1762-1839) SF1
59
Boardman, John. CWD 56 SFA
181-2
Boardman, Thomas Volney, Jr.
(1930-) ES1 54-5 IAC 57 SFE
79 SF1 59 SF2 821 SFS 15
Boas, Franz. AAL 14,158-9
EXT 7/2 32,37
Boas, George. BAA 184,205
Boas, Marcus. VES 211,266
Bobrichev-Pushkin, I.A. SIH 113
Bobrov, Sergei P. EXT 10/2 75
MSF 254
Boccaccio, Giovanni. ALW 38
FBK 26 MSF 18
Bock, Vera. FFC 54
Bockenforde, Ernst-Wolfgang.
BAA 205
Bocklin, Arnold. FBK 14
Bodart, Anne (1939-) SF1 59
Boddy, Margaret. EXT 2/1 1
Bode, Helmut. BAA 205
Bodecker, N.M. FFC 64,77
Bodelsen, Anders (1937-) AOW
146-7 HFI 15 LEX 194 NDA
185-6 SFE 79 SF1 59 SL2 845-
9 WAA 234
Bodin, Ed. STH 63 TSP 89-90, 96
Bodin, Felix. BAA 170 POE 69-
73
Bodkin, Thomas. CSF 26
Boehme, Jakob (1574-1624) CWN
31 EXT 9/2 62
Boetzel, Eric. BAA 94 CSF 44
SF1 59
Boex, Joseph Henri Honore (1856-
1940) WGT 18 see also J.H.
Rosny-Aine
Boex, Seraphin Justin Francois
(1859-1948) WGT 18
Bogardus, Emory S. BAA 205
Bogart, Humphrey. SFN 116
Bogdanov, Alexander A. (1873-
1928) EXT 10/2 74 LEX 194-5
MSF 252-3,257,260-1
Bogdanov, Fyodor M. MSF 262
Bogert, Frank S. IMS 76
Boggon, Martyn. ES1 55 HFI 15
SF1 59
Boggs, D.W. SF1 59

Boggs, Redd. IAH 1,3-5,18,34
ISW 115,154 STH 266 WAA 243
Boggs, W. Arthur. BAA 205,280
Bogoras, Waldemar pseud. of
Vladimir Bogoraz. CSF 26 SF1
59 STH 95
Bogoraz, Vladimir (1865-1936)
AOW 96,99 SFE 79 see also
Waldemar Bogoras
Boguslaw, Robert. BAA 170
MSF 60
Bohlen, Jack. LTN 177
Bohr, Niels. MFW 24 MSM 255
Bohrer, Karl Heinz. BAA 170
Boileau, Pierre Louis (1906-)
ES1 55 SF1 59 see also Thomas
Narcejac
Boisgilbert, Edmund pseud. of
Ignatius Donnelly. CSF 26 EXT
7/1 11 PST 73-4,193,232,254-
5,268,272,282,288,304,309
STH 27-8
Bok, Hannes (1914-64) ALW 8,116
CSF 138 ES1 55 FBK 73,85 FL1
87-9 FL4 1774-6 HFI 15 IMS
138 SFB 16,104-5,108 SFE 79-
80 SFW 69-70 SF1 59 SOT 261,
357-8 SRB 112 STH 266,268
VES 86,125,288,306,314 WFS
71,96,109,118 WIF 110 WSF
138,298,301 WTS ix,5,43,59,
74,76,82,93,130 see also
Dolbokgov
Boland, (Bertram) John (1913-)
BAA 128 BYS 294 ES1 55 HFI
15 SFE 80 SF1 59 SF2 821-2
WGT 18
Boland, Stuart Morton. EXT 3/1
22
Bo'ld, Paul. CSF 27 SF1 60
Boldrewood, Rolf. SFW 75
Boles, Nick. IAC 57
Bolingbroke, Henry St. John.
POE 17-22
Bolitho, Henry Hector (1897-1974)
ES1 55 SF1 60 SF2 822 WGT 18
Bolitho, T.G.G. BAA 205
Bolitho, William. WTS 121
Bolivar, Simon (1783-1830) INT 79
Bolkhovitinov, Viktor. WIF 19
Boll, Heinrich. LTN 103
Bolmer, William Brevoort. CSF
27 SF1 60
Bolognese, Don. FFC 77,171
Bolokitten, Oliver. BAA 21

Bolsover, John. IAC 57 SFS 15
Bolt, David Michael Langstone
(1927-) SF1 60 SF2 822
Bolt, William Worden (1900-) SF1
60
Bolton, Charles E. (1841-1901)
AOW 41,54 SFE 80
Bolton, F. H. CSF 27 SF1 60
Bolton, Richard. IAC 57
Bomans, Godfried. FFC 18
Bombal, Maria-Luisa (1910-) CSF
27 SF1 60
Bonaparte, Marie. FLT 44-7
Bond, Daniel. BAA 60
Bond, Frederick Drew. NWO 61
Bond, Madeleine. SF1 60
Bond, Mary Bligh. CSF 27 SF1
60
Bond, Michael. FFC 113-4,130
Bond, Nancy. FFC 160 FL4
1851-3
Bond, Nelson S(lade) (1908-) ALW
136,146 AOW 147 ASF 243 BFP
49 COT 48,235,241-2 CSC 41,
51 CSF 27 ES1 55-6 EXT 5/1
3 FFR 28 HFI 15 IAC 57-8
IMS 213 LEX 195 MSM 86 RFA
69,86,100 SFE 80 SFS 15 SF1
60 SF2 822 SOT 218 STH 84
VES 335 WGT 18 WTS 44
Bond, R. T. EXT 2/1 19
Bond, Stephen. WGT 18
Bone, J(esse) F(ranklin) (1916-)
ALW 212 BAA 137 ES1 56 FFR
28 HFI 15 IAC 58 SFE 80-1
SFS 15 SF1 60 SF2 822
Bone, Leon (1874-) SF1 60
Bonestell, Chesley (1888-) ACE
14,75 AC2 12,73 ALW 8,35,
190 ES1 56 EXT 8/1 3 KWS
65,160,208 MFW 21 MSM 57
OMN 106,225,227-8 RFA 148,
157,166-7,176,181,195,198,204
SFA 193 SFB 65 SFE 81 SOT
206 SRB 37,42 STH 267 VES
83,289-90 VFS 131,133,135
WSF 110 YTS 18,30
Bonfiglioli, Kyril. BYS 297,301-
2 ES1 56 IAC 58 TJB 44 WSF
231
Bonham, Frank. FFC 87
Bonhote, Elizabeth (1744-) SF1 60
Bonner, Anthony. MSF 153
Bonner, Paul H., Jr. RFA xiii

Bonner, Richard. SF1 60 STH
172
Bonner, William Hallam. BAA
205
Bonnet, Georges. BAA 206
Bonney, William (Billy the Kid)
CAT 24 HEN 33-4
Boole, George. EXT 7/2 33 SFN
57
Boone, Daniel. HWK 51
Boone, Lincoln. HID 145
Boorman, John (1933-) HFI 15
SFE 81 SF1 61
Boorstin, Daniel. VFS 187
Boosel, Harry. IMS 34
Booth, Arthur J. BAA 206
Booth, Bradford A. EXT 7/1 15
Booth, Charles. POE 189-90
Booth, Duane A. SF1 61
Booth, Henry Spencer see Colin
Craig
Booth, John Wilkes. WTS 130
Booth, Patrick John (1929-) SF1
61 SF2 822-3
Booth, Philip. BAA 134 EXT 2/2
28 IAC 58
Booth, Wayne C. EXT 6/1 19
Booth, (Gen.) William. BAA 41
Boothby, Guy Newell (1867-1905)
CSF 27 ES1 56-7 SIH 110 SF1
61
Borden, Mary (1886-1968) CSF 27
SF1 61 SF2 823
Borden, William Vickers (1938-)
SF1 61 SF2 823
Bordes, Francois (1919-77) see
Francis Carsac
Borders, Joe H. BAA 64
Borecky, Borivoj. BAA 206
Borel, Marguerite Appell (1883-)
WGT 18 see also Camille Marbo
Borge, Victor. WFS 256
Borges, Jorge Luis (1899-) ALW
238 AOW 118,147,298 BAA 206
BYS 257 CWN 20,46,55-6 ES1
57 EXT 8/1 16 EXT 9/1 3-17
FBK 57,134-6,143 FFR 31 FHT
43 FLT 2,52-3,93,141-2 FL3
1457-64 IAC 58 INT 64,80,88
JGB 6 KVT 28 LEX 195-6 LTN
117,176 MFW 113 MSF 29-30,
59,65,220 NWO 210,234-5 RHN
44 RSG 32,77 SFB 148 SFE 81-
2 SFS 15 SIH 53-4,59,79-81
SL4 2008-13 THM 8

Borgese, Elisabeth Mann (1918-)
BAA 138, 206 ES1 57 IAC 58
SFS 15-6 SF1 61
Borgia, Anthony V. SF1 61
Borglum, Gutzon. BAA 102
Borinski, Ludwig. BAA 206
Borman, Frank. ETN 6-8 SFB
72 VFS 77
Born, Franz. ES1 57
Borodin, A. MFW 219
Borodin, George pseud. of
George Alexis Bankoff, George
A. Milkomane. CSF 27 SF1 61
Borregaard, Ebbe. EXT 10/2 54
Borrello, Alfred. AOW 340
Borrow, George. CSF 27
Borski, Robert. IAC 58
Bortone, Leone. BAA 170
Borun, Krzysztof (1923-) LEX 196
Bosc, Robert. BAA 206
Bosch, Hieronymus. ATA 8, 10
FBK 146 ISW 221 KAU 191
VES 286
Boschine, L. M. BAA 206
Boshell, Gordon. CSF 27 SF1 61
Boshinski, Blanche. FFC 130
Bosley, Keith. ES1 57
Bossle, Lother. BAA 171
Boston, Bruce. IAC 58
Boston, Lucy Maria (1892-) ES1
57 FFC 60, 73, 174 SF1 61 SRB
24
Boston, Peter. FFC 60, 174
Bostwick, Arthur E. IAC 58
Boswell. CUA 53
Boswell, Charles. TSP 196
Boswell, Diane. BAA 91 CSF 27
SF1 61
Boswell, James. JHN 54
Bosworth, Alan R. IAC 58
Botond-Bolics, Gyorgy (1913-)
LEX 196-7
Botsford, Keith. EXT 9/1 17
Bott, Henry. IAH 132 IMS 239
ISW vi WGT 18
Bottero, Maria. BAA 206
Bottger, Heinz. BAA 280
Bottiglia, William F. BAA 206
Bottomley, Samuel. BAA 89
Bottsford, (Lord) pseud. of James
Dennis Hird. CSF 27
Bottsford, Gertrude. STH 250
Boucher, Anthony pseud. of
William Anthony Parker White.
AAL 39, 46, 96, 212 ALW 7, 33,

155, 161-2, 176, 184, 214-6, 219,
221 AOW 147-8, 287, 290, 298
ASF 215 BYS 249, 279, 284 COT
20, 105, 131, 139, 195, 253, 293,
300 CSC 170 ES1 57-8 ETN 31,
37, 46, 68-9, 160, 178 EXT 3/1
22 EXT 5/1 3, 5, 9 EXT 7/2 40-
1 EXT 8/1 6-9, 11, 13, 16 FBK
54, 122 FFR 31 FL3 1465-7
FTF 125, 191 HFI 15 HID x, 62,
75, 103, 154 IAC 58-9 IAH 19-
20, 22, 24-5, 27, 29, 35, 59-60, 81,
106, 131-2, 134 ISW 126, 128,
131, 158, 224, 228 KAU 31, 45-7,
138 LEX 197-8 MFW 145 MIH
14-5, 19 MSM xvi, 23-42, 95, 297-
9, 301 RFA 109, 114, 120, 122,
124-5, 127, 169 RSG 11 SFB 62
SFD 5, 36, 311, 314 SFE 82 SFN
80, 83 SFS 16 SFW 395-6 SF1
61-2 SOT 98, 371 SRB 13, 111
STH 18, 107, 157-8 TJB 5 VES
151, 174, 227, 330 WIF 25, 114,
226 WSF 103, 170, 185, 188, 209,
217, 358
Boucher, Sandy. IAC 59
Boughton, Willis A. EXT 5/1 9
Bouic, Frederic Vernon. BAA
121 SF1 62
Boulding, Elise. BAA 206
Boulenger, Edward George (1888-
1946) CSF 207 SF1 62
Boulez, Pierre. ETN 175
Boulle, Pierre (1912-) ALW 31,
238 AOW 148 ASF 145 CAT 90
ES1 59 EXT 10/2 110 FFR 31
HFI 15 IAC 59 LEX 198 SFB
139-40 SFE 82 SF1 62 SF2 825
SL4 1692-6 SOT 2 VES 95, 301
VFS 54
Boult, S. Kye pseud. of William
E. Cochran. AAL 85 HFI 16
IAC 59
Boumphrey, Geoffrey Maxwell
(1894-1969) CSF 27 FFC 157
SF1 62
Bounds, Sydney James (1920-) ES1
59 HFI 16 IAC 59 LEX 198-9
SFE 82 SF1 62 VES 188 WGT
18
Bourdillon, Francis William
(1852-1921) CSF 27 FL3 1096-8
SF1 62
Bourgin, Hubert. BAA 171
Bourliaguet, Leonce. FFC 24

Bourne, Arthur Mason. CSF 28
SF1 62
Bourne, Frank. CSF 28 VES 316
Bourne, John (1918-) BAA 143
SF1 62
Bourne, Lawrence R. SF1 62
Bousfield, H(enry) T(homas)
W(ishart). CSF 28 ES1 59 SF1
62
Boussenard, Louis (1847-1910)
AOW 54 CSF 28 SFE 82 SF1 62
Boutell, Clarence Burley (1908-)
CSF 149 SF1 62
Boutelle, Clarence Miles (-1903)
CSF 28 SF1 62
Boutet, F. FBK 141
Bouton, John Bell (1830-1902)
CSF 28 SF1 63
Boutwell, Edna. FFC 130
Bouve, Edward Tracy. AOW 54
CSF 28 MFW 127 SFE 82 SF1
63
Bova, Ben(jamin) (William) (1932-)
AAL 61 ALW 8, 212, 239 AOW
148-9, 288, 311, 340, 401 ASF 43,
140-52, 237-8, 252-3, 306 BAA
151, 165, 206 BFP 50-1 BYS 243,
303 COT 57, 197, 274 CSC 12,
197 ES1 59 ETN 22, 56 FFR 31
HFI 16 IAC 59-60 JHN 18, 20,
26, 60 LEX 199-200 MFW 42,
200 RGS 22 SFB 62 SFD 314
SFE 82-3 SFS 16 SF1 63 SF2
825 SIN 158 SRB 17, 357, 364,
498 WFS 265, 284-5 WSF 187,
237, 241 VES 83, 174, 217, 331
Bovet, Richard. ES1 59-60
Bowden, Etta. ES1 60 SFE 83
SF1 63
Bowden, Phil. ES1 60 SFE 83
SF1 63
Bowen, Elizabeth (1899-1973) CSC
162, 174 CSF 28 ES1 60 FL3
1468-70 IAC 60 SFS 16 SOT
305
Bowen, John Griffith (1924-) AOW
149 BYS 256 ES1 60 FFR 31
HFI 16 ISW 134-6 SFE 83 SF1
63 SF2 825-6
Bowen, Marjorie pseud. of
Gabrielle Margaret Vere
Campbell Long. CSF 28 SF1 63
Bowen, Robert Sidney (1900-77)
SF1 63
Bowen, Roger. BAA 280-1

Bowen, William Alvin (1877-1937)
CSF 28 FFC 24, 73 SF1 63
Bower, B. M. pseud. of Bertha
Muzzy Bower Sinclair. SF1 63
Bower, Herbert M. CSF 28
Bower, John Graham (1886-1940)
WGT 18 see also Klaxon
Bower, Samuel. BAA 22
Bowers, A. Herbert. BAA 58
CSF 12 SF1 64
Bowers, Margaretta K. ISW 216-7
Bowers, R. L. BAA 164 SF1 64
Bowers, William L. SF1 64
Bowes, G. K. BAA 206
Bowhay, Bertha Louisa. BAA 94
Bowker, William Rushton. SF1 64
Bowler, Jan. FFC 21
Bowles, John (1833-1900) CSF 28
SF1 64
Bowles, Paul Frederic (1910-)
ES1 60 VFS 117
Bowles, William Lisle. MFW 279
Bowman, Bill. VES 232
Bowman, Frank Paul. BAA 206
Bowman, Hildebrand. BAA 13
CSF 29
Bowman, John Stewart (1931-)
SF1 64 SF2 826
Bowman, Sylvia E. BAA 171, 206
Bowman, Thomas D. EXT 7/2 29
EXT 8/1 1 EXT 8/2 30 EXT 9/1
1
Boyce, Chris (1943-) HFI 16 SFE
83
Boyd, Felix pseud. of Harry
Harrison. IAC 60 SFS 17 VES
173
Boyd, Halbert Johnston (1872-1957)
CSF 29 ES1 60 SF1 64
Boyd, John pseud. of Boyd Brad-
field Upchurch. AOW 149 CAT
34, 121-2 HFI 16 LEX 200-1
NWO 236-42, 249 OSR 186-92
RGS 22-3 SFD 58-60 SFE 83
SF1 64 SL3 1156-60 SL4 1705-
9, 1746-50 SRB 498 VES 218
Boyd, Lyle Gifford. SFS 17 WGT
18
Boyd, Malcolm (1923-) SF1 64
SF2 826
Boyd, William Clouser (1903-)
ES1 60 SFS 17 WGT 18-9
Boyden, Polly Chase. CSF 29
SF1 64

Boye, Karin (1900-41) SF1 64
SL3 1110-3 WAA 59-60
Boyer, Mildred. EXT 9/1 16-7
Boyer, Robert H. LTN 248, 252
SRB 66, 281
Boyland, Grace Duffie (1861-1935)
CSF 29 SF1 64
Boyle, George. CSF 29
Boyle, (Ms.) John Patrick. SF1
64
Boyle, Kay. FFC 12
Boyle, Virginia Frazer (1863-1938)
CSF 29 ES1 60-1 SF1 64
Bozman, Ernest Franklin (1895-
1968) CSF 29 SF1 64
Bozza, Tommaso. BAA 171
Bozzo, Frank. FFC 45, 57, 63
Bozzo, Gianni Baget. BAA 200
Brack, Vektis (house name) SF1
65 see also Bruno G. Condray
Brackett, Leigh (1915-78) AAL
26 ALW 160 AOW 150, 399
ASF 127 BAA 126 BFP 52-4
BYS 263 COT 68, 70-1, 77, 166,
180-1, 186, 189-90, 192, 195-6,
261, 266, 278, 294, 302 CSC 29
CWD 9 ES1 61 ETN 82 FFR
31 HFI 17 IAC 60 IAH 85 IMS
45 ISW 262-4 KAU 93, 128, 134-
7, 145 KWS 54 LEX 201-2 MIH
23 MSM 139 RBY 88 RFA 104,
212 RGS 23-4, 209 SFD 308
SFE 84-5 SFS 17 SF1 65 SF2
826-7 SL3 1242-5 SL5 2201-6
SOT 80-1, 83, 218, 357, 363 SRB
116, 315, 322 TJB 49 TSF 231
VES 82, 269 WIF 114, 145, 150,
224, 230 WSF 97, 125, 135, 156,
202, 262, 283, 334, 373, 388 WTS
53 see also Leigh Brackett
Hamilton
Bradbrook, B. R. FAN 185
Bradbury, Leonard. RBY 86, 88,
157
Bradbury, Malcolm. EXT 6/1 18
Bradbury, Marguerite. RBY 87
Bradbury, Ray(mond) (Douglas)
(1920-) AAL 25-6 ACC 176
ACE 29 AC2 27 ALW 14, 34, 55,
99, 146, 160, 184, 216, 218, 233-9
AOW 150-1, 288-90, 296, 351, 394
ASF 128, 217, 223-6 BAA 120-1,
207 BFP 55-9 BYS 9, 47, 168,
177, 249, 257-9, 285 CAT xiv,
139 CEN 23-40 COT 3, 18, 52-
56, 65-6, 68-9, 71, 76, 86, 131,
134, 141, 166, 184, 206, 216-7,
252, 259, 266, 295, 298, 301 CSC
31, 40, 75, 170-1, 198, 208 CSF
29 DMK 171-82 EFP 5, 19 ES1
61-3 ETN 41, 58, 120 EXT 1/1
3 EXT 1/2 24, 29-31, 34 EXT
2/1 2, 9 EXT 2/2 28 EXT 3/1
26-7 EXT 4/2 24, 29, 31 EXT
5/1 3 EXT 6/2 51 EXT 7/2 29,
35, 47 EXT 8/1 5 EXT 9/2 25
EXT 10/1 3, 49 FAN 13, 48, 155-
6, 158-9 FBK 85, 124, 154 FFC
3, 161, 186 FFR 31-5 FHT 50
FL3 1471-81 FL4 1769-73 FTF
97-9 HEN 26 HFI 17 HID 141-
2 IAC 60-5 IAH 10-3, 19-20, 26,
48, 57-8, 60, 85, 87-9 IMS 45, 138,
200, 213, 222, 251 INT 7, 54-5,
70, 75-6, 87, 114-5, 120-1 ISW
108-13, 115, 128-9, 132, 188, 239,
245, 282 JGB 3-5, 7 JVN 70,
179-80, 182, 189, 211 KAU 74,
79, 84, 89, 91, 139, 155, 184 KWS
xiv-xv, 103-4, 121-3, 125-8, 130
LEX 203-5 MFW 11, 86, 214,
249, 282 MIH 10-2, 23, 36-7, 60-
1, 72, 89, 105, 126 MSF 68, 141
MSM 32, 80, 84, 99, 128, 132, 138-
9, 175, 304 NDA 39-41 NWO 20-
2, 31-4, 36, 47-8, 125, 186, 235
OMN 47, 127-32 POE 261 RAH
34 RFA 125, 213 RGS 24-5
SFA 266 SFB 21, 62, 102-3, 105,
152 SFD 291, 308, 314 SFE 85-
6 SFN 118 SFS 17-21 SFW 70,
171-8 SF1 65 SF2 827 SIN 19
SL2 749-55, 1008-13 SL3 1348-
52 SL4 1571-3 2042-5 SOT 3,
5-6, 80-1, 243, 298, 320, 331-2,
350, 352-74, 394, 412, 431 SRB
14, 77, 311-2, 319, 322, 498 STH
13-4, 20, 48, 50-1, 66-7, 69, 108,
118 SV2 20-9 TJB 31 TSF 55-
6, 172, 231, 235 TSO 47, 56 UFS
2 VES 68, 80-1, 147, 159, 162-3,
167-8, 170, 180, 195, 212, 226-7,
280 VFS 49, 59, 139-40, 142, 146,
151, 197 VF1 167-84, 276 WAA
94, 112, 121-2, 178, 217 WFS 17,
96, 109, 178, 200 WGT 19 WIF
91, 122, 145, 150-4, 158, 185, 188,
194, 212, 230, 245 WSF 125, 156,
173, 202, 298, 387-8 WTS 45-6,
48, 53, 58-9, 74, 93, 123, 130 YTS
19, 23 see also Brett Sterling

Bradbury, Samuel. RBY 86
Bradbury, Walter I. ASF 225
SFA 144,185 SOT 261 WFS 180-
3,192 WSF 201,203
Bradbury, Will. HFI 18
Braddock, Joseph (1902-) ES1 64
Braddon, Mary. CSF 29
Braddon, Russell Reading (1921-)
ES1 64 SFE 86 SF1 65 SF2 827
Braddy, Haldeen. NWO 61
Braden, James A. CSF 29
Bradfield, Margaret. FFC 73
Bradfield, Scott. IAC 65
Bradford, Columbus. BAA 96
CSF 29 SF1 65
Bradford, J.S. CSF 29 ES1 64
SFE 86 SF1 65
Bradford, James S. IAC 65
Bradford, Matthew C. SF1 65
Bradford, Roark (1896-1948) CSF
29 ES1 64 SF1 66
Bradford, Ronald. IAC 65
Bradford, William. NWO 35
Bradley, Albert. VES 322
Bradley, (Dr.) Charles M. BAA
101
Bradley, (Dr.) SFN 96
Bradley, F.H. FLT 115
Bradley, George. SF1 66
Bradley, Jack. CSF 29 SF1 66
Bradley, Johanna. IAC 65
Bradley, Marion Zimmer (1930-)
ALW 212 AOW 151 BFP 60-3
BYS 263 DTS 49 ES1 64-5 EXT
10/1 17,24,31 FFR 205 FL1
341-6 HFI 18 IAC 65 LEX 205-
7 RGS 25-6,209-10 SFE 86-7
SFS 21 SF1 66 SL1 488-92 VES
170,269 WSF 168,175,244-5,
262,282,330,341,388 see also
Marion Eleanor Zimmer Bradley
Breen
Bradley, Michael. FFC 174
Bradley, (Mrs.) WFS 81
Bradley, Will H. (1868-1962) CSF
29 SF1 66
Bradley, Willis T. ES1 65
Bradshaw, Steve. JGB 15
Bradshaw, William Richard (1851-
1927) AOW 54 BAA 46 CSF 29
EXT 1/1 7 EXT 5/1 4 KAU 191
MSF 165 PST 66,213,220,223,
242,250-1,262,268,272-3,284,
291 SFB 76 SFE 87 SF1 66
WIF 48

Bradwell, James. SF1 66
Brady, Adhemer. BAA 60
Brady, Charles A. BAA 207
EXT 1/2 30
Brady, Cyrus Townsend (1861-
1920) SF1 66
Brady, Franklyn. IMS 138
Bragg, Fanny Greye. WTS 23
Brahms, Caryl pseud. of Doris
Caroline Abrahams. CSF 29
SF1 66
Brahms, Johannes (1833-97) ETN
158 WFS 65
Brailowsky, Alexander. WFS 129
Brailsford, Henry Noel (1873-
1958) SF1 66
Braine, John. CWN 25
Braine, Robert D. (1861-) BAA
46 CSF 29 MSF 203 SF1 66
Brainerd, Chauncey Corey (1874-
1922) SF1 66 WGT 19
Brainerd, Edith Rathbone (-1922)
SF1 66 WGT 19
Brainin, Salomea Neumark. STH
43-4
Braithwaite, Richard (1588?-
1673) WGT 19-20
Brajer, Peter. SL2 519-23
Braley, Berton (1882-) SF1 67
Braly, Malcolm. IAC 65
Bramah, Ernest pseud. of Ernest
Bramah Smith. CSF 29 FL2
827-30 HFI 18 SFE 87 SF1 67
Brameld, Theodore. BAA 159
Bramston, Mary. BAA 49 CSF
30
Bramwell, Frank. SF1 67
Bramwell, James Guy (1911-)
BAA 171 ES1 65 SF1 67 SF2
829
Branan, John M. SF1 67
Brand, Charles Neville. CSF 30
Brand, Chris. SF1 67
Brand, Christianna. FFC 73
Brand, Jonathan. IAC 65 SFS 21
Brand, Kurt (1917-) FFR 35-7
LEX 207-9
Brand, Max pseud. of Frederick
Faust. IAC 65 RFA 98 SF1 67
TSP 85,116,132 VES 205
Brand, Thomas. IAC 65
Brandeis, Julian Walter (1875-)
CSF 30 ES1 65 SF1 67
Brandel, Marc (1919-) FFC 161
SF1 67 SF2 829

Brandenberg, Aliki see Aliki
Brandies, Ingeborg. BAA 170
Brandis, Evgeni. BAA 207 EXT
10/1 48-9 EXT 10/2 77 IAC 65
Brandis, Mark (1931-) LEX 209-
10
Brandner, Gary. IAC 65
Brandon, Henry. SF1 67
Brandon, Michael. CSF 30 SF1
67
Brandt, C.A. (1879-1947) ES1 65
STH 219-20
Brandt, (Dr.). BAA 207
Brandt, Johanna. CSF 30
Branford, Victor. BAA 86
Branley, Franklyn Mansfield
(1915-) ES1 65 SF1 67 SF2 829
Brann, Eva. BAA 207
Bransby, Emma Lindsay Squier
(1892-) WGT 20
Branstner, Gerhard (1927-) LEX
210
Brant, J. STH 75
Brant, John Ira (1872-) BAA 74
SF1 68
Brasch, Moritz. BAA 207
Brash, Margaret Maud (1880-)
BAA 99 EXT 9/2 53 WGT 20
see also John Kendall
Brauer, Theodor. BAA 207
Braun, Felix. EXT 3/2 51-2
Braun, Gunter (1928-) LEX 210-1
SL5 2357-61
Braun, Johanna (1929-) LEX 210-
1 SL5 2357-61
Brauner, Oscar. WIF 20
Braunert, Horst. BAA 171,207
Brautigan, Don. VES 135
Brautigan, Richard (1935-) BAA
145 CAT 17,27 FL4 1979-82
IAC 65 PJF 16 SFE 87 SF1 68
Bray, John Francis. AOW 19
BAA 23 ES1 65 MSF 138 SFE
87
Brayton, Gertrude E. see Edith
Bryat
Bready, Richard S. IAC 65
Brebbel, Cornelis. ASF 185-6
Brebner, Percy James (1864-
1922) CSF 30 SF1 68 WGT 20
see also Christian Lys
Brebner, Winston (1924-) BAA
129 ES1 65 HFI 183 SFE 87
SF1 68

Brecht, Bertolt (1898-1956) CAT
73-4 MSF 6-7,18,54,71,74,80,
82,278 NWO ix,26 THM 17
Breckenridge, Gerald (1889?-1964)
CSF 30 SF1 68 STH 172
Brede, Arnold. SF1 68
Bredeson, Lenore. ES1 65 SF1
68
Bredvold, Louis. BAA 207
Breedlove, Bill. SF1 68
Breen, James. EXT 5/2 42
Breen, Marion Eleanor Zimmer
Bradley (1930-) SF2 828 WGT
20 see also Marion Zimmer
Bradley
Breen Walter. SF1 68
Breggin, Peter Roger (1936-)
HFI 18 SFE 87 SF1 68 SF2 829
Brehat, Alfred pseud. of Alfred
Guezenec. CSF 30
Breines, Paul. BAA 207
Brelis, Nancy. FFC 139
Bremer, Uwe. SFB 32
Brenan, Edward Fitz-Gerald
(1894-) see George Beaton
Brenda. FFC 79
Brengle, William (house name)
WGT 20 see also Howard Browne
Brenholtz, Edwin Arnold (1859-)
SF1 68
Brennan, Alice. SF1 68
Brennan, Elizabeth. SF1 68
Brennan, Gerald Thomas (1898-)
SF1 68
Brennan, John P. UKL 117-52
Brennan, Joseph P(ayne) (1918-)
BFP 64 ES1 65 EXT 3/1 2,9,
21-2 FFR 37 IAC 65 SF1 68-
9 SF2 829-30 WTS 46-7,59-61
Brennan, Kathleen. IAC 65
Brennan, Walter. INT 39
Brenner, Anita. FFC 35
Brenner, Barbara. FFC 114
Brenner, Fred. FFC 117
Brenner, Robert (1931-) LEX 211
Brennert, Alan. COT 166 IAC
65
Brent, Jeremy. SF1 69
Brent, Loring pseud. of George
F. Worts. CSF 30
Brent, Peter (1931-) see Ludovic
Peters
Brentwood, Evelyn. SF1 69
Brereton, Cloudesley S(hovell)
H(enry) (1863-1937) CSF 30
SF1 69

Brereton, Frederick S(adleir) (1872-1957) CSF 30 SF1 69
Breslauer, Richard. TSP 201
Bretano, Clemens. FFC 53 SIH 6,18,124
Bretano, Franz. CWN 54
Bretnall, George Herbert (1871-1961) SF1 69
Bretnor, Reginald (1911-) AAL 172 ALW 7,212,216 AOW 340 ASF 58 BAA 171,207 BRS 6 COT 71,141,276 CSC 3-21 ES1 66 EXT 1/2 29 EXT 5/1 5 EXT 5/2 28 EXT 8/1 8-13,15 FHT 66 HFI 18 HID 179-80,192 IAC 65-6 ISW x,5,125-6 KAU 23 LEX 212 LTN 37 MFW 31 MSM 24,92,94,265-94 SFA 57, 285 SFD 62,85,95 SFE 87 SFN 16,31,47-8 SFS 21 SF1 69 SF2 830 SRB 70,498 TSF 245 WAA 245 WGT 20 WSF 382
Breton, Andre. FBK 26 SFB 67
Breton, Frederic. CSF 30 SF1 69
Brett, Cyril. EXT 5/2 42 EXT 10/1 24
Breuer, (Dr.) Miles J(ohn) (1889-1947) ALW 126,138 COT 23, 123-4,207-8,210 CSC 198 CSF 210 ES1 66 IAC 66 IMS 8,21, 24,68 ISW 177 LEX 213 RFA 2 SFE 87-8 SFW 145,226 SFS 22,55 SF1 69 SOT 91-2,136, 146 STH 110-2 VES 76,78,84, 124,149,153 WSF 44 WTS 51
Breughel, Pieter (the elder) [FUT]
Brewster, (Sir) David. NWO 69
Brewster, Dennis. SF1 69
Brex, John Twells (1874-1920) CSF 30 SF1 69
Brezhnev, Leonid. SIH 75
Briarton, Grendel pseud. of Reginald Bretnor. AOW 151 ASF 58 IAC 66 SFS 22
Brickell, Herschel. MSM 99
Bridge, Ann pseud. of Mary Dolling O'Malley. CSF 30 SF1 69
Bridge, James Howard (1858-1939) BAA 36-7 see also Harold Brydges
Bridges, Roy (1885-1952) CSF 30 SF1 69
Bridges, Thomas (-1775) WGT 20

Bridges, Thomas Charles (1868-) CSF 30 SF1 69 WGT 20 see also Christopher Beck
Bridgman, P.W. EXT 7/2 30 NDA 57
Brie, Friedrich. BAA 207
Briefs, Goetz A. BAA 207
Brien, Alan. BAA 148
Brigg, Peter. ACC 15-51 FL1 81-3,428-30 FL2 585-9 FL4 1757-9 FL5 2067-8,2422-46 SL1 63-6 SL2 634-8,915-20 SL3 1308-11 TSO 14 UKL 36-63
Briggs, Austin. WTS 103
Briggs, Julia. FBK 152
Briggs, Katherine. FFC 99
Briggs, K.M. EXT 10/1 24
Briggs, Philip pseud. of Phyllis Briggs. ES1 66 SF1 70
Briggs, Phyllis see Philip Briggs
Brighouse, Harold (1882-1958) ES1 66
Bright, Annie. CSF 31
Bright, Mary Chavelita Dunne (1860-1945) ES1 66 WGT 21 see also George Egerton
Bright, Robert. FFC 90
Briney, Robert E(dward) (1933-) AOW 360 BAA 171 ES1 66 EXT 3/1 2,8,21 HID x IAC 66 SF1 70 SF2 830 SRB 63 WGT 21 WSF 214 see also Andrew Duane
Bringsvaerd, Tor Age (1939-) IAC 66 SFE 88 SL3 1114-7 WAA 234
Brinig, Myron (1900-) CSF 31 SF1 70
Brink, Carol Ryrie (1895-) AOW 311 FFC 154 SF1 70 SF2 831
Brinsmade, Herman Hine. BAA 78 CSF 31 SF1 70
Brinton, Crane. BAA 207 FAN 174
Brinton, Henry (1901-) ES1 66 HFI 18 SFE 88 SF1 70 SF2 831
Brion, Marcel. FBK 16
Brisbane, Arthur. POE 112-3
Brisco, Patricia A. (1927-) HFI 18 SF1 70 SF2 831
Brisley, Joyce. FFC 84
Bristol, Michael. BAA 207
Britikov, Anatolii F. AOW 340
Britton, Lionel Erskine. BAA 96 CSF 31
Briusov, Valery (1873-1924) CSF

Briusov, Valery (cont.)
31, 33 ES1 72 EXT 10/2 74-5
FBK 42, 82 IAC 70 MSF 250-
3, 256, 260 NDA 209 SF1 70
SL4 1768-74 WGT 21
Brizzi, Mary T. SRB 79
Bro, Margueritte. FFC 130
Broch, Hermann. MFW 63
Brock, Betty. FFC 29, 61
Brock, Walter S. SF1 70
Brockes, Ferdinand. CSF 31
Brockhaus, Heinrich. BAA 171
Brockhouse, H. BAA 68
Brockies, Enid Florence (1911-)
WGT 21 see also Helene
Magriska
Brockley, Fenton pseud. of
Donald Sydney Rowland. SF1
70
Brockway, Archibald Fenner
(1888-) BAA 102 CSF 31 SFE
89 SF1 70 SF2 831
Brod, Max. FBK 128-9
Brode, Anthony. IAC 66 SFS 22
Broderick, Damien. ES1 66 HFI
19 IAC 66 SFS 22 SF1 70
Brodeur, Arthur Gilchrist (1888-)
CSF 23 SF1 70
Brodhay, Otto Chester (1875? -
1954) CSF 31 SF1 70
Brodie-Innes, John William
(1848-) CSF 31 SF1 70
Brodkin, Sylvia Z. IAC 66 SF1
70
Brodsky, Israel. IMS 52
Brodsky, Stanley. LTN 249
Brogan (the Scribe) pseud. of
Charles A. Spickler. CSF 31
Broger, Achim. FFC 103, 139
Broll, Wolfgang W. (1913-) LEX
213-4
Brome, Richard. BAA 3
Bromfield, Helen Ward. CSF 31
ES1 66-7
Bromfield, Louis (1896-1956)
ES1 67 SF1 71
Brondfield, Jerome. IAC 66
Bronk, William. IAC 66
Bronner, Stephen Eric. BAA
207
Bronowski, Jacob (1908-) ACC
129 ATA 40 ES1 67 FTF 69
Bronson, Donna. IAC 66
Bronte, Anne (1820-49) WGT 21

Bronte, Charlotte (1816-55) CSF
31 ES1 67 LTN 150, 197 SF1
71 WGT 21
Bronte, Emily (1818-48) CAT 56
FLT 137 WGT 21
Bronte (sisters). BYS 82, 92, 108
WTS 17
Brooke, (Bernard) Jocelyn (1908-
66) ES1 67 EXT 6/1 14 HFI
183 SFE 89 SF1 71
Brooke, Rupert. ATA 38-9 FLR
25 POE 225
Brooke-Rose, Christine (1923-)
BAA 140 BYS 306 ES1 67 SFE
89 SF1 71 SF2 831
Brookfield, Arthur Montagu
(1853-1940) BAA 35 SF1 71
Brookins, Dewey C. (1904-) ES1
67 SFE 89 SF1 71 SF2 831
Brookmire, Paula. LTN 269
Brooks, Byron Alden (1845-1911)
BAA 49 CSF 31 SF1 71
Brooks, C. W. , Jr. SF1 71
Brooks, Collin. BAA 207 CSF
31
Brooks, Edwy Searles (1889-1965)
CSF 31 WGT 21 see also
Robert W. Comrade
Berkeley Gray
Brooks, Mel. CSC 264 SIH 127
Brooks, Ned (pseud) see C. W.
Brooks
Brooks, Rick. EXT 10/1 18
IAC 66
Brooks, Robert E. BAA 171
Brooks, Ron. FFC 170
Brooks, Terry. FFR 37 FL4
1866-8 HFI 19 WSF 302-3, 388
Brooks, Van Wyck. FAN 13, 64
Brooks, Walter Rollin (1886-
1958) CSF 31 ES1 67 FFC 114,
130 SF1 71-2
Brooks, William Collin (1893-
1959) SF1 71
Broomhead, Reginald. BAA 88
CSF 31 SF1 72
Brophy, Brigid Antonia (1929-)
ES1 67 SF1 72
Brophy, John (1899-1965) CSF 31
SF1 72 SF2 831-2
Brophy, Liam. BAA 207-8
Brosnan, John (1947-) IAC 66
SFE 89 TSF 255
Brosnatch, Andrew. WTS 23, 62,
79-80, 82, 112, 120, 131

Broster, Dorothy Kathleen (1877-
1950) CSF 32 ES1 67 SFE 89
SF1 72 WGT 21
Brostowin, Patrick R. BAA 281
Brothers, Richard. BAA 21
Brotman, Morton. STH 149
Broughton, Bernard Lennox.
SF1 72
Broughton, Rhoda (1840-1920)
CSF 32 ES1 67 FBK 60 FL4
1989-91 IAC 66 SFS 22 SF1
72
Broun, Heywood (Campbell) (1888-
1939) CSF 32 FFC 87 IAC 66
SF1 72 WIF 175
Broussard, Louis. NWO 61
Brown. WBW 32-3
Brown, Abbie. FFC 83
Brown, Alec John Charles (1900-)
BAA 126 ES1 67 SFE 89 SF1
72
Brown, Alice (1857-1948) CSF 32
ES1 67-8 SF1 72
Brown, Alphonse. POE 139
Brown, Andrew C. CSF 32
Brown, (Sir) Arthur Whitten.
FTF 71
Brown, Beth. CSF 32 SF1 72
SF2 832
Brown, Bill. FFC 35 IAC 66
MSM 91,103 SFS 22
Brown, Brian. CSF 32
Brown, Carter. HFI 19
Brown, Charles Brockden (1771-
1810) BAA 19 BYS 44,47,52
CSF 32 ES1 68 EXT 4/1 9
FBK 27 FL5 2126-31 MSF 139
NWO 8,35-6,163,167-81,263
RBY 168-70 WTS 17
Brown, Charles Edward. CSF 32
Brown, Charles N. IAC 66 LTN
269 SRB 74,120 WFS 40 WSF
237,239,277,281,286
Brown, Charles R. CSF 143
SF1 72
Brown, Dena. SRB 74 WSF 239,
277,281,286
Brown, Douglas Frank Lambert
(1907-) BAA 109 CSF 32 SF1
72 SF2 832
Brown, Elizabeth. IAC 66
Brown, Fred H. BAA 29,49
SF1 72
Brown, Fredric (William) (1906-
72) ALW 174,185,234 AOW

151-2,290,292-3,393 BFP 65-
7 BYS 234,289 CAT 20-1 COT
139 ES1 68-9 EXT 1/2 30
EXT 5/1 3 EXT 7/2 40 FFR
37-41 HFI 19 IAC 66-8 IAH
29 INT 16-7 KAU 32,35-8,151,
175 KWS 241 LEX 214-5 MFW
24,101,103 MSM 89 RFA 130-
1,204 RGS 26-8 SFD 56,292,
308,320 SFE 89 SFN 118 SFS
22-3,98 SF1 72-3 SF2 832
SIH 185 SL3 1217-20,1362-5
SL4 1954-7 SL5 2451-4 SOT
249-50 SRB 308 STH 120-1,
157 TSF 56,231 WAA 13,23,
96,242 WGT 21 WSF 107,121,
125,200 WTS 47
Brown, George Sheldon. SF1 73
Brown, Harrison Scott (1917-)
ES1 69 HFI 166 POE 309-10
SFE 90 SF1 73 SF2 832 SIH 94
Brown, Howard V. (1878-) ES1
69 RFA 15-6,19,22,24,29,31,
37-9,41,49,54,57-8,60,63,84,
91,141 SFE 90 SRB 36 VES
287-8 WSF 34,66,120
Brown, James Cooke (1921-) AAL
194-8 AOW 152 BAA 151 HFI
19 SFE 90 SF1 73 SF2 833
Brown, James Goldie (1901-) ES1
69 IAC 68 SFE 90 SFS 23 SF1
73 SF2 833
Brown, Jeff. FFC 140
Brown, Jim. RFA 200
Brown, Joe E. STH 252
Brown, John. WTS 130
Brown, John Macmillan (1846-
1935) BAA xxi,57,65 WGT 21
see also Godfrey Sweven
Brown, John Young (1858-1921)
CSF 32 SF1 73
Brown, Joseph Mackey (1851-
1932) CSF 32 EXT 1/1 7 SF1
73
Brown, Judith. FFC 24,103,124,
167,189
Brown, Kate Clark. CSF 32
SF1 73
Brown, Lloyd W. SL1 48-52
Brown, Marc. FFC 53
Brown, Marcia. FFC 53
Brown, Morna Doris MacTaggart
(1907-) WGT 21
Brown, Norman O. KAU 91 RHN
191 WBW 59

Brown, Palmer. FFC 61,114
Brown, Peter Currell. SFE 90
Brown, Raymond Lamont. WAA 88
Brown, Reginald. CSF 32
Brown, Richard B. CSF 32
Brown, Richard Blake (1902-) SF1 73
Brown, Ritter. CSF 32
Brown, Robin. SF1 73
Brown, Roland Wilbur. MIH 70
Brown, Rosalie. FFC 35 see also Rosalie Moore
Brown, Rosel George (1926-67) AOW 213 BFP 68 BYS 263 ES1 69 HFI 19 IAC 68 IAH 128 SFE 90 SFS 23 SF1 73 SF2 833
Brown, Slater (1896-) ES1 69 SF1 73
Brown, T. K., III. IAC 69
Brown, Truesdell S. BAA 208
Brown, Wenzell. HFI 19 IAC 69
Brown, Wes (1921-) SF1 73
Brown, Zenith Jones (1898-) WGT 21-2
Browne, Barum. CSF 32 SF1 73
Browne, F. G. (1870-1954) WGT 22
Browne, George Sheldon. SFE 90
Browne, Gerald A. SF1 73
Browne, Gordon. FBK 63
Browne, Hablot Knight (1815-82) WGT 22
Browne, Helen De Guerry Simpson (1897-1940) WGT 22
Browne, Howard (1908-) ALW 127 CSF 33 ES1 69 HFI 19 IAC 14-5, 20, 24, 51 ISW 116, 133 SFE 90 SF1 74 SOT 119 WGT 22 WIF 121, 164, 178 WSF 120, 188, 300 see also Alexander Blade, William Brengle, H. B. Carleton, Lee Francis, John X. Pollard
Browne, Ray B. NWO 274
Browne, Reginald. ES1 69 SF1 74
Browne, Roscoe Lee. SL2 792-6
Browne, Thomas Alexander (1826-1915) WGT 22
Browne, Walter (1856-1911) BAA 51 CSF 33 SF1 74
Brownell, Anna Gertrude Hall (1863-) ES1 70 WGT 22
Browning, Daphne Du Maurier (1907-) WGT 22

Brown-Reed, Zealia see Zealia Brown-Reed Bishop
Browning, Gordon. BAA 208
Browning, John S. pseud. of Robert Moore Williams. IAC 69 SFS 23 STH 246
Browning, Robert. ACC 192 JGB 6 PJF 57 SFA 143 SOT 261
Browning, Tod. FBK 48 WAA 88
Browning, William Gordon. BAA 281
Brownjohn, Alan. IAC 69
Brownlow, Catherine. IAC 69 SFS 23
Brownson, Orestes. CSF 33
Brownstein, Michael. IAC 69
Brownstein, Robert. BAA 185
Broxon, Mildred Downey (1948-) AAL 107-8 FFR 41 IAC 69 LEX 215-6
Broyard. ETN 176
Broyles, Lloyd Douglas (1931-) ES1 70 SF1 74
Brubacher, J. S. BAA 208
Bruce, George. SOT 414 TSP 89
Bruce, James. MSM 125 WIF 183
Bruce, Kennedy. CSF 33 SF1 74
Bruce, Kenneth (1876-1916) WGT 22 see also Diedrick Crayon Jr.
Bruce, Muriel. CSF 33 SF1 74
Bruce, Stewart E. BAA 86 SF1 74
Bruckberger, Raymond Leopold (1907-) SF1 74
Bruckner, Karl (1906-) ES1 70 SF1 74
Bruckner, Winfried (1937-) LEX 216 WAA 235
Brueckel, Francis J. WGT 22
Bruegel, Pieter. FBK 146
Brueghel. ATA 10
Bruere, Martha Bensley (1879-) BAA 83 CSF 33 SF1 74
Bruggemann, Fritz. BAA xxii, 171, 208
Brugh, James. CSF 33
Brugmans, Henri. BAA 208
Bruller, Jean Marcel (1902-) ES1 70 VES 95 WGT 22 see also Vercours
Brumm, Charles. SF1 74
Brundage, Margaret (1903-) COT 18, 176-7, 184 CWD 32 ES1 70 STH 253-5, 257-8 VES 219 WTS

Brundage, Margaret (cont.)
ix, 5, 56, 58, 62, 64-74, 76, 78, 122-4
Brunel, Isambard K. FTF 35
Bruner, Paul. FFC 22
Brunner, John (Kilian Houston)
(1934-) AAL 50, 70, 74-6, 129-30 ALW 8, 212, 235 AOW 118,
153-5, 167, 176, 242, 252, 281,
285, 296, 300, 342 BAA 141, 143,
145, 148, 152-3, 156, 161 BFP
69-75 BYS 237-8, 257, 261, 272,
276-8, 285, 289, 296, 299, 303
COT 269 CSC 191, 216-35 DMK
243-9 DTS 7, 49 EFP 13, 19
ES1 70-2 EXT 10/1 3 EXT 10/2
50 FFR 41-2 FL4 1963-5 FTF
91, 201 HFI 19-21 IAC 69-70
IAH 103 INT 49 JHN 53 KAU
90, 93, 102, 184 LEX 216-20
MFW 14, 86, 103, 172-6, 178 MIH
129, 135, 140 MSF 27, 280 NDA
33-4 NWO 16, 125-6, 236, 254
OSR 181-5 POE 297 RGS 28-9
SFD 8, 63, 76, 264, 296, 318 SFE
90-2 SFS 23-4 SFW 104, 297-304 SF1 74-5 SF2 833-4 SIH
199 SL3 1094-7 SL4 1913-6,
1922-5 SL5 2132-5, 2140-5 SRB
14, 17, 253, 338-9, 344, 346, 354,
363, 499 STF 72-4, 78-9 TSF
59, 238 UFS 2 VF2 106-35, 201-3 WAA 27, 29, 177 WFS 75 WGT
23 WSF 205, 241, 244, 275, 387
see also K. Houston Brunner,
Gill Hunt
Brunner, K. Houston pseud. of
John Brunner. IAC 70 SFS 24
VES 75, 87, 123, 128, 136
Brunner, Robert Kendrick (1888-)
CSF 33ES1 72
Brunngraber, Rudolf (1901-) AOW
99 SFE 92
Bruno, Giordano. MSF 98
Brunswick, Ruth Mack. FLT 80,
157
Brunt, (Captain) Samuel. AOW
20 BAA 10-1 CSF 33 FTF 24-5 SFB 71 SF1 75
Brush. RFA 195
Bruss, B. R. pseud. of Roger
Blondel. ES1 72 SFE 92
Brust, John C. M. IAC 70 SFS
24
Brutus, Marcus Iunius. MSF 110,
113

Bryan, Patrick Henry Hamilton.
ES1 72 SF1 75
Bryant, Dorothy M. (1930-) SF1
75 SF2 834
Bryant, Edward (Winslow) (1945-)
ALW 212 BAA 156 BFP 76
CSC 288-9 DMK 87-92 ETN 139
HFI 21 IAC 70-1 LEX 220-1
RGS 29 SFD 57 SFE 92 SF1 75
SF2 834 VES 301
Bryant, Marguerite. CSF 33
Bryat, Edith pseud. of Gertrude
E. Brayton. SF1 76
Bryce, Lloyd S. CSF 33
Brydges, Harold pseud. of James
Howard Bridge. CSF 33 SF1 76
Bryher, Anna Winifred (1894-)
FFC 181 SF1 76
Bryning, Frank B. (1907-) ES1
72 IAC 71
Bryson, Bernard. FFC 23, 80
Bryson, Lyman. BAA 208
Buba, Joy. FFC 101
Buber, Martin. BAA 171 EXT
3/2 49 EXT 7/2 34 MSF 39
UKL 217, 220, 224
Buchan, Bryan. SF1 76
Buchan, John (1875-1940) ALW
33 CSF 33 ES1 72-3 EXT 3/1
24 FBK 100, 104-6 FFC 171
FL3 1482-4 IAC 71 SFS 24
SF1 76 STF 68 THM 39 WGT
23 see also Douglas Erskine
Buchan, Susan (1882-) WGT 24
Buchanan, Lamont. SOT 241
WTS 6, 43, 59, 93, 96
Buchanan, Marie. SF1 76
Buchanan, Robert W. CSF 33
Buchanan, Robert William (1841-1901) BAA 58 CSF 33 SF1 76
Buchanan, Thomas Gittings (1919-)
SF1 76 SF2 834
Buchard, Robert (1931-) SF1 76
SF2 834
Buchner, Hermann. BAA 171
Buchner, Ludwig. POE 86-7
Buchwald, Art. IAC 71 SFS 24
Buchwald, Emilie. FFC 46
Buck, Charles William (1844-1930) SF1 76
Buck, David. FFC 83
Buck, Doris Pitkin. ALW 212
DTS 8, 29 IAC 71 SFE 92 SFS
24
Buck, James Smith (1812-92)
WGT 24 see also Prophet James

Buck, Pearl S. (1892-1973) ES1 73

Buckingham, Emma May. CSF 33

Buckingham, James Silk. BAA 25

Buckle, Christopher Richard Sandford (1916-) SF1 76

Buckle, Richard. BAA 108

Buckle, H(enry) T(homas) EXT 7/1 17 POE 81-2 TJB 24

Buckley, Jerome. WBW 34, 37

Buckley, Robert Thompson, Jr. (1943-) COT 69 LEX 221 VES 80-1

Buckley, William F. WFS 288

Buckman, H. H. CSF 34 SF1 76

Buckmaster, Henrietta pseud. of Henrietta Henkle Stephens. SF1 76

Bucknall, Barbara J. CEN 56-69

Buckner, Bradner. VES 153

Buckner, Mary Dale. TSP 183 see also Donald Dale

Buckner, Robert Henry (1906-) ES1 73 HFI 21 SF1 76 SF2 835

Buckrose, J. E. pseud. of Annie E. Jameson. CSF 34

Budberg, Moura. FAN 189

Buddecke, Eckhart. BAA 208

Buddha, Guatama. ATA 14 CUA 12, 56 CWN 51 EXT 10/2 89 SFN 44 THM 10, 17, 23, 33, 51 VFS 6, 120, 123, 126 WBW 30

Budge. SF1 76

Budrys, Algis (1931-) AAL 21 ACC 209 ALW 212, 219 AOW 155-7, 288, 397 BAA 123, 126 BFP 77 BYS 262, 279 COT 8, 137, 281, 285, 297 CSC 34, 228 DMK 111-120 ES1 73-4 ETN 3, 21, 30, 33, 42, 46-7, 65, 67, 69, 83, 137, 142, 146, 162 EXT 4/2 27, 32 EXT 5/1 3 EXT 8/1 6 FFR 42 FTF 140-1 HFI 21 IAC 71-2 IAH 91, 124-5 ISW 122, 124-5, 199-203, 219, 266 JHN 61 LEX 221-3 LTN 12 MIH 15, 59-66, 91-2, 99-100, 125 NWO 149 RAH 55 RGS 29-30 SFD 31-2, 296 SFE 93-4 SFN 76 SFS 24-5 SFW 6, 207, 305-11, 314, 330 SF1 76-7 SF2 835 SL3 1387-90 SL4 1821-6 SL5 2474-7 SRB 329, 331-2, 371 TSF 59 TSO 3 VES 81, 157, 175, 180, 189, 193, 200, 202, 206, 328 WAA 166 WFS 202, 214 WGT 24 WSF 175, 187,

358 see also Ivan Janvier, Paul Janvier, Alger Rome

Buedeler, Werner (1928-) ES1 74

Buel, Hubert. FFC 87

Buell, John Edward (1927-) SF1 77

Buergel, Bruno H. CSF 34

Bugg, Bob. FFC 171

Buhle, Paul. BAA 208

Buhler, Theodor. BAA 171

Bulfinch, Thomas. IAC 72 SFS 25

Bulgakov, Mikhail A. (1891-1940) AOW 157 ES1 74 EXT 10/2 75 FBK 42 FL2 983-7 MSF 254 SFB 124 SFE 94 SF1 77 SL2 956-9

Bulgarin, Thaddeus. MSF 244-5, 247

Bulichev, Kirill. SFS 25

Bull, Albert E. SF1 77

Bull, Lois (1900-) CSF 34 SF1 77

Bull, R. M. VES 289, 291

Bull, Randolph Cecil. ES1 74 SF1 77

Bull, Terry pseud. of William Samuel Triplet. SF1 77

Bulla, Clyde. FFC 12

Buller, E. Reginald. IAC 72

Bullett, Gerald William (1894-1958) CSF 34 ES1 74 SF1 77

Bullivant, Cecil Henry. SF1 77

Bullock, Alice. IAC 72

Bullock, Shan F. CSF 34

Bullough, Geoffrey. BAA 208

Bulmer, (Henry) Kenneth (1921-) ALW 212 AOW 157, 288 BAA 145, 148 BFP 78-86 BYS 262, 286, 296-7 ES1 74-5 HFI 21-2 IAC 72 LEX 223-6 NDA 104 RGS 30-1 SFE 94-5 SFS 25 SF1 77-8 SF2 835 SRB 109 UFS 3 VES 157, 163, 174, 207, 315 WGT 24-5 WSF 212 see also Alan Burt Akers, Kenneth Johns, Karl Maras

Bulwer-Lytton, (Sir) Edward George (1803-73) AAL 109 ACC 174-5, 191 ALW 53, 60 AOW 9, 11, 25 BAA 29 BYS 82-4, 109, 120 CAT 22 CSF 34 ES1 75 EXT 2/2 28 EXT 3/1 29 EXT 5/1 4 EXT 7/1 2-3, 15 EXT 9/2 29 FBK 62 FL2 698-700 FL4 1843-7 FL5 2203-5 IAC 165 MSF 69, 164-5, 169, 188,

Bulwer-Lytton, Edward (cont.)
202, 220 POE 123, 139-40, 143-
4 PST 30-1, 51-4, 200, 202, 204,
224, 226, 231, 234, 250, 252, 266,
272, 283, 288 SFB 51 SFE 368
SFH 174 SF1 333 SL1 418-22
STH 1, 73, 184, 194 VES 124, 126
WGT 93 WIF 38, 48, 72
Bulwer-Lytton, Edward Robert
(1831-91) SF1 333 WGT 93 see
also Owen Meredith
Bulychev, Kirill (1933? -) HFI 22
IAC 72 LEX 226 SL4 2019-22
Bunce, Frank. TSP 71
Bunce, Oliver Bell (1828-90) BAA
39 SF1 78
Bunch, David R. ALW 212 AOW
157 BAA 152 ES1 75 ETN 28
EXT 8/1 16 HFI 22 IAC 72-3
LEX 226-7 SFE 95 SFS 25
SFW 351 SF1 78 SF2 835-6
VES 189
Bunch, John. VES 155
Bunch, Miriam. IAC 73
Bunge, Mario. BAA 208
Bunin, Ivan Alexsieevich (1870-)
ES1 75
Bunker, Ira S. BAA 65
Buntline, Ned pseud. of Edward
Zane Carroll Judson. TSP 85-6
Bunts, F. E. CSF 34
Bunuel, Luis. CSC 263
Bunyan, John. BYS 70, 73 CAT
39 COT 227 EXT 5/1 19 MSF
217 MSM 111 VES 224 WAA
27, 74 WIF 40
Buono, Victor. ASF 271-2
Bupp, Walter pseud. of Randall
Garrett. IAC 73
Burbank, Leone Clark. CSF 34
SF1 78
Burbridge, Juanita Cassil. CSF
34 SF1 78
Burckhardt, Jakob. FTF 29
Burckhardt, Lucius. BAA 208
Burdekin, Katharine. BAA 94
CSF 34 SF1 78-9
Burdett, Charles (1815-) SF1 79
Burdett, Osbert (1885-1936) CSF
34 ES1 75-6
Burdick, Eugene Leonard (1918-
65) AOW 158 BYS 55 ES1 76
FAN 168 FFR 42 IAC 73 MFW
199-200 SFE 95 SF1 79 SF2
836 TSF 131 VES 135

Burford, Daniel C. IMS 79, 116,
171 WFS 71-2
Burford, Lolah Mary (1931-) FFC
161 SF1 79 SF2 836
Burg, Leon. IMS 116, 125, 213
Burgdorf, Karl-Ulrich (1952-)
LEX 227
Burgel, Bruno H. (1875-1948)
COT 2 ES1 76 LEX 223
Burger, Dionys. ES1 76 SFE 95
SF1 79
Burger, Douglas A. FL1 45-7,
149-53
Burger, Gottfried August. FBK
44
Burger, Joanne Denise (1938-)
AOW 360 SF1 79 SF2 836 SRB
64
Burgess, Andrew J. TSF 168-76
Burgess, Anthony pseud. of John
Anthony Burgess Wilson. AAL
19, 164, 222 ACC 123 ALW 31,
99, 238 AOW 158 BAA 208 BYS
257, 298 CSC 188, 193 DTS 28
ES1 76 EXT 6/2 51 EXT 8/1
16 EXT 10/1 47 FAN 148-9
FTF 107 HFI 22 HWK 44 IAC
73 JGB 4, 13-4 LEX 227-8
MFW 23, 250 MIH 140 NDA xi,
69-72, 106-7, 121, 162-5, 208,
210-1, 216 NWO 125 POE 274-
5, 281 RAH 94, 103 RBY 24,
196, 213 SFB 92 SFD 319 SFE
95 SFW 104, 233 SF1 79 SL1
396-401 SL5 2402-6 SOT 2
STF 23, 71, 79 TSF 238 VES
262, 297 WBW 23 WSF 243, 387
Burgess, Brian. SF1 79
Burgess, Eric (1920-) ES1 76
Burgess, Eric Alexander (1912-)
SF1 79 SF2 836-7
Burgess, (Frank) Gelett (1866-
1951) AOW 54 CSF 34 EXT 1/1
7 SF1 79 SRB 11
Burgess, Leslie. CSF 34
Burgess, Mary A. FL1 4-6, 508-
10 FL2 749-56 FL4 1901-3
Burgess, M(ichael) R(oy) (1948-)
SF2 1044-5 see also Robert
Reginald
Burgess, Thornton W. FFC 115
Burgh, James (1714-75) BAA 12-
3 WGT 25
Burgin, G. G. STH 35-6
Burgin, George Brown (1856-
1944) CSF 34 SF1 79

Burgin, Richard. NWO 210
Burgoyne, Alan Hughes (1880-
1929) CSF 34 SF1 79
Burhoe, B. Alan. IAC 73
Burk, James K. JHN 61
Burke, Edmund. BYS 15, 34, 53,
99, 305 FBK 8 RAH 174
Burke, John Frederick (1922-)
BAA 126 ES1 76-7 HFI 22
IMS 200, 251 SF1 79-80 SF2
837 SOT 380 WGT 25 see also
Jonathan Burke
Burke, Jonathan pseud. of John
Frederick Burke (1922-) IAC 73
LEX 228-9 SFE 95-6
Burke, Kenneth. FLT 152, 156
MSF 51 SFN 56
Burke, Norah Eileen (1907-) CSF
34 SF1 80
Burke, Ralph pseud. of Randall
Garrett, Robert Silverberg.
SFE 96
Burke, T. Edward. STH 167
Burke, Thomas (1886-1945) CSF
35 ES1 77 SF1 80
Burkert, Nancy Eckholm. FFC
2, 63
Burkett, William R., Jr. (1943-)
ES1 77 HFI 22 SFE 96 SF1 80
SF2 837-8 VES 161
Burkhardt, Eve. SF1 80 WGT 25
Burkhardt, Francois. BAA 208
Burkhardt, Robert Ferdinand
(1892-1947) SF1 80 WGT 25
Burkholder, A. L. PST 185, 207,
267
Burkitt, Frederick Evelyn. WGT
25 see also Gregory Saben
Burkitt, William T. BAA 79
Burks, Arthur J. (1898-1974)
ALW 141 CSF 35 ES1 77-8
IAC 73 IMS 16, 77, 138, 195 RFA
13, 42, 51, 54, 57, 62-3, 66 SFE
96 SFS 25 SF1 80 SOT 45, 107,
192, 397 TSP 25, 28, 83-95, 141,
148, 189, 226 VES 103, 135, 140,
147, 340 WGT 25 WIF 88 WSF
54, 75, 122 WTS ix, 23-6, 30, 38,
40, 125 see also Esther Critchfield, E. Critchie
Burland, Cottie. ES1 78
Burland, Harris pseud. of John
Harris-Burland. BAA 67 CSF
35 EXT 1/1 7

Burleson, Donald R. FL1 203-6,
431-5 FL4 1621-8 SL1 97-101
SL3 1284-8 SL4 1973-1977
Burman, Ben Lucien (1896-) ES1
78 FFC 115 SF1 80 SF2 838
Burmeister, Kate. SF1 80
Burn, Doris. FFC 140
Burne-Jones, Edward. FBK 89
WBW 5-6, 49, 62
Burne-Jones, Georgiana. MSF
188
Burnet, Dana. CSF 35
Burnett, Frances Hodgson (1849-
1924) CSF 35 FFC 92 SF1 80
SRB 22
Burnett, Hallie Southgate (1908-)
ES1 78 SF1 80 SF2 838
Burnett, Whitney Ewing (1899-
1973) CSF 35 ES1 78 IAC 73
SF1 80
Burnford, Sheila Philip Cochrane
(1918-) FFC 3 SF1 81 SF2 838
Burnham, James. EXT 9/2 56
ISW 165 SFW 234-5
Burningham, John. FFC 144
Burns, Alan (1929-) SF1 81 SF2
838
Burns, Harvey (house name) TSP
25
Burns, Irene. FFC 180
Burns, Jim. VES 202
Burns, John Horne. WFS 154
Burns, R. C. SF1 81
Burns, Robert. ACC 119 EXT
8/2 33
Burr, Aaron. COT 38, 141
Burr, Amelia J. CSF 35
Burr, Chauncey. WAA 90
Burr, Frank. ES1 78 SF1 81
Burr, Hanford Montrose (1864-
1941) SF1 81
Burrage, Alfred McLelland (1889-
1956) CSF 35 ES1 78-9 IAC 73
SF1 81 WGT 25
Burrage, Athol Harcourt. ES1
79 SF1 81
Burrard, Gerald. CSF 35
Burroughs, Edgar Rice (1875-
1950) AAL 90, 106, 134-6 ALW
8, 33, 67, 72, 108-11, 114, 116, 125,
141, 146, 216 AOW 47, 55, 89,
349, 351-2, 394, 402-3 ASF 166,
188-9 BFP 87-95 BYS 18, 20,
139, 141, 152, 156-69, 271, 290
COT 60, 62-9, 71, 73, 77, 166, 259,

Burroughs, E. R. (cont.)
266 CSC 43, 168, 172-3, 179, 201
CSF 35-6 CWD 10, 41-2, 61 CYR
58 ES1 79-82 EXT 1/2 31 EXT
2/1 13 EXT 3/1 28 EXT 4/2 25
EXT 5/1 4, 15-6 EXT 8/1 4
EXT 10/1 34, 46 EXT 10/2 77
FAN 152 FBK 81, 112 FFR 42-
6 FHT 48 FL2 873-9 FL4 1884-
90 FTF 70 [FUT] HFI 22-4
HID 106, 120 HWK 7, 40 IAC 73
IAH 53, 141 IMS 138, 170 INT 6,
45, 59 ISW 90, 154, 197-8, 251
JVN 88-9, 188 KAU 44-5 KWS
57, 370 LEX 229-30 LTN 80
MFW 21-2, 128, 133-7 MIH 25
MSF 29, 116, 162, 178, 205, 260-1,
282 MSM 128, 132, 134, 176, 202,
304 NWO 70 OSR 229-47 OWB
85 PJF 13, 46 PST 128-9, 195,
220, 224, 317 RAH 21, 138 RBY
35, 109 RFA vi, 1-2, 63, 171, 190
RGS 31-3, 210-1 RHN 11, 81,
148, 151, 200-1 RSG 9, 31 SFB
46-7, 76 SFD 28, 41, 72, 210, 242,
273-4, 287, 305 SFE 96-7 SFS
25-6 SFW 59-64 SF1 81-3 SF2
838 SIH 48, 113 SL1 93-6, 298-
302 SL3 1130-4 SL4 1665-8,
1720-5 SL5 2229-35 SOI xiii
SOT 14, 25, 30, 70, 93, 110, 112,
123, 171, 191, 222, 294-5, 355, 399,
432 SRB 6, 253, 297 STH 41-3,
107, 255 TJB 13, 49 TSF 1-2,
52, 228 VES 70-1, 80, 97, 139,
156, 187-8, 208, 266, 273, 286,
304, 312, 322, 340 VFS 49, 140,
144, 146, 197 WAA 101-4 WFS
6, 27 WGT 25-6 WIF 23, 38, 49,
65-9, 75, 149, 178, 194, 205, 209,
211, 230, 254 WSF 24-8, 44-5,
246, 386 WTS 27, 33, 36, 42, 62,
65, 67, 86, 120 YTS 9 see also
Normal Bean, Norman Bean
Burroughs, Gail. FFC 79
Burroughs, Hulbert. RFA 63
SOT 112
Burroughs, John Coleman (1913-)
ES1 82 HFI 24 IAC 73 RFA 63
SFE 97 SF2 839 SF1 83 SOT
112
Burroughs, Joseph Birkbeck.
BAA 69 CSF 36 SF1 83
Burroughs, S. M. BAA 1

Burroughs, William S. (1914-)
ALW 31, 238 AOW 158-9 BAA
140 BYS 257, 297, 319 CSC 101
ES1 82-3 EXT 7/1 1 EXT 7/2
32 EXT 8/1 13, 17 FL3 1086-8
HFI 24 IAC 73 JGB 4, 6-7, 10,
61 MIH 16 NWO 36, 205-6, 256
POE 273-4 SFD 4 SFE 97 SF1
83 SF2 839 SIH 54 SL4 1566-
70 SOT 2 VFS 117 WGT 26
Burschell, Friedrich. BAA 208
Burstenbinder, Elisabeth (1838-
1918) WGT 26
Burt, Donald C. BAA 281
Burt, Michael (1900-) ES1 83
Burtis, Thompson (1896-) CSF
36 SF1 83
Burton, Alice Elizabeth (1908-)
BAA 116 ES1 83 WGT 26 see
also Susan Alice Kerby
Burton, Edmund pseud. of Edmund
Burton Childs. SFN 58 SF1 83
Burton, Francis George. SF1 83
Burton, (Lady) Isabel. WTS 11
Burton, John Bloundelle. CSF 36
Burton, Mary. SFN 58
Burton, Maurice (1898-) ES1 83
Burton, (Sir) Richard Francis
(1821-1920) CSF 36 EXT 10/1
26 FBK 45 PJF 49-58, 65, 73
VFS 6 WGT 26 WTS 11
Burton, Robert (1577-1640) BAA
3 EXT 2/2 33 EXT 8/1 22
WGT 26
Burton, Samuel Holroyd (1919-)
ES1 83 IAC 73 SFE 97 SF1 83
SF2 839
Burton, Virginia. FFC 1
Burtscher, Marian. INT viii
Burtt, J. Lewis. ES1 83
Bury, John B. POE 285
Busby, F(rancis) M(arion) (1921-)
BFP 96 FFR 46 HFI 24-5 IAC
73-4 RGS 33-4 SFE 97-8 SF1
83 SF2 839
Busch, Gunther. BAA 209 EXT
6/1 14
Bush, George Edward (1938-) SF1
83
Bush, Lucius M. ES1 83 SF1 83
Bush, Robert D. BAA 209
Bush, (Dr.) Vannevar. VFS 215,
221
Bushkovitch, A. K. NDA 57
Bushnell, Adelyn. SF1 83

Bushnell, David. ASF 186
Bushness, George Herbert (1896-)
ES1 83
Busoni, Rafaello. FFC 17, 73
Bussard, R.W. VES 76
Busson, Bernard. ES1 83
Busson, Paul (1873-1924) CSF 36
FBK 143-4 SF1 83
Butcher, Fanny. EXT 6/1 17-8
Butcher, Margaret. CSF 36 SF1
83
Butenko, Bohden. FBK 146
Butler, Bill. EXT 8/1 17 IAC 74
SFS 26
Butler, Canon. EXT 7/1 5
Butler, Ellis Parker. IAC 74
RAH 23 STH 138 WIF 70
Butler, Ewan. SF1 83
Butler, F.J. CSF 36
Butler, Ivan pseud. of Edward
Ivan Oakley Beuttler. ES1 83
SF1 84
Butler, Joan pseud. of Robert
Williams Alexander. ES1 83
SFE 98 SF1 84
Butler, Mary. EXT 7/1 15
Butler, Mildred. IAC 74
Butler, Octavia E. HFI 25 IAC
74
Butler, S.D. WTS 24
Butler, Samuel (1835-1902) ACC
209 ALW 53, 61 AOW 20, 55-6,
356 ASF 173 BAA xi, 29, 64
BYS 66, 84-6, 88 CAT 76 COT
166-7, 214 CSF 36 ES1 83-4
EXT 5/1 4 EXT 7/1 3-6, 9, 15
EXT 8/1 20 EXT 9/2 27, 41, 46,
47 FAN 9, 66, 90, 126, 185 FTF
100, 113, 126-7 HFI 25 IAC 74
IAH 16 MFW 85, 91, 196-8, 287
MIH 26 MSF 5, 165-6, 169, 257
MSM 244, 253 NWO 121 POE
144-5 PST 51, 53-5, 57, 62, 106,
193, 199, 217, 226, 228, 230, 234,
236, 261, 307 SFB 51 SFE 98
SF1 84 SL2 729-34 SRB 8 TRB
58 VES 124, 126, 254, 259 WAA
31 WIF 57, 223
Butler, William (1929-) ES1 84
HFI 25 SFE 98 SF1 84
Butler, (Sir) William Francis
(1838-1910) POE 183 SF1 84
Butman, Robert. EXT 3/1 22

Butor, Michel (1926-) BAA 209
BYS 95 CAT 115 MSF 147, 154
OSR 157-65, 354 SFB 16, 23, 66
SFE 98
Butters, Dorothy C. FFC 130
Butterworth, Frank Nestle see
Peter Blundell
Butterworth, Michael (1947-)
IAC 74 LEX 231 SFE 98
Butterworth, Oliver (1915-) ES1
84 FFC 87, 140 SF1 84
Buttrey, Douglas Norton (1918-)
see Densil Neve Barr
Butts, Jane Roberts (1929-) SF2
1049
Butts, Mary F. CSF 36
Buve, Sergius. BAA 209
Buzzati, Dino (1906-72) ES1 84
FBK 153 FFC 130 FFR 46
SFE 98 SF1 84
Byars, Betsy. FFC 61, 83
Byatt, Henry. CSF 36 SF1 84
STH 36
Byers, Albert F. SF1 84
Byfield, Barbara. FFC 29, 186
Bylise, Marguerite. ES1 84
Bynner, Edwin Lasseter (1842-
93) CSF 37 ES1 84
Byram, George. IAC 74 SFS 26
Byrd, Bob. SF1 84
Byrne, Cathal O. SF1 84
Byrne, Donn (1889-1928) CSF 37
ES1 84
Byrne, Jack. IMS 75 TSP 108
Byrne, Johnny. IAC 74 SFS 26
Byrne, Leon. TSP 144, 154
Byrne, Stuart James (1913-) ES1
84 FFR 46 HFI 25 LEX 231
SF1 84 SF2 839-40 WGT 26
Byrne, S.J. see Marx Kaye
Byrnes, Asher. AC2 74
Byron, (Lord) (1788-1824) ASF
182, 305 BYS 16-7, 25, 28, 31, 93
CSF 37 CWN 31 EXT 2/1 15
FBK 27, 44 INT 73 MFW 20
MSF 128, 137-8, 150, 153, 168
PJF 15, 37 POE 46 PST 28, 33-
4 RBY 58, 65, 120 SFB 32 SFN
12 SHL 38 THM 39, 45 TSO 23
WAA 87 WIF 41
Bywater, Hector Charles (1884-
1940) AOW 36, 56 CSF 37 MSM
149 SFE 98 SF1 84

C

C. C. BAA 12
C. J. T. CSF 37 SF1 506-7
Cabeen, Francis Von Albede.
  CSF 37 SF1 84
Cabell, James Branch (1879-1958)
  AOW 93-5, 402-3 BYS 266 CSC
  33-4, 185 CSF 37 ES1 84-5
  EXT 7/2 36-7 FBK 81, 98, 117-
  9 FFR 47 FL1 95-115 HFI 25
  IAC 74 IAH 82 JVN 88, 188
  LEX 232 LTN 91-2 NWO 36
  RAH 225, 227 SFD 274 SFE 98-
  9 SF1 85 SOT 342 SRB 254
  WAA 75, 98-100, 110, 230 WBW
  3 WFS 32, 116, 192 WIF 76
Cabet, Etienne (1788-1856) BAA
  xi FAN 66 MSF 138-9, 175, 177,
  248 POE 122 WGT 27
Cable, George W. CSF 37
Cabodevilla, Jose Maria. BAA
  171
Cabot, John York pseud. of David
  Wright O'Brien. STH 155
Cabral, Francisco see Gabriel
  Francois
Cabral, O. M. TSP 29
Cabral, Olga. IAC 74
Cacchioni, Marco. IAC 74
Caddy, Alice. FFC 115
Caddy, Harrison. FFC 115
Cade, Cecil Maxwell. ES1 85
Cade, Henry. IAC 117
Cade, Jack. MSF 195, 197
Cadell, Violet Elizabeth (1903-)
  ES1 85 SF1 85 SF2 840
Cadman, Harry. BAA 209
Cadman, Lawrence. TSP 71
Caen, Herb. WTS 57
Caesar, Julius. ISW 236 OWB
  70 SFN 54 VFS 129, 195

Cage, John. WFS 214
Cagney, James. HEN 18 STH 252
Cahill, Laurence J. SOT 340
  WTS 82
Cahn, Lee. IAC 74 IAH 35
Cahun, Leon. CSF 37
Caidin, Martin (1927-) AOW 159
  BAA 145 ES1 85-6 FFR 47
  HFI 25 KAU 155, 175 LEX 232-
  3 MFW 200 NDA 22-3, 25, 204
  SFE 99 SF1 85 SF2 840 VES
  102, 189, 301
Caillois, Roger (1913-) BAA 209
  ES1 86 FBK 8-9, 11, 22 SFB 21
  SF1 86 SF2 840
Cain. IAH 125 LTN 63 TDI 57
  WBW 32
Cain, Ronald. IAC 74
Caine, Hall. CSF 37
Caine, Staff (1931-) LEX 233
Caine, (Sir) Thomas Henry Hall
  (1853-1931) SFE 99 SF1 86
Caine, William (1873-1925) SF1
  86
Caine, William Ralph Hall (1865-
  1939) SF1 86
Caird, Alice Mona. CSF 37
Caird, Janet (1913-) SF1 86 SF2
  840
Cairnes, Maud pseud. of Kathleen
  H. Curzon-Herrick. CSF 37
  SF1 86
Cairnes, (Capt.) William Elliot
  (1862-1902) CSF 37 SF1 86
Caldecott, (Sir) Andrew (1884-
  1951) CSF 37 ES1 86 SF1 86
Calder, John. IAC 74
Calder, Nigel. IAC 74
Calder, (Lord) Ritchie. FTF 69,
  127

Calder-Marshall, Arthur (1908-)
ES1 86 FL2 518-9 SF1 86 SF2
840-1
Calderon, George Leslie (1868-
1915) CSF 37 SF1 86
Caldwell, Norman. IMS 15
Caldwell, Taylor (1900-) BAA 120
ES1 86 EXT 5/1 4 ISW 29-31
SFE 99 SF1 86 SF2 841
Calhoun, Mary (1926-) ES1 86
FFC 73 SF1 86 SF2 841
Calisher, Hortense (1911-) AOW
159 ES1 86 HFI 26 IAC 74
SFE 99 SF1 86 SF2 841
Calkins, Dick. SFB 109 SFE 99-
100 TRB 58 WSF 305
Calkins, Elizabeth. AOW 365
SF1 86 SRB 463 TSF 82-96
Calkins, Ernest Elmo. IAC 74
Callaghan, Stella. BAA 93
Callahan, Patrick J. OSR 147-
56,354
Callen, Larry. FFC 140
Callenbach, Ernest. BAA 161
HFI 26
Callenbach, Franz (1663-1743)
WGT 27
Callender, Julian pseud. of Austin
Lee. SF1 86
Calson, Isaac pseud. of John Wal-
ter Ledoux. SF1 86
Calthrop, Dion Clayton (1878-
1937) CSF 38 SF1 86
Calvano, Tony. SF1 86
Calvert, Robert. IAC 74
Calverton, Victor Francis (1900-
40) CSF 38 SF1 86
Calvin, John (1509-64) ATA 46
COT 98 CUA 23 CYR 7-8,11,
17,40-1,46-7,53 EXT 1/2 35
EXT 4/1 8 HEN 24,42,61 RHN
135-7 SFN 51 SHL 4,8,22,24,
42,47,50,56,59-61 TBC 12,14-
5,39 TDI 6 THM 23,45 TSO
31 VF1 88-103,267-8
Calvino, Italo (1923-) AOW 159-
60 CAT 104 ES1 86 FBK 153
FFR 47 FL3 1183-7 HFI 26
IAC 74 LEX 233-4 SFB 145
SFD 208 SFE 100 SF1 87 SIH
53 SL1 438-42 SL5 2223-8
SRB 255 WAA 235
Cameron, Alastair (1925-) ES1
86 EXT 5/1 5 SF1 87

Cameron, Berl (house name) SF1
87 see also John Glasby, Brian
Holloway, Dennis Talbot Hughes,
David O'Brien, Arthur Roberts
Cameron, Brian. VES 322
Cameron, Eleanor Butler (1912-)
AOW 312 ES1 86 FFC 29,106,
161 LTN 261,267 SF1 87 SF2
841 SRB 24 UKL 245
Cameron, Elizabeth Dorothea
Cole Bowen (1889-1973) WGT 27
Cameron, Ian pseud. of Donald
Gordon Payne. HFI 26 MFW
25 SFE 100
Cameron, John (1927-) AOW 160
SFE 100 SF1 86
Cameron, Julia Margaret. FBK
108
Cameron, Lou (1924-) HFI 26
MFW 86 SF1 87 SF2 842
Cameron, Verney Lovett (1844-
94) CSF 38 SF1 87
Cammaerts, Emile (-1953) SF1
87
Campanella, Giovanni. IAC 74
SFS 26
Campanella, Roy. WFS 222
Campanella, Tommaso (1568-
1639) ALW 43 AOW 20,344
BYS 64,66,68 EXT 3/2 48 EXT
4/2 18 EXT 8/1 23 EXT 9/1 5
EXT 10/2 76 FAN 66 FTF 99
MSF 96,100,102-3,259 POE
4-5 PST 20,25,227,230,237,
263,269,285,297 SFE 100 SIH
65,68 VES 255 WAA 49 WIF
39
Campbell, Archie. SF1 87 VES
211
Campbell, Austin (1884-) CSF 38
SF1 87
Campbell, Cliff (house name)
TSP 147-8
Campbell, Clyde Crane pseud. of
H. L. Gold. ALW 216 ASF 215
ISW 259 PST 183,195 RFA 52
STH 118
Campbell, Colin. SF1 87
Campbell, Dona. WFS 216 see
also Dona Smith
Campbell, Donald. SF1 87
Campbell, Duncan. BAA 88 CSF
38 SF1 87
Campbell, Forrest. SF1 88

Campbell, Gabrielle V. C. see
Joseph Shearing
Campbell, (Sir) Gilbert E. (1838-
99) CSF 38 ES1 86 SF1 88
Campbell, H. G. VES 108
Campbell, Hazel. CSF 38
Campbell, Herbert J. (1925-)
BAA 123 CSC 227 ES1 87 IAC
74 LEX 234 SFE 100 SF1 88
WIF 121 see also Roy Sheldon
Campbell, Hope. FFC 115 see
also G. McDonald Wallis
Campbell, Hubert J. see Herbert
J. Campbell
Campbell, J. J. EXT 6/2 51
Campbell, James L. CSF 38
SFW 39-50, 75-82, 91-100
Campbell, James Lawrence
(1889-) SF1 88
Campbell, John (1766-1840) CSF
38 SF1 88
Campbell, (John) Ramsey (1946-)
BYS 48 ES1 87 FBK 81 FFR
48 FL3 1209-11, 1485-8 FRN
58 IAC 74 LEX 237 SFS 26
SF1 89 SF2 842-3 WGT 27
Campbell, John Scott. ES1 87
IAC 74
Campbell, (Mrs.) John. IAC 75
Campbell, John W., Jr. (1910-
71) AAL 45, 49-50, 74, 109, 133-
4, 137-8, 213 ACC 62, 66, 214-5
ACE 17-8, 20, 33 AC2 15-6, 18,
31 ALW 7, 11, 31, 34, 67, 107,
126, 146-62, 166, 173, 175, 194,
211-3, 216, 219, 225, 230, 236, 239
AOW 80, 83, 85, 89, 91, 99-100,
160, 292-3, 296, 298-9 ASF 22,
31, 33, 36, 108-10, 112-3, 120,
123-6, 128, 137, 142, 148-51, 162,
168, 196-212, 216, 219, 221-4,
226, 243-4, 252-3, 260-2, 308,
313-4 BFP 97-100 BYS 217,
225-30, 233-9, 241-2, 274, 287,
314, 320 CAT xvi, 14, 16-8, 35,
43 COT 1, 16-7, 20, 24-5, 51, 57,
65, 69, 77-8, 80-1, 93, 106, 152,
156-7, 159, 165, 173-4, 176, 190-
1, 195, 211-4, 216, 219, 237, 239,
245-6, 251, 253, 278, 281, 283,
291, 294, 296, 300-1 CSC 11, 15,
28-9, 39, 58, 65, 74, 81, 102, 115,
169, 197-9, 230-1 CSF 38 CWD
61 CYR 9 ES1 87-9 ETN 2, 8,
12-3, 15-6, 18, 21, 32-3, 37, 45-
6, 54, 57, 63-9, 71-6, 95, 100, 103,
113, 120, 131, 142, 145, 159-61,
163, 178, 197 EXT 1/2 26, 30, 33
EXT 2/1 19 EXT 5/1 8, 13 EXT
7/2 39-45 EXT 8/1 2-8 EXT
10/2 112 FBK 122 FFR 48
[FJT] FLR 13, 20 FTF 68, 70,
72 HFI 26 HID 9, 18, 20-1, 23,
27-8, 52, 79, 110 HWK 8, 11, 17
IAC 74-5 IAH 13-5, 25, 29-30,
35, 45-7, 77, 87, 90, 93-4, 98-100,
102 IMS 16, 117, 124, 146-9, 170,
175-6, 182-4, 187, 195, 197, 202,
205-6, 209, 212-3, 220-1, 241
INT 7, 9 ISW xi, 34-6, 47, 60,
108, 131, 133, 139, 161, 193, 203,
217-8, 284 JVN 196, 201, 211
KAU 153, 166, 169, 191 KWS 26,
49-50, 55 LEX 234-7 LTN 229
MFW 3-5, 7-9, 11, 16, 28, 30, 39-
41, 166-7, 282, 287, 289 MIH 14-
5, 17, 22, 36, 45, 71, 86, 89, 92, 103
MSM 3-22, 24, 32-3, 53-4, 74, 77-
8, 90, 170-7, 216, 296, 298, 303,
305 OMN 12 OWB 41, 43, 79,
86, 89-101 PJF 40 RAH 16, 28,
42, 47, 60, 196, 227 RFA vi-vii,
xvi, xix, xxii, 2, 28-31, 33, 35, 41-
2, 44, 46, 48-50, 52, 54, 56-8, 60,
62-6, 72-4, 82, 84-6, 88, 96, 98,
100, 108, 117-8, 124-6, 128-9,
132-3, 138, 142-4, 152-7, 167,
176-7, 181, 183-5, 187, 192-4,
199, 202, 204, 208-9, 213, 215
RGS 34-5 RHN 27 RSG 10 SFA
26, 30-1, 34, 39, 41-7, 55, 61-3,
78, 88-9, 93, 106, 138, 142-5, 224,
232, 244, 273, 281, 294 SFB 11,
18, 21, 55, 60-2, 89, 99, 137 SFD
25, 27, 30, 55-6, 61, 64, 73, 81, 88-
9, 136, 154, 171, 209-10, 212, 232,
236, 241-2, 245, 288-9, 291, 295,
307, 309, 312, 318 SFE 100-1
SFN 25, 47, 74, 79, 83 SFS 26
SFW 114, 121, 151-9, 198, 228,
267-70, 321, 395, 397 SF1 88-9
SF2 842 SIH 12, 59, 114, 118,
165, 190, 201 SL3 1396-1400,
1444-8 SL4 2003-7 SOT 6, 10,
21, 24-46, 63, 72, 94, 97, 107, 110-
1, 115, 121, 133-4, 144, 148, 155,
157, 173, 175-7, 191, 195, 198-9,
213, 216, 222, 225, 236, 239, 253-
4, 261, 273-5, 290, 293, 296, 319,
330, 381-3, 386-7, 401, 407, 414,

Campbell, John W. (cont.)
416, 433 SRB 12-3, 44, 100, 112-3, 306, 315, 499 STH 2, 10-1, 108, 116, 158, 244-5, 260 TJB 3-6, 8-9, 12, 23 TPS 171-96 TRB 54, 56 TSF 30-1, 52, 146, 207, 228-9 TSO 29-31, 35 VES 71, 80, 87, 92, 102, 134-5, 170, 172, 179, 181-2, 204, 233, 259, 313, 317, 328, 330, 341 VFS 97 WAA 240-1 WFS 20, 43-5, 69, 75, 84-91, 96, 100, 111-2, 114, 118-9, 124, 173, 181, 188-90, 202, 216, 227, 242-3, 264-5, 296 WGT 27 WIF 20, 84, 89, 91, 95, 105, 108, 129, 138, 149, 162, 220 WSF 37-9, 47-9, 63, 68-71, 84, 91-114, 128-30, 132, 135, 139, 146, 148-57, 163-9, 182, 186, 188, 191, 211, 217-8, 233, 236-7, 272, 283, 295, 299, 305, 309, 322, 371, 386 WTS 43-4, 132 see also Arthur McCann, Don A. Stuart

Campbell, John W., Sr. OWB 89
Campbell, Joseph. INT 112, 115-8 KAU 71 PJF 13-4, 36, 45, 55 RAH 53 TDI 9 WBW 29-30
Campbell, Marion (1919-) SF1 89
Campbell, Peg. ASF 208-11
Campbell, Reginald John (1867-1956) ES1 89
Campbell, Reginald Wilfrid (1894-1950) CSF 38 SF1 89
Campbell, Spencer. SF1 89
Campbell, Thomas. CAT 2
Campbell, William Edward. BAA 172, 209
Campbell, William Edward March BAA 120
Campion, Sarah pseud. of Mary Rose Coulton. SF1 89
Campion, Sidney. CWN 3, 27
Campton, David. IAC 75
Camra, Roy. SF1 89
Camus, Albert (1913-60) CWN 7, 21, 24, 30, 42 MSF 251 MSM 88 NDA 90 RZY 94 UKL 146 WBW 18
Canaday, Nicholas, Jr. BAA 209
Canady, John. WGT 27
Canary, Robert H. BAA 209 CAT 100 KAU 129 MFW 16 SRB 499
Canby, Vincent. ACC 143
Candeze, Ernest Charles Auguste (1827-98) SF1 89

Candler, Edmund (1874-1926) CSF 38 SF1 89
Canedo, Alejandro. RFA 166 WGT 27 see also Alejandro
Caniff, Milt. SOT 85
Cannan, Gilbert (1884-1955) BAA 80 CSF 38 ES1 89 SF1 89
Canning, George. IAC 75 MSF 135
Canning, John (1920-) ES1 89
Canning, Victor (1911-) SF1 89
Cannon, Walter F. MSF 224
Cansler, Ronald Lee. BAA 209 RAH 258
Cantimori, Delio. BAA 172
Cantine, Holley. IAC 75 SFS 26
Canton, William (1845-1926) CSF 38 SF1 89
Cantor, Hal. ES1 89 SF1 89
Cantril, Hadley. CSF 38 ES1 89 SFB 36
Cantu, Gaston Garcia. BAA 177, 223
Cape, Judith pseud. of Patricia Kathleen Page. CSF 39 SF1 89
Capek, Joseph (1887-1945) CSF 39 FBK 82 FFC 130 FL2 773-5 IAC 75 MSF 270, 272, 282 SF1 89
Capek, Karel (1890-1938) ACC 136 ALW 38, 99, 105 AOW 48, 56, 100, 346 ASF 70-1, 107, 145-6, 162 BYS 26, 182-5, 229, 282, 287 CAT 106, 138 COT 203-5 CSF 39 ES1 89-90 EXT 3/1 28 EXT 4/2 25 EXT 5/1 4 EXT 5/2 2 EXT 9/1 19 FAN 95-9, 185 FBK 82 FFR 48 FL2 773-5 FTF 122, 138 HFI 26 IAC 75 ISW 11-2, 58 KAU 141, 156 LEX 237-8 LTN 80, 205 MFW 85, 195, 247 MSF 29-30, 74, 137, 229, 270-83 MSM 82 NDA 29 NWO 135-7 POE 10, 231, 261 PST 174-5 RFA 116 RHN 67, 93 SFB 45, 51, 53, 148 SFD 305 SFE 102 SFN 39, 118 SFS 26 SFW 104, 219, 583-9, 591 SF1 89-90 SIH 62, 132, 139, 147, 185 SL1 6-10 SL4 1837-43 SL5 2424-8 SOT 129, 213 SRB 293, 298 TRB 54 TSF 229 VES 92, 135, 161, 172, 175, 180, 232, 255 WAA 40 WIF 69, 88, 234, 245 WSF 87 YTS 8, 74

Capes, Bernard E(dward Joseph) (-1918) CSF 39 ES1 90 SF1 90
Capinster, Jeanette Henry. STH 183-4
Caplin, Alfred Gerald (1909-) WGT 27
Capon, (Harry) Paul (1911-69) AOW 160, 312 BAA 118, 120, 129 ES1 90 FFR 48 HFI 27 SFE 102-3 SF1 90 SF2 843 VES 122
Capone, Al. TSP 195
Capote, Truman (1924-84) CSF 39 ES1 90 ETN 176 IAC 75 MSM 103-4 SFD 208 SFS 26 STF 10 TBC 49
Capp, Al (1909-) ES1 90-1 [FUT] SFD 208
Capps, Carroll M. (1917-1971) ES1 91 WGT 27 see also C. C. MacApp
Carandell, Jose Maria. BAA 172
Caras, Roger Andrew (1928-) SF2 1063-4 WGT 27
Caravan, T. P. IAC 75-6 SFS 26
Card, Orson Scott. LEX 238-9
Cardiff, Ira D. ES1 91
Cardinal, Jane pseud. of Ethel Williamson. CSF 39 SF1 90
Carew, Henry. CSF 39 SF1 90
Carey, Cynthia. STH 62
Carey, Ernestine Moller Gilbreth (1908-) SF1 90 SF2 843
Carey, George Washington (1845-1924) SF1 90
Carey, Philip. SFN 116
Carey, Mary. SF1 90
Carfrae, Elizabeth. CSF 39
Carl, Harry. STH 260
Carleton, H. B. (house name) WGT 27-8 see also Howard Browne
Carleton, William. CSF 39 IAC 76
Carlfi, Chester H. IAC 76
Carlin, Gage. SF1 90
Carling, John. CSF 39
Carlisle, Donald T. CSF 39
Carlisle, Robert B. BAA 209
Carlisle, Robin. SF1 90
Carlisle, Samuel Hanna. SF1 90
Carlock, Nancy. BAA 281
Carloni, Giancarlo. FFC 14
Carlsen, Ruth Christoffer (1918-) AOW 312 FFC 61, 73, 140, 181 SF1 91 SF2 843-4

Carlson, Dale Bick (1935-) SF1 91 SF2 844
Carlson, Esther Elizabeth (1920-) ES1 91 IAC 76 SFS 26
Carlson, Natalie. FFC 130, 140, 154
Carlson, Ralph. TSP 22
Carlson, William. IAC 76
Carlson, William A. BAA 209
Carlsson, Peder. IAC 76
Carlton, Frank T. BAA 209
Carlton, Mary Shaffer. BAA 164 ES1 91 SF1 91
Carlton, Roger. SFE 104
Carlyle, Thomas (1795-1881) AOW 356 CSC 31-2 CSF 39 EXT 4/2 19 MSF 224 POE 129 PST 49, 103, 309 RZY 35 STF 34 TBC 45 THM 10, 12, 17, 32
Carmel, Carl. SFS 26
Carmer, Carl Lamson (1893-1976) ES1 91 IAC 94 SF1 91 SF2 844
Carmichael, Montgomery. BAA 209
Carmichael, Philip. CSF 39
Carnac, Levin pseud. of George Chetwynd Griffith-Jones. STH 200
Carnegie, Andrew. MSF 225, 229
Carnegie, Dale. RHN 57
Carneiro, Andre. IAC 76 SL1 383-5 SL4 1545-7
Carnell, E(dward) J(ohn) (1912-72) AOW 288 BYS 296-7 ES1 91-2 ETN 21 EXT 8/1 17 FTF 69 IAC 76 IMS 46, 53, 69, 73, 96-100 SFB 131 SFE 104-5 SFS 26-7 SFW 277 SF1 91 SF2 844 SIH 199 SOT 381 SRB 101 WAA 217, 230 WFS 99 WIF 121 WSF 74, 128, 147, 231, 249, 251
Carne-Ross, Joseph. BAA 37
Carnese, Levin. ALW 85
Carney, John Otis (1922-) SF1 91 SF2 844
Carnot, Sadi. FTF 36-7 VES 249
Carnson, Maxwell. CSF 39 SF1 91
Caro, Dennis R. IAC 76
Carolin, Emily Olivia. CSF 39
Carousso, Costa. TSP 206
Carpenter, Donald G. see Merlin Mesmer Merlino
Carpenter, Elmer J. ES1 92 HFI 27 SFE 105 SF1 92

Carpenter, Humphrey. SRB 81
Carpenter, John. OMN 12, 147-
51
Carpenter, Rhys. EXT 10/1 22
Carpenter, William Boyd (1841-
1918) ES1 92 SF1 92
Carpentier, Charles. SF1 92
Carpentier, Alejo (1904-) FBK
134 HFI 27 JGB 6 SF1 92
Carr, Carol. IAC 76 VES 218
Carr, Charles. ES1 92 SFE 105
SF1 92
Carr, Edward Hallett. BAA 210
Carr, John. SFW 459-65
Carr, John Dickson (1906-77)
ASF 32 CSF 39 ES1 92-3 EXT
8/1 5 FL1 184-6 HFI 27 IAC
76 IAH 106 SFE 105 SFS 27
SF1 92 SF2 845 TFC 45, 50
WGT 28 WIF 245
Carr, John F. HFI 27
Carr, Leslie. [FUT] SOT 387
Carr, Nick. SF1 92
Carr, Robert Spencer (1909-)
AOW 160 CSF 39 ES1 93 HFI
27 IAC 76 SFE 105 SFS 27
SF1 92 SOT 72 WTS ix, 5, 8, 12,
15, 24, 27, 30
Carr, Terry (1937-) AAL 82, 88
ALW 176, 212, 222 AOW 289,
291, 300-1 ASF 137 BAA 156
BYS 303 COT 195, 293 ES1 93
ETN 22, 65, 72 FFR 48 [FJT]
FRN 30 HFI 27 IAC 76-7, 252
LEX 239-40 LTN 18, 247, 250,
252-3 RGS 35-6 RZY 74 SFD
16-7, 64, 208, 321, 323 SFE 105
SFS 27 SF1 92-3 SF2 845 SRB
110, 282 VES 180 WAA 75
WGT 28 WSF 282, 389 see also
Norman Edwards
Carrel, Frederic. BAA 80 CSF
39 SF1 92 WGT 28
Carrel, Mark pseud. of Lauran
Bosworth Paine. SFE 105
Carrell, Christopher. IAC 77
SF1 93
Carrigan, Nancy. HFI 27 MFW
210 SFE 105 SF1 93
Carrigan, Richard. HFI 27
MFW 210 SFE 105 SF1 93
Carrington, Grant. COT 274
IAC 77
Carrington, Hereward (1880-)
ES1 93 SF1 93 WGT 28

Carrington, Richard (1921-) ES1
94
Carroll, Carleton W. EXT 10/1
18
Carroll, Dana. WTS 42
Carroll, Gladys Hasty (1904-)
BAA 148 HFI 27 SF1 93 SF2
845
Carroll, John M. RHN 125
Carroll, Joy. SF1 93
Carroll, Latrobe. SF1 93
Carroll, Leslie. SF1 93
Carroll, Lewis pseud. of Charles
Lutwidge Dodgson. AOW 21
BYS 104-5, 116 ES1 94 EXT
4/2 21 FBK 10, 88-9, 108-12,
114, 124 FFC 3, 174 FFR 48-9
[FJT] FLT 128-9 FL1 7-16
IAC 77 IAH 81, 83 ISW 39, 118
LTN 125 NWO 256, 321 PJF
33, 49, 56-7 RFA 115 RHN 206
SFE 105-6 SFN 40 SF1 93
SL5 2278-82 SOT 235, 331 SRB
258 UKL 186 VES 142 WAA
74, 76 WFS 41 WIF 40, 68, 149
Carroll, Nina. SF1 93
Carroll, Ruth (1899-) SF1 93
SF2 845
Carroll, Sidney. IAC 77
Carroll, Thomas Theodore (1925-)
ES1 94 SF1 93 SF2 846
Carruth, Fred Hayden (1862-1932)
CSF 40 SF1 93
Carryl, Charles Edward (1841-
1920) FFC 181 SF1 93
Carsac, Francis pseud. of
Francois Bordes. CSC 33 FFR
49 SFE 106 SL3 1435-8
Carson, Clarence B. BAA 210
Carson, DeWitt. SF1 93
Carson, John F. (1920-) SF1 93
SF2 846
Carson, Johnny. WFS 257
Carson, Rachel. COT 267 FHT
35
Carson, Robin. ES1 94 SF1 93
Carstens, Kurt. FFR 49
Carter, Angela Olive (1940-)
AOW 161 BYS 305 ES1 94 FFC
47 FFR 49 FL3 1212-5 HFI
27 IAC 77 POE 294 RGS 36
SFE 106 SF1 94 SF2 846 SRB
255 VES 220
Carter, Bruce pseud. of Richard
Alexander Hough. FFR 49 SF1
94

Carter, Diana. SF1 94
Carter, Everett. EXT 7/1 18, 26
Carter, Frederick. CSF 40 SF1 94
Carter, George Goldsmith. SF1 94
Carter, Jimmy. ETN 10 RHN 206
Carter, John. BAA 210
Carter, John Franklin (1897-1967) ES1 94 WGT 28 see also Jay Franklin
Carter, John Louis Justin (1880-) SF1 94 THM 41 WGT 28 see also Compton Irving
Carter, Lin(wood Vrooman) (1930-) AAL 157 AOW 341 BFP 101-7 BRS 7 BYS 283 CSC 48, 52 CWD 7-9 ES1 94 EXT 3/1 9, 21-2 EXT 5/1 9 FBK 81, 93 FFR 49-50 HFI 27-8 IAC 77, 136 LEX 241-2 LTN 84, 91 NWO 262 RGS 36-7, 211 SFE 106-7 SFW 179, 183 SF1 94-5 SF2 846-7 SRB 70, 283 WAA 95, 108, 245 WGT 28-9 WSF 247, 297, 302 WTS 36
Carter, Manfred A. COT 3
Carter, Margaret Louise (1948-) SF1 95 SF2 847
Carter, Margery Louise Allingham (1904-66) WGT 29
Carter, Nick (house name) SF1 95
Carter, Paul A. AAL 137-8 BRS 8 FHT 66 IAC 77 SFS 27 SRB 75 TSF 245 VES 106 WGT 29
Carter, Randolph. WTS 13
Carter, Tremlett. CSF 40 SF1 95
Cartier, Edd. BYS 217 COT 230 ES1 94-5 FBK 54, 120 IAC 77 RFA 64, 83, 142, 155, 157, 160, 166-7, 181, 186, 190, 195 SFE 107 SFS 27 VES 218, 225, 233, 289, 315, 317, 326, 335 WFS 179
Cartmell, Robert (1877-) WGT 29 see also Robert Tarnacre
Cartmell, Van Henry (1896-) ES1 95
Cartmill, Cleve (1908-64) ACE 68 AC2 66 ALW 173-4 AOW 290 ASF 85, 198 BYS 233 CAT 43 COT 24 CSC 122 ES1 95 EXT 1/2 30 FFR 50 FTF 72 HFI 29 IAC 77 ISW 226 LEX

242-3 MSM 32, 90, 141, 303 RFA 64, 109-11, 120, 132-3, 138, 211-2 SFD 9 SFE 107 SFS 27 SOT 98 STH 158 VES 107 WGT 29 WIF 91, 146 WSF 108
Carton, Sydney. SFN 116
Cartur, Peter. IAC 77 SFS 27 VES 149
Carus, Titus Lucretius. MSF 126
Caruso, Dee. SF1 95
Carver, Jeffrey A. HFI 29 IAC 77
Cary, Francine Curro. BAA 210, 281
Cary, Joyce. CSF 40 ISW 115
Cary, Richard. EXT 6/1 14
Caryl, Charles W. BAA 57 CSF 40 SF1 95
Casanova, Giacomo (1725-98) SFB 76 SFE 107
Casanova, Pablo Gonzalez. BAA 178
Casares, Adolfo Bioy (1914-) AOW 143 EXT 9/1 13-4 FBK 134-5 FFR 50 SFE 73 SF1 51 SF2 818
Case, Arthur E. BAA 172
Case, Brian David (1937-) SF1 95 SF2 847
Case, Josephine Young (1907-) CSF 40 SL1 89-92
Case, Justin (house name) TSP 132
Caseleyr, Camille Auguste Marie (1909-) ES1 95 SF2 871-2 WGT 29 see also Jack Danvers
Casewit, Curtis Werner (1922-) BAA 134 ES1 95 FFR 50 HFI 29 SFE 107 SF1 95 SF2 847
Casey, James. BAA 35-6
Casey, Kent pseud. of Kenneth McIntosh. ES1 95
Casey, Patrick. CSF 40 SF1 95
Casey, Richard (house name) SFE 107 WGT 29 see also Leroy Yerxa
Casey, Terence. CSF 40 SF1 96
Caso, Alfonso. BAA 210
Casolet, Jacques. ES1 95 SF1 96
Casparian, Gregory. BAA 69
Cassandra. SF1 96
Cassatt, Dave. SF1 96
Cassavetes, John. CSC 263-4
Cassell, Richard A. EXT 9/2 39

Cassera, Nora. CSF 40
Casserley, J. V. Langmead. SOI
109
Casserly, Gordon (-1947) SF1 96
Cassiday, Bruce Bingham (1920-)
ES1 95 SF2 847 WGT 29 see
also Carson Bingham, Con
Steffanson
Cassill, R. V. IAC 77 LTN 250
SFS 27
Cassirer, Ernst. MSF 31-2, 34-5
Cassius pseud. of Michael Mackin-
tosh Foot. CSF 40 SF1 96
Cassius-Minor. BAA 74 CSF 40
Casson, Clyde. WTS 120
Casson, Miles. SF1 96
Castell, Daphne. BYS 301 EXT
10/1 24 IAC 77-8
Castellano, Peter. VFS 117-8
Casteneda, Carlos. LTN 183
PJF 63 SFD 164, 277
Casteret, Norbert (1897-) ES1
95 SFE 107 SF1 96
Castex, P. G. FBK 137
Castier, Jules. CSF 40
Castilla, Clyde Andre. ES1 95
SF1 96
Castillo, Art. STH 248
Castle, Agnes (-1922) SF1 96
Castle, Edgerton (1858-1920)
CSF 40 SF1 96
Castle, Jeffery Lloyd (1898-)
ES1 95 HFI 29 ISW 208-9 SFE
107, 109 SF1 96
Castlemon, Harry. STH 162
Castletown, (Lord) pseud. of
Bernard E. Fitzpatrick. CSF
40 SF1 96
Castro, Fidel. MSF 38
Caswell, Edward A. BAA 62
SF1 96 WGT 29 see also
Myself and Another
Cataldi, Margherita. BAA 210
Caterinussi, Bernardo. BAA 210
Cather, Willa. RBY 40 WIF 151
Catherine (II). MSF 244
Catherwood, Mary. CSF 40
Cattell, Ann (1893-) SF1 96
Catton, Bruce. COT 89
Catullus. WFS 154
Caudwell, Christopher pseud.
of Christopher St. J. Sprigg.
MSF 212, 239-40
Cauffman, Stanley Hart. CSF 40
Caufield, Don. FFC 131

Caufield, Joan. FFC 131
Caunter, Cyril Francis (1899-)
CSF 40 SF1 96
Causey, James. IAC 78 IAH 35
SFS 27
Causgrove, Jackie. RHN 138
Causse, Charles (1862-1904) SF1
96
Cavalier, Z. Langrana. CSF 40
SF1 96
Cavanaugh, John R. BAA 210
Cave, Hugh B(arnett) (1910-)
STH 148-9 TSP 9, 15, 28, 41-3,
71, 81, 92, 102, 104, 209 WGT 29
WTS 35, 37, 69
Cavendish, Henry. ASF 187-8
Cavendish, Margaret. BAA 4-6
Cawelti, John G. CAT 44-5, 56-
7 INT 29 KAU 58-9, 229 TSF
245
Cawood, Hap. IAC 78 SFS 27
Cawthorn, James (1929-) SFE
109 VES 123
Caxton, William. VES 312
Cayce, Edgar. ACC 85 CWN
57 ES1 95
Cayley, (Sir) George. POE 75
Caylus, A. C. P. De Tubieres.
CSF 40
Cazedessus, Camille, Jr. SF1
97
Cazotte, Jacques (1719? -92) CSF
40 FBK 137 SF1 97 TFC 24,
127-8, 166
Cazotte, M. CSF 42
Cebulash, Mel (1937-) SF1 97
SF2 847-8
Cecil, Algernon (1879-1953) BAA
76 CSF 40 SF1 97
Celadon. BAA 14
Celine, Louis Ferdinand. JGB
6, 12 MIH 103, 131 WFS 295
Cellini, Joseph. FFC 95, 194
Centennius, Ralph. BAA 34 CSF
40 SF1 97
Cepeda, Alfredo. BAA 172, 210
Ception, John V. SF1 97
Cerf, Bennett Alfred (1898-1971)
ES1 95-6 CSF 41 EXT 5/1 9
ISW 15 SF1 97 SF2 848
Cerf, Christopher Bennett (1941-)
AOW 289 ES1 96 EXT 7/2 47
IAC 78 SFS 28 SF1 97 SF2 848
Cerminara, Gina. ES1 96

Cervantes. CSC 30 FFC 3 FTF
18 MSF 248 SFD 40 TFC 34
TSO 36-7 WAA 77 WIF 34, 40
Cezanne, Paul (1839-1906) [FUT]
Chabrol, Claude. CSC 264
Chadwick, Paul. TSP 81 see
also Brant House
Chadwick, Philip George. CSF
41 SFE 109 SF1 97
Chafer, Rollin Thomas. BAA
210
Chaffee, Roger B. (-1967) JGB 33
Chain, Julian pseud. of Julian
Chain May Dikty. IAC 78 IAH
35
Chakra. TSP 198
Chalfant, Fran E. FL2 543-8
FL5 2107-11
Chalker, Jack L. (1944-) AOW
362 ES1 96 HFI 29 LEX 243-
4 RGS 37, 211 SFE 109-10 SF1
97-8 SF2 848-9 SRB 80 WSF
388
Chalmers, John. AAL 115-6
Chalmers, Stephen. STH 77-8
Chalpin, Lila. BAA 210
Chamberlain, Arthur Neville
(1869-1940) WFS 98
Chamberlain, Edwin William
(1903-) ES1 96 SFE 110 SF1 98
Chamberlain, Elinor (1901-) ES1
96
Chamberlain, Henry Richardson
(1859-1911) CSF 41 PST 63,
249, 263 SF1 98
Chamberlain, Houston Stewart.
FTF 39
Chamberlen, Peter. BAA 4
Chambers, Aidan (1934-) SF1 98
SF2 849
Chambers, Dana pseud. of Albert
Leffingwell. CSF 41 SF1 98
Chambers, Elwyn Whitman (1896-)
CSF 41 SF1 99
Chambers, Isaiah Mench (1865-
1922) SF1 98
Chambers, (James) Julius (1850-
1920) CSF 41 SF1 98
Chambers, Nancy. SF1 98
Chambers, R. W. BAA 172, 210
Chambers, Robert W(illiam)
(1865-1933) AOW 42, 57, 87 BAA
79 CSF 41 CWD 39 ES1 96
EXT 1/1 2, 7 EXT 5/1 4 EXT
7/1 28 FBK 73, 80 FL2 844-7

HFI 29 IAC 78 IMS 20 JVN
88, 188 SFB 58 SFE 110 SFS
28 SFW 68 SF1 98 SIH 34
SOT 152 SRB 255 STH 75 WIF
78, 206, 283
Chambers, Wallace Jerome (1862-)
CSF 41 SF1 98
Chambless, Edgar. BAA xvii, 76
Chambon, Guy. BAA 172
Chamerovzow, Louis Alexis.
CSF 41
Champagne, Terry. IAC 78
Champion, Edouard. BAA xx
Chance, John Newton (1911-) SF2
984 see also John Lymington
Chance, Jonathan. SFE 110
Chancellor, John Walter (1876-)
CSF 41 SF1 99
Chandler, A(rthur) Bertram
(1912-) AAL 132, 157 ALW 161
AOW 161, 192 BAA 145 BFP
108-10 CSC 33 ES1 97 FFR
50 HFI 29-30 IAC 78 LEX
244-5 RFA 134, 136, 140-1, 210
RGS 37-8, 212 SFE 110-1 SFS
28 SF1 99 SF2 849-51 SIH 169
SL4 1789-93 SOT 241 VES 150,
152-3, 197 WGT 29-30 see also
George Whitley
Chandler, Helen. FBK 51
Chandler, Raymond. ALW 100
CSF 41 ETN 37, 111 FFR 50
Chaney, James M. RHN 158 SF1
99
Chaney, Lon. IAH 126 SIH 18
SRB 58 TJB 10 WAA 89
Chang, Glenn. IAC 78
Channing, Mark. CSF 41 SF1 99
Chant, Joy (1945-) FFC 174 FL2
839-43 HFI 30 SF1 99 SF2
851 SRB 255
Chanter, Gratiana. SF1 99
Chapdelaine, Perry Anthony
(1925-) IAC 78 SFE 111 SF1
100 VES 168
Chapela, Esteban Salazar Y (1902-)
ES1 97 SF1 458
Chapin, Maud Louise Hudnut
(1872-) ES1 97 SF1 100
Chaplin, Charles. CSC 264
OWB 72, 75 RFA xx
Chaplin, Saul. IAC 78
Chaplin, W. N. CSF 41 SF1 100
Chapman, Charles Hamilton
Murray. CSF 41

Chapman, D. D. HFI 30
Chapman, Edgar L. FL1 57-60
FL2 549-52, 801-4, 926-31 FL3
1142-5, 1325-31 FL4 1975-8
FL5 2171-5 SL2 564-8
Chapman, Kenneth. IMS 100, 105,
136
Chapman, Richard Marvin. BAA
81
Chapman, Samuel E. AOW 57
CSF 42 SFE 111 SF1 100
Chapman, Steve. IAC 78
Chapman, Vera (1898-) FL4 1908-
12 HFI 183
Chapman, Walker pseud. of
Robert Silverberg. RSG 23
Chappell, Connery. ES1 97
Chappell, George Shepard (1877-
1946) CSF 42 SF1 100
Chappell, Warren. FFC 3, 31
Charbonneau, Louis (1924-) AOW
160 BAA 132, 138, 141 ES1 97-
8 EXT 2/2 28 HFI 30 LEX
245-6 SFE 111 SF1 100 SF2
851
Charcot, Jean. EXT 2/1 9-10
Charcot, Paul Samuel (1907-)
BAA 138 ES1 98 SFE 111 SF1
100 SF2 851
Charlemagne (742?-814) ATA 55
WIF 34
Charles (I). ISW 91
Charles, J. A. C. FTF 26
Charles, John. SF1 100
Charles, Neil (house name) SF1
100 see also Brian Holloway,
Dennis Talbot Hughes, John W.
Jennison
Charlot, Jean (1898-) ES1 98
FFC 35, 99
Charlotte, Jean. IAC 78
Charlton, George. FFC 26
Charlton, Lionel Evelyn Oswald
(1879-1958) CSF 42 SF1 100
Charnas, Suzy McKee (1939-)
BAA 165 BFP 111 HFI 30 LTN
228 SFE 111 SF1 100
Charney, D. H. EFP 5
Charney, David. IAC 78 IMS
138, 170
Charnock, Graham. IAC 78
Charpentier, Allen R. IMS 33,
137, 213
Charques, Dorothy. SF1 100
Charrington, Charles. SF1 100

Charta, S. P. R. EXT 6/1 19
Charteris, Leslie pseud. of
Leslie Charles Bowyer Yin
(1907-) CSF 42 ES1 98 EXT
8/1 5 IAC 78 MIH 142 SF1 101
SF2 852 STH 156 TSP 145, 216
Charters, David Wilton (1900-)
ES1 98 SF1 101
Charyns. ETN 24
Chase, Adam pseud. of Paul Fair-
man, Milton Lesser. SFE 111
Chase, Borden. WFS 8
Chase, Herbert E. CSF 42 SIH
184
Chase, James Hadley pseud. of
Rene Raymond. CSF 42 ES1
98 SF1 101 THM 8
Chase, Mary (1907-73) FFC 73,
171 SF1 101, 581
Chase, Richard. CAT 48-9 NWO
22-3, 168
Chase, Stuart. BAA 93, 210 COT
261
Chatrian, Alexandre (1826-90)
CSF 69 ES1 98 SF1 101 SFS
28, 45 WGT 30 see also
Erckmann-Chatrian
Chatterton, Edward Keble. SF1
101
Chatterton, Thomas. MFW 279
Chaucer, Geoffrey. AC2 55 ACE
57 ETN 54 EXT 6/1 6 EXT
10/1 27 EXT 10/2 114 MIH 122
MSF 184 MSM 111, 279 RZY 14
SFA 10, 162 WBW 5, 50
Chauncey, Thomas. BAA 45
Chauncy, Nan. FFC 171
Chauvin, Cy. LTN 265 TJB 54
PJF 73
Chavannes, Albert (1836-1903)
BAA 46, 53 CSF 42 SF1 101
Chavis, Dom. CSF 42
Chayefsky, Paddy. AAL 57 FFR
51
Chaykin, Howard V. SFW 330
Chaytor, Henry John (1871-1954)
SF1 101
Cheetham, Anthony. IAC 78 SF1
101
Cheever, Henry Theodore (1814-
97) SF1 101
Cheever, John (1912-) CSC 25
ES1 98 ETN 176 FFR 51 IAC
79
Cheinisse, Claude F. AOW 295
IAC 79

Chekhov, Anton (1860-1904) CSC
288 FLT 73-4, 94, 104 IAH 90
LTN 234 MSF 243, 250 SFA 33
THM 45
Chenault, Nell. FFC 110
Cheney, Brainard. BAA 210
Cheney, David MacGregor. ES1
98 SF1 101
Cheney, Walter Thomas (1859-)
SF1 101
Cheng, James Chester. BAA 172
Chenneviere, Daniel (1895-) SF2
1057
Chenu, Marie-Dominique. BAA
210
Cher, Marie pseud. of Marie
Scherr. CSF 42 SF1 101
Chernyshevsky, Nikolai. AOW
88 EXT 10/2 74-8 MSF 102,
164, 247-9, 252-3, 257, 266, 268
SIH 76
Cherry, Carolyn Janice (1942-)
BFP 112 see also C. J. Cherryh
Cherry, Colin. MSF 75
Cherryh, C. J. pseud. of Carolyn
Janice Cherry. AAL 107 HFI
30 LEX 246-7 RGS 38-9, 212
SFE 111 WSF 282, 339, 388
Chesneaux, Jean. AOW 341 BAA
210 SRB 82
Chesney, (Sir) George Tomkyns
(1830-95) ALW 62, 85 AOW 35,
57 BYS 100-2, 104, 118 CSF 42
EXT 9/2 27 FAN 23, 61, 168
FTF 42 IAC 79 MSF 166 NWO
134 POE 94, 117-8, 138, 183
PST 73 SFE 111-2 SF1 101-2
SIH 47 SL1 130-2 SRB 9 STH
182 VES 101, 121, 312 WSF 21
YTS 110
Chesney, Weatherby pseud. of
C. J. Cutcliffe Hyne. CSF 42
Chesnoff, Richard Zeltner (1937-)
SF1 SF2 852
Chesnutt, Charles. CSF 42 FFC
18
Chess, Victoria. FFC 192
Chester, Alfred (1929?-71) SF1
102
Chester, George Randolph (1869-
1924) CSF 42 EXT 1/1 7 SFE
112 SF1 102
Chester, (Lord) pseud. of Cyrus
Reed Teed. CSF 42 SF1 102
Chester, Michael Arthur (1928-)
ES1 98 SF1 102 SF2 852

Chester, William L. (1907-) AOW
100 CSF 42 ES1 98-9 HFI 30
SFE 112 SF1 102
Chesterton, G(ilbert) K(eith)
(1874-1936) AOW 396 BAA 67,
80, 91 BYS 147 CSF 42-3 CWN
27 ES1 99 EXT 2/2 28 EXT
8/2 49 EXT 9/2 34-6, 39 FAN
96, 98, 145 FBK 119 FFR 51
FL2 961-5 FL3 1089-91 FTF
55, 81, 102 HFI 30 IAH 55 ISW
60, 248 MFW 249 MSF 261 POE
113, 155, 207-9 SFD 190 SFE
112 SF1 102 SIH 81 SRB 256
THM 4, 35 VES 121, 261 VFS
183 WAA 50 WTS 48
Chetwode, R. D. CSF 43 SF1 102
Chetwood, William Rufus (-1766)
WGT 30
Chetwynd, Bridget. BAA 114
ES1 99 SFE 112 SF1 102
Chetwynd-Hayes, Ronald (1919-)
FRN 31 IAC 79 SF1 102 SF2
852
Chevalier, Haakon Maurice (1902-)
ES1 99 SFE 112
Chevallier, Jean-Jacques. BAA
210
Chew, (Dr.). EXT 2/1 17
Chew, Ruth. FFC 61, 186
Cheynell, Francis. POE 54 VES
116
Chianese, Robert L. BAA 172
Chiaromonte, Nicola. BAA 210
Chiattone, Mario. [FUT]
Chichester, Imogen. FFC 193
Chikolev, V. MSF 251
Child, Frank Samuel. CSF 43
Child, Harold. BAA 211
Child, Richard Washburn. CSF 43
Childe, Wilfred Rowland. CSF 43
Childers, Ernest (1870-1922) AOW
92 BYS 145-6, 155 CSF 43 PST
85, 207 SFE 112 SFN 11 WGT
30
Childs, Bernard. IAC 79
Childs, Edmund Burton. WGT 30
see also Edmund Burton
Childs, Edward Earle. CSF 43
SF1 102
Chilson, Robert (1945-) HFI 31
IAC 79 RGS 39-40 SFE 114 SF1
102
Chilton, Charles Frederick William
(1927-) ES1 99 SFE 114 SF1 102-
3

74

Chilton, Eleanor Carroll (1898-1949) SF1 103
Chilton, Henry Herman. BAA 97 CSF 43 SF1 103
Chilton, Irma (1930-) SF1 103 SF2 852-3
Chipman, Charles Phillips (1878-) CSF 43 SF1 103
Chipman, William Pendleton (1854-1937) CSF 43 SF1 103
Chipraz, Francois. BAA 211
Chisholm, Brock. NDA 216
Chisom, Sarah pseud. of Tom Filer. SF1 103
Choate, Pearson. SF1 103
Choay, Francois. BAA 172, 211
Chojecki, Edmund. FBK 22
Cholmondeley, Mary. CSF 43
Chomsky, Noam. AAL 185-91
Chopin, Frederic (1810-49) WFS 129, 162
Chorao, Kay. FFC 187
Choron, Jacques. IAC 79 SFS 28
Chrisman, Arthur. FFC 19
Christ. CUA 20 EXT 1/1 3, 8 EXT 7/1 8 EXT 8/2 33, 44-5, 62 EXT 9/2 47, 53 EXT 10/2 74, 89 HEN 53 INT 24, 38, 47, 101, 104-6, 111, 114, 117 JGB 6 KVT 6, 51 LTN 166, 173 PJF 28, 42, 45 SHL 25, 33 TBC 45 THM 51 TJB 55 TSO 53 VMW 39 WBW 26-7, 30, 33, 49 WFS 147 WTS 11, 42 see also God, Jesus, Lord
Christ, Henry Irving (1915-) ES1 99
Christensen, John Michael. BAA 281
Christian, Catherine Mary. SF1 103
Christian, Emeline Fate. SF1 103
Christie, Agatha pseud. of Agatha Margaret Clarissa Miller Mallowan (1890-1976) COT 106 CSF 43 ES1 99-100 EXT 8/1 5 FHT 43 IAC 79 SFA 259-60, 262 SFS 28 SF1 103 SF2 853 TFC 49, 83
Christie, Douglas. SF1 103
Christie, Robert. ES1 100 SF1 103
Christie, William H. see Cecil B. White
Christin, Pierre (1938-) SFE 114

Christmas, Grace V. CSF 43 SF1 103
Christopher, Edgar E. CSF 43
Christopher, J. R. BAA 211 RHN 62, 197
Christopher, Joe R. AOW 360 RAH 195-7, 207, 213-5, 224, 258
Christopher, John pseud. of Christopher S. Youd. ALW 184, 212, 219 AOW 162, 312-3 BYS 295-6 EFP 6 FFC 42 FFR 51 HFI 31, 183 IAC 79 INT 45 ISW 169-70 JGB 18 KAU 93-4, 127, 146 LEX 247-8 MFW 23, 104 MIH 14 MSF 9 NDA 133-5, 141-2 NWO 133 RFA 174 RGS 40-1, 212 SFB 128 SFE 114-5 SFS 28 SF1 103-4 SL4 1541-4 SOT 132, 300, 377, 379, 426-7 SRB 11, 324 STH 45, 49 VES 132, 151, 233, 263, 300 WSF 185, 254
Christopher, Matthew. FFC 116
Chroust, Anton-Hermann. BAA 211
Chruszczewski, Czeslaw (1922-) LEX 248-9
Chuang, Tzu. UKL 78
Chudakova, Mariette. SIH 113
Church, Alfred John. CSF 43 SF1 104
Church, Margaret. EXT 6/1 17
Church, Richard Thomas (1893-1972) FFC 29 SF1 104
Churchill, A. T. BAA 108
Churchill, Joyce pseud. of M. John Harrison. IAC 79
Churchill, Reginald Charles (1916-) AOW 162 ES1 100 EXT 5/1 8 SFE 115 SF1 104 SF2 854
Churchill, Winston S. ASF 285 COT 120, 129, 140 FAN 78 IAC 79 IMS 159 LTN 150 MSM 124 OWB 36 VES 121 VFS 7, 222, 247 WFS 150 WIF 184, 232
Churchman, C. West. BAA 211
Churchwall, James. VES 340
Churchward, James (1854-1936) ES1 100
Chute, David. EXT 8/2 30
Chwast, Jacqueline. FFC 91, 131
Ciardi, John (1916-) CSC 173 SFS 28 IAC 79 WFS 193, 216 WGT 30 see also John Anthony Cicellis, Kay (1926-) SFE 115 SF1 104
Cicero. EXT 8/1 23

Cingoli, Guilio. FFC 14
Cioran, E.M. BAA 172, 211
Cioranescu, Alexandre. BAA
xxi, 172, 211
Cirlot, J.E. KAU 186
Clagett, John. HFI 31
Clair, Colin. ES1 100
Claire, Keith. FFC 30
Clancy, Eugene A. IMS 3 SOT
50 WTS 50
Clapp, Patricia (1912-) FFC 103
SF1 104 SF2 854
Clapperton, Jane Hume. BAA 38
SF1 104
Clare, Helen. FFC 83 see also
Pauline Clarke
Clarens, Carlos (1936-) AOW 341
ES1 100 SF1 104 SF2 854 WAA
243, 245
Clareson, Thomas D. (1926-)
ACC 52-71 AC2 74 ALW 7, 30
AOW 33-78, 81, 289, 341-2, 360
BAA 172, 211 BRS 3, 9 COT
212, 298, 300 EXT 1/1 1 EXT
1/2 29-34 EXT 2/1 1 EXT 2/2
22, 33-40 EXT 3/2 31 EXT 4/1
1 EXT 4/2 16, 23-5 EXT 5/1
1, 15-16a EXT 5/2 1, 37-9 EXT
6/1 1-21 EXT 6/2 22 EXT 7/1
1, 18-28 EXT 7/2 29, 47-8 EXT
8/1 1 EXT 8/2 30, 59 EXT 9/1
1-2, 22-3 EXT 9/2 24-5, 63 EXT
10/1 1-4 EXT 10/2 50-1, 69-115
FHT 66 IAC 79 INT 4, 29-30
KAU 44, 227 OSR ix-xvi, 1-28
PJF 73 RAH 224 RHN 62 RSG
91 SFB 7 SFE 121 SF1 104
SF2 854 SL1 369-73 SL2 591-
4 SOT 4 SRB 3-18, 68, 71, 75,
499, 514 TSF 44-51, 245-6, 250
VF1 64-87, 216-37, 265-7, 278-
80, 282 VF2 vii, 1-33, 197-8, 208
WSF 265, 270, 360, 382
Claretie, Jules. EXT 2/1 6
Clark, Alfred. CSF 43 SF1 104
Clark, Ann. FFC 131
Clark, Barrett Harper (1890-1953)
ES1 100
Clark, Catherine Anthony (1892-)
SF1 104 SF2 854
Clark, Charles Heber (1841-1915)
CSF 43 SF1 105 WGT 30 see
also Max Adeler
Clark Colin. POE 306
Clark, Cumberland. BAA 92 CSF
43

Clark, Curt. ES1 100 HFI 31
IAC 79
Clark, Cynthia Charlotte Moon
(1829-95) WGT 30 see also
Charles M. Clay
Clark, Dale pseud. of Ronal
Kayser. TSP 156 WTS 38
Clark, Dennis J. BAA 211
Clark, E. Roger. BAA 211
Clark, Evert. IAC 79
Clark, Francis Edward. BAA 39
Clark, Frederick Le Gros (1892-)
CSF 43 SF1 105
Clark, George. SRB 90
Clark, George Gordon. WFS 30-
5, 51-2, 59 IMS 33-6, 50-1, 55,
126, 213
Clark, Gideon Walter. CSF 43
SF1 105
Clark, (Dr.) John D. ASF 232,
243 CWD 10, 16, 18 ES1 100
IAC 79 IMS 84, 147, 182, 186-7,
197, 231 ISW 19, 248-9 SFD 210
SOT 154-5, 158, 164 WIF 136,
167, 294
Clark, Joseph Calvitt (1888-) see
Richard Grant
Clark, Judith A. FL2 1025-8
FL5 2185-91 SL1 213-7 SL2
605-7 SL3 1230-4
Clark, Laurence Walter (1914-)
BAA 145 SF1 105 SF2 854
Clark, Louis W. IMS 69
Clark, Roger. BAA 211
Clark, Susie Champney (1856-)
SF1 105
Clark, Thomas March (1812-1903)
SF1 105
Clark, Walter H. BAA 211
Clark, Walter Van Tilburg. FAN
168 IAC 79 SFS 28
Clark, William (1770-1838) KVT
39
Clark, William Donaldson (1916-)
SF1 105 SF2 855
Clark, William J. SF1 105
Clark, William Ronald (1916-)
ES1 100 HFI 31 SFE 121 SF1
105 SF2 855
Clarke, Alfred Charles George.
SF1 105
Clarke, Arthur C. (1917-) AAL 2,
20, 27, 41, 65-6, 97, 117 ALW 14,
29, 46, 61, 99, 161, 169, 184, 194,
215, 227-8, 230, 234, 239 AOW
89, 162-6, 286, 290, 292, 294, 296-

Clarke, Arthur C. (cont.)
7, 299, 314, 337, 353, 398 ASF 77,
123-4, 126, 128, 130, 147, 151, 161,
217, 222-3, 226-9 BAA 121 BFP
113-6 BYS 225, 259-61, 281 CAT
81, 88, 100-2, 108-10, 113, 118, 137
CEN 87-108 COT 3, 35, 49, 51, 79,
292 CSC 14, 30-1, 65-6, 121-2,
227, 233, 306, 308 EFP 10, 13, 20
ES1 100-3 ETN 32, 163 EXT 1/2
26, 29 EXT 2/2 29 EXT 3/1 26
EXT 4/2 26 EXT 5/1 3, 8 EXT
7/2 35, 47 EXT 8/1 4 EXT 9/1
19 EXT 10/2 65, 67-8, 79, 108
FAN 153-4 FFR 51-4 FRN 31-
2, 443 FTF 1, 14, 78, 114-6, 119,
134-5, 151, 153, 174-5, 184-5, 187,
189-91, 202 HFI 31-2 HWK 16,
47 IAC 79-82 IAH 54, 134, 146
IMS 100, 251 INT 51, 53, 60-1, 89,
113 ISW 129, 131, 187-92 JGB
51 KAU 4, 20, 28, 35, 50, 89-90,
92, 94, 101, 103-4, 109-16, 120,
124, 129, 137-8, 172-4, 204-5,
210, 216, 223, 235-6 KWS 66,
270 LEX 249-51 LTN 76 MFW
ix, 6-7, 18-9, 21, 86, 104-14, 167,
235, 245, 248-9, 281 MIH 36, 47-
8, 75 MSF 122 MSM xv, 28, 126,
197-220, 283, 287 NDA ix NWO
19-20, 45, 47, 62, 163-5, 265-6
OMN 10, 243 RBY 36, 83-4, 196
RFA 140, 212 RGS 41-3 SFA
266 SFB 41, 106-8, 137, 152 SFD
14-6, 19-20, 36, 60, 97, 256-7,
266, 296, 314, 318-9 SFE 121-3
SFN 31, 40, 47, 73, 110 SFS 28-
32 SFW 91, 126, 149, 313-20,
462, 522 SF1 105-6 SF2 855
SIH 118, 121, 185 SIN 47-55, 128-
30 SL1 337-42, 374-7 SL3 1019-
25 SL4 1759-63, 1926-9 SL5
2343-9 SOT 6, 28, 40, 138-9, 276,
300, 374-91, 413 SRB 6, 15, 78,
113, 314, 316-7, 319, 322, 327, 329,
335, 339, 356, 363, 375, 499 STF
79 STH 15-6, 20, 67 TJB 5, 46,
48 TPS 277-84 TRB 64 TSF 59,
133, 138-40, 238 UFS 3 UKL
105, 151 VES 71-2, 74, 77, 80-3,
92, 96, 128, 133-4, 136, 148, 153,
159, 161-3, 167-8, 183, 201, 227,
229, 239, 252, 256, 260-1, 273, 296,
318, 327 VF1 216-37, 278-80
WAA 130 WFS 17, 78, 174, 178,
200, 216, 260, 262, 289, 299-301,
305-6 WGT 30-1 WIF 91, 146,
167, 185, 202, 230 WSF 109, 121,
135, 138, 148, 200, 206, 238, 248,
283, 310, 387-8 YTS 19
Clarke, Aubrey Vincent. SF1 105
Clarke, Charles Allen (1863-1935)
CSF 44 SF1 105
Clarke, Charles Wright. ACE 11
AC2 9
Clarke, Covington pseud. of
Clark Venable. CSF 44 SF1 106
Clarke, (Gen.) F. M. BAA 46
CSF 44 SF1 106
Clarke, Francis H. BAA 58, 74
CSF 44 SF1 106 WGT 31
Clarke, George S(ydenham) (1848-
1933) WGT 31 see also A. Nelson
Seaforth
Clarke, Gerald. IMS 247
Clarke, Harry. FBK 36, 38
Clarke, I(gnatius) F(rederick)
(1918-) ALW 7, 30, 32, 64, 75-6
AOW 36, 89, 342, 360 BAA xxi,
172, 211-2 BYS 99-100, 111
ES1 103 EXT 7/1 1 EXT 8/2
64-6 EXT 9/1 1-2 EXT 9/2
24, 26-32 EXT 10/2 50 FAN
23, 145 IAC 82 NWO 134 OSR
216-28, 354 SFE 123 SF1 106
SF2 855 SRB 9, 66, 69 TSF 246
VES 116, 125, 329, 331
Clarke, Isabel Constance (-1951)
CSF 44 SF1 106
Clarke, Joan B. AOW 314 ES1
103 SF1 106
Clarke, John. IAC 82
Clarke, Marilyn. VFS 52
Clarke, Mary Victoria Cowden
(1809-1908) CSF 44 SF1 107
Clarke, Norah Mary Willis. ACE
11 AC2 9
Clarke, Olney. SFB 97
Clarke, Pauline (1921-) FFC 62,
80 IAH 106 SF1 107, 581 SF2
856 see also Helen Clare
Clarke, Roscoe. STH 258
Clarke, Shirley. VFS 117
Clarke, Thomas Ernest Bennett
(1907-) ES1 103 SF1 107
Clarke, Vinc. SRB 109
Clarkson, Helen. ES1 104 HFI
32 SFE 123 SF1 107
Clarkson, L. CSF 44
Clarkson, Paul S. EXT 5/2 2

Clarkson, Richard W. EXT 5/1 2
Claro, Joseph. SF1 107
Clason, Clyde B. ES1 104 SF1
107
Claude, Georges. EXT 2/1 6
Claudine. FFC 53
Claudius (I), (Emperor). ISW 62
RFA 139
Claudy, Carl H. (1879-1957) CSF
44 ES1 104 IAC 82 ISW 82
PJF 13 SFE 123 SFS 32 SF1
107 SOT 399 STH 174-5 WFS 7
Claxton, John G. pseud. of Donna
Brooks Beaumont. SF1 107
Claxton, Oliver Hazard Perry.
CSF 44 SF1 107
Clay, Charles M. pseud. of
Cynthia Charlotte Moon Clark.
CSF 44 SF1 107
Clayton, Alan. BAA 212
Clayton, Bertram. BAA 212
Clayton, Cecil. ALW 109
Clayton, Frederick. TSP 170
Clayton, Jo (1939-) HFI 32 LEX
251 SFE 123
Clayton, Richard Henry Michael
(1907-) ES1 104 SF2 926 WGT
31 see also William Haggard
Clayton, W. M. SFD 25-6 TSP
68
Clayton, William. RFA ix-xvi, 4,
12, 14, 182 TSP 218 WSF 52, 54-
8
Clear, Val. IAC 82
Cleary, Beverly. FFC 116
Cleary, Jon (1917-) ES1 104
Cleator, Philip E(liaby) (1908-)
COT 37-8, 42 ES1 104 IMS 96
SOT 137, 376 VES 71
Cleaver, A. V. VFS 133
Cleaver, Diane. SRB 500
Cleaver, Eldridge. [FUT]
Cleaver, Pamela. IAC 82
Cleaver, Val. VFS 76
Cleeve, Brian. IAC 82 SFS 32
Cleghorn, S. N. BAA 212
Clem, Ralph. IAC 82
Clemenceau, Georges (1841-1929)
WFS 67
Clemens, Rodgers. HFI 183
Clemens, Samuel Langhorne
(1835-1910) BAA 31, 39 ES1 104
PJF 49-58, 65 WGT 31 see also
Mark Twain
Clement, Catherine. BAA 212

Clement, Hal (1922-) pseud. of
Harry Clement Stubbs. AAL 72,
79, 81-2, 157 ALW 160 AOW
166-7 ASF 123 BYS 217, 233-4,
237 COT 71, 78, 157, 177 CSC 32-
3, 37-53, 55, 65, 136, 140, 146, 148-
9, 175, 198 EXT 3/1 26 EXT 5/1
3 EXT 7/2 40 FAN 153 FFR 55
HFI 32 HID 160 IAC 82-3 IAH
44-7, 117, 123 ISW 135, 177-8
KAU 199, 201, 209 LEX 251-3
MFW 30-1, 34, 43, 46-7, 99 MIH
10, 12, 106 MSM 217-8, 305 RFA
107-9, 125, 129, 141, 170-1 RGS
43 SFA 22 SFB 135, 137 SFD
20, 292, 315 SFE 123-4 SFN 39
SFS 32 SFW 321-7 SF1 107 SIN
13, 62-8 SL3 1424-8, 1505-9
SOT 415, 422, 428 SRB 16, 320,
500 STH 158 SV1 43-53 TSF
56, 235 VES 82, 87, 93, 96, 98,
260 WFS 148, 187-8 WIF 167,
276 WSF 103, 113, 148, 154, 173,
175, 186, 202, 387
Clements, Bruce (1931-) FFC 175
SF1 107 SF2 856
Clemm, Virginia. FBK 35
Cleopatra. WTS 42
Clery, William Edward. WGT 31
see also Austin Fryers
Cleveland, John. CSF 44
Clewes, Howard Charles Vivian
(1912-) SF1 108
Clewes, Winston David Armstrong
(1906-57) CSF 44 SF1 108
Clewett, Geoffrey Charles. SF1
108
Cliff, Catherine. AOW 295 IAC
83
Clifford, (Sir) Hugh Charles (1866-
1941) CSF 44 ES1 104
Clifford, Lucy. CSF 44
Clifford, Peggy. FFC 131
Clifford, Sarah (1916-) SF1 108
SF2 856
Clift, Denison Halley (1885-1961)
SF1 108
Clifton, Mark (1906-63) ALW 156,
212 AOW 167 BAA 131 BFP
117 BYS 234 ES1 105 ETN 36,
40, 45, 83, 126-31, 195, 197 EXT
8/1 7 LEX 253-4 MIH 121 HFI
33 IAC 83 ISW 122-3, 131 RFA
202-5, 214 SFE 124 SFS 32 SF1
108 SL5 2255-9 SRB 333 STH

Clifton, Mark (cont.)
246 VES 182, 206, 208, 335 WSF 175
Clifton, Wallace. SF1 108
Cline, Leonard Lanson (1893-1929) CSF 44 SF1 108
Cline, Linda. HFI 33
Cline, Steve. IAC 83
Clingan, C. C. IAC 83
Clingerman, Mildred (1918-) ALW 8, 212, 216 AOW 167, 285 COT 196 ES1 105 EXT 8/1 6 HFI 33 IAC 83 ISW ix, 122 SFE 124 SFS 32-3 SF1 108 SF2 856-7
Clinton, Ed(win) M., Jr. (1926-) ES1 105 IAC 83 SFS 33 WGT 31 see also Anthony More
Clinton, Jeff. HFI 33
Clock, Herbert. BAA 94 CSF 44 SF1 108
Cloete, Stuart. COT 115 IAC 83 OWB 13 SFS 33
Clonkey, Charles. VES 151
Clooney, Rosemary. SFN 82
Clopper, Jonas. BAA 18
Close, Peter. JVN 23-65, 87-8, 220, 239
Clothier, Bob. VES 289
Cloudesley, Hubert. SF1 108
Clough, Ben C. ES1 105
Clough, Fred M. BAA 88 CSF 45
Clough, Roy L., Jr. IAC 83 SFS 33
Cloukey, Charles pseud. of Charles Cloutier. ES1 105 STH 139
Clouky, Helen. IMS 186
Clouston, Joseph Storer (1870-1944) CSF 45 ES1 105 SFE 126 SF1 108
Cloutier, Charles. WGT 31 see also Charles Cloukey
Clow, Martha deMay (1932-) HFI 33 SF1 108 SF2 857
Clowes, William Laird (1856-1905) CSF 45 SF1 108 STH 191
Cluny, Thomas. CSF 45
Clute, John (1940-) ETN 69, 130 FFR 55 FL1 266-74, 324-7, 472-4, 489-96 FL2 524-5, 654-7, 848-51, 863-6 FL3 1492-5 FL4 1947-53 FL5 2383-90 IAC 83-4 SFE 126 SFW 111-7, 125-30, 243-8, 291-6, 311, 345-50, 355, 387-92, 453, 491-5, 583-9 SL2 873-7 SL3 1094-7, 1387-90 TSF 247

Clyde, Irene. CSF 45
Clyne, Ronald. ES1 105
Clynes, Manfred. FTF 118
Coakley, Timothy W. CSF 45
Coalson, Glo. FFC 144
Coates, J. B. BAA 173
Coates, John (1912-) ES1 105 SF1 108
Coates, Robert Myron (1897-1973) CSF 45 ES1 105-6 ETN 159 FL1 460-4 IAC 84 ISW 129 SFE 126 SF1 108 SF2 857
Coatsworth, Elizabeth Jane (1893-) FFC 3, 12, 19, 47, 53, 62, 80, 108, 116, 130, 141 SF1 109 SF2 857
Cobalt, Martin. FFC 30 SF1 109
Cobb, Irvin Shrewsbury (1876-1944) CSF 45 ES1 106
Cobb, Michael pseud. of Alfred Daniel Wintle. CSF 45 SF1 109
Cobb, Weldon J. EXT 7/1 20, 27 SF1 109
Cobban, James MacLaren (1849-1903) CSF 45 SF1 109
Cobbe, Frances Power (1822-1904) WGT 31-2 see also Merlin Nostradamus
Cobbold, Mirabel. CSF 45
Cobbs, Alfred L. FL4 1943-6
Cobden, Richard. MSF 146
Cober, Alan. FFC 131
Cobey, Herbert T. SF1 109
Coblentz, Catherine. FFC 62
Coblentz, Stanton A(rthur) (1896-) ALW 126 AOW 101, 167-8 BAA 93, 98, 132, 142 BFP 118-9 CSF 45 DTS 19 ES1 106 EXT 3/1 19 FL5 2115-7 HFI 33 IAC 84 IMS 21, 24 ISW 9, 12-3 LEX 254 MSM 81, 167 PST 136, 217, 229, 236, 247, 282, 288, 310 RFA 2 RGS 43-4 SFD 23-4 SFE 126-7 SFS 33 SFW 145 SF1 109 SF2 858 SOT 151, 155, 427 SRB 302, 397 VES 84, 104, 128, 140, 149, 314, 340 WFS 85 WIF 85 WSF 47, 346
Coburn, Patricia. SF1 109
Cocchiara, Giuseppe. BAA 173
Cochran, Russ. SRB 494
Cochrane, William E. ALW 212 WGT 32 see also S. Kye Boult
Cockburn, Francis Claude (1904-) ES1 106-7 WGT 32 see also James Helvick

Cockcroft, Thomas G. L. ES1
107 EXT 3/1 9, 22 SF1 109
WTS ix
Cockcroft, W. P. SF1 109
Cockerell, Sydney. WBW 40
Cockrell, Marian Brown (1909-)
SF1 109
Cockshutt, A. O. J. EXT 7/1 15
Cocteau, Jean. ATA 38 FBK 74
WFS 92
Cody, C. S. pseud. of Leslie
Waller. SF1 110
Cody, Morrill. CSF 45
Coe, Nancy Forsythe. IAC 84
Coe, Richard N. BAA 212
Coffey, Edward Hope, Jr. (1896-
1958) see Edward Hope
Coffin, Carlyn. IAC 84
Coffin, Lewis. ES1 107
Coffman, Virginia Edith (1914-)
SF1 110 SF2 858
Cogell, Elizabeth Cummins. SRB
378-452, 516 UKL 245
Coggins, Jack Banham (1911-)
ES1 107
Coggins, Jack B. VES 79
Coggs, (Dr.) pseud. of Ovidio
Giberga. SF1 110
Coghill, Nevill. SOI 8, 46
Cogswell, George Rae. IAC 84
Cogswell, Theodore R(ose) (1918-)
ALW 212 AOW 168 BAA 164
BFP 120 BYS 262, 279 ES1 107
EXT 8/1 6 FFR 55 HFI 33 IAC
84 LEX 254-5 MIH 11, 74 RFA
200 SFE 127 SFS 33 SF1 110
SF2 858 VES 111 WSF 175
Cogswell, Thomas. IAC 84
Cohen, Barney. HFI 33
Cohen, Chester. WFS 71 WGT
32
Cohen, Eli. LTN 18
Cohen, Genghis. SF1 110
Cohen, Harry. see Harry Enton
Cohen, John. MFW 193
Cohen, Marshall. BAA 231
Cohen, Octavius Roy. TSP 71
WTS 50
Cohen, Ralph. EXT 6/1 20
Cohen, Sol. WFS 249-52 WIF 111
WSF 230
Cohn, Emil Bernhard (1881-1948)
ES1 107 SF1 110
Cohn, Gary. IAC 84

Cohn, Norman. BAA 173 NWO
11-2, 101
Cohn, Roy. KVT 35 WFS 255
Cohn, Victor (1919-) ES1 107
EXT 2/1 10
Colbeck, Alfred. CSF 45 SF1 110
Colberg, Eckard. BAA 212
Colburn, Frona Eunice (1859-
1946) EXT 1/1 19 SF1 110 see
also Frona Eunice Wait
Colby, Carroll Burleigh (1904-)
ES1 107
Colby, Lincoln S. STH 145
Colby, Marie W. SF1 110
Colby, Vineta. EXT 10/1 24
Colcord, Lincoln (1883-1947) SF1
110
Cole, Adrian. IAC 84
Cole, Barry. IAC 84
Cole, Burt pseud. of Thomas
Dixon. EFP 13 ES1 107 HFI
34 NDA 22-5 SFE 127 SF1 110
Cole, Charles. CSF 45 SF1 110
Cole, Clara Gilbert. BAA 1
Cole, Cornelius (1822-1924) SF1
110
Cole, Cyrus. CSF 45 SFE 127
SF1 110 STH 53
Cole, Edward H. EXT 3/1 21
Cole, Everett B. (1910-) AOW 168
ES1 107 HFI 34 IAC 84 RFA
196, 203, 205-6, 210 SFE 127
SFS 33 SF1 110
Cole, G. D. H. BAA 212
Cole, Henry. EXT 9/2 62
Cole, Ira Albert (1883-) SF1 110
Cole, Lester. WGT 32
Cole, Olivia. FFC 195
Cole, Robert William. BAA 62
CSF 46 SFE 127 SF1 110 VES
87
Cole, Sophie. CSF 46
Cole, Susan Ablon. BAA 212, 281
Cole, Walter Randall (1933-) AOW
360 BRS 5 ES1 108 SFE 127
SF1 110 SF2 858 SOT 372
Coleman, D. C. BAA 212
Coleman, Francis Xavier J. SF1
111
Coleman, James Nelson. ES1 108
HFI 34 SFE 127 SF1 111
Coleman, Sidney. ISW xii WSF
214
Coleridge, Christabel Rose (1843-
1921) SF1 111

Coleridge, John pseud. of Earl
Binder, Otto Binder. IAC 84
Coleridge, Samuel Taylor (1772-
1834) ASF 305 CAT 48 EXT
5/1 16a, 20 EXT 10/1 45 FLT
3 FTF 1, 9 JGB 6, 23-4, 42
MSF 124, 133 MSM 96, 125 PJF
13, 57, 61 RBY 165, 168, 171
SOI 82, 84 STF 46 TDI 55 THM
32, 45 UKL 64, 67-9, 72 WIF
23, 183
Coleridge, Sara (1802-52) CSF 46
FL3 1238-40 SF1 111
Colerus, Egmont pseud. of Egmont
Colerus Von Geldern. LEX 255
Coles, Cyril Henry (1899-1965)
SF1 111 SF2 859 WGT 32 see
also Manning Coles
Coles, David. IAC 84
Coles, Manning pseud. of Cyril
Henry Coles, Adelaide F. O.
Manning. ES1 108
Coletta, Mario. BAA 173
Colin, Vladimir. IAC 84 SFB
145 SL5 2534-7
Colladay, Morrison M. CSF 46
IAC 84 SFS 33 SF1 111
Collard, Derek. FFC 14
Colledge, Edmund. EXT 10/1 24
Collens, T. Wharton. BAA 31
Collette. FLT 22
Collier, Dwight A. (1932-) SF1
111
Collier, John (1901-) ALW 216
AOW 101, 295 BAA 97, 99 BFP
121-2 CSF 46 ES1 108-9 ETN
159 EXT 3/1 27 EXT 7/2 41
EXT 8/1 5 FBK 119-20, 142,
153 FFR 55 FL2 520-3, 730-1
HFI 34 HID 2 IAC 84-5 IAH
106 ISW 13-7, 191 MSM 77, 87
SFD 16 SFE 127-8 SFN 40
SFS 33 SF1 111 SOT 127, 244,
331, 333-4, 365, 367 STH 95, 104
TSP 103 WSF 129
Colligan, Douglas. IAC 85
Collingwood, Harry pseud. of
William Joseph Cosens Lancaster.
CSF 46 SF1 111
Collins, Barnabas. SF1 112
Collins, Carroll Len. SF1 112
Collins, Charles M. ES1 109
SF1 112
Collins, Christopher. BAA 212
FAN 185

Collins, Colin. CSF 46 SF1 112
Collins, Edward James Mortimer
(1827-76) SF1 112 WGT 32
Collins, Erroll. CSF 46 ES1 109
SF1 112
Collins, Gilbert (1890-) BAA 90
CSF 46 ES1 109 SF1 112
Collins, Hunt pseud. of S. A.
Lombino. AOW 168 DTS 32
SRB 326
Collins, J. L. BAA 31 WGT 32
see also Jonquil
Collins, Mabel pseud. of Mabel
Collins Cook. CSF 46 SF1 112
Collins, Michael pseud. of Dennis
Lynds. ALW 232 HFI 34 SFE
128 VFS 78
Collins, Mortimer. CSF 46
Collins, Quentin. SF1 112
Collins, Vere Henry Gratz. CSF
46 ES1 109 SF1 112
Collins, Wilkie (1824-89) AOW 34
BYS 18, 91, 103 CSF 46-7 ES1
109 EXT 7/2 38 EXT 10/2 50
FBK 60-1, 63 FL4 1880-3 MSF
70 PST 34 SFW 69, 75-6 SF1
112 SOI 5 WGT 32 WIF 71
WTS 17
Collodi, Carlo. FFC 4, 80 SIH
141 WAA 76
Collyn, George. IAC 85
Colmore, G. pseud. of Gertrude
Renton. CSF 47
Colomb, (Sir) Philip Howard
(1831-99) CSF 47 POE 184-6
SF1 112
Colombo, John Robert. IAC 85
Colquitt, Betsey Feagan. BAA
212
Colter, Eli. STH 61-2
Colter, Elizabeth. WTS 28
Colton, Abigail. CSF 47 SF1 113
Colum, Padraic. CSF 47 FFC
24, 131, 180, 193 LTN 25
Columbus, Christopher (1451?-
1506) CAT 104 COT 29, 56 CWD
35 EXT 9/2 28 ISW 154 MSF
6, 22, 59 NWO 27-8, 138, 236
VFS 87, 149, 191
Colville, William Wilberforce
Juvenal (1862-1917) CSF 47 SF1
113
Colvin, Ian G(oodhope) (1912-75)
BAA 116 CSF 47 ES1 110 SFE
129 SF1 113

Colvin, James (house name) IAC
85 SFE 129 see also Michael
Moorcock
Colwell, Eileen. ES1 110
Colwyn, John. BAA 83 SF1 113
Combe, Andrew. EXT 6/2 27
Combe, William (1741-1823) SF1
113 WGT 32-3
Comer, Ralph pseud. of John
Sanders. SF1 113
Comfort, Paul see Paul Annixter
Comfort, Will Levington (1878-
1932) CSF 47 SF1 113
Commager, Henry Steele. COT 3
Commire, Anne. LTN 268
Commoner, Barry. COT 262
Comp, T. Allan (1942-) SF1 113
SF2 859
Compton, Arthur. IMS 220
Compton, D(avid) G(uy) (1930-)
AOW 168-9 BAA 142,151,159
BFP 123-4 BYS 303 ES1 110
FFR 56 HFI 34 IAC 85 LEX
255-6 LTN 35,108 MFW 201,
247 NDA 8-10, 42, 46-8, 203
NWO 134 RGS 44-5 SFE 133
SF1 113 SF2 859 SL5 2366-9
TSF 132 WGT 33
Compton, Michael. EXT 6/1 20
Compton-Pickett, (Sir) Joseph
(1847-1919) SF1 113
Comrade, Robert W. pseud. of
Edwy S. Brooks. CSF 47
Comstock, Sarah (-1960) SF1 114
Comte, Auguste (1798-1857) EXT
3/2 41 EXT 7/1 13 FAN 66
TJB 24-6 VFS 192-3, 203
Comyns-Carr, Barbara Irene
Veronica (1912-) ES1 110 SF1
114
Conant, James B. NDA 56-7
Conaway, J. C. SF1 114
Condit, Tom. IAC 85
Condon, Richard Thomas (1915-)
AOW 169 ES1 110 MIH 34 SFE
136 SF1 114 SF2 859
Condray, Bruno G. pseud. of
Leslie George Humphreys. SF1
114
Conesa, Lisa. IAC 85
Coney, Michael G. (1932-) BFP
125 EFP 10 FFR 56 HFI 34
IAC 85 LEX 256-7 RGS 45
SFE 136-7 SF1 114 SF2 859-
60 SL5 2218-22 VES 129, 168,
171, 210

Confucius. CUA 22
Congdon, Don. ES1 110 IAC 85
SF1 114
Congdon, Michael. IAC 85 SF1
114
Congdon, Richard. SF1 114
Conklin, Groff (1904-68) ALW 31,
175, 221 AOW 289-90, 297 BYS
244 CSF 47 ES1 110-4 ETN
56 EXT 3/1 27 EXT 5/1 9
EXT 7/2 46 EXT 8/1 5 EXT
10/1 3-4 IAC 38, 85-6 ISW vi,
220-2 KAU 237 MSM 35-6 RFA
6 SFA 226 SFE 137 SFS 33-4
SF1 114-5 SF2 860 SRB 234,
316, 500 STH 104 TSP 184
WFS 235 WGT 33 WSF 129-30,
171, 220, 358 see also Allen
DeGraeff
Conklin, Lucy (-1954) IAC 85
SF1 115
Conly, Robert Lesley (1918?-73)
see Robert C. O'Brien
Connell, Alan. ES1 114 SF1 115
WGT 33
Connell, John. CWN 3
Connell, Richard. IAC 86
Connell, Vivian. CSF 47
Connellan, Marguerite. CSF 47
Connelly, Cyril. CSC 287 CWN
3 IAC 86
Connelly, James Henderson
(1840-1903) SF1 115
Connelly, Marc. CSF 47
Connelly, Wayne. BAA 212
Conner, Mac. FFC 167
Conner, Michael. HFI 34 IAC
86
Conner, Patrick G. IAC 86
Connes, Georges. BAA 173,212
Connington, J. J. pseud. of
Alfred Walter Stewart. CSF 47
POE 229-30 SFE 137 SF1 115
Connolly, Myles (1898-1964) SF1
115
Connolly, Roy. CSF 130 SF1 115
Connor, Chris. FFC 163
Connor, Frederick W. NWO 61
Connors, James. BAA 212
Conover, Willis. IMS 64, 68, 75-
6, 85, 94, 105-6, 117, 142, 169,
200 STH 252-3 VFS 268
Conquest, Joan pseud. of Mrs.
Leonard Cooke. BAA 103 CSF
47 SF1 115

Conquest, Robert (1917-) AOW
285 BAA 212 BYS 284,320
ES1 114 EXT 6/2 51 EXT 9/1
19 FAN 152 HFI 34 IAC 33,86
IAH 135 SFE 137 SFS 34 SF1
115-6 SF2 860-1 SOI 58 SOT
2 SRB 335 WAA 124,243 WGT
33
Conrad, Earl (1912-) ES1 114
HFI 35 IAC 86 NDA 160-2,197
SFE 137 SF1 116 SF2 861
Conrad, Jane. VFS 271
Conrad, Joseph (1856-1924) CSC
8,25,112 CSF 47-8 ES1 115
EXT 2/1 18 EXT 4/2 20 EXT
9/2 39 FAN 11,64,184 FHT
15,50-1 FLT 2,12-31 IAC 86
JGB 5-6,32,44,52 MIH 60 MSF
227,276 NWO 43 RSG 51-2
SFE 137-8 SF1 116 STF 57
VES 130 VFS 127 WTS 17 see
also Josef Konrad Theodor
Korzeniowski
Conrad, Paul pseud. of Albert
King. SFE 138 SF1 116
Conrad, Pete. VFS 271
Conrads, Ulrich. BAA 173
Conreid, Hans. RFA 110
Conrow, Herbert (1874-) see
Clay Orb
Conroy, Rick. SF1 116
Conscience, Hendrik (1812-83)
FBK 146
Considerant, Victor. POE 66
Constable, F. C. CSF 48
Constable, John. MFW 21
Constance, Arthur. ES1 115
Constant, Alphonse Louis. WIF
72
Constant, Barbara. IAH 118-9
Constantine, Murray. BAA 106
CSF 48 EXT 2/2 27 SFE 138
SF1 116
Contento, William. FHT 11 SRB
67 TSF 250-1 WSF 383
Contoski, Victor. IAC 86
Converse, Frank H. CSF 48 SF1
116
Convertito, Bill. HFI 35
Conway, Gerard F. (1952-) HFI
35 IAC 86 SFE 138 SF1 116
VES 207 WGT 33
Conway, Hugh pseud. of Frederick
John Fargus. SF1 116
Conway, Laura pseud. of Dorothy
Phoebe Ansle. SF1 116

Conway, Troy (house name) SF1
116-7 see also Michael Avallone
Conyers, Bernard. SF1 117
Conyers, Dorothea. CSF 48
Coogan, Robert. BAA 212
Cook, Christine Campbell Thomson
(1897-) WGT 33
Cook, Frederick S. (1929-) ES1
115 SF1 117
Cook, Glen Charles (1944-) HFI
35 IAC 86 SF1 117 SF2 861
Cook, John Esten. VES 209
Cook, Mabel Collins (1851-1927)
WGT 33 see also Mabel Collins
Cook, Oscar. W TS 5
Cook, Peter. [FUT]
Cook, Robin pseud. of Robert
William Arthur Cook. BAA 151
SF1 117
Cook, Robert William Arthur
(1931-) SF2 861 see also Robin
Cook
Cook, Stanley J. (1935-) LTN 251
SF1 117
Cook, Stephen. IAC 86
Cook, W. Paul (1881-1948) ES1
115 EXT 3/1 8,21-2 FBK 75
ISW 224 SF1 117 WTS 15,50-2
Cook, William Wallace (1867-
1933) ALW 85,105 AOW 42,57
BAA 65 CSF 48 EXT 1/1 8
SFE 138 SF1 117 SOT 152 STH
39-40 WIF 69
Cooke, Alistair. MFW 36
Cooke, Arthur pseud. of Elsie
Balter, C. M. Kornbluth, Robert
Lowndes, John Michel, Donald
Wollheim. SFE 138 SFW 401
Cooke, David C. IAC 86 IMS 213
Cooke, David Ewin. BAA 101
Cooke, Donald Edward (1916-)
SF1 117
Cooke, Joan Conquest. WGT 33
see also Mrs. Leonard Cooke
Cooke, (Mrs.) Leonard. see
Joan Conquest
Joan Conquest Cooke
Cooke, W. Bourne. CSF 48
Cooley, Winnifred Harper. BAA
65
Coolidge, Calvin. EXT 7/2 37
RHN 211 SFN 99
Coolidge, Olivia (1908-) SF1 117
Coombe, William. CSF 48

Coombs, Charles Ira (1914-) ES1
115 HFI 35 IAC 86 SF1 117
SF2 861-2
Coombs, Francis Lovell. CSF 48
Coombs, Patricia. FFC 186
Coon, Carleton Stevens (1904-)
ES1 115 IAC 86
Coon, (Dr.) Carleton. VFS 211
Coon, Horace C. (1897-1961) ES1
115 HFI 35 KAU 138 SFE 138
SF1 117
Coon, Merlin Joseph (1917-) SF1
117
Cooney, Michael (1921-) ES1 115
SF1 117 SF2 862
Coons, Maurice. STH 136
Cooper, Anthony Ashley see Earl
of Shaftesbury
Cooper, Bryan Robert Wright
(1932-) SF1 117
Cooper, Colin Symons (1926-)
ES1 115 SFE 138 SF1 118 SF2
862
Cooper, Edmund (1926-) ALW
212 AOW 170 BAA 132,145,
151,157 BFP 126-7 BYS 303
EFP 10,14,20 ES1 115-6 FFR
57 FTF 85,88-9,165,171-2,
179-80,194 HFI 35 IAC 86-7
ISW 136-8,244-5 KAU 62,65,
71-4,90,109,125 KWS 363 LEX
257-8 MFW 104 NDA 28 RGS
46 SFE 138-9 SF1 118 SF2
862-3 SL4 1884-7 SRB 330,332
VES 74,84,95,129,131,136,169,
180, 214-5, 247-8, 256, 269-70
WGT 33-4
Cooper, Elizabeth. FFC 131
Cooper, Gary. PJF 17,36
Cooper, Giles (1918-66) SF1 118
Cooper, Hughes pseud. of George
H. Leonard. BAA 148 HFI 35
SF1 118
Cooper, J.C. SF1 118
Cooper, James Fenimore (1789-
1851) BAA 21,24 CSF 48 EXT
3/2 42 EXT 6/2 42 MSF 139,
148,156,162,193 NWO 20,36,
101, 282 RBY 35,66,123 SF1
118 WGT 34 WIF 45
Cooper, John C. pseud. of John
Croydon. SF1 118
Cooper, Ken. TSP 72
Cooper, Louise (1952-) HFI 35
SF1 118 SF2 863

Cooper, Margaret. FFC 53
Cooper, Marion. FFC 90
Cooper, Merian C. CSF 48 FFR
57 KAU 187
Cooper, Morton. SF1 118
Cooper, Parley J. HFI 36 SF1
118
Cooper, Paul Fenimore. FFC
90,175
Cooper, Ralph S. IAC 87 SFS 34
Cooper, Robert. BAA 22
Cooper, Susan (1935-) BAA 140
ES1 116 FFC 37-8 FL1 331-5
SFE 139 SF1 118 SF2 863
Cooperman, Stanley. BAA 213
Coover, Robert (1932-) BAA 142
ETN 12,141 FL3 1489-91 FL4
1995-8 IAC 87 MFW 25 RSG
77 SFD 4 SFE 139 SFH 99,171
STF 9,24
Cope, Eddie. WFS 150
Cope, Gertrude Venetta. SF1 119
Copelman, Evelyn. FFC 174
Copeman, Berger. IAC 87
Copernicus. EXT 4/2 21 FTF
18,20-1 INT 12-3 KVT 4 MFW
186,193,256 MSF 103 PST 16
RAH 65 SFH 119-20,131
Copley, Frank Barkley. AOW 58
CSF 48 EXT 1/1 8 SFE 139
SF1 119
Coppard, A(lfred) E(dgar) (1878-
1957) CSF 48-9 ES1 116-7 FBK
65,78 FL2 543-8 IAC 87 SFS
34 SF1 119 SOT 367
Coppard, Audrey Jean (1931-)
SF1 119 SF2 863
Coppel, Alfred (1921-) ALW 161
AOW 170 COT 195 ES1 117
FFR 57 HFI 36 IAC 87 RFA
155 SFE 139 SFS 34 SF1 119
SF2 863 VES 105,130,134,177,
180 WGT 34 WIF 146
Copper, Basil (1924-) ES1 117
FL2 581-4 IAC 87 SF1 119
S F2 864
Coppola, Francis Ford. CSC
243-4,263
Corbett, Chan pseud. of Nat
Schachner. RFA 41-2
Corbett, Elizabeth Burgoyne
(1846-) CSF 49 SF1 119 WGT
34
Corbett, (Mrs.) George. BAA 39

Corbett, James. CSF 49 SFE 139 SF1 119

Corbett, (Sir) Julian Stafford (1854-1922) CSF 49 SF1 119

Corbett, Scott (1913-) FFC 30, 62,87,187 SF1 119 SF2 864

Corbin, Carol Elizabeth. BAA 173

Corbin, Henry. BAA 213

Corbyn, Clara A. B. CSF 49 SF1 119

Cordell, Alexander pseud. of Alexander Graber. HFI 36 SF1 119

Corelli, Marie pseud. of Mary Mackay (1864-1924). CAT 22 CSF 49 ES1 117 EXT 9/2 62 FL3 1332-4 FL4 1784-6 MSF 69,202 SFE 139 SF1 119-20

Coren, Alan. FFC 141 IAC 87

Cores, Lucy. IAC 87

Corey, Paul Frederick (1903-) ES1 117 HFI 36 IAC 87 SFE 139 SF1 120 SF2 864-5

Coriel, Rita. ALW 8

Coriell, Vernell. ALW 8 SF1 120

Corlett, Ann. IAH 136

Corlett, William. HFI 36

Corley, Donald (1886-1955) CSF 50 ES1 118 SF1 120 SRB 256

Corley, Edwin (1931-) AOW 170 HFI 36 NDA 170-2 SFE 139 SF1 120 SF2 865

Corley, James (1947-) SFE 139-40

Cormack, Donald G. TSP 158

Cormack, Maribelle (1902-) SF1 120

Corman, Avery. SF1 120

Corman, Cid. IAC 87

Corman, Roger (1926-) FBK 35 KAU 126 SFE 140 SRB 59

Corneille. EXT 9/2 29

Cornelius, B. WTS 4-7

Cornelius, Mary Ann (1827-1918) SF1 120

Cornelius, Paul. BAA 173

Cornell, Frederick Carruthers. CSF 50 SF1 120

Cornford, F. M. MSF 25

Cornford, Leslie Cope (1867-1927) CSF 50 SF1 120

Corning, Walter D. SF1 120

Cornish, Gerald Warre (1875-1916) CSF 50 SF1 120

Cornog, Robert. HID 24 SFN 25

Cornu, Auguste. BAA 213

Cornwall, Ian Wolfram. SF1 120

Cornwallis-West, George Frederick Myddelton (1874-1951) CSF 50 SF1 120

Cornwell, David John Moore (1931-) WGT 34

Coron, Hannah. BAA 90 CSF 50 SF1 581

Correa, Hugo. IAC 87 SIH 146-7 VES 179

Correy, Lee pseud. of George Harry Stine. HFI 36 IAC 87 IAH 91 ISW 32-3,284 MIH 91 RFA 202 SFE 140 SFN 28 SFS 35 SF1 120 SF2 865-6

Corsano, Antonio. BAA 213

Corso, Gregory. TDI 10 VFS 117

Corston, Michael George (1932-) SFE 140 SF1 120 SF2 866 WGT 34

Cortazar, Julio (1914-) FBK 135, 143 SF1 120 SF2 866 SIH 54,79

Cortez, Hernando. LTN 108 STH 72

Corvaja, (Baron) Joseph. BAA 26

Corvo, (Baron) pseud. of Frederick William Rolfe. FL2 684-6

Corwin, Cecil pseud. of C. M. Kornbluth. IAC 87 IAH 35 ISW 146 RFA 191 WSF 126

Corwin, June. FFC 2

Corwin, Norman Lewis (1910-) CSF 50 ES1 118 IAC 87 RFA 138 SF1 120 SF2 866

Cory, Charles Barney (1857-1921) CSF 50 ES1 118 SF1 120

Cory, Desmond pseud. of Shaun Lloyd McCarthy. SF1 121

Cory, Howard L. pseud. of Jack Owen Jardine, Julie Ann Jardine. SFE 140

Cory, Matilda Winifred Muriel Graham. WGT 34

Cory, Vivian. BAA 103 WGT 34 see also Victoria Cross

Coryell, John Russell (1848-1924) WGT 34-5

Cosby, Eleanor. WFS 122

Cosby, Willard. WFS 122

Coser, Lewis A. BAA 213,232-3

Cosgrave, John O'Hara (1864-1947) CSF 50 SF1 121

Cosier, C. H. T. SF1 121

Cosper, Wilbert Le Roy. SF1 121

85

Cost, March pseud. of Margaret
Mackie Morrison. CSF 50 SF1
121
Costain, Thomas Bertram (1885-
1965) SF1 121 SF2 866
Costello, Dudley (1803-65) SF1
121
Costello, Frederick Hankerson
(1851-1921) CSF 50 SF1 121
Costello, Lou. INT 39
Costello, P. F. (house name)SFE
142 VES 102 WGT 35 see also
Roger P. Graham
Costello, Peter. SRB 82 TSF 249
Cotes, May. CSF 4 SF1 121
Cotgrove, Stephen. BAA 213
Cott, Jonathan (1942-) SF1 121
SF2 866
Cotton, John. IAC 87
Cotton, Jose Mario Garry Ordonez
Edmondson Y (1922-) WGT 109
see also G. C. Edmondson
Cottrell, C. L. IAC 87 MIH 91
Cottrell, G. W. , Jr. EXT 5/2 2
Couch, F. A. , Jr. FL3 1164-8
Couldrey, Oswald Jennings. CSF
50 SF1 121
Coulson, George J. CSF 50
Coulson, Juanita Ruth (1933-) ES1
118 HFI 36 IAC 87 SFE 142
SF1 121 SF2 866-7 SRB 125
WGT 35
Coulson, Robert Stratton (1928-)
HFI 36 IAC 87 SFE 142 SF1
121 SRB 125 WGT 35
Coulton, George Gordon. CSF 50
Coulton, Mary Rose see Sarah
Campion
Counselman, Mary Elizabeth
(1911-) ES1 118 IAC 87 SFS 35
WTS 37-8, 44
Counts, Ed. OWB 87
Couperus, Louis M. A. CSF 50
Coupling, J. J. pseud. of John
R. Pierce. FFR 57 IAC 87-8
RFA 167 SFS 35 VFS 261 WIF
167
Couppey, Madeleine. SF1 121
Courcelle, Pierre. BAA 213
Cournos, John (1881-1966) BAA
83-4 SF1 121
Courtenay, Luke Theophilus. CSF
50 SF1 122
Courtenay, Mitchell. SFN 105
Courtenay, Thomas G. SF1 122

Courtier, Sidney Hobson (1904-
74) SF1 122 SF2 867
Courtney, Robert. IAC 88 SFS
35
Coury, Phil. BAA 133 ES1 118
SFE 142 SF1 122
Cousins, Edmund George (1893-)
CSF 50 SF1 122
Cousins, Norman. VFS 211
Cousteau, Jacques. VFS 3, 13,
56-7
Coutts, Tristram. BAA 72
Couzyn, Jeni. IAC 88
Cove, Joseph Walter (1891-) BAA
119 ES1 118 WGT 35 see also
Lewis Gibbs
Cover, Arthur Byron (1950-) HFI
36 IAC 88 RGS 46 SFE 142
SF2 867
Coverdale, Henry Standish. BAA
36 CSF 50
Covert, Dick. RZY 9, 14
Cowan, Clyde. FTF 151
Cowan, Frank (1844-1905) AOW
42, 58 BAA 32 CSF 51 MFW
119 SFE 142 SF1 122
Cowan, James (1870-1943) AOW
58 BAA 55 CSF 51 EXT 1/1
3, 8 SFE 142 SF1 122 SRB 9
Cowden, James Seldon. BAA 46
Cowen, Laurence. CSF 51
Cowen, William Joyce. CSF 51
Cowie, Donald John. CSF 51
ES1 118 SF1 122
Cowie, George R. IAC 88 SFS
35
Cowles, Frederick Ignatius (1900-)
CSF 51 ES1 118-9 SF1 122
Cowles, John Clifford. SF1 122
Cowper, Edith E. CSF 51
Cowper, Richard pseud. of John
Middleton Murry, Jr. AOW
170-1 BYS 304 EFP 20 FFR
57 HFI 37 IAC 88 LEX 258-9
RGS 46-7 RZY 105 SFE 142-3
SF1 122 VES 203
Cox, Anne. WGT 35 see also
Annabel Gray
Cox, Anthony Berkeley (1893-
1970) CSF 51 SF1 122 WGT 35
Cox, Arthur Jean. HID 137 IAC
88 ISW 129 JVN 67-85, 184,
187, 215, 235-6, 239 SFS 35 SOT
388 WGT 35
Cox, C. B. EXT 10/1 25

Cox, Carlos Manuel. BAA 173
Cox, Donald William (1921-) ES1
119
Cox, Erle (Howard) (1873-1950)
AOW 101 BAA 90 CSF 51 ES1
119 SFE 143 SF1 122 STH
62-3, 86 WIF 52
Cox, Irving E(ngland), Jr. (1917-)
ES1 119 IAC 88 ISW 129-30
MIH 95 SFS 35
Cox, J. Sullivan. BAA 213
Cox, James M. NWO 214, 229
Cox, Jane. VMW 5
Cox, Luther. ES1 119 SFE 143
SF1 122
Cox, Steve. NWO 186
Cox, Wally. FFC 141
Cox, William R. TSP 112, 211
Coxe, (Mr.). SF1 122
Coxe, Edward D. BAA 36 SF1
123 WGT 35 see also A Fugi-
tive
Coxey, Willard D. CSF 51
Coxon, Muriel Hine. WGT 35
see also Muriel Hine
Coye, Lee Brown (1907-) ES1 119
FBK 28, 78 WTS 59, 76, 78, 82,
103, 106
Coyle, Kathleen. CSF 51
Cozzens, James Gould (1903-78)
CSF 51 ES1 119 SF1 123 SF2
867-8
Cozzi, Luigi. IAC 88
Crabapple, John. SF1 123
Crabbe, Buster. WSF 309 YTS 16
Cracken, Jael. VES 231
Craddock, Charles Egbert pseud.
of Mary Noailles Murfree. CSF
51 SF1 123
Cradock, Phyllis (1910-) SF1 123
WIF 52
Craig, A. Elsie Rundall. SF1 123
Craig, Alexander. AOW 58 BAA
58 CSF 51 SFE 143 SF1 123
Craig, Charles William Thurlow
(1901-) CSF 51 SF1 514
Craig, Colin pseud. of Henry
Spencer Booth. CSF 51 SF1 123
Craig, David pseud. of Allan James
Tucker. SF1 123
Craig, Hamilton. BAA 90-1 SF1
123
Craig, Helen. FFC 50, 55
Craig, Kent. SL5 2096-100
Craig, M. Jean. FFC 12

Craig, William. IAC 88
Craigie, David pseud. of Dorothy
M. Craigie. AOW 315 SF1 123
Craigie, Dorothy M. ES1 119
WGT 35 see also David Craigie
Craigie, William A. AAL 147-8
Craik, Dinah Maria (1826-87)
CSF 51 SF1 123 WGT 35 see
also Diana Mulock
Craine, Edith Janice (1881-) SF1
123
Crais, Robert. IAC 88
Cram, Mildred (1889-) CSF 51-2
SF1 124 SF2 868
Cram, Ralph Adams (1863-1942)
BAA 84 CSF 52 ES1 119 IAC
88 SF1 124
Cramb, John Adam (1862-1913)
see J. A. Revermort
Cramer, John D. BAA 109
Cramer, Maurice Browning
(1910-) CSF 52 SF1 124
Cramp, Leonard G. (1919-) ES1
119
Crandall, E. E. BAA 1
Crandall, Reed. ES1 120
Crandolph, Augustus J. CSF 52
Crane, Clarence. EXT 6/1 9
Crane, Frank. WTS 18
Crane, Hart. ETN 111 NWO 28,
35, 89, 263 RZY 14 WIF 135
Crane, Lillie. CSF 52
Crane, Martin. SFN 61-2
Crane, Nathalia Clara Ruth (1913-)
CSF 52 SF1 124
Crane, R. S. BAA 213
Crane, Robert pseud. of Bernard
Glemser. AOW 171 HFI 37
IAC 88 KAU 93 SFE 143 SFS
35 SF1 124
Crane, Stephen. EXT 4/1 10
EXT 9/2 39 IAC 88 JHN 23
NWO 3, 20, 84
Crane, Walter Beverly. ES1 120
FFC 3
Cranford, Hope. CSF 52 SF1
124
Cranford, Robin. SF1 124
Cranston, Ruth. WGT 35
Cravens, Gwyneth. IAC 88
Crawford, Alexander. CSF 52
Crawford, Debbie. WFS 174
Crawford, F(rancis) Marion
(1854-1909) CSF 52 ES1 120
FBK 73 FL2 836-8 FL4 2054-

Crawford, Francis Marion (cont.)
8 FL5 2136-8 HFI 37 IAC 88
SF1 124 SRB 256 WIF 71
Crawford, Gary William. FL3
1124-6, 1209-11, 1412-6, 1485-8
FL4 1600-6
Crawford, Isabell C. CSF 52
SF1 124
Crawford, Jesse. WFS 55
Crawford, Joseph H., Jr. (1932-)
BAA 173 ES1 120 EXT 5/1 5
SF1 124
Crawford, Margaret. WGT 36
Crawford, Theron Clark. BAA
51 CSF 52 SF1 124
Crawford, Thelmar Wyche (1905-)
SF1 124
Crawford, William L(evi) (1911-)
ES1 120 EXT 3/1 9 IAC 88
IMS 21-5, 30, 43, 74, 93, 95 ISW
161 RFA 54, 63 SFE 143 SF1
124 SF2 868 SOT 272, 339
WGT 36 WIF 123 see also
Garret Ford
Crawley, Rayburn. CSF 52 SF1
124
Crawshay-Williams, Eliot (1879-
1962) SF1 124-5
Crayder, Dorothy (1906-) SF1 125
Crayon, Diedrick, Jr. pseud. of
Kenneth Bruce. CSF 52 SF1 125
Creasey, John (1908-73) ES1 120
HFI 37 SFE 143-4 SF1 125,
581 SF2 868 WGT 36
Creedy, Frederick. BAA 126
Creel, George. BAA 213
Creelman, James. STH 38
Cregan, Mairin. FFC 95
Crellin, Horatio Nelson. WGT
36 see also Al Arawiyah
Cremaschi, Inisero (1928-) LEX
259-60
Cresswell, Helen (1936-) FFC 4,
30, 62-3, 154, 161 SF1 125-6
SF2 868-9
Creswick, Paul A. (1866-1947)
CSF 52 SF1 126
Crevecoeur. NWO 30 see also
J. Hector St. John
Crew, Fleming. FFC 132
Crews, Frederick. FAN 87-8
Crichton, Michael (1942-) ALW
186 AOW 171 ASF 128 CSC
76-9, 86 DTS v FFR 57 HFI
38 IAC 88 KAU 184, 189, 201

LEX 260 MFW 201 NWO 134
OMN 250-9, 269, 272-3 SFD 12-
5 SFE 144 SFH 152 SF1 126
SF2 869 SL1 63-6 SRB 354
WGT 36
Crick, Francis. SFH 141
Cridge, Alfred Denton. BAA 35
POE 162 SF1 126
Cridge, Annie Denton. BAA 28-9
Crisp, Cassius. CSF 52 ES1 121
Crisp, Frank Robson (1915-) ES1
121 SFE 146 SF1 126 SF2 869
Crisp, N. J. VES 134
Crispin, Edmund pseud. of Robert
Bruce Montgomery. ALW 7-8,
34, 144, 225, 234 AOW 290 BYS
248, 298, 304, 320 CSC 164-5
EXT 2/1 1 EXT 5/1 10 IAC 88
IAH 135 MIH 31 SFB 8 SFE
146 SFS 35 SF1 126 SOI 153
Crist, Eda Szecskay (1909-) SF1
126
Crist, Judith. EXT 10/1 25
Crist, Richard Harrison. SF1 126
Cristabel pseud. of Christine
Elizabeth Abrahamson. HFI 38
SFE 146 SF1 126
Critchfield, Esther pseud. of
Arthur J. Burks. TSP 83
Critchie, E. pseud. of Arthur J.
Burks. WTS 23
Cro, Stelio. BAA 213
Croce, Benedetto (1866-1952)
BAA 213 WBW 33
Crocker, Samuel (1845-1921) BAA
46-7 WGT 36
Crockett, Samuel Rutherford
(1860-1914) CSF 52 SF1 126
Croffts, (Mrs.). SF1 126
Croft, (Sir) Herbert (1751-1816)
POE 38-9, 44 SF1 126-7
Croft, Jason. ALW 113
Croft-Cooke, Rupert. BAA 98
Crofton, Algernon. SF1 127
Crofton, Francis Blake (1841-
1912) CSF 53 SF1 127
Crofts, Anna Helen. EXT 3/1 9
Croker, T. Crofton. IAC 88
Croly, David Goodman. POE 152
Croly, George (1780-1860) CSF
53 SFE 147 SF1 127
Croly, Herbert David (1869-1930)
WGT 36
Cromie, Robert (1856-1907) AOW
58 BAA 41 CSF 53 EXT 5/1 4

Cromie, Robert (cont.)
FTF 42 MSF 203 POE 107
SFE 147-8 SF1 127 VES 69, 80,
106, 135
Crompton, Richmal pseud. of
Richmal Crompton Lamburn
(1890-1969) CSF 53 SF1 127
Cromwell, Oliver. CAT 85 ISW
2 VFS 155-6
Cronin, Bernard Charles (1884-)
CSF 53 ES1 122 WGT 36 see
also Eric North
Cronkite, Betsy. VFS 184
Cronkite, Walter. VFS 73, 184
Crook, Compton N. WGT 36 see
also Stephen Tall
Crosby, Edward Harold (1859-
1934) CSF 53 SF1 127
Crosby, Harry C. ES1 122 WGT
36 see also Christopher Anvil
Crosby, Willard. TSP 160 WFS
104
Cross, Gene. SF1 127
Cross, J. W. EXT 5/2 27
Cross, James. IAC 88
Cross, John Kier (1914-67) AOW
315 CSF 53 ES1 122 FL3 1173-
5 HFI 38 IAC 88 SFE 148 SF1
127 SRB 26 WGT 36-7 see also
Stephen MacFarlane
Cross, Jommy. SIH 184
Cross, Martha Ruth (1887-) SF1
128
Cross, Polton pseud. of John
Russell Fearn. CSF 53 IAC 88
VES 84
Cross, Ronald A. IAC 88
Cross, Thompson. CSF 53 SF1
128
Cross, Victoria pseud. of Vivian
Cory. CSF 53 SF1 128 STH
83-4
Crossen, Kendall Foster (1910-)
BAA 123 ES1 122-3 FTF 176
HFI 38 IAC 88-9 IAH 47-8, 87-
9 ISW 91, 95-6, 232 MFW 74-
80, 90, 200 SFE 148 SFS 35 SF1
128 SF2 870 TJB 20 VES 92
WGT 37 WIF 106 see also
Christopher Monig
Crossland, John Redgwick (1892-)
CSF 154 SF1 128
Crossley, Robert. SL2 850-4
SL3 1265-9, 1429-34 SL4 1967-
72

Crossley-Holland, Kevin. ES1 123
Crottet, Robert. SF1 128
Crouch, Marcus S. EXT 10/1 25
Crouch, Nathaniel (1632? -1725?)
WGT 37
Croutch, Leslie A. IAC 89
Crow, John H. UKL 200-24
Crow, Martha Foote (1854-1924)
CSF 53 SF1 128
Crowcroft, Peter (1925-) BAA
123 ES1 123 SFE 148 SF1 128
Crowe, Catherine Stevens (1799? -
1876) CSF 53 ES1 123
Crowe, Charles. BAA 173
Crowley, Aleister pseud. of
Edward Alexander Crowley.
CSF 53 ES1 123 FBK 69 FL3
1065-7 SF1 128 WTS 45
Crowley, John (1942-) FL2 887-
90 HFI 38 LEX 261-2 RGS 47-
8 SFE 148 SL1 133-7 SL2 721-
4 SRB 365 THM 39
Crown, Peter J. WGT 37 see
also Pete Lewis
Crowninshield, Mary Bradford
(-1913) WGT 37
Croydon, John see John C. Cooper
Crozetti, Ruth G. Warner (1913-)
SF2 1117
Crozier, John Beattie. BAA 213
Cruger, Julia Grinnell Storrow
(-1920) WGT 37
Cruger, Mary. EXT 1/1 8
Cruikshank. [FUT]
Cruls, Gastao (1888-) CSF 53
SF1 128
Crume, Vic. SF2 128
Crumley, Thomas W. SF1 128
Crump, Charles George (1862-
1935) CSF 53 SF1 128
Crump, (James) Irving (1887-)
CSF 53-4 ES1 123 SF1 128
Cruse, Hans. BAA 281
Cruso, Solomon. BAA 109 CSF
54 SF1 128-9 STH 46-8
Crusoe, Robinson (pseud.) BAA
47
Cruz, Ray. FFC 196
Csernai, Zoltan (1925-) LEX 262
Csiszar, Jolan. BAA 173
Ctvrtek, Vaclav. FFC 63
Cuffari, Richard. FFC 20, 56, 61,
80, 94, 122
Culbreath, Myrna. IAC 89, 171
Cullen, Countee (1903-46) CSF
54 SF1 129

Cullen, Seamus. HFI 38
Cullen, Stephen. CSF 54 WGT 37
Cullen, Tom A. EXT 10/1 25
Culler, A. Dwight. MSF 225
Cullinan, John. CUA 11
Cullingford, Guy pseud. of
Constance Lindsay Taylor. SF1
129
Cullum, Ridgwell (1867-1943)
CSF 54 SF1 129
Culp, Mary Beth. SRB 465
Cumberland, Stuart pseud. of
Charles Garner. SF1 129
Cummings, E. E. IAC 89 MSM
92 RBY 129, 155
Cummings, Edgar L. INT 86, 88
Cummings, Monette A. ES1 123
HFI 38 IAC 89 SFE 149 SF1
129 WGT 37
Cummings, Parke. IAC 89
Cummings, (Mrs.) Ray. WGT
37
Cummings, Ray(mond) (King)
(1887-1957) ALW 60, 113-4, 124,
129, 156, 160 AOW 58-9, 101
BAA 87, 94 BFP 128-9 BYS
170 CSF 38, 54 ES1 123-4 ETN
15 FFR 58 FTF 68 HFI 38-9
HID viii IAC 89 IMS 213, 220
ISW 140 LEX 262-3 MIH 45
NWO 253 PST 129-30, 136-7,
196-7, 239-40, 248, 252, 280-1,
288-9 RFA 1-4, 6, 8, 12, 20, 57,
64-5, 70, 183 RGS 48-9 SFD
210 SFE 149 SFS 35 SF1 129
SIH 189 SL2 878-82 SOT 49,
73, 93, 111, 217 SRB 7, 296 STH
151 TJB 16 TSP 28, 62, 132,
144, 171, 175-80, 189 WFS 8,
110-1, 119 WGT 37 WIF 70, 72,
85 WSF 16, 28, 34, 54, 333, 386
WTS 28, 51, 69 VES 141, 312
see also Ray King, Gabriel
Wilson
Cummings, Sherwood. SL1 428-
32
Cummins, Harle Owen. AOW 59
CSF 54 ES1 124 EXT 1/1 8
EXT 7/1 18, 26 IAC 89 SFE
149 SF1 129
Cunha, Fausto. SL4 1545-7
Cunis, Reinmar (1933-) BAA 213
LEX 263-4
Cunliffe, W. E. EXT 10/1 19
Cunningham, Beall. BAA 105
CSF 54 SF1 129

Cunningham, Ben. IAC 89
Cunningham, John W. CSF 54
Cunningham, Julia. FFC 4, 116-
7, 131
Cuppy, Will(iam) (Jacob) (1884-
1949) CSF 54 ES1 124 EXT
3/1 22 SF1 129
Curcio, Carlo. BAA 173, 213
Curie, Marie. MFW 24
Curie, Pierre. MFW 24
Curley, Daniel. FFC 63
Curlovich, John M. IAC 89
Curran, Ronald. SF1 129
Currey, L. W. BRS 4 IAC 89,
130 RSG 91 SRB 64, 68
Currie, Jessie Monteath. CSF
54
Curry, Jane Louise (1932-) ES1
124 FFC 73, 103, 162, 187 SF1
129 SF2 870 SRB 24
Curties, (Capt.) Henry (1860-)
CSF 54 SF1 130
Curties, T. J. Horsley. CSF 54
SF1 130 WGT 37-8 see also
T. J. Horsley
Curtis, Albert Charles (1867-)
CSF 54 SF1 130
Curtis, Betsy. IAC 89 SFS 35
Curtis, Dora. FFC 93
Curtis, George William (1824-92)
SF1 130
Curtis, Jean-Louis pseud. of
Louis Lafitte. ES1 124 SFE
149 SF1 130
Curtis, Marguerite. CSF 54
Curtis, Monica Mary. BAA 101
SF1 130
Curtis, Richard Alan (1937-) ES1
124-5 IAC 89 SFE 149 SF1
130 SF2 870
Curtis, Robert G. CSF 54 SF1
130
Curtis, Wardon Allan (1867-1940)
ALW 85 CSF 54 IAC 89 SFE
149 SF1 130
Curtiss, Frank Homer (1875-1946)
SF1 130
Curtiss, Harriette Augusta (1856?-
1932) SF1 130
Curtois, Margaret Anne. CSF 54
SF1 130
Curtoni, Vittorio (1949-) LEX
264-5 SFB 145
Curval, Philippe pseud. of Philippe
Tronche. LEX 265 SFE 149-50
Curwen. WTS 44

Curwood, James Oliver. MFW 131
Curzon, Gordon Anthony. BAA
281
Curzon-Herrick, (Lady) Maud
Kathleen (1893-1965) WGT 38
see also Maud Cairnes
Cusack, Frank. ES1 125
Cusack, Isabel. FFC 141
Cushing, Harvey. EXT 7/1 15
Cushing, Paul. CSF 55

Custot, Pierre (1880-) CSF 55
SF1 130
Cuthbert, Chester D. IAC 89
IMS 29 SFS 35
Cuthbert, Estella Y. see Cuthbert
Yerex
Cutt, William Towrie (1898-) SF1
130
Cuvier, Georges. MSF 150

D

D. H. BAA 227
Da Vinci, Leonardo (1452-1519)
ES1 271 EXT 3/2 52 EXT 6/2
44, 48 FTF 18, 62 HFI 39 IMS
1 KAU 127 RZY 39 SFN 93
VFS 206
Dabbs, D. E. EXT 10/1 48
Dabbs, George H. R. (1846-1913)
CSF 55 SF1 131
Dabcovich, Lydia. FFC 19
D'Achille, Gino. FFC 9 VES
134, 147, 182, 200
Dacre, Charlotte (1782-) ALW 45
CSF 55 PST 27 SF1 131
Dadd, Richard. FBK 60
Dagmar, Peter. BAA 139 ES1
125 HFI 39 SFE 152 SF1 131
Dagron, Gilbert. BAA 213-4
Dague, Robert Addison. BAA
65-6
Daguerre, Louis Jacques (1789-
1851) EXT 6/2 30 VFS 192
Dahl, Roald (1916-) CSC 217 ES1
125 EXT 7/2 47 EXT 8/1 6
FBK 153 FFC 63 FFR 59 FTF
81-2 IAC 89 ISW 129, 221 LTN
261 SFE 152 SFH 175 SFS 36
SF1 131 SF2 870 SOT 367

Dahlgren, Madeleine Vinton (1825-
98) CSF 55 ES1 125 WGT 38
Dahlquist-Ljungberg, Ann Margaret
WAA 234
Dahrendorf, Ralf. BAA xxi, 214
Dail, Charles Curtis (1851-1902)
BAA 41 CSF 55 SFE 152 SF1
131
Dain, Alex pseud. of Alex Luke-
man. HFI 39 SFE 152 SF1 131
Daisne, Johan pseud. of Herman
Thiry. FBK 146
Dake, Charles Romyn. AOW 59
BAA 60 CSF 55 EXT 1/1 8
MFW 126 SFE 152 SF1 131
Dakers, Elaine Kidner (1905-)
BAA 140 ES1 125 WGT 38 see
also Jane Lane
Daladier, Edouard (1884-) WFS 98
Dalberg, John. FAN 115
Dalby, Richard. SF1 131
Daldorne, E. Van. CSF 55
Dale. MSM 144
Dale, Donald pseud. of Mary Dale
Buckner. TSP 144, 171, 180, 183
Dale, Harrison Clifford (1885-)
CSF 55 ES1 125-6 SF1 131
Dale, J. S. CSF 85

Dalenoord, Jerry. FFC 77
Daley, Brian. HFI 39
Daley, John Bernard. IAC 89
ISW 125-6 SFS 36 WGT 38
Daley, Richard J. (1902-76) WFS
270
Dalgliesh, Alice. EXT 10/1 25
Dali, Salvador. CUA 4 EXT 7/2
37 JGB 6 WFS 118
D'Allais, Denis Vairasse. BAA
7-8 MSF 88,107
Dallas, Ian. SF1 131
Dallas, Oswald C. C. CSF 55
SF1 131
Dallas, Paul V. ES1 126 HFI
39 SF1 131
Dalmaine, James. CSF 55 SF1
131
Dalmas, John. HFI 39 SFE 152
SF1 131
Dalrymple-Hay, John Warwick
(1928-) SF2 933
Dalsace, Lionel see Aimee Blech
Dalton, Charles Test. BAA 97
Dalton, Henry Robert Samuel.
BAA 39 SF1 131
Dalton, James. SF1 132
Dalton, John. SFH 160
Dalton, Moray. CSF 55 SF1 132
Daly, Carroll John. SFW 75
TSP 4
Daly, Marsha. IAC 89
Dameron, Louise. BAA 173
Damon, Steve. SF1 132
Damonti, Henry. AOW 295 IAC
89
Dana, Barbara. FFC 117
Dana, Francis. SF1 132
Dana, Marvin. CSF 55
Dana, Mary V. EXT 3/1 21
Danby, Frank pseud. of Julia
Frankau. CSF 55 SF1 132
Danby, Mary Heather (1941-)
SF1 132 SF2 870-1
Dance, Clifton, Jr. IAC 89 SFS
36
Dancey, Max. IAC 89
Dane, Clemence pseud. of Wini-
fred Ashton (1888-1965). CSF
55 ES1 126 EXT 1/2 30 SF1
132 WIF 17
Dane, Joan. CSF 55
Danforth, Mildred E. SFE 153
SF1 132
Dangerfield, Paul. SF1 132

Daniel, Charles S. BAA 47 CSF
55 SF1 132
Daniel, Craig. TSP 156
Daniel, Ferdinand Eugene (1839-
1914) CSF 56 SF1 132
Daniel, Gabriel. ALW 43 CSF
56 PST 20, 209
Daniel, Glyn Edmund (1914-) ES1
126 WGT 38
Daniel, Howard. ES1 126
Daniel, Jerry Clayton (1937-)
SF1 132 SF2 871
Daniel, Molly. IAC 89
Daniel, Robert. NWO 63
Daniel, Terry C. HFI 39
Daniel, Yuri M. (1925-) AOW 172
SFE 153 SF1 132 SIH 83 WAA
71 WGT 38
Daniel-Rops. BAA 214
Daniels, Alan. [FUT]
Daniels, Cora Linn. CSF 56
Daniels, David R. COT 110 SOT
136 VES 122,151
Daniels, Dorothy. SF1 132
Daniels, Jonathan Worth (1902-)
CSF 56 SF1 133 SF2 871
Daniels, Norman A. SF1 133
TSP 203
Danilova. WFS 204
Dann, Jack (Mayo) (1945-) ETN
142 FFR 59-60 [FJT] HFI 39
IAC 89 LEX 266-7 LTN 248
SFD 234 SFE 153-4 SF1 133
SF2 871 STH 45
Dannay, Frederick (1905-) SF1
133 WGT 38-9
Danrit, (Capt.) pseud. of Emile
A. Driant. CSF 56
Dante. ASF 187-8 CAT 69, 89
CUA 23, 44 EXT 8/1 23 EXT
10/2 74 FLT 5 HEN 37 INT 74
JGB 16 KVT 16 LTN 63 MIH
71 MSF 33, 55, 57, 93, 125, 132,
248 SFE 154 SFH 42-3, 203
SHL 60 STF 30, 64-5 STH 96-
7, 106 TDI 48 UKL 124 WAA
27, 74 WBW 28, 35, 50 WTS 17
Dante, Joe. RBY 240
Danton, William. IAC 90
Danvers, Jack pseud. of Camille
Auguste Marie Caseleyr. SFE
154 SF1 133
Danyers, Geoffrey. CSF 56 SF1
133

Danzig, Allan. IAC 90 SFS 36
Danziger, David. SF1 133
Danziger, Gustaf Adolf De Castro (1859-1959) ES1 126
D'Apery, Helen Burnell (1842-1915) WGT 39 see also Olive Harper
Daraul, Arkon. ES1 126
Darby, Abraham. FTF 34
Darby, Christopher Lovett see Oudeis
D'Arcos, J. Paco pseud. of Joaquim Belford Correa Da Silva. SF1 401
D'Arcy, Jack. TSP 29, 105
D'Arcy, Willard. TSP 156
Dard, Roger. SF1 133
Dardenelle, Louise. BAA 111 SF1 133
Dardis, Thomas A. SF1 133
Dare, Alan pseud. of George Goodchild. CSF 56
Dare, Marcus Paul (1902-62) CSF 56 ES1 126 SF1 133
D'Argenteuil, Paul. BAA 60
Dargon. SF1 133
Darity, William A. (1953-) SF1 133
Dark, James pseud. of James Workman. ES1 126 SF1 133, 581
Dark, Sidney. BAA 79, 173
Darling, Louis. FFC 87, 107, 116
Darlington, Andrew. IAC 90
Darlington, William Aubrey Cecil (1890-) CSF 56 SF1 134 SF2 872
Darlton, Clark pseud. of Walter Ernsting. FFR 60-2 SFB 146 SFE 154
Darnaud, Edmond. POE 191
Darnay, Arsen. HFI 39 IAC 90 SFE 154
Darrell, Gratiana. CSF 56 SF1 134
Darrington, Hugh (1940-) SFE 154 SF1 134 SF2 872
Darrow, Clarence. HWK 34
Darrow, Frank M. BAA 159 SF1 134
Darrow, Jack. ASF 243 IMS 13, 32, 34, 213, 239-40 WTS 124
D'Artois, Pierre. WTS 36
Dart, Raymond. RAH 30
Darwin, Beatrice. FFC 116

Darwin, Charles (1809-82) ACC 173-4, 178 ALW 53-4, 88, 90-1, 96, 228 AOW 87, 96 ASF 142 BYS 13, 30, 89, 110 CAT 31, 80 COT 93 CSC 167, 172 CWN 10, 31, 41 CYR 8 ETN 99 EXT 1/1 2, 17, 20 EXT 4/1 12 EXT 5/2 38 EXT 6/2 34-5 EXT 7/1 2-4, 7, 9-10, 13-4, 17 EXT 7/2 32, 37 EXT 8/2 35-6, 39, 48 EXT 9/2 33 FAN 19, 59, 70 FTF 36, 39, 49-50, 100, 129, 158 HEN 4, 61 INT 13 KVT 6, 51 LTN 219 MFW 184, 186-7, 198 MSF 30, 36, 149, 164, 166, 209-17, 223-35, 237-9, 241 MSM 247 NDA 56 NWO 24, 26, 76, 104, 126, 160-1, 166 POE 83-4, 158-9 PST 10, 23, 26, 29, 36, 44, 50-4, 56-8, 65-6, 68, 70-3, 76-9, 81, 89-93, 95, 99-101, 104-7, 110, 112, 114-5, 127, 129, 131-2, 135-45, 147-9, 153, 156, 163-4, 168, 172-3, 178-84, 215, 217-21, 232, 236, 238-9, 244, 256-7, 263, 285, 293-4, 297, 310-4, 319 RAH 139, 172 RHN 58, 95-7, 100, 187, 189 SFB 23, 100 SFH 7, 17, 56, 117, 132, 138-9, 158 SHL 14, 37 STF 35 THM 20, 44 TJB 24, 34 VES 224, 248-9, 270 VFS 199 WBW 55 WIF 52 YTS 4
Darwin, Charles Galton (1887-1962) ES1 126 POE 307-8, 310 TSO 9
Darwin, Erasmus (1731-1802) ACC 178 ALW 45, 49 BYS 13-5, 17, 24-6, 30, 36, 38, 91, 108 CAT 5-6 KAU 6 SFE 154 SFH 192
D'Astorg, Bernard. BAA 214
Dator, James Allen. BAA 214
Daubeny, Ulric. CSF 56
Daubler, Alfred. BAA 281
Daudet, Alphonse. TFC 65-6, 73
Daugherty, Walter. SRB 124 WSF 143
Daukes, Sidney Herbert (1879-) WGT 39
D'Aulaire, Edgar. FFC 109
D'Aulaire, Ingri. FFC 109
Daulton, George. IAC 90 KAU 95
Daumal, Rene (1908-44) ES1 126-7 SF1 134

Daumann, Rudolf Heinrich (1896-1957) LEX 267
Dauphine, Claude. SF1 134
D'Aurevilly, Jules Barbey (1808-88) CSF 15 ES1 30 FBK 138 SF1 33
Dautry, Jean. BAA 214
Davenport, Basil (1905-66) ALW 7 AOW 342 BAA 110-1, 174 CAT 71 COT 276 CSF 56 ES1 127 EXT 5/1 5 FAN 152 HID 179-80, 192 IAC 90 ISW x, 4-7 MIH 22, 28 SFE 154-5 SFH 238 SFN 7-13, 65 SFS 36 SFW 91, 100 SF1 134 SOT 387-8 WAA 245 WFS 174, 216
Davenport, Benjamin Rush. AOW 37, 59 BAA 53 CSF 56 SFE 155 SF1 134
Davenport, Guy. EXT 6/1 19 EXT 10/1 25
Daventry, Leonard John (1915-) BAA 141 ES1 127 HFI 39 LEX 267-8 SFE 155 SF1 134-5 SF2 872
Davey, Henry Norman (1888-) CSF 56 SF1 135
David-Neel, Alexandra Marie Louise (1868-1969) ES1 127
Davidson, Avram (1923-) ALW 8, 212, 216 AOW 118, 172-3, 287, 289 BFP 130-1 BYS 279 CSC 33 CWD 51 ES1 127-8 FFR 63 FL3 1224-6, 1250-6 HFI 39-40 IAC 90-1 IAH 128, 139 ISW 122, 127, 284 LEX 268 LTN 188 MIH 98 RGS 49-50 SFD 19, 296 SFE 155 SFS 36-7, 66 SFW 396 SF1 135 SF2 872 SL4 1930-3 SRB 256 STH 45-6 TSF 59 WAA 230 WSF 176
Davidson, Donald. BAA 214 FAN 188
Davidson, Edward H. NWO 63
Davidson, Elizabeth Sikes. FL1 401-3, 478-82 FL3 1227-9 FL4 1777-9
Davidson, Hugh pseud. of Edmund Hamilton. WTS 36
Davidson, John (1857-1909) SF1 135
Davidson, Lionel (1922-) SFE 155
Davidson, Michael. BAA 161 HFI 40
Davidson, Morrison. BAA 174

Davidson, O. IMS 169
Davidson, Sue. BAA 225
Davie, Donald. EXT 6/1 20
Davies, Christofer. EXT 8/2 30
Davies, H. Neville. BAA 214
Davies, Howell. WGT 39 see also Andrew Marvell
Davies, Hugh Sykes (1909-) ES1 128 SFE 155 SF1 135
Davies, James C. BAA 214
Davies, (Sir) John. SOI 114
Davies, L(eslie) P(urnell) (1914-) AOW 173 ES1 128-9 FFR 63 HFI 40 SFE 155-6 SF1 135 SF2 872-3 SRB 345
Davies, Mary Catherine. CSF 56 SF1 135 WGT 39
Davies, Valentine (1905-61) ES1 129 FFC 141, 154 SF1 135
Davies, Wallace Evan. BAA 214
D'Avigdor, Elim Henry (1841-95) see Wanderer
Davine. FFC 95
Davis, Bob. RFA 1 SFW 68 SOT 15 TSP 24, 176
Davis, Brian. IAC 91
Davis, Chandler (1926-) AOW 297 COT 250 ES1 129 ETN 69 IAC 91 SFS 37 WFS 204 WGT 39
Davis, David Brion. NWO 169-70
Davis, Donald. [FUT] VES 84
Davis, Dorothy Salisbury. IAC 91 SFS 37
Davis, Earle Rosco. EXT 6/1 10
Davis, Elizabeth (1936-) SF1 136
Davis, Ellis James. BAA 31
Davis, Emry. BAA 88
Davis, F. H. IAC 91
Davis, Frederick C. TSP 5, 15, 55, 79-80, 102, 143, 203
Davis, G. Brian. SF1 136
Davis, Garry. EXT 8/1 2 WIF 140
Davis, Gerry (1930-) AOW 236 FFR 63 HFI 116 LEX 504-5 SFE 156 SF1 136 UFS 4
Davis, Grania. DTS 45 IAC 91
Davis, Gwen (1936-) SF1 136 SF2 873
Davis, Hank. IAC 91
Davis, J. C. BAA 214
Davis, Jack. FFC 152 TSP 217

Davis, James (1853-1907) WGT
39 see also Owen Hall
Davis, Jerome. BAA 214
Davis, Joel. ASF 248, 253, 256,
261, 264, 323-5 WSF 287
Davis, Leopold. CSF 56
Davis, Lois Carlile (1921-) see
Lois Lamplugh
Davis, Morris. IMS 52
Davis, Natalie Zemon. BAA 214
Davis, (Capt.) Nathan. BAA 67
Davis, Nathaniel Newnham. CSF
56
Davis, Peter. SF1 136
Davis, Richard. ES1 129 IAC 91
SF1 136 SF2 873
Davis, Richard Harding (1864-
1916) CSF 56 ES1 129 SF1 136
Davis, Robert Hobart (1869-1942)
ALW 106-7, 114, 116 ES1 129
FFC 117 STH 11, 126, 135-6,
223 WSF 26, 28
Davis, Robert L. IAC 91
Davis, Sonia H. EXT 3/1 10, 22
Davis, Wesley Ford. IAC 91
Davis, William Stearns (1877-
1930) SF1 136
Davison, L. IAC 91
Davy, Catherine A. CSF 56 SF1
136
Davy, Humphrey. ASF 189 CSF
57
Davy, John. IAC 91
Dawe, William Carlton (1865-
1935) CSF 57 SF1 136
Dawes, Anna L. BAA 214
Dawley, J. Searle. WSF 307
Dawson, Alec John (1872-1951)
BAA 70-1 CSF 57 SF1 136
Dawson, Arnold. CSF 57 ES1
129
Dawson, Basil. ES1 129 SF1 136
Dawson, Carley. FFC 171 SF1
136-7
Dawson, Coningsby William (1883-
1959) BAA 77 CSF 57 SF1 137
Dawson, Emma Frances (1851-
1926) CSF 57 ES1 129 SF1 137
Dawson, Erasmus pseud. of Paul
Devon. CSF 57 SF1 137
Dawson, Forbes. SF1 137
Dawson, Francis Warrington
(1878-1962) CSF 57 SF1 137
Dawson, Mary. FFC 88, 91

Dawson, William James (1854-
1928) CSF 57 SF1 137
Dawson-Scott, Catharine A. CSF
57
Day, Benjamin H. POE 63-7
Day, Bradford M(arshall) (1916-)
AOW 361, 368 ES1 129-30 SFE
156 SF2 873 SF1 137 SRB 65
Day, Donald B(yrne) (1909-78)
ALW 184 AOW 367 ES1 130
EXT 5/1 5 FTF 13 MIH 16, 24,
40, 97 SFD 242 SFE 156 SFN
48 SF1 137 SFW 200 SRB 67
WIF 145, 175, 203 WSF 141, 212-
3, 277, 383
Day, Doris. EXT 10/2 101
Day, Emily Foster. ES1 130
DWGT 39
Day, Gerald William Langston
(1894-) ES1 130 SF1 137
Day, James Wentworth (1899-)
ES1 130
Day, Maurice. FFC 130
Day, Millard F. SF1 137
Day, Oscar Fayette Gaines (1860-)
CSF 57 SF1 137
Day, Price. IAC 91
Day-Lewis, Cecil (1904-72) WGT
39
De Acton, Eugenia pseud. of
Alethea Lewis. CSF 1
De Alarcon, Pedro. CSF 3
De Amicis, Edmondo. EXT 2/1
10
De Andrade, Oswald. BAA 168
De Balzac, Honore (1799-1850)
ALW 53, 55 AOW 19 CAT 46,
70 CSF 14 CYR 6, 9 FBK 15,
137, 141 FL2 945-7 FL3 1420-
2 IAH 23 MSF 69, 161 POE 68
PST 29, 31 SFE 58 SF1 32, 581
SHL 48 SIH 32 STF 4, 14 TFC
3, 67, 73, 124, 147, 163 THM 13,
38
De Banzie, Eric. SF1 138 WGT
39 see also Gregory Baxter
De Beaumarchais, Pierre Caron.
MSF 114
De Beauvoir, Simone (1908-)
LTN 161 SF1 40 SF2 813
De Belges, Jean Lemaire. LTN
259
De Bengoa, R. B. STH 187
De Berard, Frederick B. (1853-
1927) CSF 57 ES1 130 SF1 138

De Bergerac, Cyrano. ALW 32,
43-4 AOW 21 ASF 182 BYS
10, 61, 63-5, 79-80 CAT 69, 106
CSF 55 ES1 125 EXT 1/2 30
EXT 2/1 20 EXT 3/1 30 EXT
4/2 24, 29 EXT 5/1 15 EXT
7/2 34 EXT 8/1 23 EXT 10/2
73 FAN 10 FFR 58 FTF 21-3
IAC 91 MIH 25-6 MSF 5, 10, 12,
25, 88, 98, 100, 103-8, 111, 114,
116, 127, 162, 171, 202 MSM 203,
205-7, 213 PJF 49, 51, 54, 58
PST 18, 20-2, 26, 112, 221, 223-4,
228, 238-9, 246, 271, 274, 282,
284, 311 SFB 41, 94 SFE 152
SFN 32 SFS 37 SIH 6, 107 SOI
43 VES 79, 155, 260 WAA 17, 29
WIF 35 WSF 14, 278
De Bernardi, G. B. BAA 41
De Bertrand, Jouvenal. CSC 119
De Bibiena, Jean Galli (1710? -
1780?) CSF 23 SF1 199
De Bolt, Joe. AOW 117-301, 342
SRB 77, 80, 291-377, 516 TSF
249 VF2 106-135, 201-3, 208
De Bosschere, Jean (1878-) SF1
61
De Bougainville, Louis-Antoine.
AOW 21 MSF 59
De Broglie. EXT 7/2 30
De Bury, F. Blaze. BAA 67
WGT 39 see also F. Dickberry
De Camp, Catherine Crook (1907-)
AOW 343 IAC 91 RFA 181 SFD
244 SF1 138 SF2 873-4 WFS
216 WGT 39 WIF 129, 182, 286,
290-3
De Camp, Etta. CSF 57
De Camp, L(yon) Sprague (1907-)
AAL 14, 18, 36, 55-6 ALW 85,
155, 160, 185, 213 AOW 165, 173-
4, 343, 398 ASF 43, 148, 150, 233,
243, 252, 260-1, 324 ATA 8, 17
BAA 116, 174 BFP 132-7 BRS
7 BYS 247, 261, 264 COT 139,
185, 190, 223, 242-4, 250, 295, 298
CSC 30-2, 95, 122-3, 136, 197
CSF 57-8, 161 CWD 3, 5, 7-10,
14, 17, 24, 27, 35, 39-43, 53-6, 58
ES1 130-2 ETN 16-7, 31, 34, 160
EXT 1/2 31 EXT 3/1 22, 27
EXT 5/1 3, 5, 8 EXT 6/2 40-1,
48 EXT 7/2 40 FBK 74, 92, 94,
123-4 FFR 47-8 FL2 768-72,
870-2 FL3 1132-6 FL4 1972-4

FRN 18 HFI 40-1 HID x, 3-4,
6, 21, 152-4, 189, 192 IAC 91-3,
136 IAH 31, 53, 85, 107, 121 IMS
147, 182, 213 ISW x, 5, 19-20, 43-
5, 61, 161, 196, 259 KAU 184
LEX 269-71 LTN 262 MFW 33,
51 MIH 22-4, 26, 31-2, 35-6, 71,
99, 113, 135 MSM xvi, 32, 34, 73-
4, 77-8, 83, 119-54, 162, 172, 174,
186, 302-3 OWB 67-76, 79, 90,
93, 97-8 RFA 24, 42, 53, 55, 57,
60, 64, 66, 69-70, 83-4, 87-8, 96,
98-9, 108, 122, 155, 167, 170-1,
176-7, 181, 190, 195-6, 209, 212
RGS 50-1, 213 RHN 15 SFA 114,
229 SFB 62 SFD 9, 27-8, 63-4,
75, 243-4, 292, 308-9 SFE 158-9
SFH 176-7 SFN 28-30, 40, 47
SFS 37-8, 60, 95-6 SFW 132, 134,
137, 142-3, 149, 179-84, 262 SF1
138-9 SF2 874 SIN 8, 148-51,
153-5 SL3 1031-5, 1198-203
SL4 1827-31 SOT 6, 62, 151-66,
176, 182, 201, 218, 257-8, 330, 394,
406, 418 SRB 76, 80, 119, 257,
286, 300, 312, 334, 500 STH 103,
244 SV1 53-63 TJB 4 TSF 56,
231-2 VES 97, 116, 122, 140, 147-
8, 179, 211, 248, 269, 289, 307, 330-
1, 335 VFS 154 WAA 97-8, 243-
5 WFS 96, 111-2, 193, 216 WGT
39-40 WSF 91-3, 104, 113, 129,
134-6, 148, 154, 202, 297, 299, 386,
388 WTS 36, 48 see also Lyman
R. Lyon
De Candolle, Alphonse. POE
181-2
De Candolle, Beatrix. CSF 58
De Capoulet-Junac, Edward (1930-)
SFB 114, 140 SFE 159
De Castro, Adolphe (1859? -1959)
EXT 3/1 10 WGT 40
De Castro, Giovanni. BAA 172
De Caylus, Compte. FFC 47
De Chair, Somerset Struben
(1911-) BAA 115 ES1 132 SF1
139
De Chardin, (Pierre) Teilhard.
CWN 12 MFW 245 POE 286,
291, 315-6 SOI 6 THM 55-6
De Chatelain, Clara (1807-76)
CSF 58 SF1 101
De Chirico, Giorgio. IAC 93
JGB 6
De Cles, Jon. IAC 93

De Comeau, Alexander. CSF 58
FL3 1057-9 SF1 113
De Condillac, E. B. IAC 93
De Condorcet, (Marquis) Antoine
Nicholas. FTF 27-8, 36 MSF
117-9, 123, 128 POE 32-3
De Corte, Marcel. BAA 215
De Costa, Henry pseud. of
Frederik Pohl. IMS 169
De Courcy, Dorothy. IAC 93
SFS 38
De Courcy, John. SFS 38
De Crebillon, Claude Prosper
Julyot (1707-77) SF1 125
De Crespigny, (Mrs.) Philip Rose
Champion (-1935) SF1 99
De Cuvier, (Baron) Georges.
POE 53
De Diesbach, Ghislain. SF1 152
De Ferman, Pierre. WFS 219-20
De Foigny, Gabriel (1650? -92)
EXT 8/1 20, 23 MSF 88, 107
WGT 52 see also Jacques Sadeur
De Fontenelle, Bernard. VES 91
De Fontmell, E. V. CSF 58 SF1
191
De Ford, Miriam Allen (1888- ·
1975) AAL 89-90 ALW 212
AOW 174 BFP 138 BYS 8, 263
COT 193, 196 ES1 134 FFR 80
HFI 41 IAC 93-4 SFE 161 SFS
38 SF1 140 SF2 874-5 STH 157,
241 see also Mirian Allen De
Ford Shipley
De Forest, Eleanor. CSF 58 SF1
140
De Gandillac, Maurice. BAA 223
De Ghelderode, Michel. FBK 145-6
De Givry, Emile Grillot (1870-) ES1
194
De Gourcuff, Olivier. BAA 225
De Gourmont, Remy (1858-1915)
CSF 84 SF1 217
De Goya, Francisco. FBK 14, 45
De Graeff, Allen pseud. of Albert
Paul Blaustein. SFE 161 SFS 38
De Graffigny, Henri (1863-1942)
MSF 162 SL1 109-12
De Grainville, J. B. Cousin. CSF
85 FTF 28 MSF 137, 202 NWO
133 POE 23, 40-1 SF1 122 VES
132
De Graw, Pat. SFS 38
De Gusmao, Laurenco. SFB 31

De Hamong, (Count) Leigh. SF1
237
De Haviland, Olivia. STH 252
De Hernani, Miguel. EXT 6/1 4
De Jack, Neil. IMS 34, 239
De Jong, Adrianus (1888-1943)
SF1 284
De Jong, Dola. FFC 110
De Kobra, Maurice. CSF 58
De Kremer, Raymond Jean Marie
(1887-1964) ES1 260 WGT 82-3
see also John Flanders, Jean
Ray
De La Barra, Enrique Creel.
BAA 173
De La Bretonne, Restif. AOW 30
BYS 92-3 MSF 9, 114, 138 POE
51-2 SFB 30-1 WIF 38
De La Buque, Jean. SF1 302
De La Chavanne, Antoine. BAA
173
De La Croix, Francois Petis.
CSF 157
De La Folie, Louis G. WIF 38
De La Fuye, Marguerite Allotte.
AOW 338 EXT 2/1 5-8, 10-1
EXT 3/2 42
De La Mare, Colin. CSF 58 ES1
133 SF1 141
De La Mare, Walter John (1873-
1956) BAA 174 CSF 58-9 ES1
133 FBK 67, 69 FFC 24-5, 131
FL3 1307-10, 1492-5 FL4 1926-
9 IAC 93 SF1 141 SOT 367
WGT 40
De La Mora, Gonzalo Fernandez.
BAA 176
De La Mothe, Fenelon. MSF 45,
88, 111, 177, 244
De La Motte-Fouque, (Baron)
Friedrich H. (1777-1843) CSF
118 FBK 32 FFC 7 FL4 1992-
4 SF1 304
De La Ree, Gerry. IAC 93 SF1
142 SOT 224 SRB 494 STH 258,
266 WTS 74
De La Roche, Charles Francois
Tiphaigne (1729-74) CSF 194
SF1 515 PST 14, 276-7, 283
De La Roche, Mazo. FFC 131
De Laboulaye, Edouard Rene
Lefebure (1811-83) SF1 302
De Laforest-Divonne, Philomene
(1887-) ES1 263 WGT 84

De Lamarck, Jean Baptiste (1744-1829) AAL 214 ACC 178 COT 10 CWN 10, 41 SFH 138-9, 141, 158
De Lamartine, Alphonse. MSF 138
De LaMettrie, Julien Offray. COT 163
De Larrabeiti, Michael. FFC 42
De Larrea, Victoria. FFC 25, 29, 146
De Launay, Pierre Boaistual (-1556) WGT 17-8
De Lautremont, (Comte) pseud. of Isidore Lucien Ducasse. SF1 309
De Laveleye, Emile. BAA 240
De L'Epy, M. Heliogenes. BAA 8-9
De Levis, Pierre-Marc-Gaston Duc. POE 49, 52
De Lisieux-Pere, Zacharie (1582-1661) WGT 161
De L'Isle-Adam, Villiers (1838-89) BYS 55, 93-4, 117 CSF 200 ES2 439 EXT 10/2 110 FBK 139, 141 MSF 162, 167-71, 239 POE 104 SFB 82, 140 SFE 634 SF1 534 SIH 21, 135 SL2 735-8 TFC 31, 35, 53, 68, 73
De Lisser, Herbert George (1878-1944) CSF 59 SF1 142
De Lubicz, Isha Schwaller (1885-) SF1 465
De Mably, Gabriel Bonnot. MSF 118, 123
De Magalhaes, Benjamin Constant Botelho. EXT 6/2 37
De Maistre, Francois Xavier (1763-1852) SF1 340
De Mandiargues, Andre Pieyre. FBK 140
De Maria, Robert. BAA 281
De Marinis, Rick. HFI 183
De Marivaux, Pierre Carlet. MSF 113 STF 34
De Mars, Robert. SF1 143
De Martino, Chevalier. STH 191
De Mauny, Erik. EXT 2/1 5
De Maupassant, Guy (1850-93) AOW 34 BYS 117 CSF 136 CWN 17 ES1 133 FBK 13, 30, 82, 139 FFR 127-8 FL4 1652-6 IAC 93 IMS 2 PST 71-2, 266, 312 SF1 351 SIH 31-2 TFC 56, 81-2, 85-6, 88, 104, 143-4, 163, 174 WIF 55, 71

De Maupertuis, Pierre Louis Moreau. EXT 2/1 4
De Medici, Charles. BAA 39
De Medici, Lorenzo. ISW 62
De Mendelssohn, Peter (1908-) CSF 59 SF1 144
De Meyer, John Reed (1909-) SF1 144
De Mille, Cecil B. MSM 51
De Mille, James (1837-80) AOW 59 CSF 59 EXT 1/1 9 MFW 119 MSF 165 PST 64-6, 192, 235, 256 SFE 164 SF1 144 WGT 40
De Mille, Richard (1922-) SF1 144 SF2 876
De Mille, William C. CSF 59
De Miomandre, Francis pseud. of Francois Durand. SF1 365
De Miskey, Julian. FFC 140
De Monbron, Louis-Charles (1704-61) SF1 192
De Moncrif, Francois Augustin (1687-1770) ES2 315 SF1 368
De Montaigne, Michel Eyquem. MSF 7, 99, 114 RAH 91, 93
De Montalvo, Garcia Ordonez. STH 71-2
De Montalvo, Marie. CSF 59
De Montesquiou, Marquis. [FUT]
De Morgan, John (1848-) AOW 59 CSF 59-60 EXT 1/1 9 SF1 144 WGT 41
De Morgan, William Frend (1839-1917) CSF 60 SF1 144
De Musset, Louis Charles Alfred (1810-57) SF1 380
De Nerval, Gerard (1808-55) BYS 93 FBK 137 TFC 37-40, 61
De Orellana, Francisco. STH 71
De Paola, Tomie. FFC 19
De Patot, Simon Tyssot (1655?-1728?) WGT 144 see also Monsieur Bayle James Massey
De Pereyra, Diomedea. CSF 156 SF1 410
De Pina, Robert Albert (-1957) ES1 133
De Plancy, Jacques Simon Collin (1794-1881) WGT 32
De Planhol, Rene. BAA 188
De Pompery, Edouard. BAA 188
De Prague, L'Hermite. BAA 164

De Prat, Marie Louis Lamartine.
POE 125-7
De Queiroz, Jose Eca (1845-1900)
ES1 134 SF1 581
De Quincey, Thomas. POE 284
De Rais, Gilles. TSP 196
De Regniers, Beatrice. FFC 4,
63,105
De Reigny, Louis Abel Beffroy
(1757-1811) TGY 12
De Reyna, Diane Detzler (1930-)
SF2 877 WGT 41
De Richter, Charles. ES1 134
De Rouen, Reed Randolph (1917-)
ES1 134 SFE 165 SF1 147
De Sackville, Honoria. SF1 147
De Sade, (Marquis). ES1 134
FBK 7 FTF 30,39 MSF 114
RAH 86 SIH 16 TSP 7 WAA
27,78,80,83
De Saint-Simon, Henri. CAT 78
MSF 22,45,59,101,119-20,148,
157-8,175 POE 126 WAA 49
De Sandisson, (Mr.) pseud. of
Jean Paul Bignon. SF1 460
De Soucanton, (Baroness) Alexan-
dre. SF1 487
De Spens, Willy. BAA 268
De Tarde, Jean Gabriel (1843-
1904) AOW 74 CSF 191 PST
92-3,193,197,201,230,232,250,
252,264,268,280,282,287,296,
298,309 SFE 166 SF1 508
De Teramond, Guy (1869-1957)
CSF 191 SF1 510
De Timms, Graeme. SFE 166
SF1 148
De Tinseau, Leon (1844-1921)
CSF 194 SF1 514
De Tocqueville, Alexis. CAT 70
COT 199,252
De Trevino, Elizabeth Borton
(1904-) SF1 518 SF2 1105
De Troyes, Chretien. RAH 226
De Valda, Frederick W. (1884-)
CSF 60 SF1 148
De Vaucluse, Marianne A.
Fauques. CSF 71
De Vaucouleurs, Gerard (1918-)
ES1 134
De Veer, Willem (1865-) CSF 60
SF1 530
De Ventos, Xavier Rubert. BAA
190

De Vet, Charles V(incent) (1911-)
ES1 134 HFI 43 IAC 97 SFE
166 SFS 40 SF1 148 SF2 877
De Vitis, A.A. CUA 12,19,30,
33,51
De Voisenon, Abbe (1708-75) SF1
536
De Vos, Luk. SFE 167
De Vrankrijker, Adrianus Clemens
Johannes. BAA 196
De Vries, Peter. EXT 3/1 23
De Vries, Hugo. SFH 139-40
De Weese, (Thomas) (Eu)Gene.
IAC 93,97 EXT 9/2 25 HFI 43
SFE 167 SF1 149 WGT 41
De Weindeck, Winteler. WGT 42
see also George Z. Fighton
De Wendover, Roger. VES 232
De Wohl, Louis (1903-61) BAA
124 ES1 134 SF1 149
De Wood, C. EXT 6/1 4
Deal, Borden. IAC 93
Deamer, Dulcie (1890-) CSF 57
SF1 138
Dean, Abner. IAC 93
Dean, Joe E. IAC 93
Dean, Mal(colm) (1941-74) BYS
298,321 IAC 93 SFE 157 VES
289
Dean, Norman L. ETN 32 WSF
166
Dean, Richard. EXT 2/1 10
Dean, Roger (1944-) SFE 157
Dean, Ruth. KVT 8
Deane, Hamilton. FBK 48
Dearborn, Laura psued. of Nina
Picton. CSF 57 SF1 138
Dearmer, Geoffrey (1893-) BAA
99 CSF 57 SF1 138
Debans, Jean Baptiste Camille
(1834-) SF1 138
DeBono, Edward. TJB 29
Debout, Simone. BAA 214
Debout-Oleszkiewicz, Simone.
BAA 214
Debs, Eugene V. SFH 10
Debus, Karl. BAA 214
DeCasseres, Benjamin. EXT
5/2 42
DeCles, John. VES 207
Decobert, Jacques. BAA 214-5
Decoo, Wilfried L.J. BAA 281
Dee, Roger pseud. of Roger Dee
Aycock. ALW 161 HFI 41 IAC

Dee, Roger (cont.)
93 IAH 35 SFE 159 SFS 38
SF1 140
Dee, Sylvia pseud. of Josephine
Moore Proffitt.
Deedes, C. W. EXT 9/1 16
Deegan, Jon J. (house name) ES1
134 IAC 93 SFE 159
Deeley, Roger. IAC 93
Deeping, George Warwick (1877-
1950) CSF 58 ES1 134 SF1 140
Deer, M. J. SF1 140
Defoe, Daniel (1659-1731) ALW
38, 65, 97, 216 AOW 6, 32, 398
BAA 9-10 BYS 9, 33, 70-1, 78-9
CAT 108 CSC 217 CSF 58 ES1
134 EXT 6/2 36 FAN 23, 35
IAC 93 ISW 96, 168 MSF 111,
113 MSM 111, 213 PST 34, 58,
318 SFE 161 SFH 9 SFN 20
SFS 38 SF1 140 STF 34 VES
69
Defontenay, Charlemagne Ischir
(1819-56) HFI 41 MSF 121, 138,
202 SFE 161 SL5 2146-9
DeForest, Eleanor. BAA 107
EXT 7/1 18
Dege, Charlotte. BAA 281
Degen, Bruce. FFC 49
Degler, Claude. SRB 95
DeGraeff, Allen pseud. of Albert
Paul Blaustein. ES1 135 IAC
94 SF1 140-1
Degraw, Pat. IAC 94
DeGrazia, Alfred. BAA 151
Dehan, Richard pseud. of Clotilde
Inez Mary Graves. CSF 58 SF1
141
Dehn, Paul. IAC 94
Deighton, Len (1929-) ES1 135
HFI 41 JGB 4 NDA 174 SFE
161-2
Deitz, Thomas F. FL2 571-4,
1021-4 FL4 1774-6
Dejacque, Joseph. MSF 138
DeJouvenal, Bertrand. BAA 215
Dekhnewallah, A. SF1 141
Dekker, Thomas. IAC 94
Dekobra, Maurice pseud. of
Ernst-Maurice Tessier (1885-
1973) SF1 141
Del Martia, Astron (house name)
SFE 163 SF1 142 see also
John Russell Fearn
Del Monti, Toti. WFS 154

Del Rey, Evelyn. ISW 267 SFN
76 WFS 174, 205, 214, 216-7,
304 see also Evelyn Harrison
Del Rey, Judy-Lynn. ALW 8, 220
ASF 217, 233 ETN 79-80 IAC
94 RSG 82 SF1 142 STH 45
WFS 212, 301, 306 WSF 248, 283,
286 see also Judy-Lynn Benjamin
Del Rey, Lester (1915-) AAL 100
ALW 36, 155, 160, 173, 176, 185,
187, 213, 220-1 AOW 175-6, 221,
315-6, 343, 354 ASF 123, 146-8,
198, 211, 215, 233-4 BAA 127,
137 BFP 142-5 BYS 225, 261,
288 COT 50, 139, 164, 169, 181,
190, 250, 264, 279, 291-4, 296
CSC 65, 102, 151-2, 197 CWD 41
ES1 135-6 ETN 16-8, 105, 160
EXT 5/1 3 EXT 7/2 40, 42 EXT
10/2 102-6 FBK 124 FFR 147
FRN 30 HFI 42-3 HWK 8 IAC
94-5 IAH 35, 40, 60, 63, 67, 132
INT 46 ISW xii, 1, 42-3, 82, 119,
121-2, 131, 133, 253, 265, 267
JHN 15, 43 KAU 13, 154-5, 174,
176-7, 179, 228 LEX 273-5 MFW
29, 141, 190, 214 MIH 7, 20, 36,
38, 41, 49, 53, 56, 60, 89 MSM 136
OWB 98 PJF 40, 48, 73 RFA 50,
57, 66, 70, 76, 78, 80-1, 110, 112,
118, 120, 176-7, 205 RGS 52-3
RSG 30-1 SFB 82 SFD 36, 241,
316 SFE 163-4 SFH 169 SFN
39, 76 SFS 26, 38-9 SFW 267,
476 SF1 143 SF2 876 SIH 139
SL3 1510-5 SOT 6, 40, 62, 121,
156, 167-86, 199 SRB 13-4, 71,
119, 326, 351, 355, 365, 500 STH
11, 17, 20, 48, 260 TJB 4 VES
95, 133, 135, 158, 172, 175-6, 179,
181, 186, 195, 197, 206, 208, 227,
235, 259, 307, 316, 328, 342 WAA
165 WFS 119, 173-4, 200, 205,
212, 214, 216-7, 223-6, 264, 290,
293, 297-8, 301, 304 WGT 3-4
WIF 27, 90, 118, 226 see also
John Alvarez, Philip James,
Wade Kaempfert, Edson McCann,
Philip St. John, Charles Satterfield, Erik Van Lihn
Delaire, Jean. CSF 58 SF1 141
STH 4 SOT 9-10 VES 145
Delaney, W. S. STH 257
Del'Antonio, Eberhard (1926-)
LEX 271

Delany. WTS 6
Delany, A. FFC 88
Delany, Samuel R. (1942-) AAL
21,30,34,178-84 ACC 202-3
ALW 239 AOW 88,174-5,291,
299 ASF 147 ATA 37,52-3 BFP
139-41 BYS 303-5 CAT 15,19,
23-5,27,76,112,114,121,137
CEN 109-31 COT 192 CSC 31,
122,188,191-3,232 DMK 69-75
ES1 136-7 ETN 65, 81-2, 87-8,
96,146,180 EXT 9/2 25 EXT
10/1 1-2,8 EXT 10/2 50,52-66,
100-1 FFR 63 [FJT] FL2 798-
800 FL4 1875-9 FTF 200-1
HFI 41-2 IAC 95-6 KAU 18,93,
105-9,120,129 LEX 272-3 LTN
12,203,253 MFW 16,25,60-1,
103,146,171-2,175-6,178,215-
8 MIH 134-6,146 MSF 29,35,
52,74,121 NWO 18,21,77,92,
161,204 OSR 130-46,354 RAH
233,236 RGS ix-xii,51-2 RHN
62 RZY 105 SFA 85 SFD 4,17,
53-4,63,228,248,252-3,262,264,
280-1,301,303,319-20 SFE 162-
3 SFH 70,93-7,99,152-3,155,
157,166,171,186,188,243 SFW
329-36,355,459,486 SF1 141-2
SF2 875-6 SIN 123-5 SL1 113-
9 SL2 533-8,625-8,703-7 SL4
1560-5 SL5 2307-10 SRB 17,71,
344-5,363,369 STF 79 TSF 62-
3,238 UFS 3 UKL 69,72,166
VES 92 WAA 138,230 WBW 32
WFS 17,212 WSF 205,283,388
Delany, Selden Peabody. BAA
215
Delaro, Selina. SF1 581
Delarue, Jacques. WAA 27,74,
242
Delattre, Pierre (1930-) SF1 142
DeLay, Harold. WTS 76,88,92
Delblanc, Sven. SF1 142 WAA
234
Delcarol, Marwin. CSF 59
Delcourt, Marie. BAA 215
Delessert, Etienne. FFC 21
DelFattore, Joan. FL5 2492-500
DeLillo, Don. ETN 12 HFI 41
SFE 163
Delius, Anthony Ronald St. Martin
(1916-) SFE 163 SF1 142 SF2
876
Delius, Frederick (1862-1934)
CWN 39

Dell, Berenice V. BAA 91 CSF
59 SF1 142
Dell, Del Dow. HFI 46
Dell, Dudley pseud. of H. L. Gold.
IAC 96 SFS 38
Dell, Jeffrey. CSF 59 ES1 137
SF1 142
Dell, Joan. FFC 181
Dellbridge, John (1887-) CSF 59
SF1 142
Delmont, Joseph (1873-1935) CSF
59 LEX 273 SF1 142
Delord, Taxile. POE 73-4 see
also J. J. Grandville
Delorme, Charles pseud. of
Charles Rumball. CSF 59 SF1
142
Delray, Chester. SF1 142
Delvaille, Jules. BAA 174
Demac, Dennison. ASF 275
Demaison, Michel. BAA 215
Demaitre, Edmund (1906-) ES1
137 SF1 143
Demare, Leo. IAC 96
De'Mattei, Rodolfo. BAA 244
Demijohn, Thom pseud. of
Thomas M. Disch
John T. Sladek
SFE 164
Deming, Richard. IAC 96 SFS
39 WGT 41
Demmon, Calvin. IAC 96
Democritus. EXT 1/2 35 JGB
32 NDA 54 SF1 144
Demorgan, Augustus. IAC 96
Demoris, Rene. BAA 215
Demos, Raphael. BAA 215
Dempsey, Hank pseud. of Harry
Harrison. IAC 96
Dempsey, Jack. RFA 98
DeMurat, Ulyses Petit. EXT 9/1
17
Demuth, Michel (1939-) SFE 164
Denaerde, Stefan. HFI 43
Denham, Alice (1933-) SF1 144
SF2 876
Denison, Thomas Stewart (1848-
1911) CSF 60 SF1 144
Denmark, Harrison pseud. of
Roger Zelazny. FFR 63 RZY 10
D'Ennery, Adolphe. EXT 3/2 35,
37
Denney, Reuel. EXT 1/2 30
Denning, W. F. EXT 5/2 42
Dennis, Albert Nelson. SF1 144

Dennis, Clifford E. ES1 137 SF1 144
Dennis, Geoffrey Pomeroy (1892-1963) CSF 60 ES1 137 SF1 144
Dennis, Nigel Forbes (1912-) ES1 137 HFI 43
Dennis, Robert C. SF1 144-5
Dennis, Walter L. IMS 34 SOT 103 WGT 41
Denslow, W. W. FBK 113 FFC 174
Dent, Guy. CSF 60 SFE 164-5 SF1 145 SL2 717-20 VES 123
Dent, John Charles (1841-88) SF1 145
Dent, Lester (1905-59) ES1 137 SFE 165 SF1 145-6 TSP 86, 219 WGT 41 WSF 58 see also Kenneth Robeson
Dentinger, Stephen. IAC 96
Denton, Kit. IAC 96
Denturk, Henry Cornelius. BAA 109
Denvir, John. CSF 60
Derby, Pat. IAC 96
Derleth, August (1909-71) ALW 7, 143, 175, 184 AOW 94, 283, 343, 396, 401 BAA 215 BFP 146-55 BYS 177-8 COT 93, 292, 300 CSF 60 ES1 137-41 EXT 1/2 30 EXT 3/1 2, 5-11, 19, 21, 23, 27 EXT 5/1 10 EXT 6/2 31 FBK 78-81, 83 FL3 1496-1500 FRN 36 HFI 43 IAC 96-7, 163 IMS 18, 20, 25, 30-1, 110-1, 209, 219 ISW vi, 129-30, 133, 223-4 MSM 29, 36-7, 128, 159 NWO 262 SFB 58 SFD 289 SFE 165 SFN 15 SFS 39-40, 97 SFW 135-6 SF1 146-7 SF2 877 SOI xiv SOT 23, 73, 227, 242, 341, 343, 347 SRB 65 STH 157, 253 WGT 41 WIF 18, 78, 80 WSF 296-7 WTS ix, 26-7, 29, 37, 41-2, 44-6, 48-9, 54, 56, 59, 84, 103, 123, 125, 128, 131-2 see also Stephen Grendon, Kenvon Holmes
Dermenghem, Emile. BAA 174
Dermott, Vern pseud. of Vern D. Frye. HFI 43 SF1 147
Dern, Dorothy Louise. ES1 141 SF1 147
DeRougement, Denis. COT 130
Derrett, J. Duncan M. BAA 215

Derrick, Christopher. EXT 6/1 19 EXT 10/1 25
Desanti, Dominique. BAA 174, 215
Descartes, Rene (1596-1650) CWN 41, 54 CYR 15 EXT 2/1 6 EXT 6/2 35 FTF 21 HEN 47 HID 175 MFW 194 MSF 65, 151 PST 20-1 RHN 45, 167 SFH 129 TDI 59
Desfontaines, Pierre Francois Guyot (1685-1745) SF1 148
D'Esme(nard), Jean (1893-1966) CSF 60 SF1 173 WGT 46
Desmond, Hugh. ES1 141 SF1 148
Desmond, Shaw (1877-1960) BAA 107 CSF 60 SF1 148 SFE 165
Desmond, William H. SFD 84 SF1 148
D'Esperance, E. ES1 141 SF1 173
Desroche, Henri. BAA 174, 215-6
Dessar, Leo Charles (1847-1924) EXT 1/1 9 SF1 148
Detre, L. CSF 60 SF1 148
Detzer, Diane pseud. of Diane Detzer De Reyna (1930-) ES1 141 HFI 43 SFE 166 SF1 148
Deutsch, A. J. AOW 290 IAC 97 FAN 153 RFA 189 SFS 40 VES 153
Deutsch, Babette. FFC 13 IAC 97
Deutsch, Michel. EXT 3/1 23
Deutsch, R. H. IAC 97 SFS 40
Deutscher, Isaac. BAA 216 FAN 187
Devaulx, Noel. CSF 60 ES1 141 SF1 148
Devaux, Pierre. DTS 26 EXT 2/1 10 FFR 63
Devereux, Roy pseud. of Margaret R. Pember-Devereux. CSF 60
Devil. CUA 39, 45 CYR 30 RZY 34, 87-8 TDI 11, 23 THM 54 see also Lucifer, Satan
Devine, Andy. INT 39
Devinne, Paul. BAA 65 SF1 149
Devito, John A. SF1 149
Devon, Paul see Erasmus Dawson
DeVore, Howard. AOW 361 HID x SF1 149 SRB 65, 97, 130, 215-224, 494, 515

DeVoto, Bernard. BAA 216 COT
213,300 EXT 1/2 31 FTF 65
MSM 80-1,121 NWO 249-51
WAA 21 WFS 193 WIF 17,171,
188 WSF 359
Dewey, G. Gordon. IAC 97 SFS
40
Dewey, John. BAA 100,216 SFH
10
Dexter, John (house name) SF1
149
Dexter, Ralph W. IAC 97
Dexter, William pseud. of William
Thomas Pritchard HFI 43 SFE
167 SF1 149
Dey, Frederic Van Rensselaer
(1865-1922) SF1 149
Di Chirico, Giorgio (1888-) BYS
216,239,317
Di Fate, Vincent (1945-) SFE 170
SRB 33-55,514 VES 291
Di Fiore, Joachim. MSF 118
Di Fiori, Laurence. FFC 118,127
Di Rienzo, Constance. ASF 323
Diaconu, Emil I. BAA 281
Diaghilev, Serge (1872-1929) CUA
8 CWN 33
Diamond, Donna. FFC 6,11-2,
63,167
Diamond, Frank. CSF 60
Diamant, Alfred. BAA 216
Dibell, Ansen. HFI 43
Dick, (Mr.). BAA 49 CSF 145
SF1 149
Dick, Kay (1915-) ES1 141 SFE
167-8 see also Jeremy Scott
Dick, Philip K. (1928-) AAL 45,
50,118,177 ALW 212-3 AOW
127,176-8,288,291,299,351,394
BAA 126,129,133-4,137,140-1,
143,159 BFP 156-9 BYS 20,91,
205,258,279,285,288,310-4
CAT 26,86,105,119-22 COT
135,138,174,191,196 CSC 68,
226 DMK 145-58 DTS 33-4,36
EFP 14 ES1 141-2 ETN 33,66,
143-4,146,163 EXT 2/2 29 EXT
3/1 26 EXT 5/1 3 EXT 6/2 51
EXT 8/1 6 EXT 10/2 62 FBK
124 FFR 63-5 [FJT] FTF 138,
150-1,169-70,177 HFI 43-4,183
IAC 97-8 IAH 35 INT 55 ISW
129,228-34 JGB 7 KAU 29,184
LEX 275-8 LTN 29,80,108,132,
156,175-8,227-8,261,263-4

MFW 172,176-8,200,210-1
MSF 13,30,201-2 MSM 304
NDA 34,41-2,104 NWO 242-3,
249,263-5 OMN 22,47,184,188-
90,298-9 POE 277 RGS 53-5
RZY 12 SFB 151 SFD 131,145,
254,257-8,260,297,299,319-20
SFE 168-9 SFH 71-5,79-80,84,
177,180,243 SFS 40 SFW 337-
43,355,423 SF1 150 SF2 877
SIH 53-4,56 SL1 196,201 SL2
554-9,564-8,744-8,797-801 SL3
1323-7,1357-61 SL5 2269-73,
2350-6 SOT 424-5 SRB 78,322,
326,337,342,361 TDI 5 TSF 59,
136,238-9 VES 116,123,129,152,
174,180,207,209,227,238-9,302
WAA 138,167,230 WFS 252 WSF
175,205,244,388 YTS 21
Dick, R.A. pseud. of Josephine
A. Leslie. CSF 60
Dickberry, F. pseud. of F. Blaze
De Bury. CSF 61 SF1 150
Dickens, Bradford. SF1 150
Dickens, Charles (1812-70) ALW
97,216 AOW 356 ASF 43 BYS
82,103,120,131,150,186 CAT
56,70 COT 89,92,284 CSF 61
ES1 142 EXT 10/1 9 EXT 10/2
114 FAN 102 FBK 15,60,82
FFC 4,47 FLT 12,86 FL1 242-
7 IAC 98 ISW 136 JGB 6 KAU
27,95 LTN 21,115,118,146,172-
3,176-8,199,227,234 MSF 175,
197,208,239 MSM 25 OWB 15
RBY 168-9,183 SFD 43,66-7,
208 SFH 16 SFS 40 SF1 150
SOI 96 STH 184,226 TBC 6
THM 7 UKL 137 VES 121,145,
150 WIF 59,71,74 WTS 17
Dickeson, Alfred. SF1 151
Dickey, James. IAC 98
Dickey, William. IAC 98
Dickhoff, Robert Ernst. ES1 142
Dickie, E. Gordon. SF1 151
Dickie, James (1934-) SF1 151
SF2 878
Dickinson, Emily. KVT 8 NWO
36,44
Dickinson, Goldsworthy Lowes
(1862-1932) CSF 61 EXT 9/2
46 FAN 4,86 SF1 151
Dickinson, J.A. BAA 216
Dickinson, Joseph. IAC 98 SFS
40

Dickinson, Mike. FL1 132-6
FL2 867-9, 1007-9 FL3 1504-6
FL4 1749-53
Dickinson, Peter Malcolm (1927-)
AOW 179, 316 BAA 157 ES1 143
FFC 4, 42, 53 FFR 65 FL1 132-
6 HFI 44 LEX 278-9 SFE 169
SF1 151 SF2 878 SRB 358
Dickinson, Susan Margery (1931-)
SF1 151 SF2 878
Dickinson, Thorold. FBK 41
Dickinson, William Croft (1897-
1963) ES1 143 SF1 151 SF2 878
Dick-Lauder, (Sir) George Andrew
(1917-) SF1 150 SF2 877-8
Dicks, Terrance. SF1 151
Dickson, Gordon R. (1923-) AAL
70, 84, 108, 119, 123-4 ALW 36,
185, 212, 218, 227, 234 AOW 179,
292, 297, 316 ASF 211 ATA 11,
44 BAA 152, 157, 165 BFP 160-
3 BYS 262 COT 253 CSC 31-2,
225 DTS 7, 50 ES1 143 ETN
47, 68, 99 EXT 2/2 27 FFR 65-
6 FL1 418-22 HFI 44-5, 184
IAC 33, 99-100 IAH 124 ISW
196 JHN 18 LEX 279-81 MFW
45 MIH 4 NDA 20-1 OMN 13
RFA 210 RGS 55-6, 213 SFB 19
SFD 33, 295, 297, 312 SFE 169-
70 SFS 40-1 SFW 345-50 SF1
151-2 SF2 879 SIN 154 SL1
330-6 SRB 13, 258, 353, 500
STH 157 TSF 59-60, 234 VES
81, 102, 182, 207 WFS 171, 204,
252 WSF 172, 186, 387
Diderot, Denis (1713-84) AOW 21
MSF 30, 59, 88, 114, 123, 131, 244
SFE 170 SF1 152
Didion, Joan. HEN 9
Diebold, John. MFW 192 WFS
286
Diefendorf, David. IAC 100
Diehl, Alice Mangold (1844-1912)
CSF 61 SF1 152
Dieterle, William. STH 252
Dietz, Frank. HID x
Dietzel, H. BAA 216
Dieudonne, Florence Carpenter
(1850-) CSF 61 SF1 152
Diffin, Charles Willard. ES1
143 IAC 100 MIH 62 RFA 6-7,
11, 20, 37 SFE 170 VES 106, 135,
158 WGT 42 WSF 54, 60
Digby, Lee. SF1 152

Dighton, Ralph. IAC 100 SFS 41
Dikty, Julian Chain May (1931-)
WGT 42 see also
Julian Chain
Julian C. May
Dikty, T(haddeus) E(ugene) (1920-)
ALW 175 AOW 286-7 ES1 143-
4 EXT 5/1 9-10 EXT 7/2 46
IAC 52, 100 IMS 201, 214, 226
ISW 139 MSM 36, 96, 101, 265
SFE 170-1 SFS 41 SF1 152-3
SF2 879 SRB 320 WIF 124
WSF 135, 200, 215, 224, 263 WTS
ix
Dilbeck, Lionel. IMS 33, 111
Dilke, (Lady) Emilia Francis
(1840-1904) CSF 61 SF1 153
Dillard, R. H. W. CWN 30, 34-5,
39, 43-4
Dille, John Flint. SFB 109
Dillenback, William. IMS 34, 213
Dillingham, Peter. IAC 100
Dillon, Diane. SFE 171 SRB 52
VES 319
Dillon, Dora A. see Patricia
Wentworth
Dillon, Eilis. FFC 54
Dillon, John. IAC 100
Dillon, Leo. SFE 171 SRB 52
VES 319
Dilnot, Frank (1875-1976) CSF
61 SF1 153
Diluv, Ljuben (1927-) LEX 281
Dimeo, Steven. RBY 156-64
Dimitrov, Georgi. MSF 247
Dimmock, Frederick Haydn
(1895-1955) ES1 144
Dimondstein, Boris. SF1 153
Dines, Harry Glen (1925-) ES1
144 SF1 153
Dinesen, Isak pseud. of Blixen-
Finecke, (Baroness) Karen
Christentze (1885-1962) CSF 61
FBK 16, 53 FL3 1501-3 SFN
10 SF1 153
Dinesen, Thomas (1892-) ES1
144 SF1 153
Dingle, Aylward Edward (1874-
1947) WGT 42 see also Sinbad
Dingle, Herbert. IAC 100
Dingwall, Eric John. ES1 144
Diogenes, Antonius. MSF 87
VES 79
Dionne, Roger. IAC 100
Dionysius (of Syracuse). MSF 28

Diophantos. WFS 219
Dioscorides, (Dr.) pseud. of
Pieter Harting. CSF 61 FTF
99-100 SF1 153
Dipper, Alan (1922-) SF1 153
SF2 879
Dirac, Adrian. FTF 9
Dirac, Hugh. BAA 151 IAC 100
SF1 153
Dirac, P.A.M. IAH 101 WSF
319
Disch, Thomas M. (1940-) AAL
32-86 ALW 212, 235 AOW 180,
290, 351 BAA 139-40, 142, 145,
153-4, 157 BFP 164-5 BYS 78,
247, 298-9, 303 CAT 112 CSC
74, 173-4 DMK 9-18 DTS 7, 38
ES1 144-5 ETN 27-8, 122 EXT
8/1 16 EXT 10/2 66 FFR 66
FL3 1146-8 FTF 154-5 HFI 45
IAC 100-2 INT 15 JGB 7 KAU
93, 334 LEX 281-3 MFW 10-1,
280-1, 290 MIH 130, 145 MSF
74 NWO 125 RGS 56-7 RZY
105 SFA 85 SFB 12, 114, 132
SFD 14, 264, 301, 320 SFE 173-
4 SFH 93, 96-7, 99 SFS 41-2
SFW 351-6 SF1 153-4 SF2 879-
80 SL1 277-82 SL5 2059-64,
2274-7 SRB 353 TSF 62, 239
VES 134, 152, 154, 157, 160, 189,
237, 242, 258, 261 WAA 178 WGT
42 WSF 233, 248, 255-6, 387 see
also Thom Demijohn
Diskin, Lahna. RBY 127-55 SL2
921-5
Disney, Walt. ALW 85 EXT 2/1
13 [FUT] INT 60 MIH 13 OWB
72 SFB 66-9 VFS 61 WFS 49
YTS 21, 30
Disraeli, Benjamin (1804-81)
ACE 33 AC2 31 ASF 192 BAA
20 BYS 82, 84, 106, 108, 116, 134,
320 CSF 61 CUA 39 ES1 145
FAN 18 FL2 791-3 KAU 95
MSF 171 SFH 201, 215 SF1 154
WGT 42
D'Israeli, Isaac. CSF 61
Disrobeson, Kin I. pseud. of
Mark Stivers. SF1 154
Ditchfield, Peter H. CSF 61
Ditz, Gerhard W. BAA 216
Ditzen, Rudolf Wilhelm (1893-
1947) WGT 42 see also Hans
Fallada

Diver, Katherine Helen Maud
(1867-1945) CSF 61 WGT 42
Divine, Arthur Durham (1904-)
CSF 61 ES1 145 SF1 154 WGT
42
D'Ivoi, Paul. MSF 162
Dix, Beulah M. CSF 61
Dix, Carol. CUA 61
Dix, Maurice Buxton. CSF 61
SF1 154
Dixey, Marmaduke pseud. of
Geoffrey Howard. CSF 61 SF1
154
Dixie, (Lady) Florence C. (1857-
1905) CSF 61 MSF 203 SF1 154
Dixon, Charles (1858-1926) CSF
62 SF1 154
Dixon, Franklin W. CSF 62
Dixon, Marjorie (1887-) SF1 154
Dixon, Richard pseud. of Clifton
Reginald Walker. ES1 145 IAC
102 SF1 154 WBW 5
Dixon, Roger (1930-) HFI 46 SFE
175 SF1 154 SF2 880
Dixon, Royal Absalom (1885-1962)
CSF 62 SF1 154
Dixon, Terrence Eugene (1950-)
IAC 102 SF2 880
Dixon, Thomas (1864-1946) AOW
36, 60 BAA 74, 81 CSF 62 EXT
1/1 9 SFE 175 SF1 154
Dixon, Thomas (1930-) see Burt
Cole
Dmitravsky, Vladimir. BAA 207
EXT 10/1 48-9 IAC 102
Dmitriev-Mamonov, Fyodor I.
MSF 244
Dneprov, Anatoly pseud. of
Anatoly P. Mitskevitch (1919-)
AOW 297 FFR 66 IAC 102 LEX
283 MSF 230, 262 SFB 122
SFS 42 SIH 44, 83, 192
Doak pseud. of Hugh Rankin.
WTS 80
Doar, Graham. AAL 79 IAC 102
SFS 42
Dobbert, Marion L. BAA 157
Dobbs, Rose. FFC 4
Dobinson, Frank. IAC 102
Doblin, Alfred (1878-1957) SL1
163-7
D'Ocagne, Maurice. EXT 2/1 10
Dockweiler, Harry (Joseph Harold)
(1920?-1948?) IMS 84, 103, 111,
116, 119-20, 127-8, 142-3, 156,

Dockweiler, Harry (cont.)
169,245-6 ISW 193 WFS 24-6,
40 WGT 42 see also Paul Den-
nis Lavond, Dirk Wylie
Doctorow, E(dgar) L(aurence)
(1931-) ES1 145 HFI 46 SFE
176 SF1 154 SF2 880
Dodd, Allen Robert (1887-) see
Robert Allen
Dodd, Anna Bowman (1855-1929)
BAA 37-8 CSF 62 SF1 155
Dodge, Carlota. FFC 76
Dodge, Howard Lewis (1869-)
CSF 62 SF1 155
Dodgson, Charles L. (1832-98)
FBK 89,108 PJF 77 SFN 40
SRB 258 WGT 42-3 see also
Lewis Carroll
Dodson, Richard W. OWB 87
Doerr, Edd. SF1 155
Dogbolt, Barnaby pseud. of
Herbert Silvette. CSF 62 SF1
155,581
Dogge, Mary. IAC 102
Doherty, Brian. CSF 62
Doherty, Geoffrey Donald (1927-)
AAL 123 ES1 145 IAC 102 SFE
176 SFS 42 SF1 155 SF2 880-1
Dohrman, Richard. SF1 155
Doig, Ivan. BAA 174
Doiron, Peter. AOW vii
Doke, Joseph John (-1913) CSF
62 SF1 155
Dolan, Mike J. HFI 46 IAC 102
SF1 155
Dolbier, Maurice Wyman (1912-)
CSF 62 ES1 145 FFC 25,73,92,
154 SF1 155
Dolbokgov pseud. of Hannes Bok
and Boris Dolgov. WTS 93
Dold, Douglas M. IMS 6 RFA ix,
xii-xiii, 4,11,31
Dold, Elliott. BYS 216-7 COT
187 ES1 145 IMS 6 RFA 4,21,
25,27,31,34-5,38,40,42,126,
167 SFE 176 VES 82,193,287-
8 WSF 67,92
Dole, Stephen H. ES1 146
Dolezal, Erich (1902-) LEX 283-4
Dolgov, Boris. FBK 85 WTS 76,
93,96 see also Dolbokgov
Dolgushin, Yury A. MSF 265
Doliner, Roy (1932-) SF1 155
SF2 881

Dolinsky, Meyer (Mike) (1923-)
AOW 181 HFI 46 SFE 176 SF1
155 SF2 881
Doll, Emil. BAA 174
Dollfuss, Charles. POE 85
Dollins, Morris Scott (1920-) ES1
146 IMS 66,70-2,78-80,95,103-
6,109
Domanska, Janina. FFC 13
Dombrowski, Katrina (1881-) SF1
155
Domencq, H. Bustos. FBK 134
Domenach, Jean-Marie. BAA 216
Domhoff, G. William. BAA 216
Domingo, Pedro see Domingo
Santos
Dominik, Hans (1872-1946) ES1
146 LEX 284-7 MSF 162 SIH
183-4,202 SL3 1304-7 WAA
234
Donaho, William. RFA v,vii,xxii
WFS 39
Donahue, James J. BAA 173 SF1
155
Donaldson, Elaine. SF1 155
Donaldson, Stephen R. (1947-)
BFP 166 FHT 10 FL1 266-74
HFI 46 WSF 388
Donaldy, Ernestine. IAC 102,184
SF1 155
Donelson, Kenneth. SRB 463
Donev, Anton. IAC 102
Doney, Nina M. SF1 155
Doni, Anton Francesco. EXT 8/1
23 MSF 100
Donis, Miles (1937-) BAA 165
HFI 46 SF1 155 SF2 881
Donleavy, James Patrick (1926-)
ES1 146
Donne, John (1573-1631) ATA 42
CAT 52 EXT 1/2 38 PJF 57
SFA 58
Donnell, A.J. ES1 146 VES 76,
138,235
Donnelly, Desmond Louis (1920-
74) SF1 156
Donnelly, Ignatius (1831-1901)
ALW 88 AOW 60 BAA 41,47
CSF 62 ES1 146 EXT 1/1 3,9
EXT 7/1 11,16 MFW 121,254
MSF 178 MSM 141-3 SFE 176
SFN 92 SFW 64 SF1 156 SL1
272-6 STH 27-8,59-60 VES 127
WAA 70 WGT 43 WIF 49,56
see also Edmund Boisgilbert

Donnelly, Katherine. FFC 185
Donner, Grove pseud. of Florence Harvey. SF1 156
Donner, H. W. BAA 174
Donovan, Alexander. SF1 156
Donovan, D. J. ES1 146
Donovan, Dick pseud. of Joyce E. P. Muddock. CSF 62
Donovan, Francis. IAC 102 RFA 205 SFS 42
Donovan, John. FFC 5
Donovan, Richard. SOT 355
Donovan, W. A. EXT 6/1 19
Donson, Cyril (1919-) BAA 148 ES1 146 SFE 176 SF1 156 SF2 881
Doohan, James. IAC 102
Doolin, Joseph. STH 258 WTS 62, 80, 84
Dooner, Pierton W. (1844-1907?) AOW 36, 60 BAA 32 CSF 62 SF1 156 SRB 10 STH 210
Doppelberg, Joe. ALW 174
Doran, James. CSF 62
Dore, Gustav. FBK 82 FFC 156 SFB 15
Doremieux, Alain. AOW 295 IAC 102 MSF 239
Doren, Alfred. BAA 216
Dorman, Geoffrey (1894-) SF1 156
Dorman, Sonya. BYS 305 CEN 70-86 EXT 8/1 16 FFR 67 IAC 102 SFE 177 SFS 42
Dormer, Daniel. SF1 156
Dornberger, Walter (1895-) COT 34-5, 46, 49-50 ES1 146
Dorrance, Ethel Smith (1880-) CSF 62 SF1 156
Dorrington, Albert (1871-) CSF 62 EXT 1/1 9 SF1 156
Dorsch, T. S. BAA 216
Dorset, St. John pseud. of Hugo J. Belfour. CSF 62
Dorson, Richard M. MSF 31
Dort, Stanley. IMS 11
Dort, Wallace. IMS 11
Dos Passos, John. IAC 102 JHN 36-7, 53 MFW 14, 173 MIH 129, 139-40 MSF 280 SFD 76, 296, 318 SFH 31, 81, 91 SFN 99 SFS 42 STF 73 WFS 105
Dossi, Carlo (1849-1910) SL1 406-8
Dost, Zamin Ki pseud. of Willimina Leonora Armstrong. CSF 47 SF1 293

Dostoevsky, Fyodor (1821-81) AOW 60 CAT 138 CWN 13, 21, 24, 30, 50 EXT 9/1 18 EXT 10/2 73-6 FAN 105 FBK 34, 41 FLT 2, 48-66 FTF 97, 135 IAC 102 KVT 32 MIH 78, 121 MSF 20, 164, 243, 248-50, 256-7, 259, 274 NDA 95, 102 RAH 96 SFD 43 SFE 177 SFH 25 SF1 156 SL2 618-24 TFC 46, 48 THM 7, 32, 47 UKL 117
Dottin, Paul. BAA 174
Doty, Madelaine Z. BAA 216
Douay, Dominique (1944-) SFE 177
Doubleday, Frank Nelson. VFS 187
Doughty, Charles Montagu (1843-1926) CSC 24 SFE 177
Doughty, F. H. BAA 174
Doughty, Francis Worcester (1850?-1917) CSF 62 SF1 156
Douglas, Bryan. ES1 146 SF1 156
Douglas, David. MSF 207 SF1 156
Douglas, Donald (1893?-1966) CSF 63 SF1 156
Douglas, Drake pseud. of Werner Zimmermann. ES1 146 SF1 157
Douglas, (Sir) George Brisbane (1856-1935) CSF 63 ES1 146-7 WGT 43
Douglas, George Norman (1868-1952) SFE 177 SF1 157 WGT 43
Douglas, Mary. KAU 156
Douglas, Myrtle. IMS 137, 243-4 WIF 17 see also Morojo
Douglas, Norman. CSF 63 VFS 6 WIF 201 see also Normyx
Douglas, Stephen A. MSM 174
Douglas, Theo pseud. of Mrs. H. D. Everett. CSF 63 EXT 1/1 9
Douglass, Ellsworth. CSF 63 IAC 102 SFE 177 SF1 157 STH 32 WGT 43 see also Elmer Dwiggins
Douglass, Frederick. RHN 24, 26
Dovzhenko, Alexander P. MSF 264
Dowd, Freeman Benjamin. CSF 63 SF1 157
Dowding, A. L. WGT 43 see also Lewis Ramsden

Dowding, Henry Wallace. BAA
76 CSF 63 SF1 157
Dowling, Richard. CSF 63
Dowling, Terry. JVN 131-77,
237, 239
Dowling, Victor. FFC 72
Downey, Edmund (1856-1937) CSF
63 SF1 157 WGT 43 see also
F. M. Allen
Downing, (Mr.). VFS 235-8
Downing, Charles H. CSF 63
Downs, Michael C. UKL 117-52
Downs, Robert Bingham. EXT
6/1 9-10
Dowson, Ernest. MFW 282
Dowst, Loren. WFS 104, 122
Dowst, Loring. TSP 23, 126
Dowst, Peggy. TSP 23
Doxiadis, C. A. BAA 217
Doxiadis, Constantinos. BAA 174
Doyle, (Sir) Arthur Conan (1859-
1930) ACC 209 ALW 33, 82, 87,
100, 102 AOW 36, 43, 60-1 ASF
66-8 ATA 22 BYS 136-7, 145,
147-9, 152, 294 CAT 10 CSF
63-4 CWD 8, 55 ES1 147-8
EXT 2/1 11 EXT 3/1 28 EXT
3/2 47 EXT 4/2 20, 22, 24 EXT
5/1 4, 16 EXT 7/2 38 FFR 67
FL2 867-9 FL3 1504-6 FRN
76, 359 HFI 46 IAC 102-3 IMS
96, 142 INT 5-6 KAU 8, 44, 127,
190 LEX 287-8 MFW 21, 119
MIH 14, 127 MSF 162, 167, 279
MSM 25, 76, 136 NWO 70 OWB
13 PST 63, 90, 104, 117, 158,
163-5, 192, 204-5, 210-1, 214,
227-8, 233, 239, 256, 267, 292
RFA 110 RGS 57-8 RHN 148,
168 SFB 23, 84-7 SFD 305 SFE
177-8 SFH 90 SFS 42 SFW 45-
50, 76 SF1 157 SIH 110, 194
SL3 1270-3 SL4 1702-4 SOT
77, 399, 410 SRB 9, 11, 294 STH
122-3, 203 TFC 84 TSF 229
VES 92, 130, 137, 139-40, 209,
301, 312 VFS 5 WAA 91 WIF
55, 65, 90 WSF 22, 130 WTS 17,
52
Doyle, Charles Clay. BAA 217
Doyon, Rene-Louis. BAA 217
Dozois, Gardner R. (1947-) ALW
212 BAA 154 BFP 167 ETN
65 FFR 67 [FJT] FRN 45 HFI
46 IAC 89, 103 LEX 288-9 LTN
248 SFD 57, 265 SFE 178 SFW
393-400 SF1 157

Drabble, Margaret. LTN 1(
Draco, S. IAC 103
Drake, Alexander Wilson (1
1916) CSF 64 ES1 148
Drake, Austin Mann. CSF (
SF1 158
Drake, David. IAC 103 SF:
Drake, Frank. AAL 90, 92
201
Drake, Henry Burgess (189
CSF 64 ES1 148 SF1 158
Drake, Katharine. CSF 64
158
Drake, Leah Bodine (1914-(
148 IAC 103
Drake, Nathan. CSF 64
Drake, W. Anders. IMS 22
Drake, W. Raymond. IAC
Drakula, Voivod Tepesch (1
76) SIH 31 see also Vlad t
Impaler
Drane, Augusta Theodosia.
58
Draper, Blanche A. pseud.
Blanche A. Webb. SF1 15
Draper, Hal. IAC 103 SFS
Draper, Warwick Herbert (
BAA 83 WGT 43
Drayton, Henry Sinclair (18
1923) AOW 61 BAA 62 C
EXT 1/1 2, 10 MFW 120-:
178 SF1 158
Dreanys, J. VES 122, 153
Dreifuss, Jerome. CSF 64
158
Dreifuss, Kurt (1897-) BA
HFI 46 SF1 158 SF2 881
Dreiser, Paul see Paul Dre
Dreiser, Theodore (1871-1
CSF 64 CWD 56 EXT 10/
FTF 62 SFN 99 STF 73
222-3, 225-7, 234-6, 238-9
Drennan, Paul. BAA 161
Dresser, Mary see Mary Si
Dresser, Paul. STH 223
Dressler, (Dr.) Daniel. IA
SFS 42
Drew, Ethan. WTS 42
Dreyer, Carl. FBK 46
Dreyer, Hans P. CSF 64 :
Dreyfuss, Ernst (1908-) HI
SF1 158
Driant, (Capt.) Emile Augu
(1855-) POE 183-5 WGT
see also Captain Danrit
Drigin, S. R. TRB 58-9 V
287, 324

Dring, Nat(haniel) pseud. of R.
Curtis McBroom (1910-) ES1
148 SF1 158
Driscoll, Dennis. IAC 103 SFS
42
Drode, Daniel (1932-) SFE 179
Droke, Maxwell (1869-1957) ES1
149
Drucker, Peter F. POE 289
Drucker, R. IMS 52, 56
Druery, Charles Thomas (1843-
1917) CSF 64 SF1 158
Druillet, Phillipe (1944-) BYS 217
FBK 74 [FUT] SFE 180 SIH 181
Drummond, June (1923-) SFE 180
Drummond, V. H. FFC 136
Druon, Maurice Samuel (1918-)
FFC 13 SF1 158, 581 SF2 882
Drury, Allen Stuart (1918-) AOW
181 ES1 149 ETN 144 IAC 103
SFE 180 SFS 43 SF1 158 SF2
882 VES 262 WSF 8
Drury, Roger. FFC 117, 142
Drury, William Price (1861-1949)
CSF 64 SF1 158
Druse, Olga. WSF 312
Drussai, Garen. IAC 103 WGT
43-4
Drussai, Kirk. IAC 103
Drvota, Mojmir (1923-) SF1 159
Dryasdust pseud. of Edward Heron-
Allen. CSF 64 SFE 181
Dryden, John (1636-1700) CAT 136
CUA 61 EXT 9/2 26 VES 265
Dryer, Stan. IAC 103
Dryfoos, Dave. COT 252 IAC 103
Du Bois, Edward (1774-1850)
WGT 44 see also Count Regin-
ald De Saint Leon
Du Bois, Gaylord. CSF 120
Du Bois, Shirley Graham (1906-
77) SF1 159
Du Bois, Theodora McCormick
(1890-) CSF 64 ES1 149 HFI
46 SFE 181-2 SF1 159
Du Bois, William Sherman Pene
(1916-) AOW 317 FFC 5, 7, 35,
63, 98, 134, 142-3, 154, 156, 194
IAC 103 SFE 182 SFS 43 SF1
159 SF2 882 SOT 389
Du Bomb, Bonnee. SF1 159
Du Maurier, Daphne (1907-) AOW
291 BAA 154 CSF 65 EFP 6
ES1 149 FFR 128 FL1 465-7
FL2 749-51 HFI 47 IAC 103

SFE 182 SF1 160-1 SF2 884
Du Maurier, George (1834-96)
AAL 109 CSF 65 FL3 1227-9
FL4 1969-71 PST 115-6 SFE
182 SF1 161 STH 29, 208-9
VES 205
Duane, Andrew pseud. of Robert
E. Briney. IAC 103
Duane, Diane. SRB 258
Duane, Toby pseud. of W. Paul
Ganley. IAC 103 SF1 159
Dubanski, Ryszard. LTN 18
Dubcek, Alexander. MSF 75
Dube, Laurence. IMS 247
DuBellay. TSO 25
Dubina, Peter (1940-) LEX 289
Dubois, Claude-Gilbert. BAA
174, 217 MSF 52
DuBois, Gaylord. SF1 159
Dubos, Rene Jules. BAA 174, 217
SFH 241
DuBreuil, Elizabeth Lorinda
(Linda) (1924-) SF1 159 SF2
882-3
Ducasse, Isidore Lucien (1846-
70) WGT 44 see also Comte De
Lautreamont
Ducette, Vince see J. L. Kullinger
Duchacek, Ivo Duka (1913-) ES1
149 SF2 883 WGT 44 see also
Ivo Duka
Duchamp, Marcel. SIH 59
Duchesne, Janet. FFC 68, 107
Duchess, (The) pseud. of Margar-
et Wolfe Hungerford. CSF 64
Duchet, Michele. BAA 217
Ducovny, Allen. MSM 59
Dudbroke, M. CSF 64 SF1 159
Dudden, Arthur P. BAA 217
Dudevant, Amandine Aurore Lucie
(1804-76) see George Sand
Dudgeon, Robert Ellis. BAA 30
Dudintsev, Vladimir (1918-) AOW
181 IAC 103 SFE 182 SFS 43
SF1 159
Dudley, Eustace (1883-) CSF 64
SF1 159
Dudley, Owen Francis (1882-1952)
SF1 159
Dudley, Roy C. HFI 46 SF1 159
Dudley-Smith, Trevor (1920-)
see Elleston Trevor
Dudok, Gerard. BAA 174
Duff, Charles. CSF 65
Duff, Douglas V. (1901-) CSF 65
ES1 149 SF1 160

Duff, (Sir) Hector Livingstone (1872-1954) SF1 160
Duff-Cooper, Alfred. POE 225
Duffus, Robert Luther (1888-1972) SF1 160
Duffy, Richard. STH 222-3, 225
Duggan, Maurice. FFC 102
Duhamel, Georges (1884-1966) SF1 160
Duhamel, P. Albert. BAA 217
Duka, Ivo pseud. of Ivo Duka Duchacek. SF1 160
Dukas, Paul. ACC 136
Duke, Madelaine Elizabeth (1925-) BAA 143 ES1 149 HFI 47 SFE 182 SF1 160 SF2 883-4
Duke, Winifred (1890?-1962) SF1 160
Dulac, Edmund. FFC 17
Dulles, Allen. RHN 125
Dumas, Alexandre (1802-70) CAT 8 CSF 65 ES1 149 EXT 1/2 31 EXT 2/1 12 EXT 3/2 40 FBK 54,138 FL5 2153-5 MSF 29, 148 SFB 55 SF1 160 SIH 32 STH 160 WIF 45, 72 WSF 199 WTS 34
Dumas, Alexandre (1824-95) CSF 65 SF1 160
Dumas, Gerald. FFC 131
Dumont, Rene. BAA 174
Dunbar, William. ATA 38-9
Duncan, Bruce. ES1 149 HFI 47 SFE 182
Duncan, David (1913-) AOW 181 BYS 262 ES1 149-50 HFI 47 IAC 103 ISW 225, 255-8 KAU 33 LEX 289-90 SFE 182-3 SF1 161 SF2 884
Duncan, Graeme. BAA 217
Duncan, Isadora. EXT 7/2 37
Duncan, Lee. SF1 161
Duncan, Lois pseud. of Lois Duncan Arquette (1934-) SF1 161
Duncan, Peter. IMS 116,124,133, 182,203 see also Loki
Duncan, Robert Lipscomb (1927-) see James Hall Roberts
Duncan, Ronald F. (1914-) ES1 150 SFE 183 SF1 161 SF2 884
Dunham, Curtis. CSF 65
Dunkelberger, Walter. STH 62
Dunkerley, William Arthur (1852-1941) WGT 44 see also John Oxenham

Dunlop, Eileen. FFC 162
Dunn, Alan Cantwell (1900-74) ES1 150 IAC 103 SF1 161 SF2 884-5
Dunn, Gertrude C. pseud. of Gertrude Renton Weaver. CSF 65 SF1 161
Dunn, J. E. VFS 56
Dunn, Joseph Allan (1872-1941) CSF 65 HFI 47 SF1 161
Dunn, Philip M. (1946-) see Saul Dunn
Dunn, Saul pseud. of Philip M. Dunn. SFE 183
Dunn, Thomas. SL3 1299-1303 SL4 2046-50
Dunn, Waldo Hilary (1882-1969) CSF 65 EXT 1/1 10 SF1 161
Dunn, William B. SF1 161
Dunne, Finley Peter. SFN 98
Dunne, J. B. NWO 234-5
Dunne, John T. EXT 3/1 16
Dunne, John William (1875-1949) AOW 80 ES1 150 EXT 5/1 8 EXT 10/1 10-2,14 FTF 148,151, 153 SF1 161 SOT 60 TBJ 11 VES 149
Dunsany, (Lord) (1878-1957) ALW 143 BAA 101 BYS 176 CSC 32, 34 CSF 65-6 CWD 59 ES1 150-2 EXT 3/1 6-7,12 EXT 5/1 4 EXT 6/2 51 FBK 77-8,80,88-91,93 FFR 68-9 FL1 129-31, 161-3,232-5 FL2 557-60,625-7, 848-51 FL3 1507-10 HFI 47 HWK 40,48 IAC 103 ISW 146, 191,225-6 JGB 6 LTN 23,25-6, 83-4,88-9,91,173 MSM 86, 128 SFB 57,112 SFD 42,71 SFE 183 SFS 43 SF1 161-2 SIH 9,33 SOT 163,235,322,339, 368,384-5 SRB 274 VES 209 VFS 268 WAA 15, 75, 96,98-9, 242 WBW 3 WIF 73-9,149,158, 174,203 WSF 29,185,293 WTS 129 see also Edward John Moreton Drax Plunkett
Duntemann, Jeff. IAC 103
Duparc, Jean. BAA 217
Dupin, Aurore see George Sand
DuPont (family). KVT 59
Dupont, Victor. BAA 175 EXT 8/1 24
Dupre, Louis. BAA 217
Dupuy, Jean R. BAA 217

110

Duran, Juan Guillermo. BAA 281
Durand, Francois (1880-1959) see
Francis De Miomandre
Durand, Robert (1944-) SF1 162
SF2 885
Durant, Fred. VFS 242
Durant, William J. BAA 217
D'Urfey, Thomas (1653-1723)
BAA 8 WGT 44
Duric, Mihailo. BAA 217
Durie, A. J. L. SF1 162
Durkin, Douglas Leader (1884-)
CSF 66 SF1 162
Durning, Russell E. BAA 175
Durrani, Ahmadi Abd Allah Nadir
Khan Al-Idrisi Al (1881-1945)
WGT 104
Durrell, Gerald Malcolm (1925-)
FFC 175 SF1 162 SF2 885
Durrell, Lawrence George (1912-)
AOW 181 BAA 145-6, 151 BYS
46, 248, 257, 319 HFI 47 IAC
103 JVN 189-90 NWO ix SFE
183 SFS 43 SF1 162 SF2 885
SL5 2311-5
Durrenmatt, Friedrich. FLT
90-3, 114
Dusheck, George. STH 108
Dushkin. VFS 45
Dust, Philip. BAA 217
Duthie, Eric. ES1 152
Dutourd, Jean Hubert (1920-) ES1
152 SF1 162
Dutt, Violet L. SFS 43
Dutta, Rex. IAC 103
Dutton, Patrick. WIF 203
Duveau, Georges. BAA 175,
217-8
Duvic, Patrice (1946-) LEX 290

Dvorkin, David (1943-) HFI 47
LEX 290
Dwiggins, Elmer see Ellsworth
Douglass
Dwiggins, William Addison. BAA
113 CSF 66
Dwight, Harrison Griswold (1875-
1959) ES1 152-3
Dwinnell, Ralph Milton (1894-)
CSF 66 SF1 162
Dwyer, Bernard A. IMS 110
Dwyer, James Francis (1874-
1952) CSF 66 ES1 153 SF1 163
Dwyer, Vera G. SF1 163
Dwyer, Winifred pseud. of Wini-
fred Powell Grover. SF1 163
Dyalhis, Nictzin (-1942) ES1 153
IAC 103 IMS 3 SFS 43 SOT
305 VES 142 WTS 24-5, 29, 32,
38, 51, 120, 130
Dybek, Stuart. IAC 103
Dye, Charles pseud. of Katherine
MacLean. IAC 103
Dye, Charles (1927-1960?) ES1
153 HFI 47 SFE 183 SFS 43
SF1 163 WFS 216
Dyer, Annie Russell. SF1 163
Dyer, George. CSF 66
Dyllington, Anthony. CSF 66
SF1 163
Dyson, A. E. EXT 6/1 14
Dyson, Freeman (1923-) CSC 200-
1, 230 SFE 184 SFH 127 VFS
225, 262 WSF 319
Dyson, H. V. D. SOI 146
Dyson, S. S. BAA 98 CSF 66
Dystell, Oscar. WFS 247
Dyvirta, Tems. BAA 69 CSF 66
Dziewicki, Michael Henry. CSF
66 SF1 163

E

E. D. B. IAC 42
E. M. F. pseud. of Mrs. E. M.
Foster. CSF 66
E. W. CSF 66 SF1 538
Eade, Charles (1903-64) SF1 163
Eadie, Arlton. WTS 35, 38-9,
86, 125
Eady, Mary Aline (1912-) see
Mary Wesley
Eager, Edward McMaken (1911-
64) ES1 153 FFC 64 SF1 163
SRB 23
Eager, Frances. FFC 171
Eagle, Robin. SF1 163
Eardley-Wilmot, (Sir) Sydney
Marow (1847-1929) SF1 163
Earl, Stephen. IAC 103 SFS 43
Earle, Richard. SF1 163
Earle, Warren. IAC 104
Earley, George Whiteford (1927-)
ES1 153 IAC 104 SFE 186 SF1
163 SF2 885 WFS 264-6, 269
Earls, William. IAC 104
Early, David. IAC 104
Earnest, Ernest. EXT 4/1 9
Earnshaw, Anthony (1924-) SFE
186 SF1 164 SF2 886
Earnshaw, Brian (1929-) ES1 153
SFE 186 SF1 1705 SF2 886
Eason, Frank B. IMS 8
Easson, Robert Watson (1941-)
ES1 153 SFE 186 SF1 164
SF2 886
Eastman, Robert (-1934) WTS 5
Easton, John. CSF 66
Eastwick, James. CSF 66
Eastwood, Wilfred (1923-) ES1
153 SF1 164
Eaton, A. T. EXT 10/1 26

Eaton, Evelyn Sybil Mary (1902-)
ES1 153 SF1 164 SF2 886
Eaton, James J. CSF 66
Eaton, Tom. EXT 10/1 38
Eberhart, Richard. IAC 104
Eberhart, Sheri. IAC 104
Eberle, Joseph. WTS 111
Eberle, Matthias. BAA 208
Eberle, Merab. CSF 67
Ebers, Georg Moritz (1837-98)
CSF 67 ES1 153 SF1 164
Ebner, Dean. BAA 218
Eccles, Charlotte O'Conor. WGT
45 see also Hal Godfrey
Echard, Margaret. CSF 67 ES1
154 SF1 164
Echaurren, Roberto. IAC 104
Eckart, Chuck. FFC 112
Eckermann, Johann Peter. POE
56-7
Eckert, Allan W. HFI 47
Eckley, Grace. FL1 129-31,
383-6, 497-500 FL3 1507-10
SL1 6-10, 125-9, 133-7, 233-7,
283-7, 303-7, 386-91, 497-501
SL2 569-73, 995-9
Eckley, Wilton. FL3 1081-5
SL2 888-93 SL3 1089-93 SL4
1705-9, 1746-50, 1775-9 SL5
2159-62
Eckstein, Ernst. CSF 67
Eckstein, Gustav. CSF 67
Eckstrom, Jack Dennis. ES1
154 HFI 48 SFE 187 SF1 164
Eddington, (Sir) Arthur S. ACE
56 AC2 54 ASF 199 COT 6
FTF 69 [FUT] IAC 104 SFH
161 SOT 111

Eddison, E(ric) R(ucker) (1882-1945) BFP 174 CSC 33 CSF 67 ES1 154 EXT 5/1 3 FBK 90-1, 93, 98 FFR 70 FL5 2180-4, 2206-13 HFI 48 IAH 123 ISW 197 JVN 188 LTN 88, 90-1, 95-6 MIH 79 MSM 76, 128 SFB 112 SFD 274-5, 305 SFE 190 SFN 19 SF1 164 SOI xiv SRB 259 STH 7 THM 8 TSF 229 WAA 110 WIF 68, 81, 94, 149, 212, 231 WSF 293

Eddy, Clifford Martin, Jr. (1896-1967) SF1 164 WTS 22, 25

Eddy, (Mrs.) Clifford C. EXT 3/1 21

Eddy, Hugh M. EXT 3/1 23

Eddy, Mary Baker. COT 154 IAH 72

Eddy, Muriel. WTS 22

Eddy, William A. BAA 175

Edel, Leon. FAN 7, 182

Edelson, Edward (1932-) IAC 104 SF1 164 SF2 886

Edelstein, Scott. IAC 104

Edgar, Alfred. WGT 45 see also Barre Lyndon

Edgar, Kenneth (1925-) ES1 154 SF1 164 SF2 886-7

Edgar, Peter pseud. of Peter Edgar King-Scott (1918-) SFE 190 SF1 164

Edgell, John. SF1 164

Edgerton, (Dr.) Harold. VFS 200

Edison, Theodore. STH 164

Edison, Thomas Alva. ALW 47, 64, 73, 81, 96, 119, 126 ASF 106, 155 COT 6 EXT 1/1 14, 17 EXT 7/1 20, 24 EXT 7/2 37 FAN 88 FTF 68 MIH 101 MSF 168 PST 50, 59, 267, 302 RFA 5 RHN 10, 109 SFB 82 SFH 35 SIH 109, 189 VFS 248 WFS 110 WIF 70 WTS 28 YTS 6

Editor of Boy's Life, (The). IAC 60

Edkins, E. A. EXT 3/1 21

Edman, Irving. RHN 126

Edmonds, Harry Moreton. CSF 67 ES1 154 SFE 190 SF1 165

Edmonds, Helen Woods (1901-68) ES1 154 SF2 958 SIH 59 SRB 344 WGT 45 see also Anna Kavan

Edmonds, Thomas Rowe. BAA 20

Edmonds, Walter Dumaux (1903-) FFC 5, 117, 154 SF1 581

Edmondson, G. C. (1922-) AOW 182 BYS 304 ES1 154 HFI 48 IAC 104 SFE 190 SF1 165 SF2 887 SFS 43 see also Jose Mario Garry Ordonez Edmondson Y Cotton

Edmondson, Madeline. FFC 187

Edrich, Emanuel. BAA 218

Edson, J. T. HFI 48

Edson, Milan C. BAA 62 CSF 67 SF1 165

Edstrom, O. E. CSF 67 SF1 165

Edward (VII). FBK 100

Edwards, Amelia B. (1831-92) CSF 67 FBK 60

Edwards, Bryan. MSF 135

Edwards, Charman pseud. of Frederick Anthony Edwards. CSF 67 SF1 165

Edwards, David (1945?-) ES1 154 SFE 190 SF1 165

Edwards, Dolton pseud. of W. K. Laissing. IAC 104 RFA 140 SFS 43

Edwards, F. E. RBY 240 see also William F. Nolan

Edwards, Frank Allyn. ES1 154

Edwards, Frederick Anthony (1896-) WGT 45 see also Charman Edwards

Edwards, Gawain pseud. of George Edward Pendray. AOW 36 CSF 67 PST 157 SF1 165 VES 71

Edwards, Gunvor. FFC 153, 158

Edwards, Hamilton. VES 322

Edwards, Jonathan. COT 98, 104 NWO 35 RBY 82

Edwards, Kelley. IAC 104 SFS 43

Edwards, Malcolm John (1949-) LTN 132 RSG 91 SFE 190 SFW 197-202, 401-7, 505-11, 525-30, 543-9

Edwards, Norman pseud. of Terry Carr, Ted White. SFE 190

Edwards, Peter (1946-) HFI 48 SFE 190

Edwards, Scott. BAA 218

Edwards, Suzanne. SL1 173-7 SL5 2211-4

Eells, Elsie Spencer (1880-) ES1
155
Eenhoorn, Michael.   ES1 155
SF1 165
Effinger, George Alec (1947-)
ALW 212 AOW 182 BAA 157
BFP 175 BYS 304 ETN 65, 142
FFR 70 HFI 48 IAC 104 LEX
291 MFW 24 RGS 58 SFD 57,
265 SFE 190-1 SF1 165 SF2
887 SRB 17, 359
Efremov, Ivan see Ivan Yefremov
Egan, Thomas M. FLR 62
Egbert, Donald Drew. BAA 175
Egbert, H. M. pseud. of Victor
R. Emanuel. CSF 67
Egerton, George pseud. of Mary
Chavelita Bright. CSF 68 SF1
165
Eggeling, John. SL1 130-2, 449-
52
Eggleston, George C. VES 209
Eggleston, Katharine. CSF 68
SF1 165
Egleton, Clive Frederick (1927-)
SF1 166 SF2 888
Egner, Thor. FFC 154
Egremont, Michael. CSF 68 SF1
166
Egri, Lajos. CSC 73, 86
Ehrenburg, Ilya. EXT 10/2 75
MIH 105 MSF 253, 261
Ehrenhaft, Felix. ISW 34
Ehrenpreis, Irvin. BAA 218
Ehrenstein, Albert. CSF 68
Ehrenzweig, Anton. FLT 152
Ehrhardt, Paul Georg (1889-1961)
LEX 292
Ehricke, Krafft. WFS 262
Ehrlich, Anne H. IAC 104
Ehrlich, Max Simon (1909-) AOW
182 ASF 225 BAA 153 ES1 155
FBK 7 FFR 70 HFI 48 KAU
127 NDA 162-3 SFE 191 SF1
166 SF2 888 SRB 12 WFS 180-1
WSF 132
Ehrlich, (Dr.) Paul R. IAC 104
Ehrmann, Jacques. BAA 218
Ehrmann, Max (1872-1945) CSF
68 SF1 166
Eichenberg, Fritz. FFC 4, 21,
73, 75, 106, 117
Eichmann, Adolf. VMW 25
Eichner, Henry M. (1909-71) BAA
175 ES1 155 SF1 166 SF2 888
SRB 69

Eide, Edith. WGT 45 see also
Tigrina
Eidlitz, Walther (1892-) SF1 166
Eiger, H. R. FBK 153
Eigk, Claus (1905-) LEX 292
Eilert, Bernd. FFC 44
Einstein, Albert (1879-1955) ACC
119, 159 ATA 52 CAT 24, 31
COT 70, 109, 137, 147, 234 CSC
14, 48-9, 56-60, 66, 108, 200
CUA 55-6 ETN 99 EXT 1/2
36 EXT 7/2 37 EXT 10/2 107
FBK 129 FTF 71, 119, 166 [FUT]
HEN 31 IMS 148 LTN 163, 203
MFW 7-8, 24, 32, 184, 215-6 MIH
43, 108 MSF 14, 68, 74, 255, 269
MSM 80, 222 NDA 57 OMN 21,
53-4, 68, 78, 260 OWB 34, 84
SFH 7, 42, 47, 115, 117, 121-4, 129
SFN 20 SHL 11, 14-5, 26 STF
35-6 STH 248 TBJ 11 TDI 44-
6, 52-3, 56 THM 13, 31, 33, 62
VES 76-7, 155, 250 WFS 259,
265 WSF 5, 324, 332, 364
Einstein, Charles (1926-) ES1 155
HFI 48 SFE 191 SF1 166 SF2
888
Einzig, Susan. FFC 168
Eiseley, Loren Corey (1907-) AAL
76 COT 59, 267 CWN 50 ES1
155 EXT 10/1 26 IAC 105 IAH
133 ISW 129 MFW 24 MSF 225
THM 14, 21, 36
Eiseley, Simon. IAC 105
Eisenberg, Larry (1919-) HFI 49
IAC 105 SFS 43 SF1 166 SF2
888
Eisenberg, Lawrence B. SF1 166
Eisenberg, Monroe. TSP 30
Eisenhower, Dwight D. COT 91,
112, 135, 137-8, 267 HID 183
ISW 95, 171 POE 291 RHN 15,
67, 112, 160, 205, 211 WFS 15, 150
Eisenstat, Jane (1920-) SF2 1085
see also J. E. Sperry
Eisenstein, Alex. AC2 74 IAC
105 KAU 235 LTN 257 OSR
267-71, 354 RFA xxii
Eisenstein, Phyllis. FL4 1780-3
IAC 105
Eisenstein, Sergei M. MSF 74
SFH 102
Eisenwein, J. Berg. ALW 175
Eisermann, Gottfried. BAA 218
Eisgruber, Frank, Jr. SF1 166

Eisler, Robert (1882-1949) ES1
155
Eisner, Greta. FL1 190-2, 207-
10 FL2 710-4 SL1 363-8 SL2
574-8 SL4 1902-7
Eisner, Simon pseud. of Cyril M.
Kornbluth. IAC 105
Eisner, Steve. EXT 3/1 23
Eissler, K. R. FLT 153
Eizykman, Boris (1949-) SFE 191
Ekanayake, Hector. VFS 271
Ekberg, Carl Whitworth. SF1 166
Eklund, Gordon (1945-) AOW 182
BAA 160 BFP 176 COT 108, 285
FFR 71 HFI 49 IAC 105 LEX
292 RGS 58-9 SFD 57-8 SFE
191 SF1 166 SF2 888 VES 180
Ekstrom, Kjell M. (1920-) ES1
155
Ekstrom, William F. BAA 282
Ela, Jonathan. IAC 105
Elam, Richard Mace, Jr. (1920-)
ES1 155 FFR 71 IAC 105 SFS
43-4 SF1 166 SF2 888-9
Elchlepp, Elizabeth. FL1 1-3
FL4 1891-4, 1983-5, 2029-32
Elder, Arthur A. (1900?-1956)
SF1 166
Elder, Cyrus. BAA 29 POE 139
Elder, Joseph. AOW 291, 298
ES1 155-6 IAC 105 SFD 17
SFE 191 SF1 167
Elder, Michael (Aiken) (1931-)
AAL 138 BAA 151 HFI 49 LEX
293 SFE 191 SF1 167 SF2 889
Eldershaw, Flora Sydney Patricia
(1897-) BAA 117 SF1 167 WGT
45 see also M. Barnard Elder-
shaw
Eldershaw, M. Barnard pseud. of
Flora Sydney Patricia Eldershaw
May Faith Barnard
ES1 156 VES 261
Eldridge, Mildred. FFC 131
Eldridge, Paul (1888-) AOW 114
CSF 200 ES1 156 FL4 1918-21
HFI 152-3 SFE 191 SF1 167
SF2 889
Eldridge, Roger. FFC 42
Eleve pseud. of Mrs. H. M.
Stowe. CSF 68 SF1 167
Elg, Stefan. ES1 156
Elgin, Suzette Haden (1936-) BAA
148, 154 FFR 71 HFI 49 IAC
106 LEX 293 SFA 194 SFE
192 SF1 167 SF2 889

Eliade, Mircea (1907-) ACC 93,
107 BAA xx, 218 EXT 9/1 5-7,
16 FBK 152 FL3 1511-5 KAU
4, 88 MSF 58 SF1 167 WBW
32-3
Eliades, David. SF1 167
Elias, Albert J. HFI 49
Elias, Lee. SOT 85 WSF 306
Eliat, Helene. SF1 167
Elijah. MSM 206
Eliot, Don pseud. of Robert Sil-
verberg. RSG 11, 24
Eliot, Ethel Cook (1890-) FFC 13
SF1 582
Eliot, George pseud. of Mary
Ann Evans (1819-80) LTN 181
ETN 54 EXT 4/2 19 EXT 5/2
26-30 FLT 12, 19-20 SFH 16
SL3 1213-6
Eliot, (Maj. Gen.) George Field-
ing (1894-1971) SF1 167 WTS
31, 34
Eliot, John. BAA 5
Eliot, T(homas) S(tearns) (1888-)
CAT 136 CUA 17, 33, 50 CWN
30 ETN 119 EXT 1/2 25, 38
EXT 7/2 37 EXT 8/1 13 EXT
9/2 47 FAN 7, 138 FBK 61, 127
HEN 7, 58 IAH 65 JGB 6, 16-7
MIH 135-6 MSF 14, 141, 220
MSM 106 NDA 198 RBY 19, 157
RZY 40, 82 SFB 74 SOI xv-xvi,
28, 114, 130, 141, 144, 156 THM
5, 8, 17, 37, 39, 55, 61 TJB 52
WFS 146
Eliott, E. C. pseud. of Reginald
Alec Martin. SF1 167-8
Elisabeth (Queen-Consort of
Charles I King of Rumania)
(1843-1916) WGT 45
Elizabeth, (Queen). TSO 20-1
VFS 236-7
Elkin, Benjamin. FFC 74
Elkin, Stanley. ALW 238
Elkins, Charles L. SFW 233-41,
551-61 SL2 807-12 SL3 1073-8
SL5 2150-5
Elkins, Mary J. SL1 16-21
Ell, Richard G. (1951-) SF1 168
Ellanby, Boyd pseud. of Lyle
Boyd, William Boyd. IAC 106
SFS 44
Ellern, William B. IAC 106 SFS
44
Ellet, Elizabeth Fries Lummis
(1818-77) CSF 68 WGT 45

Ellik, Ronald D. (1938-68) ES1
156 RFA 153 SFE 192 SF1 168
SRB 81 VES 98 WGT 45
Ellin, Stanley. ES1 156 HFI 49
IAC 106
Ellinger, Geoffrey. CSF 68
Ellington, Duke. ISW 7
Elliot, Jeffrey M. FL1 146-8
Elliot, John Herbert (1918-) ES1
156 IAC 106 SFE 192 SFS 44,
61 SFW 389 SF1 168
Elliot, Lee (house name) SF1 168
see also William Henry Bird,
Dennis Talbot Hughes
Elliott, Bruce (1914?-73) EFP 11
ES1 156 HFI 49 IAC 106 SFE
192 SFS 44 SF1 168
Elliott, Carlyle. RFA 14
Elliott, Charles. EXT 10/1 26
Elliott, Don pseud. of Robert
Silverberg. RSG 11, 24
Elliott, Francis Perry (1861-1924)
CSF 68 SF1 168
Elliott, George. SF1 168
Elliott, George Paul (1918-) AOW
288 CSC 217 ES1 156 ETN 2
EXT 8/1 17 IAC 106 SFS 44
SF1 168 SF2 889
Elliott, Harry Chandler (1907?-)
BAA 126 ES1 156 HFI 49 IAC
106 ISW 69-70 SFE 192 SFS
44 SF1 168
Elliott, Hettie. SF1 168
Elliott, John. AOW 202 HFI 184
SF1 168
Elliott, Robert C. AOW 14, 343
BAA xxii, 175, 218 MSF 50, 52,
54-5, 57, 61, 108, 241 UKL 245
Elliott, Rose Bedrick. IAC 106
SFS 44
Elliott, Sumner Locke. BAA 161
Elliott, William James (1886-)
ES1 156 SF1 169
Ellis, (Mr.). BAA 18
Ellis, Charles. HFI 49
Ellis, Craig (house name) SFE
192 WGT 45 see also Lee
Rogow, David Vern
Ellis, D. E. SFE 192 SF1 169
Ellis, Dean. SRB 40, 46 VES 139,
231
Ellis, Edward Sylvester (1840-
1916) ALW 74 RHN 11 SFE 192
SFW 53-4 SF1 169 SIH 129
STH 162-3 VES 173, 322 WSF
18

Ellis, G. A. CSF 68 SF1 169
Ellis, H. F. IAC 106 SFS 44
Ellis, Havelock. BAA 62 RZY 9,
14, 26-8
Ellis, John. ALW 8 IMS 137
Ellis, T. Mullett. CSF 68
Ellis, William. POE 85-6
Ellison, Harlan (1934-) AAL 53-
4 ALW 8, 29, 35, 184, 212, 222,
224, 235-6, 239 AOW 182-3, 287,
290-1, 293, 298, 300, 363 ASF 28,
236, 306, 329-30 BAA 133, 153
BFP 177-80 BYS 286, 303-4,
306 CAT 17 COT 169, 252, 278
CSC 74, 107, 173, 198, 201, 207,
209, 236, 291 DMK 159-69 ES1
156-7 ETN 21-3, 56, 72, 105-6,
136, 179-80 EXT 9/1 21 EXT
10/1 6, 8 EXT 10/2 64 FBK 154
FFR 71-2 [FJT] FL3 1516-9
FRN 15-6 FTF 121 HFI 49-50
IAC 106-9 INT 15, 68-9, 71-2,
77, 79-80, 82-4, 88, 90-1 JGB 58
KAU 204 KVT 43 KWS 312 LEX
293-5 LTN 130, 139, 151, 254-5,
268-9 MFW 1-2, 19, 24, 152, 161,
200, 213-4 MIH 77, 131-4, 146
NDA 75, 142-5, 213 OMN 1-14,
62, 171-7 PJF 15, 40 RGS 59-
60 RHN 209 RSG 10, 15, 33
SFA 85, 182-3 SFB 117 SFE
192-4 SFH 76, 93, 106, 131-2,
171, 187 SFS 44-5 SFW 204,
207, 357-68, 459 SF1 169 SF2
889-90 SL4 1978-88 SRB 17,
108, 344, 354 STH 45, 88 SV3
9-18 TDI 7 TJB 45 TSF 60
VES 152, 174, 208, 217-20, 227,
237, 241-2, 280, 301, 339, 341
VFS 153 WAA 54 WFS 192, 240,
292, 296-9 WGT 45-6 WSF 183,
222, 234, 241, 256, 313, 388 YTS
31 see also Lee Archer, Ellis
Hart, E. K. Jarvis, Ivar Jorgensen, Clyde Mitchell

Ellison, Lee Monroe. BAA 218
Ellison, Ralph. NDA 169 NWO
9, 36, 165 SFD 32, 36, 240, 262,
297, 323
Ellmann, Mary. EXT 10/1 26
Ellmann, Richard. EXT 10/1 19
Ellora pseud. of Gideon Jasper
Richard Ouseley. SF1 510
Ellsberg, Daniel. MSF 239
Ellstein, Abraham. FBK 57

Ellsworth, Fanny. TSP 217
Ellsworth, Whitney. SOT 114
Ellul, Jacques. BAA 218 KAU
12, 160, 168, 173 POE 310
Ellwood, Gracia Fay (1938-) SF1
169 SF2 890
Elman, Dave. STH 150
Elmore, Ernest. CSF 68 SF1
169
Elmslie, Kenward. IAC 109
Elrick, George S. SL1 84-8, 144-
8
Elsbree, Langdon. BAA 218
Elshemus, Louis M. (1864-1941)
SF1 169
Elson, Jane. CSF 68
Elson, Robert. CSF 68 SF1 170
Elson, Susan. FFC 72
Elstar, Dow pseud. of Raymond
Z. Gallun. ISW 73 RFA 51
Elton, James. SF1 170
Elvin, William. EXT 10/1 20
Elwood, Roger P. (1933-) ALW
179, 222 AOW 296 COT 271
EFP 14 ES1 157 ETN 132-5,
197 FFR 72 FRN 402 IAC 109,
118, 180 LEX 295-6 LTN 250
SFE 194 SFS 87 SF1 170-1
SF2 890 SRB 359 TJB 44 WSF
249, 280-1
Ely, David (1927-) ES1 157 FFR
72 HFI 50 IAC 109 SFE 194
Ely, George Herbert (1880? -
1958) SF1 171 WGT 46 see also
Herbert Strang
Ely, Richard T. BAA 175
Emanuel, Victor Rousseau (1879-
1960) BAA 82 ES1 157-8 EXT
8/2 31-63 WGT 46 see also
H. M. Egbert, Victor Rousseau
Emanuel, Walter Lewis (1869-
1915) CSF 68 SF1 171
Emberley, Ed. FFC 87
Embree, Charles Fleming (1874-
1905) SF1 171
Embry, Margaret. FFC 187
Emersie, John. SF1 171 WGT
46
Emerson, Caroline Dwight (1891-
1973) ES1 158 FFC 171 SF1
171
Emerson, Ralph Waldo (1803-82)
ALW 52, 107, 167 COT 107 CYR
37 EXT 8/1 12 HEN 3, 7, 59, 61
HID 22 KAU 25 KVT 21 MFW

91 MSF 191 NWO 10, 36, 44, 47,
62, 280, 282 RBY 65, 100, 159
SFA 49, 143 SFB 10 SHL 4-5,
7, 40-1, 60 SOT 257
Emerson, Willis George (1856-
1918) AOW 61 CSF 68 EXT 1/1
2, 10 MFW 120 PST 110, 128,
192, 199, 205, 207, 223, 227-8,
245, 250-1, 268, 277 SFB 76 SFE
194-5 SF1 171
Emin, Fyodor. MSF 244
Emkes, Max Adolf. BAA 282
Emmens, Stephen H. BAA 55
Emmett, Elizabeth. IAC 109
SFS 45
Emmons, Winfred S., Jr. EXT
1/2 24, 35-7 EXT 2/2 22 EXT
3/1 1-25
Empson, William. EXT 9/2 59
FLT 152, 154
Emshwiller, Carol. BYS 305
ES1 158 EXT 8/1 16 FFR 73
IAC 109-10 ISW 127 MIH 96
SFE 195 SFS 45
Emshwiller, Ed(mund Alexander)
(1925-) BYS 217, 230 ES1 158
EXT 9/2 25 EXT 10/1 2 FRN
15-6 IAC 110 RFA 205, 207-11
SFE 195 SOT 247 SRB 37, 45,
112 STH 266 VES 82, 93, 96,
114, 148, 160, 175, 183, 211, 214,
217, 234, 289 WGT 46 WSF 224
Emtsev, Mikhail (1930-) HFI 50
SFS 45 SL5 2506-10 IAC 255
Enck, John Edward. SF1 171
End, Heinrich. BAA 218
Endersby, Victor. ISW 276
Endo, Hiroya. WFS 305
Endore, Guy S. (1900-70) CSF
68 ES1 158 FBK 55 FFR 73
FL5 2102-6 HFI 50 IAC 110
SFE 196 SFS 45 SF1 171 SF2
890 WAA 88
Endrey, Eugene (1891-1967) SF1
171
Enever, J. E. COT 23, 80 IAC
110
Eney, Richard Harris (1937-) ES1
158 EXT 5/1 5 SF1 171 SF2
891 SRB 109
Enfantin, Barthelemy Prosper.
MSF 157
Enfield, Hugh pseud. of Gwilym
Fielden Hughes. SF1 171
Eng, Steve. FL5 2415-21

Engdahl, Sylvia Louise (1933-)
AOW 306,317 IAC 110 SFE 197
SF1 171 SF2 891 SRB 30
Engel, Leonard (1916-64) AOW
183 CSF 68 ES1 158 SFE 197
SF1 172 VES 135
Engel, Lyle Kenyon. SFE 197
Engelhardt, Frederick. RFA 70
Engelhardt, Werner Wilhelm.
BAA 218
Engels, Frederick. BAA 175
CAT 80 EXT 3/2 48 LTN 111
MSF 23,39,112,148,199 WBW
59
Engh, Mary Jane (1933-) HFI 50
SFE 197
England, George Allen (1877-
1936) ALW 33,86,107,121,124,
156,160 AOW 61-2 BAA 80
BFP 181-2 BYS 170 CSC 168
CSF 69 ES1 158-9 EXT 1/1
10 EXT 7/1 24-5,27 HFI 50
IAC 110 IMS 23,75 MFW 23
MSM 297 PST 173-4,193,258,
278,283 RFA 1-2 RGS 60-1,
213-4 SFE 197 SF1 172 SL1
484-7 SOT 70 SRB 11 STH 40-
1, 76-7,233-4,237-8 VES 147,
160,225,232,312 WSF 24,44,
385 WTS 52 YTS 9
Englander, Sigmund. BAA 175
Engle, Eloise Hopper (1923-) ES1
159 SFE 197 HFI 50 SF1 172
SF2 891
Enguidanos, Miguel. EXT 9/1 17
Enloe, J. EXT 8/2 63
Ennis, Fred. CSF 69 ES1 159
Enright, Dennis Joseph. BAA 131
Enright, Elizabeth. FFC 5,47,92
Enright, James. OWB 87
Enright, Richard E. CSF 69
Enroth, Clyde. EXT 6/1 14
Ensley, Evangeline see Evangel-
ine Walton
Ensor, James. FBK 146
Enstrom, Robert. HFI 50
Enton, Harry. ALW 74 RHN 11
SFW 53-4 STH 45,53-4 WSF
18 see also Harry Cohen
Epicurus. MSF 106,181 NDA 54
Epperly, R.R. WTS 62
Epps, P.H. BAA 218
Epstein, J.H. BAA 218
Epstein, Samuel (1909-) ES1 159
ETN 176

Epting, K. BAA 218
Erasmus (of Rotterdam). MSF
103
Erckmann, Emile (1822-99) CSF
69 ES1 159 SFS 28,45 SF1 172
WGT 46 see also Erckmann-
Chatrian
Erckmann-Chatrian pseud. of
Alexandre Chatrian
Emile Erckmann
FBK 54,138 IAC 110 TFC 110
Erdahl, Silvert. BAA 113 SF1
172
Erdmannsdorffer, Hans Gustav.
BAA 175
Erdoes, Richard. FFC 133
Erhard, Walter. FFC 83
Ericcson. EXT 9/2 29
Erickson, Russell. FFC 118
Ericson, Marcia. IAC 110
Erie, Paul. WGT 46
Erisman, Fred. BAA 218
Erisman, Robert O. ES1 159
SOT 326,397 TSP 134 WFS 84,
100-1
Erlanger, Michael (1915-) ES1
159 SF1 172
Erlich, Richard D. FL1 447-59
SL1 409-14 SL3 1171-7 UKL
200-24
Erlich, Victor. MSF 6
Ermann, Georg. POE 190
Ermecke, Gustav. BAA 219
Ernsberger, George. ETN 72
IAC 110,252 SF1 172 SRB 290
Ernst. JGB 6
Ernst, Max. IAC 110
Ernst, Morris L. (1888-) BAA 114
ES1 159
Ernst, Paul Frederick (1902-)
COT 46 ES1 159 IAC 110 RFA
6 SFE 198 SFS 45 SF1 172-3
SOT 136,141 STH 251 TSP 28,
38,63,81,89,97,100-1,145,158,
162,215,218,220-2 VES 205
WGT 46 WTS 32,39,124-5,132
see also Kenneth Robeson, Paul
F. Stern
Ernsting, Walter (1920-) ES1 159
FFR 73 FTF 78 HFI 50 LEX
298-301 SFB 146 SIH 167 WGT
46 see also Clark Darlton
Eros, John. SF1 173
Erro. MIH 138
Erskine, Douglas pseud? of John
Buchan. CSF 69 SF1 173

Erskine, John (1879-1951) CSF 69
ES1 160 FL1 1-3 SF1 173 SOT
3
Erskine, Thomas (1788-1870) AOW
22 BAA 17-8 POE 120-2 PST
23 SFE 198 SF1 173 WGT 46
see also T. E.
Ertz, Susan (1894?-) CSF 69 ES2
892 EXT 8/1 5 OWB 13 SFN 39
SF1 173
Ervine, St. John Greer (1883-1971)
BAA 101 CSF 69 SF1 173
Erwin, Betty K. FFC 30,193 SF1
173
Erwin, John. FFC 131
Erzgraber, Willi. BAA 219
Escaich, Rene. EXT 2/1 6 EXT
3/2 46
Escalante, Manuel F. BAA 175
Eschelbach, Claire John. EXT
6/1 2,12,17
Escher, M. C. IAC 110
Eschmann, E. W. EXT 6/1 14
Eschmann, Wilhelm Ernst. BAA
219
Escott, Thomas Hay Sweet (1844-
1924) CSF 69 SF1 173
Esenwein, Joseph Berg (1867-1946)
CSF 69 ES1 160 IAC 110 MSM
36 SF1 173
Eshbach, Lloyd Arthur (1910-)
ALW 184 AOW 343 CAT 14
CSC 220,232 ES1 160 EXT 5/1
5 HFI 51 HID 192 IAC 110 IMS
16,24-5,119,125,136,147,213
MIH 22 MSM xiv OWB 9,11-2,
21-2,37-8,51-2,59,67-8,77-8,
89-90 RFA 153 SFE 200 SF1
173 SOT 23,107,218 SRB 100,
235 WFS 178 WIF 123,129,259
WSF 133-4,185,199,215 WTS
40
Eskestad, Tage (1920-) SL3 1366-9
Esmond, Sidney. SF1 173
Esmonde, Margaret P. UKL 15-
35
Essex, Rosamund Sybil (1900-)
SF1 173
Essoe, Gabor Attila (1944-) ES1
160 SF1 173 SF2 892
Estabrooks, George Hoben (1895-)
CSF 125 SF1 173
Estes, Eleanor Ruth (1906-) FFC
19,132,187 SF1 174 SF2 892
Esteven, John pseud. of Samuel
Shellabarger. CSF 69

Estival, Ivan Leon. ES1 160 SF1
174 WGT 47
Estrada, Ezequiel Martinez. BAA
244
Estrada, Francisco Lopez. BAA
241
Estridge, Robin see Philip Loraine
Eszterhas, Joe. HEN 10
Etcetera. CSF 69
Etchison, Dennis William (1943-)
IAC 110 LEX 301-2 SFS 45
Ettinger, Robert Chester William
(1918-) ES1 160 VES 148,160
WFS 48-9,252-4,256-9 WSF 167
Ettla, Katherine. EXT 9/2 25
EXT 10/1 3
Etzler, John Adolphus. BAA 21,
23-4 POE 59-60
Euclid. ATA 10 EXT 7/2 33
MSF 52 VFS 42
Euhemerus. EXT 8/1 23 MSF 87,
94
Euphues. IAH 148 TJB 58
Eurich, Nell E. AOW 344 BAA
175
Eustace, Robert pseud. of Eustace
R. Barton. ALW 85 CSF 69,137
IAC 110
Eustis, Helen. IAC 110
Evain, Elaine (1931-) SF1 174
SF2 892
Evans, Ambrose. BAA 10
Evans, Bergan. BAA 175
Evans, Bergen B. (1904-) ES1 160
Evans, Charles. WTS 33
Evans, Chris. BAA 62
Evans, Christopher Riche (1931-)
IAC 110 JGB 18 SF1 174 SF2
892-3
Evans, Cicely Louise. SF1 174
Evans, Dean. IAC 110 IAH 21
Evans, Derek. SF1 174
Evans, Don. IAC 110
Evans, Edward Everett (1893-
1958) ES1 160-1 FFR 73 HFI
51 IAC 110 LEX 302 OWB 87
RFA 153 SFE 201 SFS 45 SF1
174 SOT 24-5,320 SRB 98
VES 98,108 WGT 47
Evans, Ernestine. EXT 2/1 11
Evans, Gareth Lloyd. EXT 10/1
12
Evans, Gerald see Victor La Salle
Evans, Gladys. IAC 111
Evans, Grant. SF1 174

Evans, Gwyn. SF1 174
Evans, Oliver. POE 34
Evans, I(drisyn) O(liver) (1894-
1977) ES1 161 EXT 2/1 6 EXT
3/2 47 IAC 111 NWO 51 SFE
201 SF1 174 SF2 893
Evans, John X. BAA 219
Evans, K.W. BAA 219
Evans, Marguerite Florence
Helene Jervis (1894-) WGT 47
Evans, Mary Ann (1819-80) LTN
181 see also George Eliot
Evans, Mike. IAC 111
Evans, Mervyn. IMS 52, 72
Evans, Robert O. BAA xx, 219
Evans, Robley J. (1933-) AAL
148 SF1 174 SF2 893
Evans, Thelma D. Hamm. WGT
47
Evans, Thomas. BAA 17-8
Evans, William Harrington (1921-)
RFA 153 SFE 201 SF1 174 SF2
892 SRB 81
Evans, William M. EXT 3/1 21
Evarts, Hal G. CSF 69 FFC 143
Evarts, Richard Conover (1890-)
SF1 174
Eve. ASF 141 CYR 27 EXT 5/1
22 EXT 7/1 24 HEN 50, 59 IMS
1 INT 102, 114 JGB 17 KVT
51 NWO 23, 34, 139 SFB 53
SFE 16-7 WBW 54
Even, James Eugene. BAA 124
Everett, Catoline Whitman. EXT
10/1 27
Everett, Dorothy. EXT 10/1 27
Everett, Frances. BAA 74 SF1
174

Everett, (Mrs.) H. D. CSF 69
ES1 162 SF1 174-5 WGT 47
see also Theo Douglas
Everett, Henry Lexington. BAA
47
Everett, Walker G. IAC 111
Everitt, Nicholas. CSF 69
Everson, William Keith (1929-)
SF1 175 SF2 893-4
Everts, Lillian. ES1 162
Ewald, Carl (1856-1908) AOW 46,
62 SFE 204 SF1 175
Ewbank, David Robert. BAA 282
Ewers, H. G. (1930-) LEX 302-3
Ewers, Hans Heinz (1871-1943)
AOW 92, 102 CSF 70 ES1 162
FBK 15, 57, 141-2 FL1 26-8
SFE 204 SF1 175
Ewers-Wunderwald, Ilna. FBA 141
Ewing, Frederick R. EXT 8/2 63
MIH 73
Ex-Private X. CSF 70
Ex-Revolutionist, (An). CSF 70
Exter, Maureen. IAC 111
Eyers, Harold. SOI 130
Eyles, Allen. SF1 175
Eyles, Margaret Leonora (1889-
1960) CSF 70 SF1 175
Eyraud, Achille. WSF 18
Eyre, Katherine Wigmore (1901-
70) SF1 175
Eyton, John Seymour (1890-) CSF
70 SF1 175
Ezekiel. EXT 8/1 23
Ezo. FFC 118, 132
Ezra. SF1 175
Ezra, I. B. SF1 175

F

F. H. P. CSF 70 SF1 401
Faber, Arthur. SF1 175
Faber, (Sir) Geoffrey (1889-1961)
CSF 70 SF1 175
Fabian, Stephen E. (1930-) FRN
37-8 SFE 204 VES 291
Fabien, Jacques. POE 136
Fabre, Jean Henri. BAA 219
SOT 51
Fabregas, Juan Torrent. EXT
2/1 7
Fabre-Luce, Andre Edmond
Alfred (1899-) SF1 175
Fabricant, Noah D(aniel)(1904-64)
ES1 162 IAC 85,111 SFS 46 SF1
175
Fabun, Don. ES1 162 MSM 43-
70,301-2
Fadiman, Clifton Paul (1904-) ACC
158 ES1 162-3 IAC 111 ISW 1,
67-8 SFS 46 SF1 175-6 SF2 894
Faery, Rebecca Blevins. SL2
692-7
Fagan, Henry Allan (1889-1963)
BAA 129 ES1 163 SFE 204-5
SF1 176
Fagg, Ken(neth). KAU 121 VES
166
Fagnan, Marie Antoinette. SF1
176
Faguet, Emile. BAA 219
Faigel, M. J. EXT 4/2 16
Fainlight, Ruth. IAC 111
Fair, Charles. AOW xxi
Fairbairn, John. SF1 176
Fairbanks, Douglas. CWD 41
Fairburn, Edwin. CSF 70 WGT
47 see also Mohoao
Fairchild, Hoxie Neale. EXT 6/1
13

Fairclough, Peter. ES1 163 SF1
176
Fairfax, John (1930-) IAC 111
SF2 894
Fairfield, Frederick Pease. BAA
84
Fairman, Henry Clay. CSF 70
SFB 76 SF1 176
Fairman, Paul W. (1916-77) AOW
317 BAA 146 ES1 163-4 ETN
26 FRN 33-4 HFI 51 IAC 111
KWS 187,362 LEX 304 NDA
26-8 SFE 205 SFS 46 SF1 176
WGT 47 see also Adam Chase,
E. K. Jarvis, Ivar Jorgenson,
Paul Lohrman
Fairstar, (Mrs.). FFC 83 see
also Richard Horne
Fairweather, Mary. CSF 70 SF1
176
Fakkar, Rouchdi. BAA 175
Falconer, Kenneth pseud. of C.
M. Kornbluth. ISW 146 RFA
191
Falconer, Lanoe pseud. of Mary
Elizabeth Hawker. CSF 70 SF1
177
Falk, Doris V. NWO 68
Falk, Johann Daniel. POE 47
Falke, Rita. BAA 219,282 MSF
40
Falkiner, Caesar Litton. BAA
175
Falkner, John pseud. of E. F.
Gale. SFE 205 SF1 177
Falkner, John Meade (1858-1932)
CSF 70 SF1 177
Falkon, Felix Lance. SF1 177
Fallaci, Oriana. AOW 164

120

Fallada, Hans pseud. of Rudolf
Wilhelm Friedrich Ditzen. CSF
70 SF1 177
Fallaw, L. M. ES1 164 SF1 177
Fallowell, Duncan. JGB 40
Falter, Gustav. BAA 176
Fancett, Elizabeth. IAC 111
Fanta, Holly Roth (1916-64) WGT
47
Fanthorpe, Robert Lionel (1935-)
ES1 164 HFI 51-3 LEX 304-5
SFE 214-5 SF1 177-9 SF2 894-
5 WGT 47-8 see also Victor La
Salle, John E. Muller, Karl
Zeigfried
Faraday, Michael (1791-1867)
FTF 35 WFS 259
Faraday, Robert. SF1 179
Faraday, Wilfred Barnard (1874-
1953) CSF 70 SF1 179
Faralla, Dana (1909-) FFC 74
SF1 179 SF2 895
Farber, Jerry. IAC 111
Farber, Leslie H. SFN 76
Farber, Norma. FFC 19
Farca, Marie C. (1935-) HFI 53
SFE 215 SF1 179 SF2 895
Farcasan, Sergiu (1924-) LEX
305-6 SFB 145
Fargus, Frederick John (1847-
85) SF1 116 WGT 48
Farigoule, Louis (1885-1972) see
Jules Romains
Farina, Richard. SFH 97
Farjeon, Benjamin Leopold (1833-
1903) CSF 70 SF1 179
Farjeon, Eleanor (1881-1965) CSF
70 ES1 164 FFC 25, 54, 105 SF1
180, 582 SF2 895
Farjeon, Joseph Jefferson (1883-
1955) AOW 184 CSF 70 ES1 164
SFE 216 SF1 180 VES 135 WGT
48
Farley, Carol. IAC 111
Farley, Ralph Milne pseud. of
Roger Sherman Hoar (1887-1963)
ALW 141 AOW 102 BYS 170
COT 95, 129 CSF 70 FFR 75
HFI 53 IAC 111 IMS 16, 21, 23,
26, 136, 194, 199-200 LEX 306
RFA 33, 40 RGS 61-2 SFE 216-
7 SFS 46 SFW 145, 147 SF1 180
SOT 93, 107-8, 342, 344 STH 142
TSP 16 VES 151, 153, 156, 314
WIF 88, 209 WSF 78 WTS 32

Farley, Walter (1915-) SF1 180
SF2 895
Farmer, Penelope Jane (1939-)
ES1 164 FFC 5, 74, 163, 175
FFR 75 SF1 180 SF2 895 SRB
24
Farmer, Peter. FFC 162
Farmer, Philip Jose (1918-) AAL
13, 15-6, 30, 35-6, 77, 105, 163
ALW 212, 221 AOW 127, 184-5,
291, 296, 298 BAA 165 BFP 183-
6 BYS 262, 303 DMK 121-32
ES1 164-5 ETN 20-1, 23, 53
EXT 5/1 3 EXT 8/1 7 FFR 75-
6 FL3 1325-31 FL5 2171-5
FTF 154, 200 [FUT] HFI 53-4
IAC 111-2 IAH 139 INT 52, 110,
122 ISW 4, 8 JVN 198 KAU 3,
29, 65, 184, 186 KVT 39 LEX
306-9 MFW 12, 24, 155, 157, 160
MIH 36, 78, 122, 126, 133 MSF
239 NWO 20, 92, 236 RFA 212
RGS 62-3, 214 SFB 9, 117-8
SFD 54, 63, 253-4, 258-9, 297, 320
SFE 217-8 SFH 93, 143, 172, 178,
185-7, 243 SFS 46 SFW 369-75,
552 SF1 180-1 SF2 895-6 SIH
54, 180 SL3 1289-93 SL4 1809-
16 SL5 2190-4 SOT 6, 157, 163,
392-409 SRB 16, 79, 112, 124,
259, 333 STH 18-9, 49, 67, 87-8,
120, 265 TJB 5 TSF 60, 229
TSP 184 VES 92, 95, 123, 143,
210-1, 213, 218, 230, 232, 239, 309-
10 VF2 34-55, 198-9 WAA 117,
127, 155-6, 160 WGT 48-9 WIF
226 WSF 135, 175, 184, 242, 259,
387 see also Kilgore Trout
Farncombe, Frank E. CSF 89
SF1 181
Farnell, George. BAA 58
Farnese, A. WGT 49 see also
Franchezzo
Farningham, Marianne pseud. of
Mary Ann Hearn. CSF 71 SF1
181
Farnol, John Jeffery (1878-1952)
CSF 71 ES1 165 SF1 181 WGT
49
Farnsworth, Mona. IAC 112
ISW 131 SFS 46
Farrar, Clarence B. BAA 219
Farrar, Clyde. CSF 71
Farrar, Stewart. SF1 181
Farrell, Gage. IAC 112

Farrell, James T. EXT 7/2 37, 47 IAC 112 IAH 41 MFW 14 SFN 99 SFS 46

Farren, Mick (1943-) HFI 54 LEX 309 RGS 63-4, 214 SFE 218 SF1 181

Farrer, Reginald J. CSF 71

Farrere, Claude pseud. of Frederic Charles Pierre Edouard Bargone. CSF 71 ES1 165 EXT 2/1 6 PST 156, 158, 288, 292, 310 SFE 218 SF1 181

Farris, John. FFR 76 FL2 590-2

Farsaci, Larry B. IMS 145, 192, 199-200, 214

Farthing, Alison. FFC 175

Fast, Howard (Melvin) (1914-) ALW 212 AOW 185 ES1 165-6 FFR 76-7 HFI 54 IAC 112-3 LEX 309-10 SFE 218 SFS 46 SF1 181 SF2 896 SRB 359 STH 45 WGT 49

Fast, Jonathan. HFI 54 IAC 113 RGS 64

Fast, Julius (1919-) CSF 71 ES1 166 EXT 7/2 46 HFI 55 IAC 113 SF1 181 SF2 897

Faucette, John Matthew, Jr. (1943-) ES1 166 HFI 55 SFE 219 SF1 182 SF2 897

Faulconbridge, Philip. SF1 182

Fauley, Wilbur Finley (1872-1942) see Wilbur Fawley

Faulkner, Charles. WBW 5

Faulkner, Dorothea M. WGT 49

Faulkner, William. ALW 229 CSF 71 CUA 3-4 EXT 5/2 30 EXT 8/1 13 EXT 8/2 42 FHT 50-1 ISW 179 KVT 35 MSF 26 NWO 3-4, 35, 209-10 SFB 125 SOT 81 STF 59 WBW 4 WSF 251

Faure, Raoul Cohen (1909-) CSF 71 ES1 166 SF1 182

Faust, Alexander. TSP 162

Faust, Frederick Schiller (1892-1944) ES1 166 TSP 85, 132 VES 205 WGT 49 see also George Owen Baxter Max Brand

Faust, Johann. SFH 195

Fava, Rita. FFC 55

Favenc, Ernest (1846-1908) ES1 166 SF1 182

Fawcett, Douglas. IAC 113 SFS 46

Fawcett, Edgar (1847-1904) CSF 71 SFE 220 SF1 182 SL2 869-72

Fawcett, E(dward) D(ouglas) (1866-1960) CSF 71 MSF 162 SFE 220 SF1 182

Fawcett, Frank Dubrez (1891-1968) ES1 166 ISW 242-3 SFE 220 SF1 182 WGT 49-50 see also Simpson Stokes

Fawkes, Frank Attfield. SF1 182 WGT 50 see also X

Fawley, Wilbur pseud. of Wilbur Finley Fauley. CSF 71 SF1 182

Fax. RFA 118

Fay, William. TSP 223

Faye, Barry. SL1 78-83

Faye, Ina S. SL4 1682-6

Fayette, John B. BAA 37 CSF 71 SF1 182

Fayette, Michael. IAC 113

Feagles, Anita. FFC 74, 118 ES1 166

Fear, William Henry. SF1 182

Fearing, Kenneth (1902-61) CSF 71 ES1 166 EXT 8/1 5 HFI 55 SFE 220 SF1 182 WGT 50

Fearn, John Russell (1908-60) ALW 141 BYS 139, 220, 240-1 COT 73, 118 CSC 41-2, 51 CSF 71 DTS 14 ES1 166-7 HFI 55 IAC 113 IMS 45, 72, 75, 77, 96-7, 99, 101, 107 LEX 310-1 PST 176-7 RFA 22 SFE 220-1 SF1 182-4 SF2 897 SOT 260 STH 86 VES 75, 84, 95, 134, 142, 149, 156, 159, 179, 193, 195, 201, 205, 236, 303, 315, 324 WGT 50-1 WIF 88 WSF 116 see also Thornton Ayre, Volsted Gridban, Griff, Conrad G. Holt, Paul Lorraine, Polton Cross, Brian Shaw, Vargo Statten

Fechner, Gustav Theodor. FTF 45

Fedakh, Fatima. SF1 184

Fedeli, Ugo. BAA 176

Feder, Lillian. MFW 63

Feder, Moshe. IAC 113

Feder, Robert Arthur (1909-69) WGT 51 see also Robert Arthur

Federbush, Arnold. HFI 55 SF1 184

Federman, Donald. RBY 240

Fedor, Al. IMS 34

Feducha, Bertha. SF1 184

Feek, Lou. SRB 46
Fegan, Camilla (1939-) SF1 184
SF2 897
Fehrenbach, T. R. IAC 113 SFS
46
Feidelson, Charles, Jr. NWO 3,
37
Feiffer, Jules (1929-) ES1 167
FFC 177 IAC 113 SFS 46
Feiling, C. A. CSF 153 SF1 184
Fein, Chester. IMS 112,123,135,
137,143,148,162,167,170,175,
244
Feinberg, Gerald. VES 77
Feldman, Arthur. IAC 113 SFS
46
Feldstein, Albert B. IAC 113
Fell, Frederick. WIF 123,158
Fellini, Federico. CSC 263
Fellowes, Edward Colton (1864-
1928) CSF 72 SF1 184
Felsen, Henry Gregor (1916-)
ES1 167 IAC 113 SFS 46 SF1
184 SF2 897
Fendall, Percy. BAA 78
Fenelon, Francois. CSF 72
Fenn, George Manville (1831-
1909) CSF 72 SF1 184
Fenn, William Wallace (1862-
1932) CSF 72 ES1 167
Fenn, William Wilthew (1827?-)
SF1 184
Fennel, Eric. COT 63 IAC 113
Fenner, Phyllis Reid (1899-) ES1
167 SF1 184 SF2 897
Fennerton, William. ES1 167
SF1 185
Fennessy, J. C. BAA 119 SF1 185
Fensch, Ludwig. BAA 219
Fenton, Edward (1917-) FFC 54
SF1 185,582
Fenton, Frank. IAC 113 SFS 47,
92
Fenton, Robert W. AOW 349 ES1
167 SF1 185
Fenwick, Elizabeth. FFC 54
Ferenczi, Sandor. EXT 5/2 26-
7,30 RAH 98
Ferenczy, Arpad (1877-) SF1 185
Ferguson, Arthur B. BAA 219
Ferguson, Bird. IAC 113
Ferguson, Clay. IMS 23-4,31,
45,94
Ferguson, Dale. IAC 113
Ferguson, Ian. CSF 72

Ferguson, John. BAA 176
Ferguson, Mary. FL1 36-41
FL2 787-90 FL3 1075-80,1291-
6 FL4 1801-6
Ferguson, Merrill. BAA 134
Ferguson, Rachel. CSF 72
Ferkiss, Victor. KAU 12,169,
173
Ferlinghetti, Lawrence. CWN 46
Ferm, Betty (1926-) SF1 185 SF2
897-8
Ferman, Edward L(ewis) (1937-)
ALW 8,216 AOW 287 BYS 279
COT 277 ES1 167-8 ETN 118,
138 EXT 8/1 8 [FJT] FLR 61
IAC 113 SFE 221 SFS 47 SF1
185 SF2 898 WFS 284 WSF 235
Ferman, Harry. WTS 93
Ferman, Joseph W(olfe) (1906-
74) ES1 168 IAC 113 SFE 221
SFS 47 SF1 185 SF2 898 STH
44
Fermi, Enrico. WSF 98
Fernandes, Stanislaw. FBK 81
SRB 41,53 VES 203,239
Fernandez-Flores, Wenceslao.
CSF 72
Ferrar, William Moore. CSF 72
CWN 31 SF1 185
Ferris, Paul Frederick (1929-)
SF1 185 SF2 898
Ferris, Walter. CSF 72
Ferriss, Hugh. POE 240
Ferro, Robert. HFI 55
Ferry, W. H. BAA 176,219
Fessenden, Laura Dayton (-1924)
CSF 72 SF1 185
Fessier, Michael (1907-) CSF 72
ES1 168 IAC 113 SF1 185 SFS
47
Festinger, Leon. AOW xxi
Fetz, Ingrid. FFC 62,88,106
Feuchtwanger, Lion. SFN 23
Feuerbach, Ludvig. SIH 62
Feval, Paul. FBK 138
Feydy, Anne Lindbergh. FFC 64
SF1 582
Feynman, Richard P. FTF 10
Fezandie, Clement. CSF 72 ES1
168 EXT 1/1 10 MSM 298 SFE
221 SF1 185 SRB 10 STH 165
VES 157,160
Ffolkes, Michael. IAC 113
Fialko, Nathan (1881-) AOW 91,
102 SFE 221 SF1 185

Fialkowski, Konrad (1939-) LEX
311-2
Ficino. MFW 265
Ficke, Arthur D. CSF 72
Fidler, Kathleen pseud. of Kathleen Annie Goldie. SF1 186
Fiedler, Jean. CEN 1-22
Fiedler, Leslie A(aron) (1917-)
ALW 7,222 BAA 219 BYS 51,
55,169 COT 66 ETN 53 HFI
55 IAC 113 LTN 204,251 NWO
4,15,22,168,170 PJF 12,25,28,
48,67,73 SFB 147 SFD 82 SFH
238 SF1 186 SF2 898-9 SRB
237,500
Field, Ben (1901-) SF1 186
Field, Eugene (1850-95) CSF 72
ES1 168 SF1 186
Field, Francis J. ES1 168
Field, Julian Osgood (1849-1925)
SF1 186 WGT 51 see also X. L.
Field, Marlo. BAA 93 CSF 72
SF1 186 SRB 6
Field, Rachel Lyman (1894-1942)
FFC 80 SF1 186
Fielding, Henry (1707-54) CSF 72
EXT 9/2 29 MFW 165 SFD 43
SF1 186 SOI 143
Fielding, Howard pseud. of
Charles W. Hooke. CSF 72
Fields, W. C. HEN 16
Fienhold, Wolfgang Gunter (1948-)
LEX 312
Fifield, (Mrs.) James C. pseud.
of Effie Merriman SF1 186
Fifield, Merle. EXT 10/1 27
Fifield, William (1916-) SF1 186
SF2 899
Figge, Richard. BAA 231
Figgis, M. Darrel (1882-1925)
CSF 73 SF1 186 WGT 51 see
also Michael Ireland
Fighton, George Z. pseud. of
Winteler De Weindeck. CSF 73
Figueredo, Parra Y. IAC 189
Figuier, Louis. POE 88,104
Filer, Burt K. IAC 113
Filer, Tom see Sarah Chisom
Filkin, Roland. CSF 73 SF1 186
Filley, Alan C. BAA 176
Filmer. BAA xii
Finch, Christopher. IAC 113
Findlay, Alexander Tobias (1873-)
SF1 186
Findlay, Timothy. HFI 55

Fine, Peter see Peter Heath
Fine, Ralph Adam (1941-) SF1
187 SF2 899
Finer, S. E. BAA 220 EXT 4/2
26,28
Fingarette, Herman. BAA 220
Finger, Charles Joseph (1869-
1941) CSF 73 SF1 187
Fingesten, Peter. EXT 1/2 32
EXT 4/2 26
Finholt, Richard. SFW 459-65
Finigan, G. Lysaght. BAA 112
Fink, Conrad. BAA 220
Fink, David Harold. IAC 114
SFS 47
Fink, Howard. BAA 220
Fink, Teresina. BAA 282
Finlay, Beverly Stiles. STH 256-
7,259
Finlay, James Colin. BAA 139
Finlay, Jean Lily. STH 250
Finlay, Ruby Cole. STH 249
Finlay, Virgil (1914-71) BYS 216-
7 COT 185 ES1 169 EXT 3/1
5,18 FBK 74,103 FRN 29 IMS
77,93,109-10,221 RFA 63,70
SFB 6-7,9,20-1,28-9,104,151
SFE 222 SF1 187 SOT 328-9
SRB 112 STH 2,249-71 TRB
125 VES 105,133,169,174,184,
192,194-5,203,205-6,213,220-
1,287-8,291,313 WIF 106 WSF
124,298 WTS ix,5,40-2,44,58-
60,71-4,76,78,82,92-3,106,132
Finlay, Warden Hugh. STH 249-
51
Finley, Harry T. (1866-1940) SF1
187
Finley, M. I. BAA 220
Finn, R(alph) L(eslie) (1912-) ES1
169 SFE 222 SF1 187 SF2 899
Finney, Charles G(randison)
(1905-) ALW 146 AOW 85,230
BFP 187 CSF 73 ES1 169 EXT
3/1 28 FBK 119 FL1 282-6
FL2 948-50 HFI 55 IAC 114
ISW 128 SFE 222-3 SFS 47 SF1
187 SF2 899 SRB 259 WAA 75
Finney, Jack pseud. of Walter
Braden Finney. ALW 146 AOW
186 ES1 169 FFR 77 FL4 1938-
42 HFI 55 IAC 114 ISW 73-5,
118,123,225 KAU 49,188,191,
203 KWS 281,287 LEX 313 RHN
98 SFE 223 SFS 47 SF1 187
SL5 2283-6 SRB 328 VES 134

Finney, Lewis Erwin. BAA 83
SF1 187
Finney, Walter Braden (1911-)
BFP 188-9 SRB 328 WGT 51
see also Jack Finney
Fiorentino, Al. FFC 155
Firbank, Arthur Roland (1886-
1926) CSF 73 ES1 169 FL3
1137-41 SF1 187 THM 39
Firestone, Clark B. BAA 176
Firmin, Albert Bancroft. BAA 71
Firmin, Peter. FFC 57
Firmstone, George W. H. CSF 73
Firpo, Luigi. BAA 176, 220
Firsoff, Valdemar Axel. ES1 169
IAC 114
Firth, (Sir) Charles. BAA 220
Firth, N. Wesley. SF1 187
Firth, Violet Mary (1890-1946)
ES1 170 WGT 51 see also Dion
Fortune
Fischer, Andreas. BAA 220
Fischer, Benjamin Franklin, IV.
FL4 1989-91, 2049-53
Fischer, Bobby. ETN 132
Fischer, Bruno. TSP 127, 132,
194 see also Russell Gray,
Harrison Storm
Fischer, Fred W. IMS 200
Fischer, Harry Otto. FLR 12, 38,
60, 62 SFW 419 SOT 287, 289-
90
Fischer, John. IAC 114
Fischer, Leonard. ES1 170 SFE
223 SF1 187
Fischer, Margaret Ann Peterson
(1883-1933) WGT 52
Fischer, Marjorie (1903?-61)
CSF 73 ES1 170-1 FFC 95 SF1
187
Fischer, Michael. IAC 114 SFS
47
Fish, Robert L. (1912-) IAC 114
WGT 52
Fishbough, William. BAA 60
Fisher, Charles. SFN 76
Fisher, Clyde. IMS 8
Fisher, Eddie. LTN 89
Fisher, Gene. IAC 114 WGT 52
see also Gene Lancour
Fisher, H. A. L. VES 121
Fisher, Howard S. SF1 187
Fisher, James A. BAA 220
Fisher, James P. HFI 55 SFE
223 SF1 187

Fisher, John. EXT 4/2 15-6
EXT 6/1 1 EXT 10/1 2
Fisher, Leonard Everett. FFC
30, 66, 163 IAC 114 SFS 47
Fisher, Lou. HFI 56 IAC 114
Fisher, M. F. K. MSM 77
Fisher, Marvin. BAA 220
Fisher, Mary Ann (1839-) CSF 73
ES1 171 SF1 188
Fisher, Peter F. BAA 220
Fisher, Philip M., Jr. ES1 171
IAC 114
Fisher, Robert Thaddeus. BAA
176, 282
Fisher, Stephen Gould (1912-)
CSF 73 SF1 188 TSP 89, 218,
226 WGT 52
Fisher, Vardis Alvero (1895-1968)
CSC 27 CSF 73 ES1 171 SFE
223 SF1 188 SF2 899-900
Fishman, Robert. BAA 176
Fisk, Nicholas (1923-) AOW 318
ES1 171 FFR 77 IAC 114 SF1
188 SF2 900
Fiske, Amos Kidder (1842-1921)
BAA 44 CSF 73 SF1 188
Fiske, John. ACC 56, 65 AOW
43 EXT 1/1 3 EXT 5/2 38
Fison, Peter. EXT 1/2 31
Fissori, Valerio. BAA 220
Fitch, Anna Mariska. BAA 33
CSF 73 SF1 188
Fitch, Thomas. BAA 33 CSF 73
SF1 188
Fitschen, Marilyn. FFC 185
Fitshardinge, Joan see Joan
Phipson
Fitz Gerald, Gregory (1923-) IAC
114, 252 SF1 188 SF2 900
Fitzgerald. EXT 7/2 34
Fitzgerald. SFA 8
Fitzgerald, Ena. CSF 73 SF1 188
Fitzgerald, F. A. FFC 141
Fitzgerald, F. Scott (1896-1940)
ALW 107 CWD 56 CWN 31 ES1
171 ETN 110 FFR 77 IAC 114
ISW 128 NWO 21 SFS
FitzGerald, George F. MIH 109
Fitzgerald, James. IMS 10 WIF
134
Fitzgerald, M. FBK 60
Fitzgerald, Russell. IAC 114
Fitzgerald, Thomas P. TSP 197
Fitzgerald, Warren. SOT 103-4
SRB 89

Fitz-Gibbon, Ralph Edgerton
(1904?-) SFE 223 SF1 188
Fitzgibbon, Constantine (Robert
Louis) (1919-) BAA 134 BYS
256 ES1 171 HFI 56 IAC 114
SFE 223 SF1 188 SF2 900
Fitzhardinge, Joan Margaret
(1912-) SF2 1033 see also Joan
Phipson
Fitzhugh, George. RHN 157
Fitzpatrick, Bernard Edward
Barnaby (1849-1937) WGT 52
see also Lord Castletown
Fitzpatrick, E. D. IAC 114 SFS
47
Fitzpatrick, E. M. IAC 114 SFS
48
Fitzpatrick, Ernest Hugh. BAA
53 CSF 73 SF1 188 WGT 52
see also Hugo Barnaby
Fitzpatrick, R. C. IAC 114 SFS
48
Fitzporter, John L. BAA 44 SF1
188
Fiz, S. Marchan. BAA 220
Flach, Jacques. BAA 220
Flack, Isaac Harvey (1912-) WGT
52 see also Harvey Graham
Flack, Marjorie. FFC 118
Flackes, B. SF1 188
Flagg, Edmund (1815-90) SF1 582
Flagg, Francis pseud. of George
Henry Weiss (1898-1946) EXT
3/1 7 HFI 56 IAC 114 IMS 16,
24 RFA 9 SFE 223 SF1 188
SIH 189 SOT 107 STH 110 VES
148,179 WTS 32
Flagg, Ronald. TSP 131
Flammarion, Camille (1842-1925)
BAA 176 BYS 133 CSF 73-4
EXT 1/1 20 EXT 5/2 38,42,47
FFR 77 MSF 137,178,202-3,
220,251-3 SFE 223-4 SFH 158
SF1 189 SIH 9 SL3 1294-8 SL4
1592-5 SOT 9 VES 208 WAA
55,69,130
Flammenberg, Lawrence pseud.
of Karl Friedrich Kahlert. SF1
189
Flammenberg, Lorenz pseud. of
Karl Friedrich Kahlert. CSF 74
Flamsteed, John. FTF 23
Flanagan, Richard. HFI 56 SF1
189

Flanders, John pseud. of Jean
Ray. EXT 10/1 9 FBK 145 IAC
114 TSP 102 WTS 124
Flandrau, Macomb. FAN 186
Flanigan, Michael Cletus (1936-)
SF1 189
Flanner, Jack. SF1 189
Flashar, Hellmut. BAA 176
Flatau, Dorota. CSF 74 SF1 189
Flaubert, Gustave (1821-80) CAT
91-2 CSC 163 FL4 1891-4 HID
141 IAH 127 MFW 135 MIH 52
MSF 269 SF1 189 SOI 35 STF
47,58-9 TDI 4 TFC 163
Flechtheim, Ossip K. BAA 220
POE 291
Flechtner, Hans-Joachim. BAA
220
Fleckenstein, Alfred C. CSF 74
SF1 189
Flecker, James Elroy (1884-1915)
BAA 72 CSF 74 EXT 9/2 33
FTF 138,183,201 SF1 189
Flehr, Paul pseud. of Frederik
Pohl. IAC 115 SFS 48
Fleisher, Martin. BAA 176
Fleischer, Max (1888-) SF1 189
Fleischman, Sid. FFC 31,143-4
Fleischman, Theo (1893-) SF1 189
Fleming. IMS 239
Fleming, Andrew Magnus (1868-)
CSF 74 SF1 189
Fleming, Clifton. CSF 74
Fleming, Donald. MSF 224
Fleming, Ian (Lancaster) (1908-
64) ES1 171 FFC 144 JGB 38
SFE 225 STH 142 WAA 35
Fleming, Jiles Berry (1899-) CSF
74 SF1 189 SF2 900
Fleming, Joan Margaret. SF1
189
Fleming, Keith. CSF 74 SF1 189
Fleming, Linda. CAT 42
Fleming, May Agnes (1840-80)
CSF 74 SF1 189
Fleming, Robert Peter (1907-71)
CSF 74 IAC 115 SFE 225 SF1
189
Fleming, Roscoe. ES1 172
Fleming, Victor. WAA 90
Fleming-Roberts, G. T. TSP 15,
28,81,84,148,200,203-4
Fles, Barthold (1902-) ES1 172
IAC 115 SF2 900 SF1 189
Fletcher, Angus. CAT 68

Fletcher, David. FFC 25, 83
Fletcher, Edward Taylor. CSF 74
Fletcher, George U. pseud. of Fletcher Pratt. CSF 74 ISW 158 SRB 275 WIF 231 WSF 293
Fletcher, (Dr.) James. VFS 211
Fletcher, Joseph Smith (1863-1935) CSF 74 MSM 26 SF1 190 WGT 52
Fletcher, Lawrence. SF1 190
Flinders, Karl pseud. of Saul Milton. SF1 190
Flint, Homer Eon (1892?-1924) ALW 33, 113, 156, 160 AOW 69 BAA 86 BFP 190 BYS 170 ES1 172 HFI 56 IAC 115 ISW 22-5 LEX 313 MSM 90 RFA 1 RGS 64 SFE 225 SF1 190 SOT 49, 70, 72 SRB 313
Flint, Sam. CSF 74
Floethe, Richard. FFC 13, 93
Flood, Charles Bracelen (1929-) SF1 190 SF2 900
Flood, John Heber, Jr. (1863-) BAA 57 SF1 190
Flood, Leslie. IAC 115
Flood, R. C. S. B. EXT 10/1 28
Flora, James. FFC 19, 136
Flores, Angel (1900-) SF1 190
Florescano, Enrique. BAA 221
Florescu, Radu. AOW 355
Florez, Wenceslas Fernandez (1888?-) ES1 168 SF1 185
Flory, Claude R. BAA 176
Flournoy, Theodore. ISW 216
Flower, B(enjamin) O(range). BAA 163, 176, 221
Flowers, T. J. SF1 190
Floyd, Andress. BAA 79
Floyd, Calvin. SIH 129
Floyd, Gareth. FFC 63, 67, 161, 187
Flurscheim, Michael. BAA 55, 221
Flynn, Barbara. FFC 46
Flynn, Errol. CWD 41
Flynn, John T. BAA 221
Flynn, Thomas R. BAA 221
Flynn, William S. STH 135
Fogazzaro, Antonio. CSF 74
Fogg, Lawrence Daniel (1879-1914) CSF 74 SF1 190
Fogg, Walter E. BAA 221
Fogg, Walter L. BAA 176

Foht, Ivan. MSF 66
Foley, Charles (1861-) CSF 75 SF1 190
Foley, Dave. WGT 52 see also Gerald Hatch
Foley, George F., Jr. MSM 68-9
Foley, Joseph. BAA 221
Foley, Martha. ETN 41 IAH 128 MSM 104, 115-6 SFB 103 SOT 364
Foley, T. Raymond. STH 257
Folingsby, Kenneth. BAA 44 CSF 75 EXT 7/1 13 SF1 190
Folio, Fred. CSF 75
Follett, Barbara. FFC 13
Follett, James (1939-) SFE 226
Fon Eisen, Anthony T. (1911?-) SF1 190 SF2 901
Fontaine, Paul. BAA 221
Fontana, Dorothy C. HFI 56 SFE 226 SF1 190
Fontenay, Charles Louis (1917-) ES1 172 HFI 56 IAC 115 LEX 313-4 NDA 189-90 SFE 226 SFS 48 SF1 190 SF2 901
Foot, Michael Mackintosh (1913-) WGT 52 see also Cassius
Foote, John Taintor. CSF 75
Footman, David John (1895-) SF1 191
Foran, William Robert. CSF 75 WGT 52
Forberg, Ati. FFC 30
Forbes, Alexander (1882-) CSF 75 SF1 191
Forbes, Allyn B. BAA 221
Forbes, Archibald (1838-1900) SF1 191
Forbes, Brian. CSC 264
Forbes, Esther (1891-1967) CSF 75 SF1 191 SF2 901
Forbus, Ina. FFC 74
Forbush, Zebina. CSF 75
Ford, Charles Henri (1913-) CSF 75 ES1 172 SF1 191 SF2 902
Ford, Consuelo Urisarri (1903-) see Althea Urn
Ford, Corey. IAC 115
Ford, Don. WSF 209, 212
Ford, Douglas Morey BAA 69, 76 CSF 75 SF1 191 WGT 53
Ford, Ford Madox (1873-1939) BAA 77 CSF 75 CUA 52 EXT 9/2 38 WGT 53 see also Ford Madox Hueffer

Ford, Garret (house name) IAC 115 SFS 48 WGT 53 see also William L. Crawford
Ford, Gerald. COT 273 ETN 104 KVT 8 RHN 198
Ford, Henry. EXT 2/2 34-6 EXT 5/2 45 EXT 7/2 37 EXT 9/1 23 EXT 9/2 52-3 SFH 36 VFS 97
Ford, James Lauren (1854-1928) CSF 75 ES1 172
Ford, John J. ATA 60
Ford, Ken. SF1 191
Ford, T. Murray see Thomas Le Breton
Ford, Williston Merrick (1886-) see Williston Merrick
Fordelorrar, A. WTS 25
Foreman, Michael. FFC 3, 11, 18
Foreman, Russell. HFI 56
Forest, Jean-Claude. ES1 172 SFB 110 SIH 59
Forest, Salambo pseud. of Tina Bellini. SF1 191
Forester, C(ecil) S(cott) (1899-1966) ALW 216 AOW 102 CSF 75 ES1 172-3 FFC 154 FFR 80 FHT 16 ISW 119 SFE 227 SF1 191 SRB 14 WIF 22, 192
Forester, Elspeth Lascelles. CSF 75 SF1 191
Foriers, Paul. BAA 221
Forman, Harrison. EXT 2/1 11
Forman, Justus Miles. CSF 75
Forman, Milos. VFS 117
Formanek, Bob. IMS 214
Former Resident of the Hub, (A). pseud. of John Bachelder. CSF 75
Forrest, Aston. BAA 66 SF1 191
Forrest, Henry J. BAA 24
Forrest, Maryann. HFI 56 SF1 191
Forrester, Kent. RBY 240
Forrester, Mary. SF1 192
Forrest-Webb, Robert (1929-) SF1 192 SF2 902
Forst, S. FFC 98
Forster, E(dward) M(organ) (1879-1970) ACC 85, 214 ALW 99 AOW 288, 346 BAA 74 BYS 78, 190, 201 CAT 138 COT 214 CSC 162-3 CSF 75 ES1 173 ETN 98 EXT 1/2 37 EXT 2/2 25, 29 EXT 3/1 28 EXT 4/2 24 EXT 7/1 15 EXT 9/1 18, 22-3 EXT 9/2 39-41, 44, 46 FAN 4-5, 13, 20, 66, 82-3, 85-95, 97, 105, 109-11, 114, 126, 133, 147, 181, 184-5 FBK 66 FFR 80 FTF 102-3, 106 [FUT] IAC 115 INT 22, 28-9, 49, 79, 86-8, 91 KAU 101-5, 109, 118, 156 MFW 3, 23, 246 MSM 253 NDA 25-8, 37-8, 90, 157 NWO 125 OMN 189, 191 PST 133-4, 197, 199, 249, 262, 278, 308-10 SFB 90 SFD 274-5, 305, 307, 310, 317 SFE 227-8 SFS 48 SF1 192 SIH 93 SL3 1299-1303 SOI 112 SOT 40 VES 128, 167, 182, 261, 303 VFS 252 WSF 345 YTS 25
Forster, John. EXT 7/1 2, 15
Forsyth, Frederick. CSC 18-9
Fort, Agnes Hoy. STH 220
Fort, Anna Filing. STH 221-2
Fort, Charles (Hoy) (1874-1932) ALW 52, 136 ASF 259-60 CSC 14-5, 20, 95-6 ES1 173 EXT 1/2 30, 35 [FJT] RFA 22, 28, 31, 64, 162, 164 SFB 20 SFD 310 SFE 228 SFW 197 SOT 75-6, 133-5, 142-4 STH 218-29, 232-48 VES 333-5, 338, 340 VFS 172, 175 WFS 45 WSF 67, 391 WTS 11, 34, 43
Fort, Charles Nelson. STH 220
Fort, Clarence. STH 220, 234
Fort, John. FFC 118
Fort, Peter F. STH 221
Fort, Raymond. STH 220, 234-5
Fortey, Bryn. IAC 115
Forth, C. SF1 192
Fortnum, Peggy. FFC 23, 113
Fortune, Dion pseud. of Violet M. Firth. CSF 76 SF1 192 FL3 1375-7
Forward, Robert L. CSC 12-4, 20 WFS 262
Foss, Christopher (1946-) SFE 228 SRB 47, 51, 81 VES 74, 171, 289
Foster, Alan Dean (1946-) AAL 87 AOW 186 BFP 191-2 FFR 80 HFI 56 IAC 115 LEX 314-5 RGS 65, 215 SFE 228 SFW 200-1 SF1 192 SF2 902 WSF 314, 372
Foster, Bob. EXT 10/1 18
Foster, Clarence E. (1919-) ES1 173 SFE 228 SF1 192

Foster, David Skaats (1852-1920)
CSF 76 SF1 192
Foster, (Mrs.) E.M. WGT 53
see also E.M.F.
Foster, E.M. SF1 192
Foster, Elizabeth. FFC 101
NWO 280,293
Foster, George Cecil (1893-)
BAA 98 CSF 76 SFE 228 SF1
192 WGT 53 see also Seaforth
Foster, Hugh G. IAC 115
Foster, John. FFC 155
Foster, Lionel Brist. SF1 192
Foster, M(ichael) A(nthony) (1939-)
HFI 57 LEX 315-6 SFE 228-9
Foster, Malcolm. FFC 90
Foster, Phil. WFS 256
Foster, Reginald Francis (1896-1975) SF1 192
Foster, Robert (1949-) SF1 192
Foster, W(alter) Bert(ram) (1869-)
ALW 85 SFE 229
Foucault, Michel. AAL 183-5
MSF 131 TDI 7
Foulds, Elfrida Vipont Brown
(1902-) ES1 173 WGT 53
Fourier, Charles. BAA xi EXT
10/2 74 MSF 50-1,54,59,74,
95,102,119-21,124,138,140,
165,175,187,192,202,248 POE
55,73 SIH 68,76
Fourier, F.M.C. WAA 49
Fourier, Jean Baptiste Joseph.
SFH 133
Fournel, Victor. POE 136
Fournier, Alan. MSM 103
Foust, R.E. FL1 460-4,504-7
FL3 1052-6,1246-9 FL4 1754-6,2013-6
Foutque, Friedrich. SIH 18
Fowell, Frank. CSF 76
Fowler, Alastair. IAC 115
Fowler, Christopher. LTN 210
Fowler, Ellen Thorneycraft.
CSF 76
Fowler, George. ALW 43 BAA
17 CSF 76 KVT 28 LTN 134,
196 PST 22-3 SF1 193
Fowler, H.W. IAH 93 MIH 140
SFN 17
Fowler, Horace N. BAA 86
Fowler, John H. EXT 3/1 18
Fowler, Raymond, Jr. LTN 249
Fowler, Sidney pseud. of S.
Fowler Wright. CSF 76 STH 97

Fowles, John (1926-) CWN 47
ES1 173 FBK 153 SFD 82
Fox, David pseud. of Isabel Egenton Ostrander. SF1 193
Fox, Gardner F(ox) (1911-) ES1
173 FFR 80 HFI 57 IAC 115
LEX 316 SFE 230 SF1 193 SF2
902 WGT 53
Fox, Geoff. UKL 245
Fox, George Richard (1934-)
CWN 13 SF1 193 SF2 902
Fox, Leslie H. SF1 193
Fox, Marion I. CSF 76
Fox, (Lady) Mary. BAA 22 CSF
76 SF1 193
Fox, Matt. WTS 76,78,93
Fox, Nettie Pease. SF1 193
Fox, Paula. FFC 5,19,118
Fox, Richard A. BAA 91 SF1
193
Fox, Samuel Middleton (1856-)
SF1 193
Fox, Theodore. CSC 281
Fox, Vivian Carol. BAA 282
Fox, William. IAC 115
Fox, William McKinely. BAA
136
Fox-Davies, Arthur Charles
(1871-1928) CSF 76 SF1 193
Foxwell, H.S. BAA 221
Foyster, John. MIH 110-2
Fraenkel, Heinrich. BAA 176
Fraenkl, Gerd. EXT 8/2 63
Frame, Janet Paterson (1924-)
SF1 193 SF2 903 VES 262
Francastel, Pierre. BAA 176
France, Anatole pseud. of Jacques
Anatole Francois Thibault (1844-1924) ACC 147 CSF 76 ES1 174
EXT 3/2 49 FBK 116-7,119,154
FFR 80 FL3 1313-6 IAH 10
MSF 30,138,279 SFE 232 SF1
194 TJB 58
Frances, Stephen. SFE 232
Francesca, Piero Della. [FUT]
Franchezzo pseud. of A. Farnese.
CSF 76
Francis, Francis (-1941) CSF 76
SF1 194
Francis, H.G. (1936-) LEX 316-7
Francis, K. BAA 221
Francis, Lee (house name) VES
102 WGT 53-4 see also Howard
Browne
Francis, Marianne. SF1 194

Francis, Nigel. IAC 115
Francis, W. Nelson. AAL 31
Francke, Kuno. BAA 221
Franco, Francisco (1892-) ASF 276, 283 WFS 61, 63
Francoeur, Robert T. BAA 177, 221
Francois, Yves Regis. HFI 57
Francon, Marcel. BAA 221
Frane, Jeff. LTN 238 SRB 80
Frank, Alan G. SF1 194
Frank, Bernard. EXT 2/1 6-8
Frank, Bruno (1887-1945) CSF 76 ES1 174
Frank, Frederick S. FL1 211-6 FL4 2023-8 FL5 2126-31
Frank, Joseph (1916-) SF1 194 SF2 903
Frank, Mary. FFC 47
Frank, Pat pseud. of Harry Hart (1907-) ALW 146 AOW 186-7 BYS 284 COT 253 CSF 76 ES1 174 EXT 8/1 2 FFR 80 HFI 57 KAU 126 MSM 77 RAH 228 SFE 232 SFN 23, 40 SF1 194 SF2 903 SL1 38-42
Frank, Paul. FBK 144
Frank, Robert (1893-) BAA 103 SF1 194
Frank, S. L. BAA 222
Frank, Waldo David (1889-1967) CSF 76 SF1 194
Frankau, Gilbert (1884-1952) BAA 122 CSF 76 ES1 174 SFE 232 SF1 194
Frankau, Julia Davis (1864-1916) WGT 54 see also Frank Danby
Frankau, (Sydney) Pamela (1908-1967) BAA 121 ES1 174 SF1 194
Franke, Charlotte (1935-) LEX 317-8
Franke, Herbert W. (1927-) AOW 187 CSC 33 ES1 174 FFR 80 HFI 57 IAC 115 LEX 318-20 SFB 146 SFE 232-3 SF1 194 SIH 147 SL5 2538-42 SRB 124 VES 180 WSF 275
Franke, Jackie. VES 229
Frankel, Haskel. EXT 10/1 28
Frankenberg, Robert. FFC 14
Frankfort, H. A. KAU 185
Frankfort, Henri. EXT 9/1 5, 16 KAU 5 MFW 56
Frankfort, James. IAC 115

Frankish, H. CSF 77 SF1 194
Frankl, Viktor. CWN 54
Frankland, Edward. CSF 77
Franklin, Abraham Benjamin BAA 60-1
Franklin, Benjamin. CSC 208 FTF 26-7 VFS 213
Franklin, Donald. IAC 115
Franklin, Edgar pseud. of Edgar Franklin Stearns. AOW 42, 62 CSF 77 EXT 1/1 10 SFE 233 SF1 194
Franklin, Fabian. BAA 222
Franklin, Fredric. WFS 128
Franklin, H(oward) Bruce (1934-) ALW 7, 30-1, 54, 59-60 AOW 344 BAA 177, 222 BYS 45, 54 ES1 174 EXT 6/1 1 EXT 6/2 22-31 EXT 7/1 1 EXT 7/2 36, 48 EXT 10/1 1-2 EXT 10/2 69-115 FTF 8 IAC 115 ISW 283 JGB 51-2, 57, 60 KAU 227 NWO 19-20, 50, 62, 76, 167-8, 232, 249, 252, 273, 285, 290 OSR 199-203, 354 SFB 13 SFE 233 SFH 238 SF1 194 SF2 903 SRB 71, 500 TPS 96-99 TSF 246 VF2 82-105, 200-1, 208 WSF 265, 269-70
Franklin, Jay pseud. of John Franklin Carter. HFI 57 SF1 195
Franklin, John Hope. BAA 222
Franko, Ivan. FFC 5, 118
Franson, Donald Lewis (1916-) AOW 361 SF1 195 SF2 903 SRB 65, 130
Franthway, Burke. IAC 115
Frascino, Edward. FFC 127
Fraser, Anthea (1930-) SF1 195
Fraser, Betty. FFC 153
Fraser, Helen. ES1 175
Fraser, (Mrs.) Hugh. CSF 77
Fraser, J. T. ES1 175
Fraser, Joseph. BAA 40
Fraser, Phyllis Maurine (1915-) CSF 211 ES1 175 EXT 3/1 20 EXT 5/1 9 SF1 195
Fraser, (Sir) Ronald Arthur (1888-1974) CSF 77 ES1 175 SFE 233-4 SF1 195
Fraser, William. ES1 175
Fraser, William Alexander (1859-1933) SF1 195
Frater Viii. SF1 195

Frayn, Michael J. (1933-) BAA
146,157 BYS 257 ES1 175 FFR
80 HFI 58 SFE 234 SF1 195
SF2 904 SIH 93
Frazar, Douglas (1836-96) SF1
195
Frazee, Charles Stephen (1909-)
ES1 175 HFI 58 SF1 195 SF2
904 WGT 54
Frazer, G. S. EXT 9/2 59
Frazer, (Sir) James George (1854-
1941) IAH 53, 74 KAU 194 MFW
63 MIH 137 PJF 14,17,25 RZY
23,33,35,37,39 SFH 165 WBW
59
Frazer, James Ian Arbuthnot.
BAA 103 see also Shamus Frazer
Frazer, R. A. H. EXT 6/1 13,16
Frazer, Shamus pseud. of James
Ian Arbuthnot Frazer (1912-)
CSF 77 SF1 195
Frazetta, Frank (1928-) CWD 15
ES1 175 FRN 10 SFE 234 VES
97,326 WTS 69
Frazier, Neta. FFC 74
Frazier, Robert. LTN 238
Freas, Frank Kelly (1922-) BYS
223 ES1 175 FBK 53 KAU 228
RFA 186,202,204-6,208-11,214-
5 SFE 234-5 VES 76-7,98,104,
122,167,182-3,289,291 WSF
215,224,282 WTS 78
Frederic, George pseud. of
Charles Nuetzel. IAC 115
Frederic, Harold. EXT 4/1 10
Fredericks, S. C. MFW 16 SL3
1031-5 SL5 2190-4 SRB 500
Fredrick, Otto. SF1 195
Free, Colin (1925-) DTS 50 HFI
58 IAC 115 SFS 48 SF1 195
Freedman, Nancy (1920-) HFI 58
SFE 235 SF1 195 SF2 904
Freedman, Russell Bruce (1929-)
ES1 175 SF1 195 SF2 904
Freehafer, Paul. IMS 33,138
Freeman, Barbara. FFC 31,54,
100,163
Freeman, Don. FFC 10,131
Freeman, Gwendolen. EXT 10/1
28
Freeman, Jerry. EXT 10/2 108
Freeman, Kathleen (1897-1959)
SF1 195
Freeman, Mary E. Wilkins. CSF
77 SOT 305

Freeman, R(ichard) Austin (1862-
1943) ASF 319 CSF 77 IAC 115
PST 31,118 SFA 259-60 SFW
76 STH 123,141 WGT 54
Freeman, Robert Massie (1866-)
CSF 77 SF1 196
Freeman, T. R. FFC 172
Freese, Stanley. BAA 98
Frei, Bruno. BAA 177
Freksa, Friedrich (1882-1955)
ES1 175 LEX 320-1 SL2 639-43
Freman, Edward L. IAC 115
Fremlin, Celia Margaret pseud.
of Celia Fremlin Goller (1914-)
IAC 115 SF1 196
French, Alice (1850-1934) ES1
175 WGT 54
French, (Sir) John. POE 193
French, Joseph Lewis (1858-1936)
CSF 77 ES1 175-6 SF1 196 STH
239
French, Paul pseud. of Isaac
Asimov. ALW 169,185 SFA 185
TJB 46 WSF 203
Frenkel, James. IAC 115
Frenzel, Ivo. BAA 222
Frere, John H. IAC 115
Freschet, Bernice. FFC 119
Freschet, Gina. FFC 119
Fresco, Jacque. BAA 149
Fresco, Robert. KAU 189
Fretland, Donald John. HFI 58
SF1 196
Freud, Sigmund (1856-1939) AAL
142 ACC 103,105,128,130,139
CAT 9 COT 53,104-5,156,158,
163 CUA 36 CWN 17,37,54
ETN 84 EXT 1/1 16 EXT 2/2
35,37 EXT 7/1 21 EXT 7/2 32,
34,37 EXT 9/1 23 EXT 10/1 10
FBK 7,67 FHT 23-4,29 FLT 7-
11,32,36-7,41,49-51,55,57,71-
2,74,79-80,96,130-51 FTF 100
IAH 74 INT 111-2 ISW 164,265
JGB 6,35,58,60 KAU 20 LTN
34,63,81,84,94,149-50 MFW
185-8,252,255 MIH 45 MSF 134
MSM 238,245 NDA 56 PJF 17,
30-2,51,68 RAH 95,97-8 RBY
65,88,114 RHN 170,185,193,197
RZY 9,14 SFB 118,149 SFH 184
STH 2,132-3 TJB 37 TRB 62
VMW 38 WBW 3-4,15,32-3,51
Freudenthal, Elisabeth. SF1 196
Freund, Julien. BAA 222

Freund, Michael. BAA 222
Frew, John. RFA 60
Frewer, Glyn (1931-) SF1 196
SF2 904-5
Frewin, Anthony (1947-) AOW 344
SFE 235 SF1 196
Frey, (Mr.). VFS 234-6
Frey, Alexander Moritz. FBK 142
Freyer, Dermot J. SF1 196
Freyer, Erick pseud. of Frederick
Shroyer. IMS 123,162
Freyer, Hans. BAA 177,222
Friborg, Albert Compton. IAC
115 SFS 48
Fried, Jerome. STF 267
Friedan. LTN 161
Friedberg, Gertrude (1908-) AOW
187 ES1 176 HFI 58 IAC 115
LEX 321 SFE 235 SFS 48 SF1
196 SF2 905
Friedberg, Morris. BAA 177
Friede, Donald. STH 267
Friedell, Egon (1878-1938) HFI 58
LEX 321 SFE 235 SF1 196
Friedli, Emilie Ida (1889-) see
Lily Van Ith
Friedman, Bruce Jay. ES1 176
IAC 116 SFS 48
Friedman, Favius Louis. SF1 196
Friedman, Jerrold David (1944-)
BFP 193-4 SF2 911-2 WGT 54
see also David Gerrold
Friedman, Marvin. FFC 140
Friedman, Stuart. IAC 116 SFS
48
Friedrich II. MSF 38
Friedrich, Bruno. BAA 222
Friedrich, Caspar David. MFW
21
Friedrich, Gerhard. BAA 177
Friedrich, Herbert (1926-) LEX
321-2
Friedrich, Otto. BAA 222 FFC
54
Friedrich, Priscilla. FFC 54
Friel, Arthur Olney (1885-1959)
CSF 77 HFI 58 SF1 196
Friend, Beverly. AAL 3,105,123
AOW 365 BAA 222 FL2 561-5
FL3 1034-6 KAU 234 PJF 40
SF1 196 SL1 113-9 SL2 766-9
SL3 1317-22 SL4 1805-8 SRB
464 VF1 153-66, 275-6, 282
Friend, Oscar J(erome) (1897-
1963) AOW 107 ES1 176 HFI 58

IAC 116,171 ISW 131 SFA 77
SFE 235 SFS 48 SF1 197 SF2
905 SOT 164 STH 156-7 WGT
54 WSF 119-20 see also Owen
F. Jerome
Friers, Rowel. FFC 76
Frierson, Meade, III (1940-) SF1
197 SF2 905-6
Frierson, Penny. SF1 197
Friggens, Arthur Henry (1920-)
SF1 197 SF2 906
Frings, Ketti. CSF 77 SF1 197
Frisbie, Henry Samuel. BAA 64
CSF 77
Frisch, O. R. IAC 116 SFS 48
Fritch, Charles E. ES1 176 HFI
58 IAC 116 IAH 9-10,13, 92
SFE 235 SFS 48 SF1 197 SOT
366
Frith, Uta. IAC 116
Fritz, Jean Guttery (1915-) FFC
74 SF1 582
Froelich, J. C. BAA 222
Froeschel, Georg. CSF 77
Froman, Elizabeth. FFC 193
Frome, Nils H. IMS 64-6,111,
145,200
Fromm, Erich. ASF 278 BAA
222 FTF 129 NDA 89,199 RBY
195-6
Fromm, Lilo. FFC 157
Frost, Brian J. SF1 197
Frost, Conrad. ES1 176
Frost, Frances Mary (1905-59)
FFC 100 SF1 197
Frost, Kelman Dalgety. SF1 197
Frost, Nemi. IAC 116
Frost, Robert (1875-) ASF 305
COT 109-10 ETN 119 FTF 196
IAC 116 RBY 18, 68-9
Frost, Thomas. CSF 77
Frost, Walter A. CSF 78
Froud, Brian. FFC 179
Froude, James Anthony (1818-94)
WTS 51
Fruch, A. IAC 116
Frueh, Alfred Joseph. SF1 197
Fruhauf, Klaus (1933-) LEX 322
Frumkin, R. M. BAA 224
Fry, H. R. SF1 197
Fry, Lena Jane. BAA 68
Fry, Nicholas. SF1 197
Fry, Roger. CAT 73
Fry, Rosalie. FFC 95,106,109

Frye, Northrop. AOW 8 BAA 222 CAT xv, 49-50, 54 FAN 174 INT 113 JGB 16 KAU 88 KVT 8 LTN 81 MFW 59, 63 MSF 12, 16, 18, 26, 31-5, 46-7, 49, 51, 54-5, 60, 147 NWO 4, 10-1, 16, 28, 43, 77-8, 87, 93, 100, 102, 113-4 RAH 196, 227, 229 RZY 16 SOI 100-1, 142 SRB 500 TDI 9 TSO 8 UKL 123 WBW 3-4
Frye, Vern D. (1931-) see Vern Dermott
Fryers, Austin pseud. of William Edward Clery. CSF 78 SF1 197
Fuchs, Ernst. ACC 128
Fuchs, Klaus. MSM 226
Fuchs, Walter R. (1937-78) FFR 80 LEX 322-3
Fuchs, Wolfgang. SFH 240
Fuentes, Carlos. FBK 135-6
Fuentes, Roberto (1934-) SF1 197-8
Fueyo, Jesus. BAA 222
Fugitive, (A) pseud. of Edward D. Coxe. CSF 78
Fuhrmann, Rainer (1940-) LEX 323
Fulford, William. WBW 5
Fuller, (Lt.) Alvarado M. (1851-) AOW 62 BAA 41 CSF 78 EXT 1/1 11 MSM 144, 148 SFE 235 SF1 198
Fuller, Anne (-1790) CSF 78 SF1 198
Fuller, Buckminster. BAA 177 CSC 64, 68 [FUT] IAC 116 KAU 59 VFS 64, 100 YTS 54-5, 67-9, 72, 94
Fuller, Edmund. EXT 8/1 1 EXT 10/1 24-5, 28, 31, 37
Fuller, Frederick T. BAA 94 CSF 78 SF1 198
Fuller, Ira C. SF1 198
Fuller, J. F. C. POE 240
Fuller, John G. ES1 176-7
Fuller, Lois Hamilton (1915-) SF1 198 SF2 906
Fuller, Mary Breese. BAA 222
Fuller, Ralph. BAA 112

Fuller, Sam(uel Michael) (1911-) CSC 264 SF1 198
Fullerton, John Charles Mark (1924-) ES1 177 SF1 198
Fulthorpe, Douglas. IAC 116
Fulton, James A. BAA 80
Fulton, Robert. ASF 186 SFH 197
Fulweiler, Howard Wells. BAA 282
Fumento, Rocco (1923-) ES1 177
Funaro, Sergio F. (1922-) SF1 198
Funk, Howard. IMS 34, 239
Funk, Richard (1926-) LEX 323
Funnell, Augustine. HFI 58
Fuqua, Robert. SRB 36 TRB 60 VES 176-7, 287-8, 338-9 VFS 211, 229-30, 237, 239 WSF 114
Furbank, P. N. EXT 6/1 19
Furman, Abraham Loew (1902-) CSF 78 ES1 177 IAC 116 SF1 198
Furnas, J(oseph) C(hamberlain) (1905-) IAC 116 SFS 48 SF1 198
Furnell, John. SF1 198
Furnill, John. CSF 78 SF1 198
Furniss, Harry. FBK 109
Furter, Pierre. BAA 177, 222
Furukawa, Mel. FFC 60
Fuseli, John. RBY 169
Fuson, Ben W. BAA 222 EXT 5/2 31-6 EXT 10/1 3 OSR 282-8, 355
Futrelle, Jacques (1875-1912) AOW 62 CSF 78 EXT 1/1 11 SFE 236 SF1 198 SRB 10 STH 123, 232
Future, Steve. SF1 198
Fussell, Edwin. NWO 282-3
Fuz, Jerzy Konstanty. BAA 177
Fyfe, H(orace) B(rowne, Jr.) (1918-) AAL 120 ALW 161 BYS 37 ES1 177-8 FFR 80 HFI 58 IAC 116 RFA 164 SFE 238 SFS 48-9 SF1 198 SF2 906 WGT 54 WIF 91, 146 WSF 97
Fyfe, W. H. BAA 222
Fyne, Neal. CSF 78 SF1 198
Fysh. SF1 198
Fytche, M. Amelia. CSF 78

G

G. H. P. pseud. of George H. Putnam. CSF 78

G. P. BAA 251

Gaar, Alice Carol. RAH 64-82 RHN 178, 197

Gabbard, G. N. IAC 116

Gabor, Dennis. FTF 81-2 POE 315 SFH 241 VFS 94, 99, 253

Gabriel, Claire. IAC 116

Gabriel, Francois pseud. of Francisco Cabral. CSF 78

Gaddis, Vincent H. (1913-) AAL 63 ES1 178 SRB 500 VES 335, 339-40

Gade, Henry (house name) VES 160 WGT 55 see also Raymond A. Palmer

Gagarin, Yuri. COT 50 LTN 106 VFS 10

Gage, Wilson. FFC 64 see also Mary Q. Steele

Gahr, Robert. IMS 34

Gail, Otto Willi (1896-1956) COT 38-9, 119 CSF 78 ES1 178 FFR 81 LEX 324-5 SFE 238 SF1 199 SL5 2070-4 SOT 171 VES 71 WSF 50, 389, 391

Gaillard, Stephen. CSF 78 SF1 199

Gaines, Audrey. SF1 199

Gaines, M. C. SOT 113-4

Gaines, William M. ES1 178

Gainess, Arthur A. SF1 199

Gakov, Vl. SL2 756-60, 776-81, 950-5 SL3 1188-92 SL4 1548-54, 1934-8, 2019-22 SL5 2117-21

Galbraith, Alexander (1924-) ES1 178 WGT 55

Galbraith, John Kenneth (1908-) SF1 199 SF2 906

Galbreath, Robert. EXT 9/2 61-2

Galdone, Paul. FFC 62, 64, 71, 126, 135, 150

Gale, E. F. see John Falkner

Gale, Floyd C. ISW vi PJF 73 RSG 10

Gale, Oliver Marble (1877-) SF1 199

Gale, Zona (1874-1938) CSF 78 SF1 199

Galier, W. H. BAA 55 CSF 78

Galileo. ASF 149 CAT 73 CYR 12, 33 EXT 9/1 20 FSU 55 FTF 18-9, 21, 24 IAH 62 IMS 1 INT 13 KAU 63, 213, 233 MFW 193 MSF 6, 9, 103-4 SFB 71 SFH 42, 46, 119, 161 STF 36 VFS 43-4, 148, 190-1, 194

Gall, Alice. FFC 132

Gallagher, Buell G. BAA 177

Gallagher, Edward J. RBY 55-82

Gallagher, John. IAC 117 SFS 49

Gallagher, Ligeia. BAA 177 WAA 242, 245

Gallagher, Red. STH 153

Galland, Antoine. FBK 20 WIF 40

Gallant, Joseph (1907-57) ES1 178 IAC 117 SFS 49 SF1 199

Gallant, Roy (1924-) ES1 178

Galle. EXT 5/2 37

Gallego, Serapio Gonzalez (1883-1944) BAA 112 CSF 78 SF1 215

Gallery, Daniel V. (1901-) IAC 117 SF1 199

Gallet, Georges Hilaire (1902-) ES1 178 IAC 117 WFS 99

Gallico, Paul (William) (1897-1976) ES1 178-9 EXT 8/1 6 FFC 119 HFI 59 IAC 117 SFE 241 SF1 199, 582 SF2 907

Gallimore, F. A. CSF 78
Gallion, Jane. SF1 199
Gallishaw, John. CSC 202, 210
OWB 46
Gallizier, Nathan (1866-1927)
CSF 79 SF1 200
Gallon, Tom (1866-1914) SF1 200
Galloway, James M. BAA 57
CSF 79 SF1 200 WGT 55 see
also Anon Moore
Gallun, Raymond Z(inke) (1910-)
AAL 93-5 ALW 141 COT 42,
44, 73 CSF 155 ES1 179 EXT
5/1 3 FFR 82 HFI 59 IAC 117
IAH 45 IMS 24, 75, 77 ISW 70-
3, 133, 177, 274-5 LEX 325 RFA
30, 32, 36, 56-7 RGS 65-6 SFD
213, 240, 318 SFE 241-2 SFS
49-50 SF1 200 SF2 907 SOT
173 VES 80, 104, 163, 185, 199,
317 WGT 55 WIF 89 WSF 50,
68, 92, 125, 388 see also
Arthur Allport, Dow Elstar
Gallup, Dick. IAC 117
Galouye, Daniel F(rancis) (1920-
76) ALW 60, 212, 219 AOW 187
BFP 195 BYS 262 ES1 179
EXT 6/2 51 FFR 82 HFI 59
IAC 117 KAU 84, 128, 184 LEX
325-7 SFE 242 SFS 50 SF1 200
SF2 907-8 SL1 474-9 SRB 335
UFS 3 VES 174 WGT 55
Galpin, Alfred. EXT 3/1 9, 17-8
Galpin, J. A. see Valerius D.
Blackstone
Galsworthy, John (1867-1933)
CSF 79 ES1 179 FAN 12 WGT
55
Galt, John (1779-1839) CSF 79
SF1 200
Galvani, Luigi. ASF 106, 182-3
KAU 6
Gamini. VFS 22
Gammell, Stephen. FFC 93
Gammon, David J. SF1 200
Gamon, Richard B. SF1 200
Gamow, George Antony (1904-68)
CSF 79 ES1 179-80 IAC 117
SFE 243 SFH 241 SFS 50 SF1
200
Gamwell, (Mrs.) Phillips. EXT
3/1 5, 14
Gandhi, Indira. LTN 168 VFS 38
Gandhi, Mohandas. MFW 80
Gandon, Yves (1899-) CSF 79 ES1
180 SFE 243 SF1 200 STH 65-6

Ganley, W. Paul. FLR 60 WGT
55 see also Toby Duane
Gann, Ernest. CSC 25-6
Gann, William D. (1878-1955) CSF
79 SF1 200
Gannett, Ruth. FFC 80, 88
Ganpat pseud. of Martin Louis
Alan Gompertz. AOW 102 CSF
79 SFE 243 SF1 200-1
Gansovsky, Sever F. (1918-) IAC
117 LEX 327-8 SFB 122
Ganthony, Richard. SF1 201
Gantz, Kenneth F(ranklin) (1905-)
ES1 180 HFI 59 KAU 191 SFE
243 SF1 201
Garagnon, Jean. BAA 223
Garavaglia, Gian-Paolo. BAA 223
Garbo, Norman (1919-) AOW 187
SFE 243 SF1 201 SF2 908
Garby, (Mrs.) Lee Hawkins
(1890-) ALW 132 CSF 181 EXT
3/1 28 OWB 77, 83 PST 130-1,
194, 207, 210, 217, 220-1, 227, 236,
240, 243, 245, 265, 268, 289, 292
RFA 26 SFE 243 SF1 201 SOT
14-5 SRB 303 WSF 45
Gard, Joyce. FFC 109, 193 SF1
201
Gardener, Helen H. CSF 79
Gardner, Alan. ES1 180
Gardner, B. T. AAL 57
Gardner, Celia E. (1844-) CSF 79
SF1 201
Gardner, David S. VES 74
Gardner, E. D. WGT 55
Gardner, Erle Stanley (1889-1970)
ES1 180 FFR 83 IAC 117 PST
184-5 STH 146-8 TSP 4, 216
WGT 55
Gardner, Gerald B(rosseau) (1884-)
ES1 180 see also Scrire O. T. O.
4-7
Gardner, Gerald C. SF1 201
Gardner, John Champlin (1933-)
AOW 188 FFC 19-20 FL2 675-
9 HFI 59 MFW 58-9 SFE 243-
4 SF1 201 SIH 118
Gardner, Martin (1914-) AOW xx
ES1 180 EXT 7/2 47 FBK 114
IAC 117 SFE 244 SFH 176 SFS
50 WFS 262
Gardner, Matt. SF1 201
Gardner, Maurice Benjamin (1905-)
ES1 180 SF1 201 SF2 908
Gardner, Nellie E. STH 137
Gardner, R. A. AAL 57

Gardner, Richard. HFI 59
Gardner, Thomas D. ALW 141
COT 172,179
Gardner, Thomas H. STH 79-80
Gardner, Thomas Samuel (1908-
63) BAA 164 ES1 180 IAC 117
IMS 33, 45, 159, 170, 182, 185, 187,
197, 199-200 SFE 244 SOT 134,
327, 398
Garfield, Leon (1921-) FFC 20, 31
SF1 201 SF2 908-9
Garforth, John. SF1 201
Gargillis, Stephen. SF1 201
Garin, Eugenio. BAA 223
Garis, Cleo. STH 167
Garis, Howard Roger (1873-1962)
CSF 79 ES1 180 IAC 117 SFE
244 SF1 201-2 STH 2, 161-2,
167-70, 173-4 WGT 55-6 see
also Victor Appleton
Garis, Lilian. STH 161, 167
Garis, Roger. STH 167, 170
Garis, Simeon. STH 167
Garland, Hamlin (1860-1940) CSF
79 EXT 1/1 11 EXT 4/1 9-10
SF1 203 WTS 3
Garland, Judy. FBK 113
Garland, Rufus Cummins. SF1 203
Garner, Alan (1934-) AOW 318
ES1 180 FBK 115 FFC 38, 175
FL1 472-4 FL3 1188-90 FL5
2087-9 HFI 59 LTN 262 SFE
244 SF1 203 SRB 23-4, 260
Garner, Charles see Stuart Cum-
berland
Garner, Graham. SF1 203
Garner, R. L. SFW 63
Garner, William (1920-) SF1 203
SF2 909
Garnet, G. pseud. of Irvin Ash-
kenazy. WTS 41
Garnet, William. HFI 59 IAC
117 SF1 203
Garnett, David (1892-1981) CSF
79 ES1 180-1 EXT 2/2 30 EXT
8/1 5 FBK 53 FFC 54 FL2
863-6 SFE 244 SF1 203 SF2
909
Garnett, David S. (1947-) HFI 59
IAC 117 LEX 328 SFE 244-5
SF1 203 SF2 909
Garnett, Edward William (1868-
1937) CSF 80 ES1 181 SF1 203
Garnett, Richard (1835-1906) CSF
80 ES1 181 FL4 1986-8 IAC
117 SFE 245 SF1 203

Garnier, Charles George Thomas
BAA 177 SIH 9
Garnier, Tony. POE 174
Garou, Loup pseud. of Wallace
West. WTS 53
Garratt, Evelyn R. CSF 80 NWO
124 SF1 203
Garraty, Gail. LTN 57
Garrett, Charles Walter (1873-)
SF1 203
Garrett, David. AOW 270
Garrett, Eileen Jeanette Lyttle
(1893-) ES1 181 WGT 56
Garrett, Garet (1878-1954) CSF
80 SF1 203
Garrett, George Palmer (1929-)
SF1 203
Garrett, John Charles. BAA 177
Garrett, Randall (1927-) ALW 212
AOW 188, 236 ASF 148 BFP 196
ES1 181-2 ETN 1, 65, 68 FFR 83
FL2 894-6 HFI 59-60 IAC 117-8
IAH 29-30, 84-7, 120, 124-5, 129
ISW ix, 126 LEX 328-9 MFW
230 MIH 17, 119 RFA 196, 207-
11 RGS 66 RSG 10, 14 SFD 133
SFE 245 SFS 50, 107 SFW 505
SF1 203-4 SRB 260 VES 112,
123, 207, 235 WGT 56 WSF 172
see also Alexander Blade, Wal-
ter Bupp, Ralph Burke, David
Gordon, Richard Greer, Ivar
Jorgensen, Darrel T. Langart,
Seaton McKettrig, Clyde Mit-
chell, Mark Phillips, Robert
Randall, Leonard G. Spencer,
S. M. Tenneshaw, Gerald Vance
Garrett, William A. (1890-1967)
CSF 80 SF1 204
Garrison, Charles M. ES1 182
WGT 56 see also Charles
MacDaniel
Garrison, Wendell Phillips (1840-
1907) CSF 80 SF1 204
Garron, Marco. SF1 204
Garson, Clee (house name) SFE
245 WGT 56
Garson, Gary Paul (1946-) HFI
60 SFE 245 SF1 204 SF2 909
Garson, Vaseleos. SF1 204
Garth, Will (house name) CSF 80
HFI 60 SFE 245 VES 141 WGT
56-7 see also Henry Kuttner
Gartmann, Heinz (1917-60) ES1
182 WGT 57

Gernsback, Hugo (cont.)
20, 25, 27, 41, 68, 91, 119-21, 135,
141, 174-5, 191, 251, 253, 260, 268,
275, 280, 283 CSC 46, 55, 168
CSF 81 ES1 184-5 ETN 7, 11-3,
26, 30, 39, 82, 174 EXT 1/1 2, 11
EXT 1/2 31 EXT 3/1 28 EXT
4/2 25 EXT 5/1 3, 5-7, 15-6, 16a
EXT 7/1 25 EXT 7/2 35, 38-9,
41 EXT 8/1 17 EXT 8/2 31, 58
EXT 10/1 3-4 EXT 10/2 107, 114
FAN 7, 12, 152 FTF 65-8, 70, 76
HFI 61 HID 3 HWK 7 IAC 118
IAH 46 IMS 4-6, 10-1, 17-8, 32,
37, 40-1, 49, 52-4, 65, 159, 169,
205 ISW 35, 160-1, 283-4 KAU
17, 28, 45, 86-7, 89 LEX 331-2
MFW 282, 285 MIH 118-9 MSF
23, 65, 163, 204-5, 267, 282 MSM
xiii, 24, 29-33, 168-71, 297-8, 304
NWO ix, 50 OMN 1, 43 OWB 37
POE 243-5 RBY 83-4 RFA 1-2,
31, 63, 129, 203 RGS 67-8 SFB
9-10, 12, 42-3, 62, 152 SFD 3, 9,
12, 19-30, 63, 72, 74, 83, 134, 142,
208, 235, 239-40, 243, 276 SFE
252 SFH 36-41, 46, 107 SFN 79,
81, 106 SFS 50 SFW 6, 101, 119-
20, 126, 133-4, 140-1, 152, 181
SF1 207 SIH 9, 12, 41, 44, 54, 56,
76, 187, 189-91, 201 SL4 1751-4
SOT 10, 32, 37, 43, 75-6, 88-9,
102, 104, 109, 128, 158, 270, 357,
402, 409, 415 SRB 8, 10-2, 88,
501 STH 44, 137-44, 148-50,
154, 165, 172, 228, 237, 265 TJB
3 TRB 54, 56, 58 TSF 11, 29,
34, 36 TSP 150 VES 70, 102-3,
106, 128, 135, 155, 157, 159, 181,
205, 274-5, 279, 286-7, 305 WAA
8, 16-8, 21, 45, 200-5, 217, 219,
239 WFS 18-20, 22, 33, 35, 37-8,
45-6, 51, 84-5 WGT 57 WIF 69,
84, 116, 134, 140, 294 WSF 31-5,
39, 43-7, 49-51, 53, 64-6, 71, 73,
78-80, 123, 211, 216-7, 343 WTS
53-4 YTS 6-7, 9-10, 115 see
also I. M. Alier
Gernsheim, Helmut. FBK 108
Gerould, Katharine. CSF 81
Gerrard, Edith C. CSF 81
Gerrare, Wirt pseud. of William
Oliver Greener. CSF 81 SF1
207
Gerrold, David pseud. of Jerrold
David Friedman. AAL 122-3
ALW 212 AOW 189, 287 BYS
304 FFR 84 [FJT] HFI 61
IAC 118 KAU 175, 204 LEX
332-3 MFW 86-7, 230 RGS 68-
9 SFD 240 SFE 252-3 SFH 106
SF1 207 SL3 1333-9 SL5 2455-
8 SRB 357 SV3 19-32 VES 151,
184, 217, 230 WSF 237
Gerson, Noel Bertram (1914-)
HFI 61 SF1 207
Gerson, Villiers. ISW vi SOT 84
Gerstaecker, Friedrich (1816-72)
CSF 81 SF1 207
Gerstenfeld, Virginia. HID 7, 185
HWK 6
Gervais, Albert (1892-) SF1 207
Gervais, Edward. IMS 37-8, 94
Gervee, Baronte. WGT 57 see
also Gerve Baronte
Geston, Mark S. (1946-) AOW 189
BAA 143 BFP 199 BYS 304 ES1
185 HFI 61 LEX 333-4 RGS 69
SFE 253 SF1 207 SF2 912 SL3
1261-4
Gettman, Royal A. EXT 8/2 56
Getty, J. Paul. LTN 43-4
Ghent, W. J. BAA 224
Gheoghiu, Virgil. EXT 2/2 27
Ghidalia, Roberta. IAC 118
Ghidalia, Vic(tor Simon) (1926-)
IAC 109, 118 SF1 207-8 SF2 912
Ghose, Zulfikar (1935-) ES1 185
EXT 6/1 12 SFE 253
Ghosh, Sarath Kumar (1883-) CSF
81 SF1 208
Giachino, Enzo. BAA 224
Giamatti, A. Bartlett. BAA 178
Giannattasio, Gerard. IAC 118
Giannini, Alessandro. BAA 224
Giard, Luce. BAA 224
Gibaud, Henri. BAA 224
Gibb, Jocelyn. SOI 160
Gibbard, T. S. J. SF1 208
Gibbon, Edward (1737-94) COT
246 ISW 223 SOT 258 TJB 24
WAA 129 WBW 48
Gibbon, Perceval (1879-1926) ES1
185
Gibbons, Charles Harrison (1869-)
CSF 81 SF1 208
Gibbons, Cromwell (1893-) CSF
81 SF1 208
Gibbons, Floyd Phillip (1886-1939)

Gibbons, Floyd Phillip (cont.)
AOW 92,103 CSF 81 MSM 149-
50 SFE 253 SF1 208 SRB 294
Gibbons, Gavin (1922-) ES1 185
SF1 208
Gibbons, Robert. SF1 208
Gibbs, Angelica. EXT 1/2 31
WIF 19
Gibbs, Anthony (1902-) CSF 81
SF1 208 SF2 912
Gibbs, Barbara. BAA 161,224
Gibbs, George Fort (1870-1942)
SF1 208
Gibbs, Henry St. John. ES1 185
SF1 208 SF2 912-3
Gibbs, Lewis pseud. of Walter
Cove (1871-) CSF 81 SFE 253
SF1 208
Gibbs, (Sir) Philip Hamilton (1877-
1962) CSF 81 ES1 185 POE 240
SF1 209
Gibbs, Wolcott. IAH 126
Giberga, Ovidio see Dr. Coggs
Gibran, Kahlil (1883-1931) SF1 209
Gibson, Amanda Melvina Thorley.
WGT 57
Gibson, Colin. SFE 253
Gibson, Edmund H. SF1 209
Gibson, Floyd. SF1 209
Gibson, Joe. WGT 58
Gibson, Katharine. FFC 54
Gibson, L. S. CSF 81
Gibson, Marice Louise (1884-)
see Maryse Rutledge
Gibson, R. W. BAA xx,224 EXT
8/1 24
Gibson, (Mrs.) Walter B. WGT
58
Gibson, Walter Brown (1897-) ES1
185-6 FL3 1380-3 IAC 118
SFS 50 SF1 209 TSP 86 WGT
58 see also Maxwell Grant
Gibson, William Curtis (1857-)
SF1 209
Giddy, Eric Cawood Gwyddn
(1895-) WGT 58
Gide, Andre (1869-1951) CWN 37
SF1 209
Giedion, Siegfried. KAU 12
Gieske, Herman Everett (1892?-
1954) BAA 109 CSF 81 SF2 209
Giesy, John Ulrich (1877-1948)
ALW 113 AOW 36 BYS 170
CSF 81 ES1 186 HFI 61 IAC
118 RFA 1 SFE 253 SF1 209
SOT 49 WSF 28

Giffard, Hardinge Goulburn (1880-
1943) WGT 58 see also Earl of
Halsbury
Gifford, Clark. EXT 8/1 5
Gifford, Denis (1927-) AOW 345
SFH 240 SF1 209 SF2 913 VES
327
Gilabert, Antonio Moncho Y.
SOT 139 WGT 102
Gilbert, Dorothy. IAC 118 LTN
268
Gilbert, George Holley. BAA 224
Gilbert, John Wilmer. BAA 109
FFC 51
Gilbert, Linda S. FL4 1652-6,
1679-83
Gilbert, Mike. VES 291
Gilbert, Phil. IMS 247
Gilbert, Robert Ernest. IAC 118
SFS 51
Gilbert, Sandra. SFH 97
Gilbert, Stuart. MIH 62
Gilbert, William (1804-90) CSF
81 SF1 210
Gilbert, (Sir) William Schwenck
(1836-1911) ASF 313-4 CSF 82
ES1 186 IAH 85 SFA 89,285-7
Gilbert, William Stephen (1912-)
CSF 81 HFI 61 LEX 334 SFE
253 SF1 209-10 SF2 913
Gilchrist, Jeremy. IAC 118
Gilchrist, Robert Murray (1868-
1917) CSF 82 ES1 186 SF1 210
Gilchrist, Rosetta L. CSF 82
SF1 210
Gilden, Mel. IAC 118-9
Gilden, Stephen. IAC 119
Gilder, George. NDA 129-30
Gildon, Charles. BAA 10
Giles, Douglas pseud. of James
Hall. TSP 134
Giles, Fayette Stratton. BAA 51,
55 CSF 82
Giles, Gordon A. IAC 119 WSF
119
Giles, Herbert A. CSF 82
Giles, R. A. WGT 58
Giles, Raymond pseud. of John
Robert Holt (1926-) ES1 186 SF1
210
Gilford, Charles Bernard (1920-)
HFI 61 SF1 210 SF2 913
Gilhooley, (Lord) pseud. of
Frederick Henri Seymour. CSF
82 SF1 210
Gilien, Sasha. IAC 119 SFS 51

Gilison, Jerome M. BAA 178
Gill, Anthony K. CSF 82
Gill, Margery. FFC 14,28,37,
73,132,160
Gillanders, R.A. EXT 9/2 33
Gillen, Mollie. LTN 255
Gillespie, Alfred. IAC 119
Gillespie, Bruce (1947-) LTN 35
SFE 253 SL1 196-201,443-8
SL2 926-31 SL3 1238-41 SL5
2059-64,2520-4 SRB 78
Gillespie, Charles Coulston. SFH
241 SOI xvi
Gillespie, Jack. IMS 111,116,128,
131,135,138,140-1,143,158,170,
183,214,225,235,243-4 WFS 34,
71-2,95,117,124,174
Gillespie, Jessie. FFC 11
Gillet, Alexis Francois (1861-)
CSF 82 SF1 210
Gillet, Maturin. BAA 178
Gillette, Glen L. IAC 119
Gillette, King Camp. BAA 51,76,
90
Gilliam, Edward W. EXT 4/1 9,
12
Gilliatt, Penelope Ann (1932-)
ACC 127-8,146 ES1 186 HFI
61 SFE 253 SF1 210 SF2 913
Gillies, Margaret. FFC 83
Gillies, Robert Pearse (1788-
1858) CSF 82 SF1 210
Gilligan, Edmund. CSF 82
Gillings, Walter H. (1912-) ACC
244 AC2 74 ES1 186 FTF 69
IAC 119 IMS 75,96-7,99,101,
252 SFE 253-4 SOT 124-5,138,
147,378,381-2,387 VES 71,274
WGT 58 WIF 91 WSF 74,127
Gillmore, Inez Haynes (1878-)
CSF 82 ES1 186
Gillmore, Parker. CSF 82 SF1
210
Gillon, Diana Pleasance (1915-)
BAA 136 ES1 186 HFI 61 KAU
29 SFE 254 SF1 210 SF2 914
Gillon, Meir Selig (1907-) BAA
136 ES1 186 HFI 61 KAU 29
SFE 254 SF1 210 SF2 914
Gillon, Miriam. SFW 7
Gilman, Bradley. BAA 64
Gilman, Charlotte Perkins. BAA
77,81 COT 259 CSF 82
Gilman, Nicholas P. BAA 224
Gilman, Robert Cham. AOW 306,
318

Gilmore. RFA 74,76
Gilmore, Anthony pseud. of
Harry Bates, Desmond W. Hall.
HFI 61 IAC 119 IMS 40 RFA
8-11,18,30 SFE 254 SF1 210
WSF 55-6,59,75
Gilmour, William. HFI 62
Gilpatrick, Guy. ISW 175
Gilpin, William. BAA 41
Gilsdorf, Alethea J. Bourne.
NWO 35
Gilson, Charles. CSF 82
Gilson, Charles James Louis
(1878-1943) CSF 82 SF1 211
Gilvin, Aida M. CSF 82
Gilzin, Karl. ES1 186
Gingold, Helene E. CSF 82
Ginsberg, Allen. IAC 119 VFS
117
Ginsburg, Mirra. AOW 297 ES1
187 IAC 119 LTN 221 SFE 254
SF1 211 SF2 914 STH 45
Giordani, Pier Luigi. BAA 178
Girad, Dian. BAA 160 IAC 119
Girard, James P. IAC 119
Giraud, Jean (1938-) SFE 254
Giraud, Stephen Louis. CSF 82
Giraudeau, Ferdnand. POE 136
Giraudoux, Jean (1882-1944) SF1
211
Gironella, Jose Maria (1917-)
AOW 289 ES1 187 EXT 7/2 47
IAC 119 SFS 51 SF1 211
Girsberger, Hans. BAA 178
Girvan, Waveney. ES1 187
Girvetz, Harry K. EXT 6/1 4
Gissing, George Robert (1857-
1903) ACC 173 EXT 8/2 56 FAN
12 KAU 95 LTN 171
Giunta, John (1920?-70) ES1 187
IMS 135,171,200,213,221-2
SOT 407
Givens, Charles. CSF 82
Giventer, Abbi. FFC 74
Givins, Robert Cartwright (1845-
1915) CSF 82 SF1 211
Gjellerup, Karl (1857-1919) SF1
211
Gladish, Christine. SL4 1571-3
Gladney, Graves. RFA 62,66,68
STH 260
Glamis, Walter pseud. of Nathan
Schachner. RFA 16
Glanvill, Joseph. POE 6
Glanville, Ernest (1856-1925)
CSF 82 SF1 211

Glanzman, Louis. FFC 147
Glasby, John Stephen (1928-) HFI
62 SF1 211 SF2 914 see also
Berl Cameron, Rand Le Page,
Paul Lorraine
Glaser, Alice. IAC 119
Glasgow, Ellen (1874-1945) CSF
82 ES1 187 IAC 119 SF1 211
Glaskin, Gerald Marcus (1923-)
AOW 190 ES1 187 SFE 254 SF1
211 SF2 914-5
Glass, Bentley. EXT 1/2 31
EXT 2/1 4 EXT 7/1 18, 26
Glass, (Mrs.) Charles Wilder
(1874-) SF1 211-2
Glass, Dick. IAC 119
Glass, James M. BAA 224
Glass, L. A. BAA 151
Glass, Marvin. FFC 34
Glass, Theodore (1896-) see
Theodamus
Glasser, Allen. CSF 83 IMS 10-
1, 13-5, 19, 37, 49 ISW 160-1
SOT 102-4, 141 SRB 89 WIF
134 WSF 75
Glasson, T. F. NWO 5-6
Glebov, Anatoly G. MSF 262
Gleckner, Robert F. BAA 224
Gleig, Charles (1862-) CSF 83
SF1 212
Glemser, Bernard (1908-) ES1
187 WGT 58 see also Robert
Crane
Glendon, George. CSF 83 SF1
212
Glenn, George Alan. BAA 109
Glenn, John. LTN 106
Glenning, Raymond. SF1 212
Glicksberg, Charles I. BAA 224
EXT 6/1 14
Glicksohn, Mike. SRB 126
Glicksohn, Susan. KAU 88 OSR
334-7, 355 SF1 212 see also
Susan Wood
Glinka, Mikhail I. IAH 38
Gloag, John Edwards (1896-) BAA
100, 109 CSF 83 EXT 9/2 44
SFE 255 SF1 212
Gloeckner, Carolyn. IAC 119
Glossop, Reginald. BAA 92 CSF
83 SF1 212
Gloster, Ivan L. CSF 83
Glovatski, Alexander (1847-1912)
SF1 212
Glover, Edward. VES 130

Gluck, Sinclair (1887-) SF1 212
Glushko. VFS 45
Glut, Donald F(rank) (1944-) AOW
355 HFI 62 KWS x-xi, 37, 170,
247, 276 SF1 212 SF2 915 SRB
69
Gluyas, Constance (1920-) SF1 212
Glyn, Alice Coralie (-1928) BAA
55 SF1 212
Glyn, Elinor. CSF 83
Glynn, Alan Anthony. SFE 255
Glynn, Anthony Arthur (1929-)
HFI 62 SF1 212 see also John
E. Muller
Gnaedinger, Mary. ES1 187 STH
259, 262-3 WSF 123
Gnoli, Domenico (1933-) FFC 26
SF1 213
Gobbato, Imero. FFC 20, 73, 76
Gobetz, G. E. BAA 224
Goble, Lloyd Neil (1933-) AOW
345 SFE 255 SF1 213 SF2 915
Goble, Warwick. SFW 40 STH
204 VES 109, 286
Gobsch, Hanns (1883-) CSF 83
SF1 213
God. ASF 34, 66-7, 84, 145, 147,
151, 160, 163, 173, 183, 203, 218,
304, 307 ATA 5, 13-4, 27, 32, 37,
41-2, 46, 49-51, 57 CUA 11-4,
31, 37-8, 43-6, 55-7 CWN 8, 48
CYR 8, 26, 30, 38, 47-8 ETN 51,
74, 102 EXT 2/1 3 EXT 2/2
28, 38, 41 EXT 3/2 51-2 EXT
4/2 31 EXT 6/2 42 EXT 7/1
8, 10, 19 EXT 7/2 37, 42 EXT
8/1 23 EXT 8/2 54 EXT 9/1
10-2 EXT 9/2 39, 44, 47-9, 53,
59 EXT 10/1 36, 39 EXT 10/2
64, 67-8, 88, 93, 96 [FUT] HEN
4, 31, 44, 54, 57, 60-1 INT 6, 101,
112, 114 JGB 17, 32-3, 35, 57
KVT 4, 14, 16-20, 23, 27-9, 31-2,
36-7, 39-40, 42-3, 46, 48, 50, 55,
62-3 LTN 63, 79, 106, 121-5,
127, 139, 151, 169, 219, 224, 230
SFB 19, 35, 53, 65, 83 SFN 45,
65, 113 SHL 22, 41, 50, 59 TBC
20, 37, 43 TDI 18 THM 18-9,
27-8, 31, 49 TJB 51, 53, 55 TSO
4, 15-6, 21 VFS 5, 192 VMW 14,
20, 28, 30, 32-4, 45, 49, 54 WBW
9, 13, 16, 27, 29, 45-6, 61-2 WFS
11, 13, 40, 77, 83, 105, 111, 115,
125, 136, 138, 144, 191, 204, 217-

God (cont.)
8, 222, 227, 239, 259, 279, 283
287, 301 see also Christ, Jesus,
Lord
Godber, Noel Lambert (1881-)
CSF 83 SFE 255 SF1 213
Goddard, Richard E. CSF 83
SF1 213
Goddard, Robert H. (1882-1945)
COT 31-3, 37, 39, 41-2, 52-3, 91
EXT 7/2 37 SFN 34 VFS 43-4,
74, 81, 224, 242
Godden, Margaret Rumer (1907-)
FFC 5, 83-4, 119 SF1 213 SF2
915
Godel, Kurt. VFS 203
Godfrey, Arthur. SFN 89, 110
Godfrey, Hal pseud. of Charlotte
O'Conor Eccles. CSF 83 SF1
213
Godfrey, Hollis (1874-1936) AOW
37, 63 CSF 83 EXT 1/1 11
EXT 7/1 26 SFE 255 SF1 213
Godschalk, William L. SRB 502
Godwin, (Bishop) Francis (1562-
1633) AAL 71 ALW 42, 95 AOW
10, 13, 22 BAA 3 BYS 62, 79
CSF 83 ES1 187 EXT 3/1 30
EXT 4/2 29 FAN 10 FTF 20-2,
24 IAC 119 LTN 111 MSF 88,
100, 103 MSM 203 NWO 118
PST 17-8, 20-1, 45, 203-4, 227,
234, 238-9, 245, 274 SFB 41, 45,
70-1 SFE 257 SFS 51 SOI 43
VES 79 WAA 31 WGT 58 WIF
35 WSF 14
Godwin, George Stanley (1889-)
SF1 213
Godwin, Parke. HFI 62
Godwin, Tom (1915-) ALW 212,
231, 235 AOW 80, 190, 292, 299
CSC 106, 169, 174-5 ES1 187-8
ETN 69 FFR 84 HFI 62 IAC
119 INT 18 LEX 334 MFW 44
MIH 111-3 RFA 203 SFB 18
SFE 257 SFS 51 SF1 213 SOT
431 VES 302 WSF 176, 184
Godwin, William (1756-1836) AOW
31 BYS 15, 21, 23, 142 CSF 83
FBK 27 FL3 1347-9 MFW 195
MSF 123, 127, 129-30, 134, 136,
273 SFW 3 SF1 213 WGT 58
Goeckeritz, Felix L. STH 137-8
Goedel, Kurt. CAT 24 MFW 60,
216 TDI 44-6, 52-3, 56, 60

Goethe, Johann Wolfgang Von see
Von Goethe, Johann Wolfgang
Goff, Georgena. SF1 213
Goff, Penrith. FL3 1176-8 FL4
1575-80
Goforth, Laura. IAC 119 SFS
36, 51
Goggin, Richard. IAC 119 SFS
51
Gogol, Nikolai V. (1809-52) ETN
180 EXT 10/1 44 FBK 16, 32,
40-2, 124 FLT 2, 76-83 FL3
1520-6 IAC 119 MSF 8, 242
SFB 124 TFC 72-3, 169, 172
Gohman, Fred. IAC 119
Gold, Evelyn Paige. WFS 228,
235 WGT 58
Gold, Herbert. CSC 25 ETN 143
IAC 120
Gold, H(orace) L(eonard) (1914-)
ALW 8, 129, 162, 216-21 AOW
190 ASF 168, 212, 251, 255-6
BFP 200-1 BYS 247, 251, 279
COT 20, 22, 139, 195, 230, 251-3,
269, 279, 294 CSC 170 ES1 188-
9 ETN 1, 8, 23, 31, 37, 42, 46, 65,
68-9, 103, 140, 160, 178, 197 EXT
2/2 31 EXT 5/1 3, 10 EXT 7/2
40-1 EXT 8/1 7-8 FBK 124
FFR 85 FTF 69 HFI 62 IAC
119-20 IAH 7-8, 14-5, 19-20, 25,
29, 35, 60, 105 ISW 131, 221, 259-
60 LEX 335 MFW 289 MIH 2,
15, 19, 33, 38, 111-2 MSM 33, 39,
87, 151, 176 RFA 52, 57-8, 62,
64, 76, 199, 212 RGS 69-70 SFA
193, 273, 280 SFB 62 SFD 5
SFE 257 SFH 69, 88 SFN 79-80,
83 SFS 51-2, 69 SFW 173, 180,
204, 268, 395-6, 421 SF1 213
SF2 915 SOT 157, 176, 183-4,
263, 280, 298-9, 401, 408, 420-1
SRB 13 STH 108-9, 118-9, 158,
224, 265 TJB 5 WFS 114, 166,
183, 188-90, 194, 200-2, 214, 223-
8, 234-6, 242-3 WGT 58 WIF
115, 207 WSF 170-1, 173, 187-
8, 195, 217, 301 see also Clyde
Crane Campbell, Dudley Dell
Goldbach. WFS 220
Goldbarth, Albert. IAC 120
Goldberg, Jerry. LTN 251
Goldberg, Rube. TRB 119 YTS 6
Goldblatt, Burt. SF1 213
Golden, S. EFP 14

Goldfrap, John Henry (1879-1917)
see Captain Wilbur Lampton
Goldie, (Mrs.) Barre Bertha
(-1938) SF1 214
Goldin, Stephen (Charles) (1947-)
AAL 67 FFR 85 FL4 1848-50,
1958-62 [FJT] HFI 62 IAC 118,
120 LEX 335-6 SFE 258-9 SF1
214 SF2 916 SL3 1413-6 SL5
2429-32 VES 184
Golding, Kathleen Annie see
Kathleen Fidler
Golding, Louis (1895-1958) CSF
83 ES1 189 SFE 259 SF1 214
Golding, Morton Jay (1925-) HFI
62 SF1 214 SF2 916
Golding, William (Gerald) (1911-)
ALW 238 AOW 96,190 BAA 124
BYS 72,117,122,257 CAT 131,
138 CSC 39,51,101 ES1 189
EXT 2/2 27 EXT 3/1 26 EXT
4/1 1 EXT 5/1 4 EXT 6/2 42
EXT 9/1 19,23 EXT 9/2 45
FAN 8,25,38,163-7,188 FFR
85 FHT 15-6 FLT 123,136-7
HFI 62 IAC 120 INT 53 ISW
167-9,245 LEX 336-7 MFW 165
NDA 6,198 POE 279-80 RHN 87
SFE 259 SFH 98-9,214 SF1 214
SF2 916 SL3 1036-9,1257-60
VES 116,261
Goldman. LTN 111
Goldman, Edwin Franko. WFS 92
Goldman, Emma. UKL 77,88
Goldman, Eric. FAN 6
Goldman, Lawrence Louis. SF1
214
Goldman, Stephen H. AAL 129-
30 SL2 986-90,1014-8 SL3
1102-5,1135-9,1226-9,1274-7
SL4 1596-1602,1608-12,1730-4,
1913-6,1922-5 SL5 2132-5,
2215-7,2370-2,2455-8
Goldman, William W. (1931-)
FL3 1286-90 HFI 62 SF1 214
SF2 916
Goldmann, Lucien. CAT 32-3,
46-7 TSO 6-7,24,28,34,36
Goldring, Douglas (1887-1960)
CSF 83 SF1 214
Goldschager, B. WTS 80
Goldsmith, Cele (1933-) ES1 189
ETN 26 RZY 10 SFE 259 SFW
422,563 see also Cele Goldsmith
Lalli

Goldsmith, David H. NWO 315-6
SRB 82
Goldsmith, Harold S. TSP 3 WFS
104
Goldsmith, Howard. IAC 120
Goldsmith, John Francis. BAA
103 CSF 83 SF1 214
Goldsmith, Oliver. BAA 12
Goldsmith, Ruth M. IAC 120
Goldstein, William Isaac (1932-)
SF1 214
Goldston, Robert Conroy (1927-)
ES1 189 SF1 214 SF2 916
Goldstone, Herbert. IAC 120
SFS 52
Golffing, Francis. BAA 161,224
Goll, Reinhold Weimar (1897-)
ES1 190 SF1 214 SF2 917
Gollancz, Victor. THM 4
Goller, Celia Fremlin (1914-)
SF2 904
Gollomb, Joseph. CSF 84
Golon, Anne. SF1 214
Golon, Serge (1903-72) SF1 215
Golovine, (General). POE 240
Golub, Leon. BAA 224
Golumb, (Dr.) Solomon. VFS 249
Gombin, Richard. BAA 224
Gombrich, E. H. MFW 96
Gomery, Percy. CSF 84
Gompers, Samuel. STH 41
Gompertz, Martin Louis Alan
(1886-1951) ES1 190 WGT 58-9
see also Ganpat
Goncharov, Viktor A. MSF 261
Gondor, Lily H. BAA 225 EXT
6/2 46,48
Gonnard, Rene. BAA 178
Gonsales, Domingo. WAA 31
Gonzalez, Regino. BAA 178
Gooch, Fani Pusey. CSF 84
Good, Irving John. ES1 190
Goodacre, Henry. CSF 84
Goodale, Earl. IAC 120 SFS 52
Goodall, J.S. FFC 68
Goodavage, Joseph F. WSF 167,
233
Goodchild, George (1888-1969)
ES1 190 SFE 259 SF1 215 WGT
59 Alan Dake
Goode, Arthur Russell (1889-)
see Arthur Russell
Goode, Diane. FFC 108
Goodey, Brian. BAA 225
Goodfellow, Peter. FBK 136

Goodheart, Eugene. BAA 178, 225 EXT 9/2 52
Goodis, David. WFS 106
Goodman. LTN 111
Goodman, Abraham. STH 44 TSP 207
Goodman, Andrew. RHN 158
Goodman, Eli. EXT 9/2 61-2
Goodman, Katherine. BAA 201
Goodman, Martin. TSP 67, 133, 207
Goodman, Paul. BAA 178, 225 FSU 47 UKL 77-8, 86
Goodrich, Charles H. BAA 139 ES1 190 SF1 215
Goodrich, Samuel Griswold (1793-1860) WGT 59
Goodrich-Freer, Adela M. (-1931) CSF 84 ES1 190 SF1 215
Goodstone, Tony. AOW 81-2, 353 BYS 238-9 CWD 33
Goodwin, Harold Leland (1914-) ES1 190 FFC 53, 119, 132 SF2 819 WGT 59 see also John Blaine
Goodwin, John B. L. IAC 120
Goodwin, John pseud. of Sidney F. Gowing. CSF 84
Goodwin, John Cuthbert (1891-) CSF 84 SF1 215
Goodwin, Murray. FFC 132
Goodwyn, Burmby. BAA 23
Googendijk, Wouter. FFC 18
Goorden, Barnard. SIH 199
Gopcevic, Spiridion (1855-) SF1 215
Gor, Gennady (1907-) FFR 85 IAC 120 LEX 337 SFB 122 SFS 52 SL4 1963-6
Gordon, Caroline (1895-) SF1 215
Gordon, D. M. SF1 215
Gordon, David pseud. of Randall Garrett. RFA 208, 210 SF1 215 WSF 172
Gordon, Giles. BYS 299 IAC 120
Gordon, (Lord) Granville Armyne (1856-1907) CSF 84 SF1 215
Gordon, Irwin Leslie (1888-1954) SF1 215
Gordon, Isabel S. ES1 190 IAC 120
Gordon, Joan. SRB 79
Gordon, John (1925-) FFC 65 SF1 215 SF2 917
Gordon, Margaret. FFC 129
Gordon, Myron. RZY 9, 14

Gordon, Nancy McKay. CSF 84 SF1 215
Gordon, Neil pseud. of Archibald Gordon Macdonell. SF1 216
Gordon, Patricia see Joan Howard
Gordon, Peter. RFA 16
Gordon, Rex pseud. of Stanley Bennett Hough (1917-) AAL 77 AOW 190 BYS 9, 71 FFR 85 HFI 62 ISW 246-7 NDA 72-5, 77 SFB 18 SFE 259 SF1 216 SL2 787-91 SRB 325
Gordon, Richard. VES 150
Gordon, Richard M. IAC 120
Gordon, (Richard) Stuart (1947-) HFI 63 SFE 259 SF1 216 see also Alex R. Stuart
Gordon, Theodore J. (1930-) AOW 293 SF1 216 SF2 917-8
Gordon, W. J. J. IAC 120 SFS 52
Gorer, Geoffrey Edgar (1905-) BAA 105 CSF 84 EXT 6/1 19 FAN 122 SFE 259 SF1 216
Gores, Joe. IAC 120
Goret, J. BAA 225
Gorey, Edward St. John (1925-) ES1 190 FFC 29 IAC 120 SF1 216 SF2 918
Gorky, Maxim pseud. of Alexei M. Pyeshkov. EXT 10/2 73 MSF 17, 250
Gorman, Herbert. CSF 84
Gorman, James Thomas (1869-) SF1 216
Gossett, Thorold. IAC 120
Gorst, Harold Edward (1868-1950) SF1 216
Goshgarian, Gary. TSF 197-200
Goss, Gary L. (1934-) SF1 216
Gosse, Jeanne. SF1 216
Gosseyn, Gilbert. ALW 164
Gothein, Eberhard. BAA 225
Gotlieb, C. C. MFW 219
Gotlieb, Phyllis Fay (1926-) ES1 190 FFR 85 FRN 67 HFI 63 IAC 120 LEX 337-8 SFE 261 SF1 216 SF2 918
Gotschalk, Felix C. (1929-) BAA 161 ETN 10 HFI 63 IAC 120 RGS 70 SFE 261
Gott, Samuel. BAA 4
Gottcliffe, Harold. IMS 97, 100
Gottesman, S. D. pseud. of C. M. Kornbluth, Frederik Pohl. IAC 121 IMS 158 ISW 146, 193 RFA 191 SFE 261

Gottfried, Alex. BAA 225
Gotthelf, Ezra Gerson (1907-)
BAA 103 CSF 84 SF1 216
Gotthelf, Jeremias pseud. of
Albert Bitzius. SF1 216
Gottlieb, Alex. CSC 277-80
Gottlieb, Hinko (1886?-) AOW 191
CSF 84 ES1 190-1 SFE 261 SF1
216
Gottlieb, Seymour. SF1 216
Gottschling, Ernst. BAA 225
Gotz, Ina. BAA 178
Gouanvic, Jean-Marc. SL2 965-8
Goudge, Elizabeth De Beauchamp
(1900-) CSF 84 ES1 191 FFC
13, 65, 93 SF1 217, 582 SF2 918
Goudket, Herbert. IMS 34, 39, 55,
82-3, 143, 147-8, 150, 170-1, 175-
6, 213
Gough, Philip. FFC 26
Gouhier, Henri. BAA 178
Goulart, Ron(ald Joseph) (1933-)
ALW 212 AOW 191, 298 BAA
151 BFP 202-7 CSC 107, 228
ES1 191 FFR 85 FRN 35 HFI
63 IAC 121-2 LEX 338-9 RGS
70-1 SFE 261-2 SFS 52 SFW
499 SF1 217 SF2 918-9 SIH
142-6 VES 173 see also
Con Steffanson
Gould, Arthur Lee pseud. of
Arthur Stanley Gould Lee. CSF
84 SF1 217
Gould, F. J. BAA 44
Gould, (Sir) Francis Carruthers
(1844-1925) SF1 217
Gould, Harold. BAA 225
Gould, Jessica. WFS 122 see
also Jessica Wilson
Gould, Maggy. SF1 217
Goulding, Sybil. BAA 178
Goulemot, Jean-Marie. BAA 225
Gouraud, Aimee Crocker. CSF
84 ES1 191
Gourlay, Reginald. ES1 191
Gouschev, Sergei. ES1 191
Gouvrieux, Marc. SF1 217
Gouvy, Gertrude. SF1 217
Govan, Christine N. IAC 122
Gove, Philip Babcock (1902-72)
AOW 345 BAA xx, 178, 225 ES1
191 EXT 9/2 28, 31 MFW ix
NWO 107 SFE 262 SF1 218 SF2
919 SRB 5, 69
Gowans, Adam Luke. CSF 84 ES1
191 SF1 218

Gowing, Emilia Aylmer. CSF 84
SF1 218
Gowing, Sidney Floyd (1878-) VES
322 WGT 59 see also John
Goodwin
Gowland, John Stafford (1898-)
ES1 191 SFE 262 SF1 218
Goy, Philip (1941-) SFE 262
Goyen, William. MSM 115
Goyne, Richard. SF1 218
Goytisolo, Juan. FBK 136
Gozlan, Leon (1806-66) CSF 84
SF1 218
Graaf, Vera. AOW 345 BAA 178
Graat, Heinrich pseud. of George
Wolk. SF1 218
Graber, Alexander (1914-) SF2
864 see also Alexander Cordell
Grabinski, Stefan (1887-1936) FBK
147-8 FL3 1527-31
Grabnar, Boris. SL1 1-5
Grabowsky, Adolf. BAA 225
Grace, Stephen. CSF 85
Grace, William J. BAA 225
Grady, R. S. J. EXT 10/1 28
Graeme, Bruce pseud. of Graham
Montague Jeffries. CSF 10 SF1
218
Grafton, Samuel. EXT 10/2 103-4
Graham, Bessie. BAA 225
Graham, Daniel F. BAA 225
Graham, Donald. TSP 139-40
Graham, Harvey pseud. of Isaac
Harvey Flack. CSF 85 SF1 218
Graham, Howard W. pseud. of
Howard E. Wandrei. IAC 122
Graham, John Michael. SF1 218
Graham, Joyce Maxtone see Jan
Struther
Graham, Kenneth W. (1859-1932)
ES1 191
Graham, L. A. IAC 122
Graham, Matilda Winifred (-1950)
CSF 85 SF1 218
Graham, Peter Anderson (-1925)
BAA 88 CSF 84 SFE 262 SF1
218
Graham, Robert. JHN 12, 58-9
Graham, Roger Phillips (1909-65)
ES1 191-2 SF2 1033 WGT 59-
60 WSF 142 see also Robert
Arnette, Alexander Blade, P.
F. Costello, Rog Phillips,
Gerald Vance, Peter Worth
Graham, Victoria. SF1 218
Grahame, Edith. SF1 218

Grahame, Kenneth (1859-1932)
BAA 226 CSF 85 EXT 10/1 28
FBK 112,114 FFC 5,88,119
FL5 2132-5 LTN 125 SFN 40
SF1 582 SRB 260
Grahame-Johnstone, Janet. FFC
125
Grahame-Johnstone, Anne. FFC
125
Grahame-White, Claude (1879-
1959) CSF 85 SFE 262 SF1 218
Grainey, Michael (1947-) SF2 919
Grainger, Boyne (1882-) CSF 85
SF1 218
Grainger, Francis Edward (1857-
1927) WGT 60 see also Headon
Hill
Grams, Jay (1940-) LEX 339-40
Gramsci, Antonio. MSF 82,206
Grandville, J. J. pseud. of
Taxile Delord, Jean-Isidore-
Gerard Grandville. SL1 105-8
WAA 76
Grandville, Jean-Isidore Gerard
(-1847) POE 73-5 VES 286 see
also J. J. Grandville
Granin, Daniel. EXT 10/1 49
IAC 122
Granoski, Clarence. IAC 122
Grant. MSM 144
Grant, Allan. IAC 122
Grant, C(harles) L. (1942-) FLR
15,19,60 FL3 1191-5 HFI 64
IAC 122 RGS 71-2 SFE 262
Grant, Donald M(etcalf) (1927-)
BAA 173 CWD 14,16 ES1 192
EXT 3/1 21 SFE 262 SF1 219
SRB 286,496
Grant, Douglas Allen. CSF 85
Grant, Gary. SF1 219
Grant, Gordon. IAC 122
Grant, H. Roger. BAA 226
Grant, Isabell Francis. BAA 92
Grant, James. CSF 85
Grant, Joan pseud. of Joan
Marshall Kelsey (1907-) CSF 85
ES1 192 SF1 219
Grant, Joe (1908-) SF1 219
Grant, Lawrence Vernon. BAA
282
Grant, Marcus. SF1 219
Grant, Matthew. SFE 262 SF1
219
Grant, Maxwell (house name) SF1
219 see also Walter B. Gibson,
Dennis Lynds

Grant, Richard pseud. of Joseph
Calvitt Clarke. SF1 220
Grant, Robert (1852-1940) CSF 85
PST 73,276,286 SFE 262 SF1
220
Grant, Sebastian. SF1 220
Grant, Ulysses S. MSM 174
Grant-Watson, Elliot Lovegood
(1885-) SF1 220
Granville, Austyn W. CSF 85
SFE 262 SF1 220
Granville-Barker, Harley G.
(1877-1946) SF1 220 WGT 60
see also Granville Barker
Grass, Gunter (1927-) ETN 180
FL4 1943-6 IAC 122 SFH 180
Grasty, William K. IAC 122
Gratacap, Louis Pope (1851-1917)
AOW 63 BAA 66,76 CSF 85
EXT 1/1 2-3,11 EXT 5/2 38
MFW 121 SFE 262 SF1 220
SRB 9
Grattan-Smith, Thomas Edward.
SF1 220
Graus, F. BAA 226
Grautoff, Ferdinand Heinrich
(1871-1935) SF1 220 WGT 60
see also Parabellum, Seestern
Grave, Sergei L. MSF 261
Gravely, William H., Jr. NWO 71
Graves, Charles Larcom (1856-
1944) BAA 58 CSF 85 SF1 220
Graves, Clotilde Inez Mary (1868-
1932) ES1 192 WGT 60 see also
Richard Dehan
Graves, Emerson (house name)
TSP 132
Graves, Gordon Harwood (1884-)
SF1 220
Graves, Jocelyn. IAC 122
Graves, Peggy. WFS 108-9,113
Graves, Robert (Ranke) (1895-)
AOW 191 BAA 117 CSF 86 ES1
192 EXT 6/2 51 EXT 7/1 15
FLR 25,28 FL5 2067-8 HFI 64
IAC 122 ISW 62,182-3 MIH 12,
138 PJF 17,35,67 POE 271-2
RFA 139,155 SFD 309 SFE 262
SFS 52 SF1 220 SF2 920 VES
144,261 WIF 58,163
Gray, Alexander. BAA 178
Gray, Annabel pseud? of Anne
Cox. CSF 86
Gray, Arthur (1852-1940) see
Ingulphus

Gray, Berkeley pseud. of Edwy
Searles Brooks. SF1 220
Gray, Clarence. CSF 167
Gray, Clifford. TSP 131
Gray, Curme. AOW 192 BAA 119
ES1 192 HFI 64 ISW viii, 181-7
SFE 263 SF1 220 VES 129 WIF
212
Gray, Donald J. BAA 178
Gray, Elisha. VFS 245
Gray, Frances. SF1 221
Gray, Genevieve. FFC 31
Gray, Hector C. STH 142
Gray, J. H. BAA 226
Gray, John (1866-1934) BAA 21
SF1 221
Gray, Mary (1886-1952) SF1 221
Gray, Nicholas Stuart (1922-) ES1
192 FFC 25, 65, 176 SF1 221
SF2 920 SRB 261
Gray, Reg. FFC 170
Gray, Rod (house name) SF1 221
Gray, Russell pseud. of Bruno
Fischer. TSP 125-7, 132, 156,
209
Gray, Thomas. CAT xiii
Gray, Will H. IAC 122 SFS 52
Graydon, Robert Murray (-1937)
WGT 60
Graydon, William Murray. CSF
86 SF1 221
Grayson, Charles (1905-) ES1 192-
3
Grazier, James. HFI 64 SFE 263
SF1 221
Grazzini, Martin. LTN 216
Grean, Charles R. EXT 10/1 28
Greaves, Gordon K. SOT 99
Greaves, Margaret. FFC 93
Grebanier, Frances Vinciguerra
(1900-) WGT 60 see also Frances
Winmar
Grebnev, Grigory N. MSF 264
Greco, El (1541?-1614) EXT 6/1
7 KVT 53 VMW 50
Green, A. Lincoln. CSF 86 SF1
221
Green, A. Romney. BAA 106
Green, Alison. FFC 57
Green, David. [FUT]
Green, Edith Pinero. SF1 221
Green, Edwin. CSF 86 SF1 221
Green, Eleanor. BAA 226
Green, Fitzhugh (1888-1947) CSF
86 SF1 221 SRB 6

Green, Frederick Lawrence (1902-
52) SF1 221
Green, Gerald. IAC 122
Green, Henry pseud. of Henry
Vincent Yorke. BAA 116 MSM
281 SF1 221
Green, I. G. pseud. of Ira Green-
blatt. HFI 64 SFE 264 SF1 221
Green, J. F. BAA 226
Green, John. BAA 226
Green, Joseph Lee (1931-) AAL
101 ALW 212 BFP 208 COT 57
ES1 193 FFR 86 HFI 64 IAC
122 LEX 340-1 RGS 72 SFE
264-5 SFS 52 SF1 222 SF2 920
VES 162, 215
Green, Julien Hartridge (1900-)
FBK 67, 138-9 SF1 222 SF2 920
Green, Kathleen. FFC 25
Green, Martin (Burgess). AOW
xviii, 345 CAT 133 EXT 6/1 3,
14 FAN 6-7, 166, 189 HFI 64
Green, Nunsowe. BAA 33
Green, Peter. FAN 165-6
Green, Robert. BAA 146 SF1 222
SFE 265
Green, Robert James. SF1 222
Green, Robert M., Jr. IAC 122
SFS 52
Green, Roger Lancelyn (1918-)
AOW 346 BAA 178 BYS 36, 139,
160, 200 ES1 193 EXT 5/1 6
EXT 10/1 28 FAN 140-1, 187
FFC 25-6, 194 IAC 122 SFB 11
SFE 265 SF1 222 SF2 920-1
SOI 161 SRB 69, 261 VES 79,
329 WAA 245
Green, Roland James (1944-) HFI
64 SF1 222 SF2 921-2 WGT 60
see also Jeffrey Lord
Green, William Child. CSF 86
SF1 222
Greenbaum, Everett. FFC 141
Greenbaum, Leonard. BAA 226
Greenberg, Alvin. IAC 122 SFD
34
Greenberg, Martin (1918-) ES1
193 IAC 122-3 KAU 237 LTN
251, 263 MSM 84 SFA 90-1, 94
SFE 265 SFS 52-3 SF1 222
SOT 261 WFS 178-9, 208 WIF
123 WSF 136, 168, 199
Greenberg, Martin Harry (1941-)
ACE 75 AC2 75-6 ASF 14, 30,
318 BRS 10 ETN 180 IAC 82,

Greenberg, Martin H. (cont.)
123, 142, 172, 177, 187, 241 SFE
265 SF1 222 SF2 922 SRB 77-
80 TSF 145-56, 253
Greenblatt, Harvey. IMS 70
Greenblatt, Ira see I. G. Green
Greenblatt, Jonathan. IAC 123
Greene, Asa. EXT 4/1 12
Greene, Frederick Stuart. CSF
86
Greene, (Henry) Graham (1904-)
AOW 358 CWN 13 ES1 193-4
EXT 8/1 5 FAN 169-71 FBK
100 FFR 86 [FJT] IAC 123
JGB 4, 6, 32, 38, 44 KVT 3 SFS
53 SF1 222 SF2 922 SOI 158
SOT 242 THM 12 VES 135
Greene, James J. BAA 226
Greene, Jay Elihu (1914-) SF1
223 SF2 922
Greene, John O. CSF 86 SF1 223
Greene, Joseph Ingham (1897-)
ES1 194 SF1 223
Greene, Leslie. AOW 305
Greene, Nunsowe. CSF 86
Greene, Sonia. EXT 3/1 10 FBK
75 WTS 22
Greener, Leslie (1900-74) ES1 194
SF1 223 SF2 922-3
Greener, William Oliver (1862-)
BAA 58 WGT 60 see Wirt Ger-
rare
Greenfield, Irving A. (1928-) EFP
14 ES1 194 HFI 64 IAC 123
SFE 265 SF1 223 SF2 923
Greenfield, Louis. CSF 188 ES1
194
Greenfield, Nathan. IMS 10
Greenhough, Terence (1944-) IAC
123 SFE 265
Greening, Frank. SF1 223
Greenleaf, Sue. CSF 86 SF1 223
Greenlee, Maccowan. CSF 86
Greenlee, Sam (1930-) AOW 192
NDA 174-5, 216-7 SFE 265 SF1
223
Greenough, (Mrs.) Richard S.
(1827-85) CSF 86 SF1 223
Greenstreet, Sydney. SFH 171
Greenwald, Sheila. FFC 81, 145,
181, 189
Greenwood, Edwin. CSF 86 SF1
223
Greenwood, James. SF1 223
Greenwood, Julia Eileen Courtney
(1910-) SF2 802 WGT 60 see

also Francis Askham
Greer, Bill. FFC 161
Greer, Richard (house name)
SFE 265 WGT 60 see also
Randall Garrett, Robert
Silverberg
Greer, Tom. CSF 87 PST 60,
208, 272, 286, 296, 299 SFE 265
SF1 223
Greer, William W. IAC 123 SFS
53
Greg, Percy (1836-89) AAL 106-
7 AOW 39, 44, 63 BAA 33 BYS
141-2 CSF 87 EXT 1/1 5 EXT
5/1 4 POE 108-9 PST 67-9,
106, 192, 198, 206, 208, 224, 226-
7, 236-7, 239-40, 242-6, 256, 265,
267-9, 271, 274-6, 280, 284-6,
288, 290-1, 309 SFB 54 SFE
265 SF1 223 SL1 11-5 VES 69,
80 WIF 54
Gregg, Hilda Caroline (1868-1933)
see Sydney C. Grier
Gregg, Richard A. BAA 226
Gregor, Lee pseud. of Frederik
Pohl, Milton A. Rothman. IAC
123 SFS 53 WFS 58-9, 84 WIF
167
Gregorian, Joyce Ballou. FFC
176
Gregory (of Tours). VES 267
Gregory I, (Pope). WIF 31
Gregory, Dane. TSP 156, 173
Gregory, Franklin Long (1905-)
CSF 87 ES1 194 FBK 55 SF1
223
Gregory, H. B. SF1 223
Gregory, Jackson (1882-1943)
CSF 87 SF1 223-4
Gregory, Julian R. pseud. of Leo
Knowles. SF1 224
Gregory, Ormond. TSP 173 see
also W. Wayne Robbins
Gregory, Owen. BAA 83 CSF
87 SFE 265-6 SF1 224
Greiffenhagen, Maurice. FBK 101
Greive, Bernhard. BAA 226
Gremmels, Christian. BAA 178
Grendler, Paul F. BAA 226
Grendon, Edward. IAC 123 SFS
53
Grendon, Stephen pseud. of
August Derleth. IAC 123
Grennell, Dean A. WGT 60
Gresham, Joy Davidman. SOI 2,
11-2

Gresham, William Lindsay. IAC
123 SFS 53 WFS 216
Greshnov, M. IAC 123
Gresswell, Elsie Kay. BAA 103
CSF 87 SF1 224
Gretzer, John. FFC 39
Greve, Tora. SF1 224
Grey, Charles pseud. of E. C.
Tubb. IAC 123 VES 75
Grey, Clarence. WSF 305
Grey, Edward. SF1 224
Grey, Lynn. SF1 224
Grey, Robert Munson. SF1 224
Grey, Zane. COT 63, 66, 87, 192,
220 MFW 131 MSM 176 PJF
44 SFD 66
Gribbin, (Dr.) John. IAC 123
Gribbon, William Lancaster (1879-
1940) WGT 60-1 see also Talbot
Mundy
Gridban, Volsted (house name)
SFE 266 SF1 224 VES 75, 156
see also John Russell Fearn,
E. C. Tubb
Grier, Sydney C. pseud. of Hilda
Caroline Gregg. SF1 224
Grierson, Francis Durham (1888-)
BAA 94 CSF 87 SF1 224
Griesser, Wilhelm. BAA 88
Griff pseud. of John Russell
Fearn. SFE 266
Griff, Alan pseud. of Donald Sud-
daby. CSF 87
Griffen, Elizabeth L. SF1 224
Griffin, Anthony Jerome (1866-
1935) WGT 61
Griffin, C. S. BAA 40
Griffin, C. W., Jr. EXT 6/1 19
Griffin, Donald R. AAL 215
Griffin, Jane. CWD 3
Griffin, Lloyd W. EXT 6/1 19
Griffin, Nancy. EXT 10/1 29
Griffin, Russell. KAU 139, 142
Griffin, Sercombe. CSF 87 SF1
224
Griffin, Wilfrid. EXT 5/2 42
Griffith, A. W. SFS 53
Griffith, Alan Arnold. STH 183,
192
Griffith, Ann Warren. IAC 123
SFS 53
Griffith, D. W. ASF 295 SFH 102
Griffith, Elizabeth Brierly. STH
185

Griffith, George pseud. of George
Chetwynd Griffith-Jones (1857-
1906) ALW 85 AOW 63, 394
BAA 66 BYS 142 CSF 87 ES1
194 EXT 5/1 4 EXT 7/1 13-4,
17 FFR 86 FTF 43 IAC 123
MSF 162 POE 204 PST 74-6,
92, 112-3, 197, 199, 210, 213, 223-
4, 236, 244, 253-5, 257, 264-5, 267-
8, 271, 273, 277, 285, 287-8, 291,
301, 304 SFE 266 SIH 37, 43-4,
47, 152, 158 SL1 67-71 STH 2,
28-9, 182-217 VES 69, 101, 103,
127, 160, 312 WAA 39
Griffith, Mary (1800?-77) ALW
53, 60 BAA 21-2 CSF 88 ES1
194 HFI 184 MSF 176-7 POE
131 PST 49, 247, 263 SFE 266
SF1 225 VES 126 WGT 61 WSF
342
Griffith, Maxwell. SFN 23
Griffith-Jones, George Chetwynd
(1857-1906) BFP 209-12 SF1
225 WGT 61 see also Levin
Carnac, George Griffith, G. C.
G. Jones, Stanton Morich
Griffiths, Alan. CSF 88 SF1 225
Griffiths, Albert. IMS 159
Griffiths, David Arthur. SF1 225
see also Gill Hunt, Brian Shaw
Griffiths, Isabel. BAA 87 CSF
88 SF1 225
Griffiths, John (1934-) ES1 194
SF1 225
Grifoni, Ulisse. SIH 53 SL1 465-7
Grigg, David. IAC 123
Griggs, Sutton Elbert. BAA 61
Griggs, William N. CSF 88 POE
67
Grigoriev, Vladimir (1935-) IAC
123 LEX 341
Grigoryev, Sergei T. MSF 262
Grigsby, Alcanoan O. BAA 62
WGT 61 see also Jack Adams
Grillo, Francesco. BAA 179
Grimal, Pierre. KAU 3, 5
Grimaldi, John. EXT 10/2 110
Grimble, Rosemary. FFC 107
Grimm, Benjamin. SF1 226
Grimm, Christopher. IAC 123
SFS 53
Grimm, Reinhold. BAA 179
Grimm, Wilhelm and Jacob. FRN
130 INT 111 ISW 79 MSF 183

Grimm, W. and J. (cont.)
WAA 74 WBW 6,53,58-9 WIF
40
Grimshaw, Beatrice (1871?-1953)
CSF 88 ES1 194 SF1 226
Grimshaw, Nigel. FFC 104
Grimshaw, Robert (1850-1941)
BAA 47 SF1 226
Grimsley, Juliet. RBY 240
Grin, Alexander (1880-1932) FBK
42
Grindon, Maurice. SF1 226
Grinnell, David pseud. of Donald
A. Wollheim. IAC 123 SFS 53
Grinstead, Durwood. CSF 88
Grinstead, Gordon. SF1 226
Grip pseud. of Edgar L. Welch.
CSF 88
Gripari, Pierre. FFC 25
Gripe, Harald. FFC 5,176
Gripe, Maria Kristina (1923-)
FFC 5,176 SF1 226
Griset, Ernest. FBK 45
Grisewood, Harman Joseph (1906-)
SF1 226 SF2 923
Grisewood, Robert Norman (1876-)
CSF 88 SF1 226
Grisson, Virgil (1926-67) JGB 33
Griswold, Rufus Wilmot. FBK 37
NWO 54
Grizzard, Zenobia Qualls. WFS
142
Grlic, Danko. BAA 226
Grob, Helmut G. (1929-) LEX
341-2
Groc, Leon (1882-1956) CSF 88
SF1 226 SL5 2362-5
Groch, Judith. FFC 45
Grogan, Gerald (1884-1918) CSF
88 SF1 226
Grogg, Patrick. AOW 307
Groh, Irwin William. SF1 226
Gronau, Karl. BAA 179
Groner, Augusta (1850-) CSF 88
ES1 194-5 SF1 226
Gronlund, Laurence. BAA 226
Gronlund, Lawrence. BAA 35
Groom, Arthur John Pelham.
BAA 116 CSF 88 ES1 195 SFE
266 SF1 226
Groom, Arthur William (1898-
1964) SF1 226 SF2 923
Gropper, William. STH 239
Gross, Anna Goldmark. CSF 88
SF1 226

Gross, Marion. IAC 124 SFS 53
Gross, Werter Livingston. BAA
114
Grosser, E. A. IAC 124 RFA 86
Grosser, Morton. FFC 65 SF1
226
Grossinger, Richard Selig (1944-)
SF1 226 SF2 923
Grossinger, Tania. WFS 257
Grossman, Nancy. FFC 189 IAC
124
Groth, John. FFC 4
Grotta-Kurska, Daniel. AAL 148
SRB 81
Grouling, Thomas Edward (1940-)
ES1 195 SFE 266 SF1 226 SF2
924
Grousset, Paschal (1844-1909)
WGT 61 see also Andre Laurie
Grove, Frederick Philip (1879-
1948) SFE 266
Grove, Philip B. VES 329
Grove, W. BAA 41-2 CSF 88
SF1 226
Grove, Walt. IAC 124
Grove, Walt. SFS 53
Grover, Winifred Powell see
Winifred Dwyer
Groves, Jay Voelker (1922-) ES1
195 SFE 266 SF1 227 SF2 924
Groves, John William (1910-) BAA
146 ES1 195 HFI 64 IAC 124
SFE 266 SFS 53 SF1 227 SF2
924
Grow, Julian F. IAC 124 SFS 53
Grubb, Davis Alexander (1919-)
ES1 195 SF1 227 SF2 924
Grube, Frank. BAA 179
Grube, G. M. A. BAA 226
Gruber, Frank. AOW 353 SOT
349 TSP 24-5,89,226 WTS 44
Gruen, Von. SF1 227
Gruhn, Carrie E. (1907-) SF1 227
SF2 924
Grunert, Karl H. (1865-) IAC 124
LEX 342 SFS 54
Grunewald. ATA 10
Grunwald, Henry Anatole. BAA
226
Grushow, Ira. EXT 6/1 14
Grushvitsky, Vladimir E. see
Vladimir E. Orlovsky
Grylls, R. Glynn. SFW 7
Guareschi, Giovanni (1908-68) SF1
227

Guarnieri, Silvio. BAA 179
Gubbins, Herbert. BAA 80 CSF 88 SF1 227
Guenevere, (Queen). WBW 11, 48
Guenon, Rene. KAU 92
Guenther, Paul F. BAA 282
Guerard, Albert Joseph (1914-) AOW 192 BAA 96, 226 ES1 195 FAN 167 SFE 266-7 SF1 227 SF2 924
Guermonprez, M. EXT 2/1 6
Guernsey, H. W. pseud. of Howard E. Wandrei. IAC 124
Guest, Ernest. BAA 95 CSF 88 SF1 227
Guest, Edgar (1881-1959) KVT 25 NWO 124
Gueulette, Thomas Simon (1683-1766) CSF 89 SF1 227
Guezenec, Alfred (1823-66) WGT 61 see also Alfred Brehat
Guggenheim (family). STH 176
Guggenheim, Harry. COT 33, 36
Guhrauer, Gottschalk Eduard. BAA 226
Guieu, Jimmy. ES1 195
Guild, Leo see Arthur N. Scram
Guillen, Claudio. STF 31
Guillon-Verne, Maxime. EXT 2/1 6
Guillot, Rene (1900-69) FFC 48, 74 SF1 228 SF2 924
Guin, Wyman Woods (1915-) AOW 285 COT 252 DTS 7, 32 ES1 195 ETN 99 FFR 87 HFI 64 IAC 124 MSM 185-6 SFE 267 SFS 54 SF1 228 SF2 924-5 VES 210 WGT 61 WSF 174
Guinn, Jack. SF1 228
Guinn, Robert M. (1911-) ALW 216, 219 ES1 195 WFS 225, 234, 236-7, 241-3, 246-8, 250-2, 289, 300-2 WIF 117 WSF 170, 230
Guinta, John. WTS 93
Guiomar, Michel. BAA 179
Guirdham, Arthur. CWN 56 SF1 228
Gulbin, Suzanne. BAA 226
Gull, Cyril Arthur Ranger (1876-1923) BAA 69-70 CSF 89, 164 SF1 228 WGT 62
Gulliver, (Captain). SF1 228
Gulliver, (Capt.) Lemuel. SF1 228
Gulliver, Lemuel, Jr. BAA 15-6, 21 SF1 228

Gumpel, C. Godfrey. BAA 227
Gundran, Olive (1912-) ES1 195 SF1 228
Gunew, Sneja. UKL 178-99
Gunn, Edmund S. SF1 229
Gunn, Eileen. SL3 1362-5
Gunn, James E. (1923-) ACC 72 ALW 9, 11, 161, 219 AOW 192-3, 346, 397 BAA 126, 136-7, 164-5, 179 BFP 213-4 BRS 7 BYS 262, 288-9 CAT xvii COT 226, 299 CSC 4, 19-20, 161-77, 198-9, 214 DTS 7, 27 ES1 195-6 ETN 30, 33, 62 EXT 2/2 29 FFR 87 FHT 66 HFI 65 IAC 124-5 ISW 123, 258-9 KAU 8, 10, 12 LEX 342-4 LTN 248 MFW ix, 12, 16, 147, 249 PJF 40 RAH 137 RGS 72-3 RSG 54, 72, 92 SFA 158 SFD 238-42, 244-6 SFE 267 SFH 238 SFS 54 SFW 229 SF1 229 SF2 925 SIH 180 SL2 819-31, 855-7, 981-5, 1014-8 SL3 1226-9 SL5 2303-6, 2501-5 SRB 16, 71, 233-45, 261, 336, 502, 515-6 SV1 32-6 TSF 205-18, 246 VES 111, 128, 212, 329-31 VF1 185-215, 277-8, 282 WFS 278 WGT 62 WSF 175, 240, 265, 284
Gunn, Neil Miller (1891-1973) BAA 112-3 CSF 89 ES1 196 FL2 658-60 SFE 267 SF1 229
Gunnarson, Gunner. BAA 179
Gunness, Belle. TSP 196
Gunter, Archibald Clavering (1847-1907) ES1 196 SF1 229
Gunther, Gotthard. ES1 196 IAC 125 ISW 217-9 SFE 267-8 SOT 432
Gunther, John (1901-70) CSF 89 SF1 229 SF2 925
Gunther, Max. BAA 282
Guppy, Pauline D. IAC 125
Gurdjieff, George I. (1872-1949) CWN 30, 37 IAC 125 MIH 141 SF1 229 THM 51, 60
Gurdon, John Everard. SF1 229
Gurevich, George (1917-) LEX 344 SFS 54
Gurk, Paul Fritz Otto (1880-1953) LEX 345
Gurney, Albert Ramsdell, Jr. (1930-) SF1 229
Gurney, Bernard Gilbert. EXT 10/2 60-1

Gurney, David pseud. of Patrick Bair. SF1 229
Gurney, (Sir) Goldsworth. POE 53
Gurney, Peter. BAA 227
Gury, Jacques. BAA 227
Gusfield, Joseph R. BAA 179, 227
Gussmann, Wilhelm. BAA 227
Gustafsson, Lars. BAA 179 FBK 8, 11, 16
Gustave, Olga. SF1 229
Gutek, Gerald. BAA 227
Gutenberg, Johann. MSF 194
Guter, Josef. BAA 179
Gutherm, Frederick. EXT 9/2 46
Guthrie, Alan. VES 151
Guthrie, Ellen Jane Emma. ES1 196 SF1 229
Guthrie, Kenneth Sylvan (1871-1940) BAA 84 CSF 89 SF1 229
Guthrie, Thomas Anstey (1856-1934) ES1 196 VES 209 WGT 62 see also F. Anstey

Guthrie, Vee. FFC 110
Guthrie, W. B. BAA 179
Guttenberg, Violet. SF1 229
Gutter, Agnes. BAA 282
Gutteridge, Lindsay (1923-) HFI 65 SFE 268 SF1 229-30 SF2 925-6 VES 141
Guttin, Jacques. POE 15-6
Guttridge, Jennifer. IAC 125
Guttridge, Len. IAC 125 SFS 54
Guy, Alain. BAA 227
Guy, F. B. WBW 4
Guy, L. WGT 62 see also A Patriot
Guzman, Mauricio. BAA 179
Gwinn, D. Howard. SF1 230
Gwinn, Omar. TSP 134 see also Alan Blake
Gwynne, Paul pseud. of Ernest Slater. CSF 89 SF1 230
Gyertyan, Ervin. SIH 142
Gygax, E. Gary. SF1 230
Gyles, Gordon A. IAC 125

H

H. A. M. SF1 334
H. C. M. W. pseud. of Henry Crocker Marriott Watson. CSF 89
H. M. P. SF1 401
H. S. SFN 31
Haac, Oscar A. BAA 227
Haapenen, Gretchen. SFB 132-3
Haars, Peter. FBK 46
Haas, Benjamin Leopold (1926-77) SF2 997-8 see also Richard Meade
Haas, Charles. ES1 196 IAC 125 SF1 230
Haas, Dorothy. FFC 119
Haas, Irene. FFC 12, 47, 92
Haas, Joseph. EXT 10/1 29, 39

Haase, Donald P. FL2 720-4 FL5 2247-58
Haase, John. IAC 125
Haber, Heinz (1913-) ES1 196
Haber, Fritz. POE 226
Habib, Mohammed. CSF 89
Hacker, Andrew. BAA 227 NDA 54, 206
Hacker, Marilyn T. (1942-) EXT 10/2 54 IAC 95, 125 LTN 253 SF1 230
Hadas, Moses. BAA 227
Haden-Guest, Anthony. IAC 125
Hader, Berta Hoerner. SF1 230
Hader, Elmer Stanley (1889-) SF1 230
Hadfield, Alice Mary. EXT 9/2 47 SOI 125-38, 164

Hadfield, John Charles (1907-)
ES1 196-7 SF1 230
Hadfield, Robert L. CSF 89 ES1
197 SF1 230
Hadley, Arthur Twining (1924-)
AOW 193 BAA 132 ES1 197
HFI 65 ISW 173-4 NDA 21-2
SFE 268 SF1 230
Hadley, Franklin T. ES1 197
Hadley, George (-1798) CSF 89
SF1 230
Hadley, Thomas G. SF1 230
Hadley, Thomas P. ALW 184
EXT 3/1 21 SOT 22-3 WSF 132
Haeckel, Ernst. EXT 7/1 10, 13
EXT 8/2 48 MSF 232 POE 141
SFW 61
Haedicke, Paul. BAA 53 CSF 89
Haes, Hubert. CSF 89
Hagan, Randall. PJF 55, 73
Haggard, Andrew Charles Parker
(1854-1923) CSF 89 SF1 230
Haggard, Audrey. SF1 230
Haggard, Edward Arthur (1860-
1925) SF1 230
Haggard, H(enry) Rider (1856-
1925) ALW 33, 87, 97, 100, 102,
105, 136 AOW 46-7, 63-4, 89,
394, 396 BAA x BYS 136-9, 141,
169, 173 CAT 8 CSC 39-40, 172
CSF 89-90 ES1 197-9 EXT 1/1
3, 9, 14 EXT 1/2 24, 37 EXT
2/2 22 EXT 3/1 29 EXT 3/2
47 EXT 4/2 20 EXT 5/1 4, 16,
16a EXT 7/2 38 EXT 10/1 36
FAN 152 FBK 100-3 FFR 87-8
FL1 22-5, 486-8 FL3 1221-3,
1396-1401 FL5 2176-9 HFI 65
IMS 20 INT 5 ISW 251 KAU 44
LEX 346-8 MFW 21, 100, 122-6,
128, 133, 135, 137 MIH 81 MSF
141, 165 MSM 25 PJF 13 RGS
73-4 RSG 65 SFB 84 SFD 41
SFE 268 SFH 90 SFW 19-24, 60,
67, 75, 87, 132 SF1 231-2 SIH
185 SL4 1908-12 SOT 14, 399
SRB 6, 261 STH 196, 198, 201
THM 39 VES 140, 211 WIF 23,
51, 55, 68, 149, 231 WSF 293-4,
386 WTS 17, 123
Haggard, J. Harvey (1913-) ES1
199 IMS 45, 66-8, 83, 110-1, 182,
200, 241 SFE 268 SOT 108
WGT 63

Haggard, William pseud. of Rich-
ard Henry Michael Clayton.
SFE 268 SF1 232
Haggert, W. T. IAC 125 SFS 54
Hague, Michael. VES 233
Hahn, Arnold. BAA 179
Hahn, Charles Curtz. BAA 61
CSF 90 SF1 232
Hahn, George R. IMS 56, 72, 82-
3, 245-6 WGT 63 see also
Cyril Mand
Hahn, Istvan. BAA 227
Hahn, Otto. RHN 60
Hahn, Ronald M. (1948-) LEX
348-50
Hahn, Steve. HFI 65
Haiblum, Isidore (1935-) HFI 66
LEX 350 SFE 268 SF1 232
SF2 926 SRB 262
Haight, Gordon. EXT 5/2 27
Hail, Steve. IAC 125
Haile, H. G. FL5 2316-30
Haile, Terence. SF1 232
Hailey, Arthur (1920-) ES1 199-
200 SFE 268-9
Haines, Donal Hamilton (1886-
1951) CSF 91 SF1 232 STH 170-1
Haining, Peter Alexander (1940-)
ES1 200 FBK 150 FRN 30, 36,
95, 129-31 IAC 125 SFE 269
SF1 232-3 SF2 926 WSF 389
Hake, William Augustus Gordon.
BAA 23
Halacy, Daniel Stephen, Jr. (1919-)
AOW 318 ES1 200 SFE 269 SF1
233 SF2 926-7
Haldane, Charlotte Franken (1894-
1969) BAA 92 CSF 91 ES1 200-
1 FAN 145 FL2 1004-6 SF1 233
Haldane, J(ohn) B(urdon) S(ander-
son) (1892-1964) BAA 118 CAT
81-2, 98-9 CSC 230 CSF 91
EXT 5/1 8 EXT 9/1 23 FAN
140-3 FTF 69, 190-1 IAC 125
MIH 106 MSF 226 MSM 209
SFB 20 SFE 269 SFH 50 SFS 54
SF1 233 SOI 15-25 STH 7-8
TBJ 11, 21-2 VFS 56, 145 WFS
265
Haldeman, Gay. WFS 212
Haldeman, Jack C. (1941-) COT
55 IAC 125 JHN 60 LEX 350-1
Haldeman, Joe (1943-) AAL 27
ALW 212 AOW 193, 293 BFP
215 COT 85 ETN 44, 121 FFR

Haldeman, Joe (cont.)
88 [FJT] HFI 66 IAC 125 LEX
351-2 RGS 74-5 SFE 269 SFH
243 SF1 233 SF2 927 SL2 813-
8 SL3 1407-12 SRB 10,361,366,
372 VES 77 WFS 212 WGT 63
WSF 237,283
Haldeman, Marygay. JHN 11,15,
18,22,36
Haldeman-Julius, Emanuel (1889-
1951) SF1 582
Hale, Edward Everett (1822-1909)
ALW 53,60,87 BAA 28-9 CSF
91 ES1 201 EXT 3/2 37 EXT
5/1 4 FTF 41,44 IAC 125 MSF
162,177 MSM 29,217 PST 48
SFE 269 SFN 32 SFS 54 SF1
232-4 STH 72 VFS 221 WGT
63 WSF 18 YTS 5
Hale, John (1926-) BAA 148 SF1
234
Hale, Lucretia. FFC 145
Hale, Marice Rutledge Gibson
(1884-) WGT 63 see also
Maryse Rutledge
Hale, Martin. SF1 234
Hale, Robert Beverly. IAC 125
SFS 54 SF1 234
Hales, Alfred Greenwood. CSF 91
Hales, C. L. CSF 91 SF1 234
Hales, E. E. Y. HFI 184
Halevy, Al. HID x RFA vii
Halevy, Elie. FAN 182
Halewood, William H. BAA 227
Haley, Claude. SF1 234
Haley, Harry Franklin (1883-)
CSF 91 SF1 234
Halford, John. CSF 91 SF1 234
Halidom, M. Y. pseud. of Edward
Heron-Allen. CSF 91 ES1 201
SF1 234
Halifax, (Lord) Charles Lindley
Wood (1839-1934) ES1 201
Halifax, Clifford. CSF 137
Halifax, Robert. CSF 91
Halkin, Leon E. BAA 227
Hall, A. R. BAA 228
Hall, Angus (1932-) SF1 234 SF2
927
Hall, Anna Gertrude (1863-1961)
SF1 235
Hall, Asaph. EXT 5/2 39, 41, 43
SFH 161 WSF 15
Hall, Austin (1882? -1933) ALW
33,113,121,156 BAA 86 BFP

216 BYS 170 CSF 91 ES1 202
HFI 66 IAC 125 ISW ix, 22-5, 70
LEX 352-3 MSM 90,297 RFA 1
RGS 75-6 SFE 270 SF1 234
SOT 49,70 SRB 312 STH 259
Hall, Brian Patrick (1935-) SF1
234
Hall, Charles F. DTS 21
Hall, (Sir) Daniel. POE 236
Hall, Desmond Winter. RFA xvi,
4,10,18 SFE 270 SOT 93 WGT
63 WSF 59 see also Anthony
Gilmore, H. G. Winter
Hall, Donald. IAC 125 SFS 54
Hall, Frances. IAC 125
Hall, George Roma. CSF 91 SF1
234
Hall, Gertrude. CSF 91
Hall, Graham M. IAC 125 SF1
235
Hall, Granville Stanley (1844-1924)
BAA 85 CSF 91 SF1 235
Hall, H(albert) W(eldon) (1941-)
AOW 392-404 BRS 10 PJF 73
SFE 270 SF1 235 SF2 927-8
SRB 75,291
Hall, Hal. CSF 91
Hall, Harold Curtis. BAA 111
Hall, James. EXT 6/1 13 NWO
283 TSP 134 see also Douglas
Giles
Hall, James Norman. CSF 91
Hall, John Ryder. [FUT]
Hall, (Bishop) Joseph (1574-1656)
BAA 3 EXT 3/1 30 WGT 63
Hall, Leland Boylston (1883-1957)
CSF 91 SF1 235
Hall, Manly Palmer (1901-) ES1
202 SF1 235
Hall, Owen pseud. of James Davis.
CSF 92 IAC 125 SF1 235
Hall, Robert Lee (1941-) SFE 270
Hall, Robin. FFC 164
Hall, Ronald (1929-) SF1 235
Hall, Steve. ES1 202 IAC 125
SFS 54 WGT 63
Hall, Tord. SL1 72-77
Hall, Trevor Henry. ES1 202
Hall, William C. IAC 125
Hallahan, William H. SF1 235
Hallam, Samuel Atlantis (1915-)
ES1 202 SF1 235 SF2 928
Halle, Louis Joseph, Jr. (1910-)
BAA 139 ES1 202 EXT 10/1 29
SFE 270 SF1 235 SF2 928

Hallen, A. L. CSF 92 SF1 235
Halley, Edmund. WIF 37
Hallgren, I. BAA 282
Hallinan, Tim. SF1 235
Halliwell, Tony. SF1 235
Hallock, Robert. FFC 13
Hallowell, Priscilla. FFC 55
Hallstead, William F., III. SFS 54
Hallums, James R. SFE 270 SF1 235
Hallus, Tak pseud. of Stephen Robinett. AAL 110-1 VES 157
Halpern, Frank M. AOW 361
Halsbury, (Earl of) pseud. of Hardinge Goulburn Gifford (1880-1943) CSF 92 SFE 270 SF1 235
Halsey, Harlan Page (1839?-98) WGT 63
Halstead, William F. IAC 125
Hamada, Nobuya. BAA 87
Hamblen, Charles F. RBY 240
Hambrook, Emerson C. CSF 92 SF1 236
Hamburger, Bernard. BAA 228
Hamburger, Michael. IAC 125
Hamel, Frank. CSF 92
Hamil, Tom. FFC 54
Hamilton. JGB 6
Hamilton, Alex John. IAC 126 SF1 236 SF2 928
Hamilton, Alexander (1755-1804) COT 38,142
Hamilton, Alexander. ES1 202
Hamilton, (Count) Anthony (1645?-1719) CSF 92 ES1 202 SF1 236
Hamilton, Anthony Walter Patrick (1904-62) SF1 237
Hamilton, Bernard. SF1 236
Hamilton, Charles. WGT 63
Hamilton, Cicely Mary (1872-1952) BAA 74,87 CSF 92 POE 228 SF1 236
Hamilton, Edith. RZY 33
Hamilton, Edmund Moore (1904-77) AAL 111 ALW 126,132,136-7,169,219,239 AOW 103,108, 193 ASF 143,146 BFP 217-9 BYS 220 COT 6,45,106,145-6, 295,301 CSC 29,31,47,52,220 CSF 92 DTS 15 ES1 202-4 ETN 81-2,84,195,197 EXT 5/1 3 FFR 88 HFI 66-7 IAC 126 IAH 48,85 IMS 16,75,83,213 ISW 5, 139 KAU 121 LEX 353-5 MFW

172 MIH 23,36,39,45 MSM 77, 169,304 PST 158,198,283,288 RFA 2,6,46-7,65,110,212 RGS 76-7,215 SFA 150 SFB 39,55 SFD 25,28,210 SFE 270 SFN 30-1 SFS 54-5 SFW 115 SF1 236 SF2 928 SIH 113,165,178 SL4 1939-43 SOT 3,10,19,66-83,90,107-8,117,134-5,144,238, 309,329,359,364 SRB 5,116 STH 82-3,88,148,220,242-3, 245,251 TRB 56 TSP 189 UFS 3 VES 70,75-6,81-2,87,93,97-8,103,105,108,110,112,133-4, 139,142,150,157,173,180,185-6,191,193,307,334 WAA 144 WGT 63-4 WIF 90,136,145,150-4,161,164,192,221 WSF 29,45, 48,50,116-7,121,151,156,172, 298,312,387 WTS ix,5-6,27-9, 31-43,45-6,51-4,69,86,120,123, 125,128 see also Alexander Blade, Hugh Davidson, Brett Sterling, S. M. Tenneshaw, Robert Wentworth
Hamilton, John B. EXT 1/2 24 EXT 3/2 31 EXT 4/1 2-13 EXT 5/1 1 EXT 7/1 18,26
Hamilton, Kenneth M. BAA 228
Hamilton, Leigh Brackett (1915-78) WGT 64 WTS 53 see also Leigh Brackett
Hamilton, Marianne Lynn. CSF 92 SF1 237
Hamilton, Patrick. BAA 108 CSF 92
Hamilton, Peter. ES1 204 WIF 121
Hamilton, Ralph C. MSM xvi
Hamilton, Raphael N. EXT 10/1 29,35
Hamilton, Robert. BAA 228
Hamilton-Patterson, J. IAC 126
Hamley, Dennis (1935-) SF1 582
Hamlin, Vince. WSF 305
Hamling, William Lawrence (1921-) ES1 204 IMS 205,225,238-40 SFE 271 SOT 87 WIF 112,116, 120,207 WSF 140,300
Hamm, Charles. SOT 371
Hamm, Thelma D. IAC 126
Hammerstrom, Norman Elwood. COT 27,162 WTS 25
Hammett, Dashiell (1894-1961) AOW 84 CSC 207-8,210 CSF 92

Hammett, Dashiell (cont.)
ES1 204 ETN 38,111 EXT 3/1
19 IAC 126 MSM 26 SF1 237
WSF 103 WGT 64
Hammond, Clement M. CSF 142
Hammond, J. R. SRB 83
Hammond, H. R. VES 337 WTS
86, 96
Hammond, W. F. STH 139
Hammond, William Alexander.
EXT 4/1 9,12
Hampden, John (1898-1974) CSF
92 ES1 204 SF1 237
Hampson, Frank (1917-) SFE 271-
2 VES 327-8
Hampton, Lou. CSF 92 ES1 204
SF1 237
Hanaranda, Mulla (1882-) CSF 92
SF1 237
Hancock, Anson U. CSF 92
Hancock, Harrie Irving (1868-
1922) CSF 92 SF1 237 SRB 10
STH 171
Hancock, Niel. HFI 67
Hancock, Truda. STH 92
Handel, George Frederick (1685-
1759) CUA 39,41 LTN 88,231
Handler, Philip. SFH 241
Haney, Laura. IAC 126
Hanifin, John M. (-1889?) see
Phineas
Haniwa. IAC 126
Hankin. EXT 5/2 47
Hankinson, Charles James (1866-)
WGT 64 see also Clive Holland
Hanks, Keith (1940-) SF1 237
Hanley, Eve. FFC 74
Hanley, James (1901-) CSF 93
EXT 2/2 27 SF1 237
Hanlon, Jon. ES1 204 SF1 237
Hanmura, Ryo (1935-) SL4 1854-8
Hanna, George W. FAN 189 see
also Spirito Gentil
Hanna, W. C. ES1 204 HFI 67
SFE 272 SF1 237
Hannah, E. IAC 126
Hannan, Charles. CSF 93 SF1 237
Hannay, James Frederick Wynne
(1906-) CSF 93 SF1 237
Hannigan, D. F. IAC 126
Hano, Arnold. WFS 196
Hansard, Rene. CSF 93
Hansen, Karl. IAC 127
Hansen, Louise Taylor. COT 5
ES1 205 PST 147,229,237,266
VES 76,335,340

Hansen, Louis Ingvald (1904-)
WGT 64
Hansen, Vern. SFE 272 SF1 238
Hansman, William Donald (1913-)
ES1 205 SFE 272 SF1 238 SF2
929
Hansom, Mark. CSF 93 SF1 238
Hanson, Maurice K. IMS 97, 99
SOT 377
Hanson, Rita Mohler. SF1 238
Hansot, Elisabeth. BAA xiii-xiv,
xx-xxi,179
Hanvey, Robert E. BAA 66 SF1
238
Happel, R. V. IMS 117
Harbecke, Ulrich (1943-) LEX 356
Happy. SF1 238
Harary, F. BAA 228
Harben, William Nathaniel (1858-
1919) AOW 64 BAA 47,51 CSF
93 EXT 1/1 11 FTF 41 IAC 127
PST 66,217,250,252,267,277
SFE 272 SF1 238
Harbottle, Philip James (1941-)
BYS 240 IAC 127 SFE 272-3
SF1 238,582 SF2 929
Harcourt, Thomas A. WGT 64
Hard, Francis pseud. of Farns-
worth Wright. WTS 25
Harden, John (1902-) ES1 205
Hardesty, William H. , III. FL1
116-21, 289-93 FL4 2036-8 SL1
33-7 SL2 909-14 SL3 1444-8
SL4 1759-63 SL5 2529-33
Hardie, John Lipp. CSF 93 ES1
205 SF1 238
Hardin, Garrett James (1915-)
SF1 238 SF2 929
Harding, Allison V. WTS 45
Harding, D. W. EXT 6/1 19
Harding, Edward F. CSF 93
Harding, Ellison. BAA 71 CSF
93 SF1 238
Harding, John William. SF1 238
Harding, Lee (1937-) BYS 303
ES1 205 HFI 67 IAC 127 LTN
249,251,258,264 SFE 273 SFS
55
Harding, Ronald S. L. SF1 238
Harding, Warren G. RHN 211
Hardt, Maria Agnelies. BAA 282
Hardwick, Elizabeth. EXT 6/1 20
Hardy, David A. IAC 127 VES
289
Hardy, G. H. IAC 127
Hardy, Jerry. WFS 180

Hardy, Oliver. KVT 58-9
Hardy, Philip. SF1 238
Hardy, Thomas (1840-1928) ACC
209 BYS 9, 88-91, 109-10, 208
FL5 2107-11 IAC 127 MSF 11,
70 MSM 107 PST 78 SFH 43
TSO 34 WSF 348
Hardy, William George (1895-)
SF1 239 SF2 929
Hare, Robert pseud. of Robert H.
Hutchinson. CSF 93
Hare, William Loftus. BAA 228
Harford, Scott. SF1 239
Harfest, Betsy. ACC 87-120
TSO 4-5
Harger, Catharine. SF1 239
Hargrave, John Gordon (1894-)
CSF 93 SF1 239
Hargreaves, (Sir) Gerald. ES1
205
Hargreaves, H. A. IAC 127
Hari, Mata. KVT 25 RFA 133
Hark, Ina Rae. FL2 526-34 FL3
1311-2
Harker, Jonathan. SIH 31
Harker, Kenneth (1927-) ES1 205
SFE 273 SF1 239 SF2 929-30
Harkins, Peter J. ES1 205 WGT
64
Harkins, Philip (1912-) SF1 239
SF2 930
Harkins, William. FAN 97-8
Harkon, Franz. SF1 239
Harlan, Ethel Andrews. SF1 239
Harland, Henry (1861-1905) WGT
64-5 see also Sidney Luska
Harley, Alan. IAC 127
Harley, (Mrs.) M. CSF 93 WGT
65
Harlow, Benjamin C. BAA 228
Harlow, Jean. CAT 24
Harmon, James Judson (1933-)
ALW 212 ES1 205 HID 57 IAC
127 SFE 273 SFS 55 SF1 239
SF2 930
Harmon, Seth. IAC 127
Harmsworth, Alfred. EXT 8/2
65 STH 193
Harness, Charles L. (1915-) ALW
161, 164 AOW 194, 295 BAA 122
BFP 220 BYS 264-5, 283 ES1
205 FFR 89 HFI 67 HID 92-4
IAC 127 IAH 18, 24-5 ISW 203-
5 LEX 357-8 MFW 5, 51, 289
RGS 77-8 SFD 298, 309 SFE

273 SFS 55 SF1 239 SF2 930
SL4 1641-4, 1832-6 TSF 60, 232
VES 190, 335
Harnett, St. Clair. CSF 93
Harney, Gilbert Lane. BAA 62
Harney, W. E. ES1 205-6
Harnik, J. FLT 157
Harnishfeger, Lloyd. SF1 239
Harper, C. Armitage. CSF 93
ES1 206 SF1 239
Harper, Charles C. CSF 93
Harper, Charles George (1863-
1943) SF1 239
Harper, Harry (1880-1960) CSF
85 SFE 273 SF1 239
Harper, Jo Ann. IAC 127
Harper, Jody. IAC 127
Harper, Olive pseud. of Helen
Burnell A'Apery. CSF 93 SF1
239
Harper, Richard. IAC 127 SFS
55
Harper, Theodore A. CSF 94
Harper, Vincent. AOW 35, 64
CSF 94 EXT 1/1 12 SFE 273
SF1 239 SL3 1459-62
Harper, Wilhelmina (1884-) CSF
94 ES1 206
Harper, Winifred. CSF 94
Harre, Thomas Everett (1884-
1948) CSF 94 ES1 206 EXT 3/1
20 SF1 239 WTS 22
Harrington. EXT 8/1 20
Harrington, Alan. HFI 67 NWO
163-4
Harrington, Donald (1935-) SF1
239 SF2 929
Harrington, James. BAA 5 BYS
66 CSF 94 MSF 111
Harrington, Len. SF1 240
Harrington, Michael. BAA 176
Harrington, Richard. SF1 240
Harris. ETN 65
Harris, Ada L. CSF 94
Harris, Alfred (1928-) SF1 240
SF2 930
Harris, Arthur T. (house name)
WGT 65
Harris, Barbara S. (1927-) HFI
67 SF1 240 SF2 930
Harris, Christie Lucy (1907-)
SF1 240 SF2 930
Harris, Clare Winger (1891-)
CSF 94 DTS 12 ES1 206 IAC
127 IMS 15 ISW 177 SFD 24, 27
SFS 22, 55 SF1 240 VES 84

Harris, Frank (1854-1931) BAA
96 CSF 94 ES1 206 SF1 240
STH 238-9
Harris, J. Henry. CSF 94 SF1
240
Harris, John (1916-) EXT 10/2
50 SF1 240
Harris, John Frederick. BAA 179
Harris, John (Wyndham Parkes
Lucas) Beynon (1903-69) ALW
141 BAA 126 BFP 221-3 COT
24, 41, 125 ES1 206-8 EXT 7/2
39 IAC 127 IMS 23, 96 ISW 178
SFS 55 SF2 1135 VES 71, 150,
178, 230 WGT 65 WSF 202 see
also Lucas Parkes, Wyndhame
Parkes, John Wyndham
Harris, Larry Mark (1933-) AAL
110 IAC 127 IAH 30 SFE 273
SFS 55 SF2 950-2 WGT 65 see
also Laurence M. Janifer,
Mark Phillips
Harris, Marilyn pseud. of Mari-
lyn Harris Springer (1931-) SF1
240
Harris, Rosemary Jeanne. FFC
20, 42, 108 SF1 240 SF2 931
Harris, T. George. WFS 287
Harris, Thomas Milner (1865-)
SF1 242
Harris, W. T. BAA 228
Harris, Walter (1925-) SF1 240
Harris, (Rev.) William Shuler
(1865-) BAA 68 CSF 94 SF1
240 SOT 10 STH 4
Harris-Burland, John B. (1870-
1926) CSF 94 IAC 127 SF1 240
WGT 65 see also Harris Bur-
land
Harrison, Ada. FFC 74
Harrison, Eva. CSF 94
Harrison, Evelyn. WFS 205 see
also Evelyn Del Rey
Harrison, George Bagshawe
(1894-) ES1 208 SF1 240 SF2
931
Harrison, Harry (1925-) AAL 2
ALW 136, 176, 212, 222 AOW
194-5, 291-4, 299, 394 ASF 211
BAA 137, 140-2 BFP 224-30
BYS 20, 241-3, 247, 252, 286, 296,
302, 308-10 COT 268-9 CSC
106-7 DTS 8, 34 ES1 208-9
ETN 22, 26, 30, 45, 128 EXT 6/2
22 EXT 10/1 6 FFR 89-90 FHT

10, 43, 45, 48, 54 [FJT] FRN 14,
36, 95 FTF 85 [FUT] HFI 67-8
IAC 29, 127-9, 226 KAU 61, 67,
69-72, 74, 84, 93 LEX 358-9
LTN 250 MFW 24, 44, 230, 249
MIH 7, 16, 18-9, 39, 62, 115-6
NDA 158-9 NWO 125 OMN 143-
6 POE 296-7 RAH 228 RGS 78-
9, 215 RSG 60-1 SFB 100 SFD
31-2, 34-5, 54-6 SFE 273-4 SFH
92, 150 SFS 55 SFW 203 SF1
240-2 SF2 931 SIH 94, 118, 185
SL1 223-7 SL2 519-23 SL3
1235-7, 1312-6 SL5 2136-9,
2324-8 SOT 146, 183 SRB 75,
333, 336, 347, 356 STH 45 TRB
66 TSF 248 VES 82-3, 87, 108,
112, 123, 129, 136, 148, 157, 165,
168, 173-4, 227, 253, 317, 329-30
WAA 27, 58, 69, 117 WFS 39, 174,
205 WGT 65-6 WIF 118, 140
WSF 4, 174, 187, 241, 346, 387
see also Felix Boyd, Hank
Dempsey, Wade Kaempfert
Harrison, Helga (1924-) BAA 137
ES1 209 SF1 242
Harrison, James A. NWO 54
Harrison, Jane Ellen. MSF 25
Harrison, Liz. IAC 129
Harrison, Mary St. Leger Kings-
ley (1852-1931) WGT 66 see
also Lucas Malet
Harrison, Michael (1907-) CSF 94
ES1 209 EXT 3/1 23 SFE 274
SF1 242 WGT 66
Harrison, M(ichael) John (1945-)
AAL 40 AOW 195 BFP 231
BYS 298 FL4 1826-30 HFI 68
IAC 129 LEX 359-60 RGS 79-
80 SFE 274-5 SF1 242 SF2
931-2 SL4 1655-9 see also
Joyce Churchill
Harrison, Rex. SFN 82
Harrison, T. Milner. CSF 94
Harrison, William (1933-) AOW
293 HFI 68 IAC 129 SF1 242
SF2 932
Harrower, Jack. PST 118
Harry, Wilfried Antonius (1947-)
LEX 360-1
Harryhausen, Ray (1920-) OMN
216, 222-3 SFE 275 SRB 58, 99
Harshaw, Ruth. CSF 94 EXT
10/1 29
Harshman, Tom. SF1 242

Hart, Bernard Liddell. POE 239-40

Hart, Dale. IMS 137, 156, 182, 213, 243

Hart, Edward (1854-) ES1 209

Hart, Ellis pseud. of Harlan Ellison. SFS 55

Hart, Francis M. CSF 94

Hart, Harry (1907-) WGT 66 see also Pat Frank

Hart, James S. IAC 129

Hart, Jeffrey. EXT 6/1 19

Hart, Johnny. IAC 129

Hart, Lawrence. MSM 102

Hart, Moss. OWB 70

Hart, Steve. SF1 242

Harte, (Francis) Bret (1836? -1902) ALW 82 CSF 94 EXT 4/1 10 FBK 72 STH 203 WGT 66

Harting, Pieter (1812-85) POE 134-6 WGT 66 see also Dr. Dioscorides

Hartl, Harold W. SF1 242

Hartley, George Innes. CSF 94

Hartley, Harry Livingston (1900-) SF1 242 SF2 932

Hartley, L(eslie) P(oles) (1895-1972) BAA 134 BYS 256 CSF 94 DTS 7, 27 ES1 209 EXT 2/2 29 EXT 6/2 51 EXT 10/1 47 FAN 149-51 FBK 72, 78 FTF 107 HFI 68 NDA 92-4, 209-10 NWO 125 POE 280 SFE 275 SF1 242 SF2 932 VES 261

Hartlib, Samuel (1600? -62) ES1 209 SFE 275

Hartman, Darlene (1934-) SF2 968 WGT 66 see also Simon Lang

Hartman, Emerson B. (1890-) CSF 95 SF1 242

Hartman, Lee Foster. CSF 95

Hartman, Louis E. SF1 242

Hartmann, Franz (1838-1912) CSF 95 SF1 242-3 WGT 66 see also Student of Occultism

Hartmann, Geoffrey H. MFW 112 SOI 95

Hartmann, Helmut Henry (1931-) see Henry Seymour

Hartridge, Jon (1934-) BAA 151 BYS 304 HFI 68 IAC 130 SFE 275 SF1 243

Hartshorne, Henry. BAA 33

Hartwell, David G. BYS 283 IAC 130 LTN 18

Hartwick, Harry. FFC 13

Harun-Al-Rashid. MSF 195

Harvey, Alexander (1868-1949) CSF 95 ES1 209 SF1 243

Harvey, Florence see Grove Donner

Harvey, Frank Laird (1913-) ES1 209 IAC 130 SFE 275 SFS 55 SF1 243 SF2 932

Harvey, James Clarence (1859-1917) SF1 243

Harvey, Walter. CSF 95 SF1 243

Harvey, William Fryer (1855-1937) CSF 95 ES1 209-10 FL3 1532-5 IAC 130 SF1 243 SOT 368 TSP 105

Harvey, William Hope. BAA 90

Harvey, William Wirt (1866-) CSF 95 SF1 243

Harwood, Henry Cecil (1893-1964) IAC 130 SF1 243

Harwood, John. SF1 243

Hasek, Jaroslav. MSF 282 SFN 50

Haselkorn, Mark P. LTN 268

Haselriis, Elsie. FFC 19

Hasford, Gustav. IAC 130 WFS 277

Haskin, Byron (1899-) SFE 275

Hass, Hans. VFS 3

Hassan, Ihab. NWO 4, 9-10, 13 STF 8

Hasse, Henry L. (-1977) ALW 60, 141 ES1 210 HFI 68 IAC 130 IMS 29, 33, 45 RBY 105 SFE 275 SFS 56 SF1 243 SOT 108, 358-9 VES 153 WGT 66 WIF WTS 19, 41

Hasselblatt, Dieter (1926-) LEX 361 SFE 275-6

Hassler, Donald M. FL2 616-8 SL3 1036-6, 1257-60 SL5 2056-8, 2392-5

Hassler, Kenneth Wayne (1932-) HFI 69 SFE 276 SF1 243 SF2 932-3

Hasson, James. ES1 210

Hastings, Archibald C. G. CSF 95

Hastings, Basil. THM 41

Hastings, Christel. IAC 130

Hastings, George Gordon. CSF 95 EXT 1/1 12 SF1 243

Hastings, Macdonald (1909-) SF1 243 SF2 933

Hastings, Michael (1938-) CWN 25 SF1 243
Hastings, Milo (1884-1957) AOW 64 BAA 85 COT 120 CSF 95 SFE 276 SF1 243
Hatch, David Patterson (1846-1912) CSF 95 SF1 243-4 WGT 66
Hatch, Eric Stowe (1901-73) SF1 244
Hatch, Gerald pseud. of Dave Foley. ES1 210 HFI 69 SFE 276 SF1 244
Hatch, Joseph. IMS 33
Hatch, Mary R. Platt (1848-1935) CSF 95 SF1 244
Hatch, Richard Warren (1898-) SF1 244
Hatcher, Jack. IAC 130 SFS 56
Hatfield, Frank pseud. of John Stevens. CSF 95 SF1 244
Hatfield, Richard (1853-) AOW 64 BAA 72 CSF 95 EXT 1/1 2,12 MFW 120 SFE 276 SF1 244
Hathaway, Alan. SF1 244 see also Kenneth Robeson
Hathaway, Hanson. BAA 101
Hathaway, Louise pseud. of Maria Metlova. CSF 95 ES1 210 SF1 244
Hatton, Joseph (1841-1907) CSF 95 SF1 244
Haubold, Herman Arthur. EXT 4/1 12 see also Ivan Trepoff
Hauff, Wilhelm (1802-27) CSF 95 ES1 210 FBK 64 FFC 48,74, 91,145 SF1 244
Hauman, Doris. FFC 7
Hauman, George. FFC 7
Haun, Blair A. SF1 244
Hauptmann, Gerhart (1862-1946) CSF 95 SF1 244
Haus, I. N. FL2 973-5
Hausenstein, Wilhelm. BAA 179
Hauser, Heinrich (1901-60) ES1 210 LEX 362 WGT 66-7 see also Alexander Blade
Hauser, Richard. BAA 228
Hauskeer, Herman. BAA 228
Hausmann, Raoul. IAC 130
Havers, Theodora (1847-89) WGT 67
Haweis, Stephen. CSF 96 SF1 244
Hawke, Napier. SF1 245

Hawker, Caleb. SF1 245
Hawker, Mary Elizabeth (1865-1908) WGT 67 see also Lanoe Falconer
Hawkes, Jessie Jacquetta (1910-) AOW 196 ES1 210 POE 286-7 SFE 276 SF1 245 WGT 67
Hawkesworth, John (1715?-73) CSF 96 SF1 245
Hawkey, Raymond. SF1 245
Hawkin, Martin pseud. of Martin Hawkins. SFE 276 SF1 245
Hawkins, Bruce A. SF1 245
Hawkins, John. ES1 210 STH 256 TSP 185
Hawkins, Lee. ASF 218
Hawkins, Martin. BAA 112 see also Martin Hawkin
Hawkins, Peter. IAC 130 SFS 56 SF1 245 see also Karl Maras
Hawkins, Ward. STH 256
Hawkins, Willard E. BAA 103 COT 265 HID 13 SOT 108 WTS 5,19
Hawkins, William. IAC 130 SFS 56
Hawks, Chester. SF1 245
Hawkwood, Allan pseud. of H. Bedford Jones. CSF 96
Hawley, Cameron. WFS 198
Hawliczek, I. A. EXT 7/1 17
Hawthorne, Julian (1846-1934) ALW 55 BAA 49,228 CSF 96 ES1 210-1 EXT 1/1 12 SF1 245
Hawthorne, Nathaniel (1804-60) ACC 136,140 ALW 33,53-4,87, 92 AOW 7,13,22-3,343-4,351 BAA 25 BYS 44,47,52,117 CAT 4-6,8 COT 86 CSC 166 CSF 96 ES1 211 ETN 11 EXT 4/1 5,8,9 EXT 6/2 23,27,29 EXT 7/1 18 EXT 7/2 38,48 FAN 10 FBK 26-9,82 FLT 2,12-31,75-6,85 FL3 1536-43 HEN 3 IAC 130 IMS 2 ISW 129 MSF 139-40,143, 162,176-7 NDA 47 NWO 20,23, 35-8,101,269-71,282-3 PST 30, 32 RBY 84,124,168,172 RHN 193 RZY 58 SFE 276 SFS 56 SF1 245 SL4 2035-41 SOT 333 VES 172
Hawton, Hector (1901-) ES1 211 SFE 276 SF1 246 SF2 933
Hay, Colin. [FUT] VES 131
Hay, George (1922-) ES1 211 IAC 130 LTN 250 SFE 276-7 SF1

Hay, George (cont.)
246 see also King Lang, Roy
Sheldon
Hay, George Albert. SF1 246
Hay, Ian pseud. of John Hay Beith.
CSF 96 SF1 246
Hay, Jacob (1920-) HFI 184 SFE
277 SF1 246 SF2 933
Hay, John pseud. of John Warwick
Dalrymple-Hay (1928-) SFE 277
SF1 246
Hay, William Delisle. BAA 33
CSF 96 EXT 7/1 12,17 MSF 177
POE 109-10,156-9 SFE 277 SF1
246
Hayakawa, Hiro. WFS 305
Hayakawa, S.I. AAL 178
Haycock, Christine. IAC 130
Hayden, J.J. SF1 246
Haydn, Franz Joseph (1732-1809)
LTN 88
Hayes, E. Nelson. EXT 10/1 29
Hayes, Frederick William (1848-
1918) BAA 49 CSF 96 SF1 246
Hayes, Gabby. INT 39
Hayes, Geoffrey. FFC 81,120,123
Hayes, Hiram Wallace (1858-1939)
SF1 246
Hayes, Jeff W. (1853-1917) BAA
79 SF1 246
Hayes, Lilian. CSF 97 SF1 246
Hayes, Noreen. EXT 10/1 30,39
Hayes, Ralph Eugene (1927-) HFI
69 SF1 246 SF2 933
Hayes, William D. SF1 246
Hayford, Harrison. NWO 282
Hayles, Brian (1931-) SF1 247
Hayles, N.B. UKL 97-115
Hayman, Art. SF1 247
Haynes, Betsy. FFC 31
Haynes, Dorothy Kate (1918-) ES1
211 SF1 247
Haynes, Jean. WFS 205
Haynes, Renee. BAA 228
Hayward, Abraham (1801-84) SF1
247
Hayward, William Stephens. CSF
97 SF1 247
Haywood, Caroline. FFC 5
Haywood, Eliza Fowler (1693?-
1756) CSF 97 SFE 277 SF1 247
Hazard, R.H. CSF 97 SF1 247
Hazlitt, Henry (1894-) BAA 119
ES1 211 EXT 8/2 33 SFE 277
SF1 247 SF2 933-4

Hazlitt, William. CSF 97 POE
42
Head, Richard (1637?-86?) BAA
7 WGT 67
Heal, Edith. FFC 74
Heald, Hazel. EXT 3/1 3,6,10
IMS 110 WTS 37,39,128
Healy, Dominic. CSF 97 SF1
247
Healy, Raymond J(ohn) (1907-)
ALW 175,179,215 AOW 293
BYS 244 CSF 97 ES1 211-2
ETN 56 EXT 3/1 27 EXT 5/1
10 EXT 7/2 46 EXT 8/1 5 HID
6 IAC 130 IAH 59 MSM 35-6,
265 RFA 56 SFD 309 SFE 277
SFS 56 SF1 247 SOT 46,180
SRB 234,304 STH 18,102-3
WSF 130,385,389
Heaphy, Thomas. CSF 97
Heard, Gerald pseud. of Henry
Fitzgerald Heard. AOW 196
EXT 5/1 8 IAC 130 MSM 243-
64,306 SFE 277 SFS 56 SRB
502 Heard, H(enry) F(itzgerald)
(1889-1971) BAA 115 BYS 282
CSF 97 ES1 212 EXT 6/2 51
EXT 7/2 41 EXT 8/1 5 FL3
1544-6 HFI 69 IAC 130 SF1
247-8 SF2 934 SFS 56 STH 13,
107 WGT 67 WIF 58 see also
Gerald Heard
Hearn, Betty Holland. BAA 282
Hearn, Lafcadio (1850-1904) CSF
97 ES1 212-3 FBK 150 FL2
859-60 IAC 130 NWO 8,36,44
SF1 248 WGT 67
Hearn, Mary Ann (1834-1909)
BAA 47 WGT 67 see also
Marianne Farningham
Hearne, Betsy. FFC 5,97
Hearst, William Randolph, Sr.
EXT 8/2 65 STH 260
Heath, Peter pseud. of Peter
Fine. HFI 69 SFE 277 SF1
248
Heath, Thomas Edward. CSF 97
ES1 213 SF1 248
Heath-Stubbs, John. IAC 130
Heaton, John Langdon. CSF 97
Hebraud, Raymonde. BAA 228
Hecataeus (of Abdera). MSF 87
Hecht, Ben (1893-1964) CSF 97
ES1 213 FL2 535-8 IAC 130
KWS 86 PJF 61-2 SFE 277 SF1
248 STH 237,240 WTS 3

Hecht, Friedrich (1903-) WGT 67
Heckel, Frederick C. SF1 248
Heckel, Joseph. BAA 282
Hedgeland, Isabella Kelly (-1813) WGT 67-8
Hedges, Doris. ES1 213 SF1 248
Hedges, Sidney George (1897-1974) CSF 97 SF1 248
Heeley, Maureen. SF1 248
Heffelfinger, Charles. FL4 1954-7
Hefner, Hugh. ETN 44 WFS 54 WTS 129
Hegel, Georg Wilhelm Friedrich. CAT 91 COT 223 MSF 21, 78, 80 SFH 32 VFS 191
Heidegger, Martin (1889-) CWN 41, 60 EXT 7/2 34 UKL 220, 224
Heidenry, John. IAC 130
Heifetz, Jascha (1901-) LTN 88
Heilbroner, Robert L. BAA 228
Heilbrun, Carolyn G. (1926-) WGT 68
Heilman, Robert. EXT 6/2 27 RZY 41
Heim, Michael. HFI 69 SF1 248
Heine, Heinrich. ACC 147 FLT 52
Heine, Irving. SF1 248
Heine, William C. (1919-) HFI 69 SF1 248
Heinisch, Klaus J. BAA 228
Heinlein, Bam Lyle. RHN 6
Heinlein, Harvey Wallace. RHN 8
Heinlein, Leslyn McDonald. HID 5
Heinlein, Oscar. RHN 6
Heinlein, Rex Ivar. RHN 6-8, 139
Heinlein, Robert A. (1907-) AAL 31, 44, 139, 173-6 ACC 119 ACE 23 AC2 21 ALW 7-8, 14, 29, 31, 34, 36, 48, 98-9, 118, 125-6, 146, 154-5, 160, 162-3, 169-71, 173, 185, 190, 213-4, 216, 218, 222, 226-8, 239 AOW 85, 89, 128, 186, 196-8, 261, 288, 290, 292-3, 296, 300, 302, 319-20, 351, 353, 395 ASF 27-8, 44, 76, 85, 123-4, 126, 128-9, 147-8, 150, 161, 198, 205, 215, 217-20, 222, 226, 229, 233, 252, 301 ATA 8 BAA 116, 122, 131, 133, 136, 140, 151, 157, 228 BFP 232-6 BYS 9, 53, 56, 96, 228-9, 257, 270-5, 280, 283, 308 CAT 15-9, 27, 37, 41, 60-2, 72, 76, 83, 88, 100, 102-4, 108, 114, 139 CEN 144-75 COT 3, 12, 23, 62, 96, 98, 106-9, 192, 217-

22, 245-6, 250, 266, 276, 284, 292-3 CSC 11, 30, 39, 42, 44, 46-7, 51-2, 66-8, 93, 102, 116, 132, 164, 169-70, 172-3, 182, 184, 186, 188, 193-4, 220, 232, 281 CSF 97 DTS 24 EFP 6, 11, 15, 20 ES1 213-6 ETN 16-7, 23, 31-2, 34-5, 54-5, 59, 64, 68, 71, 83, 121, 159-60, 163 EXT 1/2 30 EXT 3/1 27 EXT 4/2 29 EXT 5/1 3, 10 EXT 5/2 28 EXT 6/2 51 EXT 7/2 40 EXT 8/1 5, 7, 15 EXT 8/2 31, 58 EXT 10/2 55, 64-5, 110 FBK 122 FFR 91-2 FHT 15-6, 42, 52, 58 [FJT] FLR 20 FL2 942-4 FSU 10-1 FTF 69, 87-8, 91-2, 116-7, 119-21, 135-6, 141-2, 153, 157-62, 174 [FUT] HFI 69-70 IAC 131-2 IAH 28, 43, 54, 68-79, 90, 146 IMS 159 INT 50-1, 120 ISW ix, 1, 4-5, 9, 32-3, 61, 70, 76-91, 117-21, 132, 189, 232, 258 JGB 51 JHN 15, 33-4, 60-2 JVN 180-1, 186, 198, 216-7 KAU 4-5, 8, 17, 27, 59, 61-5, 72, 74, 84, 89, 104, 129, 154, 203, 233 KWS xiv, 2-6, 143-5 LEX 362-5 LTN 27 MFW ix, 8-10, 16, 30, 34, 41, 43, 46, 86, 143-7, 164-8, 170-1, 173, 175, 178, 201, 232, 245, 281-2, 290 MIH 13, 16, 22-3, 28, 30, 36, 39-40, 49, 51-8, 60, 73, 117, 121, 125-6 MSF 13, 22, 78, 143, 193, 201, 218, 242, 279 MSM 19-20, 32, 34, 68, 84, 87, 132, 172, 180, 287 NDA ix, 108, 110-1 NWO 12, 24-5, 46, 149-56, 165-6, 235, 255 OMN 6, 20, 25, 102-6, 225 OWB 11-9, 79, 87, 90, 97 POE 297 RBY 36, 83, 156, 159 RFA 59, 64, 69-70, 74, 76-7, 79-82, 86-91, 93, 96-7, 99-100, 106, 108, 110, 112, 118, 124, 134, 138, 141, 145, 155, 162, 170-1, 176-7, 184, 187, 194-5, 206-7, 212-4 RGS 80-2 SFA 25, 28, 94, 200 SFB 14, 36, 62, 98-100, 114 SFD 4, 9, 16, 28, 64, 73-5, 93-101, 109-28, 131-95, 208-10, 222, 232-3, 235-6, 240, 242, 244, 250, 266, 291-2, 294, 296, 308-10, 312, 315, 319-20, 322 SFE 277-9 SFH 41, 51-9, 62, 65-6, 84, 90, 92, 106, 116, 132, 144, 165, 169, 177-8, 184-5, 188-9, 243 SFN 8-9, 11, 14-48, 70, 83, 90-1, 110-3, 115 SFS 56-7 SFW 3, 157, 185-

Heinlein, Robert (cont.)
196,335 SF1 248-9 SF2 934
SIH 47,59,185,190 SIN 87-92
SL1 207-12,363-8 SL2 587-90
SL3 1439-43 SL4 1645-54,1730-
4 SL5 2173-8,2195-200 SOI 45
SOT 2-3,6,44,62,80,82,98,159-
60,163,167,178,182,187-212,
218,220-1,255,258-9,293,300,
313,316,330,357,394,412-3,431
SRB 5,13,26,79,99,115,126,262,
308,310,312,314,319,323-5,330,
332,334,339,349,357,503 STF
79 STH 6,9-12,19-20,116,158,
178-9,212,245 TDI 6,31 TJB 4,
23-6,46-8 TPS 3-28,199-204,
238-58 TSF 56,134-5,232,235-
6 TSO 38,43-4 VES 68,73,77,
80-1,95,102,106,108,114,116-7,
119,124,128,134-5,143,151,153,
156,158,160-3,168,184,199,202,
210,217,219,225,227,229,231,
235-6,256,259,294,300,307,313,
316-7,328-9 VFS 49,152-3 VF1
104-52,268-75 WAA 56,64-5,67-
8,96,117,121,125,133-6,178
WFS 78,87,111-2,178,192,240,
291-2,300 WGT 68 WIF 90,
107,122,145,149-55,194,225,
238,259,272,284 WSF 95-100,
102,104,114,116,130-1,133,
135,146,148,150-2,167,173,
176,183,185,201-4,212,215,
224,234,237,242,248,251,256,
285,309,321,329,336,356,372,
387-8 WTS 47 YTS 18,23,28
see also Anson McDonald, Lyle
Monroe, John Riverside, Caleb
Saunders, Simon York
Heinlein, Samuel E. RHN 7-8
Heinlein, Virginia Gerstenfeld.
HID 7,185 RHN 14,209
Heinly, John. FFC 188
Heinrich, Carl (1880-1955) CSF
98 SF1 249
Heins, Ethel L. EXT 10/1 30
Heins, H(ardy) H(enry) (1923-)
ES1 216 SF1 249 SRB 78 WAA
102
Heins, Paul. LTN 261
Heintz, Bonnie L. IAC 132
Heisenberg, Werner Carl. COT
109 EXT 7/2 30,37 [FUT]
KAU 43 MFW 7-8,231 RHN 52
SFH 115,128-9,131 TBJ 11
WSF 326

Heiserman, A. R. BAA 228
Heiss, Robert. BAA 180
Heitman. WTS 79
Hekking, Avis. CSF 98 SF1 250
Held, Felix Emil. BAA 228
Held, John, Jr. (1889-1958) CSF
98 SF1 250
Held, Serge Simon. ES1 216
Helders, (Major) pseud. of Robert
Knauss. SF1 250
Heldreth, Lillian M. FL1 341-6
Heliodoros. WIF 28
Helleiner, Karl F. BAA 229
Hellens, Franz. FBK 146
Heller, Astra. BAA 201
Heller, Frank pseud. of Martin
G. Serner. CSF 98
Heller, Joseph. COT 135 NWO
9,36,211 RHN 126-7 WAA 230
WFS 42,230
Hellin, F. P. BAA 229
Helm, Philip. EXT 10/1 18
Helm, Rudolf. BAA 180
Helm, Thomas. ES1 217
Helms, Randel (1942-) AOW 346
SF1 250 SF2 934
Helps, (Sir) Arthur (1813-75) SF1
250
Helson, Ravenna. SRB 30
Helvick, James pseud. of Francis
Claud Cockburn. SF1 250
Helwig, Hans. FFC 114
Hemesath, James B. (1944-) ALW
212 IAC 132 SFE 279
Heming, Jack. SF1 250
Heming, John Winton (1900-53)
CSF 98 ES1 217 SFE 279 SF1
250
Hemingway, Ernest. CSC 28,163
CWN 17,23,30,40 CYR 23 ETN
20,111 EXT 7/2 37 FHT 16,51
[FJT] FSU 20 HEN 21-3 IAH
83 INT 63 JGB 6 JHN 23,35,
47 KVT 5,19,36,40 LTN 149,
182 MSM 111,128,281 NWO 21
RBY 56,160 SFH 81 SOT 361,
368 TBC 4,6,49-50 THM 8,12,
39 VFS 180,270 VMW 45 WAA
138 WIF 152,212,245,255 WTS
45
Hemming, Norma Kathleen (1927-
60) ES1 217 STH 85 WGT 68
Hemyng, Bracebridge (1841-1901)
CSF 98 SF1 250 STH 162
Henderson, Bill (1941-) SF2 1116
see also Luke Walton

Henderson, Gene L. IAC 132 SFS 57
Henderson, Joseph L. KAU 215
Henderson, Keith. SFB 112
Henderson, Le Grand see Le Grand
Henderson, Phillip Prichard (1906-77) ES1 217 SF1 250 SF2 934 WBW 32
Henderson, Thomas. SFH 117
Henderson, Walter B. D. CSF 98
Henderson, William J. IAC 132
Henderson, Zenna (1917-) ALW 212, 216 AOW 198-9 BFP 237 BYS 263, 279 COT 196 ES1 217 EXT 8/1 6 FFR 92 HFI 70 IAC 132-3 ISW 123-4, 126 LEX 365-6 RGS 82-3 SFE 279 SFS 58 SFW 148 SF1 250 SF2 934-5 SL4 1682-6 SRB 335 VES 95 WSF 174
Hendow, Z. S. BAA 57 CSF 98 SF1 250
Hendrich, Paula. FFC 65, 163
Hendrickson, Walter B., Jr. HFI 70
Hendrix, Pjotr. BAA 229
Henham, Ernest George (1870-) BAA 77 CSF 98 SF1 250 WGT 68 see also John Trevena
Henie, Sonja. OWB 18
Henkin, Leo J. MSF 225
Henley, Carra Depuy. BAA 64 CSF 98 SF1 250
Henley, Samuel. FBK 20
Henley, William Earnest. ALW 92, 101
Henneberg, Charles (1899-1959) CSC 33 ES1 217 IAC 133 LEX 366-7 SFE 279 SFS 58 SL3 1472-5 WGT 68
Henneberg, Nathalie (1917-77) LEX 366-7 SFB 139 SFE 279 WGT 68
Henneberger, Jacob Clark. STH 44 WTS 3-6, 21-2, 134
Henneberger, Robert. FFC 92, 154
Hennig, Richard. BAA 180
Hennings, Joseph P. SF1 250
Henningsen, Charles Frederick (1815-77) MSF 138 SF1 251
Henningsen, Jurgen. BAA 229
Hennissart, Martha. WGT 68
Henot, Georges (1848-1918) see Georges Ohnet

Henri, Adrian. IAC 133
Henricksen, Henry Christian (1869-) SF1 251
Henry, Bruce. TSP 138
Henry, Edgar pseud. of Albion Winegar Tourgee. CSF 98 SF1 251
Henry, Jan. FFC 75
Henry, John Louis. STH 183
Henry, Joseph. FTF 35
Henry, Judy. EXT 10/1 32
Henry, O. pseud. of William S. Porter. ACC 54 ETN 40-1, 120 IAC 133 IAH 37 RFA 88 SFS 58 STH 126 TBC 6 WIF 71
Henry, Patrick (1736-99) CYR 26
Henry, Paul-Marc. SF1 251
Henry, (Dr.) Walter O. BAA 80
Henry IV (1050-1106) CUA 53
Henry VIII (1491-1547) CUA 39 SFN 35
Hensel, C. F. EFP 14 IAC 133
Hensley, Joe Louis (1926-) ALW 212 HFI 70 IAC 133 SFE 279
Henson, William Samuel. POE 75-6
Henstra, Friso. FFC 19, 52, 58
Hentoff, Nat. EXT 10/1 30
Henty, G. A. SFW 75
Hepburn, Audrey. SFN 82
Hepworth, George Hughes (1833-1902) CSF 98 ES1 217 SF1 251
Heraclitus. SFB 15
Herbert, Alan Patrick (1890-1971) SF1 251
Herbert, Auberon. BAA 42
Herbert, Beda. BAA 229
Herbert, Benson (1912-) BAA 105 CSF 98 DTS 14 ES1 217 IAC 133 SFE 279-80 SF1 251 SOT 124
Herbert, Edward Geisler. BAA 76
Herbert, Frank (1920-) AAL 6, 53 ALW 30, 212, 239 AOW 128, 199-200, 394 ASF 128, 144 BAA 141, 148, 154, 229 BFP 238-40 BYS 217, 258, 274-6 CAT 37, 139 CEN 41-55 COT 82, 225, 266-7, 271 CSC 31-2, 66, 68, 76, 79, 81, 86, 121, 135-6, 192 DMK 183-92 DTS 38 EFP 11, 15-6 ES1 217-8 FFR 92-3 HFI 70-1 IAC 132-4 INT 16, 52-3, 116-8 JVN 131 KAU 4, 44-5, 47-50, 79, 105, 175

166

Herbert, Frank (cont.)
LEX 367-9 MFW 11,15,34,104,
211-2,224,230-2 MIH 6 NDA
111,113-6 NWO 17,90 OMN 13
RFA 204-5 RGS 83-4,216 RSG
86 SFA 22,244 SFD 253-4,298,
315,320 SFE 280 SFH 59-60,
116,146,169,243 SFS 58-9 SFW
377-85 SF1 251 SF2 935 SIN
77-87,101,133-41 SL1 343-8
SL2 595-9,647-64 SL4 1859-62
SOT 427-8 SRB 14,80,262,325,
342,367,503 STF 67-8,70,78
TSF 60,132-3,140-1,236,239
VES 102,165,229,232 WSF 168,
175-6,236,242,284,387
Herbert, George. THM 28
Herbert, Hugh. STH 252
Herbert, James. HFI 71 SF1 251
VES 220
Herbert, Larry. STH 267
Herbert, William. BAA 47 SF1
251
Herbruggen, Hubertus Schulte.
BAA xxi,191 MSF 40,46-7
Herbst, Steve. IAC 134
Hercourt, Raymond. BAA 283
Hering, Henry Augustus (1864-)
CSF 98 ES1 218 SF1 251
Herlitschka, Herberth E. EXT
6/1 7-8
Herman, Henry. CSF 98
Hermand, Jost. BAA 179,229
Hermes pseud. of Benjamin Lum-
ley. CSF 98
Hermstein, Rudolf. FBK 74
Hernaman-Johnson, Francis (1879-
1949) AOW 41 CSF 98 SFE 280
SF1 252
Hernandez, Felisberto. FBK 135
Hernhunter, Albert. IAC 134
SFS 59 WGT 69
Hernlund, Patricia. BAA 229
Hero (of Alexandria). SFH 114
Herodotus. IAC 134
Herodotus. MSM 125 STF 13
STH 70
Heron, E. pseud. of Hesketh
Prichard, Kate Prichard. CSF
99
Heron-Allen, Edward (1861-1943)
FL4 1999-2001 SF1 252 VES
220 WGT 69 see also M. Y.
Halidom, Dryasdust, Christopher
Blayre

Herr, Daniel J. (1917-) SF1 252
SF2 935
Herrick, Robert (1868-1938) BAA
100 CSF 99 EXT 6/2 51 PST
152-3,222-3,228-9,232,274,285,
290-1,298,306,320 SF1 252
SRB 10
Herrick, Thornecliff (house name)
WGT 69
Herriman, George. SFH 107
Herrman, Louis. CSF 99 SF1
252 VES 139
Herrman, Paul (1905-) ES1 218
Herrmann, Wolfgang. BAA 178
Herron, Don. FL1 193-6 FL2
1015-20
Herron, Edna (1904-) WGT 69
Herron, Ron. [FUT]
Herron, Don. JVN 87-102,236-
7,239-40
Herschel, (Sir) John Frederick.
FTF 32-3 NWO 71 POE 62-7
PST 46,205 WAA 92 WIF 43
Herschel, William. FAN 10
FTF 27
Herscholt, Wolfe. CSF 99 SF1
252
Hersey, Harold B. (1892-) ALW
121 AOW 353 ES1 218 RFA
viii,xii,4,31 TSP 67-8,78
WGT 69 WTS 50
Hersey, John (Richard) (1914-)
ALW 31,238 AOW 200 BAA
134,141,160 ES1 218 EXT 2/2
27,40-1 EXT 4/1 1 EXT 6/2
51 HFI 71 SFE 281 SFH 153
SF1 252 SF2 935-6 SL1 325-9
SOT 426 VES 123
Hershey, Harold. IMS 3,6,72-3
Hershman, Morris (1920-) HFI
71 IAC 134 SF1 252 SF2 936
Hertz, Heinrich Rudolph. OWB
28 VES 91
Hertzberg, Lee. IMS 63
Hertz-Garten, Theodore pseud.
of Mrs. De Mattos. CSF 99
Hertzka, Theodor (1845-1924)
AOW 65 BAA 51 BYS 88 EXT
6/2 41 FAN 10,66 FTF 101
POE 164-5,178 PST 57,262-3,
270,304 SFE 281-2 SF1 252
Hertzler, Joyce Oramel. BAA
xii,xx,180,229 EXT 8/1 23-4
FAN 184 MSF 41-2 PST 319
Hervey, Harry Clay (1900-51)
SF1 252

Hervey, Michael (1920-) SF1 252 SF2 936
Herwer, Chris. SF1 252
Herzberg, Max. SOT 3
Herzl, Theodor. EXT 3/2 49 EXT 6/2 41
Herzog, Arthur (1927-) AOW 206 BAA 283 EXT 6/1 19 HFI 71 SFE 282 SF1 252 SF2 936
Herzog, Bert. BAA 229
Herzog, Emile Salomon (1885-1967) WGT 69 see also Andre Maurois
Herzog, Jesus Silva. BAA 266
Herzog, Tom. IAC 134 SFS 59
Herzog, William Peter (1918-) LEX 369
Hesiod. AOW 10 MSF 187
Hesky, Olga L. (-1974) ES1 218 SF1 253 SF2 936
Heslop, Val. CSF 99 SF1 253
Hess, Dirk (1946-) LEX 369
Hesse, Hermann (1877-1962) AOW 200 CSF 99 CWN 30, 55-6 ES1 218 EXT 2/2 29 EXT 9/2 61 FAN 188 FFR 94 FHT 16 FL2 619-24 FL4 1821-5 POE 256-8 SFE 282 SF1 253 SL2 899-904 WAA 24, 230
Hessen, Sergius. BAA 229
Hessenstein, (Countess) Gabrielle CSF 99 SF1 253
Heston, Charlton. SFH 103
Hetschel, Dick. IAC 134
Hettinger, John (1880-) BAA 97 WGT 69 see also Johnhett
Hettner, Hermann. BAA 180
Hetzel, Pierre Jules. ALW 66-7 POE 92-6, 104 SFB 66-7
Heuer, Kenneth (1927-) ES1 218-9 EXT 5/1 8
Heuffer, Ford Maddox. CUA 52 see also Ford Madox Ford
Heuston, Benjamin F. BAA 44
Heuvelmans, Bernard. ES1 219
Hevelius, Johann. FTF 21
Hevesi, Ludwig. BAA 180
Hewelcke, Geoffrey. WGT 69
Hewett, Anita. FFC 20, 132
Hewison, J. STH 185
Hewlett, Maurice Henry (1861-1923) BAA 229 MIH 64 SF1 253
Hewlett, William. CSF 99
Hewson, Irene Dale see Jean Ross
Hexter, J. H. BAA 229-30

Heydon, Joseph Kentigern. SFE 282 VES 140 WGT 69
Heyer, Georgette. MIH 73
Heyerdahl, Thor. VES 266
Heymann, Robert (1879-1963) LEX 370
Heyne, William P. (1910-) BAA 132 ES1 219 SF1 253
Heynes, Amy E. CSF 99
Heynick, Louis. IMS 52, 56
Heyward, Du Bose (1885-1940) CSF 99 SF1 253
Heywood, D. Herbert. BAA 40
Heywood, Rosalind. ES1 219
Heywood, Victor D. HFI 71 SF1 253
Hibbard, Addison. BAA 95
Hibbs, Ben. ISW 170 SOT 426
Hichens, Robert Smythe (1864-1950) CSF 99 ES1 219 SF1 253 WTS 17
Hicken, Una see Asta Kindler
Hickey, H. B. pseud. of H. Livingston. IAC 134 SFS 59
Hickey, James. INT 73-4
Hickey, Richard. RFA vii, xxii
Hickey, Rosemary. RFA vii, xxii
Hickey, T. Earl. ES1 219 HFI 71 SFE 282 SF1 253
Hickling, Reginald Hugh (1920-) SF1 253
Hicks. RFA 195
Hicks, Betsey. CSF 1
Hicks, Clifford B. (1920-) ES1 219 SF1 253 SF2 936
Hicks, George L. BAA 230
Hicks, Granville (1901-) BAA 109 COT 259 CSF 99 FAN 120 SF1 253
Hicks, Harvey. STH 162
Hidley, Charles. COT 237-8
Heinger, Jorg (1927-) AOW 343 BAA 180 SFE 282
Hieronimus, Ekkehard. BAA 230
Higdon, Hal (1931-) SF1 253 SF2 936
Higginbottom, J. W. FFC 34, 114
Higginbottom, William Hugh (1881-) BAA 81 SF1 253
Higgins, Charles Eli see Mulier
Higgins, Jimmy. WFS 64
Higgins, Margaret. SF1 254
Higginson, H. W. CSF 99 SF1 254

Higginson, Thomas Wentworth (1823-1911) BAA 180 ES1 219 IAC 134 RHN 193
High, Philip E(mpson) (1914-) BAA 142 ES1 219-20 HFI 71 IAC 134 LEX 370-1 SFE 282 SFS 59 SF1 254 SF2 937 VES 199
Higham, Charles (1931-) ES1 220 SF1 254 SF2 937
Highet, Gilbert. EXT 6/1 18 IAC 134 TBC 3
Highland, Harry Joseph. BAA 283
Highsmith, Patricia. IAC 134
Highstone, H. A. IAC 134 SFS 59
Higuchi, Kichiro. STH 48-9
Hildebrand, Tim. EXT 9/2 25
Hildebrandt (brothers). VES 175, 186
Hilder, Rowland. FFC 76
Hildick, E. W. FFC 90
Hildreth, Charles Lotin (1858?-96) CSF 99 SF1 254
Hile, William H. BAA 78
Hill, Albert Fay. HFI 72
Hill, Barney. WFS 267-8
Hill, Betty. WFS 267-8
Hill, David C. HFI 72
Hill, David R. BAA 283
Hill, Dorothy. SF1 254
Hill, Douglas Arthur (1935-) BYS 298 ES1 220 IAC 134 SF1 254 SF2 937
Hill, Elizabeth Starr (1925-) FFC 66 SF1 254 SF2 937
Hill, Ernest (1915-) ES1 220 HFI 72 IAC 134 SFE 282 SFS 59 SF1 254 SF2 937-8
Hill, H. Haverstock pseud. of James Morgan Walsh. CSF 99
Hill, (Miss) Harrison. EXT 10/2 103, 105-7
Hill, Headon pseud. of Francis Edward Grainger. CSF 99 SF1 254
Hill, John. HFI 72
Hill, Merton A. SF1 254
Hill, Reginald see Dick Morland
Hill, Richard. BAA 154 IAC 134
Hill, Robert. SF1 254
Hill, Teddy. WFS 78
Hill, Warren. CSF 100
Hill, William Boyle. BAA 105 CSF 100 SF1 254

Hillam, S. A. SF1 254
Hillegas, Mark R. (1926-) ACC 198 ALW 7, 30, 75, 98 AOW 346-7 BAA 180, 230, 283 BYS 214, 319 CAT 131-2, 135-6, 138-40 ES1 220 EXT 1/2 24-8, 31 EXT 2/1 1, 4-16 EXT 3/1 1, 26-30 EXT 3/2 31-47 EXT 4/1 1 EXT 4/2 16, 26-33 EXT 5/1 2-14 EXT 5/2 37 EXT 7/2 29 EXT 8/1 1 EXT 8/2 30, 56 EXT 9/1 18-23 EXT 9/2 24-5, 63 EXT 10/1 2, 5, 18 FAN 182-3 MFW 6-7 MSF 147, 222 NDA x, 204 NWO 18, 100 OSR 272-81, 355 SFE 282 SFH 238 SF1 255 SF2 938 SOI xi-xvii, 41-58 SOT 4 SRB 69, 76, 503 TSF 97-101, 246 VES 128, 329 WSF 269
Hilliard, A. Rowley. IAC 134 IMS 14 SFS 59 SOT 141
Hilliard, Maurice (1931-) SF1 255
Hilliers, Ashton pseud. of Henry Marriage Wallace. CSF 100 SF1 255
Hillkowitz, Max. BAA 230
Hillman, Alex. WFS 189-90
Hillman, Arthur F. EXT 3/1 23
Hillman, Harry W. BAA 70 CSF 100
Hillman, Martin. IAC 134
Hillquit, Morris. BAA 180
Hills, Baldwin pseud. of Burton Wohl. SF1 255
Hilton, A. C. IAC 134
Hilton, James (1900-54) AOW 93, 103 BAA 100 BYS 208, 256 COT 259 CSF 100 ES1 220 EXT 9/2 45 FFC 176 FFR 94 FL2 920-5 HFI 72 MFW 123, 131 PST 122, 150-1, 198, 255 SFD 41, 70 SFE 282 SFW 75 SF1 255 SIH 81 SL3 1265-9 VES 137 WAA 51 WGT 70
Hilton, Margery. SF1 255
Hilton-Young, Wayland. IAC 134 SFS 59
Hilts, Philip J. IAC 134
Hilzinger, John George. CSF 100 SF1 255
Himler, Ann. FFC 120
Himler, Ronald. FFC 67, 120, 139
Himmelfarb, Gertrude. BAA 230 RAH 148
Hind, Charles Lewis (1862-1927) ALW 92 CSF 100 SF1 255

Hindin, Nathan. WTS 55
Hine, Al(fred Blakelee) (1915-)
ES1 220 SF1 255 SF2 938
Hine, Muriel pseud. of Muriel
Coxon. BAA 114 CSF 100 ES1
220-1
Hinge, Mike. VES 150
Hingley, Ronald Francis (1920-)
AOW 201 BAA 129 ES1 221
SFE 282 SF1 255 SF2 938
Hinrichs, James V. IAC 134
SFS 59
Hinterhauser, Hans Heinrich.
BAA 180
Hinton, Charles Howard (1853-
1907) CSF 100 ES1 221 EXT
5/1 4 SFE 282-3 SF1 255
Hinton, Edward H. VES 83
Hintze, Naomi A. (1909-) SF1
255 SF2 938
Hipolito, Jane. FL1 331-5 IAC
134 OSR 186-92,355 SF1 255
SL1 298-302 SL2 792-6 SL3
1084-8 SL4 1555-9,1720-5
SL5 2168-72
Hippocrates. MIH 6 TJB 35
Hirai, Kazumasa. SFB 142
Hirai, Taro (1894-) see Edogawa
Rampo
Hird, James Dennis (1850-1920)
BAA 51 WGT 70 see also Lord
Bottsford
Hirdler, Edgar. IMS 69-70
Hirsch, Foster. FLR 60
Hirsch, Walter. BAA 230 COT
96 ES1 221 EXT 1/2 32
Hirschfeld, Burt (1923-) SF1 255
Hirschhorn, V. MSF 262
Hirshfield, Henry I. IAC 134
SFS 59,82
Hiscock, Leslie (1902-) see
Patrick Marsh
Hitchcock, Alfred (1899-) ASF
323 CSF 100 ES1 221-3 ETN
109-10 FBK 154 FFR 94 SF1
256 SOT 335,347,350
Hitchcock, Raymond John (1922-)
SFE 287 SF1 256 SF2 938-9
Hitler, Adolf (1889-1945) ASF
114,260,282-3,292 ATA 11
CAT 12 COT 47,117,119,122-
3,126,129-31,136-8,140,237,
266 EXT 1/2 37 EXT 2/2 40
FAN 4,124,147 FTF 57,82,105,
127,161,200-1 LTN 146,214

MSF 276-7,281 MSM 11 OWB
72 RBY 99 RHN 17,41,57,75-
6 STH 43 WFS 61,63,67,98-9,
120,124-5 WIF 16,71,218
Hix, J. Emile. BAA 59
Hjortsberg, William (1941-) AOW
201 HFI 72 NDA 67-8 SFE
288 SFH 168,186,188-9 SF1
256 SF2 939 SL2 921-5 SRB
352
Hoadley, H. Orlo. WGT 70
Hoag, Jonathan E. EXT 3/1 18,
20
Hoagland, Clayton. NWO 61
Hoagland, Richard C. COT 69
IAC 134
Hoar, Roger Sherman (1887-1963)
BFP 241 ES1 224 WGT 70 WTS
32 see also Ralph Milne Farley
Hoban, Abrom. FFC 120
Hoban, Lillian. FFC 6
Hoban, Russell (Conwell) (1925-)
FFC 6,120,145-6 HFI 72 SF1
256,582 SF2 939
Hobana, Ion (1931-) LEX 371 SIH
12 SL2 644-6 SL3 1340-3 SL4
1613-6
Hobbes, Thomas (1588-1679) ACC
128,146 BAA xii CWN 54 MSM
257 NDA 54,56 RAH 148 TBC
17 UKL 65,173-5
Hobson, (Sir) Harold (1904-) EXT
6/1 19 SF1 257
Hobson, J.A. BAA 230
Hobson, Pearson. AOW 37
Hocart, A.M. KAU 200
Hoch, David D. AC2 75
Hoch, Edward D. (1930-) FFR 94
FRN 36-7 HFI 72 IAC 134 SFE
288 SF1 257 SF2 939
Hochart, Patrick. BAA 230
Hochstein, Peter (1939-) see
Jackson Short
Hock, David G. ACC 244
Hockett, Charles F. AAL 14-5,
69,73-4,78-9,81,97,121,123
IAC 134 SFS 59
Hocking, Joseph (1860-1937) CSF
100 SF1 257
Hocking, Silas Kitto (1850-1935)
SF1 257
Hodder, William Reginald. CSF
100 EXT 1/1 12 SF1 257
Hodder-Williams, C. IAC 134
Hodder-Williams, Frank Garfield
(1881-1960) SF1 560

Hodder-Williams, John Christopher (1926-) ES1 224 HFI 72 LEX 371-2 MFW 200-1 SFE 288 SF1 257 SF2 939-40 WGT 70

Hodes, Robert M. WSF 247

Hodgart, Matthew John (1916-) BAA 149, 230 EXT 10/1 30, 34 SF1 257 SF2 940

Hodge, Frederick Arthur. VES 104

Hodge, T. Shirby pseud. of Roger Sherman Tracy (1841-1926) CSF 100 SFE 288 SF1 257

Hodgell, Pat. IAC 134

Hodgens, Richard. OSR 248-62, 355

Hodges, A. L. STH 145

Hodges, C. Walter (1909-) ES1 224 FFC 54, 65, 183

Hodges, Elizabeth. FFC 55

Hodgins, Roderic C. IAC 134 SFS 59

Hodgkins, Russell J. IMS 137-8, 214, 227-8, 232

Hodgson, John Laurence. BAA 95 CSF 100 SF1 257

Hodgson, William Earl (-1910) BAA 15 CSF 100 SF1 257

Hodgson, William Hope (1877-1918) ALW 86 BFP 242-4 BYS 171-4, 177, 203 CSF 101 ES1 224-5 EXT 3/1 14 EXT 5/1 3 FBK 64-5, 78 FFR 94 FL1 143-5, 193-6 FL2 601-4, 744-8 FL3 1105-10 HFI 72 IAC 134 IMS 20 JVN 192 RGS 84-5 SFE 288-9 SFS 59 SFW 76 SF1 257-8 SIH 9 SL2 524-8 SOT 262 STH 5, 7, 128 VES 148 WAA 94 WIF 48 WTS 46

Hodus, Mike. IAC 134

Hoen, Richard A. HID 52 RFA 176-7 SOT 182 WSF 113-4

Hoess, Rudolf. VMW 25

Hoffer, Eric. MIH 49

Hoffman, Arthur Sullivant. STH 223, 225

Hoffman, Charles G. EXT 6/1 15

Hoffman, Daniel. NWO 71, 176

Hoffman, David (1784-1854) CSF 101 SF1 258 VES 232

Hoffman, Eleanor. FFC 75, 132

Hoffman, Everett (1921-) SF1 258

Hoffman, Felix. FFC 57

Hoffman, Frederick J. BAA 230

Hoffman, Kurt. CSF 101 SF1 258

Hoffman, Lee pseud. of Shirley Bell Hoffman. (1932-) BAA 154 ES1 225 HFI 72 IAC 134-5 SF1 258 SRB 104

Hoffman, Shirley Bell (1932-) SF2 940 see also Lee Hoffman

Hoffman, Stuart. SF1 258

Hoffmann, E(rnst) T(heodor) A(madeus) (1776-1822) AOW 23 BYS 93-4 CSF 101 ES1 225 EXT 3/2 41 EXT 10/1 44 FBK 13-6, 32-5, 37, 40, 42, 124, 137, 141-2 FFR 95 FL1 387-90 FL2 831-5 FL4 1547-53 FLT 2, 22, 32-47, 53-8, 83, 109 MSF 131, 168, 245, 282 RHN 193 SFB 82 SFE 289 SFH 182 SF1 258 SIH 6, 21, 33, 124 SL4 1848-53 TBC 3, 12 TFC 35-6, 40, 45, 54, 56, 69, 72-3, 82-3, 103, 121-3, 143-4, 150-1, 154 THM 15, 38-9, 58 VES 172 WAA 16, 234 WTS 121

Hoffmann, Franz. CSF 101

Hoffmann, Gerhard. BAA 230

Hoffmann, Horst (1950-) LEX 372

Hoffmann, Oskar (1866-) LEX 372-3

Hoffner, Joseph. BAA 230

Hofmann, Hellmut W. (1928-) LEX 373

Hofstadter, Richard. RAH 138, 171

Hogan, James P. (1941-) HFI 73 LEX 373 TSF 133, 135

Hogan, Patrick G. Jr. BAA 231 MFW 15

Hogan, Robert J. (1897-1963) ES1 225 SF1 258 TSP 89 WFS 106

Hogan, William. EXT 6/1 19

Hogarth, Grace Allen (1905-) WGT 70

Hogarth, Paul. FFC 51

Hogg, James (1770-1835) CSF 101 ES1 225 FL3 1291-6 SF1 258-9 WGT 70

Hogg, Thomas J. IAC 135

Hogrogian, Nonny. FFC 70

Hohoff, Curt. BAA 231

Hoke, Helen L. (1903-) ES1 226 FFC 86 SF1 259

Hoke, Travis. BAA 98

Holberg, Ludwig (1684-1754) ALW 32,67 AOW 9,23 BYS 68-70, 79,162-3 CSF 101 ES1 226 EXT 3/1 30 FTF 25 IAC 135 KAU 191 MSF 114,165,244 PST 15-6, 204,206,227,233-4, 239,242,250-2,263 SFB 75-6 SFE 289 SFS 59 SF1 259 SIH 85 SRB 3 VES 137 WAA 27, 131 WGT 70 WIF 37-8

Holbrook, Stewart H. BAA 180

Holbrooke, Joseph C. IAC 135

Holcomb, Claire. EXT 1/2 32

Holcombe, William Henry. BAA 29 EXT 4/1 9,12

Holden, Angus William Eden (1898-1951) see Lord Holden

Holden, Beatrice Inez. CSF 101

Holden, Edward S. EXT 5/2 42

Holden, Fox B. IAC 135

Holden, Larry. IAC 135

Holden, (Lord) pseud. of Angus William Eden Holden. SF1 259

Holden, Richard Cort. ES1 226 HFI 73 SFE 289 SF1 259

Holder, Charles Frederick (1851-1915) SF1 259

Holder, Geoffrey (1930-) SF1 259

Holder, Mary. CSF 101

Holding, Elisabeth Sanxay (1889-1955) ES1 226 IAC 135 SF1 259

Holdridge, Herbert Charles (1892-) SF1 259

Holdstock, Robert P. (1948-) ASF 17 FFR 95 HFI 73 IAC 135 LEX 374 LTN 262 SFE 289 TSF 246

Hole, Dorothy Christina Stanley (1896-) ES1 226

Holford, Castello N. BAA 53 CSF 101 SF1 259

Holgate, Jerome Bonaparte. SF1 259

Holland, Cecelia (1943-) HFI 73 LEX 376-7 SFE 289

Holland, Clive pseud. of Charles James Hankinson. CSF 102 SF1 259

Holland, Ena. CSF 102

Holland, Hester. IAC 135

Holland, Janice. FFC 62

Holland, Josiah Gilbert. EXT 4/1 9,12

Holland, Ralph M. EXT 5/1 6 IMS 46

Holland, West Bob (1868-1932) CSF 102 ES1 226 SF1 259

Hollander, Carl. FFC 189

Hollander, John. BAA 231 FFC 55 IAC 135

Hollander, Paul. BAA 231

Holledge, James. ES1 226

Hollerer, Walter. BAA 231

Holliday, Don. SF1 582

Hollinger, Deanne. FFC 186

Hollins, Dorothea. BAA 180

Hollis, H. H. pseud. of Ben Ramey. AAL 157 ALW 212 DTS 7, 46 IAC 135 SFD 16 SFE 289

Hollister, Bernard C. (1938-) AOW 365 FHT 67 IAC 135 SF1 259-60 SF2 940-1 SRB 464

Hollister, C. Warren (1930-) SF1 260

Hollow, John. AC2 75 WBW 24-5

Holloway, Brian. SF1 260 see also Berl Cameron, Neil Charles, Rand Le Page

Hollowell, Lillian. EXT 10/1 30

Hollriegel, Arnold pseud. of Richard Arnold Bermann. SF1 260

Holly, J(oan) Hunter pseud. of Joan Carol Holly (1932-) HFI 73 IAC 135 LEX 377 SFE 289 SF1 260

Holly, Joan Carol. AAL 120 ES1 226-7 IAC 135 SF2 941 WGT 70 see also J. Hunter Holly

Holm, Else Anne (1922-) FFC 171 SF1 582

Holm, John Cecil (1904-) CSF 102 ES1 227 SF1 260

Holm, Sven (1940-) LEX 377-8 SFE 289 SF1 260 SF2 941-2 SL5 2245-9

Holman, Felice (1919-) FFC 120, 146,155,194 SF1 260

Holmberg, John-Henri (1949-) SFE 289-90

Holme, Constance. CSF 102

Holmes, Charles M. EXT 6/1 12,15

Holmes, Clara H. CSF 102 ES1 227 SF1 260

Holmes, David C. ES1 227
Holmes, F. Ratcliffe. CSF 102
SF1 260
Holmes, H. H. pseud. of William
A. P. White. ALW 215 COT
105 IAC 135 IAH 35 ISW vi
MSM 23 RFA 110,116,122 SFS
59 STH 157-8 VES 174 WIF
114
Holmes, John Eric. HFI 73 SRB
53 VES 210
Holmes, Kenyon pseud. of August
Derleth. IAC 135 SFS 59
Holmes, Larry W. SF1 260
Holmes, Lawrance. SF1 260
Holmes, Oliver Wendell (1809-94)
AOW 34 BYS 47,53-4,117 CSF
102 EXT 4/1 5-9,12-3 EXT
6/2 23 EXT 7/1 18 FL1 475-7
PST 33-4 SF1 260
Holmesby, John. CSF 102
Holquist, J. Michael. BAA 231
MSF 3,52
Holroyd, Stuart. CWN 25
Holst, Gustave. IAH 76
Holst, Spencer. SF1 260
Holt, Conrad G. pseud. of John
Russell Fearn. SFE 292
Holt, George. VES 195
Holt, Isabella. FFC 55
Holt, John Robert (1926-) see
Raymond Giles
Holt, Lee Elbert. BAA 231
Holt, Marilyn J. SFW 483-90
Holtan, Gene. FFC 71
Holtby, Winifred (1898-1935) BAA
Holten, Knud. WAA 234
Holt-White, William Edward Brad-
den (1878-) CSF 102 SF1 261
Holynski, A. BAA 231
Holz, Hans Heinz. BAA 180
Holzer, Hans W. (1920-) ES1 227
SF1 261 SF2 942
Holzhausen, Carl Johan (1900-)
SFE 292
Home-Gall, Edward Reginald. SF1
261
Home-Gall, W. B. WGT 70 see
also Reginald Wray
Homer. ALW 32,39,47,239 ASF
22-3,35,181,242 COT 31,53,79,
174 CSC 6,22-4,26,33-5,201,
204,219 DTS 3 EXT 5/1 19
FBK 12,44 FLT 96 FTF 1 [FUT]
IAC 135 IAH 38,82 INT 4-5,16,

28 ISW 82 LTN 92 MFW x,5,51
MSF 25,92,97,145,153,187,275
NWO 252 RHN 148 SFD 47,240
SFE 292 SFH 176 TFC 34 TSO
6,25,34,41,56 VFS 12 VMW 45
WAA 14 WBW 21-2 WIF 27
WSF 13,291 WTS 17
Hompf, Alois. WGT 70
Homunculus. SF1 261
Honda, Ishiro. SFB 142
Honey, Frederic R. EXT 5/2 42-3
Honeycombe, Gordon (1936-) SF1
261
Honncher, E. BAA 231
Hood, Archer Leslie (1869?-1944)
SF1 261 WGT 70-1 see also
William Leslie
Hood, Hugh. IAC 135
Hood, Thomas (1835-74) CSF 102
SF1 261
Hood, Thomas (1799-1845) CSF
102 ES1 227 POE 46,73 SF1
261
Hooke, Charles Witherle (1861-
1929) WGT 71 see also Howard
Fielding
Hooke, S. H. EXT 9/1 16
Hooker, Fanny. WGT 71 see
also Erniest Hoven
Hooker, Fanny. WGT 71
Hooker, Le Roy (1840?-1906) SF1
261
Hookham, Albert E. CSF 102 SF1
261
Hooper, Albert W. CSF 102
Hooper, Walter. FAN 187 IAC
135
Hoopes, Ned Edward (1932-) ES1
227 SF1 261 SF2 942
Hoor, Martin Ten. BAA 271
Hooton, Earnest A. IAC 135
Hoover, Ernest L. BAA 283
Hoover, H. M. AOW 320 SF1 261
Hoover, Ham. HFI 73
Hoover, Herbert. RHN 211 WFS
1,14-5,64 WTS 13
Hope, Andree. STH 32-3
Hope, (Sir) Anthony. BYS 137,270
Hope, Coral. SF1 261
Hope, Edward pseud. of Edward
Hope Coffey Jr. SF1 261
Hope, Francis. EXT 10/1 31
Hopf, Alice Martha (1904-) SF2
977 WGT 71 see also A. M.
Lightner

Hopkins, Alice Kimball (1839-)
CSF 102 SF1 261 WGT 71 see
also A. K. H.
Hopkins, Bill. CWN 25 THM 4
Hopkins, Eric. COT 166
Hopkins, Gerard Manley. SOI 89
Hopkins, Jeune. SF1 262
Hopkins, Kenneth (1914-) SF2 988
see also Warwick Mannon
Hopkins, Robert Thurston (1884-
1958) ES1 227-8 SF1 262
Hopley, George pseud. of Cornell
Woolrich. CSF 102
Hopley-Woolrich, Cornell George
(1906-68) see George Hopley,
Cornell Woolrich
Hopp, Zinken. FFC 75
Hopper, Nora (1871-1906) SF1 262
Horan, Keith. SF1 262
Horbiger, Hans. WIF 50
Horgan, Paul (1903-) SF1 262
SF2 942
Horkheimer, Max. BAA 231
Horler, Sydney (1888-1954) CSF
102-3 SF1 262 WGT 71
Horn, Edward Newman (1903-)
SF1 262
Horn, Holloway. IAC 135
Horn, Peter (house name) SFE
292 WGT 71 see also Henry
Kuttner, David Vern
Hornby, Nicole. FFC 77
Horne, Richard Henry (1803-84)
SFE 292 see also Mrs. Fairstar
Horner, Donald William. CSF
103 SF1 262 VES 84
Horner, Jacob W. BAA 77
Hornig, Charles D. (1916-) ALW
156, 180, 184 ASF 118, 219 COT
119 ES1 228 IMS 14, 18-20, 32,
34-6, 39-41, 45, 49-51, 54, 56-7,
71, 84, 94, 138-9, 191, 195-7, 213,
221-2, 231, 244 ISW 161 MSM
173 RFA 18, 50, 64 SFB 152
SFE 292-3 SIH 190 SOT 17, 328
SRB 90 WGT 71 WIF 135 WSF
67, 74, 123, 138
Hornik, Henri. LTN 259
Horniman, Roy (1874-1930) CSF
103 SF1 262
Hornsby, Samuel. BAA 231
Horowitz, Irving Louis. BAA 231
Horowitz, M. G. LTN 268
Horrell, Joseph. MSF 242
Horsburgh, H. J. N. BAA 231

Horseman, Elaine (1925-) ES1
228 FFC 75 SF1 262 SF2 942
Horsford, Howard C. NWO 294
Horsley, T. J. pseud. of T. J.
Horsley Curties. CSF 103
Horsnell, Horace (1882-1949)
CSF 103 SF1 263
Horstmann, Hubert (1937-) LEX
378
Hort, Richard (1803?-57) SF1 263
Horvath, Barna. BAA 231
Horwitz, Elinor. FFC 188
Horwood, Harold. ES1 228
Horwood, William (1944-) FL1
436-40
Horzelski, Jerzy. EXT 6/1 4
Hosea. EXT 8/1 23
Hosea, Lucy R. CSF 103
Hosemann, Theodor. FBK 33
Hoshi, Shin-Ichi. SFB 142
Hoskin, Albert A. BAA 62-3
Hoskin, C. H. see Tuesday Lub-
sang Rampa
Hoskins, Robert (1933-) ETN 78
HFI 73 IAC 135 LTN 209, 253,
263 SFE 293 SF1 263 SF2 942-3
Hostovsky, Egon. ISW 12
Hotchkin, F. E. BAA 167 SF1 263
Hotson, Cornelia Hinkley. ES1
228 SF1 263
Hottinger, Mary. ES1 228
Houblon, Grahame. SF1 263
Houdini pseud. of H. P. Lovecraft
EXT 3/1 6
Houdini pseud. of Ehrich Weiss.
WIF 77 WTS 4, 21-2
Hough, Charlotte. FFC 26
Hough, Emerson (1857-1923) SF1
263 WTS 3
Hough, Graham. FLT 152, 156
Hough, Richard Alexander (1922-)
ES1 228 SF2 846 WGT 71 see
also Bruce Carter
Hough, Robert L. BAA 180
Hough, Stanley Bennett (1917-)
BAA 126, 142 BFP 245-6 ES1
228 SF2 917 SRB 325 WGT 71
see also Rex Gordon
Hough, (Rev.) T. W. BAA 231-2
Houghton, Claude pseud. of Claude
Houghton Oldfield. CSF 103 SFE
293 SF1 263
Houghton, J. A. SF1 263
Hougren, Robert. SFB 140
House, Brant pseud. of Paul
Chadwick. ES1 228 TSP 81

House, Edward Mandell (1858-
1938) BAA 78 CSF 103 SF1 263
Household, Geoffrey (1900-) CSF
103 ES1 228 FFR 95 IAC 135
SFS 60 SF1 263
Houser, Lionel Louis. CSF 103
SF1 263
Housman, A. E. IAC 135 KAU
180,182 VFS 129
Housman, Clemence Annie (1861-
1955) CSF 103 SF1 264
Housman, Laurence (1865-1959)
CSF 103 ES1 228-9 FFC 20,
95 SFE 293 SF1 264
Houston, James D. (1933-) IAC
135 SFS 60 SF1 264
Houston, Libby. IAC 135
Houtain, George. WTS 49
Hoven, Erniest pseud. of Fanny
Hooker. CSF 103
Hovorre, M. Auberre pseud. of
Albert Waldo Howard. CSF 103
SF1 264
Howard, Albert Waldo. BAA 54
WGT 71-2 see also M. Auberre
Hovorre
Howard, Allan. ISW 223
Howard, Charles F. BAA 26
CSF 103 SF1 264
Howard, Dana. ES1 229 SF1 264
Howard, Daniel F. EXT 7/1 15
Howard, Ebenezer. BAA 59 POE
176-8,180
Howard, Edward. BAA 7
Howard, Elizabeth Jane (1923-)
ES1 229 SF1 264 SF2 943
Howard, Geoffrey (1889-1973) see
Marmaduke Duke
Howard, George Fitzalan Bronson.
CSF 104
Howard, Hayden. IAC 136
Howard, Hilda Glynn. BAA 86
Howard, I. M. CWD 4 WTS 22
Howard, Ivan. ES1 229 IAC 136
SFE 293 SFS 60 SF1 264
Howard, James. IAC 136
Howard, Joan. FFC 75,132-3,
181,194
Howard, John Hayden. AOW 201
BFP 247 ES1 229 HFI 73 SFE
293 SF1 264 WGT 72
Howard, Katharine (1858-) SF1
264
Howard, Keble pseud. of John
Keble Bell. CSF 104 SF1 264

Howard, Marghanita Laski (1915-)
WGT 72
Howard, Maude Lesseur. CSF
104 SF1 264
Howard, Milford Wriarson (1862-)
SF1 582
Howard, Paul pseud. of Henry
Treat Sperry. TSP 134
Howard, Richard Christopher.
SF1 264
Howard, Robert E. (1906-36) AOW
87, 94,104,114 BFP 248-54
COT 124,176 CSF 104 ES1 229-
31 EXT 1/2 33 EXT 3/1 3,12-3
EXT 5/1 3-4 FBK 78, 81, 83, 93-
5,124 FFR 95-6 FLR 38 FL1
300-7 HFI 73-5,184 HID 106
IAC 136 IMS 16, 19, 21-2, 24, 30-
1, 75,137 ISW 19-20,159 JVN
41-3 LEX 378-80 MSM 128,137,
303 RFA 64,171 RSG 31 SFB
58,113 SFD 288 SFE 293-4
SFH 37,172 SFS 37-8,60-1 SFW
142, 179,182-3 SF1 264-5 SOT
52, 73,164-5, 291,304,309,321,
326,334,340,363 SRB 263,341
STH 152 TSF 53 TSP 29,34
VES 140, 211, 266,314 WAA 97-
8,106-7 WGT 72 WIF 27,68,78,
113, 136, 158,190, 224, 229 WSF
135-6, 248, 294-5, 297-8,386
WTS ix, 15, 25-6, 28, 30-43, 49-
52, 63, 68-9, 71, 80,123-6,128,132
Howard, William Lee. EXT 4/1
9, 13
Howatch, Susan (1940-) SF1 265
SF2 943
Howe. ETN 24,176
Howe, Bea (1898-) CSF 104 SF1
265
Howe, Cliff. TSP 131
Howe, Frederic C. BAA 94
Howe, Irving. BAA 180, 232 NDA
89, 209
Howell, George Rogers (1833-99)
CSF 104 SF1 265
Howell, Joseph. IAC 136
Howell, Scott. SF1 265
Howells, David. FBK 151
Howells, William Dean (1837-1920)
ALW 62 AOW 35,65 BAA 51,71,
232 CSF 104 ES1 231 EXT 1/1
12 EXT 4/1 9 EXT 4/2 19 EXT
7/1 18,26 FAN 66 MSF 172,177-
8, 197 NWO 101 PST 57-8,193,

Howells, William Dean (cont.) 198, 231, 237, 268, 291 SFE 294-5 SF1 265 VES 126
Howells, William White (1908-) ES1 231
Howes, Alan B. ACC 149-171
Howes, Margaret. IAC 136
Howett, John Newton. TSP 22
Howland, Marie. BAA 31
Howorth, Muriel K. SF1 265 SF2 943
Hoy, John S. STH 221
Hoyenga, Betty Ritchie. BAA 283
Hoyle, (Sir) Fred (1915-) ALW 212 AOW 201-2 ASF 151 BAA 151 BFP 255 BYS 303 ES1 231-2 EXT 3/1 26 EXT 5/1 3 EXT 9/2 63 FFR 96 FTF 166 HFI 75-6 IAC 136-7 KAU 19, 127 LEX 380 MFW 210, 271 RGS 85-6 SFB 136-7 SFE 295 SFS 44, 61 SFW 387-92 SF1 265-6 SF2 943 SL1 228-32 SL4 1574-82 SRB 328 VES 96, 123, 259-60, 302 VFS 68-9 WSF 200
Hoyle, Geoffrey (1941-) AOW 202 BAA 151 ES1 232 MFW 271 SFB 137 SFE 295 SF1 266 SF2 943-4
Hoyne, Thomas Temple (1875-1946) AOW 91, 104 BAA 101 CSF 104 SFE 295 SF1 266
Hrolda, Jean. IAC 137
Hubalek, Felix. BAA 232
Hubbard, Elbert. STH 126
Hubbard, L(afayette) Ron(ald) (1911-) AAL 110, 176 ALW 155, 158, 160, 164, 172, 213 AOW 118, 202 BFP 256-7 BYS 227, 238, 242, 274 COT 23, 106, 158-9, 235, 237-40, 250 CSC 29, 60-2, 170, 197 CSF 104 ES1 232-3 ETN 17, 33, 68, 83, 159-60 EXT 5/1 3 EXT 7/2 40 FBK 122 FFR 96 FL4 1763-5 FTF 200 HFI 76 IAC 137 IAH 18, 84-5 ISW xii, 34, 37-40, 61, 233, 272 KAU 166, 228 LEX 381-2 MSM 131, 138 OWB 14-5, 99 RGS 86 RFA 52, 57, 64, 76-8, 80, 84, 100, 108, 110, 148, 155, 165, 172, 188, 192-3, 196, 208 SFB 20, 62-3, 89 SFD 135 SFE 295 SFH 159 SFS 61 SFW 158, 212, 214-5, 397 SF1 266 SIH 165 SL2 761-5 SOT 62, 164,

195, 218, 224-5, 330, 414-5 STH 116-7 TSP 90 VES 76, 207-8, 210, 313, 333, 341-2 VFS 154 WFS 118-9 WGT 72 WIF 90, 93-6, 203 WSF 93-4, 97, 104, 132, 135, 162-4, 171-2, 386 see also Rene Lafayette Kurt Von Rachen
Hubbard, P. M. IAC 137 SFS 61
Hubbard, Richard see Chris Stratton
Hubbard, Stanley. TSP 68
Hubbard, Thomas O'Brian (1882-) BAA 100 SF1 266
Hubbard, Walter W. TSP 68
Hubbard, Wynant Davis (1900-61) CSF 104 SF1 266
Hubert, Fred (1930-) LEX 382
Hubner, Herbert. BAA 283
Huddleston, George (1862-1944) SF1 266
Hudleston, Gilbert Roger (1874-1936) WGT 72
Hudson, Jeffrey S. IAC 137
Hudson, Robert. SF1 266
Hudson, W(illiam) H(enry) (1841-1922) ALW 61 AOW 65 BAA 38, 67 CSF 104 CAT 78 ES1 233 EXT 5/1 4 EXT 7/1 9-10, 16 FAN 26, 34 FL1 328-30 FL2 670-4 FTF 100 LTN 111 MSF 187-8, 193 POE 146-9 PST 55, 223, 226, 232, 234, 247, 255, 297-8, 314 SFE 295-6 SF1 266, 582 SL1 449-52 SOT 235 SRB 8 VES 126
Hueffer, Ford Madox (1873-1939) CSF 48, 104 EXT 9/2 38-9 SFE 296 SF1 266 see also Ford Madox Ford
Huemer, Dick (1898-) SF1 266
Huey, Guy L. IMS 22
Huffaker, Sandy. FFC 76
Hufford, Liz. IAC 137
Huggins, Roy. IAH 20-1
Hughart, Sarah. SF1 267
Hughes, Arthur. FFC 50
Hughes, Daniel. SOI 81-96
Hughes, David Y. BAA 232 EXT 6/2 22, 32-8
Hughes, Dennis Talbot. SFE 296 SF1 267 see also Berl Cameron, Neil Charles, Lee Elliot, Gill Hunt, Brad Kent, John Lane, Van Reed, Russell Rey

Hughes, Dorothy Belle (1904-)
CSF 104 SF1 267
Hughes, Gwilym Fielden (1920?-)
SF2 891 see also Hugh Enfield
Hughes, Howard. ETN 20 VFS
117,184
Hughes, James (1937-) HFI 76
SF1 267
Hughes, John Cledwyn (1920-)
SF1 267 SF2 944
Hughes, Merritt Y. BAA 232
Hughes, Pennethorne. ES1 233
Hughes, Peter T. FFC 48 SF1
267
Hughes, Richard Arthur (1900-
76) CSC 30 CSF 104 ES1 233
EXT 10/1 31 FFC 26 IAC 137
SF1 267 SF2 944
Hughes, Riley. ES1 233 HFI 76
SFE 296 SF1 267
Hughes, Robert J. EXT 9/2 25
Hughes, Rodney. HFI 76 SF1 267
Hughes, Rupert (1872-1956) CSF
104 SF1 267
Hughes, Shirley. FFC 28,51, 72,
84,105,191
Hughes, Ted (1930-) FFC 26, 97
IAC 137 SFE 296
Hughes, Thomas J. BAA 81-2
Hughes, W. J. BAA 113 EXT 9/2
25
Hughes, Walter Llewellyn (1910-)
ES1 233-4 SF2 1116 WGT 72-3
see also Hugh Walters
Hughes, William. SF1 268
Hughes, Zach pseud. of Hugh
Zachary. AAL 28, 92,135 HFI
76 RGS 86-7 SFE 296 SF1 268
Hugi, Maurice Gaspard pseud. of
Eric Frank Russell (1904-47)
COT 167,288 ES1 234 IAC 137
RFA 86 SFD 316 SFS 61 SF1
268 SOT 145 VES 141
Hugli, Edwin E. H. BAA 137,140
Hugo, C. BAA 192
Hugo, Victor (1802-85) CAT 8
CSF 105 FBK 82 MSF 153 POE
170-1 SF1 268 TFC 163
Huidobro, Vicente (1893-1948)
CSF 105 SF1 268
Huizinga, Johann. RZY 75
Hulbert, Homer B. CSF 105
Hulke, Malcolm (1924-) SF1 268
SF2 944

Hull, E(dna) Mayne (1905-75) ALW
160 CSF 198 ES1 234 FFR 96
HFI 76 IAC 137 ISW 61 LEX
382 OWB 52 RFA 112,117,122-
3,127,130,139 SFS 61 SF1 268
SF2 944-5 SOT 219 SRB 99 VES
123 WIF 163 see also Edna
Mayne Hull Van Vogt
Hull, Gerald. IAC 137
Hull, Paul E. IAC 137
Hulme, T. E. CAT 52 THM 17,
33, 54-6, 58, 61
Hulme-Beaman, Emeric. SF1 268
Hume, Cyril (1900-66) CSF 105
ES1 234 SF1 268
Hume, David (1711-76) BAA 11
CWN 54 MFW 7 SFB 16-7,19
UKL 65
Hume, Fergus(on Wright) (1859-
1932) BAA 48 CSF 105 ES1
234 SFW 76 SF1 268-9 WGT 73
Humiston, Fred. WTS 93, 96
Hummel, William Castle. EXT
6/1 10
Hummert, Paul A. BAA 232
Humphrey, Hubert. ETN 105
Humphrey, William. AAL 68
Humphreys, Emyr. IAH 106
Humphreys, John R. CSF 105
Humphreys, Leslie George see
Bruno G. Condray
Humphreys, M. L. WTS 20, 23
Humphries, George Rolfe (1894-
1969) CSF 73 ES1 234 SF1 269
SF2 945
Huneker, James Gibbons (1857-
1921) SF1 269
Hunger, Anna. HFI 103 SF1 269
Hungerford, Margaret Wolfe
(1855?-97) CSF 105 SF1 269
WGT 73 see also The Duchess
Hunt, Barbara (1907-) CSF 105
SF1 269 SF2 945
Hunt, Douglas. ES1 234
Hunt, Everette Howard, Jr. (1918-)
see David St. John
Hunt, Gill (house name) SFE 300
SF1 269 see also John Brunner,
David Arthur Griffiths, Dennis
Talbot Hughes, John William
Jennison, E. C. Tubb
Hunt, H. L. BAA 134,143 WFS
255
Hunt, Isobel Violet (1866-1942)
ES1 234 SF1 269

177

Hunt, James Henry Leigh (1784-1859) SF1 269 CSF 105
Hunt, Laura Shellabarger. SF1 269
Hunt, Marigold. FFC 99
Hunt, Violet. CSF 105
Huntemann, Georg H. BAA 232, 283
Hunter, Alan (1923-) ES1 234
Hunter, Bluebell Matilda (1887-) BAA 103 WGT 73 see also George Lancing
Hunter, Doris. BAA 232
Hunter, Evan pseud. of S. A. Lombino. AOW 168, 321 ES1 234-5 HFI 76-7 SFE 300 SF1 269 SRB 326 WSF 176, 260
Hunter, Helen. SF1 269
Hunter, Howard. BAA 232
Hunter, Jim (1939-) BAA 142 SF1 270 SF2 945
Hunter, Mel (1929-) ES1 235 SFS 61 VES 174, 289
Hunter, Mollie pseud. of Maureen Mollie McIlwraith. FFC 86, 93, 95, 102, 108, 188, 194 SF1 270
Hunter, Norman (1899-) SFE 300
Hunter, Norman Charles (1908-1971) SF1 270
Hunter, Paul. IMS 71
Hunter-Blair, John. SF1 270
Hunter-Duvar, John (1830-99) SF1 270
Hunting, Henry Gardner (1872-1958) CSF 105 PST 160-1, 249, 278 SF1 270
Huntington, Charles. SF1 270
Huntington, Edward Stanton. WGT 73 see also Edward Stanton Hunting, Gardner (1872-1958) ES1 235 SFE 300
Huntington, John. ACC 82, 211-22 AC2 75 BAA 232 CAT 59 KAU 15 TSO 4, 6 UKL 245
Huntley, Florence (-1912) CSF 105 SF1 270
Hurbon, Laennes. BAA 180
Hurd, Douglas Richard (1930-) ES1 235 SF1 270 SF2 945-6
Hurlbut, Kaatje. IAC 137 SFS 61
Hurley, Richard James (1906-) ES1 235 IAC 137 SF1 270
Hurrell, Francis Gordon (1885-) SF1 270

Hurst, Fannie (1889-1968) CSF 105 SF1 270 SF2 946 STH 41
Hurt, Freda (1911-) FFC 133 SF1 270
Hurtado, Luis. CSF 105
Hurwood, Bernhardt Jackson (1926-) ES1 235 SF1 270-1 SF2 946
Huss, Roy Gerard (1927-) SF1 271 SF2 946
Husserl, Edmund (1859-1938) CWN 8-10, 27, 41, 54 THM 7, 60
Hussey, S. S. EXT 10/1 31
Hussingtree, Martin pseud. of Oliver Ridsdale Baldwin. CSF 105 SF1 271
Huston, John. CSC 264 RBY 20, 97
Hutchins, John K. EXT 6/1 19
Hutchins, Laurence. FFC 146
Hutchins, Maude. MIH 96
Hutchins, Pat. FFC 146
Hutchins, Robert Maynard. BAA 181, 232 EXT 6/1 9
Hutchins, Roy. IAC 137
Hutchinson, Alfred L. BAA 71
Hutchinson, H. N. EXT 6/2 33
Hutchinson, Horace Gordon. CSF 106
Hutchinson, Loring (1912-) SF1 271
Hutchinson, Mary Louise. BAA 283
Hutchinson, Ray Coryton (1907-75) CSF 106 SF1 271 SF2 946
Hutchinson, Robert Hare (1887-) WGT 73 see also Robert Hare
Hutchinson, Tom (1930-) BAA 181 SF1 271
Hutchinson, Vere. CSF 106
Hutchinson, William. CSF 106 FFC 180
Hutchison, Graham S. CSF 106
Huttenhower, Helen Graham. BAA 283
Hutton, Amy. IAC 137
Hutton, Clarke. FFC 166
Huxley, Aldous (1894-1963) ACC 29, 32, 209 ALW 30, 99, 118, 143-5, 228 AOW 85, 88, 96, 104-5, 203, 343, 346 ASF 108, 174 BAA xxi, 98, 116, 132, 137, 232-3 BYS 18, 43, 67, 75, 94, 192-6, 212-3, 254-5, 273 CAT xiv, 78, 131, 138-9 COT 115, 130 CSC 14, 25-7,

Huxley, Aldous (cont.)
30-1, 58, 73, 75, 93-7, 100, 107,
121, 124, 126, 131-2, 163, 165-7,
170, 174, 200-6, 212, 220 CSF
106 CUA 3-4 CWN 37 DTS 5-
6, 10, 13, 28 EFP 6, 16, 21 ES1
235-6 EXT 1/2 27, 32 EXT 2/2
22, 24, 26-7, 29, 33-41 EXT 3/1
28 EXT 4/1 1 EXT 4/2 24 EXT
5/1 1, 4, 18 EXT 5/2 38 EXT
6/1 2-21 EXT 6/2 39, 41-2, 51
EXT 7/1 25 EXT 7/2 41 EXT
8/1 5-6, 20 EXT 8/2 59 EXT
9/1 19, 21-3 EXT 9/2 30, 52-5,
59 EXT 10/1 9, 31, 47 EXT 10/2
100 FAN 3-5, 9, 12, 20, 34, 38,
47-8, 52, 66, 75, 82-3, 100, 105,
110-23, 125-6, 129, 132-4, 146-9,
156-8, 161, 167-8, 174-5, 178-9,
186 FFR 96 FTF 44-5, 60, 85,
97, 102, 104-6, 136, 193 HFI 77
IAC 137 IAH 16, 141-2 INT 49
ISW 2, 136 JGB 6 JVN 218 KAU
44, 101 KVT 9 LEX 382-3 LTN
106, 205 MFW 23, 81, 89, 207,
249, 287 MIH 13 MSF 83, 279
MSM 29, 166, 259 NDA xi, 6-7,
17, 38-9, 42, 45, 52, 61, 63, 89, 96-
8, 102, 115, 121, 154, 181-5, 189,
205, 214 NWO 113, 125-6, 183
OWB 18 POE 228, 235, 244-7,
261-2, 267-8, 270, 287 PST 11,
122, 154-6, 193, 197, 228, 232,
236-7, 249, 259, 261, 274, 281-2,
285, 290, 293, 307, 309-10, 318
RAH 139 RBY 17, 196, 213 RFA
158 SFB 91-2 SFD 57, 208,
274, 305 SFE 300-1 SFH 28, 33-
5, 70, 143-4, 151, 155, 174, 216
SFN 12, 40, 117 SFS 61-2 SFW
101-8, 234 SF1 271 SIH 62, 88,
94, 185 SL1 33-7, 78-83, 247-53
SL3 1073-8 SOI xiii, 161 SOT
1, 222, 395 SRB 10-1, 296 STF
24, 79 STH 6, 108 TJB 22 TPS
231-7 TSF 229 VES 124, 128,
136, 165, 188, 195, 202, 212-3,
254, 256, 259, 341 VMW 11 WAA
27, 49, 53, 59, 119 WFS 78 WIF
58, 82, 152, 212 WSF 87, 260,
345, 386 WTS 16
Huxley, (Sir) Julian (1887-) BAA
101 BYS 182 ES1 236 EXT
6/1 9 IAC 137 KAU 11 MSF
226 MSM 263 POE 291 SFD
208 SFS 62 VES 205

Huxley, T(homas) H(enry). ACC
174-6, 185, 188 ALW 54, 90
CAT 132, 141 EXT 6/2 35-6
FAN 14, 18-21, 24, 30, 32, 36-7,
59, 79, 177, 182 FTF 49-50, 53-
4, 62, 95, 130, 133-4, 136, 163, 183
INT 13 MSF 23, 209, 222-31,
233, 238-9, 242 MSM 247, 263
NDA 61, 207 POE 87 SFB 27,
35 SFH 17 SFN 47 UKL 81-2,
87 WSF 19
Huygens, Christian. SIH 107
Huysmans, Joris Karl (1848-
1907) CSF 106 FBK 117 FL2
861-2 MFW 279-80 SF1 271
TDI 9 THM 39 WFS 32, 116
Huzarski, Richard. TSP 200
Hyams, Edward Solomon (1910-
75) BAA 161 ES1 236 SFE 301
SF1 271 SF2 946
Hyberger, Hy. RBY 240
Hyde, Alan. TSP 134 see also
Taylor Ward
Hyde, Christopher. SF1 271
Hyde, Gavin. IAC 137 SFS 62
Hyde, Mark Powell. CSF 106
SF1 271
Hyde, (Mrs.) Nelson Waldorf
(1893-) WGT 73
Hyde, William J. BAA 233
Hyde-Chambers, Derek. SF1 271
Hyder, Alan. CSF 106 SF1 271
Hyers, M. Conrad (1933-) SF1
582
Hyland, M. E. F. see Kythe Wyl-
wynne
Hyman, Shirley (1919-65) WGT
73 see also Shirley Jackson
Hyman, Stanley Edgar. IAH 20
MSF 26, 31, 224 NWO 4
Hyman, Trina Schart. FFC 12,
19, 65-6, 82, 97, 100, 162, 178,
188, 191, 194
Hynam, John Charles (1915-74)
ES1 236 SF2 962 WGT 73 see
also John Kippax
Hynd, Lavinia Leitch. ES1 236
WGT 73 see also Lavinia Leitch
Hyndman, H. M. BAA 181
Hyndman, Jane see Lee Wyndham
Hyne, C(harles) J(ohn) Cutcliffe
(1865-1944) ALW 85 CSF 106
ES1 236-7 FL2 916-9 HFI 77
IAC 137 SFE 301 SFW 60 SF1
271-2 SRB 9, 264 VES 140
WGT 73-4 WIF 50, 212 WSF 23

Hyne, C. J. Cutcliffe (cont.)
see also Weatherby Chesney
Hynek, J. Allen. VFS 144,176
WFS 268

Hyre, K. M. EXT 9/2 61-2
Hytes, Jason. SF1 272
Hythloday, Jr. (pseud.) BAA 48

I

I. A. EXT 3/1 22
I. S. pseud. of Isidor Schneider.
CSF 106
Iambulus. EXT 8/1 23 MSF 87,
94-5,100 WIF 30,39
Ianni, Lawrence. EXT 9/2 25
Ibbotson, Eva. FFC 31
Ibsen, Henrik (1828-1906) FLT
41-2 FL3 1216-20 MSF 11
STF 33 THM 34
Idiotes. BAA 233
Iggers, Georg. BAA 181
Iggulden, John Manners (1917-)
ES1 237 SFE 303 SF1 272 SF2
947
Iles, Robert L. BAA 283
Iliowizi, Henry (1850-1911) SF1
272
Illes, Theodora (1946-) SF2 947
Illing, Werner (1895-) LEX 384
Ilsley, Velma. FFC 21,106
Ilton, Paul (1901-58) SF1 272
Imaz, Eugenio. BAA 181,233
Imbert, Enrique Anderson (1910-)
ES1 237 IAC 138 SF1 14 SF2
799
Imbert-Terry, (Sir) Henry. CSF
106
Inca-Pablo-Ozollo pseud. of
Alfred Francis Sears. SF1 272
Ince, Richard Basil (1881-) BAA
233 CSF 106 ES1 237 SF1 272
Inchfawn, Fay. FFC 133
Indick, Benjamin P. RBY 240

Infeld, Leopold. THM 62
Ing, Dean. IAC 138
Ingalese, Isabella (1855-) CSF
106 SF1 272
Inge, Thomas M. TSF 251
Inge, W. R. BAA 97
Ingelo, Nathaniel. BAA 6
Ingelow, Jean. FFC 93
Ingerflom, Claudio. BAA 233
Ingerman, Charles. TSP 81,89
Ingher, Maurice Z. IMS 10,15
SOT 107 WSF 75
Inglefield, Eleanor. SF1 272
Inglis, James. IAC 138 SFS 62
Ingraham, Erick. FFC 46
Ingraham, Joseph Holt (1809-60)
SF1 273
Ingraham, (Col.) Prentiss. STH
28 TSP 85-6 see also Frank
Powell
Ingram, Anne (1937-) SF1 273
SF2 947
Ingram, Archibald Kenneth (1882-
1965) SF1 273 SF2 947 BAA 90
CSF 107
Ingram, Eleanor Marie (1886-
1921) CSF 107 FL4 1901-3 SF1
273
Ingram, Thomas Henry (1924-)
FFC 48,163 SF1 273
Ingram, William. STH 199
Ingrey, Derek. ES1 237 SFE 308
SF1 273

Ingulphus pseud. of Arthur Gray.
SF1 273
Inman, Herbert Escott. SF1 273
Innes, David. ALW 109-10
Innominatus. BAA 37
Inouye, Jon. IAC 138
Institoris, Henricus. ES1 237
Ionel pseud. of Yuval Ronn. SF1
273
Ionesco, Eugene (1912-) BYS 188
ES1 237 FL3 1317-9 IAC 138
SFS 62 SF1 273 SF2 947 SIH
54 WAA 75
Ipcar, Dahlov (1917-) FFC 93,176,
194 SF1 273 SF2 948
Irby, James E. BAA 233 EXT 9/1
3,17
Ireland, M.J. WGT 74
Ireland, Michael pseud. of Darrell
Figgis. CSF 107
Ireland, William Henry (1777-
1835) CSF 107 SF1 273 WGT 74
Ireson, Barbara (1927-) FFC 20
SF1 273 SF2 948
Irvine, Andrew Alexander (1871-
1939) SF1 274
Irvine, Amy Mary (1866-) CSF
107 SF1 274
Irvine, Gilbert Marshall. CSF
107 SF1 274
Irving, Clifford. ETN 20 VFS 117
Irving, Compton pseud. of John L.
J. Carter. CSF 107
Irving, David. KVT 48
Irving, Edith. VFS 117
Irving, Washington (1783-1859)
ALW 60 CSF 107 ES1 237 FBK
27,29,82 FFC 66 FL4 1554-62
IAC 138 IMS 2 ISW 112 MSF
139,177 SFH 166-7,200 SF1
274 VES 148,160 WGT 74-5
WTS 17
Irwin, Bernice Piilani. SF1 274
Irwin, Constance. ES1 237

Irwin, G.H. (house name) WGT
75 see also Raymond A. Palmer,
Richard S. Shaver
Irwin, H.C. see Mark Time
Irwin, Inez Haynes (1873-1970)
CSF 107 SF1 274 WGT 75
Irwin, James. ACC 52
Irwin, Margaret E. (1889-1967)
CSF 107 ES1 237-8 FL4 1898-
1900 IAC 138 SFS 62 SF1 274
Irwin, W.R. EXT 8/1 1 EXT
10/1 31 SOI 139-49 SRB 71
Irwin, Wallace. CSF 107
Irwin, William Henry (1873-1948)
SF1 274
Isaacs, (Dr.) John. VFS 226
Isaacs, Leonard (1939-) BAA 181
IAC 138 JHN 61 SFE 314 SRB
464
Isaacs, Linda Irene (1944-) LEX
384
Isaacs, Neil David (1931-) EXT
10/1 22,24,28,31-3,38-41,45
SF1 274 SF2 948-9
Isaacs, Reginald R. BAA 233
Isaiah. ASF 173 EXT 9/2 48
MSF 117-8
Isherwood, Christopher. EXT
6/1 15 IAC 138 ISW 109 VES
149
Ish-Kishor, Sulamith (1896-1977)
FFC 6 SF1 274
Isihara, Fuzio. SFB 142
Isip (brothers). RFA 118
Isosaki, Arata. [FUT]
Israeli, Nathan. BAA 233
Istvan, Hegedus. SFB 12,97,148-9
Itin, Vivian A. EXT 10/2 75 MSF
253
Ivan (the Terrible). MSF 243
Ivanov, Vsevolod V. EXT 10/2
75 IAC 138 MSF 254
Iverson, William J. AOW 307
Ivie, Larry. ES1 238
Iyer, Raghavan N. BAA 196,233

J

J., Jezebel. CSF 107
J. A. C. K. FTF 42 SF1 285
J. F. H. BAA 227
J. G. BAA 223
J. J. J. SF1 274
J. K. R. BAA 256
J. S. BAA 8
J. W. L. pseud. of J. W. Lethaby.
CSF 107
J. W. M. SF1 334
Jackel, Eberhard. BAA 233
Jacks, Lawrence Pearsall (1860-
1955) CSF 107 ES1 238 SF1
274-5
Jackson, A. A., IV. IAC 138
Jackson, Alan Stewart. BAA 283
Jackson, Ambrose Lester. CSF
107 SF1 275
Jackson, Andrew (1767-1845)
CYR 13
Jackson, Basil. HFI 77
Jackson, Birdsall. ES1 238
Jackson, Charles Loring (1847-
1935) CSF 107 ES1 238 SF1
275 VFS 117
Jackson, Clive. IAC 138 SFS 62
Jackson, Edward Payson (1840-
1905) SF1 275
Jackson, George Gibbard (1877-)
SF1 275
Jackson, George Russell. SF1
275
Jackson, Holbrook. BAA 181
Jackson, Irene. IAC 138
Jackson, J. H. EXT 3/1 23 EXT
10/1 31
Jackson, Jacqueline. AOW 321
Jackson, James W. CSF 108 SF1
275

Jackson, John William, Jr. (1945-)
WGT 75 see also William T.
Silent
Jackson, Noel (1917-) SF1 275
Jackson, Shirley (1919-65) AOW
295 ES1 238 FL2 710-4 FL4
1563-7 HFI 77 IAC 138 IAH
106 ISW 122,129,226-7 MSM
104-7 SFE 317 SFH 83 SFS 62
SF1 275 SF2 949 see also
Shirley Jackson Hyman
Jackson, Stephen pseud. of John
Stevenson. CSF 108 SF1 275
Jackson, (Sir) Thomas Graham
(1835-1924) CSF 108 ES1 239
SF1 275
Jackson, Winifred. EXT 3/1 14
Jacob, Joseph. SRB 22
Jacob, Piers Anthony Dillingham
(1934-) BAA 146 BFP 258-60
ES1 239 WGT 75 see also Piers
Anthony
Jacob, Sylvia. VES 173
Jacob, T. Evan. BAA 70
Jacob, Violet K. CSF 108
Jacobi, Carl Richard (1908-)
ALW 143 COT 154 CSF 108
ES1 239 EXT 7/2 39 FFR 97
IAC 138-9 IMS 112,169 ISW
129-30 SFE 317 SFS 62 SF1
275 SF2 949 TSP 29,105 WTS
34-5,37-8,46,54-5,132
Jacobi, Jolande. LTN 64
Jacobs, David Michael. VFS 176-8
Jacobs, Fred. EXT 10/1 3
Jacobs, Harvey Jay (1930-) AAL
16 BYS 303 IAC 139 SFE 317
SFS 62 SF1 275 SF2 949
Jacobs, Joseph. WBW 48-9

Jacobs, Sylvia. IAC 139 SFS 62
Jacobs, T. C. H. (1889-) SF1 275
see also Jacques Pendower
Jacobs, William Wymark (1863-1943) ASF 303-4 CSF 108 ES1 239 FBK 64
Jacobsen, Helen. IAC 139 SFS 62
Jacobsen, Jens Peter. ATA 57
Jacobson, A. EXT 2/1 6
Jacobson, Dan (1929-) SF1 275 SF2 949
Jacobson, Edith. TSP 153
Jacobson, Ejler. TSP 153 see also Ejler Jakobsson
Jacobson, Sid. SF1 275
Jacomb, Charles Ernest (1888-) BAA 92 CSF 108 SFE 317 SF1 275
Jacquemard, Simonne (1922-) SF1 275
Jacques, Dennis A. IMS 97
Jacques, Norbert (1880-1954) SF1 275
Jacques, Robin. FFC 98, 166, 170, 178, 182
Jaeger, Cyril Karel Stuart. CSF 108 ES1 239 SF1 276 SF2 949-50
Jaeger, Muriel. BAA 92 CSF 108 SFE 317 SF1 276
Jaffe, Hyman (1882-) BAA 107 WGT 75
Jaffee, Irving Lincoln. SF1 276
Jaffee, Mary Flora. SF1 276 SF2 950
Jaffray, Norman R. IAC 139 SFS 62
Jagendorf, Moritz A. CSF 108
Jago, Wendy. UKL 245
Jaher, Frederic Cople. BAA 181
Jahnig, Dieter. BAA 233
Jakes, John (William) (1932-) ALW 212 BAA 139 ES1 239 FL1 166-8 HFI 77-8 IAC 139 LEX 385-6 RGS 87-8 SFB 19 SFE 317 SFS 62 SF1 276 SF2 950 SRB 265 STH 68 VES 195 WSF 172
Jakob. LTN 140-1
Jakober, Marie (1941-) SFE 317
Jakobsen. TDI 6
Jakobsson, Ejler (1911-) ALW 220 [FJT] ISW 131 SFE 317-8 TSP 154, 160, 183 WFS 303

WSF 126, 230, 280 see also Ejler Jacobson
Jakoby, Hans. BAA 233
Jakubowski, Maxim (1944-) BYS 321 IAC 139 SFE 318 SF1 276
James, Andrew. CSF 108
James, Clive. IAC 139
James, D. L. SFS 62
James, Daniel B. ASF 146 IAC 139
James, Daniel Lewis. IAC 139
James, David John. ES1 240 SF1 277 SF2 950
James, Dolan. SF1 276
James, E. R. IAC 139 SFS 63
James, Edward (1907-) SF1 276
James, Francis. TSP 33, 60, 209-11
James, George Payne Rainsford (1801?-60) CSF 108 SF1 276 WGT 75
James, George Wharton (1858-1923) SF1 276
James, Gunthar. SF1 277
James, Henry (1843-1916) ALW 88-9, 102 AOW 34 BAA 63 BYS 51, 53, 78, 114, 128 CAT 8 CSC 162-3 CSF 108 ES1 239-40 ETN 54, 98, 136 EXT 4/1 9 EXT 4/2 19 EXT 5/1 19 EXT 5/2 30 EXT 9/1 21 EXT 9/2 29, 39 EXT 10/2 50 FAN 5, 7, 11, 64, 184 FBK 15, 67 FLT 2, 12, 42 FL4 1568-74 ISW 129 MSF 49 MSM 25 NWO 95 SFH 11, 18-9 SF1 277 SOI 112 SOT 370 SRB 11 STF 6, 47, 58-9 STH 29 TFC 43, 105, 139, 166 THM 5 VES 149 WIF 55, 71
James, Henry pseud. of L. C. Kellenberger. IAC 139
James, Howard. CSF 108
James, Laurence. IAC 139 SFE 318 SF1 277
James, Leigh. SF1 277
James, Lionel (1871-1955) SF1 277
James, M(ontague) R(hodes) (1862-1936) BFP 261-2 CSF 108-9 ES1 240 EXT 10/1 44 FBK 60, 63, 65-6, 77 FL1 289-93 IAC 139 SF1 277 SOT 368 WTS 103
James, Philip pseud. of James H. Beard, Lester Del Rey. IAC 139

James, Rowland (1885-) BAA 98
CSF 109 SF1 277
James, Vernon. TSP 148
James, William (1842-1910) AAL
133 COT 100-1,104 CWN 10,
54 FAN 64,184 LTN 251 NDA
178 SF1 277 THM 32
Jameson, Annie Edith (1868-1931)
WGT 75-6 see also J. E. Buck-
rose
Jameson, Frederic. BAA 233
Jameson, Fredric R. MSF 76
UKL 245
Jameson, Malcolm (1891-1945)
AOW 321 BAA 110 BFP 263
CSF 109 ES1 240 ETN 64,68
EXT 5/1 3 EXT 7/2 40 FFR
97 HFI 78 IAC 139-40 IMS 45,
213,231 MSM 32,126 RFA 52,
57,60,62,78,83,90,110,114,
125,138,141 SFE 318 SFS 63
SF1 277 SOT 218 STH 155
WFS 112-3,118 WGT 76 WIF
185 WSF 93-4,97,103 WTS 54
Jameson, Margaret Storm pseud.
of Mrs. Guy Chapman (1897-)
BAA 105,111,117 CSF 109 ES1
240-1 EXT 2/2 27 SFE 318
SF1 277 WGT 30
Jameson, Twiggs pseud. of James
Twiggs. SF1 278
Jameson, Vida. IMS 213 WFS
119
Jamieson, Walter. IMS 68
Janacek, Leos. SIH 185
Jane, Frederick Thomas (1865-
1916) AOW 66 BFP 264 CSF
109 SFE 318 SF1 278 STH 183,
191-2,200-1,203 VES 156,312
Janes, Henry Hurford. SF1 278
Janes, Henry P. CSF 116 SF1
278
Janet, Paul. BAA 233
Janeway, Elizabeth. EXT 10/1
26 FFC 155
Janifer, Laurence M. pseud. of
Laurence Mark Harris (1933-)
ALW 212 AOW 236,397 BAA
160 ES1 241 ETN 65-6,97
HFI 78 IAC 140 IAH 49 MIH
119 RFA 210 RGS 88 SFE 318
SFS 63 SF1 278 STH 45 VES
207
Janney, Russell (1884-1963) CSF
109 SF1 278

Jannone, Claudia. PJF 60,62,73
Janson, Hank. SF1 278
Janssen, Jorn. BAA 233
Jansson, Tove. FFC 98-9,174
WAA 76
Jantsch, Erich. POE 313-4
Janvier, Ivan pseud. of Algis
Budrys. IAC 140 SFS 63
Janvier, Paul pseud. of Algis
Budrys. IAC 140 STH 120
VES 206
Janvier, Thomas Allibone (1849-
1913) AOW 66 CSF 109 ES1
241 EXT 1/1 12 SFE 318 SF1
278 WIF 48
Japy, Gaston. BAA 181
Jardine, Jack Owen (1931-) ES1
241 SF2 987 WGT 76 see also
Howard L. Cory, Larry Maddock
Jardine, Julie Ann (1926-) ES1
241 SF1 278 SF2 952 WGT 76
see also Howard L. Cory
Jaritz, Kurt. BAA 181
Jarmon, Mary Dolores. SF1 278
Jarrell, Randall (1914-65) FFC
6,66,120 SF1 278 SF2 952-3
Jarrett, Cora Hardy (1877-) CSF
109 SF1 278 WGT 76
Jarry, Alfred (1873-1907) EXT
8/1 16 FL4 1859-62 HFI 78
IAC 140 JGB 6 SFE 319-20
SFS 63 SIH 37,43-4,48,54,79,
109,138-9,146,181,184 WAA
75,136
Jarvis, Bob. IAC 140
Jarvis, E. K. (house name) SFE
320 WGT 76 see also Harlan
Ellison, Paul W. Fairman,
Robert Silverberg
Jarvis, Frederick Gordon, Jr.
(1930-) SF1 279 SF2 953
Jaspers, Karl. KAU 48
Jaures, Jean. BAA 181
Jauss, Anne. FFC 130
Jauss, Hans Robert. MSF 80
Javary, Auguste. POE 85
Javor, Frank A. ES1 241 HFI
78 IAC 140 SFE 320 SFS 63
SF1 279
Jay, Eric. SF1 279
Jay, Martin. BAA 233
Jay, Mel. ES1 241
Jay, Victor. SF1 279
Jayne, Mitchell F. SF1 279
Jean, Marie Joseph Albert (1892-)
CSF 165 SF1 279

Jean-Paul. THM 15
Jean-Aubrey, G. FAN 182
Jeanmarie, Henri. BAA 181
Jeanniere, Abel. BAA 233
Jeans, (Sir) James. COT 154
FTF 69 NDA 57 SFH 241 SOT
111 WFS 113
Jeeves, Byron Terry. SF1 279
Jefferies, John Richard (1848-87)
BAA 36 BYS 106-8 CSF 109
FAN 62,168 FTF 41 JGB 20
MSF 187-8,193 POE 146-8
PST 76-7, 88,192,200,255 SFE
320 SF1 279 THM 12 VES 127
Jeffers, Axel (1917-) LEX 386
Jeffers, Donnan Call. IAC 140
Jeffers, Robinson. EXT 10/2
109 IAC 140
Jeffers, Susan. FFC 169
Jefferson, Thomas. ASF 104-5
COT 38,123,142,235,242-4
CSC 111-2 MSF 38,175 VFS
163,211 VMW 6
Jeffries, Graham Montague see
Bruce Graham
Jemzew, Michail (1930-) LEX
388
Jenkin, Leonard. SF1 279
Jenkins, Alan. BAA 233
Jenkins, Alan Charles (1914-)
ES1 241-2 SF1 279
Jenkins, Esther Bigger (1894-)
SF1 279
Jenkins, Geoffrey (1920-) SF1
279 SF2 953
Jenkins, Will F(itzgerald) (1896-
1975) ALW 8,114,140-1 BAA
98,117 BFP 265-70 CSF 109
ES1 242-4 EXT 8/1 5 FFR 98
IAC 140 ISW 120 MIH 23 OWB
13 RFA 5 SFD 288 SFS 63
SF2 973 TSF 53 VES 107,173
VFS 154 WFS 205 WGT 76-7
WIF 145,147,155,192 WSF 54
see also Murray Leinster
Jenks, Almet (1892-1966) SF1
279
Jenks, Anton Shrewsbury. SF1
276
Jenks, George Charles (1850-
1929) WGT 77
Jenks, Tudor (1857-1922) ES1
244 SF1 279
Jenner. ETN 48
Jenner, Edward. POE 3,40-2

Jennings, Gary. IAC 140 SFS
63
Jennison, John William. SF1
279 see also Neil Charles, Gill
Hunt
Jens, Walter. ES1 244 POE 259
SFB 92
Jensen, Axel (1932-) AOW 203
BYS 307 ES1 244 SFE 321 SF1
279 SIH 93 SL2 725-8 WAA
234
Jensen, Johannes Vilhelm (1873-
1950) AOW 66 CSC 27 CSF 109
SFE 321 SF1 280
Jensen, Norman. SF1 280
Jenson, L. M. IMS 33
Jenyns, Soame. NDA 113-4
Jeppson, Janet Opal (1926-) HFI
78 SF1 280 SF2 953 see also
Janet Asimov
Jepson, Edgar Alfred (1863-1938)
CSF 109 SF1 280
Jepson, Rowland Walter (1888-
1954) CSF 109 SF1 280
Jepson, Selwyn (1899-) SF1 280
Jeremiah. EXT 8/1 23 HEN 18
Jerome, Jerome K. (1859-1927)
BAA 44-5 CSF 109 ES1 244
FTF 101 IAC 140 SFS 63 SF1
280 STH 35 VES 172
Jerome, Owen F. pseud. of Oscar
J. Friend. CSF 109
Jerrold, Douglas William (1803-
57) BAA 24, 96 CSF 109 SF1
280
Jersild, P. C. WAA 234
Jesby, Edward. AAL 15 IAC 140
Jeschke, Susan. FFC 103,188
Jeschke, Wolfgang (1936-) IAC
140 LEX 388-9
Jesse, Fryniwind Marsh Tennyson
(1889-1958) ES1 244 SF1 280
Jessel, John pseud. of Stanley G.
Weinbaum. IAC 140 RFA 36
Jessup, Morris K. ES1 244-5
Jesus. CUA 44,49 ETN 83 EXT
2/2 38 FHT 9-10,29-30,37,51,
54-6 FTF 158,195 IAH 10,57-
60,74 INT 79 ISW 31,51,182
KVT 6-7, 46,62 LTN 80,114,
124 MIH 136 MSM 14,232 NDA
61 NWO 4-6,31, 48,124,237,240,
274,293-4,303,331 SFN 116
THM 56 TJB 52 VMW 47 WFS
88,202 WTS 28 see also Christ,
God, Lord

185

Jeter, K.W. HFI 79
Jeury, Michel (1934-) LEX 390
SFE 321
Jevons, H. Stanley. BAA 234
Jewett, Sarah Orne. EXT 4/1 9
IAC 140
Jinadasa. VFS 18-21
Joachim (of Floris). ATA 14
NWO 101
Joachimson, Paul. BAA 234
Joad, Cyril E(dward) M(itchison)
(1841-1953) BAA 234 CSF 110
POE 253-4 SF1 280
Joan (of Arc). ETN 157
Job. HEN 4
Jobling, Peter. IAC 140
Joedicke, Jurgen. BAA 234
Johannesson, Olof pseud. of
Hannes Olof Goesta Alfven
(1908-) AOW 203 ES1 245 HFI
79 IAC 140 KAU 175 SFE 321-
2 SF1 280 SL4 1844-7 VES 182
Johannis, Luigi Rapuzzi (1905-68)
SL1 322-4
Johannot, Tony. FBK 82
John, Augustus. BAA 234
John, E. Roy. AAL 110
John, Jasper pseud. of Rosalie
Muspratt. CSF 110 ES1 245
SF1 280
John, Owen (1918-) SF1 280
John-Martin pseud. of William
Morris, Morgan Shepard. SF1
281
John (the Baptist). CWD 54
Johnhett pseud. of John Hettinger.
CSF 110 SF1 281
Johns, Kenneth pseud. of Kenneth
Bulmer, John Newman. SFE
322
Johns, Marston pseud. of Robert
L. Fanthorpe. ES1 245
Johns, William Earl (1893-1968)
CSF 110 ES1 245 SF1 281
Johns, Willy. BAA 124 ES1 245
HFI 79 SF1 281
Johnson, B.S. ES1 245
Johnson, Bill. IAC 140
Johnson, Carl. IMS 37
Johnson, Crockett pseud. of
David J. Leisk. CSF 110 FFC
26, 48
Johnson, David. SF1 281
Johnson, Doris. FAN 189 IAC
140 SFS 63

Johnson, Dorothy. SF1 281
Johnson, Dorothy. CSF 110 SF1
281
Johnson, E.A. BAA 67
Johnson, Edgar (1901-72) CSF
110 SF1 281 SF2 953
Johnson, Edna. EXT 10/1 24, 32
Johnson, Elizabeth. FFC 55, 66,
75, 100
Johnson, Frank R. BAA 111
Johnson, Frosty (1935-) SF1 281
Johnson, George Clayton. AOW
233 BAA 144 ES1 245 IAC 140
KAU 90 NDA 213 SFE 322 SF1
281 SRB 344
Johnson, George Lindsay (1853-
1943) CSF 110 SF1 281
Johnson, Gordon (1943-) SF2 954
Johnson, Henry T. SF1 281
Johnson, Holly. FFC 92
Johnson, Hugh S. IAC 140
Johnson, Jack. IMS 186
Johnson, James W. BAA 181
ES1 245
Johnson, Josephine W. ES1 245
IAC 140
Johnson, L.P.V. (1905-) ES1
245 SFE 322 SF1 281
Johnson, L.T. AAL 25
Johnson, Larry. FFC 116
Johnson, Leslie T. IAC 140 IMS
33, 97 RFA 42, 91 SOT 137, 139
VES 148, 156
Johnson, Lynda Bird. EXT 10/1
26
Johnson, Lyndon B. ETN 8 INT
122
Johnson, Maud Lalita (1875-) see
Lalita
Johnson, Owen McMahon (1878-
1952) AOW 42, 91, 105 BAA 97
CSF 110 SFE 322 SF1 282 STH
81-2
Johnson, Pamela. FFC 175
Johnson, Ray W. (1900-) ES1
245 SFE 322 SF1 282
Johnson, Robbin S. BAA 181, 234
Johnson, Robert Barbour. IAC
140 ISW 131 SFS 64 VES 317
WTS 39, 43-4, 56-9
Johnson, Ronald. IAC 140
Johnson, Rossiter (1840-1931)
CSF 110 ES1 245 SF1 282
Johnson, Russell. VES 148, 156
Johnson, S.S. IAC 141 SFS 64

Johnson, Sally. FFC 48
Johnson, Samuel (1709-84) AAL
164-5 BAA 12 BYS 76, 78 CAT
4 NDA 113 SFE 322 SOI 11,
153-4 STF 34 WIF 97
Johnson, Stanley Patrick (1940-)
AOW 207 SF1 282 SF2 954
Johnson, Thomas Marvin (1889-)
CSF 158 SF1 282
Johnson, Vera. IAC 141
Johnson, W. Cairnes. SF1 282
Johnson, W. R. IAC 141
Johnson, W. Ryerson. SOT 362
Johnson, Wayne L. CEN 23-40
Johnson, William B. (1927-)
AOW 347 EXT 5/2 37-48 SF1
282
Johnston, A. S. IMS 137, 213
Johnston, George. IAC 141
Johnston, George Burke. EXT
10/1 32, 34
Johnston, Gunnar. SF1 282
Johnston, Johanna. FFC 133
Johnston, Mary (1870-1936) BAA
85 CSF 110 SF1 282
Johnston, Thomas. FFC 182 SF1
282
Johnston, William (1924-) SF1 282
Johnstone, Charles (1719?-1800?)
SF1 282 WGT 77
Johnstone, David Lawson. CSF
110 SF1 283
Johnstone, Ted (1939-77) see
David McDaniel
Jokai, Maurus (1825-1904) ES1
246 MSF 162 SFB 45 SFE 322
SF1 283 SIH 40
Jolas, Eugene (1894-1952) CSF
110 SF1 283
Jolly, Stratford D. CSF 110
Jonas, Gerald. AOW 291 BAA
151-2, 234 ETN 45 EXT 10/1
32 IAC 141 LTN 204 SFS 64
Jonchere, Ernest. POE 136
Jones, A. Ernest. FLT 139-41
SFS 64
Jones, Adrienne (1915-) FFC 176
SF1 283 SF2 954 WGT 77 see
also Gregory Mason
Jones, Alan Price. EXT 6/1 20
Jones, Alice Eleanor. IAC 141
Jones, Alice Ilgenfritz (-1906)
BAA 49 SF1 283 WGT 77 see
also Two Women of the West
Jones, Charlotte Rosalie. ES1
246

Jones, Clara Augusta. WGT 77
Jones, Constance Bridges. CSF
110 ES1 246 HFI 79 SF1 283
Jones, D(ennis) F(eltham) (1915?-)
AOW 204 BAA 142-3, 160 BFP
271 ES1 246 FFR 98 HFI 79
KAU 155, 174-5 LEX 390 MFW
86, 200 RGS 88-9, 216 SFE 322
SF1 283 SL1 409-14 VES 182
Jones, Diana Wynne (1934-) FFC
43, 66, 120, 164, 188 SF1 283
Jones, Dorothy. SF1 283
Jones, Dupre Anderson (1937-)
ES1 246 SF1 283
Jones, Eddie (1935-) BYS 217 IAC
141 SFE 322-3 SRB 124 VES
291
Jones, Elias W. CSF 110
Jones, Elis Gwyn. IAC 141 SFS
64
Jones, Elizabeth Orton. FFC 81,
93
Jones, Ernest. ISW 265
Jones, Ewart Charles. BAA 132
ES1 246 SF1 283
Jones, Francis. WGT 77
Jones, Frank Earl. SF1 582
Jones, G. C. G. pseud. of Griffith-
Jones, George Chetwynd. BAA
54, 70 EXT 7/1 13
Jones, George Alfred. STH 183-4
Jones, Glyn. ES1 246
Jones, Gonner. BAA 146 ES1
246 SFE 323 SF1 283
Jones, Gordon. EXT 2/1 11, 13
Jones, Guy Pearce. CSF 110 ES1
246 HFI 79 SF1 283
Jones, H. Bedford see Allan Hawk-
wood
Jones, (Sir) Harold Spencer (1890-
1960) ES1 246
Jones, Ira L. SF1 283
Jones, J. A. HFI 79
Jones, Jack Ray (1934-) ES1 246
SF1 284
Jones, James. SFN 43
Jones, John Beauchamp (1810-66)
SF1 283
Jones, John T. pseud. of H. P.
Lovecraft. EXT 3/1 15
Jones, Joseph. BAA 234
Jones, Judith P. BAA 234
Jones, Kenneth. IMS 69
Jones, L. Q. SF1 284
Jones, Langdon (1942-) BYS 298,
321 DTS 46 ETN 21, 23 HFI 79

Jones, Langdon (cont.)
IAC 141 LEX 391 SFB 132 SFD
35 SFE 323 SF1 284 VES 153
Jones, Leroi. IAC 141
Jones, Lillian B. BAA 82
Jones, Louis. FFC 20
Jones, Louis Clark (1908-) ES1
246
Jones, McClure. FFC 43
Jones, Margaret. ES1 246-7 HFI
184 SFE 323 SF1 284
Jones, Mervyn (1922-) ES1 247
SFE 323 SF1 284 SF2 954
Jones, Myrtle K. see Morojo
Jones, Neil R. (1909-) ALW 136
AOW 105 COT 163 ES1 247
HFI 79 IAC 141 IMS 76 ISW
153, 276 LEX 391 MFW 37
RFA 41, 91 RGS 89-90, 216
SFE 323 SFS 64 SF1 284 SF2
954-5 SOT 74 STH 141 VES
83, 93, 117, 185, 187 WFS 47-9
WIF 120, 146 WSF 49, 99
Jones, (Prof.) P. SF1 284
Jones, Randy. FFC 156
Jones, Raymond F. (1915-) AOW
204 BAA 137 BFP 272-3 COT
61, 83 ES1 247-8 EXT 5/1 3
HFI 79-80 IAC 141-2 IAH 29-
30, 123 KWS 229-30 LEX 392
MSM 75 NDA 103 RFA 96, 104,
116, 120, 126, 130, 140, 198, 200,
205 RGS 90 SFE 323-4 SFS
64 SF1 284 VES 80, 105, 188,
195, 314, 342 WGT 77-8 WIF
90, 146, 167, 233 WSF 106-7
Jones, R(ichard) Glyn (1946-)
SFB 133 SFE 255
Jones, Richard L. (1948-) SF1
284
Jones, Robert Francis (1934-)
BAA 160 HFI 80 SF1 284 SF2
955
Jones, Robert Gibson. SFE 324
VES 238, 291, 333 WSF 115
Jones, Robert L. KAU 92
Jones, Robert Webster. CSF 111
ES1 248 SF1 284
Jones, Roger. IAC 142
Jones, Stephen K. BAA 234
Jones, Susan Carleton (1864-
1926) WGT 78
Jones, Tupper (1909?-) ES1 248
Jones, Vernon H. IMS 33 WGT
78
Jones, William M. EXT 6/1 15

Jong, Erica. COT 181
Jonklass, Rodney. VFS 6, 27
Jonquil pseud. of J. L. Collins.
CSF 111 SF1 284
Jonson, Ben. EXT 6/1 6 NWO
11 SFA 9
Jonsson, Runer. FFC 155
Joos, Donald A. IAC 132, 142
Jordan, Alice M. EXT 10/1 32
Jordan, Elizabeth Garver (1867-
1947) CSF 111 ES1 248 SF1
285
Jordan, F. Dormer. CSF 111
SF1 285
Jordan, Owen. WFS 23
Jordon, Chester. IMS 137
Jorgensen, Ivar (house name)
ES1 248 SFE 324 WGT 78 see
also Harlan Ellison, Randall
Garrett, Robert Silverberg
Jorgenson, Alf A. WGT 78 see
also Aaron Arne
Jorgenson, Ivar (house name)RSG
11 SFE 324 WGT 78 see also
Paul W. Fairman, Robert Silver-
berg
Jorgensson, A. K. IAC 142 SFS
64
Joscelyne, Cyril. CSF 111 SF1
285
Joseph, Gentle. BAA 82 SF1 206
Joseph, Marie Gertrude Holmes.
BAA 114
Joseph, Michael Kennedy (1914-)
AOW 204 BYS 38 ES1 248 HFI
80 SFE 324 SF1 285 SF2 955
Joslin, Sesyle. ES1 248
Jourdan, D. A. IAC 142
Jourdain, Eleanor Frances (1863-
1924) ES1 248
Jowett, Benjamin. EXT 7/1 16
VFS 188
Joyce, James (1882-1941) ACE 56
AC2 54 CAT 51, 73, 136 CSC 8,
163, 197, 201, 204, 218 CUA 3-4,
6, 61 CWD 55-6 CWN 36 EXT
2/1 18 EXT 7/2 32 EXT 8/1 13
EXT 10/2 65 IAH 81, 89, 116
INT 40 ISW 150, 272 MFW 281
MIH 66, 71-2, 122, 129, 135, 139-
41, 143 MSF 280 MSM 114 NWO
187, 255-6 OWB 15 RAH 16, 228
SFD 43, 66-7, 76, 87, 295, 298
SFH 60, 88, 91 SFN 42, 79 SIH
56 STF 3, 6, 49, 59 TBC 6 THM
8, 13 WFS 41, 290 WSF 251, 261

Joyce, Michael. CSF 111 IAC
142 SFS 64
Judas. SHL 31
Judd, Cyril M. pseud. of Cyril M.
Kornbluth, Judith Merril. IAH
50 MSM 76 RFA 199 SFE 325
SFW 402-3 WFS 182
Judd, Sylvester. BAA 24
Jude, Christopher. SF1 285
Judge, William Quan (1851-96)
SF1 285
Judson, Edward Zane Carroll
(1823-86) TSP 86 WGT 78 see
also Ned Buntline
Judson, Jeanne Margaret (1890-)
CSF 111 SF1 285
Judson, Lyman Spicer Vincent.
BAA 157
Judson, Ralph. WGT 78
Juenger, Ernst (1895-) ES1 248
POE 260-1 SFE 325 SF1 285
SL2 960-4
Juffe, Mel. SF1 285
Juhre, William. VES 287
Juin, Hubert. BAA 234
Jules-Verne, Jean. AOW 347
Julesz, (Dr.) Bela. VFS 143
Julie, (Sister). BAA 234
Julius. SF1 285

June, Harold. WGT 78
Jung, Carl G. (1875-1961) ACC
88-9, 103, 107, 128, 185, 191 ACE
30-1 AC2 28-9 CSC 55, 125-6
CWN 54 ES1 248 EXT 7/1 12,
17 EXT 8/2 65-6 EXT 10/1 15
EXT 10/2 109 FBK 101 FHT
23-4, 29-30, 52 FLT 141-2 IAH
60 INT 112-3, 118 ISW 272
JGB 17, 35, 42, 49-50 KAU 19-
20 KVT 4 LTN 12, 34-5, 47, 62-
7, 77-9, 81, 84, 123, 167 MSM
238, 246 RAH 95, 175 RBY 103,
164 RZY 9, 14, 19, 48, 50-1, 83
TJB 54 TSO 5 UKL 16-20, 25,
27, 35-6, 97-9, 180, 186-7, 201-3,
205, 207-8, 216, 220 WBW 3-4,
32-3, 41-2, 46, 51
Jungk, Robert. ALW 14, 174
BAA 234 POE 307, 313
Junius (Junior). SF1 285
Just, Klaus Gunther. BAA 181
Juster, Norton (1929-) ES1 248
FFC 26, 177 IAC 142 SF1 285
SF2 955
Justinian I. SFN 39
Justus, Douglas R. SRB 483-8,
516
Justus, James H. BAA 234

K

Kacewgari, Romain (1914-) see
Romain Gary
Kael, Pauling. CSC 281 KAU 93
Kaempfert, Wade (house name)
SFE 326 see also Lester Del
Rey, Harry Harrison
Kaempffert, Waldemar Bernhard.
BAA 234 EXT 2/1 13 IAC 142
SFS 64
Kaestner, Erich. CSF 111

Kafka, Franz (1883-1924) BYS 48,
183, 185-8, 317 CSC 171 CSF
111 CUA 11 ES1 248-9 EXT
2/2 41 EXT 8/1 5, 12 FBK 16,
41, 128, 131 FFR 99 FHT 50-1
FLT 1-2, 67-92, 119, 133 FL1
207-10 FL4 1575-80, 1966-8
HEN 15-6, 18, 60 IAC 142 JGB
6, 9, 26 KAU 30, 32 LTN 176
MIH 11, 103 MSF 26, 29-30, 65,

Kafka, Franz (cont.)
282 MSM 107 NWO ix, 207 RFA
162 SFB 124, 145 SFD 88-9
SFE 326 SFN 85 SFS 64 SF1
286 SOI xiii, 35-6, 49 TFC 169-
75 THM 8 UKL 137 WAA 229
WSF 251, 348
Kagan, Norman. ETN 65-6 EXT
8/1 16 IAC 142 SFE 326 SFS
64
Kagarlitski, Julius (1926-) AOW
347 BAA 234 BYS 281 EXT
10/1 48-9 FAN 177, 189 OSR
29-52, 355 SFE 326-7 WFS
305-6
Kahler, Erich. BAA 234
Kahlert, Karl Friedrich (1765-
1813) WGT 79 see also Lawrence
Flammenberg
Kahn, Alec. CSF 111
Kahn, Bernard I. IAC 142 SFS
64
Kahn, Herman (1922-) BYS 245
CSC 133 ES1 249 FTF 127, 129
SFE 327 VFS 60
Kahn, Joan. ES1 249 SF1 286
Kainen, Ray pseud. of Ray Kainu-
lainen. SF1 286
Kaiser, George. FAN 95 MSF
282
Kaiser, Helmut Horst. BAA 283
Kai-Shek, Chiang. ASF 287
Kaldor, Steve. IAC 142
Kaler, James Otis (1848-1912)
WGT 79 see also James Otis
Kaletsky, Milton. IAC 142 IMS
84, 93
Kalin, Martin G. BAA 181
Kallas, Aino. SF1 286
Kallman, Chester. FLT 49
Kamin, Nick pseud. of Robert J.
Antonick (1939-) HFI 80 SFE
327 SF1 286
Kamlah, Wilhelm. BAA 181
Kampf, Harold Bertram (1916-)
SF1 286
Kandel, I. L. BAA 235
Kandel, Michael. IAC 142
Kane, Bob. SFB 110 SFH 108
VES 237, 326
Kane, Gil. HFI 80
Kane, Harry. SFS 64
Kane, James Johnson (1837-1921)
SF1 286
Kane, Wilson (house name) SFE
327 see also Robert Bloch

Kaner, Hyman. CSF 111 ES1
249 SFE 327 SF1 286
Kangilaski, Joan. HFI 80 SRB
265
Kangrga, Milan. BAA 235
Kanin, Garson. IAC 142 SFS 65
Kant, Immanuel (1724-1804) COT
104 FTF 44-5 MFW 7, 51 MSF
60, 83, 202 THM 10 UKL 72, 212
Kanters, Robert. BAA 235
Kantor, Hal. SF1 286
Kantor, MacKinlay (1904-77) AOW
204 ES1 249 HFI 80 IAC 142
SFE 327 SFN 40 SF1 286 SF2
956 SOT 425
Kantorowicz, Alfred. BAA 235
Kantrowitz, Arthur. VFS 225
Kapetansky, Seymour. COT 25-
6, 28, 212, 218
Kaplan, Barry see Bettina Kings-
ley
Kaplan, M. M. WGT 79
Kapp, Colin (1929?-) AAL 80-1
ES1 249 FFR 99 HFI 80 IAC
142 LEX 393 RGS 90-1 SFD 16
SFE 327 SFS 65 SF1 287 VES
105, 108, 174
Karig, Walter (1898-1956) CSF
111 ES1 249 FL5 2214-6 MSM
82 SFE 327 SF1 287
Karinthy, Frigyes (1887-1938)
BYS 189-90 ES1 249-50 FL4
2046-8 LEX 393 SFB 45 SFE
327 SF1 287 SIH 135
Karl, Frederick R. EXT 6/1
13, 15, 17-8, 20
Karl, Jean E. IAC 142 LTN 57
Karlins, Marvin (1941-) BAA 160
HFI 80 SF1 287 SF2 956
Karloff, Boris pseud. of William
Henry Pratt (1887-1969) ALW
47 AOW 355 CSF 111 EXT
3/1 20 FBK 26 ISW 220 OMN
4, 60, 69, 79, 257 SFB 8-9, 33
SFH 101, 183 SF1 287 SIH 17,
34 WAA 86 WFS 55 WSF 308
Karlova, Irina. CSF 111 SF1
287
Karlson, Hans. CSF 111 SF1
287
Karlsson, Ewert. FFC 155
Karp, David (1922-) AAL 32-3
AOW 205 BAA 122 ES1 250
EXT 2/2 29 EXT 5/1 4 EXT
6/2 51 FAN 148 HFI 80 ISW
66-9 NDA 95-6, 105, 210 SFE

Karp, David (cont.)
327 SF1 287 SF2 956-7 VES
261 WAA 62
Karp, Marvin Allen. ES1 250
SF1 287
Karpf, Fritz. BAA 235
Karpov, Nikolai A. MSF 262
Kasack, Hermann (1896-1966)
SF1 287
Kasanzew, Alexander (1906-)
LEX 393-4
Kaschnitz, Marie Luise. FBK
152
Kashiwagi, Isami. FFC 172
Kasper, Walter. BAA 235
Kassil, Leo (1905-) SF1 287
Kassirer, Norma. FFC 171
Kasson, Helen Weinbaum. IAC
142 WGT 79
Kasson, John F. BAA 235
Kast, Pierre. FL4 2008-12
Kastel, Warren (house name)
SFE 327 see also Chester S.
Geier, Robert Silverberg
Kastle, Herbert David (1924-)
ES1 250 FFR 99 HFI 80 SFE
327 SF1 287 SF2 957 SOT
367 STH 45
Kastner, Erich. FFC 13,104,156
Katayev, Valentin P. EXT 10/2
75 MSF 253-4
Katcha, Vahe. ES1 250
Kateb, George. AOW 347 BAA
xix,181,231,235,283 FAN 173-
4,178 NDA 54,62-5,206 TSF
246-7
Kateley, Walter. VES 139
Katz, Harvey A. IAC 142 LTN
251 SF1 287
Katz, Jack. HFI 81
Katz, Steven (1935-) SF1 287
SF2 957
Kauffmann, Stanley. WFS 197-8
Kaufholz, Elaine. BAA 235
Kaufman, George S. OWB 70
STH 41
Kaufmann, (Rev.) A. BAA 235
Kaufmann, Moritz. BAA 181,235
Kaufmann, John. FFC 69,74,181
Kaufmann, V. Milo. BAA 235
EXT 5/1 1,17-24
Kaul, A.N. NWO 23
Kaul, Fedor. CSF 111 SFE 327
SF1 287
Kaupp, Peter. BAA 235

Kautsky, Karl. BAA 182
Kavan, Anna pseud. of Helen
Woods Edmonds. AOW 205 BYS
316-7 FFR 99 HFI 81 SFE 327
SF1 287-8 SIH 59 SL2 1000-3
SRB 344
Kavanagh, Herminie Templeton.
WGT 79 see also Herminie
Templeton
Kaverin, Veniamin A. FBK 41
MSF 254
Kawalec, Julian. AOW 289 EXT
7/2 47 IAC 142 SFS 65
Kawin, Bruce. IAC 142
Kaye, Marx (house name) WGT 79
see also S.J. Byrne
Kaye, Nora. WFS 204
Kaye, Pamela. SF1 288
Kaye-Smith, Sheila (1887-1956)
CSF 111 SF1 288
Kayser, Martha. BAA 87 SF1
288
Kayser, Ronal. WGT 79 WTS 38
see also Dale Clark
Kazantsev, Alexander P. IAC 142
MSF 264-5 SFS 65 SIH 199 SOT
431
Kazin. ETN 24,176
Kealing, Ethel Black. SF1 288
Kearney, C.B. SF1 288
Kearney, Chalmers (1881-1966)
BAA 112 CSF 111 PST 151-2,
198,200,209,222-3,227,230,236,
269,279,285,291,305 SFE 328
SF1 288
Kearns, Winn. IAC 142
Kearney, Peter. STH 186-8,193,
205
Keating, Eliza H. SF1 288
Keating, Lawrence. IMS 26,80
Keaton, Buster. ETN 60
Keats, Ezra Jack. FFC 129
Keats, John. CAT 68 CUA 61
FBK 27 JGB 42,59 LTN 140
MFW 279 MSM 280 NDA 24-5
RZY 48 TDI 10 TSO 10-2,40
Keck, Maud. SF1 288
Kedabra, Abby. ES1 250
Kee, Robert (1919-) BAA 126-7
ES1 250 SFE 328 SF1 288
Keefer, Lowell B. SF1 288
Keel, John A. pseud. of John Alva
Kiehle. ES1 250 SF1 288
Keeler, Clinton Clarence. BAA
283

Keeler, Harry Stephen (1890-1967) CSF 111 IAC 142 SF1 288

Keenan, Hugh T. EXT 10/1 31-2

Keene, Day. BAA 134 ES1 250 HFI 81 IAC 142 SFE 328 SFS 65 SF1 288

Keeping, Charles. FFC 25, 57, 65, 95, 98, 176

Kefauver. CWN 4

Kegel, Charles H. BAA 236

Kegel, Walther (1907-45) LEX 394

Keightley, David Noel (1932-) ES1 250 SF2 960 SOT 62 WGT 79 see also Noel Keyes

Keilty, James. BAA 153 IAC 143

Keith, Brandon. SF1 288

Keith, Eros. FFC 16, 47, 155

Keith, John. IAC 143

Keith, Leigh. COT 124

Keith, Samuel James. SF1 288

Kellam, Ian. FFC 182 SF1 288

Kelland, Clarence Budington (1881-1964) CSF 112 SF1 288

Kellar, Von. SF1 288

Kelleam, Joseph E(veridge) (1913-) COT 202, 205, 248 ES1 250 HFI 81 IAC 143 SFE 328 SFS 65 SF1 288-9 SF2 958 VES 179

Kellenberger, L. C. see Henry James

Keller, B. L. IAC 143

Keller, (Mrs.) David H. see Cynthia Carey

Keller, David H. (1880-1966) ALW 126 AOW 394 BAA 94 BFP 274-5 COT 9-10, 23, 216 CSF 112, 181 DTS 13, 23 ES1 250-1 EXT 3/1 23 FL1 374-6 FL4 1581-5 HFI 81 IAC 143 IMS 16, 20-5, 31, 45, 76, 83, 107, 138, 159, 200, 213, 221 LEX 394-5 MSM 304 RFA 2, 63 SFD 23-4, 27 SFE 328 SFS 65 SFW 119-23, 145 SF1 289 SOT 73, 92, 107-8, 277, 338 SRB 98, 305 STH 2, 12-3, 61-2, 78-9, 109-16, 118, 120, 139-40, 143-4 VES 103-4, 128, 132, 173, 182, 185, 211, 232, 314 WGT 79 WIF 88, 135 WSF 45 WTS 28, 32-3, 35, 38, 42, 44, 132

Keller, Donald G. [FJT]

Keller, Gottfried. CSF 112

Keller, I. MSF 262

Keller, Marc F. BAA 96-7 CSF 17 SF1 289

Keller, Teddy. IAC 143 SFS 65

Kellermann, Bernhard (1879-1951) CSF 112 LEX 395-6 PST 157 SFE 328 SF1 289 SL5 2316-20

Kellett, Ernest Edward (1864-1950) CSF 112 SF1 289

Kelley, DeForest. IAC 143

Kelley, Francis Clement (1870-1948) CSF 112 SF1 289

Kelley, Joseph. EXT 10/1 19

Kelley, Leo P(atrick) (1928-) BAA 182 HFI 81 IAC 143 SFE 328-9 SF1 289 SF2 958 VES 230 WGT 79

Kelley, Martha Mott. WGT 79-80

Kelley, Maurice W. BAA 236

Kelley, Thomas P. ES1 251 IMS 199 SF1 289 WTS 41-3

Kelley, William Melvin. AOW 205 SFE 329

Kellino, Pamela pseud. of Pamela Ostrer Mason. SF1 289

Kellner, Wolfgang (1928-) LEX 396

Kellogg, Grace. CSF 112

Kellogg, Steven. FFC 106, 112, 126

Kelly, Frank K. (1914-) COT 121 ES1 252 IAC 144 RFA 24, 32

Kelly, Isabella. CSF 112

Kelly, James Paul. CSF 112 EXT 1/1 12 SF1 289

Kelly, Kathryn. IMS 63

Kelly, Mary Quella. EXT 10/1 31-2

Kelly, R. Gordon. BAA 236 KAU 13

Kelly, Robert (1935-) HFI 81 PJF 74 SFE 329 SF1 289-90 SF2 958

Kelly, Teague M. SF1 290

Kelly, Walt (1913-) COT 131 ES1 252 IAC 144 SIH 121

Kelly, (Col.) William Patrick (1848-) BAA 64 CSF 112 SF1 290

Kelsall, Charles. BAA 18 WGT 80

Kelsey, Franklyn. CSF 112 SF1 290

Kelsey, Joan Marshall (1907-)
SF2 919 see also Joan Grant
Kelton, Aryan (1892-) SF1 290
Kemble, Fanny. NWO 282
Kemp, Earl (1929-) ES1 252 ETN
93 EXT 5/1 6 IAC 144 ISW
xii, 181 SFD 64, 250 SFS 65
SF1 290 SF2 958 WSF 215
Kemp, Harold Curry (1896-) ES1
252
Kemp, Robert (1908-) ES1 252
Kemper, William E., Jr. SF1
290
Kempster, James Aquila (1864-)
CSF 112 SF1 290
Kendall, Carol (1917-) ES1 252
FFC 104 SF1 290 SF2 958-9
Kendall, John pseud. of Margaret
Maud Brash. CSF 112 EXT
6/2 51 EXT 9/2 53 SFE 329
SF1 290
Kendall, May. CSF 112 SF1 290
Kendrick, Bayard. TSP 215-20
Keneally, Thomas Michael (1935-)
SF1 290
Kenealy, Arabella. CSF 112
Keniston, Kenneth. BAA 236
Kenkel, William F. BAA 236
Kennaway, James pseud. of
James Ewing Peebles (1928-)
HFI 81 SFE 329 SF2 959
Kennedy, Arthur. TSP 216
Kennedy, Bart (1861-1930) CSF
112 SF1 290
Kennedy, Charles Rann. CSF 113
Kennedy, Craig. WTS 39, 71
Kennedy, Edgar Rees. SF1 290
Kennedy (family). JGB 27
Kennedy, Jacqueline. JGB 12
Kennedy, John F. DTS v INT
79 KAU 21 POE 283 RHN 73,
115-7, 124, 158, 160, 211 VFS 9,
229
Kennedy, Paul. FFC 25, 193
Kennedy, R. A. CSF 113 SFE
329 SF1 290 WGT 80
Kennedy, Richard. FFC 6, 54, 67
Kennedy, Robert F. KVT 48
NDA 215 RHN 172
Kennedy, X. J. EXT 10/1 33
IAC 144
Kenneth, Bruce see Diedrick
Crayon, Jr.
Kenneth-Brown, Kenneth. CSF
113
Kenney, Douglas C. SF1 290

Kenny, Herbert A. FFC 177
Kennicott, Donald (1881-) ES1
252 ISW 131
Kensch, Otto. CSF 113 SF1 290
Kensett, Percy F. CSF 113 SF1
290
Kent, Brad (house name) SF1 291
see also Dennis Talbot Hughes
Kent, Edward. BAA xvi, 25
MSF 177
Kent, George. EXT 2/1 13
Kent, Jim. SF1 291
Kent, Kelvin pseud. of Arthur K.
Barnes, Henry Kuttner. IAC
44 SFE 329 VES 147 WIF 157
Kent, Morgan. IAC 144 SFS 65
Kent, Russell. IAC 144
Kent, Ryland. CSF 113 SF1 291
Kent, Saul. SF1 291
Kenton, Bernard J. pseud. of
Jerome Siegel. IMS 15
Kenton, Edna. NWO 161
Kenton, L. P. SF1 291
Kenward, James Macara (1908-)
CSF 113 SF1 291 SF2 959
Kenwood, Robin. BAA 157
Kenworthy, Joseph. FAN 96
Kenyon, Charles Richard. CSF
113 SF1 291
Kenyon, Ernest M. HFI 81
Kenyon, Paul. SF1 291
Keon, Miles Gerald (1821-75)
SF1 291
Keown, Anna Gordon (1902-57)
CSF 113 SF1 291
Keown, Eric. EXT 6/1 19
Kepler, Johannes (1571-1630)
ALW 32, 42, 95 AOW 24 BYS
61-2, 79-80 EXT 1/2 30 EXT
2/1 15, 20 EXT 3/1 30 EXT
3/2 52 EXT 4/2 29 EXT 7/2
34 FAN 9, 51 FTF 19-20 IAC
144 INT 12-3 KAU 10 MIH 26
MSF 88, 100, 103, 219 MSM 29,
201 PST 11, 17-8, 21-3, 244
RZY 48 SFB 41, 44, 70-1, 74
SFE 329 SFH 117, 119-21, 160-
1 SFN 32 SFS 65 SIH 107 SOI
42-3 SRB 3 VES 69, 260 WIF
34, 61 WSF 14
Keppel-Jones, Arthur Mervyn
(1909-) AOW 205 BAA 115 ES1
252 SFE 329 SF1 291
Ker, Anne. CSF 113
Ker, David (1842-1914) CSF 113
SF1 291

Kerby, Susan Alice pseud. of Alice Elizabeth Burton. CSF 113 SF1 291

Kerenyi, Karl. BAA 236

Kermode, Frank. EXT 6/1 18-9 FAN 188 NWO 4,11-3,15,36

Kern, Gary. SL1 28-32,138-43, 378-82 SL2 618-24 SL4 1768-74,1837-43,1879-83 SL5 2373-7,2433-41

Kern, Gregory pseud. of E. C. Tubb. FFR 99 SIH 169 VES 202-3

Kern, Helmut. BAA 283

Kernahan, John Coulson (1858-1943) BAA 68 CSF 113 ES1 252 SF1 291 WGT 80

Kernan, Alvin. NWO 9

Kerouac, Jack. EXT 7/2 32 EXT 8/1 13 FTF 194

Kerr, Alvah Milton (1858-1924) CSF 113 SF1 292

Kerr, Andrew William (1848-) BAA 79 SF1 292

Kerr, Artemus P. CSF 113 SF1 292

Kerr, David. IAC 144

Kerr, Frank Robinson. BAA 113

Kerr, Geoffrey (1895-) ES1 252 HFI 82 SF1 292

Kerr, Sophie (1880-1965) SF1 292

Kerr, Stephen Thomas. BAA 283-4 SF1 292

Kerr, Walter H. IAC 144 ISW 124,242 SFS 65

Kerrigan, Anthony. EXT 9/1 17

Kerruish, Jessie Douglas. CSF 113 ES1 252 FBK 55 SF1 292

Kersh, Gerald (1911-68) ALW 146 CSF 114 ES1 252-3 EXT 7/2 41 EXT 8/1 5 FFR 99 HFI 82 IAC 144 SFE 329 SFS 65-6 SF1 292

Kesey, Ken. CAT 37 KAU 4

Keshishian, John M. (1923-) SFE 329 SF1 292 SF2 959

Kessel, J. EXT 2/1 13

Kessler, Martin. BAA 236 EXT 9/2 59

Kessler, Merle. IAC 144

Kessler, Meta. BAA 284

Kesten, Herman. CSF 114

Kesting, Hanno. BAA 236,284

Ketterer, David (1942-) ACC 244 AOW 8,348 BAA xx-xxi,182,

236 CAT 7 FHT 67 FRN 20 KAU 87 LTN 13,34,259 MFW 96 NWO ii-iii,71,270 RAH 258 SFE 330 SFH 9,239 SFW 6 SF1 292 SF2 959 SRB 72,504 UKL 245 VES 330

Kettle, Leroy. IAC 144

Kettle, Pamela (1934-) BAA 149 SFE 330 SF1 292

Kevles, Bettyann. IAC 144

Key, Alexander Hill (1904-) AOW 321 ES1 253 FFC 164,177 SF1 292 SF2 959

Key, David. SF1 292

Key, Ellen. EXT 8/2 48

Key, Eugene George. CSF 114 ES1 253 IAC 144 IMS 23 SFE 330 SF1 292 STH 142

Key, Samuel Whittell (1874-) CSF 114 SF1 292

Keyes, Daniel (1927-) ALW 239 AOW 205,207,299,354 ASF 144, 308 BFP 276 BYS 262 COT 162 CSC 224 ES1 253 FFR 99-100 HFI 82 IAC 144 INT 58 LEX 396-7 MFW 44,46 NWO 165 OMN 10 RGS 91 SFB 23 SFD 19-20,86 SFE 330 SFH 243 SFS 66 SF1 293 SF2 959-60 SL2 802-6 SOT 262 STF 54-8,78 VES 177,239,242 WFS 228

Keyes, Kenneth S., Jr. BAA 149

Keyes, Noel pseud. of David Noel Keightley (1932-) IAC 145 SFE 330 SF1 293

Keyes, Thom. BYS 301 IAC 145

Keyhoe, Donald E. (1897-) ES1 253 EXT 5/1 8

Keynes, (Lord) John Maynard. ETN 47 MSF 219 WFS 203

Keyserling. EXT 9/2 62

Khachaturian, Aram. ACC 124

Khaldun, Ibn. COT 254

Khan, Genghis. VFS 254

Khanna, Lee Cullen. BAA 236

Kharafra, Ramon. SF1 293

Kheraskov, Mikhail M. MSF 244

Khosrofian, Harry (1924-) ES1 253 SF1 293

Khouri, Nadia. BAA 236

Khrushchev, Nikita S. EXT 10/2 77 ISW 171 RHN 147,152 WFS 66

Kidd, Benjamin. POE 190

Kidd, Virginia (1921-) COT 271
IAC 109,145 IAH 57 LTN 18,
57,228,238,249 MIH 65 SFS
66 SF1 293 SF2 960-1 SRB
373 TJB 43-4 WGT 80
Kiehle, John Alva see John A.
Keel
Kierkegaard, Soren (1813-55)
CUA 17 CWN 31 EXT 7/2 33
EXT 8/1 12 EXT 9/2 47 JGB
6 THM 51
Kikutake, Kiyonoru. [FUT]
Kilburn, David. IAC 145
Kilby, Clyde S. EXT 8/1 1 EXT
9/2 25 EXT 10/1 2,19 SOI 70-
80
Kiley, Frederick S. EXT 6/1 18
Kilker, Dorothy K. SL3 1417-23
SL4 1827-31
Killough, Lee. LEX 397-8
Killy, Jean-Claude. HEN 13-4, 23
Kilmartin, Joanna. NWO 186
Kilworth, Garry (1941-) IAC 145
LEX 398 SFE 330 VES 226
Kimball, Ellen A. STH 167
Kimball, Grace Lucia Atkinson
(1875-1923) WGT 80
Kimball, Harold Clive. BAA 124
Kimball, Richard Bowland. WGT
80
Kimberly, Gail. HFI 82 IAC 145
VES 226
Kimmel, Margaret. FFC 188
Kimmerle, Heinz. BAA 236
Kimoy, Ernest. SFA 55-6
Kincaid, C. A. CSF 114
Kinder, Stephen. CSF 114 SF1
293
Kindermann, Eberhard Christian.
FTF 25 SFB 71 WAA 32-3
Kindler, Asta pseud. of Una
Hicken. SF1 293
King, Albert (1924-) SF1 293 see
also Paul Conrad
King, Alexander. FFC 133
King, Arthur. FFC 157
King, C. A. EXT 6/1 15
King, Charles Daly (1895-1963)
CSF 114 WGT 80
King, Christopher. SF1 293
King, Clive. FFC 133
King, Cynthia (1925-) SF1 582
King, Frank Harvey. BAA 137
SF1 293

King, Harold. HFI 82
King, J. Norman. MFW 16
King, John pseud. of Ernest
Lionel McKeag (1896-) SF1 293
King, John Robert (1948-) SFE
330
King, Mac. IAC 145
King, Marshall. IAC 145 SFS 66
King, Martin Luther, Jr. KVT
48 MFW 80 RHN 158,172
King, Ray pseud. of Ray Cummings.
TSP 132
King, Rufus Frederick (1893-)
CSF 114 SF1 293
King, Stephen (1947-) BFP 277
FBK 7,46 FFR 100 FL1 197-
202,350-4 FL2 553-6 FL3
1040-3,1116-20,1350-4,1402-6
FL4 1801-6 FRN 10 KWS xvi
SFE 330 SF1 293 SF2 961
King, Tappan. HFI 82
King, Valerie. IAC 145
King, Vincent pseud. of Rex
Thomas Vinson (1935-) AOW 206
BYS 304 HFI 82 IAC 145 SFE
330 SFS 66 SF1 293
King, William (1663-1712) BAA
11-2 WGT 80
King, William Benjamin Basil
(1859-1928) CSF 114 ES1 253-4
SF1 293 WGT 80
King-Hall, Louise Olga Elizabeth
(1897-) BAA 113 CSF 114 SF1
293
King-Hall, Magdalen (1904-71)
CSF 114 SF1 293 SF2 961-2
King-Hall, William Stephen
Richard (1893-1966) SF1 294
King-Hele, Desmond. BYS 4, 36,
38, 282
Kingman, Lee pseud. of Mary Lee
Natti. SF1 294
Kingsbury, R. H. SF1 294
King-Scott, Peter. WGT 80 see
also Peter Edgar
Kingsford, Anna Bonus (1846-88)
CSF 114 EXT 7/1 16 SF1 294
Kingsland, William (1855-1936)
CSF 114 SF1 294
Kingsley, Bettina pseud. of Barry
Kaplan. SF1 294
Kingsley, Charles. AOW 304
BYS 102,109 CSF 114 EXT 4/2
21 FBK 112,114 FFC 94 FL5
2074-8 KAU 95 SRB 265

Kingsmill, Hugh pseud. of Hugh
Kingsmill Lunn (1889-1949) CSF
114 SFE 331 SF1 294 TJB 31
Kingston, John pseud. of Keith
Roberts. IAC 145 SFS 66 VES
208
Kinkade, Kathleen. BAA 236
Kinkaid, Mary Holland. BAA 66
Kinley, George. SF1 294
Kinnaird, John. SL2 832-9 SL5
2085-90
Kinnison, Kimball. ALW 134
Kin'nosuke, Natsume (1867-1916)
see Soseki Natsume
Kinross, Albert (1870-1929) CSF
114 SF1 294
Kinsolving, May R. IAC 145
Kip, Leonard (1826-1906) CSF
114 ES1 254 IAC 145 SF1 294
Kipling, Arthur Wellesley. CSF
114 SF1 294
Kipling, Leonard. IAC 145
Kipling, Rudyard (1865-1936) ACC
119 ACE 11 AC2 9 ALW 33,82-
3,88 AOW 66,356 ATA 44-5,49
BAA 74,78 BYS 120,123,138,
146-7,152 COT 220 CSC 25,
27,31,217 CSF 114-5 ES1 254
EXT 2/1 11 EXT 2/2 30 EXT
4/2 20,22 EXT 9/2 36 FBK 55,
65,112 FFC 21,35,96,133 FL2
822-6 FL4 1586-8 HID 191
IMS 2 ISW 35,189 LEX 398-9
MFW 281 MSF 214,231,276
MSM 145-6,148 OWB 13-4,18
PST 85-6,117-8,200,215,235,
263,271-2,305,318 RHN 12 RSG
51 SFE 331-2 SFS 66 SF1 294-
5 SFW 60,75 SIH 37 SL5 2051-
5 STH 105,203 VES 266 VFS
116,180 WAA 36 WIF 54,66,
85,149,199 WSF 22,350 WTS
130 YTS 5
Kippax, John pseud. of John
Charles Hynam. IAC 145 SFE
332 SFS 66 SF1 295
Kippenberg, August. BAA 182
Kirban, Salem. SF1 295
Kirby, Hayward S. IMS 78,104
Kirby, Jack (1917-) IAC 145 SFE
332 VES 326
Kirby, Josh (1928-) IAC 145 SFE
332-3
Kirby, Richard. IAC 145

Kircher, Athanasius (1601-80)
BYS 62,68 SFB 75 SFE 333
SFW 13 WIF 37-8,47
Kirchhoff, Frederick. WBW 27
Kirchmann, George H. BAA 284
Kirde, Kalju. FBK 69
Kirk, Clara Marburg. BAA 182
Kirk, Eleanor pseud. of Eleanor
Maria Ames. CSF 115 SF1 295
Kirk, Ellen Warner Olney. CSF
115 BAA 97
Kirk, George Willard. EXT 3/1
15
Kirk, Hyland Clare (1846-1917)
CSF 115 SF1 295
Kirk, Laurence pseud. of Eric
Andrew Simson. SF1 295
Kirk, Russell Amos (1918-) COT
229 ES1 254 FL4 1863-5 IAC
145 RBY 240 SF1 295 SF2 962
Kirk, Tim. IAC 145 VES 282,
291
Kirkby, John (1705-54) BAA 11
SF1 295
Kirkegaard, Ole. FFC 67
Kirkham, Nellie. CSF 115 SF1
295
Kirkland, Jack. IAC 145 ISW
131 SFS 66
Kirkup, James. IAC 145
Kirkwood, Daniel. EXT 5/2 43
Kirmess, C.H. CSF 115 SF1
295
Kirs, Alex. IAC 145 SFS 66
Kirschner, Gabriel. IMS 11-2
Kirshenblit, Harold W. IMS 33,
35-6,52,55-7 WFS 52,59
Kirst, Hans Hellmut (1914-)AOW
206 ES1 254 FFR 100 HFI 82
SFE 333 SF1 295
Kirwan, Thomas (1829-1911) BAA
75 WGT 80 see also William
Wonder
Kishor, Sulamith see Sulamith
Ish-Kishor
Kissling, Dorothy Hight Richard-
son (1904-) ES1 254 WGT 80-1
see also Dorothy Langley
Kita, Morio. IAC 145
Kitchell, Joseph Gray (1862-1947)
CSF 115 SF1 296
Kitman, Marvin (1929-) SF1 296
Kjelgaard, James Arthur (1910-
59) SF1 296 WTS 55
Klages, Helmut. BAA 236

Klainer, Albert S. SF1 296
Klainer, Jo Ann. SF1 296 see
also L. T. Peters
Klainer, Robert see L. T. Peters
Klapper, Paul. EXT 7/2 29 EXT
8/1 24
Klarmann, Andrew Francis (1866-
1931) SF1 296
Klass, Morton. IAC 145
Klass, Philip (1920-) ALW 161,
218 BAA 118-9, 127, 129, 132,
141 BFP 278-9 ES1 254-5
ETN 44, 46, 65, 142-4 EXT 6/2
22 EXT 10/2 104-7 ISW 266
SFD 300 TSF 56 VFS 176-8
WFS 194 WGT 81 WSF 144, 265
see also William Tenn
Klaus, Carl. LTN 252
Klaw, Spencer. BAA 236
Klaxon pseud. of John Graham
Bower. CSF 115 SF1 296
Klee, Paul. IAC 145 MSM 92
Kleier, Joe. VES 185
Klein, Edward. SF1 296
Klein, Gerard (1937-) AOW 206,
294 CAT 33-5 FFR 100 HFI
82 IAC 145-6 LEX 399-400
MIH 15 MSF 161 SFB 139 SFE
333 SF1 296 SF2 962-3 TSO
24-5, 36 UKL 245
Klein, Jay Kay (1931-) ASF 60
SF1 296 SF2 963 SRB 115, 125
Klein, Mary Ann. BAA 284
Klein, Melanie. FLT 49-50, 140,
143
Klein, Robert. BAA 236
Klein, Sidney. IAC 146 SFS 37,
66
Klein, T. E. D. IAC 146
Kleiner, Harry. AOW 134
Kleiner, Rheinhart. EXT 3/1 10,
15-6, 23 WGT 81
Kleinsinger, George. VFS 117
Kleinwachter, Friedrich. BAA
182
Kleist, Heinrich. FLT 67-8, 74
Klement, Otto. AOW 134
Klemm, Heinrich. BAA 284
Klemperer, Otto. RAH 97
Klette, Charles Herman Bruno
(1861-) CSF 115 SF1 296
Kleven, Arthur. SF1 296
Kley, Heinrich. ES1 255 FBK 83
Klimius, Nicholas. ALW 67
Kline, Allen. IMS 84

Kline, Milton V. ISW 216-7
Kline, Nathan. FTF 118
Kline, Otis Adelbert (1891-1946)
AOW 105 BFP 280 BYS 170
CSF 115 CWD 8, 41 ES1 255-6
EXT 5/1 3 HFI 82-3 IAC 146
IMS 16, 75, 84, 147, 213 ISW 131
LEX 400 MSM 304 PST 131-2,
220, 266, 270 RFA 1, 63 RGS 91-
2 SFE 333 SFS 66 SF1 296
SIH 189 SOT 73, 76, 93, 107, 110,
337 SRB 295 STH 142, 162 VES
92 WIF 66 WFS 8 WTS 3-6, 8-
10, 14, 16, 19-23, 29, 32-3, 35-6,
51-2, 67, 119-22
Kline, T. F. IAC 146
Kling, Bernt Bernhard (1947-)
LEX 400-1
Klinkowitz, Jerome. AOW 348
SRB 83
Klise, Robert S. (1928-78) SF1
296
Kloor, Mary Conway. SFE 333
SF1 296
Klopfer. EXT 6/2 48
Klossowski, Pierre. BAA 236
Kloster, Bill. LTN 238
Kloten, Norbert. BAA 237
Kluyeva, Bella. SIH 114, 199
Knapp, Adeline (1860-1909) BAA
51 SF1 297
Knapp, Friedrich. BAA 237
Knapp, George Leonard (1872-)
CSF 115 SF1 297 SOT 171-2
Knapp, Lawrence. PJF 73
Knapp, Mary Clay. SF1 297
Knatchbull-Hugessen, Edward H.
CSF 115
Knauss, Robert (1892-1955) WGT
81 see also Major Von Helders
Kneale, Nigel (1922-) AOW 206
BAA 149 BFP 281 ES1 256
EXT 1/2 37 IAC 146 ISW 129
KAU 192 KWS 248-9, 253-4, 298,
314, 316, 330, 338-40, 342-3, 403
NWO 265 SFB 120 SFE 333
VES 302-3 WGT 81
Knebel, Fletcher (1911-) AOW
207 ES1 256 NDA 172-4 SFE
333-4 SF1 297 SF2 963
Kneifel, Hans (1936-) LEX 401-3
Knepper, Bill Garton. BAA 237,
284
Knerr, Michael E. SF1 297
Knight, Charles. POE 88, 205

Knight, Damon (Francis) (1922-)
AAL 30, 52, 79-80, 95 ACC 204,
244 ALW 7, 143, 160, 184, 186,
191, 218, 221-2 AOW 106, 207-8,
289, 293-5, 348, 400 BAA 127,
133, 182, 237 BFP 282-7 BYS
170, 179, 224, 262, 264, 281, 289,
303-4, 315 CAT xvi COT 165
CSC 68, 90, 102, 146 DMK 193-
204 ES1 256-8 ETN 2, 22, 33,
36, 45, 56, 64, 72, 99, 138, 140, 158,
160 EXT 2/1 1 EXT 3/1 24
EXT 5/1 3, 6, 17-8, 21 EXT 8/1
7, 13, 16 EXT 9/1 21 EXT 10/1
6, 8, 47 FFR 101-2 FRN 46 HFI
83 HID viii, 9, 17, 30, 33, 69-70,
92, 140, 147, 170, 190, 192 IAC
146-7 IAH 3, 13, 17-9, 28, 31-2,
38-9, 65, 87, 89, 92, 102, 111, 124,
132 JHN 18 JVN 57 KAU 31, 90
LEX 403-5 LTN 12, 134, 238,
249, 253-4, 257, 260-1, 265 MFW
28, 289 MIH 5, 7, 15-6, 19-22, 28,
31, 38, 56, 110, 112, 121, 125-6
MSF 36, 143 MSM 180, 301 NDA
121-2, 187, 195 NWO 21 RAH 16,
111, 174-5, 202, 258 RBY 83 RFA
163, 198 RGS 92-3 RSG 10 SFA
114, 117, 203, 233, 237 SFB 7, 19,
21, 23, 89, 152 SFD 17, 27, 34-6,
63, 74, 86, 94, 96, 111, 128, 242-3,
259, 293, 315 SFE 334-5 SFH
54, 239 SFN 15, 47, 56, 74-6, 105,
117 SFS 67-8 SFW 293-4, 393-
401 SF1 297-8 SL1 48-52 SOT
182 SRB 72, 287, 374, 504 TJB
4-6, 37-9, 41, 44 TPS 62-9, 163-
7, 218-28 TSF 56, 236, 247 VES
114, 149, 152, 209, 227, 248, 258,
316, 329-30, 334-5 WAA 140, 245
WFS 2, 34, 39, 71, 135, 187, 189-
90, 227, 273-4, 276-8 WGT 81
WSF 74, 127, 140-1, 176, 214, 222-
3, 225, 249, 256, 261, 268, 358
WTS 93 see also Donald Laverty
Knight, David C. IAC 147 SFS 68
Knight, Eric Mowbray (1897-1943)
CSF 116 ES1 258 IAC 147 SFN
19 SF1 298
Knight, Helen. ISW 266
Knight, Hilary. FFC 19, 68, 75,
113, 148
Knight, Isabel F. BAA 237
Knight, J. Richard. BAA 284
Knight, Kate Wilhelm (1928-) WGT
81 see also Kate Wilhelm

Knight, Leonard Alfred (1895-)
SF1 298
Knight, Norman L(ouis) (1895-
1970?) AOW 146 BAA 143 BYS
56, 253 COT 184 ES1 258-9
HID 13 IAC 52, 147 IAH 28 IMS
213 KAU 93 MFW 86 NDA 156-
8, 188, 215 RFA 42, 57, 60, 79-
80, 96, 109 SFE 335 SFS 68 SF1
298 SF2 963-4 SOT 136 TJB
16, 35 VES 261
Knight, Randy. SF1 298
Knight, W. Kobold. CSF 116
Knight-Adkin, J. H. CSF 116
Knighten, Merrell A. SL1 318-21
SL3 1476-9 SL4 2003-7
Knittel, John (1891-1970) CSF 116
SF1 298
Knoblock, Edward (1874-1945)
CSF 116 SF1 298
Knoles, William see Clyde Allison
Knopf, Alfred. LTN 28
Knott, William Cecil (1927-) AOW
322 SF1 298 SF2 964
Knott, William Wilson. SF1 298
Knotts, Don. SFH 107
Knowles, Leo see Julian R.
Gregory
Knowles, Mabel Winifred (1875-)
WGT 81 see also Lester Lurgan,
May Wynne
Knowles, Vernon (1899-1968) CSF
116 ES1 259 FL4 1589-91 SF1
299
Knowles, William Plenderleith.
BAA 100 CSF 116 SF1 299
Knowlson, James R. BAA 237
Knowlton, Don. EXT 2/1 13
Knowlton, James Albert. SF1
299
Knox, Calvin M. pseud. of Robert
Silverberg. IAC 148 RSG 11-2,
24, 26
Knox, George. BAA 237
Knox, Gordon Daniell. CSF 208
SF1 299
Knox, Hugh Randolph (1942-) SF1
299 SF2 964
Knox, John H. TSP 9, 15, 28, 41,
55, 81, 105, 144, 200, 202
Knox, R. A. IAC 148
Knox, Ronald Arbuthnot (1888-
1957) CSF 116 BAA 88 EXT
9/2 38 SFE 335 SFN 7-8 SF1
299
Knust, Herbert. BAA 237

Kobler, John. TSP 152,195
Kobylinski, Szymon. FBK 66
Koch, Eric (1919-) HFI 83 LEX 405-6 SF1 299
Koch, Fritz. BAA 284
Koch, Howard (1902-) ES1 259 IAC 148 SFS 68
Koch, Kenneth. IAC 148
Koch, Richard (1895-1970) LEX 406-7
Kocher, Paul Harold (1907-) AAL 149 AOW 348 SF1 299 SRB 81
Kocsis, J. C. FFC 109,183
Koebel, William Henry. BAA 72
Koebner, Richard. BAA 237
Koenig, H. C. EXT 3/1 12 IMS 20, 25, 30, 115, 182, 191 PST 259
Koepsel, Louis Herman. BAA 84
Koering, Ursula. FFC 107
Koerner, James David. BAA 284
Koester, Frank (1876-1927) CSF 116 SF1 299
Koester, Otto. BAA 201
Koestler, Alfred G. VFS 56
Koestler, Arthur (1905-) ACC 114 ACE 31 AC2 29 AOW 208 BAA 237 CSF 116 ES1 259 EXT 2/2 27 FAN 147 IAC 148 ISW 2, 30, 66-7, 69, 165, 263 NDA 32-3, 38, 54-5, 207 SFB 16 SFE 335 SFW 234-5, 237 SF1 299
Kofler, Leo. BAA 237
Kohler, Bernhard. BAA 237
Kohler, Wolfgang. STF 35
Kolar, Heinz. BAA 284
Kolda, Helena (1928-) SF1 299
Kolesnikov, Leonid. IAC 148
Kolliker. RFA 118
Kolnai, Aurele. BAA 237
Kolpakow, Alexander (1925-) LEX 407
Kolupayev, Victor. IAC 148
Komarov, N. S. MSF 251
Komatsu, Sakyo (1931-) BYS 281 HFI 83 SFB 142 SFE 335 SIH 85 SL1 508-12
Komoda, Kiyo. FFC 131-2
Komroff, Manuel (1890-1974) CSF 116 SF1 299 SF2 964
Konecci, (Dr.) Gene. VFS 55
Konigsburg, Elaine Lobl (1930-) SF1 299
Konstantinove, Elka. SIH 9-10
Konvitz, Jeffrey (1944-) SF1 299 SF2 964
Kooiker, Leonie. FFC 189

Koomoter, Zeno pseud. of Joseph Marnell. SF1 299
Koontz, Dean R. (1945-) AAL 51-2 ALW 212 AOW 208 BAA 149 ES1 259 ETN 28 HFI 83-4 IAC 148 LEX 407-8 NDA 42, 48-9 RGS 93-4 SFD 240 SFE 335-6 SF1 299-300 SF2 964-5 WGT 81-2
Koontz, Gerda see Gracie Amber
Kopf, Seymour O. SF1 300
Kopley, Richard. FL3 1092-5
Korda, Alexander. CAT 83 FAN 16 FTF 62 SFB 28-9 SFH 103
Korinman, Michel. BAA 237
Korn, Friedrich (1803-50) WGT 82
Kornbluth C(yril) M. (1923-58) AAL 9, 15, 29, 70-1, 162 ALW 99, 156, 160, 184, 217, 239 AOW 208-10, 238-9, 285, 288, 294, 297, 299 ASF 174, 242 BAA 119, 122-3, 125, 127, 133, 136, 237 BFP 288-90 BYS 79, 249-50, 283, 304 CAT 72, 139 COT 140-1, 252, 267, 276, 295 CSC 224, 310-1 DMK 103-9 EFP 17 ES1 259-60 ETN 31, 34-5, 40, 45-6, 55, 83, 103, 126, 128, 130, 144, 195-7 EXT 2/2 27 EXT 3/1 26 EXT 4/2 29 EXT 5/1 3 EXT 6/2 51 EXT 8/1 7 FAN 48, 155-8 FFR 102 FTF 3-7, 12, 15, 69, 78, 86, 88, 106-7, 128, 132 HFI 84 HID 179 IAC 148-9, 192 IAH 16, 26-7, 35, 49-50, 102-3, 147-8 IMS 112, 138, 158, 170, 183, 210, 214, 225, 234, 243, 245 INT 49 ISW 4-6, 8, 118-9, 125-6, 146-9, 157, 166, 193, 196-7, 266, 268 LEX 408-10 LTN 99 MFW 11, 169, 207, 251 MIH 28-9, 33-4, 53, 60 MSF 27, 78 MSM 132 NDA 30-1, 118-22 NWO 125 POE 277-8 RAH 234-5 RFA 191, 199-200, 213 RGS 94 SFB 13, 23, 151 SFD 74, 260, 293-4, 313-6 SFE 336 SFH 66-7, 150, 152 SFN 8, 10-1, 39, 49-76, 83-4, 117 SFS 68, 94-5 SFW 293, 351, 394, 396, 401-7, 433, 475-6 SF1 300 SIH 44, 94, 178 SL1 178-85 SL2 894-8 SL5 2211-4 SOT 184, 252, 258, 418-20 SRB 14, 218, 322, 331 STH 45 TJB 4 TSF 56-7, 236 VES 81, 105, 123, 128-9, 151, 160,

Kornbluth, C. M. (cont.)
167, 201, 215, 238, 253, 256, 260,
275, 309, 328 WAA 27, 61, 140,
242-3 WFS 34, 71-3, 75, 80, 92,
99-100, 117, 151, 161, 182-3, 187,
194-5, 201-2, 216, 224, 226-7, 229,
233-4, 283-5 WGT 82 WIF 202,
218, 230, 233 WSF 5, 126, 172,
184-5, 206, 215, 246, 346, 387
YTS 12 see also Gabriel Barclay, Arthur Cooke, Cecil Cor-
win, Simon Eisner, Kenneth
Falconer, S. D. Gottesman,
Cyril Judd, Paul Dennis Lavond,
Scott Mariner, Martin Pearson,
Ivar Towers
Kornbluth, Mary G. (1920-) ES1
260 IAC 149 SFN 76 SFS 69
SF1 300 WFS 194, 216
Korolov, Sergei. VFS 45
Korshak, Erle Melvin (1923-)
ES1 260 IAC 149 IMS 205, 213,
222-3, 226, 237-9, 241 MSM 101
WFS 178 WIF 124, 130 WSF 135
Korzeniowski, Josef Konrad
Theodor (1857-1924) WGT 82
see also Joseph Conrad
Korzybski, (Count) Alfred (1879-
1950) AAL 171, 173-6 CSC 11-2
CYR 29-30, 40 EXT 7/2 37 HID
184 ISW 55 MSM 187, 291 RFA
137 SFB 89 SFE 336 SFN 47
SFW 212-3 SOT 221 TBJ 11
WSF 321
Kosinski, Jerzy (1933-) AOW 210
HFI 84 KAU 238 SFE 336-7
Kosow, Irving. IMS 34, 36, 52, 56
Kostikov. VFS 45
Kostkos, Henry J. STH 63 VES
189
Kostolefsky, Joseph. EXT 1/2 32
Kostrowicki, Guillaume Apollinaire
Albert (1880-1918) WGT 82 see
also Guillaume Apollinaire
Kotzwinkle, William. FBK 153
FFC 26 HFI 84 SFE 337
Kovaly, Pavel. BAA 238
Kracauer, Siegfried. FBK 58
ISW 222
Kraeling, Carl. EXT 9/1 16
Kraft, David A. PJF 73
Kraft, Robert (1870-1916) ES1
260 MSF 162
Kraft-Ebbing. EXT 10/1 10
Kragalott, Robert. BAA 238

Kramer, F. RFA 100 VES 107,
179
Kramer, Nora. ES1 260 SF1 300
Kramer, Stanley. KAU 126
Kramer-Badoni, Rudolf. BAA 182
Krantz, Edwin Kirker (1949-)
HFI 84 SF1 300 SF2 965
Kranzle, Karl. BAA 182
Krapivin, Vladislav. AOW 297
IAC 149
Krappe, Alexander H. BAA 238
Krarup, Soren. BAA 182
Kraspedon, Dino. ES1 260
Krassnoff, Peter N. (1869-1947)
CSF 116 SF1 300
Kraus, Michael. BAA 238
Krause, Gerd. BAA 238
Krausnick, Michail (1943-) LEX
410
Krauss, Werner. BAA 238
Kredel, Fritz. FFC 135
Kreeft, Peter. SOI 161-78
Kreisheimer, (Mrs.) H. C. ES1
260
Kreisheimer, H. C. BAA 127
SF1 300
Kremser, Rudolf. BAA 182
Krenkel, Roy G. (1918-) BYS
217 ES1 260 IAC 149 SFE 337
SFS 69 VES 326
Krensky, Stephen. FFC 21, 49, 88
Krepps, Robert Wilson (1919-)
ES1 260-1 IAC 149-50 SFS 51,
69 WGT 83
Kressing, Harry. ES1 261
Kretzman, Edwin M. J. BAA 238,
284
Kreuder, Ernst (1903-) SF1 300
Kreupp, W. SF1 300
Krey, Friedrich. BAA 195
Kreymborg, Alfred (1883-1966)
SF1 300
Kriegel, Bobby. VFS 29-30
Krige, Uys (1910-) ES1 261
Kristol, Irving. BAA 238
Kritschewsky, S. B. BAA 238
Krleza, Miroslav. MSF 127
Kroeber, A. L. LTN 14
Kroeber, Alfred. LTN 259
Kroeber, Karl. LTN 26-7, 248
Kroeber, Theodora. FFC 81
LTN 14, 259
Krog, Fritz. BAA 238
Kroger, Alexander (1934-) LEX
410-1

Kroitor, Harry P. FHT 67
Kroll, Harry Harrison. CSF 116
Kronenberger, Louis. EXT 6/1 9
Kropotkin, Peter Alexander (1842-1921) BAA xii, 238 EXT 9/2 54 LTN 111 POE 178 UKL 77-96, 116-7, 150
Kropp, Lloyd Edward (1936?-) HFI 84 SF1 300-1 SF2 965
Krueger, John R. AAL 12, 107
Krulfeld, M. RFA 96
Krupa, Julian S. IMS 205, 241 KAU 117 VES 73, 287, 338-9 WSF 115
Krupkat, Gunther (1905-) LEX 411 SL3 1468-71
Kruse, Clifton B. ES1 261 IAC 150 IMS 29 SFS 69
Krush, Beth. FFC 74, 104, 106, 181
Krush, Joe. FFC 74, 104, 106, 171, 181
Kruss, James (1926-) ES1 261 FFC 182
Krutch, Joseph Wood. BAA 238 COT 267 FAN 6, 175 NDA 51, 54-7, 61-4, 206
Krutenych, Aleksey. SIH 53
Krysmanski, Hans-Jurgen. BAA xxi, 182, 238 EXT 9/2 31 MSF 47-8, 60 SFB 17
Kryzhanovskaia, Vera I. MSF 251
Ksanda, Charles F. IMS 213
Kubilius, Walter (1918-) ES1 261 IAC 150 IAH 51 IMS 37, 86, 94, 111, 150, 169, 175, 183 ISW 118-9 SFE 337 SFS 70, 95 SOT 252 WFS 34, 71, 117 WGT 83
Kubin, Alfred (1877-1959) FBK 36, 82, 141, 143-4 FL3 1176-8 SF1 301 SL4 1627-31
Kubinyi, Laszlo. FFC 17, 93, 134, 184
Kubrick, Stanley (1928-) ACC 103, 122-6, 137 ACE 11, 14, 38, 75 AC2 9, 12, 36, 73 ALW 46 BYS 261 CSC 263 CUA 36, 40 EXT 10/2 67, 108 FTF 115-6 KAU 22, 60, 80, 126, 155 KWS 213-4, 261 MSF 76 OMN 8, 10, 20-3, 31, 46-8, 57, 71, 73, 82, 130, 215, 218-20, 238-45, 255, 269, 287, 289 PJF 61 POE 9, 278, 295 SFB 14, 90-1, 106-7, 125, 128 SFE 337 SFH 102-4, 132 SRB 59

TRB 93 TSO 35, 57 VFS 51-2, 55, 73, 151, 176, 250 WSF 310 YTS 19
Kuczka, Peter. SIH 193 SL2 708-11 SL3 1118-21 SL4 1892-5
Kudlay, Robert R. SF1 301
Kuebler, Harold W. ES1 261 IAC 150 SFS 70 SF1 301
Kuer, Dorothy. BAA 157-8
Kugan, Frank L. BAA 176
Kuhlhoff, Pete. WTS 76
Kuhn, Johannes. BAA 239
Kuhn, Thomas S. CAT 125, 127 KAU 14-5 MSF 222 SFH 241 TJB 28
Kulemann, W. BAA 239
Kullinger, J. L. pseud. of Vince Ducette. SF1 301
Kumin, Maxine W. IAC 150
Kummer, Frederic Arnold Jr. (1873-1943) CSF 116 IAC 150 SFA 34, 37 SFS 70 SF1 301 WGT 83
Kung, Emil. BAA 239
Kunitz, Stanley. IAC 150
Kunlaschke, Horst. BAA 225
Kunos, Ignaz. IAC 150
Kunst, Earle. CSF 117 SF1 301
Kunz, Hans. BAA 182
Kupferberg, Tuli. IAC 150
Kuppord, Skelton pseud. of J. Adams. CSF 117 SF1 301
Kuprin, Alexander I. (1870-1938) MSF 251 SFE 338
Kurelek, William. FFC 118
Kurka, Anton. VES 178
Kurland, Michael (Joseph) (1938-) ES1 261 HFI 84 IAC 150 RGS 94-5 SFE 338 SF1 301 SF2 965-6
Kurosaka, Bob. IAC 150 SFS 70
Kurten, Peter. TSP 196
Kurtz, Katherine (Irene) (1944-) FL1 360-5 HFI 85 LEX 411-2 LTN 95 SFE 338 SF1 301 SF2 966 SRB 265 WSF 247, 302
Kurtzman, Harvey. ES1 261 ISW 236
Kusenberg, Kurt. FBK 142
Kushkin, Karla (1932-) FFC 136 SF1 301 SF2 966
Kuslan, Gertrude. IMS 184, 200, 213, 247
Kuslan, Louis. IMS 126, 128, 135, 184, 192-3, 200, 213-6, 227, 244, 247

Kuttner, Catherine Lucille (1911-)
ETN 16-7, 35, 68-9, 137, 140, 158-
9 ISW 119 WGT 83 see also
C. L. Moore, Lewis Padgett

Kuttner, Henry (1914-58) AAL
72, 106, 175 ALW 85, 143, 160-1,
174, 213 AOW 210-1, 285, 288,
292-3 BAA 115, 124 BFP 291-
4 BYS 55, 236-7, 242 COT 106,
160-1, 180, 190, 206, 250 CSC
29-30 ES1 261-2 ETN 16-7, 31,
35, 55, 68-9, 103, 126, 139-40,
142, 158-9, 195, 197 EXT 3/1 7,
27 EXT 5/1 3 EXT 7/2 40 EXT
8/1 5 EXT 10/2 108 FFR 103
FL2 980-2 FL4 1592-6 FRN
255 [FUT] HFI 85 IAC 150-1
IAH 12-3, 18, 85-6, 89-91 IMS
25, 30, 76, 110, 138, 200, 213 ISW
78, 84, 119, 122, 129, 139-45, 151,
219, 249-50 JGB 5 JVN 14, 198
KAU 31-2, 128, 157-8, 185-6, 191,
216-7 KWS 150-1 LEX 412-3
MIH 23-4, 36, 60 MSM 85, 114,
132, 172, 298 RBY 157 RFA 109,
112, 114-5, 120, 127, 138, 145, 155,
172, 184, 194, 201-2, 211-2 RGS
95-7 SFB 23, 83 SFD 56, 289,
293, 309-10 SFE 338-9 SFN 83,
90 SFS 70-1, 85-6 SFW 148,
161-7 SF1 301-2 SF2 966 SL1
191-5 SOT 6, 81, 108, 110-1, 121,
155, 276, 290, 296, 311-7, 319-34,
339, 343-4, 357, 360, 365, 397-8,
431 SRB 13, 310, 319 STH 45,

117, 121, 152, 157, 254, 257-9, 262
TJB 13 TSF 57, 232 TSP 25, 29,
144, 190 VES 81, 95, 133, 140,
147, 167, 173, 179, 187, 197, 206,
210, 258, 261, 326, 334-5 VF1
185-215, 277-8 WAA 94 WFS
111-2, 118, 200 WGT 83-4 WIF
78, 107, 136, 145, 151, 156-9, 229,
238, 272, 276 WSF 104-5, 111,
119, 121-2, 135, 148, 152, 156, 185,
200, 206, 386, 388, 391 WTS ix,
37, 39-40, 42-5, 48-9, 53, 55-6,
93, 122-4, 128, 132 see also
Edward J. Bellin, Will Garth,
Peter Horn, Kelvin Kent, Lawrence O'Donnell, Lewis Padgett
Kuykendall, Roger. IAC 151 SFS
71
Kuypers, Julien. BAA 239
Kvacala, J. BAA 239
Kyd, Thomas. SFD 4
Kyffin-Taylor, (Lady) Bessie
(1880?-1922) CSF 117 ES1 262-
3 SF1 302
Kyle, Arthur C. WFS 178
Kyle, David A. (1912?-) BAA 182
BRS 8 DTS 21 ES1 263 IAC 151
IMS 56, 70, 78-80, 82-3, 103, 105,
107, 115-6, 119, 125, 135, 137, 150-
1, 158, 174, 185, 213, 216, 218, 221,
232, 234, 241, 244-5 SFE 339 SFS
71 SIH 41 SRB 72, 102 VES 330
WFS 51, 59, 71, 117-8, 124, 161,
174, 178 WSF 136, 144
Kyle, Richard. BYS 139

L

L. W. J. S. pseud. of V. Thisted.
CSF 117
La Bossiere, Camille. BAA 239
La Due, Russell. BAA 157-8
La Farge, Oliver Hazard Perry
(1901-63) ES1 263 IAC 151 ISW
129 SFS 71
L'a Fausset, Hugh. EXT 10/1 27
La Guardia, Fiorello. COT 87
TSP 211
La Master, Slater (1890-) CSF
117 SFE 340 SF1 303
La Mettrie, Julien. MFW 194
La Place. EXT 6/2 35
La Prade, Ernest (1889-) SF1 307
La Rochefoucauld. EXT 5/1 22
La Salle, Victor (house name)
SFE 342 SF1 307 see also
Gerald Evans, R. L. Fanthorpe,
John Glasby
La Spina, Celia. WTS ix, 4
La Spina, Greye Bragg (1880-
1969) ES1 263 IAC 151 IMS 77
SF1 307 SF2 969 WGT 85 WTS
23, 25, 35, 49-50, 65, 129
La Spina, Robert. WTS 23
La Tourrette, Jacqueline (1926-)
SF1 308 SF2 969
Labougle, Eduardo. BAA 182
Labry, Michel. SF1 302
Lacan, Jacques. FLT 73, 132, 135
Lacas, M. M. BAA 239
Lachevre, Frederic. BAA 182
Lach-Szyrma, Wladislaw Somer-
ville (1841-1915) BAA 34, 38
CSF 117 IAC 151 SFE 339 SF1
302 STH 4 WGT 84 see also
W. S. L. S.

Lack, G. L. IAC 151 SFS 71
Lacombe, M. M. BAA 239
Lackow. VES 229
Laddy, Thyril L. EXT 3/1 24
Lady, (A). CSF 117
Lafargue, Paul (1842-1911) CSF
117 MSF 262 SF1 303
Lafargue, Philip pseud. of Joseph
Henry Philpot. CSF 117 SF1
303
Lafayette, Rene pseud. of L. Ron
Hubbard. ALW 155 RFA 84,
148, 165, 172 WIF 94
Lafferty, Perry. SFN 81
Lafferty, R(aphael) A(loysius)
(1914-) ALW 212 AOW 212-3
BAA 142, 146 BFP 295-6 BYS
304 CSF 117 DTS 42 ES1 263
ETN 27-8, 65, 106 EXT 8/1 16
FFR 105-8 [FJT] FL1 380-2
HFI 85 IAC 151-3 LEX 414-5
NDA 74-7 MFW 24, 229, 267,
270, 290 RGS 97-8 SFA 85 SFD
9, 17, 35, 58, 134, 208, 233, 240,
263, 302, 321 SFE 339-40 SFS
71 SF1 303 SF2 966 SL2 574-
8 SRB 265, 345 TSF 63, 239
VES 150, 153 WFS 240, 285 WSF
187
Lafitte, Louis (1917-) see Jean-
Louis Curtis
Lafleur, Lawrence J. EXT 2/1 13
Lafond. SF1 303
Laforgue, Jules (1860-87) ES1
263 SF1 303
Lagerkvist, Par Fabian (1891-
1974) SF1 303 SIH 27
Lagerlof, Selma (1858-1940) CSF
117 FFC 105 SF1 303

Lagin, Lazar I. MSF 262
Lahman, Damon. ES1 263 SF1 303
Laidler, Harry W. BAA 182-3
Laimgruber, Monika. FFC 48
Laing, Alexander Kinnan (1903-) CSF 117, 153 ES1 263-4 PST 184, 207 SFE 340 SF1 303 SF2 966-7
Laing, Janet. CSF 117
Laing, R. D. CAT 18 CWN 54
Laing, Samuel. POE 188
Laird, Charlton. AAL 56
Lake, David John (1929-) HFI 86 RGS 98 SFE 340
Lake, Leonard M. IAC 153
Lakewizc. IMS 239
Lalande, Andre. BAA 239 MSF 43-4, 52, 54
Lalita pseud. of Maud Lalita Johnson. SF1 303
Lalli, Cele Goldsmith (1933-) EXT 8/1 8 LTN 28, 50 SFW 351-2 WGT 84 see also Cele Goldsmith
Lama, Francesco. FTF 23, 25 WAA 32-3, 73
Lamb, Harold (1892-1962) CSF 117 CWD 51, 61 MSM 128 SF1 303
Lamb, Hugh (1946-) SF1 304 SF2 967
Lamb, Lynton. FFC 68
Lamb, William. CSF 117
Lambert, Diane. BYS 298
Lambert, J. K. FFC 7, 47
Lambert, John S. LTN 251
Lambert, Leslie Harrison (-1940) WGT 84 see also A. J. Alan
Lambert, R. S. ES1 264
Lambert, S. H. pseud. of Stephen Southwold. CSF 117
Lambert, Saul. FFC 20, 70
Lambert, William J., III. SF1 304
Lambourne, John pseud. of John Battersby Crompton Lamburn. CSF 118 SFE 340 SF1 304
Lamburn, John Battersby Crompton (1893-) SF2 967 see also John Lambourne
Lamburn, Richmal Crompton (1890-1969) ES1 264 SF2 870 WGT 84 see also Richmal Crompton
Lamont, Archibald. CSF 118

Lamont, Duncan. VES 183
Lamont, Gilvan Derwent (1947-) IAC 153 SF1 304 SF2 967
Lamont, H. EXT 2/1 14
Lamorisse, Albert. FFC 6
Lamour, Dorothy. VFS 185
Lampa, Anton. BAA 183
Lampen, Charles Dudley (1859-1943) CSF 118 SF1 304
Lampland. EXT 5/2 40
Lamplugh, Lois pseud. of Lois Carlile Davis. SF1 304 SF2 967
Lampman, Ben Hur (1886-1954) SF1 304
Lampman, Evelyn Sibley (1907-) ES1 264 FFC 35, 87, 182 SF1 304, 582 SF2 967
Lampo, Hubert. BAA 183 FBK 146
Lamport, Felicia. IAC 153 SFS 71
Lamport, Richard Fifield. CSF 118 SF1 305
Lampton, Christopher. HFI 86 IAC 153
Lampton, (Capt.) Wilbur pseud. of John Henry Goldfrap. SF1 310
Lamszus, Wilhelm (1881-) CSF 118 SF1 305
Lancaster, Albert Edmund. SF1 305
Lancaster, Clay. FFC 75
Lancaster, Osbert. FFC 55
Lancaster, William Joseph Cosens (1851-1922) WGT 84-5 see also Harry Collingwood
Lancelot. WBW 11
Lancing, George pseud. of Bluebell M. Hunter. CSF 118
Lancour, Gene pseud. of Gene Fisher. HFI 86 SFE 340 SF1 305
Land, (Dr.) Edwin. VFS 241
Landauer, Gustav. EXT 3/2 49
Landberg, Edward. IMS 116
Landers, Clifford E. LTN 268
Landis, Arthur H. HFI 86
Landis, Simon Mohler. BAA 29-30 CSF 118 SF1 305
Landolfi, Tommaso (1908-) ES1 264 IAC 153 SF1 305
Landon, Alfred Mossman. WFS 63

Landon, Brooks. FL1 61-2 FL2 728-9, 773-5, 938-41 FL3 1468-70, 1489-91 FL4 1611-5, 1938-42 FL5 2197-9

Landon, Melville De Lancy (1839-1910) WGT 85 see also Eli Perkins

Landon, Michael. WAA 89

Landon, Percival (1869-1927) CSF 118 ES1 264

Landow, George P. FL2 852-4 FL3 1268-70 FL4 1831-3 FL5 2176-9

Landshut, S. BAA 239

Lane, Jane pseud. of Elaine Dakers. SFE 341 SF1 305

Lane, Jeremy. CSF 118

Lane, John (house name) SF1 305 see also Dennis Talbot Hughes, John D. MacDonald

Lane, Mary E. Bradley. BAA 40 MSF 165 SFE 341 WGT 85 see also Princess Vera Zarovitch

Lane, Spencer (house name) VES 198 WGT 85

Lane, Temple pseud. of Mary Isabel Leslie. CSF 118 SF1 305

Laney, Francis Towner (1914-58) ES1 264 EXT 3/1 21, 24

Lang, Allen Kim (1928-) ES1 264 HFI 86 IAC 153 SFE 341 SFS 71 SF1 305 SF2 967

Lang, Andrew (1844-1912) CSF 90, 112, 118 ES1 264 FFC 49 IAC 153 SFE 341 SF1 305 SRB 22, 262 WBW 59 WGT 85

Lang, Daniel (1913-) ES1 264 IAC 153 SFS 71

Lang, Fritz (1890-1976) COT 36 EXT 8/2 58 [FUT] KAU 11, 17, 87, 95, 103, 105 KWS 2, 41, 281 MFW 113 OMN 3, 5, 19, 43-6, 62, 69-71, 79, 85-9, 130, 152, 182, 216, 225 POE 234-5 SFB 74 SFE 341-2 SFH 102-4 SRB 57 TRB 108 WAA 192 WFS 301 WSF 308 YTS 15

Lang, Gregor pseud. of Faber Birren. SF1 305

Lang, Hans-Joachim. BAA 239

Lang, Herrmann. BAA 26-7 CSF 118 MSF 166 POE 147 SFE 342 SF1 305

Lang, King (house name) SFE 342 SF1 306 VES 75 see also David

Griffiths, George A. Hay, Brian Holloway, John Jennison, E. C. Tubb

Lang, Leoni. BAA 183

Lang, Simon pseud. of Darlene Hartman (1934-) HFI 86 RGS 98-9 SFE 342 SF1 306

Lang, Wilbert Jason. BAA xx, 284

Lang, William Dickson. MFW 63

Langart, Darrel T. pseud. of Garrett Randall. IAC 153 CSC 144-5 IAH 120 SFS 71

Langbaum, Robert. MFW 10-1

Langdon, George. SFS 71

Langdon, John. IAC 153 SFS 71

Langdon, Norman Earle (1888-) SF1 306

Langdon-Davies, John. ES1 264

Lange, Ernest Charles. AOW 85, 106

Lange, Hellmuth (1903-) LEX 415

Lange, John Frederick, Jr. (1931-) BFP 297-8 ES1 264-5 HFI 86 SF2 1017 WGT 85 see also John Norman

Lange, Oliver. AOW 213 BAA 153 SFE 342 SF1 306

Langelaan, George (1908-) ES1 265 IAC 153 LEX 415 SFE 342 SFS 72 SF1 306 VES 153, 156

Langer, Suzanne. INT 100 MSF 32

Langford, David. IAC 153

Langford, George (1876-1964) CSF 118 SF1 306

Langguth, Arthur John (1933-) SF1 306 SF2 968

Langland, William. EXT 10/2 74 MSF 184, 248

Langley, Dorothy pseud. of Dorothy Hight Kissling. SF1 306

Langley, Fredric. SF1 306

Langley, Kenlis. CSF 119 SF1 306

Langley, Nina. FFC 133

Langley, Noel A. (1911-) IAC 153 SF1 306 SF2 968

Langlois, Dora. SF1 306

Langner, Lawrence. BAA 109

Langrenus, Manfred (1903-) LEX 416

Langton, Jane Gillson (1922-) FFC 67 SF1 583 SRB 23

Langton, Joy. SF1 306

Lang-Tung. SF1 306
Lanier, Sterling E. (1927-) AAL
19 ALW 212 AOW 213 BFP
299 FFC 133 HFI 86 IAC 153
LEX 416-7 RGS 99-100 SFE
342 SFS 72 SF1 306 SF2 968-9
SRB 358
Laning, Caleb B. HID 22,186
Lanning, George William, Jr.
(1925-) ES1 265 SF1 307 SF2
969
Lanos, H. STH 58 VES 312
Lansac, Maurice. BAA 183
Lansdell, Sarah. CSF 119
Lansinger, John M. WTS 3-4
Lanza, Clara Hammond (1859-
1939) SF1 307
Laplace, Pierre Simon. KAU 14
SFH 129
Lapouge, Gilles. BAA 183
Lapp, Ralph E. NDA 203 VFS 41
Lardner, Dionysius. POE 54
Lardner, Ring. ISW 195 SFN 98
Large, Ernest Charles (-1976)
CSF 119 ES1 265 EXT 8/1 5
IMS 216 SFE 342 SF1 307
Larionova, Olga (1935-) IAC 153
LEX 417 SL3 1188-92
Larkin. EXT 5/2 47
Larnach, S. L. EXT 3/1 24 SF1
307
Larri, Yan. EXT 10/2 75 MSF
253
Larsen, Egon pseud. of Egon
Lehrburger (1904-) ES1 265 SF1
307 SF2 969
Larsen, Suzanne. FFC 189
Larson, Jean. FFC 107
Larson, Randall. WTS 55
Larsson, Gosta (1898-) SF1 307
Lasell, Fen. FFC 183
Lasker, Joe. FFC 78
Laski, Audrey. BAA 146
Laski, Marghanita (1915-) BAA
116 ES1 265 SFE 343 SF1 307
Lasky, Melvin J. BAA 183,239
Lasser, David (1902-) ES1 265
IMS 8,11,18 ISW 160 SOT 104,
376 STH 45,142,242-3 VES 71
WGT 85 WSF 50,64,87
Lassmann, Alfred. BAA 239
Lasswell, Harold D. IAC 153
Lasswitz, Kurd (1848-1910) ALW
13 AOW 66 BYS 143,154 ES1
265 EXT 1/2 31 EXT 3/1 29
EXT 4/2 32 EXT 5/1 14 FAN

10,153 FFR 109 FTF 43-6,56-
7 HFI 86 IAC 153 LEX 417-9
MSF 252,261 MSM 211,305
OSR 289-306 POE 111 RBY
109 SFB 42 SFE 343 SF1 307
SIH 9,12,39 SL5 2334-8 SOI
51 WAA 234 WIF 69
Lath, J.A. CSF 119 SF1 308
Latham, Philip pseud. of Robert
S. Richardson. AOW 322 EXT
1/2 32 FFR 109 HFI 86 IAC
153 IAH 85 MSM 82 RFA 139,
175,195 SFE 343 SFN 28 SFS
72 VES 335 WIF 167
Lathom, Francis (1777-1832)
CSF 119 SF1 308
Lathrop, Dorothy P. FFC 75,80,
84,131
Lathrop, George Parsons. BAA
57 IAC 153
Lathy, Thomas Pike. CSF 119
Latimer, John (1937-) SF1 308
Latter, Simon. SF1 308
Latzer, Milton J. IMS 34
Laubenthal, Sanders Anne (1943-)
HFI 86 SF1 308 SF2 969-70
SRB 266
Laucour, Harold. EXT 6/1 17
Laughlin, Clarence John. ES1
265
Laughlin, Florence. FFC 189
Laumer, (John) Keith (1925-)
ALW 212 AOW 213-4,400 BAA
143-4 BFP 300-3 BYS 304 ES1
265-6 FFR 109-10 HFI 87 IAC
153-5 JHN 18 LEX 419-21
MFW 25 NDA 124-5 RGS 100-
1,216-7 SFB 19 SFE 343-4
SFH 172,180 SFS 72 SF1 308-
9 SF2 970 SL4 1687-91,1775-
9 SL5 2511-5 SRB 14,352 TPS
215-7 UFS 1,3-4 VES 105,123,
143,147,301 WFS 292 WGT 85-
6 WSF 186
Laumer, March. SF1 309 WGT
86
Laune, A. MSM 206
Laurance, Alice. IAC 155 LTN
253
Laurel, Stan. KVT 58-9
Laurence, John pseud. of John
Laurence Pritchard. SF1 309
Laurence, Margaret. FFC 133
Laurens, Marshall. HFI 88 SF1
309

Laurent-Cely, Jacques (1919-) WGT 86

Laurentz, Townsend. SF1 309

Lauria, Frank Jonathan (1935-) SF1 309 SF2 970-1

Laurie, Andre pseud. of Paschal Grousset (1844-1909) ALW 85 CSF 119 EXT 3/2 40 MSF 162 POE 104 SFE 344 SF1 309 SOT 68 WAA 39

Laurie, Robin. FFC 58

Lauterbach, Edward S. BAA 211 EXT 1/1 1 EXT 1/2 29-34

Lavaivre, Noelle. FFC 137

Laver, James (1899-1975) BAA 240 SF1 309 SF2 971

Laverty, Donald pseud. of James Blish, Damon Knight. SFE 344

Lavigne, Robert. IAC 155

Lavond, Paul Dennis (house name) IAC 155 ISW 193 WGT 86 see also Joseph H. Dockweiler, Robert W. Lowndes, C. M. Kornbluth, Frederik Pohl

Lavrenyev, Boris A. EXT 10/2 75 MSF 254, 261

Lavrin, Nora. FFC 164

Law, Richard Kidson. BAA 183

Law, William. CWN 31 EXT 9/2 55 THM 10

Law, Winifred. CSF 119 ES1 266 SF1 310

Law-Abiding Revolutionist, (A) pseud. of Bert J. Wellman. CSF 119

Lawler, Amy C. FL3 1343-6

Lawler, Donald L. FL1 95-115, 336-40, 410-7, 501-3 FL2 680-3, 776-80, 961-5 FL3 1216-20, 1257-61, 1343-6, 1396-401 FL4 1703-11, 1733-43, 1826-30, 2017-22 LTN 251 SL1 178-85, 191-5, 502-7 SL2 554-9 SL3 1019-25, 1333-9, 1510-5 SL4 1574-82, 1655-9, 2023-9 SL5 2383-8, 2424-8, 2511-5

Lawlor, Harold. IAC 155 WTS 130

Lawlor, John. SOI 7

Lawrence. FBK 63, 104, 119 VES 97

Lawrence, Ann (1942-) FFC 49, 75 SF1 583

Lawrence, Charles Edward (1870-1940) CSF 119 SF1 310

Lawrence, D(avid) H(erbert) (1885-1930) BYS 43, 54 CAT 51 CSF 119 CWN 37, 50 ES1 266-7 EXT 6/1 9 EXT 9/2 50-2, 59 FBK 100 FLT 153 FL2 959-60 FTF 141 IAC 155 MSF 127 NWO 4, 8, 43 SFS 72 SF1 310 THM 5-9, 11-2, 24, 39, 49, 51, 53, 61

Lawrence, Harriet. FFC 76 SF1 310

Lawrence, Henry Lionel (1908-) ES1 267 SFE 344 SF1 310 SF2 971

Lawrence, J. A. IAC 155

Lawrence, James Cooper (1890-1932) BAA 17, 99 CSF 119 POE 120 SF1 310

Lawrence, John. FFC 10

Lawrence, Josephine. BAA 140 NDA 132-3, 141-2 SF1 310

Lawrence, Judith Ann. IAC 155 TJB 45

Lawrence, Louise pseud. of Elizabeth Rhoda Wintle. FFC 32, 39 SF1 310

Lawrence, Margery (-1969) CSF 119 IAC 155 SFS 73 SF1 310

Lawrence, St. Leger. WFS 216

Lawrence, Stephen pseud. of Lawrence Sterne Stephens. SFE 344

Lawrence, T. E. (1888-1935) CWN 30 STF 68 THM 59, 61 VFS 5

Lawson, Alfred William (1869-1954) SF1 310

Lawson, Jack B. IAC 155 SFS 73

Lawson, John Shults. FFC 7, 171 SF1 310

Lawson, Robert (1892-1957) CSF 120 ES1 267 FFC 58, 77, 96, 105, 121, 134, 139, 147, 154 SF1 310, 583

Lawson, Robert Neale (1873-1945) SF1 310

Lawson, W. B. pseud. of Edward Stratemeyer. STH 162

Lawton, Cliff. ES1 267

Lawton, H. W. BAA 240

Layland-Barratt, Frances (-1953) CSF 120 SF1 310

Layne, Stan (1899-) ES1 267

Layton, Frank George (1872-1941) WGT 86 see also Stephen Andrew

Layzell, Bob. [FUT] VES 70

Lazarevich, Mila. FFC 75

Lazarus. SHL 60
Lazarus, Henry. BAA 52 CSF 120 SF1 311
Lazarus, Keo Felker (1913-) FFC 147 SF1 311 SF2 971
Lazenby, Norman Austin. SF1 311
Lazlo, Gustave. SF1 311
Lazo, Hector (1899-1965) SF1 311 SF2 971-2
Le Blanc, Maurice. CSF 120
Le Blond, Marius-Ary. CSF 120
Le Breton, Thomas pseud. of T. Murray Ford. SF1 311
Le Cain, Errol. FFC 2, 45
Le Clezio, Jean-Marie (1940-) SFE 345
Le Conte, Caroline E. CSF 120
Le Corbusier. [FUT]
Le Fanu, J(oseph) Sheridan (1814-73) BYS 18, 91, 102-3 CSF 121 ES1 267 EXT 10/1 44 FBK 13, 44, 46, 49, 60-1, 69, 78 FL4 1600-6 IAC 155 SF1 313 SIH 31 SOT 347 WGT 86-7 WIF 72 WTS 103
Le Faure, Georges (1858-1935) SL1 109-12
Le Grand. FFC 155-6
Le Guin, Elisabeth. LTN 146
Le Guin, Ted. LTN 174
Le Guin, Ursula K. (1929-) AAL 9, 19, 57-60, 67, 83, 127-8, 135, 203-8 ACC 192 ALW 239 AOW 170, 214-5, 291, 306, 351, 354 ASF 127, 300-4 BAA 149, 158, 160, 162, 165-6, 183 BFP 304-6 BYS 37, 291, 305-6 CAT 37, 58, 63-7, 86-7, 116, 137, 139 CEN 56-69 COT 178, 183, 190-1, 198-200 CSC 31, 84, 119, 121, 190-1 CWD 14 EFP 16 ES1 269 ETN 55, 65, 121-2, 146 FBK 115 FFC 21, 39 FFR 111-2 FHT 67 [FJT] FLR 39, 41 FLT 79 FL1 81-3, 447-59 FL4 1607-10 HEN 19 HFI 88 HWK 48 IAC 155-6 INT 15, 52, 65, 97-8, 122 JGB 7 KAU 9, 29, 44, 105, 208, 227 LEX 422-4 MFW 11-2, 24, 46-7, 102, 104, 109, 112, 114, 157-60, 228 MSF 29-30, 68, 74, 79, 121, 193, 199-200, 280 NWO 48-9, 75-90, 119, 194 PJF 33 POE 287-9 RAH 170-1, 236 RGS 102-4, 217 RSG 86 SFB 151 SFD 17-8, 84, 131,
134, 188, 208, 224, 240, 280, 302, 321 SFE 345-8 SFH 45, 64, 71, 75-80, 95, 98-9, 116, 146, 155-6, 165, 186, 189, 226-30, 243 SFW 91, 107, 351, 377, 409-17, 591 SF1 314 SF2 972-3 SIH 79 SIN 101-11 SL2 548-53, 681-6, 692-7 SL3 1161-4, 1171-7 SL5 2492-6 SRB 16, 29, 80, 126, 267, 342-3, 346, 351, 360, 363, 504 STF 79-99, 104 TDI 6-7 TSF 21-5, 63, 239-40, 247 TSO 32-3 VES 95, 169, 171, 215, 245, 258-9, 261, 280, 319 VF2 154-79, 204-5 WFS 285 WSF 205, 233, 243, 262, 337, 348, 387
Le May, Jean. SFE 352
Le Page, Rand (house name) SFE 352 SF1 316 see also William Henry Bird, John Glasby, Brian Holloway, David O'Brien, Cyril Protheroe, Arthur Roberts
Le Plongeon, Alice. CSF 122
Le Plongeon, Augustus. CSF 122
Le Pretre, William. SF1 316
Le Queux, William Tufnell (1864-1927) AOW 67 BAA 76 BYS 102, 112, 126, 145, 154-5 CSF 122 ES1 267 IAC 156 SFE 352 SF1 316-7 STH 183, 193, 200, 205 VES 312
Le Rouge, Gustave. MSF 162 SIH 41
Le Sage, Alain Rene (1668-1747) CSF 123 SF1 317
Le Sueur, Theodore. BAA 183
Lea, Alec Richard. ES1 267 SF1 311
Lea, Dave. SF1 311
Lea, Homer. CSF 120
Lea, Terrea see Terry Stacy
Leach, Bailey Kay. CSF 120 SF1 311
Leach, Christopher. FFC 32
Leach, Decima. BAA 137 SFE 344 SF1 311
Leach, Edmund. KAU 179
Leach, Marie. FFC 21
Leacock, Stephen Butler (1869-1944) BAA 99 CSF 120 ES1 267-8 EXT 2/2 30 IAC 156 SFE 344 SF1 311
Leadabrand, Russell A. FFC 76 IMS 68, 134
Leadbeater, Charles W. CSF 120
Leader, Mary. SF1 311

Leahy, John Martin (1886-) ES1 268 HFI 88 IAC 156 SFE 344 SFS 73 SF1 311 WTS 28-9
Leakey, Louis. ACC 128
Leamy, Edmund. CSF 120
Lean, David. VFS 121
Lear, Edward. MSF 215 SRB 20
Learmonth, David. CSF 120
Learoyd, Cyril G. CSF 120
Leary, Daniel J. BAA 240
Leary, Francis. ES1 268
Leary, Paul M. BAA 284
Leary, Timothy. EXT 10/1 26
Leatham, Moyra. FFC 48
Leatherwood, Hank. SF1 311
Leavis, F. R. CAT 132-3 FAN 6 FLT 13
Leavitt, Hart Day. IAC 156
Leavitt, Harvey. BAA 240
Lebar, John pseud. of Gilbert Munger Wright, Harold Bell Wright. CSF 212 SF1 311
Lebeck, Oskar. CSF 120 SF1 311
Lebedev, Vladimir. COT 50
Lebenson, Richard. FFC 195
Leblanc, Georgette. FFC 14
Leblanc, Maurice (1864-1941) ES1 268 IAC 156 SFS 73 SF1 311
Leblond, Marius-Ary. BAA 183
Lecale, Errol. SF1 311-2
Lechtliner, Ruth. IAC 156
Leckie, Peter Martin (1890-) ES1 268 WGT 86 see also Peter Martin
Leclair, (Sister) St. Ida. BAA 183
LeConte, John. EXT 5/2 43
LeCroix, Jacques. WFS 173
Lederberg, Joshua. EXT 4/1 1 POE 296
Lederer, Richard. BAA 240
Lederman, Frank. SF1 312
Ledoux, John Walter (1860-1932) see Isaac Calson
Ledoux, Nicolas. [FUT]
Lee, Arthur Stanley Gould (1894-1975) ES1 268 WGT 86 see also Arthur Lee Gould
Lee, Austin (1904-) SF2 841 see also Julian Callender
Lee, Christopher (1923?-) ES1 268 FBK 48,51,105 IAC 156 WTS 55
Lee, David. SF1 312

Lee, Doris. FFC 52
Lee, Edgar. CSF 120
Lee, Edmund. CSF 120
Lee, (Mrs.) Eliza. CSF 120
Lee, Elizabeth. ES1 268-9 SF1 312
Lee, Elsie. SF1 312
Lee, Henry Boyle. WGT 86 see also Theophilus McCrib
Lee, Jennette Barbour (1860-1951) CSF 120 SF1 312
Lee, Josephine. FFC 194
Lee, Manfred Bennington (1905-71) SF1 312 WGT 86
Lee, Marguerite Du Pont. ES1 269
Lee, (Mrs.) Norman. CSF 121 SF1 312
Lee, Raymond. SF1 312
Lee, Robert Corwin, Jr. (1931-) ES1 269 FFC 155,164 SF1 312 SF2 972
Lee, Robert E. WTS 130
Lee, Sophia. CSF 121
Lee, Stan (1922-) SFE 345
Lee, Stanislaw G. IAC 156
Lee, Tanith (1947-) FFC 21,49, 55 FFR 111 FL1 116-21 FL2 988-92 FL4 2036-8 HFI 88 IAC 156 LEX 421-2 RGS 101-2 SFE 345 SF1 583 SIH 79 SRB 265 WSF 282
Lee, Thomas. BAA 37 CSF 121 SF1 312
Lee, Vernon pseud. of Violet Paget (1856-1935) CSF 121 EXT 6/1 14 FL4 1597-9 SF1 312-3
Lee, Walt(er William, Jr.) (1931-) AOW 361 BRS 11 ES1 269 EXT 5/1 6 FRN 103-4 KWS x,150 MSM 302 SFE 345 SF1 313 SF2 972
Lee, Wayne Cyril (1917-) ES1 269 SF2 1072 WGT 86 see also Lee Sheldon
Lee, William M. IAC 156 SFS 73
Leech, Joseph. SF1 313
Leeds, Arthur. IMS 84
Lee-Hamilton, Eugene (1845-1907) CSF 121 SF1 313
Leek, Sybil (1923-) AOW 323 ES1 269 SF1 313 SF2 972
Leeming, John Fishwick (1900-) CSF 121 SF1 313 SF2 972
Leeper, Geoffrey. BAA 240

Lees, Gene. IAC 156 SFS 73
Lees, Robert J. CSF 121
Lefebure, Molly. FFC 134
Lefebvre, Henri. BAA 240
Lefevre, Edwin. CSF 121
Leffingwell, Albert (1895-1946) WGT 87 see also Dana Chambers
Leflamanc, Auguste. BAA 183
Leftwich, Robert. CWN 56
Leger, Raymond Alfred (1883-) SF1 313 WGT 87 see also Raymond McDonald
Legg, W. Dorr see Auctor Ignotus
Legge, James Granville (1861-1940) BAA 92 CSF 121 SF1 313
Legge, Ronald. CSF 121 SF1 313
Leggett, Mortimer Dormer (1821-96) BAA 42 SF1 313
Legman, Gershon. IAH 84 NDA 214-5 SFB 110 SOT 392,398
Legoyt, Alfred. POE 173-4
Lehmann, Rudolf C. CSF 122
Lehmann, W. P. AAL 72
Lehman-Wilzig, Sam N. AC2 75
Lehouck, Emile. BAA 183
Lehr, Paul. SRB 46,48
Lehrburger, Egon (1904-) BAA 131 see also Egon Larsen
Lehrman, Herb. IAC 156 VES 173
Lehtimaki, Konrad. SIH 81
Leiber, Fritz, Jr. (1910-) AAL 141 ACE 53 AC2 51,75 ALW 160,217 AOW 118,215-6,291, 296,300 BAA 118,122,133,136, 149,240 BFP 307-9 BYS 262, 279 COT 112,135,195,252,278, 295 CSC 30,188-9 CSF 122 ES1 269-70 ETN 28 EXT 3/1 11,24 EXT 5/1 3,10,16 EXT 7/2 40, 42 EXT 8/1 6-7,16 EXT 9/1 21 EXT 10/1 6,8 FBK 94,154 FFR 112-5 [FJT] FL1 314-8 FL2 511-7 FL4 1611-5 FL5 2200-2 FTF 157 [FUT] HFI 88-9 HID 103 HWK 40 IAC 156-8 IAH 22,106,129-30 ISW ix,40-2,121,127-8,182,223-4,226,258 JGB 5 JVN 207-8 KAU 127 LEX 424-6 LTN 91-2 MIH 17, 23,36,80 MSM 132,184-6 NWO 16-7 RFA 119-21,123,125,134, 137-8,191,194-5,213-4 RGS 104-6 SFB 23,58,62,113 SFD 14-6,22,28,86,251-2,293,310-1

SFE 348-9 SFH 84,156,172,177, 243 SFN 16,117 SFS 73-4 SFW 419-24 SF1 314 SF2 973 SIN 7, 55-62 SL1 218-22 SL4 1958-62 SL5 2396-401 SOT 6,96-7,196, 283-302,316,320,323,344,412 SRB 80,127,267,312,319,340 STH 12,157 SV1 37-43 TJB 40 TSF 57,134,236 VES 83,122, 128,136,142,150,174,207,238, 318 WAA 94,97,103,106-7 WFS 161,200,216,227,240 WIF 113, 145,157,194,229 WSF 105-6, 148,152,200,283,386,388 WTS 56,58
Leiber, Fritz, Sr. FLR 9,11-2
Leiber, Jonquil. FLR 9-10,12-4
Leiber, Justin. AAL 102 FLR 9,29,36-7,61
Leiber, Virginia. FLR 9,11
Leibich, Andre Leonard. BAA 284
Leibniz, Gottfried Wilhelm. KAU 222-3
Leibscher, Walt. IAC 158
Leiby, Joan. SF1 314
Leichman, Seymour. FFC 13
Leiden, Mark. EXT 6/1 19
Leif, Evelyn. IAC 158
Leigh, Bill Colston. VFS 183
Leigh, Edmund. SF1 314
Leigh, Stephen. IAC 158
Leight, Edward. FFC 193
Leighton, Frances Spatz. SF1 314
Leighton, Peter. ES1 270 SF1 314 VES 79
Leighton, Robert (1859-1934) SF1 314
Leimert, John. IAC 158 MSM 94,107-10 SFS 74
Leinster, Murray pseud. of Will F. Jenkins (1896-1975) AAL 13,26,73,90 ALW 8,114,121, 129,136,141,146,154,213,218, 234 AOW 217-8,285,290,292 ASF 175 BYS 210,234 CAT 102 COT 81,109-10 CSC 44-5, 51,65,91-2,234 CSF 122 EXT 5/1 3,10 EXT 7/2 39 EXT 10/1 3 FFR 115-6 HFI 89-90 HID 3,18-9,23,71,122,128,148,193, 195 IAC 158-60 IMS 16,24 INT 9 ISW 120,136-9,221-2 KAU 59,104,191,195,198,206-7 LEX 426-8 MFW 17,85,97,99,

Leinster, Murray (cont.)
102 MIH 23,36 MSF 268 MSM
30, 77, 87, 90, 101, 131-2, 139,
298, 303 OWB 79 PST 165-6,
199, 213, 258, 266, 289 RFA xiii,
xviii, 1, 5-6, 12-3, 24, 28, 31-2,
36, 39, 110, 134-6, 165, 183, 205-8,
210-2, 214 RGS 106-7, 217 RSG
26 SFB 114 SFD 19, 23, 27, 211,
288, 313 SFE 349-50 SFN 28
SFS 74-5 SFW 111-7 SF1 314-
5 SIH 114, 117, 189 SL4 2030-
4 SOT 3, 47-65, 71, 73, 155, 320,
334, 430-1 SRB 12, 16, 115 STH
117-8, 147-8 TSF 53 VES 71,
75, 87-8, 92, 107, 121-3, 132, 141-
2, 145, 147, 156, 161-2, 173, 197,
301, 326, 328 WFS 200, 205 WIF
155 WSF 28-9, 44, 54, 59, 67, 69,
109, 120-1, 152, 156, 329-30, 332,
388 WTS 26, 36, 51, 85
Leipiar, Louise. WGT 87
Leisk, David Johnson (1906-)
WGT 87 see also Crockett
Johnson
Leitch, Lavinia pseud. of Lavinia
Leitch Hynd. CSF 122 SF1 315
Leitch, Patricia (1933-) ES1 270
FFC 107 SF1 583
Leitenberg, Barbara. BAA 284
Leitfred, Robert. WTS 44
Leithauser, Joachim G. BAA 240
Leivick, Halper. FBK 57
Leland, Charles Godfrey (1824-
1903) CSF 122 SF1 315
Leland, Samuel Phelps. BAA 45
Lem, Stanislaw (1921-) AAL 101-
2, 138 AOW 218-9 ASF 127
BYS 289, 307 CAT 81, 104-5,
122-30, 140 COT 194 ES1 270
ETN 121 EXT 10/2 79-80 FFR
116 HFI 90 IAC 160 INT 106,
122 KAU 9-10, 23, 34, 158, 189,
227 LEX 428-31 LTN 12-3, 81,
117-8, 131, 256-7 MFW 205-6
MSF 3, 29-30, 36, 67, 74, 83, 202,
230, 269, 280 NWO 185-202 OMN
47, 288-9, 292 OSR 307-25, 355
POE 298-301 RGS 107-9 SFB
12, 16, 23, 83, 114, 120, 122, 148-9
SFE 350-2 SFH 71, 84-7, 181-2
SFW 91, 104, 591-8 SF1 315-6
SIH 118, 142, 144, 202 SL1 457-
61 SL2 905-8 SL3 1050-6, 1370-
4 SL5 2107-12 SRB 16, 349, 358,
362 UKL 69 VES 96, 190, 197,
261, 297 VFS 256 WAA 214, 233,
237-9
Lemaitre, Jules (1853-1914) CSF
122 ES1 270-1 SF1 316
Leman, Alfred (1925-) LEX 431
Leman, Bob. SF1 316
Leman, Grahame. IAC 160
LeMay, (Gen.) Curtis. MIH 144
NWO 257 VFS 225
Lemberg, Eugen. BAA 240
Lemieux, Pierre. BAA 101-2
Lemire, Charles. EXT 2/1 6-7,
14
Lemkin, William. ES1 271 IMS
11 ISW 160
Lemon, Don Mark. IAC 160 SOT
397
L'Engle, Madeleine (1918-) AOW
306, 323 ES1 271 FFC 164 FFR
73 SF1 316 SF2 973-4
Lengyel, Cornel Adam (1915-) ES1
271 HFI 90
Lengyel, Peter. SIH 141
Lenin, Vladimir/Nikolai (1870-
1924) EXT 10/2 75 FAN 100
FTF 104 ISW 199 LTN 13 MSF
38, 158, 219, 247, 253, 260 RHN
165 SFH 14 WFS 68
Lenski, Lois. FFC 67
Lent, Blair. FFC 2
Lentini, A. IAC 160
Leo, Bessie. SF1 316
Leo, Robert Joseph. BAA 284
Leo XIII, (Pope). SFB 67
Leonard, Gene. WFS 255-6
Leonard, George H. HFI 90, 184
see also Hughes Cooper
Leonard, J.N. COT 32
Leonard, John (1939-) IMS 69
SF1 316 SF2 974
Leone, Sergio. CSC 264 FFC 9
VES 147
Leonhart, Raphael W. pseud. of
Peter F. Wybraniec. CSF 122
Leonhart, Rudolph. BAA 38, 49
Leonov, Aleksandr. SIH 13
Leonov, Alexei. VFS 226
Leonov, Leonid M. EXT 10/2
77, 93 MSF 264
Leopold, Aldo. COT 267
Leopold, Friedrich (1772-1801)
see Novalis
Leourier, Christian (1948-) AOW
219 HFI 90 SFE 352 SF1 316
LePire, Joe H. SF1 316

Lerman, Rhoda (1936-) IAC 160 SF1 317 SF2 974
Lermontov, Mikhail (1814-41) FBK 41
Lerner, Alan J. CSF 122
Lerner, Fred. SF1 317
Lerner, Laurence. BAA 240
Lerner, Max. NWO 127
Lernet-Holenia, Alexander (1897-) ES1 271 FBK 144 IAC 160 SFS 75 SF1 317
Lerond, Dennis. SF1 317
LeRouge, Gustave (1867-1938) SL4 1726-9
Leroux, Gaston (1868-1927) CSF 122-3 ES1 271 FBK 139 IAC 160 SF1 317 SOT 73 WTS 32, 34, 124
Leroux, Pierre. BAA 240
Leroy, Gaylord C. BAA 240
Leroy, Maxime. BAA 183
Leshner, Ben. WFS 122
Leshner, Felice. WFS 122
Leskov, Nikolai. FFC 13
Leslie, Cecil. FFC 68
Leslie, Delia. IAC 160
Leslie, Desmond Arthur (1921-) ES1 271 SFE 352 SF1 317 SF2 974
Leslie, Josephine Aimee Campbell (1898-) SF1 317 WGT 87 see also R. A. Dick
Leslie, Mary Isabel (1899-) WGT 87 see also Temple Lane
Leslie, Norman. IAC 160
Leslie, Peter (1922-) SFE 352 SF1 317 SF2 974 WGT 87
Leslie, (Sir) Shane (1885-1971) CSF 122 ES1 271 SF1 318
Leslie, William pseud. of Archer L. Hood, Violet Perkins. CSF 123
Lesperance, David. WGT 87
Lesser, Milton (1928-) ES1 271-2 HFI 91 IAC 160 ISW 32 LEX 431-2 SFE 352 SFS 75 SF1 318 SF2 974 VES 95 WGT 87 see also Adam Chase, Stephen Marlowe, S. M. Tenneshaw, C. H. Thames
Lessing, Bruno. STH 128
Lessing, Doris May (1919-) ALW 238 AOW 220 CAT 17-8, 27 CSC 101 CWN 25, 47 HFI 91 LEX 432-3 POE 294-5 SFE 352 SFH 66, 99 SF1 318 SF2

974-5 SL1 254-9 STF 23-4
Lessing, Gotthold. NDA 10
Lessner, Erwin Christian (1898-1959) BAA 113 CSF 123 SF1 318
Lester, Edward. SF1 318
Lester, Horace Frank (1853-) CSF 123 SF1 318
Lester, Irving. DTS 12 MSM 302 VES 104
Lester, Teri. SF1 318
LesTina, Dorothy. WFS 133, 135, 140, 151, 155-6, 161-3, 170, 207
L'Estrange, C. James (1880?-1947) SF1 318 see also Herbert Strang
L'Estrange, Henry. BAA 49 CSF 123 SF1 318
L'Estrange, Miles. CSF 123 SF1 318
Letcher, Owen. CSF 123
Lethaby, John W. WGT 87-8 see also J. W. L.
Lethbridge, Katharine Greville. ES1 272
Lethbridge, Thomas Charles. ES1 272
Letsche, Curt (1912-) LEX 433
Letson, Russell. FL2 642-5 FL3 1132-6 FL4 1633-9, 1895-7, 1922-5 PJF 25, 28, 74 RAH 194-221 RSG 39, 92 SL2 600-4, 665-70 SL3 1289-93 SL4 1809-16
Lettau, Reinhard Adolf. BAA 284-5
Lettieri, Dan J. DTS iii
Letts, Barry. SF1 318
Levak, J. H. SRB 82
Levehgi, Riccardo. WAA 235
Level, Maurice (1875-1926) CSF 123 ES1 272 WTS 35
Levene, Malcolm (1937-) BAA 146 ES1 272 HFI 91 SFE 353 SF1 318 SF2 975 VES 128
Levene, Philip. ES1 272
Levenson, S. FFC 171
Leventman, Herman. IMS 34, 36, 52, 56, 183 WFS 71
Leverentz, Alan C. SF1 318
Levett, Arthur. SF1 318
Levi, Albert William. BAA 240
Levi, Lazar. TSP 149
Levie, Rex Dean (1937?-) ES1 272 HFI 91 SFE 353 SF1 318

Levin, Barry Raymond (1946-) SF2 975

Levin, Betty. FFC 164 SF1 319

Levin, Harry. BAA xix-xx, 183, 240 MSF 26 NWO 22

Levin, Ira (1929-) AAL 39-40, 50-1 ALW 186 AOW 220, 225 BAA 152 ES1 272 ETN 144 FBK 7 FFR 118 FL3 1338-42 HFI 91 IAC 161 MFW 87-90, 141-2, 202 NDA 96-7, 126, 128-30, 209 SFE 353 SF1 319 SF2 975 SRB 350 TSF 127 WSF 295

Levin, Jeffrey. LTN 14, 237-8 UKL 245

Levin, Meyer (1905-) SF1 319 SF2 975

Levin, Richard. IMS 245-6 WGT 88 see also Cyril Mand

Levin, Sol. IAC 161

Levine, David. EXT 10/1 30 FFC 74

Levi-Strauss, Claude. ACC 85 KAU 110 MFW 104, 112, 184 MSF 59, 233 STF 35 TDI 3

Levitin, Alexis. EXT 10/1 24, 33-4

Levitin, Sonia. FFC 147

Levitt, Israel Monroe (1908-) ES1 272

Levrero, Mario. SL1 383-5

Levshin, Vassily A. MSF 244

Levy, Brigid Antonia Brophy (1929-) WGT 88

Levy, Clifton Harby. STH 257

Levy, David (1913-) BAA 240 HFI 91 SF1 319 SF2 975

Levy, Jessica. FFC 125

Levy, Joseph Hiam. BAA 78

Lewandowski, Herbert (1896-) WGT 88

Lewi, Charlotte Armstrong (1905-69) WGT 88

Lewin, Albert (1894-1968) SF1 319

Lewin, Leonard Case (1916-) BAA 144, 154 ES1 272 HFI 91 NDA 78-82 SFD 187, 190 SFE 353 SF1 319

Lewis, Albert. ES1 272 IAC 161 SF1 319

Lewis, Alethea Brereton (1749-1827) WGT 88 see also Eugenia De Acton

Lewis, Anthony R. IAC 161 SF1 319

Lewis, Arthur O(rcutt), Jr. (1920-) BAA 183, 241 EXT 2/1 1, 20-1 EXT 2/2 27-32 EXT 4/1 1 MFW 183 SF1 319 SF2 976

Lewis, Benn E. SF1 319

Lewis, Beth. FFC 55

Lewis, Brian (1929-78) ES1 272 SFE 353 VES 89, 98, 240, 289

Lewis, Cecil Day (1904-72) SF2 819 see also Nicholas Blake

Lewis, Charles. SFE 353

Lewis, Charles Bertrand (1842-1924) see M. Quad

Lewis, C(live) S(taples) (1898-1963) AAL 153, 199 ACC 85, 209 ALW 99 AOW 89, 93, 96, 220, 324, 346-8, 353, 356, 360, 396 ATA 10, 54 BAA 107, 112-4, 241 BFP 310-2 BYS 3, 88, 106, 119, 196-201, 205, 210, 286, 289, 305, 307, 320 CAT xv, 22-3, 58-9, 81, 83, 138 COT 64 CSC 34, 119, 163 CSF 123 ES1 272-3 EXT 1/2 25, 27-8 EXT 2/2 26, 30 EXT 3/1 27-8 EXT 4/2 28-31 EXT 5/1 4, 22-3 EXT 6/2 22, 51 EXT 7/2 41 EXT 8/1 1, 5 EXT EXT 8/2 30 EXT 9/1 19, 22-3 EXT 9/2 47, 61 EXT 10/1 18-9, 31, 33, 39-40, 43, 45 FAN 5, 13, 133-44, 164 FBK 65, 88, 91, 97-8, 100, 115, 126, 132 FFC 177 FFR 118 FL1 248-55 FL2 635-7 FL3 1363-8 FL4 1790-7, 1933-7 FTF 187-9 HFI 91 IAC 161 IAH 57-8, 71 INT 40-1, 114 ISW 226, 259, 267 KAU 58, 204-5 LEX 433-4 LTN 256 MFW 51, 95, 229, 266, 270 MIH 3, 15 MSF 26, 69, 138, 178, 189, 193 MSM 200-1, 204 NDA xi, 10-6, 122-3, 203 NWO 18, 44, 47-8, 92 OSR 147-56 POE 274 PST 123-4, 196, 198, 203, 214, 220-1, 224, 242-4, 259, 275 RBY 84, 109, 156 RFA 158 RGS 109-110, 218 SFB 11, 20, 64-5 SFD 305 SFE 353-4 SFH 43-51, 87, 168, 226 SFN 20, 32, 40 SFS 75 SFW 75, 243-8 SF1 319-20 SL4 1632-6, 1669-73 SL5 2250-4 SOT 290, 410-2 SRB 268 STF 80-2, 85 STH 3, 6-9, 12-3, 19-20 THM 39 TPS 119-31 TSF 229 VFS 49, 76,

Lewis, C. S. (cont.)
268 WBW 3, 25, 48, 57 WGT 88
WIF 81, 86, 223 WSF 10, 129
Lewis, David. FL3 1304-6 FL4
1869-71 SL1 508-12 SL3 1040-
4, 1106-9 SL4 1854-8
Lewis, Dewitt F. BAA 78
Lewis, Elisabeth R. IAH 35
Lewis, Ernest Michael Roy (1913-)
BYS 217 KAU 184 SFE 354 SF1
321 SF2 976-7 WGT 88
Lewis, G. M. FTF 30
Lewis, Gogo. SF1 320
Lewis, H. Milo. SF1 320
Lewis, Harve Spencer (1883-1939)
CSF 122 SF1 320
Lewis, Helen Prothero. CSF 123
Lewis, Henry Harrison. ALW
105 BAA 100 SF1 320
Lewis, Hilda Winifred (1896-1974)
FFC 164 SF1 320, 583
Lewis, Irwin (1916-) ES1 273 HFI
91 SFE 354 SF1 320 SF2 976
Lewis, Jack. IAC 161 SFS 75
SF1 320
Lewis, Jerry. WAA 90
Lewis, Jerry Lee. HID 150
Lewis, Joan. BAA 183
Lewis, John L. WFS 197
Lewis, L. A. CSF 123 ES1 274
SF1 320
Lewis, Leon (1833-1920) CSF 123
SF1 320
Lewis, Mary Christianna Milne
(1907-) WGT 88 see also
Christianna Brand
Lewis, Matthew Gregory (1775-
1818) ALW 45 BYS 17, 25 CSF
123-4 ES1 274 FBK 23-4, 33, 44
FL1 36-41 RBY 167-8, 170, 179
SF1 320 SIH 14 TFC 42, 126,
129 WAA 27, 80, 82, 243 WGT
88
Lewis, Meriwether (1774-1809)
KVT 39
Lewis, Monk see Matthew Gregory
Lewis
Lewis, Myron R. IAC 161
Lewis, Naomi. EXT 10/1 33
FFC 2
Lewis, Oscar (1893-) AOW 288
ES1 274 IAC 161 SFE 354 SFS
76 SF1 320 SF2 976 VES 123
Lewis, (Percy) Wyndham (1884-
1957) CSF 124 ES1 274 FAN

4, 124, 181 JGB 6 SFE 354 SF1
321 THM 61
Lewis, Pete pseud. of Peter J.
Crown. SF1 320
Lewis, Philip C. SF1 320
Lewis, R. M. CSF 124 SF1 320
Lewis, R. W. B. NWO 3-4, 9-10,
15, 274
Lewis, Richard O. COT 96, 98
IAC 161
Lewis, Roy. IAC 161
Lewis, Sinclair (1881-1951) AOW
106 BAA 103, 241 COT 120, 122,
136 CSF 124 DTS 3 ES1 274
ETN 1 EXT 1/2 31 EXT 7/1
18 EXT 7/2 37 FAN 6 IAC 161
MSF 280 MSM 303 SFE 354
SFN 8, 16-7, 39, 51, 99-100 SF1
321 SL3 1089-93 SOT 190
WIF 21, 216 WSF 4
Lewis, W. H. EXT 10/1 33 SOI
2-3, 37, 146
Lewisohn, Ludwig (1882-1955)
CSF 124 SF1 321 STH 41
Ley, Olga. IAC 161 WFS 124,
216
Ley, Robert Arthur Gordon (1921-
68) BFP 313 ES1 274 SF2 1068
WGT 88-9 see also Arthur
Sellings
Ley, Sandra. IAC 161
Ley, Willy (1906-69) AAL 15 ASF
260-2 BAA 174 BYS 264 COT
16, 33-4, 37-8, 51-3 ES1 274-6
ETN 74 EXT 5/1 8 EXT 8/1
3-4 FTF 69 HID 13 IAC 161
IMS 2, 8-9, 17, 182, 197, 222, 231
KWS 208 MIH 26 MSM 70, 119,
125-6, 208, 211-2, 305 RFA 42,
57, 69, 84, 122, 125, 136, 167, 176,
181 SFB 73 SFE 354 SFN 24,
29, 31, 47 SFS 76 SOT 163, 178,
206 SRB 112 STH 178, 267
VES 71, 149, 289, 300 VFS 131-
6, 191 WFS 124, 173-4, 193, 205,
216, 264 WGT 89 WIF 115, 140,
185, 196 WSF 37, 70, 98, 103,
107, 164, 218, 312 YTS 30 see
also Robert Willey
Ley, Xenia. WFS 216
Leyburn, Ellen Douglass. BAA
183
Leydenfrost, A. FBK 106 SFE
354-5 VES 288
Leyland, V. B. FTF 51

Ley-Piscator, Maria (1905-) SF1 321
Leys, John K. STH 200
Leyson, (Capt.) Burr W. IAC 161 SFS 76
Lezra, Giggy. FFC 134
Licata, Tony. ES1 276 IAC 161 SF1 321
Lichtenberg, George. IAC 161
Lichtenberg, Jacqueline (1942-) HFI 91 LEX 434-5 SF1 321
Lichtenberger, Andre. BAA 183
Lichtig, E. H. IMS 46
Lichty. IAC 161
Liddell, Alice. FBK 108
Liddell, C. H. IAH 13
Liddy. G. Gordon. LTN 214-5
Lie, Jonas Lauritz Idemil (1833-1908) CSF 124 ES1 276
Lieber, Maxim (1897-) ES1 276 SF1 321
Lieberman, Rosalie. SF1 321 SF2 977
Lieblich, Irene. FFC 8
Liebscher, Walt. HFI 91 SF1 321
Lief, Evelyn. IAC 161
Lief, Ruth Ann. BAA 183
Lifton, Betty. FFC 14, 35, 134, 147
Ligeti, Gyorgy. ACC 124
Light, John. CSF 124
Lightner, A(lice) M. pseud. of Alice Martha Hopf (1904-) AOW 324 BAA 149 ES1 276 HFI 92 IAC 161 SFE 356-7 SFS 76 SF1 321
Lilienthal, David. CSC 133-4
Liljegren, Sten Bodvar. BAA 184
Liljencrantz, Ottilie A. (1876-1910) SF1 321
Lilly, John C. AAL 61-6
Lima, Robert. EXT 9/1 17
Limbo. SF1 321
Lincoln, Abraham (1809-65) MSF 175 RFA xvii SFN 50 SHL 21 VFS 199
Lincoln, Maurice. CSF 124 SF1 322
Lindbergh, Anne Morrow. MSM 192
Lindbergh, Charles A. COT 33, 45 EXT 7/2 37
Lindbohm, Denis. SIH 179
Linde, Gunnel. FFC 76
Lindgren, Carl C. ES1 276

Lindelof, Otto Julius Swenson (1852-) SF1 322
Linden, Margaret. SF1 322
Lindgren, Astrid. FFC 7, 104, 147, 182
Lindner, Robert Mitchell (1914-56) AOW 94 BYS 179 ES1 276 ETN 171 IAC 161 SFE 357 SFS 76 STH 107-9
Lindon, (Dr.) C. E. BAA 85
Lindop, Audrey. FFC 134
Lindsay, (Capt.) Charles McDonald. CSF 124 SF1 322
Lindsay, David (1876-1945) AAL 76, 132 BFP 314 BYS 199 CSF 124 CWN 40, 47, 50-1, 55, 57 ES1 276 EXT 5/1 3 EXT 9/1 19 FBK 126 FFR 118 FL1 391-5 FL2 701-9 FL4 2033-5, 2039-45 HFI 92 KAU 189, 210 LEX 435 MSM 201 RSG 59 SFB 65 SFD 306 SFE 357 SFH 49, 156, 169-70, 191, 207-12, 223, 226 SF1 322 SL5 2383-8 SOI xiv, 49 SRB 269 TSF 229 VES 153, 208 WAA 110
Lindsay, David T. CSF 124
Lindsay, Douglas. SF1 322
Lindsay, Jack. WBW 20-1
Lindsay, Kathleen (1903-) CSF 124 SF1 322
Lindsay, Norman (1879-1969) FFC 134 SF1 322
Lindsay, Vachel (1879-1931) BAA 85 IAC 161 SF1 322
Lindsay, William. CSF 124
Lindskoog, Kathryn Ann. SF1 322
Linebarger, Paul Myron Anthony (1913-66) ALW 212 BFP 315-6 ES1 277 ETN 114 SFB 150 SFD 222, 300, 316 SF2 1078-9 TSF 61-2, 240-1 WFS 244, 292 WGT 89 WSF 172 see also Cordwainer Smith
Lines, Kathleen Mary. ES1 277 SF1 322
Lingeman, Richard Roberts (1931-) SF1 322 SF2 978
Lingfeld, Norbert (1942-) AOW 352 BAA 187 SFE 357
Linington, Barbara Elizabeth (1921-) WGT 89
Link. IAC 161
Linklater, Eric Robert (1899-1974) CSF 124 ES1 277 EXT

Linklater, Eric R. (cont.)
8/1 5 FFC 182 SFE 359 SF1
322 VFS 118
Linkroum, Richard. SF1 322
Linnaeus. SFB 22-3
Linnekogel, Otto. FBK 82
Linnett, Peter. IAC 161
Linton, Anne. FFC 26
Linton, (Dr.) Charles Ellsworth
(1865?-1930) BAA 85 CSF 124
SF1 323Linton, Elizabeth Lynn
(1822-98) CSF 124 ES1 277
SF1 323
Lipkin, Beth see Beth Lewis
Lipow, Arthur Sherman. BAA
285
Lippard, George (1822-54) CSF
125 SF1 323
Lippincott, David McCord (1925-)
SFE 359 SF1 323 SF2 978
Lippmann, Walter. BAA 241
Lipscomb, Winifred Lawrence.
BAA 285
Lipton, Robert see Barry Sterling
Lipton, Seymour. RBY 195
Lisle, Charles Wentworth. SF1
323
Lisowski, Gabriel. FFC 8
Lissenden, George B. SF1 323
Lissner, Ivar (1909-) ES1 277
Lissovoy, P. MSF 264
Lister, R. P. IAC 161
Lister, Stephen. BAA 116 ES1
278 SF1 323
Liston, Edward J. BAA 116-7
CSF 125 ES1 278 SF1 323
Liszt, Franz. IAH 75 WFS 162
Littell, Janie. WFS 103-4
Littell, Philip (1868-1943) CSF
125 SF1 323
Littell, Robert. BAA 92 SF1
323
Littke, Lael J. IAC 161
Little, Jane. FFC 164,189 SF1
323
Little, Margaret. IAC 161
Little, Paul H. (1915-) SF2 1028
see also Hugo Paul
Little, William John Knox (1839-
1918) BAA 57 SF1 323
Littledale, Freya Lota (1929-)
SF1 323 SF2 978
Littlefield, Henry M. BAA 241
Lively, Penelope (1933-) FFC 14,
32,40,67,165 SF1 323,583 SF2
978

Liveright, Horace. STH 235
Livesey, Eric M. SFE 359 SF1
323
Livia. ISW 62
Livingston, Armstrong (1885-)
CSF 125 SF1 323
Livingston, Berkeley (1908-) ES1
278 SFE 359 SF1 324 WGT 89
WIF 120 see also Morris J.
Steele
Livingston, Dennis. BAA 241
TSF 200-2
Livingston, Harold (1924-) ES1
278 HFI 92 SFE 359 SF1 324
SF2 978
Livingston, Herb (1916-) ES1 278
WGT 89 see also Alexander
Blade, H. B. Hickey
Livingston, Marjorie Prout
(1893-) CSF 125 SF1 324
Livingstone, David (1813-73)
TSO 40
Livy. STF 13
Ljoka, Daniel John (1935-) HFI
92 SF1 324 SF2 978-9
Ljungquist, Kent P. FL2 976-9
FL4 1665-78
Llewellyn, (David William) Alun
(1903-) BYS 291 CSF 125 SFE
359 SF1 324
Llewellyn, Richard. IAC 162
Lloyd, Daniel. IAC 162
Lloyd, Harold. RFA xx
Lloyd, Jeremy. SF1 324
Lloyd, John Seaton. ES1 278
SF1 324 WIF 48
Lloyd, John Uri (1849-1936) AOW
42,67 CSF 125 EXT 1/1 13
FL1 497-500 HFI 92 MFW 120
PST 108-9,192,200,207,225-6,
250,252,265 SFB 76 SFE 359-
60 SF1 324
Lloyd, John William (1857-) BAA
67 SF1 324
Lloyd, (Mr.). VFS 232-3
Lloyd, Noel. ES1 278
Lloyd, Norris. FFC 88
Lloyd, Roger Bradshaigh (1901-)
SF1 324
Lo Medico, Brian T. IAC 162
Lobachevsky, Nikolai I. EXT
7/2 33 VFS 42
Lobato, Monteiro. SIH 11
Lobdell, Jared C. EXT 10/1 34
Lobeira, Joam. CSF 125
Lobel, Arnold. FFC 6,194

Lobo, George Edmund. WGT 89
Lobo, George Oliver see Oliver
Sherry
Lobsenz, Norman Mitchell (1919-)
ES1 278 STH 45
Loch, J. M. SF1 324
Locke, A. T. STH 152
Locke, Ashley. SF1 583
Locke, Charles F. WGT 89
Locke, David M. IAC 162
Locke, E. L. RFA 167
Locke, George Walter (1936-)
AOW 349 BAA 184 IAC 162
SFE 360 SF1 324 SF2 979
SRB 65-6
Locke, John (1632-1704) CWN 54
EXT 8/1 21 INT 108 UKL 64,
71, 118
Locke, Richard Adams (1800-71)
ALW 51, 56, 121 AOW 24 CSF
125 EXT 3/1 29 EXT 5/1 4
FTF 32-3 NWO 71 POE 63-7
PST 46-7, 204-5, 220 SFE 360
SFW 14 SF1 324 WAA 92 WGT
89-90 WIF 43
Locke, Robert Donald. IAC 162
SFS 76 WGT 90
Locke, William John (1863-1930)
CSF 125 ES1 278 SF1 325
Locke-Elliot, Sumner. VES 262
Lockhard, Leonard pseud. of
Theodore L. Thomas. IAC 162
SFS 76
Lockhart, (Mr.). EXT 3/1 6, 18
Lockhart-Mummery, John Percy.
BAA 105
Lockhart-Ross, H. S. CSF 125
SF1 325
Lockley, Ronald Mathias (1903-)
FFC 108 HFI 92 SF1 325 SF2
979
Lockridge, Norman. ES1 278
Lockridge, Richard Orson (1898-)
CSF 125 SF1 325
Lockwood, Ingersoll (1841-1918)
BAA 55 CSF 125 SF1 325
Lockwood, Thomas (1956-) LEX
436
Lodge, David. BAA 241 FTF 102
WAA 53
Loe, Gladys St. John. CSF 125
Loeb, Jacques. KAU 190
Loew, (Rabbi) (1512?-1609) ASF
145, 161, 183 FBK 57
Loewenstein, Bernice. FFC
116, 118

Loewenthal, Eduard. BAA 184
Loffler, Henner. BAA 184
Lofting, Hugh (1886-1947) AOW
304 FFC 67, 122, 148 ES1 278
SF1 583
Lofts, Norah Ethel (1904-) ES1
278 SF1 325 SF2 979 WGT 90
Logan, Charles (1930-) SFE 360
Lohrman, Paul (house name)
SFE 361 WGT 90 see also
Paul W. Fairman, Richard
Shaver
Lohwater, A. J. IAC 162
Loki pseud. of Peter Duncan.
IMS 124, 203-4
Lokke, Virgil L. BAA 241
Lombard, Louis (1861-1927) SF1
325
Lombardi, Cynthia (-1942) CSF
125 SF1 325
Lombino, S(alvatore) A. (1926-)
BAA 129 SF2 945 WGT 90 see
also Hunt Collins, Evan Hunter
London, Jack (1876-1916) ACC
128 ALW 33, 85, 88, 216 AOW
67 BAA 71-2 BYS 117, 149-52,
313 CAT 75 COT 120, 148, 192,
220, 231-2, 234, 240, 252 CSC 27
CSF 125-6 ES1 278-9 EXT 1/1
2, 13-4 EXT 3/1 28 EXT 4/1
8 EXT 7/1 11 FAN 168 FBK
16 FFR 120 HFI 92 IAC 162
KAU 127, 186 LEX 437-8 MFW
129 MIH 96 MSF 10, 25, 27, 178,
185, 193, 199, 207, 230, 240, 250,
255, 262, 276 MSM 143 NWO
vi, 36, 118, 126-33, 161-3, 263
OWB 15 PJF 16, 50, 53 PST
89-90, 197, 239, 257, 308, 314
RHN 12, 45, 51, 55, 124, 183 SFB
125 SFD 272 SFE 361 SFH 27,
36 SFS 76 SFW 60 SF1 325
SIH 47, 99 SL1 144-8 SL3 1068-
72 SL5 2159-62 SRB 11 STH
126 VES 211, 266 WIF 53, 223,
233 WSF 20
Long, Amelia Reynolds (1904-)
CSF 28 ES1 279 IAC 162 IMS
23, 199 RFA 69 SFS 76 VES
316 WGT 90
Long, Charles Russell (1904-)
ES1 279 HFI 93 SFE 361 SF1
325 SF2 979
Long, (Mrs.) F. R. WTS 52
Long, Frank Belknap (1903-) ALW
143, 185 AOW 94, 401 BAA 140

Long, Frank Belknap (cont.)
BFP 317-9 COT 90,121,156
CSF 126 ES1 279-80 EXT 3/1
7 FBK 78,81 FFR 120 FL4
1616-20 HFI 92-3 IAC 162-3
IMS 24-5,34,147 ISW 161 KAU
155 LEX 438-9 MIH 23-4,91
RFA 111 RGS 110-1 SFB 58
SFE 361-2 SFS 76-7 SF1 325-
6 SF2 980 SOT 52,73,305,309-
10,347 STH 156,219 TSP 29,
148,190 VES 96,132 WGT 90-1
WIF 78,135,145,158 WSF 241
WTS ix, 23-5, 29-30, 32-3, 35, 42,
45, 48-9, 52, 54, 62, 84, 120, 130,
132 see also Leslie Northern
Long, Gabrielle Margaret Vere
Campbell (1886-1952) ES1 280-1
WGT 91 see also Marjorie
Bowen
Long, George. CSF 126 SF1 326
Long, Haniel Clark (1888-1956)
SF1 326
Long, Huey. STH 114
Long, John. THM 41, 43
Long, Paul. SF1 326
Long, Wesley pseud. of George
O. Smith. RFA 130,134
Longdon, George pseud. of Francis
G. Rayer. IAC 163 SFS 77
Longfellow, Henry Wadsworth.
IAH 48 ISW 214 MSF 146 PJF
13, 42-3, 45 SOT 173
Longley, Alcander. BAA 42
Longley, Mary Theresa (1853-)
SF1 326
Longman, Harold. FFC 56
Longmate, Norman Richard
(1925-) SF1 326 SF2 980
Longo, Chris. HFI 93 SF1 326
Longstreth, Thomas Morris
(1886-) ES1 281 SF1 326 SF2
980
Longueville, Peter. WGT 91
Longworth, Nicholas (1844-90)
SF1 326
Longyear, Barry B. TSF 75-81
Lonnerstrand, Sture (1919-) ES1
281
Lonsdale, Bernard J. AOW 307
Lonsdale, H.M. SF1 326
Lookup, Alexander. BAA 27
CSF 126
Loomis, Noel Miller (1905-69)
BAA 111 ES1 281 HFI 93 IAC
163 SFE 362 SFS 77 SF1 326

SF2 980-1 VES 151,180 WGT
91
Loos, Anita. EXT 6/1 15
Lopate, Phillip. IAC 163
Lopez, Antony. SFE 362
Lopez, Hank. SF1 327
Lopez-Morillas, Juan. BAA 241-2
Loraine, Philip pseud. of Robin
Estridge. SF1 327
Loran, Martin. IAC 163 SFS 77
Lord. EXT 3/2 51 EXT 8/2 53
TBC 47 see also God, Christ,
Jesus
Lord, Beman (1924-) AOW 325
ES1 281 FFR 120 SF1 327 SF2
981
Lord, Glenn. CWD 3 ES1 281
SFS 77 WTS ix
Lord, Jeffrey (house name) SF1
327 see also Roland Green
Lord, Mindret. CWD 33 IAC
163 TSP 144,171,173-8 WTS 69
Lord Commissioner pseud. of
John McCoy. CSF 126
Lorensen, Charles E. CSF 126
SF1 327
Lorentz, Hendrik A. EXT 7/2
34 MIH 109
Lorenz, Jakob. BAA 242
Lorenz, Peter (1944-) LEX 439
Lorenzen, Coral E. (1925-) ES1
281
Lorenzen, Jan A. SF1 327
Lorenzetti. [FUT]
Lorenzini, Carlo see Carlo
Collodi
Lorimer, George Horace. CSF
126 EXT 1/1 14
Lorimer, Norma Octavia (1864-
1948) SF1 327
Loring, Ann. SF1 327
Lorraine, Lilith pseud. of Mary
M. Wright (1894-) CSF 126 ES1
281 IMS 8 ISW 32 SF1 327
Lorraine, Paul (house name) BAA
122 SFE 362 SF1 327 see also
William Henry Bird, John
Glasby, John Russell Fearn,
Arthur Roberts
Lorraine, Walter. FFC 57 STH
270
Lorre, Peter. STH 229
Lory, Robert Edward (1936-) HFI
93 IAC 163 SFS 77 SF1 327-8
SF2 981
Lot. KVT 50

Lothar, Ernst. CSF 126 SF1 328
Lotman, Jurij. MSF 70, 74
Lott, Stanley Makepeace. IAC 163 SFE 364 SF1 340
Loubere, Leo. BAA 184
Louden, Leo. IAC 163
Loudon, Jane Webb (1807-58) AOW 12, 25 CSF 126 SFE 364-5 SF1 328
Loughlin, Richard L(awrence) (1907-) ES1 281 IAC 163 SFS 77 SF1 328 SF2 981
Lougy, Robert E. BAA 242
Louis, Gustave. BAA 184
Louis XIV. VFS 62
Louis XV. [FUT]
Louis XVI. ISW 91
Louit, Robert. JGB 12
Lounsberry, Lionel. SF1 328
Loutrel, Anna Gregson. BAA 131
Louvancour, Henri. BAA 285
Louys, Pierre (1870-1925) FL1 48-50
Love, E. C. IMS 37
Love, Edmund George (1912-) FFC 171 SF1 328 SF2 981
Love, Joseph L. BAA 242
Lovecraft, H(oward) P(hillips) (1890-1937) ALW 55, 59, 121, 136, 141-3, 180, 184-5 AOW 6, 89, 94, 106-7, 342, 349, 352, 358, 394, 396, 401, 404 BFP 320-35 BYS 45, 146, 176-8 CAT 22 COT 7-8, 18, 67, 93-6, 137-9, 111, 242, 259, 291-2, 298 CSC 230 CSF 60, 126-7 CWD 3-4, 13-4, 17, 25, 27, 29, 47, 53-4, 56-8, 61 CWN 35, 46 ES1 281-5 EXT 1/2 24, 35-7 EXT 2/2 22 EXT 3/1 1-25, 27-8 EXT 4/2 25 EXT 5/1 3-4, 15-6 EXT 6/2 22 EXT 7/2 38-9, 42 EXT 9/2 61-2 EXT 10/1 44 EXT 10/2 107 FBK 7, 12-3, 19, 63, 65, 69, 74-8, 80-1, 85, 143-4, 146-7, 154 FFR 120 FLR 9, 12-3, 15, 19, 38, 42, 60-1 FL1 203-6, 431-5 FL4 1621-8 IAC 163-4 IAH 52-3, 141 IMS 3, 16, 18-25, 30-1, 66, 68, 75-6, 83, 93, 107, 109-11, 123, 133-4, 189, 219 INT 7, 68-9, 71, 73, 77-8 ISW 19, 26, 111, 159, 178, 223-6 KAU 194, 198-9 KWS 138 LEX 439-41 LTN 262 MFW 19 MIH 79-80 MSF 8, 68, 141 MSM 37, 74, 128, 304 NWO 19, 51, 261-3 OWB 79, 81-2 PJF 54 PST 178-81, 187, 198, 207, 246, 249, 259, 265, 281, 318 RFA 39, 41, 116 RGS 111-3 RSG 9 SFA 85 SFB 21, 56-9 SFD 275, 288 SFE 365 SFH 36-7, 65, 167, 169 SFN 60 SFS 77 SFW 15, 70, 131-7, 142 SF1 328-9 SIH 32-3 SIN 14, 19 SL1 97-101 SL3 1284-8 SL4 1973-7 SOI xiv SOT 52, 68, 73-4, 108, 135, 290, 293, 296, 304-5, 308-9, 321-3, 326, 328, 334, 338-42, 347-8 SRB 72, 80-1, 88, 269 STH 152, 249, 252-3 TSF 53 TSP 34 VES 137, 139, 142, 144, 273, 280, 313-4, 316, 338 WAA 16, 94-6, 243 WGT 91-2 WIF 18, 38, 75-80, 135, 158, 206, 224, 253, 288 WSF 44, 69, 76, 135, 296-7, 386 WTS ix, 4, 13-5, 20-35, 37-44, 46-52, 55-8, 76, 78-80, 82, 84, 92, 106, 120-1, 123-6, 128-9, 131-2 see also Lawrence Appleton, Houdini, John T. Jones, Henry Paget-Lowe, Ward Phillips, Ames Dorrance Rowley, Edgar Softly, Theobald, Lewis Theobald Jr., Albert Frederic Willie
Lovejoy, Arthur O. BAA 184 KAU 222-3, 225
Lovejoy, Jack. FFC 190
Lovelace, Delos Wheeler (1894-1967) CSF 127 HFI 93 SF1 329 SF2 981-2
Lovell, A. C. B. EXT 1/2 32
Lovell, (Sir) Bernard. IAC 164 POE 290
Lovell, James. SFB 72
Lovell, Marc pseud. of Mark McShane (1930-) SF1 329
Lovell, Tom. TSP 22
Loveman, Samuel. EXT 3/1 10, 18, 24 IMS 25 WIF 135
Lovesey, Andrew (1941-) SFE 365
Lovett, Margaret Rose (1915-) FFC 56 SF1 329
Lovin, Roger. IAC 164
Low, (Prof.). WSF 265
Low, Archibald Montgomery (1888-1956) CSF 127 ES1 285 IMS 96, 99 SFE 366 SF1 329 SOT 377 VES 71
Low, David. COT 120
Low, Joseph. FFC 131, 135

Low, Judah (1525?-1609) SFB 53
Lowe, Arthur. SF1 329
Lowe, Charles (1848?-1931) POE
184-6 SF1 329
Lowell, Amy. EXT 10/2 114
Lowell, Jan. SF1 329
Lowell, Percival (1855-1916)
ACE 19 AC2 17 ALW 109,122
BYS 141,163,168 COT 65 EXT
1/1 3 EXT 5/2 37-41, 43-4, 46-
7 EXT 7/1 27 HID 51 IAC 164
MIH 27 MSF 260 OSR 229-47
RBY 109 SFH 118 SFW 61
SOI 50-1 TJB 48 VES 70, 80,
97 VFS 140,142-4,197-8 WSF
328
Lowell, Robert. SF1 329
Lowenell, Johann Wilhelm. SF1
329
Lowenkopf, Shelly. IAC 164 SFS
77
Lowes, John Livingston. MSM
125 WIF 183
Lowndes, Marie Belloc (1868-
1947) CSF 127 ES1 285 EXT
2/1 14 SF1 329
Lowndes, Robert A(ugustine)
W(ard) (1916-) ALW 156,180,
184 AOW 145 ASF 119-20 BFP
336 COT 265,297 ES1 285
ETN 44 FBK 85 HFI 93-4 IAC
164 IAH 49-51, 65-7 IMS 23,
33, 45, 83-4, 106, 110, 115, 128,
131, 142-3, 154, 160-1, 168, 183,
185, 188-93, 199, 205, 209-10,
214, 216, 223, 225, 244, 246, 248-
51 ISW xii, 118-9, 131, 162, 277
LEX 441-2 MIH 39, 95-7 RFA
60 SFD 83 SFE 366 SFS 77
SFW 293, 393, 401 SF1 329-30
SF2 982 SOT 182, 241, 252 STH
249, 265 TJB 4, 15, 33-4 TSP
150 WFS 32, 34, 51-2, 58, 71-2,
95, 97, 116, 192, 230-1 WGT 92
WIF 113 WSF 74, 123, 138, 144,
146, 188, 195, 231 WTS 30, 53
see also Arthur Cooke, Paul
Dennis Lavond, John MacDougal
Lowry, C. B. BAA 242
Lowry, Robert. IAC 164
Lowther, George Francis (1913-
75) CSF 127 SF1 330
Luban, Milton (1909-56) ES1 285
SF1 330
Lubbock, Percy. ALW 231
Lubin, David. BAA 63
Lubin, Leonard. FFC 19
Lubke, Anton. POE 240
Lucas, Charles (1769-1854) CSF
127 SF1 330
Lucas, Edward Verrall (1868-
1938) BAA 58 CSF 85 SF1 330
Lucas, Frank Laurence (1894-
1967) CSF 127 SFE 366
Lucas, George (1944-) ETN 10,
104 FFR 120 HFI 94 KAU 43,
228, 237 KWS 143 OMN 11-2,
14, 58, 74, 94, 99, 167, 187-92,
221-3, 237, 269, 271, 291, 293
SFE 366 SFH 103-4 SRB 59
TRB 112 WSF 370, 372-3 YTS
20-1
Lucas, Mary R. EXT 10/1 34
Lucas, Reginald Jaffray (1865-
1914) SF1 330
Lucas, Saint John Welles. CSF
127
Lucatelli, Luigi. CSF 127
Luce, Henry. IAH 141 TSP 195
Lucian. BAA 82 SF1 330
Lucian (of Samosata). ACC 136
ALW 32, 41, 47, 95 AOW 11, 13
ASF 24 BYS 10, 58-61, 79 CAT
69, 104, 106, 140 COT 31, 53
EXT 2/1 20 EXT 7/2 34 FTF
16-7, 27 IAC 164 IMS 2 MFW
282 MIH 35 MSF 5, 10, 12, 25,
54, 74, 87-8, 97-8, 107, 116, 211,
219 MSM 29, 127-8, 203-5, 305
PST 16, 18, 23, 209, 221 RAH
229 SFB 13, 29-30, 41, 70, 74
SFE 366-7 SFH 6, 117 SFN 32
SFS 77 SIH 6, 105, 107 SOI 43
VES 79, 155, 224, 260 WAA 17,
20, 28-9, 170 WIF 30 WSF 13,
328 see also Loukianos
Lucientes, Francisco Jose De
Goya Y (1746-1828) EXT 6/1 7
Lucie-Smith, (John) Edward
(McKenzie) (1933-) ALW 38
AOW 295 IAC 164 SFE 367
Lucifer. ASF 213-4 ATA 41
INT 114 LTN 64-5 SHL 61
TBC 16 TJB 53 TSO 53 see
also Devil, Satan, Mephistopheles
Luckmann, Thomas. KAU 85
Lucky, Robert Montfort. SF1 330
Lucretius. NDA 191
Ludlam, Harry. ES1 285 SF1
330
Ludlow, Edmund (1898-) BAA
141 ES1 286 SFE 367 SF1 330

Ludlow, Phill. SF1 330
Ludtke, Franz. BAA 242
Ludwig, Albert. BAA 242
Ludwig, Boris. CSF 127 SF1 330
Ludwig, Edward William (1920-) COT 216 HFI 94 IAC 164 SF1 330 SF2 982
Ludwig, R. M. EXT 9/2 39
Ludz, Peter Christian. BAA 242
Lugosi, Bela. FBK 48,51 SFB 8-9 SFH 101 SIH 22-5 WAA 88 WSF 308 YTS 24
Luif, Kurt (1942-) LEX 442
Luigi, Belli. CSF 127 SF1 330
Lukacs, Georg. CAT 91-3 MSF 14, 73, 222
Lukeman, Alex see Alex Dain
Lukermann, Fred E. BAA 255
Lukodyanov, Isai B. (1913-) IAC 164 SFS 77, 120 SF1 331 SF2 982-3
Lull, (Rev.) D. BAA 71 SF1 331
Lull, Ramon. MFW 193
Lum, Peter (1911-) ES1 286
Lumley, Benjamin (1812-75) BAA 30 CSF 127 SF1 331 WGT 92 see also Hermes
Lumley, Brian (1937-) FBK 81 HFI 94 IAC 164 SF1 331
Lumley, William. EXT 3/1 3 IAC 164 IMS 30, 110 WTS 42
Luna, Kris (house name) SF1 331 see also William Henry Bird, David O'Brien
Lunacharsky, Anatoly V. MSF 262
Lunan, A. Duncan (1945-) IAC 164 LEX 442-3 VES 157 VFS 173-4
Lunatic, (Sir) Humphrey pseud. of Francis Gentleman. SF1 331
Lunatic, Nicholas. SF1 331
Lund, Ivar. SF1 331
Lundberg, Knud (1920-) ES1 286 SF1 331
Lunde, David. IAC 164
Lundin, Claes (1825-1908) FTF 41 SFE 367 SL4 1637-40 WAA 43, 144
Lundwall, Sam J. (1941-) ALW 30 AOW 80, 349 BAA 184 BRS 8 BYS 266, 283, 304 ES1 286 FFR 120 FRN 20-1 HFI 94 IAC 164 KAU 23, 158 LEX 443-4 MFW 28, 161 NWO 196 RBY 40, 83 RGS 113 SFE 367 SFH 150, 239 SF1 331 SF2 983 SL1 105-8, 153-6 SL2 956-9 SL3 1110-3, 1344-7 SL4 1592-5, 1637-40, 1817-20 SL5 2339-42 SRB 72, 505 TSF 247
Lunn, Brian Holdsworth (1893-) CSF 81 SF1 331
Lunn, Hugh Kingsmill (1889-1949) ES1 286 WGT 92-3 see also Hugh Kingsmill
Lunn, Janet Louise (1928-) FFC 165 SF1 331
Lunts, Lev N. (1901-24) EXT 10/2 75 MSF 254 SL1 378-82 SL5 2373-7
Lupoff, Pat. IAH 1, 63 MIH 7
Lupoff, Richard A. (1935-) AOW 221, 291, 349 BAA 154 BFP 337-8 BYS 141, 154, 178 DTS 36 ES1 286 EXT 10/1 34 FL4 1869-71 FRN 69-70 HFI 94 IAC 164 IAH 1, 63 LEX 444-5 MIH 7 RFA vii, xxii RGS 113-4 SFE 367-8 SF1 331 SF2 983-4 SRB 78, 117 SV2 3-7 SV3 32-43 WAA 243, 245
Lupton, J. H. BAA 242
Lupton, Thomas. BAA 2
Lurgan, Lester pseud. of Mabel Winfred Knowles. CSF 127 SFE 369 SF1 332
Luria, S. E. SFH 241
Luska, Sidney pseud. of Henry Harland. CSF 127 SF1 332
Lusty, G. H. CSF 128 SF1 332
Luther, Martin (1483-1546) ASF 104 CUA 23
Luther, Ray. ES1 286
Lutwin, Theodore. IMS 34
Lvov, Arkady. IAC 164
Lvov, Pavel I. MSF 244
Lyall, Edna pseud. of Ada Ellen Bayly. SF1 332
Lyapunov, Boris. SIH 75
Lyell, (Sir) Charles (1797-1875) AOW 87 MFW 187 MSF 227 TJB 42
Lyle, Alva E. RHN 6-7, 78, 195-6
Lyle, David. IAC 164
Lyle, Peter. HFI 94
Lymington, John pseud. of John Newton Chance (1911-) ES1 286 FFR 121 HFI 94-5 ISW 225-6

Lymington, John (cont.)
SFE 368 SF1 332 VES 134
Lynch, (Col.) Arthur Alfred
(1861-1934) BAA 88 CSF 128
SF1 332
Lynch, Arthur T. SFD 24
Lynch, Hal. ASF 246 IAC 164
Lynch, Jane Gaskell (1941-)WGT
93 see also Jane Gaskell
Lynch, John Gilbert Bohun (1884-
1928) ES1 286 SFE 368 SF1 332
Lynch, Miriam. SF1 332
Lynch, Patricia. FFC 100
Lynde, Francis. EXT 1/1 14
Lyndon, Barre pseud. of Alfred
Edgar. HFI 95 SF1 332
Lynds, Dennis (1924-) SF1 332
SF2 859 WGT 93 see also
Maxwell Grant, Michael Collins
Lyne, Standford. IAC 165
Lynen, John F. NWO 36-7
Lynes, Joseph Russell, Jr.
(1910-) SF1 332
Lynn, David. SF1 333

Lynn, Elizabeth A. (1946-) FL1
275-81 IAC 165 LEX 445 LTN
18
Lyon, Edmund David. CSF 128
SF1 333
Lyon, Harris Merton. STH 38-9
Lyon, Jean. BAA 184
Lyon, Laurence Gill. BAA 285
Lyon, Lyman R. pseud. of L.
Sprague de Camp. RFA 66
Lyons, Edgar Albion. BAA 105
CSF 128 SF1 333
Lyons, John O. BAA 242
Lyons, Victor Sam. SF1 333
Lys, Christian pseud. of Percy
Brebner. CSF 128
Lysenko, T. D. CSC 111 SFH
139
Lytle, Andrew Nelson (1902-)
CSF 128 SF1 333 SF2 984
Lytle, B. J. IAC 165
Lyttleton, George (1709-73) SF1
333

M

M. B. K. EXT 10/1 23
M. E. W. S. BAA 260
M. L. BAA 239
Maas, Dorothy. FFC 193
Mabbott, Thomas. EXT 3/1 7, 24
Mabie, Hamilton Wright (1846-
1916) SF1 334
Maby, Joseph Cecil. CSF 128
ES2 287 SF1 334
McAlister, Patricia. IAC 165
McAllister, Bruce Hugh (1946-)
AAL 29-30 BAA 153 BYS 304
HFI 95 IAC 165 SFE 368 SFS
77 SF1 352 SF2 993-4
MacAlpine, Margaret. FFC 96

Macao, Marshall. SF1 334
MacApp, C. C. pseud. of Carroll
M. Capps (1917-71) HFI 95 IAC
165 LEX 446 SFE 368 SFS 77-
8 SF1 334 VES 82
Macardle, Dorothy (1889-) CSF
128 ES2 287 SF1 334
MacArthur, Arthur (1896-) CSF
128 SF1 334
MacArthur, (Gen.) George. WFS
15
Macartney, Clem. SF1 334
Macassey, Kenneth. BAA 105-6
Macauley, Charles Raymond
(1871-1934) SF1 334

Macaulay, Clarendon pseud. of
Walter Marsham Adams. SF1
334
Macaulay, Rose (1881-1958) CSF
128 EXT 6/2 42 EXT 9/2 39,
45 FAN 145 SFE 368 SF1 334
Macaulay, Thomas Babington.
MFW 5, 9 MSF 42 POE 58, 81
Macauley, Charles R. CSF 15,
128
Macauley, George W. EXT 3/1
12, 24
McAuley, Jacquelin Rollit (1925-)
SFE 368 SF1 352
Macauley, L. BAA 95 SF1 334
Macauley, Robie. WFS 54
MacBeth, George. EXT 8/1 17
IAC 165 SFS 78
McBride, Melchior. CSF 128
McBroom, R. Curtis (1910-)
SF2 881 see also Nat Dring
MacBryde, James. FBK 65
McCabe, Joseph. BAA 118-9
McCaffrey, Anne (1926-) AAL 47
ALW 212 AOW 221 ASF 127,
146 BFP 339-40 BYS 305 COT
166, 180 CSC 33 ES2 287 ETN
2 FFC 89 FFR 121 FTF 118-9
HFI 95 IAC 165 KAU 59, 78, 80-
4 LEX 460-2 LTN 228, 264
MFW 33, 142, 145, 235 PJF 33
RAH 111 RGS 117-8, 218 SFD
75 SFE 368-9 SFH 186 SFW
3 SF1 352 SF2 994 SL2 605-7
SL4 1917-21 SRB 348, 369, 374,
505 VES 92, 187, 199, 207-8
WAA 154, 165, 244 WFS 212
WSF 168, 175, 187, 235, 246, 262,
387
McCain, George Nox. CSF 128
McCall, Marie (1909-) ES2 287
McCall, Robert. [FUT] SRB 43
McCann, Arthur pseud. of John
W. Campbell. COT 65
McCann, Edson pseud. of Frederik
Pohl, Lester del Rey. ALW 217
AOW 221 ISW 260-2 MIH 53
SFE 369 SFN 105 WFS 225
McCardell, Roy L. IAC 165
McCarthy, Eugene. ETN 105
McCarthy, (Sen.) Joseph R. ASF
277-8 CAT 71 COT 140-1 CWN
4 ETN 34, 39, 48 EXT 8/1 2, 6
EXT 10/2 86 IAH 114 KVT 35
LTN 214 MIH 34, 121 RHN 97
SFN 99 TJB 23 WFS 63

MacCarthy, Justin Huntly (1860-
1936) CSF 128 SF1 352
McCarthy, Mary Theresa. BAA
117
McCarthy, Shaun Lloyd (1928-)
see Desmond Cory
McCarthy, Shawna. ASF 21, 41,
253-4, 256, 264
McCauley, Harold W. (1913-)
COT 183 ES2 287 VES 230, 287
WSF 115
McCauley, Motly Ranke. CSF
128 SF1 353
McCay, Winsor. VES 324-5
McClary, Thomas Calvert. AOW
107 CSF 128 ES2 287 HFI 95
IMS 117 LEX 462 RFA 15, 20,
50 SFE 369 SF1 353 SOT 175
SRB 302 WGT 94 WSF 66 see
also Calvin Peregoy
McClelland, Mary Greenaway
(1853-95) CSF 128 SF1 353
WGT 94
McClintic, Winona. IAC 165-6
SFS 78
McClintock, Michael William.
BAA 285 FHT 67 SL5 2396-401,
2411-5
McCloskey, Robert. FFC 127
McCloud, Richard. IAC 166
McCloy, Helen Worrell (1904-)
ES2 287 IAC 166 SFS 78
MacClure, Victor (1887-1963)
CSF 129 ES2 287 SFE 369 SF1
335 WIF 54
McClusky, Thorpe. COT 125, 291
IAC 166 VES 193
Maccoll, Hugh. AOW 44 BAA 40
CSF 129 SFE 369 SF1 335
McComas, J(esse) Francis (1910-)
ALW 161-2, 175, 214-5 AOW 287,
293 BYS 244 CSC 170 CSF 97
ES2 287-8 ETN 31, 37, 56 EXT
3/1 27 EXT 5/1 10 EXT 7/2
46 EXT 8/1 5-6 FFR 121 HID
6, 62, 154 IAC 58, 130, 166 IAH
24-5, 27, 29, 35, 81-4 ISW vi, 131,
158 MSM 33, 33, 35, 96, 297 RFA
56, 169 SFD 5, 309 SFE 369
SFS 56, 78 SFW 395 SF1 353
SOT 81, 180 SRB 13, 234, 304
STH 102-3 TJB 5 WGT 94 WIF
25, 114, 226 WSF 130, 170, 385,
389 see also Webb Marlowe
McCombs, Larry. DTS 7, 30
McConnel, Gerald. VES 213

MacConnell, Colum. HFI 95
McConnell, James V. (1925-)
ES2 288 IAC 166 SFS 78 TPS
175-96
McCord, Peter B. (-1908) CSF
129 SF1 353
MacCormac, John. IAC 166 OWB
76
McCormack, Ford. IAC 166
McCormack, Win. LTN 128, 268
McCowan, Archibald. CSF 129
SF1 353
McCoy, John. BAA 55-6 SF1
353 WGT 94 see also Lord
Commissioner
McCoy, Nathaniel P. CSF 129
McCrea, Paul. BAA 107
MacCreigh, James pseud. of
Frederik Pohl. IAC 166 ISW
193-4 SFS 78, 83
McCrib, Theophilus pseud. of
Henry Boyle Lee. BAA xvi
CSF 129 SF1 356
McCullough, Ken. ALW 212 IAC
166
McCully, Emily. FFC 25, 128,
146, 165
MacCurdy, Edward. EXT 6/2 48
McCutchan, Philip Donald (1920-)
BAA 146 ES2 288 SFE 369
SF1 353 SF2 994
McCutchen, Duval. BAA 99
McCutcheon, Elizabeth. BAA
242
McCutcheon, George Barr (1866-
1928) SF1 353 WGT 94
MacDaniel, Charles pseud. of
Charles M. Garrison. SF1 335
McDaniel, David Edward pseud.
of Ted Johnstone (1939-77) BAA
160 IAC 166 ES2 288 HFI 95
SFE 369 SF1 353-4 SF2 994-5
WGT 94
McDermot, Murtagh. AOW 13,
25 CSF 129 MSM 207-8 SFB
73 SFE 370 SF1 354
McDermott, Aubrey. IMS 8-9
McDermott, Paul. IMS 34 WGT
94
MacDonald, Anson pseud. of
Robert A. Heinlein. ALW 173
ASF 85 COT 245 CYR 9, 35
HID 5, 22-3, 34, 52, 123, 193-4
IAC 166 OWB 11, 93, 95 RFA
84, 86-7, 91, 94, 96, 104, 106, 108,
112, 176-7 SFB 100 SFD 145,

147, 150, 154-5, 162, 315, 319
SFH 54 SFS 78 STH 10-1 VES
117 WIF 155 WSF 99-100
McDonald, Bernard (1923-) see
Brian Macdonnaill
MacDonald, Betty. FFC 148
McDonald, Christie V. BAA 242
MacDonald, Donald K. SF1 335
McDonald, Dwight. CWN 27-8
McDonald, Edward Richard
(1873-) SF1 354 WGT 94 see
also Raymond McDonald
McDonald, Francis Charles
(1874-1952) CSF 129 SF1 335
MacDonald, Frederika. ES2 288
McDonald, George (1824-1905)
AOW 396 BYS 102 CSF 129
ES2 288 FBK 88-9, 91, 112, 126
FFC 7, 49-50 FL1 63-5 FL2
880-6 FL3 1241-5, 1271-5,
1280-5 FL4 1629-32 HFI 96
SFE 370 SF1 335, 583 SOI 4, 6
SRB 22, 269 STH 7 THM 38
VES 143 WIF 40
McDonald, Greville. FFC 76
MacDonald, John D. (1916-) AOW
222 BAA 124 CSC 33 DTS 23
ES2 288-9 EXT 7/2 47 EXT
8/1 6 FFR 121 HFI 96 IAC
166 LEX 446-7 SFD 66 SFE
370 SFH 56 SFS 78-9 SF1 335
SF2 984 SL2 883-7 TSP 28
WGT 94 see also John Lan
McDonald, Leslyn. HID 5
MacDonald, Philip (1896-) EXT
8/1 5 IAC 166 SFS 79 TSP
145 WGT 94
McDonald, Raymond pseud. of
Edward McDonald, Raymond
A. Leger. CSF 129
MacDonald, Robert MacLaughlan
(1874-) CSF 129 SF1 335
MacDonald, Ross. SFH 56
MacDonell, Archibald Gordon
(1895-1941) WGT 94 see also
Neil Gordon
Macdonnaill, Brian pseud. of
Bernard McDonald. SF1 335
McDonnell, T. P. EXT 6/1 19
MacDougal, John pseud. of James
Blish, Robert A. W. Lowndes.
SFE 370
McDougald, Roman. WTS 58
MacDougall, Jeannie Craig. OWB
78

Macdougall, Margaret (-1943)
see Margaret Armour
MacDougall, Ranald. KAU 126
McDougall, Walter Hugh (1858-1938) CSF 129 SF1 354
McDougall, William. BAA 86
McDougle, William. ES2 289
McDowell, Emmett. IAC 166 SFS 79
Mace, Elisabeth. FFC 43,165
McElhiney, Gaile Churchill. BAA 114 SF1 354
McElroy, Joseph. HFI 96
McEvoy, Seth. IAC 166
MacEwen, Gwendolyn Margaret (1941-) SF1 335 SF2 984
MacEwen, Mary E. SF1 335
Macey, Peter. SFE 370 SF1 335
MacFadden, Bernarr. COT 6 TSP 68 WSF 47
MacFadden, Gary. BAA 242
MacFadyen, A., Jr. IAC 166
MacFadyen, Virginia. SF1 335
Macfall, Chambers Haldane (1860-1928) SF1 335
Macfarlane, Claire (1906-) SF1 335
MacFarlane, Stephen. FFC 182 see also John Kier Cross
MacFarlane, Wallace. AAL 116 IAC 166-7 RFA 175 SFS 79 VES 274
McGarry, Jim. SF1 354
McGaughy, Dudley Dean. ES2 289 WGT 94-5 see also Dean Owen
McGavin, Moyra. FFC 84
McGee, Jane Agorn. IAC 132, 167
McGhan, Barry Robert (1939-) AOW 362,365,369 SF1 354 SF2 995 SRB 463 TSF 82-96
McGhan, Harlan Perry. SRB 130-214,515
McGillis, Roderick. FL2 880-6 FL3 1238-40,1369-71,1392-5 FL4 1784-6
McGinley, Phyllis. FFC 7
McGivern, Patrick. IAC 167
McGivern, William Peter (1927-) ES2 289 SFE 370 VES 102 WGT 95 WIF 120 WSF 116
McGlathery, James M. FL1 387-90 FL2 831-5,970-2 FL3 1234-7 FL4 1718-23
McGowan, Roger A. KAU 151

McGowen, Thomas (1927-) FFC 104,122,194 SF1 354 SF2 995
McGrady, (Rev.) Thomas (1863-) BAA 64 CSF 129 SF1 354
McGrath, Thomas (1916-) BAA 131 ES2 289
McGraw, Eloise. FFC 165
MacGregor, Ellen (1906-54) AOW 325 ES2 289 IAC 167 SF1 336
MacGregor, Geddes pseud. of John Geddes MacGregor. BAA 124
MacGregor, James Murdoch (1925-) BAA 122,146 BFP 341-2 ES2 289 EXT 6/2 51 SF2 995-6 SRB 320-1 WGT 95 see also J. T. McIntosh
Macgregor, John. SF1 336
MacGregor, John Geddes (1909-) SF1 336 SF2 984-5
McGregor, Reginald James. IAC 167 SFS 79 SF1 354
MacGregor, Richard. ES2 289 SFE 370 SF1 336
McGuire, John Joseph (1917-) COT 244 ES2 289 IAC 167 IAH 39 RFA 200 SFB 19 SFD 16 SFE 370 SFS 79 SF1 354 STH 157
McGuire, Patrick L. ATA 23 FL1 137-42 FL3 1160-3, 1250-6 FL4 1607-10 IAC 167 JHN 61 SL2 813-8 SL3 1407-12 SL5 2506-10
McHale, John. BAA 184 IAC 167 RZY 73
MacHarg, William Briggs (1872-1951) AOW 52 EXT 1/1 5 SF1 336 STH 123-6,132-3,138
McHargue, Georgess. ES2 290 FFC 68 IAC 167 SF1 354,583 SF2 995 WGT 95
Machen, Arthur (1863-1947) BYS 44 CSF 129-30 CWD 60 ES2 290-1 EXT 3/1 22 EXT 5/1 4 EXT 9/2 62 FBK 13,69-70,80 FLR 15 FL2 642-5 FL4 1633-9,1895-7,1922-5 HFI 96 IAC 167 ISW 223 SFB 57 SFE 370-1 SF1 336 SOT 309 THM 3 WGT 95 WIF 73,77,206,246
McHenry, James (1785-1845) CSF 130 WGT 95
Machiavelli, Niccolo (1469-1527) HEN 14 MFW 268 RHN 57 SIH 63,65 TJB 16,20

Machovcova, Marketa. BAA 184

Macht, Norman L. IAC 167

McHugh, Christine. BAA 285

McHugh, Vincent (1904-) AOW 85,107,222 CSF 130 ES2 291 EXT 8/1 5 HFI 96 RAH 225, 227,230,232-3 SFE 372 SFN 23,40 SF1 354 SL2 991-4

McIlraith, Frank. CSF 130 SF1 354

McIlvaine, Charles (1840-1909) WGT 95

McIlwain, David (1921-) BAA 154 BFP 343-4 ES2 291-2 IMS 200, 251 LEX 462-3 SF2 987 SRB 323 WGT 96 see also Charles Eric Maine

McIlwraith, Dorothy. COT 184 ES2 292 FBK 83 ISW 131 SFW 419 WIF 117 WSF 296 WTS 6, 43-4, 46-7, 56, 58-60, 74, 119, 129-30

McIlwraith, Maureen Mollie (1922-) SF2 945 see also Mollie Hunter

McInnes, Graham Campbell (1912-70) ES2 292 HFI 96 SFE 372 SF1 355 SF2 995

McIntosh, J. T. pseud. of James Murdoch MacGregor. ALW 212, 219 AOW 222 BYS 262,295 EXT 8/2 66 FFR 122 FTF 132 HFI 96 IAC 167 IAH 105-6 ISW 64-6,169 KAU 61,94 LEX 463 RGS 118-9 SFD 86 SFE 372-3 SFS 79 SF1 355 SOT 201 SRB 320-1 STH 120 VES 176, 180,182,208 WSF 172

McIntosh, Kenneth. WGT 96 see also Kent Casey

McIntosh, Kinn Hamilton (1930-) WGT 96

MacIntyre, Alasdair. EXT 6/1 18

McIntyre, Margaret A. SF1 355

McIntyre, Vonda N. (1948-) ALW 212 BFP 345 COT 197 FFR 122 [FJT] HFI 96 IAC 167 LEX 464 LTN 131,192,228,242, 259,269 RGS 119 SFD 265 SFE 373 SL2 739-43 SRB 372 TSF 190-3 WSF 262

MacIsaac, Frederick John (1886-1940) CSF 130 ES2 292 HFI 96 SFE 373 SF1 337

McIver, G. M. BAA 52 CSF 130 SF1 355

McIvor, Allan. CSF 130 SF1 355

Mack, Thomas. CSF 130 STH 148

MacKail, J. W. WBW 10,34

Mackarness, Matilda Anne (1826-81) SF1 337

Mackay, Charles. BAA 30 IAC 167

MacKay, Donald. CSF 130

McKay, Harold B. VES 103

Mackay, (James Alexander) Kenneth (1859-1935) CSF 130 SF1 337

McKay, Lewis Hugh (1897-)WGT 96 see also Hugh Matheson

Mackay, Mary (1855-1924) CSF 130 WGT 96 see also Marie Corelli

MacKaye, Harold Steele (1866-1928) CSF 130 SF1 337

McKeag, Ernest Lionel (1896-) SF2 961 see also John King

McKechnie, Neil Kenneth (1873-) SF1 355

MacKellar, William (1914-) FFC 32, 36,107,148,190 SF1 337

Mackelworth, Ronald Walter (1930-) HFI 97 IAC 167 SFE 373 SFS 79 SF1 337 SF2 985

McKenna, Richard (1913-64) AOW 223,294 CSC 97 ES2 292 ETN 120 EXT 8/1 16 HFI 97 IAC 167-8 ISW 127-8 MIH 99 SFE 373 SFS 79 SF1 355 SF2 996 SF1 308-12 TPS 285-300 WGT 96

McKenna, Stephen (1888-1967) BAA 97 CSF 130 SF1 355 SF2 996

McKenney, Kenneth. HFI 97

Mackenroth, Nancy J. HFI 97 IAC 168

McKenty, Jack. IAC 168 SFS 80

McKenzie, A. R. (1908-) ES2 292

McKenzie, Allan. BAA 242

McKenzie, Barbara. LTN 251

Mackenzie, (Sir Edward Montague) Compton (1883-1970) BAA 134 ES2 292 EXT 6/2 51 SFE 373 SF1 337 SF2 985

McKenzie, Ellen Kindt. ES2 292 FFC 56,178 SF1 355

MacKenzie, Garry. FFC 129, 132-3,136,181

MacKenzie, Jeanne. AOW 349 SRB 83 TSF 249

MacKenzie, Jonathan Blake. IAC 168 SFS 80

MacKenzie, Nigel. ES2 292-3 SF1 337

MacKenzie, Norman Ian. AOW 349 ES2 293 SRB 83 TSF 249

McKesson, Charles L. CSF 130 SF1 355

McKettrig, Seaton pseud. of Randall Garrett. IAC 168 SFS 80

Mackey, Douglas A. SL1 354-7 SL2 744-8 SL4 1999-2002

McKie, Angus. [FUT] VES 75, 170, 174

Mackie, J. L. BAA 242

McKillip, Patricia Anne (1948-) FFC 32, 43-4 FL2 566-70 FL4 1813-20 HFI 97 SF1 355 SF2 996 SRB 270

McKim, Audrey. FFC 134

McKimmey, James. IAC 168 SFS 80

Mackin, Edward. ES2 293 IAC 168 SFS 80

McKinley, Mary C. IAC 168

McKinley, Robin. FFC 50

MacKinnon, Allan. ES2 293 SF1 337

McKinstry, Lohr. SF1 355

MacKintosh, Elizabeth (1896-1952) WGT 96

Mackintosh, Helen K. AOW 307

Macklin, Edward. SFS 80

Macklin, John. ES2 293

McKnight, John P. IAC 168

MacKnight, Ninon. FFC 35

Mackworth, John Dolben (1887-1939) CSF 130 SF1 337

McLachlin, Steve. FFC 118

Maclagan, David T. (1932-) SF1 337

McLandburgh, Florence (1850-) CSF 131 SF1 355

MacLane, Mary (1881-1929) SF1 337

MacLaren, Bernard. ES2 293 SFE 373 SF1 337

McLaren, Florence V. CSF 131 SF1 355

McLaren, (Mrs.) Jack. CSF 131 SF1 356

McLaren, Jack (1887-1954) ES2 293 SF1 356

McLaughlin, Bernard. IAC 168

McLaughlin, Dean (Benjamin, Jr.) (1931-) ALW 212 COT 273 ES2 293 HFI 97 IAC 168 IAH 124-8 LEX 465 RFA 209 SFE 373 SFS 80 SF1 356 SF2 996 WIF 217

McLaughlin, Dennis. VES 327

McLaughlin, Lorrie. FFC 156

McLaughlin, Nathan Monroe. SF1 356

McLaughlin, Richard. EXT 6/1 17, 19

McLaughlin, Venard. ISW 126

MacLean, Alistair (1922-) ES2 293 WGT 96

MacLean, Charles Agnew. ALW 105 STH 222-3, 225

MacLean, Katherine (1925-) AAL 53, 67, 121 ALW 161 AOW 223 BAA 153, 158 BFP 346 BYS 263 CSC 136-58 ES2 293 ETN 17, 47 FFR 122 FTF 179 HFI 97 IAC 168 ISW 127 LEX 447 MSM 81 RFA 175, 195 SFB 114 SFE 373-4 SFS 80 SF1 337 SF2 985-6 VES 96, 342 WFS 216 see also Charles Dye

MacLeish, Archibald. BAA 242 INT 89-90, 114 MIH 9

MacLennan, Phyllis. AAL 102 IAC 168 SF1 337

MacLeod, Angus M. (1906-) ES2 293 HFI 97 SFE 374 SF1 337-8 SF2 986

McLeod, Emilie. FFC 190

Macleod, Fiona pseud. of William Sharp. CSF 131 FL4 1754-6 SF1 338

Macleod, Joseph Todd Gordon (1903-) CSF 131 SF1 338

MacLeod, Sheila. SFE 374 SF1 338

McLociard, George. ES2 293 PST 159-60, 203, 237, 258, 278

McLoughlin (brothers). ALW 175

McLuhan, Marshall. CSC 68 EXT 9/2 27 FLR 43 LTN 261 MFW 248, 287 NDA 49-51, 206 NWO 12, 24 POE 191, 274 THM 7

McMahon, (Senator) Brian. MSM 224-5

McMahon, Jeremiah. IAC 168 LTN 269 SF1 356

McMahon, Thomas Patrick. HFI
97 SF1 356
McManus, L. BAA 83
MacManus, Seumas (1869-1960)
ES2 293-4 EXT 3/1 12 IAC 168
McMartin, Donald. BAA 63 CSF
131
McMasters, William Henry. CSF
131 SF1 356 SRB 10
McMichael, R. Daniel (1925-)
BAA 144 SF1 356
McMichael, R. David. HFI 97
Macmillan, John Armour. CSF
131 SF1 338
McMorrow, Fred. IAC 169 SFS
80
McMorrow, Thomas. IAC 169
SFS 80 SOT 205
McMorrow, Will. ES2 294 TSP
39
McMurdie, Annie Laurie. SF1
356
McMurray, Clifford. JHN 37, 61
McNail, Stanley. ES2 294
Macnair, Everett W. BAA 184
McNally, Raymond T. (1931-)
AOW 355 SF1 356 SF2 996
McNaught, Kenneth. BAA 242
McNaughton, Brian J. IAC 169
McNaughton, Charles, Jr. SF1
356
McNaughton, Mildred. SF1 356
McNear, Robert. IAC 169
McNeely, J. A. BAA 242
McNeely, Jerry. CSC 281, 286
McNeer, May Yonge (1902-) SF1
356 SF2 996-7
McNeil, (Henry) Everett (1862-
1929) CSF 131 SF1 356
McNeile, Herman Cyril (1888-
1937) SF1 356 WGT 96 see
also Sapper
McNeill, Janet (1907-) FFC 76,
106, 182 SF1 583
McNeillie, John. ES2 294 WGT
97 see also Ian Niall
McNeilly, Wilfred Glassford
(1921-) SF2 805 WGT 97 see
also Peter Saxon
McNelis, James I., Jr. BAA 242
McNelly, Willis Everett (1920-)
AAL 2 AOW 365 BYS 321 FL2
951-4 FL4 1995-8 IAC 127,
134, 169 OSR 193-8, 355 RBY
17-24, 240 RSG 66, 92 SFE 374
SFW 171-8, 251-8, 283-90, 377-

85 SF1 356 SF2 997 SL1 202-
6, 223-7, 288-93 SL2 529-32,
587-90, 595-9, 647-58, 671-5,
687-91, 721-4, 749-55, 840-4
SL3 1156-60, 1261-4, 1323-7
SL4 1764-7, 1784-8 SL5 2311-5
SRB 464, 505 VES 330 VF1 167-
75, 276, 282
MacNie, John (1836-1909) BAA
34 MSF 177 POE 140 WGT 97
see also Ismar Thiusen
McNight, John P. SFS 80
MacOrlan, Pierre. MSF 279
Macowan, Norman. BAA 107
McPhail, Daniel. IMS 69-70, 72,
79-80, 115, 123, 130-1, 145, 151,
153, 214
McPhail, David. FFC 122, 180
McPharlin, Paul. RZY 33
McPhee, John. VFS 225
Macpherson, Donald. CSF 131
SF1 338
Macpherson, Ian. CSF 131 SF1
338
Macpherson, John F. CSF 131
SF1 338
MacQuitty, Bill. VFS 153
MacRae, Donald. EXT 6/1 10
MacReady, R. G. IAC 169
McReynolds, Cliff. [FUT]
McReynolds, Douglas J. FL3
1471-81 SL3 1217-20 SL4 1944-
7, 1954-7, 2042-5 SL5 2324-8,
2451-4
Macrow, Brenda Grace Joan
(1916-) SF1 338
McShane, Mark (1930-) ES2 294
SF2 982 see also Marc Lovell
McSpadden, Joseph Walker (1874-
1970) CSF 131 ES2 294 SF1 357
MacTyre, Paul pseud. of Robert
James Adams (1924-) ES2 294
HFI 98 SFE 374 SF1 338
MacVey, John Wishart (1923-)
ES2 294 SF1 583
MacVicar, Angus (1908-) ES2 294
SF1 338 SF2 986 VES 302
McWilliams, James Aloysius
(1882-) ES2 294 SF1 357
McWilliams, Wilson C. EXT
10/1 30
Macy, John. BAA 243
Madarevic, Vlado. BAA 243
Madariaga, Salvador pseud. of
Salvador de Madariaga y Rojo
(1886-) SF1 338

Madden, Samuel (1686-1765) CSF
131 POE 16 PST 24, 195 SF1
338-9 VES 116
Maddison, Michael. BAA 243
Maddock, Larry pseud. of Jack
Owen Jardine (1931-) HFI 98
LEX 447-8 SFE 374 SF1 339
VES 147
Maddock, Reginald Bertram
(1912-) ES2 294 SF1 339
Maddock, Stephen. CSF 131
Maddocks, Melvin. COT 55 EXT
6/1 17-8
Maddox, Carl. VES 75
Maddux, Rachel (1912-) BAA 131
ES2 294-5 HFI 98 IAC 169 SFE
374 SFS 80 SF1 339
Mader, Friedrich-Wilhelm (1866-
1947) CSF 132 LEX 448 SFE
374 SF1 339
Maderas, John. IMS 34
Madison, Charles A. BAA 243
Madison, J. J. SF1 339
Madle, Robert A. (1920-) ES2 295
IMS 64, 67, 70-3, 82, 84-5, 87, 93,
95, 103, 106, 115-7, 127-8, 136,
142-3, 145, 147, 153, 155-6, 176,
186, 188, 200, 204-5, 213, 222, 233,
235 SRB 96, 126 STH 115 WFS
58 WIF 131
Madler, Johann. FTF 21
Madonia, Gail. IAC 169
Madreyhijo, L. CSF 132
Madsack, Paul. FBK 142
Madsen, Alan L. SF1 339
Madsen, Svend Age. IAC 169
Maestro, Guilio. FFC 31
Maeterlinck, Maurice (1862-1949)
ES2 295 FBK 146 FFC 14
WTS 17
Magalaner, M. EXT 6/1 13, 17-8,
20
Magidoff, Robert (1905-70) ES2
295 FAN 189 IAC 169 SFE
377 SFS 81 SF1 339 SF2 987
Magill, Frank N. SRB 63 TSF
247
Maginn, William (1793-1842) SF1
339
Magnaini, Joe. VES 245
Magnus, Albertus. EXT 6/2 28
IAH 59
Magnus, Leonard Arthur (1879-
1924) BAA 68 SF1 339
Magor, Nancy. SF1 339

Magriska, Helene pseud. of Enid
Florence Brockies. CSF 132
SF1 339
Magritte, Rene. IAC 169 JGB 6
NWO 30
Magroff, R. VES 180
Magroon, Vector. SF1 339
Maguire, Don. CSF 132 SF1 339
Maguire, Gregory. FFC 166
Maguire, John Francis (1815-72)
CSF 132 POE 130-1 SFE 377
SF1 339
Mahaffey, Beatrice (1926-) ASF
118 ES2 295 WIF 112
Maher, Richard Aumerle. SF1
340
Mahl, Hans-Joachim. BAA 184
Mahlman, Maude Mary. WFS
22-3
Mahlmann, Theodor. BAA 243
Mahner-Mons, Hans see Hans
Possendorf
Mahomet. THM 51
Mahoney, Patrick (1911-) ES2 295
Mahr, Kurt (1936-) FFR 123-5
LEX 448-51
Maiden, Cecil. FFC 68
Maiewski, Shirley S. IAC 169
Mailer, Norman. COT 3, 135
ETN 141 IAC 169 JGB 33 LTN
47, 104 NDA 129 NWO 26-31
SFD 66 STF 9-10 VFS 117, 152
WTS 48
Maine, Charles Eric pseud. of
David McIlwain (1921-) ALW
212 AOW 223 BYS 262, 295
CAT 18 FFR 125 HFI 98 IAC
169 IAH 134 ISW 97-100 KAU
20, 146, 184 KWS 148-9, 236
MIH 107-10 SFE 377 SF1 340
SRB 323 STH 89 UFS 4 VES
132, 215
Maine, (Sir) Henry. POE 124
Mair, George Brown (1914-) ES2
295 SF1 340
Mair, Mary. WFS 173
Maitland, Antony. FFC 17, 77
Maitland, Edward (1824-97) BAA
30 CSF 132 EXT 7/1 10, 16
MSF 177 POE 139 SFE 378
SF1 340
Malaguti, Ugo (1945-) ES2 295
LEX 451-2 LTN 262 SFB 145
SL4 1863-5 WAA 235

229

Malamud, Bernard. FL4 1640-
4 IAC 169 SFS 81 STH 45
Malaquais, Jean (1908-) SF1 340
Malaval, Suzanne. IAC 169
Malcolm, David. CWN 27
Malcolm, Donald (1930-) ES2 295
HFI 98 IAC 169 SFE 378 SFS
81
Malcolm, Ed. SF1 340
Malcolm, Mary (1918-) SF1 340
Malcolm, Sibbald. SF1 340
Malcolm-Smith, George (1901-)
CSF 132 ES2 295 HFI 98 SF1
340-1
Malcom, Grant. SF1 341
Malden, Richard Henry (1879-
1951) CSF 132 ES2 295 SF1 341
Malec, Alexander B. (1929-) ES2
296 HFI 98 IAC 169 SFE 378
SFS 81 SF1 341
Malet, Lucas pseud. of Mary St.
Leger Harrison. CSF 132 SF1
341
Malet, Oriel pseud. of Auriel
Rosemary Malet Vaughan. CSF
132 SF1 341
Malkin, Lawrence. BAA 243
Malko, George. IAC 169
Malkus, Alida Sims (1895-) SF1
341
Mallan, Lloyd (1914-) ES2 296
Mallardi, William C. SF1 341
Mallarme, Stephane. SFB 67
TDI 5 WFS 32,116
Malleson, Constance. THM 62
Malleson, Lucy Beatrice (1899-
1973) WGT 97
Mallette, Mose. IAC 169 SFS 81
Mallock, W. H. BAA 243
Mallock, William Hurrell. BAA
32 FAN 64
Mallory, Arthur. SF1 341
Mallory, George Leigh. EXT
6/2 47-8
Mallowan, Agatha Margaret
Clarissa Miller (1890-1976)
WGT 97 see also Agatha Christie
Mally, R. M. WTS 62
Malone, Dumas. COT 142
Malone, Richard F. CSF 132
Malone, Walter (1866-1915) ES2
296
Maloney, Francis Joseph Terence
(1917-) ES2 296 WGT 97
Maloney, Russell. IAC 169

Malory, (Sir) Thomas. EXT 10/1
35 FBK 120 INT 4 LTN 89
MFW x MIH 79 MSF 195,197
NWO 227,229,231 RAH 226
RZY 53 WBW 5-6
Malpass, E. L. IAC 169 SFS 81
Malraux, Andre. MFW x
Malstrom, Robert C. IAC 169
Malthus, Thomas Robert (1766-
1834) EXT 2/2 28 EXT 5/2 36
EXT 6/2 36 EXT 7/1 12 MSF
229 POE 41-5,55,119,308
SFH 148-9 SIH 94 TJB 34,36
Malyn, Thomas. SF1 341
Malzberg, Barry N. (1939-) ALW
212 AOW 223-5,292 BAA 154,
158,162 BFP 347-52 BYS 303
COT 283-5 CSC 226 DMK 77-
86 ES2 296 ETN xi,96,113,118,
190 FFR 125 [FJT] HFI 98-9
IAC 113,169-71 JGB 3,60 LEX
452-3 RGS 114-6 RSG 64,66
SFD 35,57-8,63,77,233,247-8,
265,321 SFE 378-9 SFH 186
SF1 341 SF2 987-8 SIH 57 SL1
202-6 SL2 972-6 SRB 359,367
TSF 240 VES 81,152,210 WGT
97 WSF 237 see also K. M.
O'Donnell, Robin Schaeffer
Mammone, Gaetano. TSP 196
Mamoulian, Rouben. WSF 308
Man of the People, (The) pseud.
of W. Thomson. CSF 132
Manabe, Hiroshi. BYS 217
Manchel, Frank (1935-) SF1 342
SF2 988
Mand, Cyril pseud. of George
Hahn, Levin Richard. IMS 199-
200,245 STH 258
Mandel, Siegfried. EXT 1/2 32
Mandeville, Bernard. EXT 9/2
44
Mandeville, (Sir) John. ASF 23
MSF 94
Manfred, Ernest. CSF 132 ES2
296
Mangan, Sherry. EXT 9/1 17
Manganelli, Giorgio. FBK 74,77
Mangels, Arthur C. SF1 342
Manhattan, Avro. IAC 171 SFS
81
Manhood, Harold Alfred (1904-)
CSF 132 ES2 296
Mani, Lakshmi. NWO 36

Manicardi, Luigi. BAA 243
Mankiewicz, Herman J. CSC 264
Mankiewicz, Joseph L. CSC 264
Mankowitz, Cyril Wolf (1924-)
SF1 342
Manley, David L. SF1 342
Manley, Elizabeth. CSF 132
Manley, Mary de la Riviere
(1663-1724) SF1 342 WGT 97-8
Manley, R. M. CSF 132 SF1 342
Manley, Seon. SF1 342
Manlove, C. N. FBK 12 FHT 67
SRB 76
Manly, William M. NWO 171, 173
Mann, A. Philo. SF1 342
Mann, Abby. CSC 263
Mann, Charles. EXT 8/1 24
Mann, Edward Andrew. SF1 342
Mann, Francis Oscar. CSF 132
IAC 171 SF1 342
Mann, Fritz Karl. BAA 243
Mann, George. SOT 296
Mann, Jack pseud. of Evelyn
Charles Vivian (1882-1947)CSF
132-3 FBK 55 FL2 596-600
Mann, John Harvey. SF1 343
Mann, Klaus Heinrich Thomas
(1906-49) SF1 343
Mann, Thomas (1875-1955) CSF
133 CUA 3 FBK 129 FLT 54
RZY 14 SF1 343
Mann, William-Edward. BAA 285
Manners, Alexandra pseud. of
Anne Rundle. SF1 343
Mannes, Marya (1904-) BAA 146
ES2 296 HFI 99 NDA 138-43
SFE 380 SF1 343 SF2 988
Mannheim, Karl. BAA x-xi, 184,
243 MSF 39, 48 NWO 98 SF1
343
Mannin, Ethel Edith (1900-) BAA
113, 184 SF1 343 SF2 988
Manning, Adelaide Frances (-1959)
SF1 343 WGT 98 see also
Manning Coles
Manning, Edie. WFS 217
Manning, Laurence (1899-) AAL
23-4 ASF 83-4 BAA 100 COT
38, 208-9, 214, 258, 260-1, 264-5
ES2 296 HFI 99 IAC 171 IMS
34, 47, 66, 83 KAU 61, 69 LEX
453-4 MFW 40 MSM 214 SFE
380 SFS 81 SFW 181 SOT 78,
128, 201, 387 VES 71, 73, 80,
140, 178, 188 WFS 217 WSF 64,
386

Manning, P. L. SF1 343
Manning, Rosemary. FFC 90
Manning-Sanders, Ruth (1895-)
ES2 296
Mannion, Michael. HFI 99
Mannon, Warwick pseud. of
Kenneth Hopkins. SF1 343
Mano, D. Keith (1942-) BAA 158
HFI 99 LEX 454 NDA 168-70,
174 SF1 343 SF2 988-9
Mansfield, Charlotte (1881-) CSF
133 SF1 343
Mansfield, Roger Ernest (1939-)
ES2 296 IAC 171 SFE 380 SF1
343 SF2 989
Mansford, Charles Jodrell. ES2
296-7 SF1 343
Manson, Charles. BYS 273-4,
284 CAT 37 KAU 4 NWO 12
RAH 51, 53 RHN 127, 137, 173
SFB 100 WFS 301
Manson, Margaret. MIH 40
Manson, Marsden (1850-1931)
SF1 343
Mantley, John Truman (1920-)
ES2 297 HFI 99 LEX 454-5
SFE 380 SF1 344
Manuel, Frank Edward (1910-)
AOW 350 BAA xi-xii, xix-xx,
184, 243 ES2 297 FAN 178, 184,
189
Manuel, Fritzie P. BAA 184, 243
Manus, Willard (1930-) ES2 297
Manvell, (Arnold) Roger (1909-)
AOW 225 ES2 297 SFE 380
SF1 344 SF2 989
Manzalauoi, Mahmoud. BAA 243
Manzin, Isadore. IMS 28
Maple, Eric (1915-) ES2 297
Mapple, Nelson. CSF 133 SF1
344
Maras, Karl (house name) SF1
344 see also Kenneth Bulmer,
Peter Hawkins
Marasco, Robert. SF1 344
Maravall, Jose Antonio. BAA
184, 243
Marbarger, John Porter. ES2
297
Marbo, Camille pseud. of Mar-
guerite Borel. CSF 133
Marcault, J. E. EXT 7/1 17
Marceau, Felicien. ES2 297
Marcelin, Philippe Thoby (1908-)
CSF 192 ES2 297 SF1 344

Marcelin, Pierre Thoby (1904-75) CSF 192 ES2 297 SF1 344
Marcellinus, Ammianus. VES 181
March, Eric. JHN 61
March, Fredric. WFS 56-7 WSF 308
March, R. NWO 124
March, William. AOW 225
Marchant, Ella. SF1 344 WGT 98 see also Two Women of the West
Marchant, M. A. CSF 133
Marchioni, Mark. RFA 38, 63 VES 101-2, 158, 210, 287-8
Marcks, Marie. FFC 157
Marconette, Walter E. IMS 131, 134-6, 145, 200-1, 232-3, 240
Marconi, Guglielmo. EXT 7/2 37 SFN 92
Marcucci, Edmondo. EXT 2/1 5, 7
Marcus, Robert P., Jr. HFI 100
Marcus, Steven. RHN 197
Marcuse, F. L. ISW 216
Marcuse, Herbert. AOW 348 BAA 184, 244 FAN 178
Marcuse, Katherine. IAC 171
Marcuse, Ludwig. BAA 244
Marcy, Mary E. CSF 133
Marden, William Edward (1947-) HFI 100 SF1 344 SF2 989
Mardrus, Joseph Charles Victor (1868-1949) SF1 344
Marfax, Clyde. SF1 344
Margolies, Joseph Aaron (1889-) CSF 133 ES2 297-8 SF1 344
Margrie, William (1877-) BAA 92-3 SF1 344
Margroff, Robert Ervien (1930-) AOW 133 BAA 146 ES2 298 HFI 100 IAC 171 NDA 107 SFE 381 SF1 344 SF2 989-90
Margulies, Cylvia. ETN 108
Margulies, Leo (1900-75) ALW 127, 136 AOW 107 ASF 118 ES2 298-9 ETN 108 FBK 82 IAC 171 IMS 45, 53-4, 147, 172-3, 175-6, 183, 209, 213, 219 MSM 31 SFA 77 SFE 381 SFS 82 SF1 344-5 SF2 990 SOT 82, 109-12, 114, 279, 405, 407 STH 41, 44, 152-3, 267 TSP 17, 24-7, 30, 89, 204 WFS 200-1, 231 WSF 146 WTS ix, 52, 134

Marie, Anne. SF1 345
Marie, (Queen of Roumania) (1875-1938) CSF 133 SF1 345
Mariella, Raymond Peel. IMS 71
Marin, Louis. BAA 185, 244
Marin, Peter. RAH 85
Mariner, David pseud. of David MacLeod Smith. SF1 345
Mariner, Scott pseud. of C. M. Kornbluth, Frederik Pohl. SFE 381
Marinetti, Filippo Tommaso. SIH 53
Markham, Russ. ES2 299 VES 176
Markham, Virgil. CSF 133
Markov, Walter. BAA 244
Markow, Ralston J. BAA 76
Marks, Percy Leman (1867-) SF1 345
Marks, William Dennis (1849-1914) BAA 68 CSF 133 SF1 345
Marks, Winston K(itchener). ALW 212 IAC 171 RFA 97 SFE 381 SFS 82 WGT 98
Markwick, Edward. CSF 133 SF1 345
Marlow, Louis pseud. of Louis Umfreville Wilkinson (1881-1966) CSF 133 FL1 377-9 SFE 381 SF1 345
Marlowe, Christopher. MFW 193 SFD 4 SFH 195 WFS 92
Marlowe, Stephen pseud? of Milton Lesser. ES2 299 IAC 171 SFS 82
Marlowe, Webb pseud. of J. Francis McComas. ALW 215 IAC 171 SFS 82 WSF 130
Marnell, Joseph. ES2 299 WGT 98 see also Zeno Koomoter
Marokvia, Artur. FFC 57
Marple, J. Clarence. SF1 345
Marquez, Gabriel Garcia (1928-) FBK 134 LTN 113 SF1 201 SF2 908
Marquis, Don (1878-1937) CSF 133 ES2 299 EXT 8/1 5 FL1 54-6 IAC 171 SFS 82 SF1 345
Marquis, Roy. SF1 345
Marraud, Pierre. EXT 2/1 9
Marriott, Crittenden (1867-1932) CSF 133 SF1 345
Marriott, Herbert Philip Fitzgerald. CSF 133

Marriott, J.W. BAA 244
Marriott, Mudge. VES 198
Marriott, Pat. FFC 138,194
Marriott, Ronald. SF1 345
Marryat, Florence Church (1837-99) CSF 133 ES2 299 SF1 345
Marryat, (Capt.) Frederick (1792-1848) CSF 133 ES2 299 FBK 54,64 FL3 1246-9 SF1 345
Mars, Alastair (1915-) SF1 345-6
Mars, W. T. FFC 129,153-4
Marsch, Wolf-Dieter. BAA 244
Marschner. FBK 44
Marsden, Antony pseud. of Graham Sutton. CSF 133
Marsden, Bob. IAC 171
Marsden, Richard. BAA 88
Marsh, Carl David. SF1 346
Marsh, George Perkins. COT 257
Marsh, John (1907-) CSF 134 ES2 299 SF1 346 SF2 990 WGT 98
Marsh, Joyce. IAC 171
Marsh, Patrick pseud. of Leslie Hiscock. ES2 299 SF1 346
Marsh, R. P. SOI 161
Marsh, Richard (1867-1915) CSF 134 ES2 299 IAC 171 SF1 346 STH 3 WTS 17
Marsh, Willard. IAC 171 ISW 122 SFS 82
Marshak, David. IAC 171
Marshak, Sondra. IAC 171
Marshall, Alfred. POE 188-9
Marshall, Archibald (1866-1934) CSF 134 FL4 2005-7 SFE 383 SF1 346
Marshall, Armine. BAA 109
Marshall, Arthur Hammond. BAA 81
Marshall, Bruce (1899-) CSF 134 ES2 299 SF1 346 SF2 990
Marshall, Chris. IAC 171
Marshall, Constance. FFC 90
Marshall, Edison Tesla (1894-1967) CSF 134 ES2 300 HFI 100 IAC 172 ISW 276 MFW 21, 129-30 SFE 383 SF1 346 SF2 990 VES 122
Marshall, James Scott. BAA 84 FFC 122 SF1 346
Marshall, James Scott. BAA 129
Marshall, Lenore. IAC 172
Marshall, Luther. CSF 134 SF1 346
Marshall, M. CSF 134

Marshall, Margaret Scott. BAA 84 SF1 346
Marshall, Robert (1863-1910) CSF 134 ES2 300 SF1 346
Marshall, Sidney John (1866-) CSF 134 EXT 1/1 14 MFW 126 SF1 346
Marson, Gerald Francis. CSF 134 SF1 347 ES2 300
Marsten, Richard. AOW 325 FFR 126
Martel, E. A. EXT 2/1 9
Martel, Suzanne Chouinard. AOW 325 ES2 300 HFI 100 SF1 347
Marten, Ambrose. CSF 134
Martens, Paul pseud. of Stephen Southwold. CSF 134
Martensson, Bertil (1945-) IAC 172 SFE 383
Marti-Ibanez, Felix (-1972) IAC 172 SFS 82 SF1 347 STH 108
Martin, Albert Harry (1897-) ES2 300 SF1 347
Martin, David A. BAA 244
Martin, David Stephen (1913-) ES2 300 SFE 383 SF1 347 SF2 991
Martin, Dick. INT 39
Martin, Don. SF1 347
Martin, Edgar A. SF1 347
Martin, Eva M. SF1 347
Martin, George R. R. (1948-) ASF 203 BFP 353 FFR 126 HFI 100 IAC 172 LEX 455-6 RGS 116 SFE 383 WFS 17
Martin, Harold. IAC 172
Martin, Harrison Pillsbury (1911-) SF1 347
Martin, Harry Stratton. BAA 285
Martin, Henry Laster (1917-) SF1 347
Martin, James. MFW 192
Martin, Jay. BAA 244
Martin, John. BYS 83,108 MFW 20-1
Martin, John Stuart (1900-) CSF 134 SFN 39 SF1 347 SF2 991
Martin, Kay. SF1 347
Martin, Kingsley. FTF 95,163
Martin, Larry W. IAC 172
Martin, Lew. IMS 192
Martin, Margaret Rhett. ES2 300
Martin, Mario, Jr. IAC 172
Martin, Nettie Parrish. BAA 72 CSF 134 SF1 347

Martin, Peter pseud. of Peter
Martin Leckie (1890-) BAA 114
CSF 134 SFE 383 SF1 347
Martin, Prestonia Mann. BAA 99
Martin, Quinn. SFH 105-6
Martin, Ralph. SF1 347
Martin, Ray. SF1 347
Martin, Reed. SF1 347
Martin, Reginald Alec (1900-)
ES2 300 WGT 98 see also E. C.
Eliott
Martin, Roland. EXT 9/1 5
Martin, Stefan. FFC 12
Martin, Thomas Hector (1913-)
ES2 300 SF2 1099 WGT 98 see
see also Peter Saxon, Martin
Thomas
Martin, William McChesney. CSF
134
Martindale, Cyril Charles (1879-
1963) CSF 135 SF1 348
Martineau, Louis. BAA 136
Martinez. RFA 209-10
Martinez, Diana. SF1 348 SRB
464
Martini, Virgilio (1903-) SF1 348
SF2 991
Martin-Magog, Adler. CSF 135
SF1 348
Martino, Joseph P. (1931-) IAC
172 LEX 456 SFS 82
Martinson, Harry E. (1904-78)
BYS 307-8 ES2 300 HFI 100
IAC 172 LEX 457 SFE 383 SL1
72-7 SRB 326 WAA 117
Martyn, Edward (1859-1923) WGT
98 see also Sirius
Martyn, Wyndham (1875-) SFE
383-4 SF1 348
Martynow, Georgij (1906-) LEX
457-8
Marvell, Andrew pseud. of Howell
Davies. BAA 107 CAT 85 CSF
135 EXT 10/2 74 IAC 172 MSF
248 SFE 384 SF1 348 VES 217
Marwick, Edward. BAA 56
Marx (brothers). HEN 16, 18
PJF 16
Marx, Groucho. HEN 16 ISW 117
VMW 31
Marx, Karl. CAT 80 COT 98,
141, 210, 223, 238, 254, 259 EXT
1/1 12, 17 EXT 2/2 34 EXT
3/2 48 EXT 8/2 35-6, 39, 60
EXT 9/2 48, 55, 59 EXT 10/2
78 IMS 192, 205, 211, 216, 245

ISW 95, 117, 164 JGB 10, 51 LTN
98, 111 MSF 21, 39, 68, 73-4, 77,
112, 118-9, 121, 175, 199, 230,
247, 256, 266 NDA 56 POE 78
PST 294-5 RAH 189 RHN 96,
118, 148 SFB 67 SFH 10, 148,
174 SFN 59 SOI 20 TJB 24-5
TSO 7, 28, 36 VES 254 WBW 4,
25, 33, 45, 51, 58-9, 61-2 WFS
16, 68, 116, 120, 305 WSF 348-9
Mary. LTN 76
Mary Catherine, (Sister). SF1
348 see also S. M. C.
Mary Charitina, (Sister). SF1
348Marye, Beatrissia. SF1 348
Masaryk, Thomas G. MSF 281
Maschler, Tom. CWN 26
Masefield, John Edward (1878-
1967) CSF 135 ES2 301 FFC
76 IAC 172 SFS 82 SF1 348
Masefield, Lewis Crommelin.
SF1 348
Mashburn, W. Kirk, Jr. (1900-
68) ES2 301 WGT 98 WTS 34
Maskwitz, Bernard. IMS 201
Maslow, Abraham. CWN 17, 52,
54, 59 WBW 32-3
Mason, Alfred Edgar Woodley
(1865-1948) CSF 135 ES2 301
IAC 172 SF1 348
Mason, Arthur (1876-) CSF 135
FFC 96 SF1 348
Mason, Bill. WFS 7
Mason, C. P. WGT 98
Mason, Carol. IAC 172 SF1 348
Mason, Colin (1926-) SF1 348
Mason, David (1924-74) CSC 154-
6 FL4 1777-9 HFI 100 SFE
385 SF1 348 SF2 991 SRB 270
Mason, Douglas Rankine (1918-)
BFP 354-6 ES2 301 FFR 126
HFI 100-1 IAC 172 LEX 458
NDA 97-8 SFE 385 SFS 82
SF1 348-9 SF2 991-2 UFS 4
WGT 98-9 see also John Rankine
Mason, Eveleen Laura (1838-)
CSF 135 SF1 349
Mason, Francis Van Wyck (1901-
78) SF1 349 WGT 99
Mason, Gregory pseud. of Doris
Meek, Adrienne Jones. BAA
129 ES2 301 HFI 101 SFE 385-
6 SF1 349
Mason, H. A. CSF 135 SF1 349
Mason, Hugh Churchill. CSF 135
SF1 349

Mason, John Edward (1892-) SF1 349
Mason, John Keith. IAC 172
Mason, Lowell Blake (1893 -) BAA 144 ES2 301 SF1 349
Mason, Miriam. FFC 134
Mason, Pamela Ostrer (1915-) ES2 301 WGT 99 see also Pamela Kellino
Masquerier, Lewis. BAA 32
Massey, James pseud. of Simon Tyssot De Patot. CSF 135
Massey, Kathleen. FL4 1872-4 FL5 2214-6
Massey, Raymond. WFS 57
Massie, Chris. SF1 349
Massie, Douglas. CSF 135 SFE 386 SF1 349
Massingham, Harold John. BAA 185
Masso, Gildo. BAA 185
Masson, David Irvine (1915-) BFP 357 ES2 301 IAC 172 NWO 207, 235 SFD 35 SFE 386 SFS 82 SF1 349 SF2 992 TJB 39 VES 150
Masterman, Charles Frederick. FAN 41, 182 POE 164, 210
Masterman, Walter Sidney (1876-) CSF 135 SF1 349
Masters, Dexter (1908-) ES2 301 SF1 583
Masters, Edgar Lee. PJF 61
Masters, John (1914-) ISW 170 SFE 386 SF1 350
Masters, R. E. L. SOI 161
Masters, W. W. CSF 135
Masterton, Whit. ES2 301
Mastin, John (1865-1932) BAA 71 CSF 135 SFE 386 SF1 350
Mata, Soria Y. [FUT]
Matania, Fortunio. SFS 82 SOT 123
Mateyko, G. M. IAC 172 SFS 59, 82
Mather, Cotton. NWO 35 WIF 37
Mather, Increase. NWO 35
Mathers, Helen Buckingham pseud. of Helen B. M. Reeves (1853-1920) CSF 135 SF1 350
Matheson, Hugh pseud. of Lewis Hugh Mackay. ES2 301-2 SF1 350
Matheson, Jean. SF1 350
Matheson, Joan (1924-) SF2 1104 WGT 99 see also Jacob Transue

Matheson, Richard (1926-) ALW 212, 216 AOW 225-6 BFP 358-9 BYS 48, 262, 279 EFP 16 ES2 302 EXT 5/1 3 EXT 8/1 6 FBK 46, 124, 153 FFR 126-7 FL1 90-4 FL2 725-7 FL4 1645-51 FL5 2112-4 FTF 157-8, 191 HFI 101 IAC 173-4 ISW 8, 63-4, 96, 239-40, 278-83 JGB 5-6 KAU 90, 121, 152, 184, 201 KWS 352-5, 357-8, 360, 401 LEX 458-9 OMN 41 RGS 116-7 SFD 22, 311 SFE 387-8 SFH 105 SFN 74 SFS 82-3 SFW 425. 31 SF1 350 SF2 992 SL2 986-90 SOT 300, 332, 366, 395, 409 SRB 114 STH 119 VES 130, 141, 174, 180, 231, 235 WAA 88 WGT 99 WSF 172 YTS 37 see also Logan Swanson
Mathew, Frank J. CSF 135 ES2
Mathews, Frances H. SF1 350
Mathews, R. D. BAA 185
Mathews, Richard Barrett (1944-) FL2 701-9, 897-915 FL3 1307-10 FL4 1854-8 FL5 2090-6, 2165-70 SF2 992 SL1 313-7 SL2 579-82 SL3 1144-50 SL5 2223-8 SRB 76-7, 82
Mathewson, Joseph. EXT 10/1 35
Mathieu, Joe. FFC 187
Mathiews, Franklin K. (1873? - 1950) CSF 135 ES2 302 SF1 350
Mathison, Volney G. CSF 136 SFD 21
Matisse, Henri (1869-1954) TBC 44
Matlaw, Ralph E. FAN 185
Matschat, Cecile Hulse. IAC 94 SFS 83 SF1 350
Matson, Norman Haghelm (1893-1965) CSF 136, 182 ES2 302 ISW 20-1 SF1 350
Mattes, Arthur S. (1901-) SFE 389 SF1 350 SF2 992
Mattes, William Ward. BAA 244, 285
Matthewman, S. CSF 136
Matthews, Brander (1852-1929) CSF 136 ES2 303 SF1 350
Matthews, Carleton. BAA 115
Matthews, E. Paul. SF1 351
Matthews, Ronald de Couves (1903-67) BAA 119 SF1 351
Matthews, Thomas. CSF 136

Matthiessen, Peter. FFC 134
Mattingly, Sidney. SF1 351
Maturin, Charles Robert (1780-1824) CSF 136 ES2 303 FBK 26, 53, 93, 137 FL2 998-1003 SFE 389 SF1 351 SIH 25, 185 TFC 161 WAA 82 WGT 99 WIF 41
Matus, Greta. FFC 31
Matzke, Gerhard (1925-) LEX 459-60
Maude, Frederic Natusch (1854-1933) POE 184-6 SF1 351
Maudslay, Henry. FTF 34
Maugham, Robert Cecil Romer (1916-) SF2 992 see also Robin Maugham
Maugham, Robin pseud. of Robert Cecil Romer Maugham. BAA 112 SF1 351
Maugham, W(illiam) Somerset (1874-1965) CSF 136 ES2 303 FFC 14 FFR 127 IAC 174 ISW 189 JGB 5, 45 POE 205 RFA 212 SFA 153 SFN 119 SF1 351 SF2 993 VFS 118, 270 WFS 78 WIF 219
Maurice, F. J. POE 184-6
Maurice, John Frederick (1841-1912) SF1 351
Maurice, Michael pseud. of Conrad Arthur Skinner. CSF 136 SF1 351
Maurin, Peter. BAA 244
Mauro, John Francis (1911-) CSF 136 SF1 351
Maurois, Andre pseud. of Emile Herzog (1885-1967) AOW 108 BAA 93 CSF 136 ES2 303 EXT 2/2 30 EXT 9/1 17 FAN 6 FTF 92 FL5 2084-6 HFI 101 IAC 174 PST 181-2, 207 SFB 140 SFE 389 SFS 83 SF1 351, 583 SF2 993 SIH 110 SL3 1521-5 VES 107 WAA 119, 173
Mauzy, Peter. FL2 631-4
Mawson, L. A. BAA 79 CSF 136 SF1 351
Max, Nicholas pseud. of Bernard Asbell (1923-) SF1 351
Maxim, Hiram Stevens. STH 189, 197-8, 208
Maxim, Hudson. BAA 72-3 POE 216-7
Maximov, Herman. IAC 174

Maximovic, Gerd (1944-) LEX 460
Maxon, P. B. (-1934?) CSF 136 ES2 303-4 SF1 351 STH 149-51
Maxton, James. BAA 103
Maxwell, Ann. HFI 101
Maxwell, Edward. BAA 131 ES2 304 SFE 389 SF1 352
Maxwell, James Clerk. OWB 28 SFH 137 STF 85
Maxwell, John C. HFI 101 SF1 352
Maxwell, Mary Elizabeth Braddon (1837-1915) WGT 99
Maxwell, May. CSF 136 SF1 352
Maxwell, Perriton (1868-1947) SF1 352
May, Ernest R. SF1 352
May, John R. NWO 36, 100
May, Julian C. pseud. of Julian Chain May Dikty (1931-) ES2 304 IAC 174 RFA 197 SFS 83 WIF 110
May, Rollo. CWN 54 SOT 211
Mayakovsky, Vladimir (1893-1930) EXT 10/2 75-7 MSF 127, 254-5, 258, 260-1, 264, 266 RHN 67 SFE 389 SIH 53-4, 74-5, 77, 85-6 SL1 138-43
Mayan, Earl E. IAC 174 SFS 83
Mayer, Douglas W. F. IMS 35, 97, 99-100, 102, 216, 252 SOT 378
Mayer, Hans. BAA 244-5
Mayer, Mercer. FFC 11, 52
Mayfield, Marilyn. ACE 12 AC2 10
Mayne, Isobel. IAC 174 SFS 83
Mayne, John Dawson (1828-1917) BAA 73 CSF 136 SF1 352
Mayne, Richard. EXT 6/1 19
Mayne, William James Carter (1928-) AOW 325 ES2 304 FFC 32, 68, 76, 94, 166, 172 SF1 352 SF2 993 SRB 24, 270
Mayo, Clark. FL1 228-31 FL2 794-7 SL3 1449-52 SL4 1697-1701 SL5 2260-3, 2447-50
Mayo, Robert D. AOW 81
Mayo, William Starbuck (1812-95) CSF 137 EXT 4/1 9, 13 SF1 352
Mayoe, Franklin pseud. of Frank Rosewater. CSF 137
Mayoe, Marian pseud. of Frank Rosewater. CSF 137

Mayor, Flora MacDonald (1872-)
CSF 137 ES2 304 SF1 352
Mayor, Theodor Heinrich (1884-
1949) LEX 460
Mays, Julia Webb. SF1 352
Mays, Milton A. OSR 171-80,
355
Mazelish, Bruce. MFW 185-7,
218
Mazer, Charles Litten. BAA 285
Mazer, Norma. FFC 166
Mazzeo, Henry J., Jr. ES2 304
SF1 352
Mead, Edward Shepherd (1914-)
AOW 226 BAA 124 ES2 304
EXT 6/2 51 EXT 9/2 62 HFI
101 MFW 81-2 NDA 42-6, 123-
4 SFE 389 SF1 357 SF2 997
SL1 213-7 SRB 321 WGT 99
Mead, Harold (1910-) AOW 226
BAA 127, 131 ES2 304 EXT
2/2 30 HFI 101 ISW 241-2 LEX
465-6 SFE 389 SF1 357 SF2
997 SRB 324
Mead, Margaret. BAA 245 EXT
5/1 6, 8 EXT 7/2 37
Meade, L. T. pseud. of Elizabeth
Thomasina Smith. ALW 85 CSF
137 IAC 174 SF1 357
Meade, Richard pseud. of Benjamin
Leopold Haas (1926-77) HFI 101
SF1 357
Meader, Gerald. IMS 247
Meadley, Robert. IAC 174
Meadows, Dennis L. IAC 174
INT 48
Meadows, Donella H. IAC 174
INT 48
Meadows, Patrick. IAC 174 SFS
83
Meagher, George Edward (1895-)
SF1 357
Meagher, Maud. SF1 357
Meaney, J.W. BAA 245
Mears, Amelia Garland. BAA 54
CSF 137 SF1 357
Mearson, Lyon (1888-1966) SF1
357
Mebane, Banks. RZY 105
Meckauer, Walter (1889-) SF1
357
Meckier, Jerome. BAA 245
Medawar, (Sir) Peter Brian
(1915-) ES2 304 VFS 187
Meech, Shirley. IAC 174

Meek, Doris. WGT 99 see also
Gregory Mason
Meek, (Capt.) S(terner St.)
P(aul) (1894-1972) AAL 88 ALW
10 CSF 137 ES2 304-5 HFI 101
IAC 174 LEX 466 MFW 39 RFA
5-6, 183 SFD 23-4, 210, 306 SFE
392 SF1 357 SF2 998 SOT 306
STH 141 WGT 99-100 WIF 167
WSF 54
Meeker, Nathan Cook (1817-79)
WGT 100
Meeker, W. Johns. WGT 100
Meeus, Jean. VFS 35-6
Mehmet (the Conqueror). FBK 49
Meier, Paul. BAA 185
Meigs, Cornelia. FFC 76
Meiji (Emperor of Japan). SFB 67
Meik, Vivian Bernard (1895-)
CSF 137 SF1 357
Meinhold, Johann Wilhelm (1797-
1851) CSF 137 SF1 357 WGT
100
Meir, Golda. LTN 168
Meise, Fred. FFC 161
Meisler, Maurice J. IMS 216, 218
Meisner, Maurice. BAA 245
Meitner, Lise. COT 189 RHN 60
Mejerow, Alexander (1915-) LEX
466
Melchior, Hathaway Kate. EXT
10/1 26
Melchior, Ib. IAC 174
Melchiorre, Virgilio. BAA 185,
245
Melde, G. R. SF1 358
Mele, Jim. CEN 1-22
Melies, Georges (1861-1938) ES2
305 OMN 2, 4, 19, 47-8, 67, 102,
130, 214-6, 218-9, 221 SFB 10,
72-3, 138-40 SFE 392 SFH 102,
104 SRB 57 WAA 191 WSF 307
YTS 15
Meline, Jules. POE 178
Mellen, Philip A. BAA 185
Mellersh, H. E. L. CSF 137
Melling, Leonard (1913-) BAA
127 SF1 358
Mellon (family). KVT 59
Mellon, John. EXT 10/1 5
Mellows, Suzanne. SF1 358
Melnyk, Bohdan. FFC 118
Meltzer, David (1937-) SFE 392
SF1 358 SF2 998
Meltzoff, Stanley. SRB 39

Melville, Herman (1819-91) ACC 136,140 ALW 53,60 AOW 26 BAA 24 CAT 6,27 CSC 24-5 CSF 137 ETN 11,98 EXT 4/1 9 EXT 7/2 48 EXT 9/1 6,16 FBK 29 FL1 308-13 FL2 976-9 HEN 3-4,60 IAC 174 INT 77, 79,106-9 JGB 6,24-6 KVT 28 LTN 75 MIH 141 MSF 137,139, 143-4,170 MSM 278 NWO 3,5, 8,20,35,94-5,209,266-95 PJF 43,65 RBY 17-19,56,84,97,192 RHN 118,193 SFE 392-3 SFN 52-4 SL4 1989-93 THM 32,62 VMW 28

Melville, John. BAA 122

Melvin, Kenneth. LTN 249

Menard, Guy. BAA 245

Mencinger, Janez. SL1 1-5

Mencken, H. L. BAA 245 FAN 6,56 FBK 72 HEN 10,13-4 SFN 98-9 WIF 170

Mencken, J. B. IAC 174

Mendel, Ann. LTN 128,268

Mendel, Gregor J. (1822-84) EXT 1/1 17 SFH 139 TJB 8

Mendel, S. EXT 4/2 26

Mendelsohn, Felix, Jr. (1906-) HFI 102 SFE 393 SF1 358 SF2 998

Mendelson, Drew. IAC 174

Mendes, Catulle Abraham (1841-1909) ES2 305 SF1 358

Mendes, Henry Pereira (1852-1937) BAA 61 SF1 358

Mendham, Clement A. CSF 137 SF1 358

Mendoza, George. ES2 305 FFC 106

Menen, Salvator Aubrey Clarence (1912-) ES2 305 EXT 10/1 26, 35 SF1 358 SF2 998

Mengeling, Marvin E. RBY 83-109,240 Menger, Lucy. CEN 87-108

Menninger, William. EXT 4/1 7

Mentor, Lillian Frances. CSF 137 SF1 358

Menville, Douglas Alver (1935-) IAC 174 SF2 998-9

Menzel, Donald Howard (1901-76) COT 11,301 ES2 305 EXT 5/1 8 MSM 285-6 WFS 267

Menzies, John. MIH 130

Menzies, William Cameron. SFH 103

Meozzi, Antero. BAA 185

Mephistopheles. KVT 26 TJB 34 see also Devil, Lucifer, Satan

Merak, A. J. ES2 305 HFI 102 SFE 393

Mercer, Archibald Henry. SF1 358

Mercer, Cecil William (1885-1960) WGT 100 see also Dornford Yates

Mercer, Derwent. AAL 93

Mercer, Henry Chapman (1856-1930) CSF 137 ES2 305-6 SF1 359

Mercer, Johnny. IAC 174

Merchant, Ella. BAA 49

Mercier, Alfred. EXT 4/1 9,13

Mercier, Louis-Sebastien (1740-1814) ALW 43 AOW 26 CSF 138 EXT 9/2 29 FAN 26 FTF 28 IAC 174 MSF 27,118,177, 179,245 PST 26-7,49,56,197, 222,226,247-8,263,279-80,284-5,297,302 POE 2,15,23,26-30, 35,55,71 SFD 41 SFE 393 SFW 7 SF1 359 SRB 3 STH 1 VES 125-6

Mercier, Mario. SF1 359

Meredith. SFA 8

Meredith, Edgar. BAA 106 CSF 138 SF1 359

Meredith, Ellis (1865-) SF1 359

Meredith, Geoffrey. SF1 359

Meredith, George (1828-1909) CSF 138 FL3 1392-5 HFI 102 ISW 240 MSM 25 SF1 359

Meredith, James Creed, Jr. (-1942) BAA 108 CSF 138 SFE 393 SF1 359

Meredith, Owen pseud. of Edward Robert Bulwer-Lytton. CSF 138

Meredith, Richard C. (1937-) AAL 20 ETN 27-8 HFI 102 IAC 174 RGS 120 SFE 393 SF1 359

Meredith, Scott. SOT 181-2 TJB 5-6,11 WSF 221

Merian, Paul. BAA 185

Merimee, Prosper. CSF 138 FBK 44,138 TFC 43,80,87,163

Merlaud, Andre. BAA 245

Merle, Robert (1908-) AAL 66-7 AOW 226-7 HFI 102 INT 45 KAU 204 LEX 467 MFW 23 SFB 140 SFE 393 SF1 359 SL3 1317-22

Merlin. ASF 142
Merlino, Merlin Mesmer pseud.
of Donald G. Carpenter. SF1
359
Merliss, R. R. IAC 174 ISW 122
SFS 83
Merlyn, Arthur pseud. of James
Blish. TJB 7
Merriam, Alexander R. BAA
245
Merrick, Williston pseud. of
Williston Merrick Ford. SF1
359
Merril, Judith (1923-) AAL 2, 74,
138 ALW 161, 184, 235 AOW
227, 295-6 BFP 360-3 BYS 264,
279, 281, 284 CEN 70-86 COT
141, 195, 293 CSC 138 ES2 306-
9 ETN 41, 45 EXT 5/1 3, 10
EXT 6/2 22 EXT 7/1 1 EXT
7/2 29-48 EXT 8/1 1-19 EXT
9/1 1, 21 EXT 9/2 25, 62 EXT
10/1 1-2, 6-8, 47-8 EXT 10/2
50, 69, 85, 95, 98, 105 FFR 128
FHT 67 FLR 11, 13-4, 61 FTF
89 HFI 102 HID 13 IAC 174-5
IAH 50, 118 ISW ix, 104-5, 120,
122-8, 146, 249 JGB 3 KAU 31,
34, 75 LEX 467-8 MFW 212-3
MIH 21-2, 37-8, 124-6, 128, 130,
146 MSM 36, 81 OSR 53-95, 356
PJF 25, 74 RFA 158, 163, 199
RGS 120-1 RSG 15, 26 SFD 3, 311
SFE 393-4 SFH 41-2, 69-70, 89
SFS 78, 83-4 SFW 395, 433-9
SF1 359-60 SF2 999 SL4 2014-8
SOT 241, 247, 366, 419 SRB 311,
317, 324 STH 45 VES 195, 212
WFS 71, 135, 173-4, 182, 192, 194,
196, 200, 202, 204-8, 214, 273, 299-
300, 305 WGT 100 WIF 202 WSF
144, 222, 252-3, 256
Merrill, Albert Adams. BAA 61
CSF 138 SF1 360
Merrill, Jean Fairbanks (1923-)
FFC 14, 122, 148 SF1 360 SF2
999
Merrill. Stuart (1863-1915) CSF
138 SF1 360
Merriman, Effie see Mrs. James
C. Fifield
Merriman, Henry Seton. SFW
75-6
Merritt, A(braham) (1884-1943)
ALW 33, 59, 114-6, 137, 141, 156,
183, 186 AOW 83, 108, 394 BFP

364-6 BYS 146, 174-6 CSC 33,
168, 172 CSF 138 ES2 309-10
EXT 1/2 33 EXT 3/1 3, 28
EXT 4/2 25 EXT 5/1 3, 10, 15-6
FBK 103 FFR 128 FL1 181-3,
504-7 FL3 1060-4, 1407-11
HFI 102-3 IAC 175 IAH 82, 141
IMS 2, 14, 16, 24, 45, 67, 83, 134,
221 ISW 19, 25, 37, 159 JVN 188
KAU 190 LEX 468-70 MFW 19,
138 MIH 79-85, 98, 103, 107, 121
MSF 68 OWB 79 RFA 1-2, 39,
46-7, 157, 169 RGS 121-3 SFA
85 SFB 16, 48-9, 104-5 SFD 72,
210, 242, 273, 289, 306 SFE 394
SFS 84 SFW 65-71, 76, 158, 161,
226 SF1 360-1 SIN 12-4, 19
SL3 1449-52 SOT 67-8, 70, 72,
76, 87-8, 90, 93, 106-7, 110, 152,
261, 292, 296, 304, 328, 334 SRB
271, 294, 296 STH 97, 255-62
TJB 13 TRB 54, 56 TSF 53,
229 VES 93, 137, 142, 179, 305,
314 WAA 109, 243 WFS 8 WIF
70, 84, 89, 135, 149, 151, 231 WSF
27-8, 44, 278, 294, 385-6 WTS
27, 36-7, 42-3, 64, 123
Mershon, Helen L. LTN 269
Merson, Alick James (1885-)
ES2 310
Mertens, Karl R. SF1 361
Mertins, Gustave Frederick
(1872-) CSF 138 SF1 361
Mertz, Barbara Gross (1927-)
ES2 310 SF2 999 WGT 100 see
also Barbara Michaels
Mervan, Rencelof Ermagine.
CSF 138
Merwin, Samuel, Jr. (1910-)
ALW 31, 127 ES2 310 EXT 5/1
3 FFR 128 HFI 103 IAC 175-6
IAH 47 ISW 155 LEX 470 RGS
123 SFA 143-4, 273 SFE 395
SF1 361 SFS 84 SOT 261 TJB
6 VES 123 WFS 174 WGT 100
WIF 116, 232 WSF 120, 156, 174,
188
Meskys, Edmund R. EXT 10/1
18-9
Mesmer, Franz Anton (1734-1815)
CWD 27 SFH 157
Mesnard, Pierre. BAA 245
Messac, Regis (1893-1943) BAA
185, 245 ES2 310-1 SL4 1742-5
Messineo, A. BAA 245

Messman, Jon. HFI 103 see also Claudette Nicole
Mesterhazi, Lajos (1916-) SL4 1892-5
Meston, Jack. CSC 281-2
Metcalf, Eleanor Melville. NWO 268
Metcalf, John. IAC 176
Metcalf, Norman (1937-) AOW 367-8 ES2 311 MIH 40 RFA vii, 190 SFE 397 SF1 361 WAA 245
Metcalf, Thomas Newell. ALW 108-10
Metcalfe, John (1891-1965) CSF 138 ES2 311 SFS 84 SF1 361
Metchim, D. Bridgman. CSF 138 SF1 361
Metchnikov, Elie. EXT 8/2 49, 62
Metchnikov, Ilya. EXT 8/2 62
Methold, Kenneth. EXT 1/2 33
Metlova, Maria. WGT 100 see also Louise Hathaway
Metraux, Rhoda. EXT 5/1 6
Mettais, Henri. POE 136-7
Mette, John Allen. BAA 93
Metzger, Arnold. BAA 246
Metzger, Lois. IAC 176
Meunier, Denise. EXT 6/1 4
Meuriot, Paul. POE 173-4
Meyer, Bill. ES2 311 SF1 583
Meyer, Dorothy Quick (1900-) WGT 100
Meyer, John Joseph (1873-1948) BAA 103 CSF 139 SF1 361
Meyer, Joseph A. SF1 361
Meyer, Karl Ernest. BAA 246 NDA 199
Meyer, Richard I. IMS 205, 238-41
Meyerhold, Vsevolod E. MSF 255
Meyer-Oldenburg, Christian (1936-) LEX 470-1
Meyers, Carolyn Hodgson. BAA 285 EXT 6/2 22, 50
Meyers, Jeffrey. BAA 185, 246
Meyers, John Myers (1906-) FL4 1749-53
Meyers, Robert E. SFW 225-31
Meyers, Roy Lethbridge (1910-74) ES2 311 HFI 103 SFE 398 SF1 362 SF2 999
Meyers, Valerie. BAA 185
Meyers, Walter E. FL1 66-8, 154-60, 314-8 FL2 520-3, 635-7, 649-53, 675-9, 1010-4 FL3 1286-90, 1384-6 FL4 1592-6, 1744-8, 1790-7, 1963-5 FL5 2063-6, 2481-91 SL1 53-7, 93-6, 168-72, 242-6 SL2 787-91, 977-80 SL3 1130-4, 1151-5, 1353-6, 1505-9 SL4 1566-70, 1617-21, 1665-8, 1687-91, 1789-93, 1939-43, 1958-62 SL5 2122-6, 2136-9, 2250-4
Meyerson, Martin. BAA 246
Meyerstein, Edward Harry William (1889-1952) ES2 311
Meynell, Esther Hallam (-1955) CSF 139 SF1 362
Meynell, Laurence Walter (1899-) BAA 97 CSF 139 SF1 362
Meyrick, Geraldine. BAA 246
Meyrink, Gustav (1868-1932) CSF 139 ES2 311 FBK 58, 128, 143 FL2 628-30 MSF 282 SFB 53 SFH 183 SF1 362 SIH 135 WAA 86 WIF 42
Mezieres. [FUT]
M'Guire, Sean. CSF 129 SF1 362
Mian, Mary Lawrence. FFC 190 SF1 362
Micah. MSF 118
Michael, Cecil (1909-) ES2 311 SF1 362
Michael, John. IAC 176
Michaelis, Richard C. (1839-1909) BAA xxii, 42 CSF 139 EXT 2/2 30 FAN 34 PST 57 SF1 362
Michaels, Barbara pseud. of Barbara Mertz. SF1 362, 583
Michaelson, L. W. EXT 1/2 33 SL2 991-4
Michaud, Alfred Charles (1876-) BAA 119-20 SF1 362
Michaux, Henri. IAC 176 SFB 67
Michel, Aime (1919-) ES2 311
Michel, John B. (1917-69) COT 265 ES2 311 IMS 34-42, 48-9, 51, 55-6, 58, 68, 82-3, 86, 103, 114, 116, 118-9, 125-6, 129-31, 137, 140, 142, 148-9, 153-4, 158-9, 170, 179, 183, 185, 188, 190-3, 215-6, 225, 227, 244-6 MIH 97 SRB 90 WFS 34-5, 37-8, 51-3, 59-60, 63, 67-8, 70-3, 80, 83, 95, 97, 116 WGT 100-1 WIF 137 see also Arthur Cooke, Hugh Raymond
Michel, Milton Scott (1916-) SF1 362 SF2 999
Michelangelo. VFS 148

240

Michelet, Jules (1798-1874) ES2
311-2 MSF 153
Michelmore, Reg. CSF 139 SF1
362
Michels, Nicholas. BAA 61 WGT
101 see also Nicolai Mikalowitch
Michelson, Miriam (1870-1942)
CSF 139 EXT 1/1 14 SF1 362
Michener, C. WTS 20
Middleton, Frances Bragg. TSP
183, 200
Middleton, John B. BAA 68-9
CSF 139 SF1 362
Middleton, Richard Barham (1882-
1911) CSF 139 ES2 312 FBK 64
IAC 176 SFS 84 SF1 362
Middleton, William. BAA 45
Miehe, Ulf (1940-) LEX 471
Mieke, Anne. FFC 175
Mielke, Thomas R. P. (1940-)
LEX 471-3
Miesel, Sandra Louise (1941-)
BAA 245 EXT 10/1 35 IAC 176
SF1 363 SF2 1000 SL5 2236-40
Mighels, Ella Sterling (1853-1934)
SF1 363
Mighels, Philip Verrill (1869-
1911) CSF 139 EXT 1/1 14 SF1
363
Miglieruolo, Mauro Antonio (1942-)
SL1 415-7
Mihilakis, Ulysses George. WGT
101
Mikalowitch, Nicolai pseud. of
Nicholas Michels. CSF 139
SF1 363
Mikes, George (1912-) SF1 363
Mikolaycak, Charles. FFC 19,
137
Miksch, William F. SF1 363
Mildred, E. W. CSF 139 SF1 363
Miles pseud. of Stephen Southwold.
CSF 139
Miles, Charles A. ES2 312 SFE
398 SF1 363
Miles, Hamis. IAC 176 SFS 84
Miles, Josephine. IAC 176
Miles, Lois. WFS 174
Miles, Patricia. FFC 8
Miles, Robert. SF1 363
Milkomane, George Alexis (1903-)
BAA 113 WGT 101 see also
George Borodin
Mill, Garrett pseud. of Margaret
Miller. CSF 139 SF1 363

Mill, John Stuart (1806-73) CSC
117 CWN 54 EXT 7/1 13 NDA
64 TJB 24-5, 27, 55, 59 WBW 19
Millais. WBW 46
Milland, Ray. KAU 126
Millar, H. R. FFC 21, 69, 103, 182
Millar, Jeff. IAC 176
Millar, Kenneth (1915-) WGT 101
Millard, Joseph John (1908-) ES2
312 HFI 103 SFE 398 SF1 363
SF2 1000
Millay, Edna St. Vincent. IAC
176
Millay, Margaret. RZY 72, 75-6
Mille, Pierre. AOW 295 IAC 176
Miller. HEN 9
Miller, Alan. CSF 139 SF1 363
Miller, Arthur. CSC 280 SFD
45, 50 VFS 117
Miller, Chris. IAC 176
Miller, Clarence H. BAA 246
Miller, David M. EXT 9/2 25
EXT 10/1 2, 19, 34-5, 37 SRB 80
Miller, Elizabeth Jane (1878-)
CSF 139 SF1 363
Miller, Elizabeth York. CSF 140
Miller, Eugenia (1916-) FFC 172
SF1 363
Miller, George Noyes. BAA 42,
45 CSF 140 MSF 203
Miller, Glenn. MIH 144
Miller, H. Billy (1920-61) WGT
101
Miller, Henry. ETN 24 EXT
7/2 32 EXT 8/1 13 FBK 100-1
NWO 36, 44 PJF 78 RAH 228
SFN 42
Miller, Ian. VES 94
Miller, Irene. SF1 363
Miller, Jane. BAA 246
Miller, Jessie. IAC 176
Miller, Jimmy. HFI 103 SFE
398 SF1 363
Miller, Joaquin (1841-1913) BAA
49-50 CSF 140 SF1 363
Miller, Leo Edward (1887-1952)
CSF 140 SF1 364
Miller, Lion. IAC 176 SFS 84
Miller, Margaret see Garrett
Mill
Miller, Marilyn. FFC 32
Miller, Marjorie M. (1922-) AOW
362 BAA 185 SFA 7, 9 SFD 83
SF1 364 SF2 1000 SRB 77
Miller, Marvin. IMS 36

Miller, Miriam Youngerman.
FL2 732-9 FL4 1908-12
Miller, Mitch. ETN 34
Miller, Mitchell. FFC 10,145
Miller, Morris. IMS 52
Miller, P(eter) Schuyler (1912-
74) AAL 95-6,178-9 ALW 184
AOW 173,228,293 BYS 264
COT 107,185,244-5,266-7,296
CSC 29 CWD 10,16-8 ES2 312
EXT 5/1 3,6 HFI 103 HID 31
IAC 176 IAH 113,132-3 IMS
8-9,16,21-4,45 ISW vi,10,19
LEX 473 MIH 21,25-8 NWO
234 OWB 74 RFA 2,46,66,70,
84,87,90,114,127,181,197-8
RSG 10,12,26 SFD 55,308SFE
398-9 SFS 84 SFW 179 SF1
364 SF2 1000-1 SOT 96,107,
154,164,177 VES 92,95,142,
147 WFS 112 WGT 101 WIF
88,134,136,151,161,222 WSF
51,174,220,358 WTS 43
Miller, Richard DeWitt (1910-58)
ES2 312 HFI 103 IAC 176 IMS
22 ISW 119 SFE 399 SFS 84
SF1 364 WSF 336,368
Miller, Ron. RHN 89
Miller, Russ. SF1 364
Miller, Stanley. SFH 140-1
Miller, Stephen O. SF1 364
Miller, Sutro. SF1 364
Miller, Walt. RFA 191,195,198
VES 183-4,341-2
Miller, Walter M., Jr. (1923-)
AAL 21,140-1 ALW 212,239
AOW 228-9 BAA 134-5 BFP
367 BYS 278-81 CAT 100-1,
121,138-9 COT 46,253 CSC
75,123-4 EFP 6 ES2 312-3
ETN 46,56,137,160,174 EXT
3/1 26 EXT 4/2 29 EXT 5/1 3
EXT 8/1 6,11 EXT 9/1 19 FAN
13,167,171-3 FFR 129 FTF
75,129-30,194-6 HFI 103 HID
45,145 IAC 176-7 IAH 13-4,
60,102 INT 21,23-5,34,42,97
ISW 122 JGB 7 KAU 62,128,
137-46 LEX 473-5 MFW 11,
23,86,251 MIH 14,62 MSF 27
NDA 151-5 NWO 44-5,48,140-
8 PJF 74 RFA 196,200,205,
212,214 RGS 123-4 SFD 19,
252,298,316 SFE 399 SFH 50,
165,221-6,243 SFS 84-5 SFW
106,441-8 SF1 364 SF2 1001

SIN 68-76 SL1 288-93,423-7
SOT 196,413 SRB 12,334 STF
60 STH 16-7,22-3,265 TSF
60-1,236 VES 95,167,175,195,
200,206,224,227,232,258 VF2
56-81,199-200 WSF 177,340,
387
Miller, Ward S. EXT 10/1 3
Miller, Warren (1921-66) ES2
313 NDA 167-8 SFE 399 SF1
364
Miller, William Amos. BAA 59
CSF 140 SF1 364
Miller, William H. IMS 47,64,66,
70,72,79-80,84,103-4,106,113,
129,133,141,153,178
Millers, Rheinhold R. HFI 103
SF1 364
Millet, Francis Davis (1846-1912)
CSF 140 ES2 313 SF1 364
Millett, Kate. COT 194 LTN 161
Millhiser, Marlys Joy (1938-)
FL3 1034-6 SF1 364 SF2 1001
Millies, Susan. SRB 464
Milligan, Alfred Lee (1893-) ES2
313 SFE 399 SF1 364 SF2 1001
Millikan, Robert. IMS 220
Millin, Leslie. EXT 10/1 35,39
Mills, Arthur. CSF 140
Mills, (Lady) Dorothy Rachel
(1889-1959) CSF 140 SF1 364
Mills, Elliott Evans. CSF 140
SF1 364
Mills, Frances M. CSF 140
Mills, Godfrey Hope Saxon. CSF
140 SF1 462
Mills, Janet Melanie Ailsa (1894-)
CSF 140 SF1 364
Mills, Robert E. HFI 103
Mills, Robert P. (1920-) ALW 54,
187,216 AOW 287 ASF 250-1,
261 BYS 279 ES2 313 EXT 5/1
10 EXT 8/1 8 IAC 113,177 MIH
28,98,100 SFE 399 SF1 365
SF2 1001 SFS 85 SOT 407 SRB
333
Mills, Weymer Jay (1880-1938)
CSF 140 SF1 365
Milne, A(lan) A(lexander) (1882-
1956) ES2 313-4 FBK 112 FFC
56,81 SF1 365
Milstead, John W. IAC 123,177
SF1 365
Milton, John (1608-74) ASF 67,
160 ATA 38 BYS 10,26-7,31,
67-8,199,213 CAT 69,81,89,

Milton, John (cont.)
136 CYR 7 DTS 3 EXT 4/2
22 EXT 5/1 22 EXT 9/2 26
ISW 149 JGB 16 MFW 282
MSF 33, 70, 122, 132, 134, 217
NWO 43, 111, 232 RBY 18, 166,
179 RZY 34, 37 SFA 57, 125
SFH 42-3, 48-9 STH 6 VES 224
WTS 17
Milton, Saul see Karl Flinders
Milward, Virginia. CSF 140 SF1
365
Minattus, Joseph. BAA 246
Minder, Robert. BAA 246
Miner, Horace. AOW 299
Mines, Samuel S. (1909-) ES2
314 ETN 20-1 IAC 177 IAH
11, 47 PJF 18 SFE 400 SFS 85
SF1 365 SF2 1001-2 SOT 78,
393, 401 STH 45 TJB 6 WAA
233, 244 WIF 106, 119 WSF 174
Mingston, R. Gresham pseud. of
Roger Stamp. SF1 365
Mink, A. R. IMS 68
Minkowski, Helmut. BAA 285
Minnett, Cora. CSF 140 SF1 365
Minor, Horace M. IAC 177
Minor, John W. CSF 140 SF1 365
Minor, Thomas Chalmers (1846-
1912) CSF 140 SF1 365
Minot, Stephen (1927-) ES2 314
HFI 104 SF1 365 SF2 1002
Minsky, Gloria. VFS 241
Minsky, Marvin. MFW 209 VFS
241 WFS 262
Minto, William. CSF 140
Miranda, Vincent. SRB 56-62,
514-5
Mirbeau, Octave (1850-1917) ES2
314
Mirdrekvandi, Ali. SF1 365
Miro, Joan. IAC 177
Mirrielees, Edith R. IAC 177
MSM xiii, 79 SFS 85 WIF 171
Mirrlees, Helen Hope (1887-
1978) CSF 141 FL2 926-31 HFI
104 SFE 400 SF1 366
Mish, Charles C. BAA 246
Miske, J. Chapman. IMS 169,
199, 201
Mistral, Bengo (house name) SF1
366
Misuse, Ryu. IAC 177 SFB 142
Mitcham, Alison. BAA 246
Mitchell, Adrian (1932-) BAA 152
IAC 177 SFE 400 SF1 366 SF2

1002
Mitchell, Albert. CSF 141
Mitchell, Clyde (house name) SFE
400 WGT 101 see also Harlan
Ellison, Randall Garrett, Robert
Silverberg
Mitchell, Ed. ALW 232 WFS 262
Mitchell, Edgar D. CSC 15-6
Mitchell, Edmund (1861-1917)
CSF 141 SF1 366
Mitchell, Edward Page (1852-
1927) HFI 104 IAC 177 MSF
167 SFE 400 SFW 39 SF1 366
STH 187, 202 VES 145, 150, 156,
180, 209
Mitchell, Gladys Maude Winifred
(1901-) WGT 101
Mitchell, Isaac. CSF 141
Mitchell, J. Calvin. BAA 83
CSF 141
Mitchell, J. Calvin. BAA 83
CSF 141
Mitchell, James Leslie (1901-35)
BAA 102 CSF 141 ES2 314 HFI
104 POE 231 SFE 400-1 SF1
366 STH 263 WIF 51, 54
Mitchell, John Ames (1845-1918)
AOW 68 CSF 141 ES2 314
EXT 1/1 14 IAC 177 PST 77,
314 SFE 401 SFS 85 SF1 366
SRB 10-1 VES 127
Mittelholzer, Edgar Austin (1909-
65) BAA 120 ES2 314
Mix, Tom. PJF 50, 53
Mizener, Arthur. ALW 236
Moberly, Charlotte Anne Eliza-
beth (1846-1937) ES2 315
Mobley, Jane. LTN 252 SRB 287
Mobus, Gerhard. BAA 185
Mockler-Ferryman, Augustus F.
CSF 141
Modder, Montagu Frank. STH 49
Modelmog, Ilse. BAA 185
Moebius. [FUT]
Moers, Ellen. SFW 6
Moffat, W. Graham. BAA 50 SF1
367
Moffatt, Adah Terrell. SF1 367
Moffatt, James. HFI 104 SF1
367
Moffett, Cleveland Langston
(1863-1926) AOW 36, 68 CSF
141 EXT 1/1 14 EXT 7/1 24
SFE 401 SF1 367
Moffitt, Donald. HFI 104
Mogridge, Stephen. SF1 367
Mohamet. IAH 72
Mohammed. HWK 32 INT 118

Mohler, Will. IAC 177
Mohoao pseud. of Edwin Fairburn.
SF1 367
Mohs, Mayo. AOW 296 IAC 177
SFD 35 SF1 367
Moilin, Tony. POE 136
Moldenhauer, Joseph J. NWO 61
Mitchell, John B. ETN 104
Mitchell, Linda. SF1 366
Mitchell, M. E. CSF 141 SF1 366
Mitchell, Milton. CSF 67
Mitchell, R. BAA 246
Mitchell, Ronald Elwy (1905-)
CSF 141 SF1 366
Mitchell, Silas Weir (1829-1914)
AOW 26 CSF 141 ES2 314
EXT 4/1 8-9, 13 IAC 177 SFE
401 SF1 366
Mitchell, Stephen O. EXT 1/2 33
Mitchell, William. IMS 63
Mitchell, (Prof.) Willis. BAA 54
SF1 366
Mitchell-Hedges, Frederick
Albert (1882-1959) SF1 366
Mitchison, Gilbert Richard (1890-
1970) SF1 366
Mitchison, Naomi (1897-) AAL
76-7, 83-4 AOW 228 BAA 162
BYS 305 ES2 314 EXT 10/1
31, 35 HFI 104 IAC 177 RGS
124-5 SFE 401 SF1 366 SF2
1002 SRB 16, 339 VES 136,
202, 214
Mitford, Bertram (1855-1914)
CSF 141 SF1 366-7
Mitgang, Herbert (1920-) SF1
367 SF2 1002-3
Mitskevitch, Anatoly P. see
Anatoly Dneprov
Molesworth, Mary Louisa (1839-
1921) CSF 142 ES2 315 FFC
26, 178 SF1 367 WGT 102
Molesworth, Voltaire (1924-64)
CSF 142 ES2 315 SF1 367
Moliere pseud. of Jean-Baptiste
Poquelin. MSF 114
Molin, Charles. ES2 315 SF1 367
Molk, Ulrich. BAA 246
Moller, Per Stig. BAA 182
Molloy, Hercules. SF1 367
Molnar. EXT 10/1 14
Molnar, Eugene Frank (1891-)
CSF 142 SF1 367
Molnar, T. S. NWO 101
Molnar, Thomas. BAA 185, 246-7

Molson, Francis J. AOW 302-34
FL1 7-16, 256-61, 483-5 FL3
1297-300 SL5 2298-302 SRB 19-
32, 514
Moltruhn, Maximilian. SF1 368
Mommers, Helmuth W. ES2 315
Monahan, James L. ES2 315
Monath, Elizabeth. FFC 76
Mondadori, Arnoldo (1889-1971)
ES2 315
Mondrian, Piet. ISW 115
Mongardini, Carlo. BAA 247
Mongelard, Joseph Cyril. SF1 368
Monig, Christopher pseud. of
Kendell F. Crossen. IAC 177
SFS 85
Moniz, Milton. BAA 185
Monk, Samuel H. BAA 247
Monkhouse, Bob. VES 327
Monro, Harold. POE 215-6
Monroe, Donald (1885-) ES2 315
SF1 368 WGT 102
Monroe, Keith (1917-) SF1 368
Monroe, Lyle pseud. of Robert
A. Heinlein. HID 18, 22-4, 31,
44, 193-4 IAC 177-8 OWB 11
RFA 187 RHN 23 SFD 145, 150,
152, 170 SFH 54 SFS 85 WSF
126, 167
Monroe, Marilyn. HEN 51 JGB 27
Monsarrat, Nicholas (1910-) ES2
315 HFI 104 SFE 402 SF1 368
Monsell, Margaret Emma Irwin.
WGT 102
Monsma, John Clover. ES2 315-6
Montague, C. E. BAA 93
Montague, Charles Howard. CSF
142
Montague, Edward. CSF 142 SF1
368
Montague, Nell St. John. CSF 142
Montalenti, Giuseppe. BAA 247
Montalvo, Garcia O. IAC 178
Montanari, Gianni (1949-) LEX
475-6 SFB 145 SFE 403-4 SL1
102-4, 322-4, 406-8, 415-7, 462-
7 SL3 1380-2 SL4 1739-41,
1863-5, 1896-7 SL5 2321-3
Monteleone, Thomas F. (1946-)
BAA 162 HFI 104 IAC 178 LEX
476-7 RZY 96, 105 SFE 404
Monterroso, Augusto. SF1 368
Montesquieu, Charles De Secondat
(1689-1755) EXT 8/1 21 MSF
114, 245

Montgolfier (brothers). FTF 26
PST 14, 271 WAA 33
Montgolfier, Jacques Etienne
(1745-99) EXT 9/2 29 TBC 44
see also Montgolfier brothers
Montgolfier, Joseph Michel
(1740-1810) EXT 9/2 29 TBC
29 see also Montgolfier brothers
Montgomerie, F. W. CSF 142
Montgomery, Bruce. MIH 31
Montgomery, Frances T. (1858?-
1925) AOW 304 CSF 142 SF1
368
Montgomery, L. M. LTN 255
Montgomery, Richard R. AOW
41 SF1 368
Montgomery, Robert Bruce (1921-
78) ES2 316 SFN 81 SF2 869
WGT 102 see also Edmund
Crispin
Montgomery, Rutherford George
(1894-) ES2 316 SF1 368 SF2
1003
Montgomery, T. H. EXT 7/1 27
Monti, Alessandro. BAA 247
Montresor, Beni. FFC 48, 126
Montresor, Frances T. CSF 142
Montrose, Anne. FFC 26
Moody, H. A. CSF 142 SF1 368
Moody, L. D. EXT 10/1 5
Moon, Eric. CWN 35
Moon, Sheila Elizabeth (1910-)
FFC 182 SF1 368 SF2 1003
Moon, Sun Myung. RHN 134
Mooney, James. IMS 138 SOT
328 STH 257
Mooney, Leo F. SF1 369
Moorcock, Michael (1939-) AAL
17-8, 122 ALW 212, 234-5 AOW
229, 296 ATA 16-7 BAA 154
BFP 368-76 BYS 230, 252, 264,
282, 296-8, 302-3, 308, 321 CAT
17 CSC 226 CWD 61 DMK 205-
13 DTS 39 ES2 316-7 ETN 7,
21, 65, 178-9 EXT 8/1 17 FBK
94-5, 124 FFR 129 FL1 489-96
FTF 69, 158 HFI 104-6 IAC
178 JGB 4, 10-1 LEX 477-9
MFW 56-8, 215 MIH 128-30,
136 NWO 48, 303 OMN 11, 14
RGS 125-7, 218-9 SFB 131-2
SFD 320 SFE 405-7 SFH 88-
93, 170-1 SFS 85 SFW 252,
277, 352, 423, 449-57 SF1 369-
70 SF2 1003 SIH 54, 59 SL1
157-62, 433-7, 468-73 SRB 271,

347-8 STH 5 VES 131, 143-4,
147-8, 212, 215, 227, 237, 242,
261-2 WAA 106, 109, 160, 243-
4 WGT 102 WSF 231, 251-2,
255 see also Michael Barring-
ton, James Colvin
Moore, Anne Carroll. EXT 10/1
35
Moore, Anon pseud. of James M.
Galloway. CSF 142
Moore, Arthur. SF1 370 see
also Antrim Oriel
Moore, B. S. SFD 22
Moore, Bidwell (1917-) SF1 370
Moore, Brian (1921-) AOW 229
FL2 646-8 HFI 106 SFE 407
SF1 370 SF2 1004
Moore, C. E. BAA 131
Moore, C(atherine) L. (1911-)
ALW 8, 143, 161 AOW 211, 230,
285, 288, 292, 401 ASF 127 BAA
124 BFP 377-9 BYS 237, 263
COT 64, 111, 165-6, 180-3, 186-
7, 195-6, 248-9, 292 CSC 29-30
ES2 317-8 ETN 137, 139, 142
EXT 3/1 3, 27 EXT 5/1 3 EXT
7/2 39 EXT 8/1 6 FBK 94 FFR
129-30 FL2 805-7 HFI 106 IAC
150, 178-9 IAH 12 IMS 16, 23-4,
134, 178 ISW 4, 122, 144-5 KAU
157-8 LEX 479-80 MIH 23-4,
36 MSM 81, 298 OWB 15, 79
RFA 28, 31, 36, 38, 68, 102, 109,
112, 115, 118, 124-5, 131, 140,
183, 195, 201, 212 RGS 127-9
SFD 56, 213, 289, 293, 309-10
SFE 407-8 SFS 70-1, 85-6 SFW
70, 161-7 SF1 370-1 SF2 1004
SL1 173-7 SOT 6, 52, 81, 178,
254, 303-18, 324, 329-31, 343
SRB 13, 272, 310, 319, 329 STH
121, 245, 258 TSF 53, 229 VES
81, 105, 173, 179, 187, 210, 261,
334-5 VF1 185-215, 277-8 WFS
200 WIF 24, 145, 157, 159, 230
WSF 67-8, 80, 108, 262, 283, 388
WTS ix, 12, 37-43, 48, 53, 56, 70,
85, 125 see also Catherine Kut-
tner, Lawrence O'Donnell, Lewis
Padgett
Moore, C. R. VES 202
Moore, David Albert (1914-) BAA
26 SF1 371
Moore, Erica Maria see Akira
Moore, Fenworth. CSF 142

245

Moore, Frank Frankfort (1855-
1931) BAA 71 CSF 142 SF1 371
Moore, George (1852-1933) SF1
371 STF 40
Moore, Hal R. IAC 179 SFS 86
Moore, Harris. HFI 106
Moore, Isabel. SF1 371
Moore, John W. BAA 247
Moore, M. Louise. BAA 48 CSF
142 SF1 371
Moore, Margaret. FFC 134
Moore, Mary. BAA 247 FFC 100
Moore, Maxine. KAU 158, 175-6
VF1 88-103, 267-8, 282
Moore, Patrick Alfred (1923-)
AOW 350 ES2 318 EXT 5/1 6
IAC 179 SFE 408 SF1 371-2
SF2 1004 VES 289, 330
Moore, Raylyn Thyrza (1928-)
IAC 178 SF2 1004
Moore, Rosalie. MSM 91-118,
303 SRB 505
Moore, Silas L., Jr. SF1 372
Moore, Stanley. BAA 247
Moore, Thomas (1779-1852) CSF
142 SF1 372
Moore, Thomas Emmet (1861-
1950) SF1 372
Moore, W. George. BAA 247
Moore, Ward (1903-78) AAL 88-
9 ALW 212-3 AOW 172, 230
BYS 20, 262, 279 COT 110 CSC
94-5 CSF 142 ES2 318 EXT
3/1 26 EXT 8/1 5 FFR 130
HFI 106 IAC 179 ISW vi KAU
191 LEX 480-1 MFW 165 NWO
236, 249 POE 293 SFE 408
SFN 105 SFS 86 SF1 372 SF2
1004-5 SL1 260-4 SOT 425
SRB 318 STH 45 VES 123, 132,
144, 187 WAA 69, 117, 126 WIF
113 WSF 8, 174
Moore, Wilbert E. BAA 247
Moorman, Charles. EXT 8/1 1
EXT 10/1 31, 35, 39 FAN 138
SOI 59-69, 161-2
Moos, Rudolf. BAA 185
Moosdorf, Johanna. SF1 372
Moote, A. Lloyd. EXT 6/1 18
Mor, Jokai. POE 139
Mora, Jose. CSF 143
Moran, John C. FL2 836-8 FL4
2054-8 FL5 2136-8
Moran, Kathryn. BAA 285
Morand, Hubert. EXT 2/1 9

Morand, Paul (1888-1976) SF1
372
Moravia, Alberto pseud. of
Alberto Pincherle. RAH 228
SFN 42 SF1 372
Moray, Clifford. CSF 143
Mordaunt, Elinor. CSF 143
ES2 318
Mordvinoff, Nicolas. FFC 130
More, Anthony pseud. of Edwin
M. Clinton. CSF 143 SF1 372
More, Enoch Anson, Jr. (1854-
1932) CSF 143 SF1 372
More, Marcel. BYS 95
More, (Sir) Thomas (1478-1535)
AAL 208 ALW 32, 43 AOW 11,
27, 343 ASF 173 BAA x-xii,
xiv-xv, 1-2 BYS 65-6 CAT 69,
77, 87 CSF 143 EXT 2/2 33
EXT 3/2 48 EXT 4/2 23 EXT
6/2 39-49 EXT 8/1 20-1, 23-4
EXT 9/2 28-9 EXT 10/2 76
FAN 4, 59, 66 FFR 130 FTF 18,
99 IAC 179 INT 12, 49 LTN
111 MFW 254, 267-8, 270, 274-
5 MSF 10, 12-3, 37, 40-3, 48, 50-
4, 58, 60, 73-4, 83, 88, 90-103, 106-
7, 110-1, 113, 115-6, 123, 131, 165,
171, 179-80, 213, 222, 230, 235,
237, 242, 244-5, 249, 257, 267
MSM 159-60 NWO 97, 99, 100-2
POE 4, 35, 119, 274 PST 11, 24,
237, 239, 261-2, 297 SFB 17 SFD
70 SFE 408-9 SFH 6, 42, 80, 173
SFN 111 SFS 86 SIH 6, 60, 62,
65, 68, 74, 77, 79 SRB 3 STF 30,
39 STH 1 UKL 125-7, 137, 141,
152 VES 124-5, 165, 247, 254,
261-2, 270, 312 WAA 47-8 WBW
31 WIF 38, 227 WSF 341-2
Moreana. BAA 247
Morehouse, William Russell
(1879-1937) SF1 372
Morel, Dighton pseud. of Kenneth
Lewis Warner (1915-) BYS 295
SF1 372
Morel, Eugene. EXT 2/1 14
Morell, Charles pseud. of James
Ridley. CSF 143
Moresby, (Lord) Charles. SF1
372
Moresby, Louis pseud. of L. Adams
Beck. CSF 143 MFW 128-9, 131
SFW 68
Moreton, John. FFC 76

Morey, Leo. COT 175 ES2 318-9 ISW 284 SRB 36 TSP 30 VES 136, 286-8 WSF 49, 126
Morf, Otto. BAA 247
Morgan, Albert Edward (1920-) SF1 373 SF2 1005
Morgan, Alice B. BAA 247
Morgan, Alison. FFC 134
Morgan, Arthur E. BAA 131, 185-6, 247 CSF 143 MSF 177 SF1 373
Morgan, Bassett. WTS 27, 30-1, 37
Morgan, Chris. FLR 61 FL1 71-3, 161-3, 173-7, 436-40 FL2 605-6, 768-72, 855-8 FL3 1301-3, 1387-91, 1417-9, 1482-4 FL4 1662-4, 1913-7, 1933-7, 2002-4 IAC 179 SFW 321-7, 433-9, 497-503, 519-24
Morgan, Dan (1925-) AOW 242 BYS 262 ES2 319 HFI 106 IAC 179 LEX 481 SFE 409 SFS 86 SF1 373 SF2 1005-6 VES 160
Morgan, Edwin. IAC 179-80
Morgan, Elaine. CSC 154 JGB 53
Morgan, H. Wayne. BAA 247
Morgan, Helen. FFC 105
Morgan, Helene. SF1 373
Morgan, Jacques. ES2 319 FTF 66 WIF 70
Morgan, John Minter (1782-1854) BAA 19-20 CSF 143 SF1 373
Morgan, Joseph. MSF 139
Morgan, Lewis H. WBW 59
Morgan, Louisa. SF1 373
Morgan, Sophia. EXT 10/2 111
Morice, Charles (1861-1919) CSF 143 SF1 373 STH 229
Morich, Stanton pseud. of George Chetwynd Griffith-Jones. EXT 7/1 17
Morison, Frank pseud. of Albert Henry Ross. CSF 143 SF1 373
Morland, Dick pseud. of Reginald Charles Hill (1936-) BAA 160 SFE 409 SF1 373
Morland, Harold. EXT 9/1 3, 16-7
Morland, Nigel (1905-) SF1 373 SF2 1006
Morley, Christopher (1890-1957) CSF 143 ES2 319 EXT 2/1 14, 16 FL4 1930-2 IAC 180 IAH 6 ISW 112, 274 SF1 373
Morley, Felix Muskett (1894-) BAA 129 ES2 319 HFI 106 SFE 409

SF1 373
Morley, Henry. CSF 143 ES2 319
Morojo pseud. of Myrtle Douglas, Myrtle K. Jones. IMS 138-9, 213-4, 222, 225-6, 228, 236, 243 WFS 96
Morphett, Tony. IAC 180
Morra, Gianfranco. BAA 247
Morressy, John (1930-) AAL 13 AOW 326 FFC 172 HFI 107 RGS 129 SFE 409-10 SF1 373 SF2 1006
Morrill, Fred Brown (1858-) BAA 83 CSF 143 SF1 373
Morrill, Leslie. FFC 117
Morris, Alfred. BAA 48 CSF 143 FTF 101 SF1 374
Morris, Anthony P. SF1 374
Morris, Gouveneur (1876-1953) AOW 46, 68 BAA 77 CSF 143 ES2 319 EXT 1/1 14 IAC 180 SFE 410 SFS 86 SF1 374 SRB 9 STH 126
Morris, Gwendolen Sutherland see Morris Sutherland
Morris, Henry O. BAA 57 CSF 143 SF1 374
Morris, Humphrey. FLT 152
Morris, Janet E. (1946-) HFI 107 SFE 410
Morris, Joe Alex (1904-) SF1 374
Morris, John. SF1 374
Morris, Kenneth (1879-1937) CSF 143 ES2 319 FL2 539-42 FL3 1372-4 LTN 88, 91-2, 95, 111 SF1 374
Morris, Martha Marlowe (1867-) BAA 108 CSF 144 SF1 374
Morris, May. WBW 22, 36, 43
Morris, Ralph. ALW 43 AOW 27 CSF 144 FTF 25 SFE 410 SF1 374 WGT 102
Morris, Robert. HID 113
Morris, Rosamund. ES2 319 SF1 374
Morris, Vic. IAC 180
Morris, William (1834-96) ACC 85-6, 209 ACE 33 AC2 31 ALW 62 AOW 356 BAA 37, 42 BYS 3, 86-8, 137-8 CAT 8, 10, 50, 63, 78, 95 CSF 144 EXT 2/1 2 EXT 2/2 27 EXT 5/1 4 EXT 6/2 41 EXT 9/2 31, 46, 51 FAN 26, 34, 65 FBK 88, 91, 93 FFR 131 FL4 1831-3, 1854-8 FL5 2069-73, 2090-6, 2165-70 FTF 100-1, 103, 109 HFI 107 HWK

Morris, William (cont.)
40 KAU 97 MSF 9, 38, 45, 50-1,
54, 76, 95, 113, 169, 171, 175, 177-
94, 198-9, 201, 203, 212, 217, 219-
20, 230, 235-7, 240, 266 POE 153,
165-6 PST 57, 93, 236 SFB 112
SFD 42, 71 SFE 410 SFH 11,
149, 174 SFN 12 SF1 374-5
SL3 1516-20 SOT 235 SRB 272
UKL 134, 136, 150-1 VES 124,
126, 255 WSF 293 see also
John-Martin
Morrish, Leslie Furze. SF1 375
Morrison, Arthur. CSF 144 ES2
319-20
Morrison, D. A. C. BAA 124 IAC
180 SFS 86
Morrison, Emmeline. CSF 144
SF1 375
Morrison, Henry. RSG 23
Morrison, Margaret Mackie (-1973)
WGT 102-3 see also March Cost,
Peggy Morrison
Morrison, Peggy pseud. of Mar-
garet Mackie Morrison. ES2
320
Morrison, Seon. FFC 57
Morrison, William pseud. of
Joseph Samachson. DTS 25
FFR 131 HFI 107 IAC 180
ISW 120-1 SFS 86 WFS 200
Morrissey, James Lawrence
(1905-) SFE 410 SF1 375 WGT
103 see also Richard Saxon
Morrough, E. R. CSF 144 ES2
320 SF1 375
Morrow, Glenn R. BAA 186
Morrow, Gray. VES 102, 142,
184, 189, 209, 231, 234
Morrow, Lowell Howard. CSF
144 IMS 23 SF1 375
Morrow, W. C. IAC 180 WTS 37
Morrow, William Chambers
(1853-1923) CSF 144 ES2 320
EXT 1/1 15 EXT 7/1 18, 26
SF1 375
Morsberger, Katharine M. FL1
262-5 FL2 873-9 FL3 1127-31
FL4 1568-74 FRN 109 SL1
396-401 SL3 1531-6 SL5 2101-
6, 2184-9
Morsberger, Robert E. FL2 873-
9 FL4 1554-62, 1712-7, 1904-7
FL5 2118-21, 2159-61 FRN 109
SL2 1008-13 SL4 1908-12, 1989-
93, 2035-41 SL5 2229-35

Morse, Albert Reynolds (1914-)
ES2 320 SF1 375 SF2 1006-7
Morse, Elizabeth A. EXT 10/1
36
Morse, J. Mitchell. EXT 6/1 19
Morse, Katharine Duncan (1888-)
WGT 103
Morse, Richard Ely. EXT 3/1 7
Morse, Samuel F. B. FTF 35
MSF 194 SFN 92
Mortimer, Edward James. BAA
31
Mortlock, Bill. IAC 180
Morton, A. L. BAA 247 EXT
8/2 60 FAN 91, 184 VES 127
Morton, A. S. CSF 144 SF1 375
Morton, Arthur Leslie. BAA 186
Morton, F. IMS 25
Morton, Frank (1869-1923) CSF
144 SF1 375
Morton, Henry Canova Vollom
(1892-) BAA 111 CSF 144 SF1
375
Morton, James F. EXT 3/1 21
ISW 224
Morton, John B. CSF 144
Morton, (Cardinal) John. MSF 29
Morton, K. M. CSF 144
Mosca, Mariangela. BAA 247
Moschkowskaja, J. BAA 247
Mosely, Oswald. RAH 179
Moser, Simon. BAA 247
Moses. CYR 6 INT 118 JGB 19
VF1 88-103, 267-8
Moses, Bernard. BAA 248
Mosig, Dirk W. SL1 97-101
Moskowitz, Alfred. IMS 137
Moskowitz, Sam (1920-) ACC 244
AC2 75 ALW 7-8, 31, 58, 74, 107,
110, 122, 180, 183, 187 AOW 68,
81-2, 283, 296, 350 ASF 241-2
BAA 186, 248 BFP 380-4 BRS
9 BYS 41, 54, 176, 213, 242 CAT
xv, 131 COT 18, 238, 285, 299-
300 ES2 320-2 ETN 22, 53, 82,
85 EXT 3/1 24 EXT 4/2 24-5
EXT 5/1 6, 15-6a EXT 6/2 22
EXT 7/2 47-8 EXT 8/2 32, 58,
62 EXT 9/2 63 EXT 10/1 46
EXT 10/2 102 FAN 7 FBK 82
FFR 131 FHT 67 FLR 61 FRN
21, 47 FTF 139 HID 12, 189, 192
IAC 109, 180, 184 IAH 57 ISW ix,
12, 25, 33, 91, 128, 130-3, 160-3,
284 KAU 165 MIH 6, 8, 16, 25-
8, 35-9, 80, 120 NDA 214-5 NWO

Moskowitz, Sam (cont.)
50-2 PJF 12, 74 RAH 52, 258
RBY 240 RFA xxii RHN 16, 62
SFB 8, 55, 97, 152 SFD 29, 63,
209 SFE 410-1 SFH 39, 52 SFN
14 SFS 87 SFW 91, 100, 117, 123,
148-9, 178, 184, 211, 214, 276 SF1
376-7 SF2 1007-11 SIH 191 SL1
22-7 SL2 698-702, 878-82 SRB
72, 76, 92, 239, 341, 505 TSF 247
VES 330, 335, 341 WAA 133, 161,
244, 246 WFS 59, 74, 94-5 WIF
17, 116, 131, 138 WSF 74, 78, 142-
3, 146, 213-4, 224, 263, 278, 281,
383, 389 WTS ix, 54, 134 see
also Robert Bahr, Robert San-
ders Shaw, William M. Weiner,
Fred Wollonover
Mosley, Maboth (1906-) BAA 102
SF1 376
Moss, Robert F. SF1 377
Mosse, George L. BAA 248
Moszkowski, Alexander (1851-
1934) CSF 144 SFE 412 SF1
377
Mott, Frank Luther. ALW 116
Mott, Lawrence (1881-) ES2 322
Motta, Luigi (1881-1955) CSF 144
SF1 377 SL5 2321-3 WAA 235
Mottley, Charles C. HFI 107
Mottram, Ralph Hale (1883-1971)
BAA 114 CSF 144 ES2 322 SFE
412 SF1 377
Moudy, Walter Frank (1929-73)
ES2 322 HFI 107 IAC 180 SFE
412 SFS 87 SF1 377 SF2 1011
Moulton, Forest Ray. COT 34
Mountbatten, (Lord). VFS 120
Mowshowitz, Abbe. IAC 180
Moxley, Frank Wright (1889-1937)
CSF 144 EXT 10/2 100, 107 PST
174-5, 255, 288 SFE 412 SF1 377
Moy, Seong. FFC 130
Moylan, Tom. AC2 75 SL2 894-
8 SL5 2307-10
Moynihan, Daniel Patrick. WFS
74-5
Moynihan, Roberta. FFC 9
Mozart, Wolfgang Amadeus (1756-
91) CWN 39 FLT 32 LTN 88
THM 60
Mozley, Charles. FFC 74
Moyer, Mildred. EXT 9/1 3
Mrozek, Slawomir (1930-) AOW
230 BYS 307 IAC 180 SFE 412
SF1 377 SF2 1011

Mucchielli, Roger. BAA 186, 248
Muddock, Joyce Emmerson Pres-
ton (1843-1934) CSF 145 ES2
322 SF1 377 STH 123 WGT 103
see also Dick Donovan
Mudgett, Herman W. pseud. of
William Anthony Parker White.
IAC 180 TSP 197
Mudrick, Marvin. EXT 9/2 51-2
Muggeridge, Malcolm (1903-) SF1
377
Mugnaini, Joseph. FFC 161 SFS
87
Muhammad, Elijah. RHN 158-9
Muhlbach, Louisa pseud. of Klara
Mundt. SF1 377
Muir, Charles S. CSF 145
Muir, Edwin. EXT 10/1 36 IAC
180 POE 266
Muir, John. BAA 158
Muir, John Ramsay Bryce (1872-
1941) BAA 95 SF1 377
Muir, Ward (1878-1927) BAA 84
CSF 145 SF1 377
Muirden, James (1942-) ES2 322
SF1 377
Mukerji, Dhan Gopal. CSF 145
Mukhanov, N. I. MSF 261
Mulier pseud. of Charles Eli Hig-
gins. SF1 377
Mulisch, Harry. SFS 87
Mullaly, Frederic. COT 138
Mullen, Richard D. AAL 14
ALW 109 BAA 239, 248 BYS
167, 179 COT 221 EXT 7/2 29
EXT 8/1 1 EXT 8/2 31-63 EXT
10/1 48 EXT 10/2 50 IAC 180
KAU 129 LTN 256, 262, 264
MSF 239 OSR 229-47, 356 SFE
412 SFH 60, 239 SRB 72
Mullen, Stanley B. (1911-73?)
CSF 145 ES2 322 HFI 107 IAH
18 ISW 26-9 MIH 20, 90-1 SFE
412 SF1 377 WGT 103
Mullenbrock, Heinz-Joachim.
BAA 248
Muller, Al. SL3 1463-7
Muller, Ernst see Julian West
Muller, G. EXT 6/1 7
Muller, Gert H. BAA 248
Muller, Herbert J. AOW 356
BAA 248
Muller, (Dr.) Herman. VFS 127
Muller, Hermann Joseph. EXT
5/1 6 IMS 159
Muller, Horst (1923-) LEX 481-2

Muller, John E. (house name)
ES2 322-3 SFE 412 SF1 378
see also Robert L. Fanthorpe,
A. A. Glynn
Muller, Julian. VFS 41
Muller, Julius Washington (1867-)
CSF 144 SF1 378
Muller, Max. WBW 59
Muller, Paul (1924-) SF1 378
Muller, Robert (1925-) SF1 378
Muller, Wolf Dietrich. BAA 285
Muller-Stormsdorfer, Ilse. BAA
248
Mulligan, Bob. SOT 372
Mulock, (Miss). ISW 275
Mulock, Diana. FFC 50, 86
Mumford, Edwin Embree (1932-)
SF1 378-9
Mumford, James E. CSF 82
Mumford, Lewis. BAA x, xix,
xxi, 186, 248 COT 221, 223
EXT 7/1 15 EXT 9/1 3, 5, 16
FAN 66, 174, 184 [FUT] KAU
10-1, 59, 86-8, 97, 193, 200, 222
MFW 183 MSF 12, 73, 93, 131,
141, 180-1 NDA 199 SFD 189
Muminovic, Rasim. BAA 249
Munby, Alan Noel Latimer (1913-
74) ES2 323 SF1 379 SF2 1011
Munby, Lionel M. BAA 249
Munch, Edvard. FBK 47
Munch, Paul George (1877-) SF1
379
Munchen, A. Langer. EXT 6/1 7
Munchhausen, Karl. FFC 156
Muncker, Franz. BAA xxii
Mund, E. S. VES 199
Munday, John William see Charles
Sumner Seeley
Mundis, Jerrold J. IAC 180-1
Mundo, Oto. CSF 145 SF1 379
Mundt, Klara (1814-73) see
Louisa Muhlbach
Mundt, Theodor. BAA 186
Mundy, Talbot pseud. of William
Lancaster Gribbon (1879-1940)
AOW 108, 394 CSF 145 CWD 6,
53 ES2 323-4 FBK 103 FL2
801-4 FL3 1142-5 FL4 1975-8
HFI 107-8 MSM 128 SFD 41
SFE 412-3 SF1 379 WTS 62
Munkittrick, Richard Kendall
(1853-1911) ES2 324
Munn, Bertram. CSF 145 SF1
379

Munn, H(arold) Warner (1903-81)
ES2 324 FBK 53 FL2 1015-20
HFI 108 IAC 181 LEX 482 SFE
413 SF1 379 SF2 1011 SRB 273
WTS 12, 25-6, 28, 30, 33, 37, 43,
50-2
Munro, Duncan H. WIF 221
Munro, H(ector) H(ugh) (1870-
1916) BYS 145-6 CSF 145 ES2
324-5 IAC 181 SF1 379 WGT
103 see also Saki
Munro, John (1849-1930) BAA 57
CSF 145 IAC 181 SFE 413 SF1
380
Munro, Kirk. IAC 181
Munsey, Frank Andrew (1854-
1925) ALW 80-2, 85, 106-7, 110,
118, 156 ES2 325 ETN 11 SFE
413 STH 39-41 WFS 8 WSF 23,
29 YTS 9
Munson, Donald. SF1 380
Munson, Gorham. WIF 171
Munson, Ronald. BAA 249
Munster, (Countess of). ES1 118
Munzer, Thomas. MSF 38
Muralto, Onuphrio. FBK 18
Murch, A. E. SOT 249
Murdoch, Iris. BAA 249 SOI xiii,
158
Murdock, B. IMS 30
Murfree, Mary Noailles (1850-
1922) WGT 103 see also Charles
Egbert Craddock
Murillo, L. A. EXT 9/1 17
Murnau, F. W. FBK 48 WAA 88,
192
Murphy, Brian. SL3 1516-20
SL4 1669-73
Murphy, Gardner. CWN 59
Murphy, George Read. CSF 145
SF1 380
Murphy, James. CSF 146
Murphy, Robert William (1902-
71) IAC 181 SFS 87 SF1 380
SF2 1012
Murphy, Shirley Rosseau. FFC
44, 50, 122, 135 HFI 108 IAC 181
Murphy, Walter F. BAA 249
Murphy, Warren. AOW 246 SF1
380
Murray, Alfred. CSF 146 SF1
380
Murray, (Dr.) Bruce. VFS 139,
211
Murray, (Sir) Charles Augustus
(1806-95) SF1 380

Murray, Colin Middleton (1926-)
WGT 103
Murray, David Christie (1847-
1907) SF1 380 STH 188
Murray, David Leslie (1888-1962)
SF1 380
Murray, George Gilbert Aime
(1866-1957) BAA 40 CSF 146
SF1 380
Murray, Gilbert. MSF 25
Murray, Grenville. BAA 30
Murray, Henry. CSF 33
Murray, Jacqueline. SF1 380
Murray, Kate. CSF 146
Murray, Margaret Alice (1863-
1963) ES2 325 EXT 1/2 36
Murray, Matthew. BAA 249
Murray, Patricia Hagan. SF1 380
Murray, Robert. IAC 181
Murray, Robert H. BAA 249
Murray, Violet Torlesse (1874-)
CSF 146 ES2 325 SF1 380
Murray, (Rev.) William. BAA 93
Murrow, Edward R. COT 141
EXT 10/2 86
Murry, John Middleton, Jr. (1926-)
BAA 144,249 BFP 385 ES2 325
SF2 867 see also Richard Cow-
per
Musa, Gilda. LEX 483
Muslin, E. IAC 181

Muspratt, Rosalie Helen (1906-76)
CSF 146 SF1 380 WGT 104 see
also Jasper John
Musser, Joseph L. (1936-) SF1
380 SF2 1012
Mussino, Attilio. FFC 80
Mussolini, Benito. ASF 282-3
COT 120-1 WFS 61,63,146
WTS 58
Mussorgsky, Modest P. MSF 243
Muybridge, Eadweard. VFS 199-
200
Myers, Charles F. (1922-) ES2
325
Myers, F.W. H. AAL 132
Myers, Henry (1893-) ES2 325
HFI 108 SF1 381
Myers, Howard L. HFI 108 IAC
181 SFE 415
Myers, John. HID 30
Myers, John Myers (1906-) ES2
325 HFI 108 SF1 381 SF2 1012
SRB 273
Myers, L. H. THM 8,10
Myers, Robert E. TSF 177-83
Myers, William Wilshire. CSF
146 SF1 381
Myra, Harold Lawrence (1939-)
SF1 381
Myself and Another pseud. of
Edward A. Caswell. CSF 146

N

N. N. SF1 381
Nabokov, Vladimir (1899-1977)
ALW 31,238 BAA 115 BYS 128,
257 CSC 95,101 CUA 3-4 DTS
v ETN 90 FAN 147 FLT 2,93-
110,124,141 KAU 26 KVT 28
LTN 175 MIH 60 RHN 192 SFD
4 SFE 418-9 SFH 97 SF1 381
SF2 1012 SIH 43 SL1 16-21
SOI xiii

Nace, Pierce. HFI 108
Nadel, Aaron. VES 181
Nader, George. HFI 184
Nader, Ralph. JGB 27
Nadler, Maggie. IAC 181
Nadler, Robert. FFC 97
Nagel, Ernest. IAH 133
Nagera, Humberto. FLT 153
Nagl, Manfred (1940-) BAA 186
SFE 419

Nagpal, Veena. SF1 381
Naha, Ed. OMN 232-8, 260-7
Najera, Fernando Vida. BAA 195, 273
Nanovic, John. TSP 221
Nansen, Fridtjof. CSC 23
Napier, Carson. ALW 109, 111
Napier, Eva M. CSF 146
Napier, Melissa. SF1 381
Napoleon (1769-1821) ASF 102, 245 CUA 61 EXT 4/1 3 EXT 8/2 33 INT 79 ISW 276 LTN 157 MSF 119, 150, 153, 245, 273
Napoli, James Vincent. VES 92 WTS ix, 86, 103
Narayan, R. K. IAC 181
Narcejac, Thomas pseud. of Pierre Ayraud, Pierre Boileau. SF1 381
Narodny, Ivan. CSF 146
Nash, Mary (1925-) FFC 148 SF1 381 SF2 1013
Nash, Ogden (1902-71) ES2 326 IAC 181 SFS 87
Nast, Thomas. SFH 107
Natas, Eth. SF1 381
Nathan, Richard. SF1 381
Nathan, Robert Gruntal (1894-) CSF 146 ES2 326 FFC 195 FL3 1276-9 FL4 1766-8 IAC 181 ISW 110, 112, 126 SFE 419 SFS 87 SF1 381-2 SF2 1013 STH 48, 51 VES 144
Nathanson, Isaac. STH 45
Nation, Terry (1930-) HFI 108 SFE 419 VES 303
Natsume, Soseki pseud. of Natsume Kin'nosuke. SF1 382
Natti, Mary Lee (1919-) see Lee Kingman
Natti, Susanna. FFC 70
Naude, Gabriel. BAA 186
Naujack, Peter. ES2 326
Naval Officer, (A). CSF 146
Navarchus pseud. of Patrick Vaux, Lionel Yexley. CSF 146
Navasky, Victor S. (1932-) SF1 382 SF2 1013
Naviglio, Luigi (1936-) LEX 484 WAA 235
Nayfack, Nicholas (1909-58) ES2 326
Naylor, Charles. IAC 100, 181 SFW 354-5
Neal, H. C. IAC 181 SFS 87

Neal, John (1793-1876) CSF 146 SF1 382
Neale, Arthur. CSF 146 ES2 326 SF1 382
Nearing, (Prof.) Homer, Jr. (1915-) ALW 216 AOW 231 CSC 50, 52 ES2 326 HFI 108 IAC 181 MSM 92, 126 SFE 421 SFS 87 SF1 382 WIF 185, 226
Neaum, Radford A. CSF 147
Nebel, ("Long") John (1911-) ES2 326 SOT 185, 246 WFS 14-5, 255-7, 264
Necker, Claire Kral (1917-) SF1 382 SF2 1013
Nedram. BAA 86 CSF 147 SF1 382
Needham, Joseph. VFS 189
Neele, Henry. CSF 147
Neeper, Carolyn. HFI 109 WGT 104
Neesam, Malcolm. SF1 382
Neff, M. A. BAA 80
Negley, Glenn Robert (1907-) BAA xvii, xxi, 186, 249 ES2 326-7 EXT 8/1 23-4 EXT 9/1 16 EXT 9/2 31, 63 FAN 184 MSF 46-7, 54 NDA 51-2, 54 SF1 382 SF2 1013
Negri, Rocco. FFC 44, 65
Neibuhr, Reinhold. KVT 50
Neill, Alexander Sutherland (1883-1973) CSF 147 SF1 383
Neill, Peter (1941-) SF1 383
Neill, Robert. ES2 327 SF1 383
Neill, T. P. BAA 249
Neilson, Keith. FL1 143-5, 187-9, 197-202, 294-9, 465-7 FL2 553-6, 581-4, 590-2, 607-11, 638-41, 715-7, 740-3, 955-8 FL3 1040-3, 1105-10, 1116-20, 1191-5, 1338-42, 1358-62, 1402-6, 1536-43 FL4 1616-20, 1729-32 FL5 2122-5, 2150-2 SL2 749-55 SL3 1480-7 SL4 1871-8 SL5 2350-6, 2416-23
Nelson, Alan. IAC 181 MSM 93 SFS 87-8
Nelson, Albert D. BAA 106 CSF 147 SF1 383
Nelson, Albert Francis Joseph Horatio (1890-1957) ES2 327
Nelson, Arthur A. CSF 147 IMS 137 SF1 383 SRB 9
Nelson, James. EXT 3/1 20
Nelson, Kam. HEN 14

Nelson, R(ay) F(araday) (1931-)
DTS 36, 47 ES2 327 HFI 109
IAC 181 LEX 484-5 SFE 423
SFS 88 SF1 383 SF2 1013-4
WGT 104
Nelson, Richard H. STH 18
Nelson, Robert. IMS 30 WTS 126
Nelson, William. BAA 186, 249
Nembhard, Mabel. SF1 383
Nemerov, Howard. EXT 10/1 26
IAC 181
Nemo, Omen pseud. of Warren S.
Rehm. CSF 147
Nemtsov, Vladimir I. MSF 265
Nepean, Hubert. CSF 83 SF1 383
Nepolis, Ivan pseud. of Wilson
Shepard. IMS 28, 30
Nergert, Heinz. BAA 285
Neri, Nicoletta. BAA 249
Nero, (Emperor). MSF 121 NWO
6, 27
Nero, Lucius Domitius. ISW 236
Nesbit, Edith pseud. of Edith
Nesbit Bland (1858-1924) AOW
304 CSF 147 ES2 327 EXT 1/2
37 FBK 114 FFC 21, 68-9, 89,
103, 166, 182 FL1 483-5 FL3
1297-300 IAC 181 SF1 383, 583
SRB 23
Neset, Malvin. FFC 75
Ness, Evaline. FFC 14, 45, 47,
116, 131, 135, 168
Nesvadba, Josef (1926-) AOW 231
BYS 189, 307 COT 217 ES2 327
EXT 7/2 47 FFR 133 HFI 109
IAC 181 LEX 485 SFE 423 SFS
88 SFW 583, 591 SF1 383 SF2
1014 SOT 431
Netherclift, Beryl. FFC 36 SF1
383
Nethercot, Arthur H. EXT 9/2 62
Netherwood, Bryan Arthur. ES2
327 SF1 383
Netterville, Luke pseud. of Stan-
dish James O'Grady. CSF 147
SF1 383
Nettlau, Max. BAA 186
Neufeld, John Arthur (1938-) SF1
383 SF2 1014
Neumann, Erich. ISW 6
Neususs, Arnhelm. BAA 187, 249
Neutzell, Albert A. VES 288
Neville, Derek. BAA 115 CSF
147 SF1 383
Neville, Henry (1620-94) BAA 6-7
CSF 147 WGT 104-5

Neville, Kris (Ottman) (1925-)
ALW 212, 216 AOW 231 BAA
158 BYS 262 ES2 327-8 HFI
109 IAC 182 LEX 485-6 SFE
423 SFS 88 SF1 383-4 SF2 1014
VES 134 WGT 105
Neville, Lil. BAA 158 IAC 182
Neville, Pierre. BAA 249
Nevins, W. Varick. IMS 29
Nevinson, Christopher Richard
Wynne (1889-1946) CSF 195 SF1
384
Nevinson, Henry Wood (1856-
1941) ES2 328
Newbolt, Henry John (1862-1938)
BAA 249 FL1 4-6 HFI 109 SF1
384
Newby, Percy Howard (1918-)
HFI 109 SF1 384 SF2 1015
Newcomb, Cyrus Flint (1831-1905)
SF1 384
Newcomb, (Prof.) Simon (1835-
1909) AOW 37, 69 BAA 63 CSF
147 EXT 1/1 2, 15 EXT 5/1 4
EXT 7/1 23, 27 IAC 182 MSM
189-90, 211-2, 305 PST 84, 201,
264-5, 270, 287, 290, 296, 299
SFE 423 SF1 384
Newcomen, Thomas. FTF 34
Newell, Charles Martin (1821-
1900) CSF 147 SF1 384
Newell, Peter E. BAA 249
Newfield, Jack (1939-) SF1 384
SF2 1015
Newill, Henry. ES2 328
Newman, A. pseud. of Herbert
M. Pim. CSF 147
Newman, Bernard Charles (1897-
1968) CSF 147 ES2 328 SFE
424 SF1 384 STF 22 VES 107
WGT 105
Newman, H. E. BAA 78
Newman, Howard (1911-) SF1 384
SF2 1015
Newman, James. VES 181
Newman, John. ES2 328 SFE 424
WGT 105 see also Kenneth Johns
Newman, John Henry. CWN 31
Newman, Louis. IAC 182 SFS 88
Newman, Philip. EXT 10/1 36
Newman, Robert Howard (1909-)
FFC 39, 195 SF1 384 SF2 1015
Newman, Sharon. FFC 50
Newnes, George. ALW 80 EXT
10/1 46 STH 186

Newquist, Roy (1925-) see Carl Sterland
Newsom, Tom. VES 73
Newte, Horace Wykenham (1870-1949) BAA 71 CSF 147 SF1 385
Newton, Bertha. SF1 385
Newton, Douglas. STH 136, 140
Newton, (Sir) Isaac (1642-1727) ASF 187 CAT 73 CSC 59, 66, 167, 219 EXT 4/2 21 EXT 7/2 33 EXT 10/2 107 FTF 19, 23 MFW 193 MSF 87, 109, 122, 210 OWB 31 POE 24 PST 15, 17 SFH 42-3, 120-1, 123, 125, 129, 131, 148 SFN 34 THM 44 TSO 10 VFS 81, 196, 199 WFS 259 WSF 14, 332, 364
Newton, John H. SF1 385
Newton, Joseph Emerson. SF1 385
Newton, Julius P. ES2 328 HFI 109 SFE 424 SF1 385
Newton, Rita. FFC 82
Newton, Wilfrid Douglas (1884-1951) CSF 148 ES2 328 SFE 424 SF1 385
Neyroud, Gerald E. IAC 182 SFS 88
Niall, Ian pseud. of John McNeillie. HFI 109 SF1 385
Nichol, (Mrs.) C. A. Scrymsour. BAA 73 SF1 385
Nicholas, Brian. BAA 249-50
Nicholas II. ISW 91
Nicholls, Peter (1939-) BYS 319 ETN 56, 62-3 FL4 1787-9, 1813-20 IAC 182 JGB 60 KWS 5 LTN 22, 36, 210, 263 SFE 426-7 SFW 185-96, 305-11, 355, 358, 425-31, 449-57, 563-70 SL1 277-82, 308-12 SL2 770-5 SL4 1622-6, 1821-6 SL5 2163-7 SRB 64, 73, 506 TJB 17 TSF 247
Nichols. WTS 25
Nichols, Joanna Ruth (1948-) FFC 69, 178 SF1 385 SF2 1015
Nichols, Mike. CSC 309
Nichols, Nichelle. IAC 182
Nichols, Robert Malise Bower (1893-1944) CSF 148 ES2 328 FL2 524-5 SF1 385
Nichols, Thomas Low. BAA 27
Nicholson, Celia Anna. CSF 148 SF1 385
Nicholson, Daniel. SOI 130
Nicholson, John pseud. of Norman Howe Parcell. CSF 148 ES2 328 IAC 182 SF1 385
Nicholson, Joseph Shield (1850-1927) BAA 38 CSF 148 SF1 385 WGT 105
Nicholson, Norman. FAN 17, 33-4, 36, 183
Nicholson, Normen. BAA 187
Nicholson, William. FFC 80
Nickl, Peter. FFC 123
Nicklaus, Carol. FFC 139, 141, 149
Nickless, Will. FFC 135
Nicol, Charles. JGB 58
Nicolaides, Nicholas. BAA 106
Nicolas. FFC 140, 151-2, 154
Nicole, Claudette pseud. of John Messman. SF1 385
Nicoletti, Manfredi G. BAA 250
Nicoli, Fabio. FBK 153
Nicoll, Henry Maurice Dunlop (1884-1953) WGT 105 see also Martin Swayne
Nicolson, (Sir) Harold George (1886-1968) CSF 148 POE 248-9 SFE 427 SF1 385 SF2 1015 VES 121
Nicolson, John Urban (1885-) CSF 148 SF1 386 VES 77
Nicolson, Marjorie Hope (1894-) ALW 30 AOW 44, 350 BAA 187 BYS 11, 35, 65 COT 53-4, 300 ES2 328 EXT 4/2 29 EXT 7/1 1 EXT 9/1 2 EXT 9/2 28 FAN 9-10, 51, 183 MSM 199, 207 NWO 148 SFB 73 SFE 427 SFH 239 SF1 386 SF2 1016 SOI 42, 46, 49 SRB 5, 69 VES 79, 329 WBW 26
Nicolson, Norman. EXT 8/2 56
Niculescu, Mihai (1909-) SF1 386
Niebuhr, Reinhold. BAA 250
Nielsen, Helga. ES2 328 SF1 386
Nielsen, Leslie. KAU 199
Nielsen, Lin. IAC 182
Nielsen, Niels E. IAC 182 SIH 147
Nielson, Jon. FFC 50
Niemann, August (1839-1919) CSF 148 SF1 386
Niesz, Anthony. BAA 201
Nietzsche, Friedrich Wilhelm (1844-1900) ACC 161 ASF 142 ATA 54 CAT 58 COT 148-9, 161 CUA 36 CWN 13, 18, 23-4,

Nietzsche, Friedrich W. (cont.)
30-1, 43 EXT 1/1 17 EXT 3/1
13 EXT 7/1 14 EXT 9/2 33, 51
EXT 10/2 109 FTF 47, 138 HEN
57 LTN 77 MSF 22, 229, 272,
275 POE 160-1 RAH 74 SFH
32 TBC 31 THM 20, 23, 38, 44,
51, 56 VES 265
Nightingale, Charles. IAC 182
Nijinsky, Vaslav Fomich (1890-
1950) CWN 13, 33
Nikolsky, V. D. MSF 253, 264
Nile, Dorothea see Michael Angelo
Avallone
Nimoy, Leonard. EXT 10/1 28
FRN 261 IAC 182 KWS 193 OMN
18, 77, 214, 260-7 WSF 314, 371
Nims, John Frederick. IAC 182
Nin, Anais (1903-77) SF1 386
Nipperdey, Thomas. BAA 187, 250
Nisbet, Hume (1849-1921?) BAA
54 CSF 148 ES2 328-9 SF1 386
Nisot, Mavis Elizabeth Hocking
(1893-) WGT 105 see also Wil-
liam Penmare
Nissenson, Hugh. IAC 182 SFS 88
Niswonger, Charles Elliott. CSF
148 SF1 386
Nitchie, Elizabeth. SFB 125
Niven, Frederick J. CSF 148
Niven, Larry (1938-) AAL 4-5,
16-7, 24-5, 27-8, 47-8, 113-4, 120-
3, 165-6 ALW 212 AOW 231-3,
286, 291, 400 BAA 146, 158 BFP
386-7 BYS 304 COT 78 CSC
31, 45-6, 52, 55, 65, 178-94, 230
DTS 47 ES2 329 ETN 65-6, 121,
178 FFR 133-5 FHT 32, 50
[FJT] FLR 33 FL2 938-41 HFI
109-10 IAC 182-3 JVN 131 KAU
20, 28, 60, 146, 184 LEX 486-8
LTN 98 MFW ix, 16, 34, 147-8
RGS 129-31 SFA 22, 46, 194
SFB 55, 137 SFD 9, 35, 240, 302,
321 SFE 428-9 SFH 127, 243
SFS 88 SFW 326-7, 459-65 SF1
386 SF2 1016 SIN 101, 111-20
SL3 1463-7 SL4 1799-804, 2023-
9 SRB 5-6, 361, 366, 371 SV2 9-
19 TSF 63, 240 VES 68, 74, 76,
81-2, 84, 87, 96, 112-3, 131, 156-
7, 160, 163, 260, 328 WFS 17, 240,
292, 295-6 WSF 234, 246, 335,
337, 375, 387-8
Nixon, Joan. FFC 123

Nixon, Richard M. COT 272 ETN
xi, 48, 104, 107, 162 HEN 13 LTN
218 MIH 146 RHN 198 SIH 83
WBW 44
Nizer, Louis. SOT 116
Nizzi, Guido (1900-) ES2 329 SF1
386 SF2 1016
Noah. EXT 3/2 52 EXT 7/1 24
JGB 19
Noakes, Aubrey. BAA 250
Noakes, Donald. IAC 183
Nobes, Patrick. SF1 387
Noble, Edward (1857-1941) SF1
387
Noble, William. SF1 387
Nock, Albert Jay. BAA 250
Nodier, Charles (1780-1844) FBK
22, 44, 82, 137 TFC 43, 46, 84, 90
Nodvik, Stan. IAC 183
Noel, L. pseud. of Leonard Noel
Barker. CSF 148 SF1 387
Noel, Sterling (1903-) ES2 329
HFI 110 SF1 387 SF2 1016
Nolan, David F. EXT 4/2 24
Nolan, Lewis. SFN 58
Nolan, William F. (1928-) AAL
45 AOW 233, 351 BAA 144 ES2
329 FFR 135 FRN 73-4, 110-1
HFI 110 IAC 183-4 KAU 90
LEX 488-9 NDA 213 SFE 429-
30 SFS 88 SF1 387 SF2 1017
SRB 77, 344 VES 129 WGT 105-
6 see also Frank Anmar, F. E.
Edwards
Nolane, Richard D. SL2 560-3
SL3 1435-8, 1472-5, 1501-4 SL4
1537-40, 1588-91 SL5 2146-9,
2241-4, 2516-9
Nona. VFS 18, 25
Noname pseud. of Phillip Luis
Senarens, Wilson Shepard. IMS
27 PST 96, 273 SFW 53-4
Novalis pseud. of Friedrich
Leopold, Friedrich Von Harden-
berg. FL2 720-4 THM 15, 38
Noonan, Julia. FFC 20, 44, 52
Noordung, Hermann. COT 41
Norbert, W. pseud. of Norbert
Wiener. IAC 184
Norburn, Hope Robertson. BAA
121
Nordau, Max. EXT 9/2 33
Norday, Michael. SF1 387
Norden, Eric. HFI 110 SFE 430
SF1 387
Norfolk, William. PJF 14

Norman, Adrian R.D. MFW 192
Norman, Alfred. BAA 103
Norman, Alfred Lorn. BAA 154
Norman, Barry. SFE 430
Norman, Doreen. SF1 387
Norman, Eric. SFE 430
Norman, (Sir) Henry (1858-1939)
CSF 148 ES2 329 SF1 387
Norman, James pseud. of James
Norman Schmidt (1912-) ES2
329 SF1 387 STH 155
Norman, John pseud. of John
Frederick Lange (1931-) AAL
31 FFR 135 FL2 631-4 HFI
110 LEX 489-90 MIH 106 RGS
131-2, 220 SFE 430 SF1 387-8
SIH 170, 177-8 VES 122
Norman, Marty. FFC 149
Norman, Philip. EXT 10/1 37
Normano, J. F. BAA 250
Normyx pseud. of Norman Douglas.
CSF 148
Norris, Darrell. BAA 250
Norris, Frank (1870-1902) CSF
148 HFI 110 ES2 330 EXT 4/1
8-10 SF1 388
Norris, Frank Callan (1907-67)
ES2 330 SF1 388
Norris, Kathleen (1880-1966) ES2
330 HFI 110 SF1 388
Norris, Mary Harriott (1848-1919)
SF1 388
Norstadt, George. NWO 61
North, Andrew. IMS 23
North, Delaval. CSF 149
North, Eric pseud. of Charles
Bernard Cronin (1884-) HFI 111
SFE 430 SF1 388
North, Franklin H. SF1 388
North, Joan Marian (1920-) FFC
76, 172, 183 SF1 388 SF2 1017
North, N. E. P. pseud. of Wilson
Shepard. IMS 28, 30
North, Sterling (1906-74) CSF 149
ES2 330 SF1 388 SF2 1018
Northbourne, (Lord). BAA 250
Northcote, Amyas. ES2 330 SF1
388
Northern, Leslie (house name)
WGT 106 see also Frank Belk-
nap Long
Northmore, Thomas. BAA 15
Northrop, Caleb. COT 17, 239-40
Northrup, Edwin Fitch (1866-)
IAC 184 MSM 209-10 PST 124

WGT 106 see also Akkad Pseudoman
Northumberland, (Duke of) pseud.
of Alan Ian Percy. SF1 388
Norton, Alden H. (1903-) ES2 330
IAC 184 ISW 131 SF1 388 SF2
1018 SOT 359 STH 262 TSP
206, 226 WFS 104, 132-4
Norton, Alice Mary (1912?-) ES2
330-2 SFD 299 WSF 204 see
also Andre Norton
Norton, Andre pseud. of Alice
Mary Norton. ALW 36, 185 AOW
234, 326-7 BAA 158 BFP 388-
95 BYS 263 COT 196 EFP 3, 7
EXT 9/2 61 FFC 39, 44, 69, 166-
7, 178-9 FL5 2139-49 HFI 111-3
IAC 184 LEX 490-2 LTN 53-4
RAH 226 RGS 132-4, 220-1 SFD
27, 299 SFE 430-1 SFS 88-9
SF1 389-90 SF2 1018-9 SL2
969-71 SL5 2156-8 SOT 81 SRB
273 TSF 61 VES 198, 269 WGT
106-7 WSF 127, 132, 387
Norton, Henry. IAC 185 SFS 89
Norton, John. EXT 10/1 37
Norton, Mary (1913-) FFC 69,
104, 179 FL1 164-5 SF1 390
Norton, Natalie. FFC 110
Norton, (Rev.) Philip. BAA 42
see also Artegall Smith
Norton, Ralph. IAC 185
Norton, Ray. EXT 7/1 22
Norton, Roger Howard. TSP 45,
103 see also Robert C. Black-
mon
Norton, Roy (1869-1942) AOW 37,
69 CSF 149 EXT 1/1 15 SFE
431 SF1 390
Norton, Seymour F. BAA 45
Norton, W. W. WSF 243
Norvil, Manning. HFI 113
Norway, Nevil Shute (1899-1960)
BAA 122 ES2 332-3 WGT 107
see also Nevil Shute
Norwood, Rick. IAC 185
Norwood, Victor George (1920-)
SFE 431 SF1 390 SF2 1019
Norwood, William D. EXT 10/1
34, 37
Nostlinger, Christine. FFC 149
Nostradamus. RFA 122
Nostradamus, Merlin pseud. of
Frances Power Cobbe. CSF 149
SF1 390
Noto, Cosimo. BAA 66 SF1 390

Nott, Kathleen Cecilia. SFE 431
Nottingham, Ernest. SOI 130
Nourse, Alan E. (1928-) ALW 212,
219 AOW 327-8,398 BAA 250
BFP 396 BYS 262,279,285,288
CSC 73-88 ES2 333 EXT 8/1 6
FFR 135 HFI 113 IAC 185 LEX
492-3 RGS 134-5 SFD 9 SFE
431 SFS 89,111 SF1 391 SF2
1019-20 SRB 336,507 VES 82,
153,206,302,309
Novak, Maximillian E. BAA 250
Novotny, John. IAC 185 SFS 89
Nowlan, Philip F. (1888-1940)
ALW 126,173 AOW 109 BYS
210 ES2 333 HFI 113 LEX 493-
4 RFA 2,79 RGS 135 SFB 109
SFE 431 SFH 107,202 SF1 391
SL1 84-8 SOT 102 TRB 58
WAA 181 WGT 107 WSF 46,304-
5,386 YTS 9 see also Frank
Phillips
Noy, John. CSF 149 SF1 391
Noyelle, Henri. BAA 187
Noyes, Alfred (1880-1958) CSF 149
ES2 333-4 EXT 8/1 5 OWB 13
SFE 431-2 SF1 391
Noyes, Pierrepont Burt (1870-
1959) CSF 149 ES2 334 SF1 391
Noyes, Sherman A. SF1 391
Noyga. RFA 195
Nozick, Robert. BAA 160
Nuallain, Brian O. (1911-66) SF2
1022 see also Flann O'Brien,
Brian O'Nolan
Nudel'man, Rafail. MSF 67-8,
79 UKL 245

Nuetzel, Charles A(lexander)
(1934-) ES2 334 FFR 136 HFI
113 IAC 185 SFE 433 SF1 391
SF2 1020 WGT 107 see also
George Frederic
Nuita, Seija. BAA 250
Nulisch, Harry. IAC 185
Nunes, Claude (1924-) ES2 334
HFI 113 SFE 433 SF1 391 SF2
1021
Nunes, Rhoda Gwylleth (1938-)
SF1 391 SF2 1021
Nunez, Guido Donoso. BAA 216
Nurnberger, Joseph. POE 67-8
Nutt, Charles (1929-1967) ES2
334-5 SF2 813 WGT 107 see
also Charles Beaumont
Nutt, Lily Clive (1888-) WGT 107
see also Clive Arden
Nuttall, Jeff. IAC 185
Nuverbis pseud. of Dillon Jordan
Spotswood. CSF 149
Nyberg, Bjorn (1929-) CWD 7-9
ES2 335 FBK 93 IAC 136,185
SFW 179,182-3 SF1 392 SF2
1021-2 SOT 165 WSF 297 WTS
36
Nydahl, Joel Mellin. BAA 250,285
Nye, Cassandra. BAA 162 IAC
185
Nye, Robert (1939-) ES2 335 FFC
22,50 FL2 1007-9
Nygaard, Jacob. FFC 135
Nykoruk, Barbara. LTN 269
Nyland, Theo. SF1 392

O

O. Henry's Ghost. CSF 150
Oakes, Philip Barlow (1928-)
HFI 114 SF1 392 SF2 1022
Oakhurst, William. SF1 392
Oakley, Graham. FFC 49, 150
Oaks, Priscilla. SL1 402-5 SL3
1122-5
Oates, Joyce Carol (1938-) CWN
47 ETN 175 FL3 1124-6
Oates, Whitney J. BAA 250
O'Bannon, Dan. [FUT]
Obendorf, Clarence P. EXT 4/1
7 EXT 6/2 23
Ober, Frederick Albion (1849-
1913) CSF 149 SF1 392
Oberth, Hermann Julius (1894-)
COT 33, 36, 39 ES2 335 IMS 17
MSM 199, 209, 213 SFN 31, 34
SOT 16, 171 VES 71 VFS 44,
224 WSF 5, 50
Obligado, Lilian. FFC 115
Obloy, Elaine. BAA 187
Oboler, Arch (1907?-) CSF 149
ES2 335 IAC 186 KAU 126 MSM
57-8 SF1 392 WSF 311
Obrant, Susan. FFC 25
O'Brien, Clancy. IAC 185
O'Brien, Clifford Edward. ES2
335 WGT 108 see also Larry
Clinton O'Brien
O'Brien, David Wright (-1944)
ES2 335 IAC 185 SFE 433 SF1
392 WGT 108 WIF 120 WSF
116 see also John York Cabot,
Berl Cameron, Rand Le Page,
Kris Luna, Brian Shaw
O'Brien, Fitz-James (1828-62)
ALW 53, 59-60, 74, 87, 113, 121
AOW 27-8, 34 CAT 5 CSF 149

ES2 335 EXT 3/1 29 EXT 4/1
1 EXT 4/2 24 EXT 5/1 4, 16-
16a EXT 7/2 48 EXT 10/2 99
FBK 30, 41 FL4 1657-61 IAC
185-6 IMS 2 MFW 18-9 MSF
144, 201 MSM 29 NWO 20, 251-
3 PST 33, 36, 129, 208, 252, 266
RHN 193 SFE 433 SFS 89 SFW
68 SF1 392 SL4 1944-7 STH
24-5 TJB 16 VES 140, 173, 205
WIF 71 WSF 16
O'Brien, Flann pseud. of Brian
O. Nuallain. FL1 61-2 SFE
434 SF1 392
O'Brien, Florence Roma Muir
Wilson (1891-1930) WGT 108
O'Brien, Joseph. SF1 392
O'Brien, Larry Clinton pseud. of
Clifford Edward O'Brien. SF1
392
O'Brien, Robert Carroll pseud. of
Robert Lesley Conly (1922-73)
AOW 306, 328-9 FFC 123, 179
LTN 265 SFE 434 SF1 392
SRB 365 VES 280
O'Brien, Seumas (1880-) SF1 392
O'Brien, Willis H. (1886-1962)
SFE 434
Obrist, Jurg. FFC 49
O'Bruchev, Vassily A. MSF 263
Obruchev, Vladimir A. (1863-
1956) ES2 335 LEX 495 SFE
434 SF1 393 SOT 431
Obtulowicz, Marek. IAC 186
Obukhova, Lydia. SF1 393
O'Cluny, Thomas. SF1 393
O'Connell, Charles Christopher.
ES2 336 SF1 393
O'Connell, Daniel. EXT 1/1 16

257

O'Connell, Jean. FFC 81
O'Connor, Barry. CSF 149
O'Connor, Edwin (1918-68) ES2
336
O'Connor, Flannery. ETN 63
O'Connor, Frank. IAH 35
O'Connor, Paul Dennis. SOT 261
O'Connor, William Douglas (1832-
89) CSF 149 ES2 336 SF1 393
VES 180
O'Connor, William Van. FAN 181
Odegard, Holtan P. BAA 187, 286
Odell, Samuel W. (1864-1948)
BAA 59 CSF 149 SFE 434 SF1
393
Odell, William. SF1 393
October, John. SFE 434
Octogenarian, (An). BAA 30
O'Den, Daniel. BAA 110
Odle, E. V. AOW 69 CSF 149
SFE 434 SF1 393 SL1 392-5
O'Donnell, Charles. NWO 63
O'Donnell, Elliott (1872-1965)
CSF 150 ES2 336 SF1 393 SF2
1022
O'Donnell, K. M. pseud. of Barry
N. Malzberg. IAC 186
O'Donnell, Lawrence pseud. of
Henry Kuttner, C. L. Moore.
ALW 161, 174 CSC 29-30 ETN
137 IAC 186 RFA 112, 115, 118,
140, 145, 195, 201 SFD 310 SFS
90 SL2 855-7 STH 245 VES 81,
334 WIF 159 WSF 105, 110-1
O'Donnell, Peter. SF1 393
O'Donnevan, Finn pseud. of
Robert Sheckley. IAC 186 SFS
90
O'Donoghue, Michael. ES2 336
O'Donovan, Patrick. EXT 6/1 19
Odoyevsky, Vladimir F. (1803-
69) EXT 10/2 73 FBK 41 MSF
137, 245-7 SIH 76
O'Duffy, Eimar (1893-1935) BAA
94 CSF 150 SFE 434 SF1 393
Oechsli, Kelly. FFC 91, 177
Oersted, Hans Christian. FTF 35
O'Faolain, Eileen. FFC 101
O'Farrell, Eddy. SF1 394
O'Farrell, William (1904-) SF1
394
Offenbach, Jacques. FBK 32, 34
SIH 24 WAA 162
Offin, Thomas William, Jr. CSF
150 SF1 394

Offutt, Andrew J. (1936-) ALW
212 AOW 329 BAA 165 BYS
304 CWD 8, 61 HFI 114 IAC
186 LEX 495-6 RGS 136 SFE
435 SFS 90 SF1 394 SF2 1022
SRB 287 VES 180 WGT 108 see
also J. X. Williams
O'Flannagan, Phineas. SF1 394
Ofshe, Richard. ALW 30, 179
SFE 435
Ogden, Antoinette. SF1 394
Ogden, George Washington (1871-
1966) SF1 394
Ogilvy, G. S. IAC 187
O'Gorman, Edmundo. VFS 187
O'Grady, Rohan pseud. of June
Margaret O'Grady Skinner. SF1
394
O'Grady, Standish James (1846-
1928) BAA 63 WGT 108 see
also Luke Netterville
O'Hanlon, Jacklyn. FFC 179
O'Hanlon, James. SOT 206
O'Hara, John. ETN 176
O'Hara, Kenneth pseud. of Bryce
Walton. IAC 186
Ohle, David. SF1 394
Ohlson, Hereward. SF1 394
Ohlsson, Ib. FFC 13
Ohmann, R. M. EXT 6/1 18
Ohnet, Georges pseud. of Georges
Henot. CSF 150 SF1 394
O'Kelly, Seumas (1881-1918) SF1
394
Okhotnikov, Vadim. IAC 187
SFS 90
Okunev, Yakov M. EXT 10/2 75
MSF 253
Olander, Joseph D. ACE 75 AC2
75-6 BRS 10 IAC 123, 177, 187
LTN 251 SF1 394-5 SRB 77-80
Oldale, Peter. IAC 187
Oldfield, Claude Houghton (1889-
1961) SFE 293 WGT 108 see
also Claude Houghton
Oldmeadow, Ernest James (1867-
1949) CSF 150 SF1 395
Oldrey, John. CSF 150 SF1 395
Olds, Charles Burnell. SF1 395
Oldsey, Bernard. EXT 9/1 23
FAN 164, 189
Ole Luk-oie pseud. of Ernest D.
Swinton. CSF 150
O'Leary, Con. SF1 395
O'Leary, Timothy J. IAC 186

Oleck, Jack (1914-) SF1 395
SF2 1022
Olemy, P. T. pseud. of George
Baker. HFI 114 SFE 435 SF1
395
Olerich, Henry (1851-) BAA 50,
81, 88 CSF 150 SFE 435 SF1
395
Olesha, Yury K. MSF 264
Oleszkiewicz, Antoine. BAA 251
Olexa, Joseph Stephen. BAA 286
Olfson, Lewy. SF1 395
Olgivy, Arthur James. SF1 394
Olinick, G. O. WTS 80
Oliphant, Margaret O. (1828-97)
CSF 150 ES2 336 FL1 84-6
SFE 435 SF1 395 WGT 108
Oliphant, Ronal. WTS 50
Oliver, Amy Roberta Ruck (1878-)
WGT 108
Oliver, (Dr.) Bernard. VFS 211,
263-4
Oliver, Egbert S. NWO 280, 282
Oliver, Frederick Spenser (1866-
99) WGT 108 WIF 50 see also
Phylos
Oliver, George (1873-1961) WGT
108-9 see also Oliver Onions
Oliver, H. J. EXT 9/2 39-40
Oliver, J. T. IAC 187 SFS 90
VES 177
Oliver, Jane pseud. of Helen
Christina Easson Rees. CSF
150 SF1 396
Oliver, Jerome (1886-) CSF 150
SF1 396
Oliver, John A. W. CSF 151
Oliver, John Rathbone (1872-
1943) CSF 151 SF1 396
Oliver, Kenneth. BAA 251
Oliver, M. BAA 146
Oliver, Owen. IAC 187
Oliver, (Symmes) Chad(wick)
(1928-) AAL 97-100, 157, 179
ALW 212 AOW 234 BAA 124,
127 BFP 397 ES2 336-7 EXT
5/1 3 EXT 8/1 7 FFR 136 HEN
18-9 HFI 114 IAC 187 IAH 15,
99-100, 103 ISW 192-3 KSU 61,
67, 203, 206-8 LEX 496-7 MFW
272, 274 RFA 200, 203, 205, 211
RGS 136-7 SFE 435 SFN 28
SFS 90 SFW 467-73 SF1 395
SF2 1023 SL4 1898-901 SOT
282 SRB 16, 321, 327 WGT 109
WSF 172

Olivier, Edith Maud (-1948) CSF
151 SF1 396
Olivier, Olivier. IAC 187
Ollero, Andres. BAA 251
Ollivant, Alfred (1874-1927) BAA
93 CSF 151 SF1 396
Olmstead, Dvora. IAC 187
Olmstead, Frederick Law. WFS
28
Olney, Clark. EXT 1/2 33 NWO
50-2
Olney, Ross Robert (1929-) IAC
187 SF1 396 SF2 1023
Olsen, Alfred John (1884-1956)
ES2 337 HFI 114 IAC 187 IMS
16 RFA 2 SFD 24, 27 SFS 90
SF1 396 SOT 107, 401 STH 110,
145-6 WGT 109 WSF 80
Olsen, Bob see Alfred John Olsen
Olsen, Ib Spang. FFC 135
Olsen, Robert R. IAC 187
Olsen, Tillie. ETN 99
Olson, Eugene E. (1936-) SF2
1087 WGT 109 see also Brad
Steiger
Olson, Ruby. RZY 9, 14
O'Malley, Frank (1916-) WGT 109
see also Frank O'Rourke
O'Malley, Mary Dolling (1891-
1974) ES2 337 WGT 109 see
also Ann Bridge
O'Meara, James. WSF 215
O'Meara, Walter Andrew (1897-)
SF1 396 SF2 1023-4
Omen, Edward. BAA 73 SF1 396
Onassis, Aristotle. LTN 43
Oncken, Hermann. BAA 187, 251
Onderdonk, Matthew H. EXT 3/1
21, 24
One of the Unemployed. CSF 151
O'Neil, Dennis Joseph (1939-)
BAA 158 HFI 114 IAC 186 SF1
396 SF2 1024
O'Neil, Henry Nelson (1817-80)
POE 147 SF1 396
O'Neil, Russell. SF1 396
O'Neill, Eugene (1888-1953) AOW
34 EXT 7/2 37 FL2 638-41
SFN 114
O'Neill, (Dr.) Gerald. VFS 211,
231-2
O'Neill, Gerard K. [FUT] SFH
128 WSF 322 YTS 58
O'Neill, Henry J. BAA 66
O'Neill, John (1869-) CSF 151
SF1 396

O'Neill, Joseph (1886-1953) BAA
104 CSF 151 SFE 436 SFW 69
SF1 396 VES 139
O'Neill, Rose. CSF 151
O'Neill, Scott. ES2 337 IAC 186
Ong, Walter J. MSF 242
Onions, Oliver (1873-1961) BAA
83 CSF 151 ES2 337 FBK 63
FL1 294-9 IAC 187 SF1 397
see also George Oliver
O'Nolan, Brian pseud. of Brian
O. Nuallain (1911-66) ES2 337
WGT 109
Onspaugh, Carl. IAC 187
Oppel, Horst. BAA 251
Oppenheim, Edward Phillips (1866-
1946) CSF 151 SFE 437 SF1 397
WGT 109
Oppenheim, Garrett. MSM 94
Oppenheim, Ralph. TSP 4,156
Oppenheim, Shulamith. FFC 108
Oppenheimer, Robert. IMS 159
LTN 111
O'Quinn, Vithaldas H. pseud. of
Hans Stefan Santesson. IAC 186
Oram, John pseud. of Jack Thomas.
SF1 397
Orb, Clay pseud. of Herbert Con-
row. ES2 337 SF1 397
Orban, Paul. BYS 217 COT 202
ES2 337-8 RFA 62,66,118,123,
143,157,164,167,174,181,195,
198,200 SFE 438 TSP 22 VES
92,114,199 WSF 104,108
Orbison, Olive. SF1 397
Orcutt, Emma Louise. CSF 151
SF1 397
Orcutt, Harriet E. CSF 151 SF1
397
Orcutt, William Dana. CSF 151
Orczy, (Baroness) Emmuska
(1865-1947) CSF 151 SF1 397
Ord, Robert. SOT 106
Ordway, Frederick I. KAU 151
O'Reilly, Bridey M. CSF 158
O'Reilly, John (1906-) SF1 397
O'Reilly, John Boyle (1844-90)
CSF 85 MSM 144 SFE 438 SF1
397
O'Reilly, Timothy. CEN 41-55
FHT 67 SL1 330-6,343-8 SL2
647-64 SL3 1401-6
Orgel, Doris. FFC 74
Orgill, Michael. IAC 187-8
Oriel, Antrim pseud. of Arthur
Moore. SF1 398

Origen. IAH 72
Orkow, Ben (Harrison) (1896-)
ES2 338 HFI 114 SF1 398 SF2
1024
Orlans, Harold. BAA 187
Orlovsky, Vladimir E. Pseud. of
Vladimir E. Grushvitsky. MSF
262
Ormesson, Jean (1925-) SF1 398
Ormondroyd, Edward. FFC 14,
33,108,167 SF1 398,583
Orna, Adolphe O. CSF 152 SF1
398
Orndorff, Frank. SF1 398
Ornstein, Robert. CWN 59
O'Rourke, Frank pseud. of Frank
O'Malley. ES2 338 HFI 115
SF1 398
Orpen, Adela E. BAA 57
Orpen, (Mrs.) G. H. CSF 152
Orr, Paul Wright (1904-) BAA
146-7 SF1 398 SF2 1024
Orr, Violet May (1904-) BAA 146-
7 SF1 398 SF2 1024
Orr, William F. IAC 188
Orrick, Allan H. BAA 178
Ortega, Felix. BAA 187
Ortlieb, Heinz-Dietrich. BAA 251
Orton, Arthur W. IAC 188
Orwell, George pseud. of Eric
Blair. AAL 33,163-5,198-9
ACC 209 ALW 31,97,99,145
AOW 118,235,346 ASF 174,275-
89 BYS 67,75,124,131,254-6,
281-2 CAT xiv,36,70,75-6,80,
114,131,138 COT 252 CSC 107,
119,121-2,131,189 CSF 152
CUA 61 EXT 1/2 34 EXT 2/2
25,30,41 EXT 3/1 27 EXT 3/2
49 EXT 4/1 1 EXT 4/2 24 EXT
5/1 4 EXT 6/2 40-1,51 EXT
8/1 5-6,20 EXT 8/2 66 EXT
9/1 19,22-3 EXT 9/2 29,31,55-
7,59-60 EXT 10/1 47 FAN 3,
5-6,12,20,38,47,66,82-3,100,
106,110-1,115,123-7,129-34,
147-9,151,155-6,158,161,163,
174,181,186-7 FFR 137 FLT
93 FL1 45-7 FSU 20 FTF 1,7,
30,84,86,92,104-6,127 [FUT]
HFI 115 IAC 188 IAH 141-5
INT 49 ISW 2,6,8,19,30,67,69,
136,172,242,267 KVT 9 KWS
298,302 LEX 497-9 LTN 106,
205 MFW 23,78-9,287 MIH 29
MSF 76,83,112,129,242,256

Orwell, George (cont.)
MSM 29, 74, 88, 90, 166 NDA xi,
11, 30, 59, 88-93, 95-8, 102, 118,
122-3 NWO 97, 113, 125-6, 183
OMN 59, 107-11, 128, 189, 298
POE 261, 263, 268-70 RAH 165
SFB 90, 92 SFD 57, 310 SFE
440 SFH 28, 34-5, 156, 169, 216
SFN 12, 39, 66-71, 106, 117 SFW
233-41 SF1 398 SIH 88 SL3
1531-6 SOI xiii SOT 2, 195 STF
24, 71, 79 STH 6, 105, 108 TSF
162-4 VES 124, 128, 159, 212-3,
225, 254, 256, 261-2, 269, 302
VFS 59, 94 VMW 11 WAA 59,
242 WIF 24 WSF 129, 346 YTS
12, 20, 25
Osborn, Edward Bolland (1867-
1938) CSF 152 SF1 398
Osborn, John. CWN 25
Osborn, Laughton (1809-78) SF1
398
Osborn, Scott C. EXT 4/2 15-6
EXT 5/1 1 EXT 6/1 1 EXT 9/1
2 EXT 10/1 2 EXT 10/2 69
Osborne, Chester Gorham (1915-)
SF1 398
Osborne, David pseud. of Robert
Silverberg. RSG 11-2
Osborne, Maurice. FFC 135
Osborne, Robertson. AAL 120
IAC 188 SFS 90
Osborne, Samuel Duffield (1858-
1917) CSF 152 EXT 1/1 15
MFW 126-7 SF1 398
Osbourne, Lloyd (1868-1947) CSF
152 EXT 1/1 15 SF1 398
Osburn, Joseph. SF1 398
Oscarsson, Per. SIH 129
Osgerby, J. R. BAA 251
O'Shaughnessy, Arthur. FTF 203
O'Shaughnessy, Marty. WFS 99
O'Sheel, Shaemas (1886-1954)
BAA 99 CSF 152 SF1 398
Osheroff, Alex. IMS 103-4, 115,
128, 141, 145, 150, 171-2, 180,
229, 236
Oshikawa, Shunru (1877-1914)
SIH 40 SL3 1106-9
Oshinsky, Abraham. IMS 111, 170
Osinovsky, Igor N. BAA 251
Osler, (Sir) William (1921-) ES2
338 EXT 7/1 8, 15 SF1 398
Osmond, Andrew (1938-) ES2 338
SF1 399 SF2 1024
Ossian, John. IAC 188

Ossolinski, Jozef Maksymilian.
FBK 147
Osterbaan, N. ES2 338
Osterwalder, Hans Ulrich. FBK
69, 76-7
Osterwalder, Ute. FBK 69, 76-7
VES 239
Ostrander, Isabel Egenton (1885-
1924) WGT 110 see also David
Fox
Ostrander, Sheila. CSC 16
O'Sullivan, James Brendan (1919-)
SF1 399
O'Sullivan, Jack. ES2 338 WIF
115
O'Sullivan, Maureen. WFS 56
O'Sullivan, Vincent (1872-1940)
CSF 152 ES2 338 SF1 399
Oswald, Dave. SF1 399
Oswald, Elizabeth Jane. CSF 152
SF1 399
Otis, James pseud. of James
Otis Kaler. CSF 152 SF1 399
Otling, Joan K. AOW 360
O'Toole, George. SF1 399
Otterbourg, Edwin Max (1885-
1967) SF1 399
Otto, Frei. [FUT]
Otto, Herbert. CWN 59
Ottolengui, Rodrigues (1861-1937)
CSF 152 SF1 399
Ottum, Robert K. Jr. HFI 115
IAC 188 SFS 90 SF1 399
Oudeis pseud. of Christopher
Lovett Darby. SF1 399
Oursler, Charles Fulton (1893-
1952) ES2 338 SF1 399 WGT
110
Ousdal, Asbjorn Pederson (1879-)
SF1 399
Ouseley, Gideon Jasper (1835-
1906) BAA 35 EXT 7/1 8 WGT
110 see also Ellora, Theosopho
Ouspensky, Petr D. (1878-1947)
CSF 152 EXT 1/2 36 EXT 10/1
10-2, 14 FFR 137 FL4 1840-2
FTF 151 MIH 141, 143 NWO
234, 257 SF1 524
Outcault, Richard. SFH 107
Overton, Grant Martin (1887-
1930) CSF 152 ES2 338 SF1 399
Ovid. FTF 16 UKL 99
Owen, Albert Kimsey. BAA 57
Owen, Betty M. ES2 338 SF1 399
Owen, Dean pseud. of Dudley
Dean McGaughy. HFI 115 SFE

Owen, Dean (cont.)
444 SF1 400
Owen, Evelyn. CSF 152
Owen, Frank pseud. of Roswell
Williams (1893-1968) CSF 110,
152 HFI 115 SFE 444-5 SF1
400 WGT 110 WTS 21, 28, 130
Owen, George W. SF1 400
Owen, George Washington (-1916)
SF1 400
Owen, Harry Collinson (1882-
1956) BAA 89 WGT 110 see
also Hugh Addison
Owen, Mably Ceredig (1912-69)
ES2 338 SFS 90-1, 126 SF1
400 SF2 1025
Owen, Maurice Leslie Lloyd
(1925-) SF1 400 SF2 1025
Owen, Olin Marvin (1847-1918)
SF1 400
Owen, Richard. HFI 184
Owen, Robert. BAA xi, 17, 26
EXT 8/1 21 EXT 10/2 74 MSF
165, 248 SIH 68, 76 WAA 49

Owen, Rye. CSF 152 SF1 400
Owen, Sidney Cunliffe. CSF 152
Owen, Walter. CSF 153
Owen, Thomas. FBK 146
Owen, Walter (1884-) ES2 338
SF1 400
Owen, Wilfred. POE 226
Owens, Gail. FFC 102, 112, 159
Owens, Tommy. WFS 144-5
Ower, John B. AC2 76 FHT 67
SFW 441-8
Owings, Mark Samuel (1945-)
AOW 362 ES2 338-9 IAC 188
SFE 445 SF1 400-1 SF2 1025
SRB 79-80
Owsley, Cliff. IAC 188 SFS 91
Oxenford, John (1812-77) CSF 153
SF1 401
Oxenham, John pseud. of William
Arthur Dunkerley. CSF 153 SF1
401
Ozick, Cynthia. IAC 188
Ozman, Howard. BAA 187
Ozmon, Howard A. BAA 251

P

Paalen, Wolfgang. IAC 188
Pacini, Kathleen. IAC 188
Padberg, Majie. BAA 193
Paddock, Paul (1907-) ES2 339
NDA 165-6, 208, 214, 216
Paddock, William (1921-) ES2 339
NDA 165-6, 208, 214, 216
Paderewski, Ignacy Jan. OWB 18
Padgett, Lewis pseud. of Henry
Kuttner, C. L. Moore. ALW 161
ETN 137 EXT 3/1 27 EXT 6/2
51 FFR 138 IAC 188 IAH 86,
89-90 ISW 217-9, 249-50 LTN
27 MSM 32, 58, 85, 298, 302
OWB 99-100 RFA 109-12, 114-
5, 117-8, 120, 125-7, 131, 134, 136,
138-9, 142, 165-6, 172, 187, 201

SFD 209, 293, 309-10, 312 SFS
91 SRB 319 TJB 30 VES 173,
179, 187, 261 WIF 157 WSF 105,
109
Padgett, Ron. IAC 188
Page, Francis. SF1 401
Page, Gerald W. (1939-) IAC 188
SFS 91 WGT 111
Page, Norvell (1904? -61) COT
148-9 ES2 339 HFI 115 IAC
188 ISW 37, 279 RFA 64, 81
SFE 445 SFS 91 SF1 401 TSP
9-11, 15, 57-9, 82, 89, 139, 158,
203 WGT 111 WSF 336 see
also N. Wooten Poge, Grant
Stockbridge.

Page, Patricia Kathleen (1916-)
SF2 843 see also Judith Cape
Page, Thomas Walker (1942-)
HFI 115 SFE 445 SF1 401 SF2
1025
Page, Will A. IAC 188
Paget, Victoria. BAA 251
Paget, Violet (1856-1935) ES2 339
FBK 60 WGT 111 see also
Vernon Lee
Paget-Fredericks, J. FFC 53
Paget-Lowe, Henry pseud. of H.
P. Lovecraft. EXT 3/1 3-4, 9,
16
Pagetti, Carlo. AOW 351 SFE
445
Paige, Leo. IAC 188 SFS 92
Pain, Barry Eric (1865-1928)
BAA 78-9 CSF 153 ES2 339-40
FL4 1662-4 SF1 401
Paine, Albert Bigelow (1861-1937)
AOW 35, 69-70 BAA 64 CSF 153
EXT 1/1 2, 15 MFW 121-2 SFE
445 SF1 401 SRB 9, 11 STH
60-1
Paine, Doris M. SF1 402 SRB
464
Paine, J. Lincoln. IAC 188
Paine, Lauran Bosworth (1916-)
ES2 340 SF1 402 SF2 1025 see
also Mark Carrel
Paine, Thomas (1737-1809) CYR
25-6 WFS 162
Painter, Thomas. CSF 153 SFE
445 SF1 402
Painton, Frederick C. IMS 213
STH 155-6
Pairault, Pierre (1922-) SF2 1135
see also Stefan Wul
Paisley, Tom see T. Ernesto
Bethencourt
Pakula, Alan. SOT 372
Pal, George (1908-) ALW 96, 145,
171, 190, 194 ASF 195 COT 93
ES2 340 ISW 277 KAU 200 KWS
2-6, 10-1, 58, 60-6, 144, 151-63,
176, 198, 201, 208-14, 233, 257,
311 MSM 51-2, 54-8, 62-3, 302
OMN 9, 24, 39, 56, 224-32 RFA
195, 205 SFE 445 SOT 206 SRB
59 TSO 30-1 VFS 141 YTS 18
Pal, (Dr.) Yash. VFS 258
Palazzo, Tony. FFC 137
Paley, Abram R. MSF 254
Paley, Grace. ETN 99
Palladini, David. FFC 23-4

Pallander, Edwin. CSF 153 IAC
189 SF1 402
Pallen, Conde Benoist (1858-1929)
AOW 70 BAA 84 CSF 153 EXT
6/2 45, 48 SFE 445 SF1 402
Palm, Gene pseud. of Luigi
Palmisano. SF1 402
Palmer, Bernard Alvin (1914-)
ES2 340 SF1 402 SF2 1025-6
Palmer, C. H. STH 105
Palmer, Charles H. IAC 189
Palmer, Cuthbert A. SF1 402
Palmer, Frederick (1873-1958)
BAA 99 COT 233 CSF 153 SF1
402
Palmer, Geoffrey. ES2 340
Palmer, John. CSF 153
Palmer, John H. CSF 153
Palmer, John Horsley. BAA 106
SF1 403
Palmer, John Leslie (1885-1944)
CSF 154 EXT 9/2 53-4 SF1 403
WGT 111 see also Francis
Beeding
Palmer, Juliette. FFC 53
Palmer, L. D. (1956-) LEX 500
Palmer, Leonard R. EXT 9/1 16
Palmer, Lucile. SF1 403
Palmer, Mary. FFC 56, 76, 183
Palmer, P. K. (-1973?) see
Keith Parnell
Palmer, Ray(mond A.) (1910-77)
ALW 125, 127, 156, 186 ASF 117-
8 COT 170, 290 ES2 340 ETN
26 EXT 1/2 29 IMS 5, 8-9, 15-
7, 26, 30, 33, 38, 48, 75, 80-1, 83-
4, 93, 194, 205, 216 ISW 284 RFA
10, 63, 169, 191-2 SFA 31 SFE
446 SOT 28, 103, 107-8, 148, 342,
344 SRB 88-9 STH 50-1, 261
VES 102, 135, 147, 160, 313, 337-
9 WFS 140-1, 231 WGT 111
WIF 87, 92, 112, 116, 120, 134,
137, 140, 164 WSF 51, 56, 74-5,
78, 114-9, 138, 149, 161-2, 166-7,
188, 298-300 WTS 54 see also
Henry Gade, G. H. Irwin, Frank
Patton, A. R. Steber, Morris J.
Steele, Rae Winters
Palmer, Robin. ES2 340
Palmer, Roy C. IMS 8
Palmer, William. IMS 37 SF1
403
Palmer, William J. (1890-) BAA
147 ES2 340 SFE 446 SF1 403
SF2 1026

Palmgren, Raoul. BAA 187
Palmisano, Luigi see Gene Palm
Paltock, Robert (1697-1767) AOW
28 BYS 63,68 CSF 154 EXT
3/1 30 FTF 25 IAC 189 MSF
88,127,165 PST 14,21,191,239,
242-4,272 SFB 75 SFE 446
SF1 403 SRB 3 WGT 111 WIF
36 see also R. S.
Paludan-Mueller, Frederik
(1809-76) CSF 154 SF1 403
Palumbo, Donald. FL2 619-24
FL3 1086-8 FL4 1966-8 FL5
2465-80
Pan pseud. of Leslie Beresford.
CSF 154
Panage, John H. BAA 286
Panati, Charles. CSC 10,16
Pangborn, Edgar (1909-76) ALW
212 AOW 235,398 BAA 122
BFP 398 BYS 262,279 ES2
340-1 EXT 8/1 6-7 FFR 138
HFI 115 IAC 189 ISW 198-9
LEX 500-2 NWO 139 RGS 137
SFD 16,299,321 SFE 446 SFH
243 SFS 92 SF1 403 SF2 1026
SL1 493-6 SL3 1417-23 SOT
422-3 SRB 320,340 TSF 61,
240 WGT 111-2 WSF 174,387
Pangborn, Frederic W. CSF 154
Panhard, Rene. FTF 66
Panizza, Oskar (1853-1921) FBK
141-2
Pankhurst, Emmeline. LTN 161
Panshin, Alexei (1940-) AAL 17,
128,175-6 ALW 30,184,212
AOW 8,326,351 BAA 187,251
BFP 399 BYS 271,273,283-4
COT 68,108,299 CSC 172,187
CYR 3-5,8,23,25 DTS 7,43
ES2 341 ETN 64,82-3 FFR 138
FHT 67 HFI 115 HWK 13 IAC
189 KAU 77,84 LEX 502-3
LTN 12,201 MFW 145-6,164-5
MIH 39-40 OSR 326-33,356
RAH 16,33,38,48,64-5,86,106,
109,125,155,200,222,234-6,
258 RGS 137-8,221 SFE 447
SFH 54-7,150,187,243 SF1 403
SF2 1026 SIN 9,92-101 SL4
1805-8 SRB 73,79,507 TSF
52-64,228-41 VES 168,316
WSF 215
Panshin, Cory (1947-) COT 68,
108,299 IAC 189 LTN 12,201
MFW 164-5 SFD 303 SFE 447

SRB 73 TSF 52-64,228-41
Pantell, Dora F. AOW 325 SF1
403-4
Paolozzi. JGB 6
Papademetriou, Costas Basileiou.
BAA 187
Papashvily, Helen. WIF 279
Pape, Frank. FBK 117,119
Pape, Richard Bernard (1916-)
ES2 341 SFE 447 SF1 404 SF2
1026-7
Papp, Desiderius (1897-) ES2 341
SFE 447
Pappazisis, Evangelos pseud. of
Angelos Pappas (1883-) SF1 404
Parabellum pseud. of Ferdinand
F. Grautoff. CSF 154
Paracelsus. EXT 3/2 52 EXT
6/2 28
Paradyne. EXT 5/2 47
Paraf, Pierre. BAA 187
Parcell, Norman Howe. WGT 112
see also John Nicholson
Pardoe, Julia. CSF 154
Pardoe, Margot Mary (1902-) ES2
341 FFC 172 SF1 404
Pardon, Tom. EXT 5/1 9
Paredes, Horacio V. IAC 189
Parekh, Bhiku. BAA 251
Pareto, Vilfredo. COT 223
Pargeter, Edith Mary (1913-)
CSF 154 ES2 341 SF1 404,584
SF2 1027 WGT 112
Paris, Bernard J. EXT 5/2 26-
30
Paris, John pseud. of Frank Tre-
lawny Arthur Ashton-Gwatkin.
CSF 154 SF1 404
Paris, Matthew. IAC 189 VES
232
Pariset, Georges. BAA 187
Park, James W. BAA 251
Park, Mary C. BAA 286
Park, W. B. FFC 149
Parke, Jean. SF1 404
Parkenham, Ivo. SF1 402
Parker. EXT 5/2 48
Parker, Dorothy. EXT 6/1 19
Parker, Douglass. EXT 10/1 37,
44 SOI xv
Parker, E. Frank. SF1 404
Parker, Edgar. FFC 56,90,135
Parker, Hershel. NWO 287
Parker, Joseph D. SF1 404
Parker, Joseph W. BAA 104
Parker, Norton S. SF1 404

Parker, Richard (1915-) ES2 341
FFC 69,167 IAC 189 SFE 451
SF1 404
Parkes, Lucas pseud. of John
Wyndham Parkes Lucas Beynon
Harris. IAC 189 SFS 92,129
Parkhirst, Douglas. SF1 404
Parkinson, C. Northcote. CSC
108,118 EXT 6/1 19 WFS 206
Parkinson, Ethelyn Minerva
(1906-) SF1 404
Parkinson, Harold Frederick.
CSF 154 SF1 404
Parkinson, Robert C. FHT 67
Parkman, Sydney Muller (1895-)
SF1 404
Parks, George B. BAA 251
Parmele, Mary Platt (1843-1911)
SF1 404
Parmenter, Ross. EXT 6/1 15
Parnall, Peter. FFC 124,128,
136,182
Parnell, Frank. WGT 112
Parnell, John. BAA 37 SF1 404
Parnell, Keith pseud. of P. K.
Palmer. SF1 405
Parnov, Eremei I. (1935-) BYS
281 IAC 189 LEX 503 SFS 45,
92 SL5 2506-10 WFS 305
Parr, Christie. IAC 189
Parr, Julian (1923-) ES2 341
Parrinder, Edward Geoffrey
(1910-) ES2 341
Parrinder, Patrick. BAA 251-2
Parrington, Vernon Louis, Jr.
(1871-1929) BAA 187,286 ES2
341-2 EXT 5/1 6 NDA 199
Parrish, Anne (1888-1957) CSF
154 FFC 84,156 SF1 405
Parrish, George Dillwyn (1894-)
CSF 154 SF1 405
Parrish, John Maxey. CSF 154
ES2 342 SF1 405
Parrish, Maxfield. SFB 105
VES 288 WTS 74,93
Parrish, Randall (1858-1923) CSF
154 EXT 1/1 15 SF1 405
Parry, David MacLean (1852-1915)
AOW 70 BAA 70 CSF 154 EXT
1/1 2,15 EXT 7/1 28 MFW 120
SFE 451 SF1 405 VES 140
WIF 51
Parry, Dennis Arthur (1912-)
CSF 154 SF1 405
Parry, Michael Patrick (1947-)
HFI 116 IAC 189 LTN 249

SF1 405 SF2 1027 WGT 112
Parsons, Coleman O. EXT 2/1
15 FAN 51,183
Parsons, Eliza. CSF 154
Parsons, Philip B. VES 148
Parssinen, Terry Mitchell. BAA
252,286
Partington, Charles. IAC 189
Partridge, Edward Bellamy (1877-
1960) SF1 29 WGT 112 see also
Thomas Bailey
Pascal, Blaise (1623-62) COT 143
CWN 31 MFW 194 MSF 106
SHL 60 TSO 9,19,21,61
Pascal, Francine. FFC 167
Pass, Rudolf A. BAA 252
Passingham, W. J. SOT 124 VES
139
Pasternak, Boris. EXT 10/2 75
LTN 215 MSF 253
Pasteur, Louis. EXT 8/2 49
MFW 283 SFH 7 VFS 195
Pastor, Rosita. FFC 91
Patai, Daphne. BAA 252
Patch, Howard Rollin. BAA 187
Patchen, Kenneth. IAC 189
Patchett, Mary Elwyn (1897-) ES2
342 SFE 453 SF1 405 SF2 1027
Pater, Roger. CSF 154 ES2 342
WBW 34
Paterno, Domenica. SF1 405
Paternoster, George Sidney (1866-)
SF1 405
Paterson, Arthur Elliott. SF1 405
Paterson, Isabel. CSF 154
Patnaik, (Mr.). VFS 38
Paton, Andre Archibald (1811-74)
CSF 155 SF1 406
Paton, Jane. FFC 77,105,129
Paton, J. Noel. FBK 114
Paton, Raymond. CSF 155 SF1
406
Patrick, J(ohn) Max (1911-) BAA
xii, xvi, xx, 186-7, 224, 252 ES2
342 EXT 8/1 1, 20-4 EXT 7/2
29 EXT 9/1 16 EXT 9/2 31
FAN 184 MSF 46-7,54 NDA 51-
2, 54 SF1 406 SF2 1027-8
Patriot, (A) pseud. of L. Guy.
CSF 155
Patrizi. EXT 8/1 23
Patrouch, Joseph F. , Jr. (1935-)
AOW 351 SFE 453 SF1 406 SF2
1028 SRB 77
Pattee. RFA 195
Patten, Brian. FFC 100 IAC 189

Patten, Clinton A. WGT 112
Patten, Frederick. SL3 1198-203
Patten, Gilbert (1866-1945) WGT
112 see also Emerson Bell,
Burt L. Standish
Patten, J. Alexander. WGT 112
Patten, William (1861?-1936) ES2
342 SF1 406
Patterson, James Ernest William.
BAA 147 SF1 406
Patterson, Robert Hogarth. BAA
252
Patton, Frank (house name) STH
261 VES 102 WGT 112 see
also Raymond A. Palmer, Richard
S. Shaver
Patton, (Gen.) George. HWK 37
RHN 205
Patzer, Sidney. CSF 155
Pauer, Louis. BAA 89
Paul, Auren pseud. of Auren Uris.
SF1 406
Paul, Barbara. IAC 189
Paul, Elliot. IAC 190
Paul, Frank R. (1884-1963) ALW
120 ASF 243 BYS 216-7 COT
2, 6, 11, 30, 43, 74, 79, 116, 162,
172, 175, 258, 280 ES2 342-3
IAC 190 IMS 182, 195, 207, 213,
220, 222, 231 ISW 130 KAU 86-
7, 89, 116-7, 202 SFB 46, 104
SFE 453 SIH 187, 191 SOT 88,
355 SRB 34, 36, 92 STH 137-8,
263, 269 TRB 56-7 VES 72, 77,
93, 95, 103, 121, 126-7, 136, 149,
151, 158, 161, 166, 169, 185, 286-
8, 307, 326 WIF 17, 107 WSF 34,
43, 49-50, 73, 115, 126, 145 YTS
6-7, 9-10, 56
Paul, Herb. IAC 190
Paul, Hugo pseud. of Paul H.
Little. SF1 406
Paul, Phyllis. SF1 406
Paul, Saul W. TSP 61
Paulding, James Kirke (1778?-
1860) BAA 20 CSF 155 WGT
112-3
Pauli, Wolfgang. FTF 151 IAC
190 SFH 129
Pauling, Linus. ISW 172
Paull, Grace. FFC 130
Pauls, Theodore. SF1 406
Paulsen, Gary. HFI 116
Paulsen, Kathryn. IAC 190
Paulton, Edward Antonio (1868-
1939) SF1 406

Pauwels, Louis (1920-) ES2 343
NWO 11
Pavlenko, Piotr A. (1899-1951)
CSF 155 MSF 265 SF1 406
Pavlov, Ivan. EXT 2/2 34-5, 37
EXT 7/2 34 FAN 118, 186 [FUT]
NDA 54, 106-7 SFH 151-2
Pavlova, Vera. SIH 76
Pawelka. RFA 200, 202
Pawle, Hanbury (1886-1972) BAA
127 SF1 406
Pawley, Martin. JGB 53
Paxton, Joseph. ALW 60 EXT
5/2 31-6 FTF 36
Payes, Rachel Ruth Cosgrove
(1922-) BAA 162 ES2 343 IAC
190 LEX 503 SF2 800 WGT 113
see also E. L. Arch
Payne, A. R. Middleton. BAA 25
Payne, Charles. SF1 406
Payne, Donald Gordon (1924-) ES2
343 SF1 406 SF2 1028 WGT 113
see also Ian Cameron
Payne, Joan. FFC 88, 100, 135, 149
Payne, Joseph Frank. EXT 5/2 28
Payne, Paul Lawrence. IAH 58, 60
STH 18
Payne, (Pierre Stephen) Robert
(1911-) HFI 39 SF1 407 SF2
1028
Payson, Dale. FFC 28, 179
Peabody, Francis G. EXT 5/2 2
Peabody, George. EXT 8/2 63
Peabody, Joel R. SF1 407
Peacey, Howard Marriott (1880-)
CSF 155 SF1 407
Peacock, Lucy. CSF 155 SF1 407
Peacock, Thomas Love (1785-
1866) BYS 18, 37, 82, 86 FAN 64
SF1 407
Peake, Mervyn (1911-68) AOW
118 BFP 400-1 BYS 266-9, 299
CSF 22 ES2 343 FAN 188 FBK
130-2 FL4 1947-53 HFI 116
IAC 190 ISW 8, 246 LEX 504
LTN 125 SFE 453 SFH 99 SFW
455 SF1 407 SF2 1028 SOI xiv
SRB 274 THM 8 WAA 98, 110,
230
Peake, Richard Brinsley. SFB
32, 35
Peal, S. E. EXT 5/2 45
Pearce, Ann Philippa. FFC 14,
76, 168 SF1 407 SF2 1029 SRB
24

Pearce, Brenda (1935-) SFE 453 VES 81-2
Pearce, Gerald. STH 120
Pearce, Joseph Henry. CSF 155 SF1 407
Peardon, Thomas P. BAA 252
Peare, Catherine O. EXT 2/1 7
Pearl, Clinton. IAC 190
Pearl, Jacques Bain (1923-) ES2 343 SF1 407 SF2 1029
Pearlman, Gilbert. SF1 407
Pearn, Violet. CSF 25
Pearson, Andrew Russell (1897-1969) SF1 407 SF2 1029
Pearson, C. Arthur. STH 186, 188, 191-3, 195-6, 198, 202-8, 210, 212
Pearson, Charles Henry. BAA 50 POE 190-1
Pearson, Edward Max (1908-) HFI 116 SF1 407 SF2 1029
Pearson, Elizabeth J. IAC 66 SF1 407
Pearson, Hesketh. FAN 187
Pearson, Karl. POE 219
Pearson, Martin pseud. of Donald A. Wollheim, C. M. Kornbluth. IAC 190 IAH 35 SFE 453 SFS 92
Pearson, Michael Edward (1941-) IAC 190, 248 SF1 407 SF2 1029
Peart, Noel. IAC 190 SFS 92
Peary, Robert Edwin (1856-1920) EXT 1/1 3
Pease, Harlan Trask. SF1 408
Pease, Howard (1863-) CSF 155 ES2 343 SF1 408
Pease, M. C. IAC 190 MIH 89-90 RFA 198 SFS 92
Pease, Tom. BAA 136
Peattie, Elia M. BAA 48
Peattie, Elia Wilkinson (1862-1935) CSF 155 ES2 343-4 SF1 408
Pechel, Rudolf. BAA 252
Pecirka, Jan. BAA 252
Peck, Bradford. BAA 63 CSF 155 SF1 408
Peck, George Washington (1817-59) BAA 25 WGT 113 see also Cantell A. Bigley
Peck, Ira. ES2 344 SF1 408
Peck, Richard E. (1936-) BAA 155 FFC 33 HFI 116 IAC 190 SFE 454 SF1 408
Peck, Robert. FFC 149
Peck, Vernon. SF1 408

Peckham, William C. EXT 5/2 45
Peddie, James Anderson. SF1 408
Peddiwell, J. Abner pseud. of Harold R. W. Benjamin. CSF 155
Pedersen, Con. IAC 190 SFS 92
Pederson, John. VES 80
Pedler, Christopher (1927-) SF2 1030 see also Kit Pedler
Pedler, Kit pseud. of Christopher Pedler. AOW 236 FFR 139 HFI 116 IAC 190 LEX 504-5 SFE 454 SF1 408 UFS 4 VES 303
Pedley, (Rev.) Hugh. BAA 79 CSF 155 SF1 408
Pedroso, Elizabeth. BAA 115
Pedroso, Felix. BAA 115
Peebles, H. P. BAA 252
Peebles, James Ewing (1928-68) ES2 344 WGT 113 see also James Kennaway
Peek, Bertrand M. ES2 344
Peek, Hedley. CSF 155 ES2 344 SF1 408 Peeke, Margaret Bloodgood (1838-1909) CSF 155 SF1 408
Peel, Charles V. CSF 155
Peel, Robert. CWN 28
Peeples, Edwin Augustus, Jr. (1915-) SF1 408, 584
Peeples, Samuel Anthony. SFS 92 SOT 349-50
Peet, Bill. FFC 123
Peew, Dimiter (1919-) LEX 505
Pehlke, Michael (1943-) AOW 352 BAA 187 SFE 454
Pei, Mario Andrew (1901-78) AAL 178 ES2 344 SF1 408 SF2 1030
Peirce, Charles Sanders. MIH 139 MSF 77
Peirce, Hayford. IAC 190
Pelcher, Anthony. RFA 5
Pelham, David (1938-) SFE 454 VES 189, 246, 289
Pell, Sarah-Warner J. RBY 186-94
Pellaert, Guy. SFB 110
Pellerin, George. POE 139
Pelley, William Dudley. CSF 156
Pelot, Pierre (1945-) LEX 505-6 SFE 454
Pelton, Guy Cathcart. SF1 408
Pelz, Bruce E. EXT 9/2 25 EXT 10/1 18

Pember-Devereux, Margaret Rose
Roy McAdam (1877-) WGT 113
see also Roy Devereux
Pemberton, Elizabeth Leigh. EXT
10/1 38
Pemberton, (Sir) Max (1863-1950)
CSF 156 MSF 162 SFE 454-5
SF1 408 SIH 194 STH 33-4, 183
Pemberton, Robert. BAA 26
Pendarves, G. G. pseud. of Gladys
Graves Trenery. STH 253-4
WTS 27, 30, 41-3, 128
Penden, William. IAC 190
Pendered, Mary Lucy (1858-1940)
CSF 156 SF1 408
Pendergast, Thomas. RHN 12
Pendexter, Hugh. EXT 6/1 15
Pendleton, Don(ald Eugene) (1927-)
BAA 165 HFI 116 SFE 455 SF1
409 SF2 1030 VES 136 WGT 113
Pendleton, John. CSF 156 SF1
409
Pendleton, Louis Beauregard
(1861-1939) CSF 156 SF1 409
Pendower, Jacques pseud. of T. C.
H. Jacobs (1899-) SF2 949
Pendray, Gawain Edwards (1901-)
COT 33, 37-8 ES2 344 IMS 11
ISW 160 SFE 455 VES 71 WGT
113
Pengreep, William. CSF 156 SF1
409
Penman, Thomas. IAC 190
Penmare, William pseud. of Mavis
Elizabeth Nisot. CSF 156 SF1
409
Penney, Roger. IAC 190
Pennington, Bruce (1944-) BYS
217 FBK 81 SFE 455 VES 109,
289
Penny, David G. SFE 455
Penny, Fanny Emily (1857?-1939)
CSF 156 SF1 409
Penrice, Arthur. CSF 156 SF1
409
Penrose, (Mrs.) H. H. CSF 156
Penta, Clement Della. BAA 188
Penzoldt, Peter. AOW 84, 92, 352
ES2 344 EXT 5/1 6 FBK 69 SF1
409 SRB 73
Peple, Edward Henry (1869-1924)
SF1 409
Pepys, Samuel. VFS 196
Perce, Elbert (1831-69) SF1 409
Percival, (Dr.) C. SF1 409

Percy, Alan Ian (1880-1930) see
Duke of Northumberland
Percy, H. R. IAC 190
Percy, Walker (1916-) ALW 238
AOW 236 BAA 153, 252 ETN
174-5 FFR 139 HFI 116 SFE
457 SFH 99 SF1 409 SF2 1031
SL3 1278-83 STF 23
Peregoy, Calvin pseud. of Thomas
Calvert McClary. IAC 190 SOT
238
Pereira, N. G. O. BAA 252
Pereira, Wilfred Dennis (1921-)
SF1 409 SF2 1031
Perelman, S. J. CSC 220 MIH 90
MSF 264 SFH 97
Perera, (Dr.) N. M. VFS 184
Peresvetov, Ivan S. EXT 10/2
73 MSF 243
Peretz, Martin. BAA 252
Pericles. [FUT] MSF 38
Peril, Bruce. CSF 156 SF1 410
Perkins, D. M. SF1 410
Perkins, Eli pseud. of Melville
De Lancey Landon. CSF 156
SF1 410
Perkins, Frederick Beecher
(1828-99) CSF 156 IAC 190 SF1
410
Perkins, Lawrence A. IAC 190
Perkins, Maxwell. IAH 87-8
SFA 143
Perkins, Merle L. BAA 252
Perkins, Michael (1942-) SFE 458
SF1 410 SF2 1031
Perkins, Violet Lilian. SF1 410
WGT 113 see also William
Leslie
Perl, Susan. FFC 56
Perlini, Tito. BAA 253
Perlman, William J. IMS 119,
125, 187
Perlmutter, William. AOW 321
Perrault, Robert. SF1 410
Perrault, Charles. SRB 21 TFC
35, 54, 64-6, 73, 83, 131, 135-6
Perret, Jacques (1901-) ES2 344
SF1 410
Perri, Leslie pseud. of Doris
Baumgardt. IMS 218, 238, 245
Perrier, Francois. BAA 253
Perrin, Alice (1867-1934) CSF 156
SF1 410
Perrin, Jeffery. IAC 190
Perrott, Roy. BAA 253
Perry, A. T. (1887-) WGT 113

Perry, Abner. ALW 110
Perry, Alvin Earl. IMS 33
Perry, Dick (1922-) see Dick Winfield
Perry, Donald Robert. BAA 93
Perry, James Raymond. BAA 65
Perry, Richard (1944-) SF1 410
Perry, Ted (1931-) SF1 410
Perry, Walter Copland (1814-1911) CSF 157 SF1 410
Perry-Coste, Frank Hill. BAA 188
Persinger, Clark Edmund. BAA 63
Persky, Stan. IAC 190
Persons, Stow. BAA 175
Pertwee, Roland (1885-1963) CSF 157 SF1 411
Perutz, Leo (1882?-1957) CSF 157 ES2 344 FBK 82,144 SF1 411
Pesch, Ludwig. BAA 253
Peschke, Hans (1923-) LEX 506-7
Pesek, Ludek (1919-) AOW 329 FFR 139 LEX 507-8 SFE 458-9 SF1 411 SF2 1031
Pesic-Golubovic, Zagorka. BAA 253
Pesin, Harry (1919-) SF1 411 SF2 1031
Pestum, Jo (1936-) LEX 508
Petagno, Joe. [FUT]
Petaja, Emil Theodore (1915-) ALW 160 BYS 304 ES2 344-5 EXT 3/1 7 FFR 139 HFI 116-7 IAC 190 IMS 30, 94, 110 LEX 508 MIH 136 SFB 105 SFD 63 SFE 459 SF1 411-2 SF2 1031-2 WGT 113
Peter, Laurence J. BAA 166
Peter (the Great). MSF 245
Peterkiewicz, Jerzy (1916-) SFE 459 SF1 412 SF2 1032
Peters, Alan. SF1 412
Peters, H. F. RZY 26
Peters, L. T. pseud. of Albert Klainer, Jo Ann Klainer. HFI 117
Peters, Ludovic pseud. of Peter Brent. BAA 144 SFE 459 SF1 412
Peters, Robert. BAA 253
Petersham, Maud. FFC 22, 24
Petersham, Miska. FFC 22, 24
Petersilea, Carlyle (1844-1903) BAA 61 CSF 157 SF1 412 WGT

113-4 see also Ernst Von Himmel
Peterson, Ephraim. BAA 69, 75
Peterson, Houston. FAN 20
Peterson, John Victor. HFI 117 IMS 213 SF1 412 WGT 114
Peterson, Margaret Ann (1883-1933) CSF 157 ES2 345 SF1 412
Peterson, Bob. ES2 345
Peterson, Robert C. SF1 413 STH 157
Peterson, Russell C. (1943-) SF1 412
Peterson, Sidney (1912-) SF1 412
Pethebridge, Denis. IAC 190
Petracca, Joseph. IAC 190 SFS 47, 92
Petrarch(a, Francesco) (1304-74) MSF 43 OWB 71 WFS 80
Petre, M. D. BAA 253
Petrescu, Cezar. SIH 139
Petrie, C. Barker, Jr. WTS 63-4
Petrie, Flinders. POE 218-9
Petrie, Stuart. FFC 156
Petrol. CSF 157
Petronius. SIH 32
Pettee, Florence Mae. CSF 157
Pettersen, Rena Oldfield. BAA 90 CSF 157 SF1 412
Petty, John (1919-) BAA 142 ES2 345 SFE 459 SF1 412
Petworth, Algernon. BAA 80
Petzler, John. BAA 42
Peyton, Green pseud. of G. Peyton Wertenbaker. IAC 190 SFS 92
Peyton, K. M. FFC 33
Peyton, Roger G. SF1 412
Pezet, Alfonso Washington (1889-) CSF 157 SF1 412
Pfaelzer, Mary Jean. BAA 286
Pfeiffer, Fred. SRB 47
Pfeiffer, Gunter. BAA 253
Pfeiffer, Johann Gregor (-1723?) WGT 114
Pfeiffer, John R. 117-301, 362 FL1 42-4 FL5 2074-8 SFW 101-8, 297-304 SF1 413 SL1 120-4 SL2 899-904 SL3 1383-6
Pfeiffer-Belli, W. BAA 253
Pfeil, Don(ald J.). HFI 117 SFE 459 WGT 114 WSF 231 see also William Arrow
Pflaezer, Jean. BAA 253
Phaleas. EXT 8/1 23
Phelan, James Leo. CSF 157
Phelan, R. C. IAC 190 SFS 92
Phelon, Mira M. SF1 413

Phelon, William P. CSF 157
SF1 413
Phelps, Corwin. BAA 54 CSF
157
Phelps, Elizabeth Stuart pseud.
of Elizabeth Stuart Phelps Ward
(Mrs. Herbert Ward) (1844-
1911) CSF 157 ES2 345 SF1
413
Phelps, George Hamilton (1854-)
BAA 75 WGT 114 see also
Patrick Q. Tangent
Phelps, Gilbert Henry (1915-)
ES2 345 HFI 117 SF1 413 SF2
1032
Phelps, Robert. EXT 10/1 38
Phelps, Sydney. CSF 158
Phelps, William Lyon (1865-1943)
SF1 413
Philbrook, Rose Miriam (1911-)
SF1 413
Philip, Alexander John (1879-)
SF1 413
Philips, Judson Pentecost (1903-)
CSF 158 SF1 413 WGT 114
Philips, Mary Alice. SF1 413
Philips, Peter. STH 117
Philipson, Morris. EXT 6/1 6
Phillifent, John T(homas) (1916-
76) BAA 155 ES2 345 HFI 117-
8 IAC 190-1 SFE 459 SFS 92
SF1 413-4 SF2 1032-3 WGT 114
Phillips, Alan Meyrick Kerr
(1916-) SF2 1033 see also
Mickey Phillips
Phillips, Alexander Moore (1907-)
COT 17, 91 CSF 158 ES2 345-6
HFI 118 IAC 191 OWB 74 RFA
64 SFS 92 SF1 414 SOT 136
VES 131, 175 WSF 134
Phillips, Forbes. SF1 414
Phillips, Frank pseud. of Philip
F. Nowlan. RFA 79
Phillips, Jonas B. CSF 158
Phillips, Leslie. EXT 6/2 48
Phillips, Louis. IAC 191
Phillips, Lundern M. CSF 158
SF1 414
Phillips, Mark pseud. of Laurence
M. Janifer, Randall Garrett.
AOW 236 RFA 210 SFE 459
VES 207
Phillips, Mickey pseud. of Alan
Meyrick Kerr Phillips. SF1 414
Phillips, Peter (1921-) ALW 161
COT 159 IAC 191 SFE 459-60

SFS 92-3 VES 180, 210 WGT
114 WSF 4
Phillips, R. CSF 158
Phillips, R. A. J. IAC 191 SFS 93
Phillips, Rog pseud. of Roger
Phillips Graham (1909-65) DTS
26 FFR 139 HFI 118 IAC 191
LEX 509 SFE 460 SFS 93 SF1
414 STH 120 VES 135, 302, 338
WIF 91 WSF 142 see also A. R.
Steber
Phillips, Roland Ashford. CSF
158 SF1 414
Phillips, Vic. IAC 191 RFA 60,
84
Phillips, Ward pseud. of H. P.
Lovecraft. EXT 3/1 2, 4, 6, 10,
14-5, 17
Phillips, Wendell. UKL 87
Phillpotts, Eden (1862-1960) CSF
158 ES2 346 FL1 51-3, 355-7
SFE 460 SF1 414 SL4 1866-70
WGT 114-5
Philmus, Lois C. SF1 414
Philmus, Robert M. (1943-) AAL
198-9 ALW 30 AOW 3-32, 352
BAA xx, 188, 193, 253 BYS 112
MSF 65, 67, 76, 80, 222, 232 NWO
xi-xii, 18, 46 SFB 10 SFE 460
SFH 239 SF1 414 SF2 1033 SL3
1079-83 SL5 2287-92 SRB 73,
83, 507 VES 330
Philpot, Joseph Henry (1850-1939)
WGT 115 see also Philip Lafar-
gue
Phineas pseud. of John M. Hanifin.
SF1 414
Phipson, Joan pseud. of Joan Mar-
garet Fitzhardinge (1912-) FFC
168 SF1 414
Phylos (the Tibetan) pseud. of
Frederick Spencer Oliver. CSF
158 SF1 415
Physick, Edward Harold (1878-
1972) WGT 115 see also E. H.
Visiak
Picard, Barbara. FFC 22, 26
Picard, Charles. FFC 137
Picard, Don. IAC 191
Picasso, Pablo (1881-) CWN 49
ETN 123-4 MSF 74
Piccone, Paul. BAA 253
Picht, Georg. BAA 188
Pick, John Barclay (1921-) SF1
415 THM 10, 13-4, 40, 46, 54, 61
Pickens, Thomas. IAC 191

Pickering, William H. COT 34
EXT 5/2 38-9, 40-1, 45, 47
Pickersgill, Frederick. ES2 346
SF1 415
Pickersgill, Joshua, Jr. CSF
158 SF1 415
Pickman, Richard Upton. WTS
103
Picton, J. A. BAA 253
Picton, Nina. WGT 115 see also
Laura Dearborn
Pienkowski, Jan. FFC 16
Pieper, Annemarie. BAA 253
Pier, Arthur Stanwood (1874-1966)
BAA 104 CSF 158 SF1 415
Pier, Garrett Chatfield (1875-
1943) CSF 158 SF1 415
Pieratt, Asa B., Jr. AOW 348
SRB 83
Pierce, Caldwell. TSP 134
Pierce, Earl, Jr. SOT 342 WTS
40-1
Pierce, Hazel. RBY 165-85 SL2
797-801 SL3 1246-50
Pierce, John Jeremy. IAC 191
SFD 3 WSF 37, 280
Pierce, (Dr.) John Robinson
(1910-) BAA 253 BYS 320 ES2
346 EXT 1/2 33 EXT 8/1 4
IAC 191 SFE 461 SFS 93 VFS
211, 241, 261 WGT 115 WIF 167
see also J. J. Coupling
Pierce, Roy. BAA 253
Piercy, Marge (1936-) HFI 118
IAC 191 NDA 142-3, 145 SF1
415 SF2 1033-4 SL5 2488-91
Pierik, Robert. IAC 191
Pierret, M. BAA 188
Pierson, Ernest De Lancey. SF1
415
Pieterse, Jan Nederveen. BAA
253
Pietrkiewicz, Jerzy. ES2 346
Pietzak, Marek. FBK 136
Piffard, Harold. STH 204
Piggin, Julia R. EXT 10/1 38
Piggott, William (1870-1943)
WGT 115 see also Hubert Wales
Pigott, Percy. CSF 158 SF1 415
Pike, Judith. SF1 415
Pilate, Pontius. TDI 49
Pilgrim, John. BAA 254
Pilgrim, (The). BAA 254
Pilibin, (An) pseud. of John Hack-
ett Pollock. CSF 159 SF1 415

Pilkington, Mary Hopkins (1766-
1839) CSF 159 SF1 415 WGT
115
Pilkington, Thomas Roger Edward.
SF1 415
Piller, Emanuel S. (1907-) AOW
183 CSF 68 SFE 462 SF1 415
VES 135
Pim, Herbert M. see A. Newman
Pincher, (Henry) Chapman (1914-)
ES2 346 HFI 118 SFE 462 SF1
415 SF2 1034 WGT 115
Pincherle, Alberto (1907-) see
Alberto Moravia
Pinchin, Frank J. SF1 415
Pinckard, Terri E. IAC 191
Pinckney, Josephine (1895-1957)
ES2 346 MSM 77 SF1 416
Pinero, A. W. IAH 26
Pines, Ned. IMS 45, 53 SOT 110
STH 44 TSP 24, 28
Pines, Robert A. TSP 24
Pinkerton, Thomas A. BAA 65
SF1 416
Pinkney, Dorothy C. IAC 191
Pinkwater, D. Manus. FFC 123,
149, 168
Pinto, Ralph. FFC 100, 120
Piotrowski, Sylvester Anthony.
BAA 286
Piper, H(orace) Beam (1904-64)
AAL 42 AOW 236 BFP 402
BYS 37 COT 244 CSC 33 ES2
346-7 ETN 126, 191 FFR 139
HFI 118 HID 45, 122, 180 IAC
191 IAH 39 ISW 217, 248-9 KAU
204 LEX 509-10 MIH 87, 89
MSM 74, 132 RFA 144, 155, 158,
163-4, 190, 195-7, 200, 204, 207
RGS 138-9 SFB 19 SFD 16 SFE
462 SFS 79, 93 SF1 416 SL3
1230-4 SOT 431 SRB 338 STH
157, 246 VES 81, 122, 144, 147,
335 WFS 161, 202 WIF 91, 232
WSF 111-2, 148, 172, 184, 233,
244, 324, 333, 387
Piper, Walter. SF1 416
Pirandello, Luigi (1867-1936) FL4
1757-9
Piranesi, G. B. BYS 16, 37 FBK
8, 11
Pirie, David Tarbat (1946-) SF1
416 SF2 1034
Pirie-Gordon, Charles Henry
Clinton (1883-1969) CSF 170
SF1 416 WGT 115 see also
Prospero and Caliban

Pirker, Theo. BAA 188
Piroschow, Vera. BAA 188
Pirsig, Robert M. MFW 188
    UKL 145-6
Piruli, Madigan. SF1 416
Piserchia, Doris (Elaine) (1928-)
    AAL 27 ALW 212 AOW 237
    FFR 139-40 HFI 118 IAC 191
    RGS 139-40 SFE 462 SF1 416
    SF2 1034
Pitcairn, John James. WGT 115
Pitkin, Walter B. TSP 218
Pitman, Patricia. CWN 34-5
Pitocca, Francesco. BAA 188
Pitt, Stanley. VES 289
Pittard, Helene Dufour (1874-)
    WGT 115 see also Noelle Roger
Pittock, (Mrs.) M. A. BAA 42
Piyadasa. VFS 22
Pizarro, Francisco. STH 71
Pizer, Laurette Naomi. ES2 347
    SF1 416
Pizor, Faith K. (1943-) SFE 462
    SF1 416
Place, Marian Templeton (1910-)
    FFC 191 SF1 416
Plachta, Dannie. IAC 191 SFS
    93 VES 151
Planchat, Henry-Luc. IAC 191
Planck, Max (1858-1947) FTF 71
    TBJ 11
Plank, Robert. AAL 1-2 ACC
    121-48, 244 AC2 76 AOW 86
    BAA 188, 229, 254 EXT 2/2 40-
    1 EXT 3/2 48-52 EXT 4/1 1
    EXT 6/2 22, 25-6, 39-49 EXT
    8/2 64-6 EXT 10/1 49 FAN
    185 KAU 205 MFW 255 NWO
    121, 166 OSR 265-7, 356 RAH
    53, 83-106, 125 SFH 183-5, 239
    SOI 26-40, 45 STH 108 TSF 157-
    67 UKL 245
Plath, David W. BAA 188
Plath, Sylvia. IAC 191
Plato. ALW 32, 39-41, 47, 53, 98-
    9 AOW 10-1 ASF 173 ATA 5
    BAA xi, xiv-xv, xxi BYS 58, 65
    CAT 48 COT 163 EXT 4/2 18,
    23 EXT 7/1 16 EXT 7/2 34
    EXT 8/1 20, 23 EXT 8/2 33
    EXT 9/2 50 FAN 4, 59, 66-7, 72
    FLT 48 FTF 48, 99-101 [FUT]
    HEN 22 HID 97 IAC 192 INT
    12, 49 JGB 32 LTN 146, 150
    MFW 262-3, 268 MSF 28, 37, 39,
    42, 45, 83, 87-8, 93-4, 97, 101-2,

111, 118, 123, 166, 168, 176, 220,
    229-30, 246, 257, 267 MSM 13,
    29, 125, 127-8, 136, 159-60 NWO
    96, 98-9, 101-2, 223 POE 4, 214,
    255 PST 11, 24, 123-4, 308 RFA
    172 SFB 13, 75 SFE 464 SFH
    6-7, 10, 26, 173, 218 SFS 93 SHL
    39 SIH 65, 79, 86 TBC 31 THM
    27 TSO 48 UKL 98-9, 116-7,
    125, 127, 133-4, 137, 141, 145-6
    VES 124-5, 140, 269-70 VFS 69
    WAA 45-6, 242 WBW 3, 7, 41
    WIF 29, 37, 39, 47-50, 184 WSF
    342 WTS 12
Platonov, Andre. FBK 41
Platt, Charles (1943?-) AOW 237
    BYS 298-9 DMK 281-2 ES2 347
    FFR 140 HFI 118 IAC 178, 192
    LEX 510-1 SFB 132 SFE 464
    SF1 416-7 SF2 1034-5 SRB 76
    UFS 4 VES 129, 289 WSF 255
Platt, James, Jr. CSF 159
    SF1 417
Platt, Kin (1911-) ES2 347 SF1
    417
Plattel, Martin G. BAA 188, 254
Plattes, Gabriel. BAA 3-4
Platts, W. Carter. CSF 159
Plauger, P. J. (1944-) IAC 192
    LEX 511 SFE 464 VES 232
Plautus, Titus Maccius. OWB 71
Pleasance, Alice Liddell. PJF
    49-58
Plenn, Doris. FFC 135
Plimpton, George. EXT 6/1 13
    FAN 186 FFC 156
Pliny (the Elder). ASF 23 FBK
    12 STH 70 VFS 189
Pliny (the Younger). COT 28
Plockhoy, Pieter. BAA 5-6
Plotinus. COT 154 MFW 265
Plotz, Richard D. EXT 10/1 18,
    26, 38
Plum, Werner. BAA 188
Plummer, Kathleen Church. BAA
    254
Plummer, William F. CSF 159
Plunkett, Edward John Moreton
    Drax (1878-1957) BFP 168-73
    WGT 115-6 see also Lord Dun-
    sany
Plutarch. SFB 70
Plym, Don. SF1 417
Plym, Thea. SF1 417
Pocock, Bryant Walker. SF1 417
Pocock, George. POE 52-3

Pocock, Roger S. (1865-1941) CSF
159 SF1 417
Podhoretz. ETN 176
Podojil, Catherine. CEN 70-86
Podolny, Roman. IAC 192 SFS 93
Podwell, Jerry. SRB 52
Poe, Edgar Allan (1809-49) ACE
58, 73 AC2 56, 71 ALW 13, 33,
53, 55-9, 62, 65-6, 68, 72, 76, 82,
87, 120, 216 AOW 10, 28-9, 34,
54, 344, 351 ASF 165, 184, 191
BAA 25 BYS 18, 36, 40-57, 68,
87, 93, 117, 168 CAT xvi, 2, 7, 10,
41, 63, 107-8, 110 COT 27, 92
CSC 40, 166, 172, 208-9 CSF 159
DTS 3 ES2 347-50 EXT 1/1 8-
9, 14 EXT 1/2 25, 30, 33, 38 EXT
2/1 11, 15 EXT 3/1 5, 18, 24, 29-
30 EXT 3/2 33, 39, 44 EXT 4/2
24 EXT 5/1 4, 15-6, 16a EXT
7/1 14 EXT 7/2 38, 48 FAN 10,
12 FBK 13, 15-6, 27, 29, 32, 35-
9, 41, 72, 74-5, 80-2, 137, 141 FFR
140 FLT 13, 32-47, 49-50, 114
FL3 1092-5 FL4 1665-78 FTF
31-3, 41 HEN 3, 12, 29, 59 IAC
192 IAH 55 IMS 2, 189 INT 6-7
ISW 112, 220 JGB 6, 59 KAU 7-
8, 34, 127, 158, 194 LEX 511-3
MFW 17, 21, 117, 126, 280-1 MSF
22, 36, 82, 124, 132, 137, 139-43,
148-9, 162, 165, 168, 201, 204, 220,
251 MSM 25, 29-30, 103, 128, 210,
297, 304 NWO 8, 10, 17, 20, 25, 35,
44, 49-75, 88, 95, 148, 203-5, 263,
282 PJF 57 POE 65, 76-7, 97
PST 11, 29-36, 42-7, 50, 64-5, 67,
107-9, 120, 178-9, 205, 208-9, 211,
215, 228, 241, 243, 250-3, 259, 264,
268-9, 271, 274-6, 283, 318 RBY
18, 51-2, 72, 80, 111, 168-70, 172,
174-6, 179-80, 185 RFA 39 SFA
261 SFB 20-2, 42, 57, 96-7 SFD
23, 72, 87, 287 SFE 464-5 SFH
8-10, 14, 37, 106, 157, 182-3, 199
SFN 32 SFS 93-4 SFW 11-8, 31-
2 SF1 417-21 SHL 48 SIH 14,
33 SL3 1480-7 SL4 1871-8 SOI
44 SOT 14, 361, 367, 410 STH
52, 122, 130, 254 TBC 3, 33, 49
TFC 39-40, 47-9, 56, 70, 73, 82,
86-7, 163 THM 39 TSF 49 TSP
43 VES 130, 145, 173, 205, 249,
260, 305, 312 WAA 90-3 WBW
6, 11 WGT 116-7 WIF 42-5, 77,
144, 149 WSF 15-6, 43, 130, 211
WTS 3, 16-8, 25, 45, 48, 56, 59, 120-
1, 123, 128, 130 YTS 2-3
Pofford, W. IMS 33
Pogany, Willy. FFC 180
Poge, N. Wooten pseud. of Norvell W. Page. TSP 58
Poggenmiller, Helmuth. EXT
10/1 19
Poggioli, Renato. BAA xxi, 188
Pogorelski, Antony (1787-1836)
FBK 41
Pohl, Ann. WFS 206-7, 214, 216
Pohl, Carol. IAC 192 SF1 421
WFS 147, 205, 214-5, 217, 228-9,
250, 279, 281-2, 295, 297, 299, 301,
304-8 see also Carol Metcalf
Ulf, Carol Stanton
Pohl, Ernst. WFS 4-5
Pohl, Frederik (1919-) AAL 15,
48-9, 56-7, 79, 86 ALW 36, 99,
140, 156, 160, 162, 176, 179, 184,
212, 217, 219, 239 AOW 221, 237-
9, 285, 295, 297, 400 ASF 43, 112,
120, 174, 242 BAA xvi, 123-5,
127-9, 133, 136, 139, 141, 149
BFP 403-8 BYS 79, 224, 226,
230, 245, 249-51, 279, 281, 289,
296 CAT 72, 86, 139 COT v, 14,
134, 140-1, 163, 165, 238, 252, 268-
70, 275-6, 296 CSC 186-7, 198,
201, 214-5, 224, 292-311 DMK
57-67 DTS 7, 22 EFP 17 ES2
350-2 ETN 3, 30-1, 34, 40, 42,
45, 47, 64-5, 72, 123, 126, 163, 178
EXT 2/1 21 EXT 2/2 27, 31
EXT 3/1 26 EXT 4/2 29 EXT
5/1 3, 10 EXT 6/1 1 EXT 6/2
22, 51 EXT 8/1 7-8, 15 EXT
10/1 1-2 EXT 10/2 69-115 FAN
9, 155 FFR 140-1 [FJT] FTF
3-8, 12, 69, 78, 86-8, 90, 106-7,
124-5, 128, 132, 179 HFI 118-9
IAC 192-5 IAH 16, 103-5, 113,
123, 132-3, 147 IMS 36, 45, 52,
55-8, 68, 82-3, 85, 103, 111, 113-
4, 116, 119-20, 126-8, 137, 140,
142-3, 149, 151, 153, 156, 158, 170-
2, 179, 183, 192, 199, 210, 214, 225,
234, 244-5, 252 INT 28, 49, 61-2,
84-5, 93-4 ISW 8, 119, 121-2,
146, 166, 189, 193-7, 221 JGB 5
KAU 185, 200, 204 LEX 513-6
MFW 11, 169, 251 MIH 6, 20, 29,
33, 41, 53, 103 MSF 13, 27, 78,
218, 242 NDA xi, 19-20, 25, 30-
1, 42, 116-22, 130 NWO 76, 125

Pohl, Frederik (cont.)
OMN 90-6, 214 POE 277-8 RFA
64, 191, 212-3 RGS 140-1 RSG
23, 32, 39 SFA 26, 31, 41, 47, 62,
144-5, 220-1 SFB 151-2 SFD
74, 234, 260, 293-4, 313, 315-6
SFE 465-7 SFH 62, 65-7, 69, 84,
150, 152 SFN 72-3, 76 SFS 68-
9, 94-5 SFW 229-30, 351, 396,
401, 406, 433, 475-82 SF1 417-22
SF2 1035 SIH 44, 94-5, 178, 190
SL2 858-64, 894-8 SL3 1328-32
SL4 1948-53 SL5 2127-31 SOT
119, 182-4, 197, 241, 252, 254-5,
296, 359, 418-20 SRB vii-viii,
12, 14, 125, 318, 331, 367, 370, 376,
513 STH 121, 157 SV1 26-32
TJB 4 TSF 57, 147, 236, 249 UFS
4 VES 75, 77-8, 81, 105, 124, 128-
9, 167, 170, 174-5, 190, 201, 212,
215, 253, 256, 260, 275, 303, 307
WAA 25, 61, 137-8, 154, 209, 242
WGT 117 WIF 218 WSF 4-5, 11,
74, 125, 138, 144, 146, 167, 174,
176, 183-4, 187, 206, 221, 229, 232,
236-7, 241, 246, 276, 283, 346, 387-
8 YTS 12 see also Elton V. An-
drews, Henry De Costa, Paul
Dennis Lavond, Paul Flehr, S.
D. Gottesman, Lee Gregor,
Edson McCann, James MacCreigh,
Scott Mariner, Charles Satter-
field, Allen Zweig
Pohl, Frederik, III. WFS 228
Pohl, Frederik, IV. WFS 229
Pohl, Julius. IMS 137, 213
Pohlman, Edward Wendell (1933-)
SF1 422 SF2 1035
Poincare, Raymond. EXT 3/2 43
Poisson, Ernest. BAA 188
Polak, Frederick L. BAA xx, 188,
254 MFW 184, 221-2
Polanski, Roman. FBK 44 WAA
88 WFS 301
Polanyi, Michael. KAU 12-4
Polese, Carolyn. FFC 102
Poleshchuk, A. IAC 195
Polidori, John William (1795-
1821) ALW 45 CSF 159 FBK
44 FL4 2013-6 SFB 32 SF1
422 SIH 28 WAA 87 WIF 41
Polin, Raymond. BAA 254
Politella, Joseph. RZY 65
Politi, Leo. FFC 131
Poll, Max. BAA 254
Pollack, Jackson. RBY 195

Pollack, Rachel. IAC 195
Pollack, Reginald. FFC 55
Pollack, Richard A. IAC 195
Polland, Madeleine. FFC 57
Pollard, Alfred Oliver (1893-)
CSF 159 SF1 422
Pollard, John X. (house name)
WGT 117-8 see also Howard
Browne
Pollard, Leslie. CSF 159 SF1
422
Pollexfen, Muriel A. CSF 159
SF1 422
Pollock, Arthur Williamson
Alsager (1853-1923) CSF 159
SF1 422
Pollock, Frank L. IAC 195
Pollock, George H. BAA 254
Pollock, John Hackett (1887-)
WGT 118 see also An Pilibin
Pollock, Walter Herries (1850-
1926) CSF 118 SF1 422
Polo, Marco. MSF 243 VFS 118,
152
Polya, G. IAC 195
Pomeau, Rene. BAA 254
Pomerance, Irwin. BAA 286
Pomerantz, Charlotte. FFC 70,
149
Pomeroy, John. WIF 140
Pomeroy, William C. BAA 52
CSF 159 SF1 422
Pompen, Aur. BAA 254
Ponchielli, Amilcare. OWB 72
Ponder, Zita Inez. SF1 423
Pong, Hoy Ping pseud. of Wilson
Tucker. IMS 19, 43, 203, 241
Ponnamperuma, (Dr.) Cyril.
VFS 164, 171
Pons, Emile. BAA 254-5
Pons, Maurice (1927-) SFE 470
SF1 423 SF2 1036
Ponsot, Georges. SF1 423
Poole, Josephine (1933-) SF1 423,
584 SF2 1036
Pooley, Robert Cecil (1898-) ES2
352-3
Poor, Katharine Hillwood. SF1
423
Poore, Charles. EXT 6/1 19
NDA 53
Pope, Alexander (1688-1744) CAT
135 EXT 1/2 38 EXT 10/2 113
IAC 195 NWO 9 SHL 6
Pope, Carl. IAC 195

Pope, Elizabeth Marie (1917-)
FFC 94,168 SF1 584
Pope, Gustavus W. AOW 70 BAA
52 CSF 160 EXT 1/1 3,16 MFW
127-8 SFE 470 SF1 423 SRB
9 VES 80-1
Pope, Marion Manville (1859-)
SF1 423
Popham, Hugh. FFC 150
Popham, Melinda (1944-) SF1 423
SF2 1036
Popp, Lilian. SFS 95 SF1 423
Popp, Max. EXT 2/1 5,7
Popper, Karl R. BAA 188,255
CWN 12 NDA 54,206-7 SFB
14-5 UKL 116-7
Popper-Lynkeus, Josef. EXT
3/2 49
Poquelin, Jean-Baptiste see
Moliere
Porges, Arthur. ALW 212,216
ES2 353 IAC 195 SFE 470 SFS
95 STH 45 VES 147,226 WGT
118
Porges, Irwin. AOW 352 SRB
78 STH 43
Porges, Paul Peter. IAC 195
Porphyrius. MSF 242
Portegal, Aleck. WFS 104,108-9
Porter, Andrew. LTN 34,47-8,
53 WFS 40 WSF 276,286
Porter, David Dixon (1813-91)
SF1 423
Porter, David L. BAA 255 UKL
224,245
Porter, Edwin S. SFH 102
Porter, Gene Stratton. MFW 131
Porter, Jane. ALW 109
Porter, Katherine Anne. TBC 6
WIF 151
Porter, Linn Boyd (1851-1916)
BAA 43 WGT 118 see also
Albert Ross
Porter, Pat. FFC 147
Porter, Peter. IAC 195
Porter, Philip W. BAA 255
Porter, Sylvia. WFS 287
Porter, William S. (1862-1910)
WGT 118 see also O. Henry
Portmann, Adolf. BAA 255
Portnoy, Howard N. SFE 470
Portundo, Jose Antonio. EXT
2/1 15
Portune, Robert. ES2 353
Portwin, E. T. CSF 160 ES2 353
SF1 423

Posey, M. N. NWO 71
Posnack, Emanuel Robert. BAA
111,115
Posner, Richard. IAC 195
Possendorf, Hans pseud. of Hans
Mahner-Mons. SF1 423
Post, George. TSP 89
Post, Jerry Benjamin (1937-) SF1
423 SF2 1036
Post, Joyce (1939-) SF1 423 SF2
1036
Post, Melville Davisson (1871-
1930) CSF 160 SF1 423
Poster, Mark. BAA 189,255
Poster, William. EXT 3/1 24
Posteritas. CSF 160 SF1 424
Posten, Tom. WTS 45
Postgate, Oliver. FFC 57
Potocki, (Count) Jan Hrabia (1761-
1815) ES2 353 FBK 21-2,26,147
FL3 1355-7 SF1 424 TFC 27,
79,85,136,144
Potter, Beatrix (1866-1943) FBK
114 FFC 124
Potter, Doug. RHN 155
Potter, Margaret Horton (1881-
1911) CSF 160 SF1 424
Potter, Martin H. CSF 160 SF1
424
Potter, Miriam. FFC 135-6
Potter, Robert. CSF 160 SFE
470 SF1 424
Potter, Zenas. FFC 135
Poulat, Emile. BAA 255
Poulin, A., Jr. IAC 195
Poulson, Theodore Frederick.
CSF 160 SF1 424
Poulton, Peter. VES 205
Pound, Arthur. COT
Pound, Ezra. CAT 89 CSC 126
ETN 119 IAH 3 ISW 150 MFW
281 MIH 8,21 MSM 288 RZY
49
Pournelle, Jerry (Eugene) (1933-)
AAL 1-5,27-8 ALW 212 AOW
232 BFP 409 CSC 104-20,170,
185-6,191,193-4 ETN 121,178
FFL 141 FLR 33 HFI 119-20
IAC 195 KAU 146 LEX 516-7
MFW 16,147-8 RGS 141-2 SFD
302 SFE 470-1 SFW 335,459,
461,463 SF1 424 SF2 1036-7
SL3 1463-7 SRB 6,13,361,371
SV3 53-64 VES 68,112 WSF
335,388

Powe, Bruce (1925-) BAA 162
HFI 120 SF1 424 SF2 1037
Powell, Dick. STH 252
Powell, F. Inglis. CSF 160 SF1
424
Powell, Frank pseud.? of Prentiss Ingraham. CSF 160 SF1
424 SRB 6
Powell, Gerald. CSF 160
Powell, J. M. BAA 255
Powell, Jep. STH 85
Powell, Talmage (1920-) SF1
424 SF2 1037
Powell, Van. CSF 160 SF1 424
Powers, J. F. IAC 195
Powers, J. L. ES2 353 HFI 120
Powers, Ralph. TSP 131
Powers, Richard M. (1921-) BYS
217 IAC 195 SFE 471 SRB 48
VES 289 WSF 225
Powers, Timothy. HFI 120
Powers, William T. IAC 195
SFS 95
Powys, John Cowper (1872-1963)
BYS 9, 110 CSC 6 CSF 160
CWN 40 ES2 353 FL1 71-3
FL3 1068-70 KAU 26 SFE 472
SF1 425 SRB 275 STH 240 THM
8, 13, 39
Powys, Theodore Francis (1875-
1953) CSF 160 FL3 1047-51
SF1 425
Poyer, Joseph John (1939-) ES2
353 HFI 120 IAC 195 RHN 161
SFE 472-3 SF1 425 SF2 1037
SFS 95
Poynet, Quintin. CSF 160 SF1
425
Praed, Rosa Caroline (1851-1935)
CSF 160-1 SF1 425 WGT 118
Prager, R. L. BAA 189
Pragnell, Festus (1905-) CSF 161
ES2 353 HFI 120 IAC 195 IMS
75, 96-7, 99 LEX 517-8 SFE
473 SF1 425 SOT 124 SRB 298
VES 141 WSF 64
Pratchett, Terry. HFI 120 IAC
195
Prather, Hugh (1938-) SF1 425
SF2 1037
Pratt, Ambrose (1874-1944) CSF
161 SF1 425
Pratt, Cornelia Atwood (-1929)
CSF 180 SFE 473 SF1 425

Pratt, (Murray) Fletcher (1897-
1956) AAL 22-3 ALW 123, 126,
185 AOW 118, 165, 173-4 ASF
148 ATA 8, 17 BAA 116 BFP
410-1 BYS 262, 264 COT 38,
208-9, 214 CSF 58, 161 DTS 12
ES2 353-4 EXT 1/2 34 EXT
5/1 3 EXT 6/2 51 FBK 91, 123-
4 FFR 141 FL1 137-42 FL2
768-72, 870-2 FL5 2097-101
HFI 120 HWK 40 IAC 91, 195-6
IAH 53, 63, 107 ISW 158-9, 196,
225, 248-9 LEX 518-9 MFW 51
MIH 15, 71, 135 MSM xiii, 29, 34,
73-90, 136, 302-3 OWB 68 RGS
142-3, 213 SFD 28, 292, 309 SFE
473 SFS 38, 70, 95-6 SFW 181
SF1 425-6 SF2 1037 SIN 8, 148-
51, 153-5 SL3 1031-5 SOT 158-
9, 163 SRB 257, 275 TJB 14
TSF 231-2 TSP 64 VES 71, 104,
289, 318 WFS 174, 178, 193, 215-
8, 274 WGT 118 WIF 20, 23, 27,
85, 101, 124, 170, 174, 196, 202,
231 WSF 129, 135, 293, 299, 386
see also George U. Fletcher
Pratt, Inga. WFS 193, 215, 218
Pratt, Parley Parker. BAA 33
Pratt, Theodore (1901-69) CSF
161 FL3 1044-6 SF1 426 SF2
1038 WGT 118-9
Pratt, William Henry (1887-1969)
ES2 354-5 EXT 3/1 20 WGT
119 see also Boris Karloff
Pratter, Frederick Earl. BAA
286
Praviel, Armand. EXT 2/1 15
Praz, Mario. EXT 4/2 19
Preece, Harold. CWD 3
Prentice, Harry. CSF 161 SF1
426
Prentice, Patrick H. IAC 196
Prescott, Harriet Elizabeth
(1835-1921) SF1 426
Prescott, Henry W. BAA 255
Prescott, Orville. IAH 132 NDA
39, 53
Presland, John pseud. of Gladys
Skelton. SF1 426
Presley. ETN 48
Presley, Elvis. CUA 39 SFN
109 VFS 18 WAA 90
Presley, James T. BAA 255
EXT 7/1 16 POE 139-40

Pressey, Edward Pearson. BAA 75

Presslie, Robert. ES2 355 IAC 196 SFS 96

Prest, Thomas Pecket (1810?-79?) CSF 161 FBK 44-5 FL4 2017-22 SF1 426 SIH 28-9

Prestigiacomo, A. TRB 58

Preston, Edna Mitchell. SF1 426

Preston, Hayter. CSF 161

Preston, James R. PJF 74

Preston, John Hyde. BAA 255

Preston, L. E. IAC 196

Preu, James. BAA 255

Preussler, Otfried. FFC 36, 156, 191, 195 SF1 426

Prevost, Andre. BAA 255

Prevost, Antoine-Francois. MSF 49

Prevot, Francis Clare. CSF 161 SF1 426

Price, Christine. FFC 74, 172

Price, Cornell. WBW 5, 21

Price, D. M. IAC 196

Price, (Dr.) Derek. VFS 190

Price, E(dgar) Hoffmann (1898-) CWD 4, 6, 53 ES2 355 EXT 3/1 8, 11, 24 HFI 120 IAC 196 IMS 16, 25, 75, 93, 110 SFS 96 SF1 426 SF2 1038-9 SOT 76, 108, 303, 309, 323 WAA 107 WGT 119 WTS ix, 4-5, 7, 23-4, 27, 29, 31-2, 36-8, 43, 49, 51-3, 56-8, 64, 69, 80, 82, 123, 126

Price, Garrett. FFC 75, 148

Price, George W., Jr. HID x, 27, 63 WSF 215, 284

Price, Roger Damon (1941-) SF1 426 SF2 1039

Price, Roger Taylor (1921-) ES2 355 IAC 196 SFS 96 SF1 426 SF2 1039

Price, Susan. FFC 40

Price, Theodore. SF1 426

Price, Vincent (1911-) ES2 355 IAC 196 SFB 97 WAA 93

Prichard, Hesketh Vernon (1876-1922) ES2 355 SF1 426 WGT 119 see also E. Heron

Prichard, Kate O'Brien. ES2 355 SF1 426 WGT 119 see also H. Heron

Prickett, Marmaduke A. CSF 161 SF1 427

Prickett, Stephen. FL1 63-5 FL3 1241-5 FL4 1629-32 FL5 2369-82 SRB 73

Priddle, Michael. FBK 151

Priest, Christopher (1943-) ALW 8, 212 AOW 239 BAA 152, 155 BFP 412 BYS 295, 301, 304 CAT 116 CSC 230 FFR 141 FRN 445 [FUT] HFI 120 IAC 196 LEX 519-21 LTN 262 RGS 143-4 RHN 44 SFE 474-5 SF1 427 SF2 1039 SL1 480-3 SL3 1045-9 SRB 361, 369 VES 186, 219, 246, 259

Priestley, J(ohn) B(oynton) (1894-) ALW 144, 216 AOW 80 BYS 208, 257, 298 CSF 161 ES2 355-6 EXT 1/2 34 EXT 7/2 41 EXT 8/1 5 EXT 10/1 9-16 FFR 141 FTF 139, 151 HFI 121 IAC 196 ISW 172 NWO 234 SFE 475 SFN 40 SFS 96 SF1 427 SF2 1039-40 VES 142, 149

Priestley, Lee. IAC 196

Prime, Alfred. WSF 134

Prime, (Lord) pseud. of Walter Doty Reynolds. CSF 126 SF1 427

Primrose, Jean. FFC 84

Prince, Don. CSF 161 SF1 427, 584

Prince, Edward. BAA 77 SF1 427

Prince, J. F. T. BAA 255

Pringle, David. SL1 453-6

Pringle, Rita. WFS 205

Prior, Ann (1949-) SF1 427 SF2 1040

Pritchard, John Laurence (1885-1968) see John Laurence

Pritchard, John Wallace (1912-) SF2 1114-5 see also Ian Wallace

Pritchard, William Thomas (1909-) ES2 356 WGT 119 see also William Dexter

Pritcher, Jacob Leon. BAA 107

Pritcher, Leon. SF1 427

Pritchett, E. Blanche. SF1 427

Pritchett, Victor Sawdon (1900-) BAA 256 ES2 356 NWO 95

Privat, Edmond. BAA 189

Proby, William C. CSF 161 SF1 427

Proctor, George W. IAC 197

Proctor, H. B. CSF 161
Proctor, Henry. CSF 161 SF1
427
Proctor, Mary. EXT 5/2 45
Proctor, Richard A. EXT 5/2
45-6
Proffitt, Josephine Moore (1914-)
see Sylvia Dee
Progoff, Ira. BAA 256
Prokofiev. WFS 65,129
Prokofieva, R. SFS 96
Prokop, Gert (1932-) LEX 521
Pronzini, Bill. ETN 15,38 IAC
197 WGT 119
Prophet James pseud. of James
Smith Buck. SF1 428
Propp, Vladimir. CAT 54-7
Prosperi, Piero (1945-) LEX 521-
2 SL1 102-4
Prospero, Peter. BAA 22
Prospero and Caliban pseud. of
Charles Harry Pirie-Gordon,
Frederick W. Rolfe. CSF 162
Prosser, Harold Lee, II. SF1 428
Protheroe, Cyril. SF1 428 see
Rand Le Page
Protter, Eric (1927-) ES2 356
SF1 428
Proust, Marcel (1871-1922) BYS
89, 93, 109-10 CWN 13 [FJT]
INT 40 MSF 49 SFD 43 SFN
119 STF 4
Prout, B. VES 104
Prout, Mearle. WTS 37
Proxmire, William. EXT 10/1 26
Proysen, Alf. FFC 22
Prudhommeaux, Jules. BAA 189
Prud'hommeaux, Rene. ES2 356
SF1 428
Pruning Knife pseud. of Henry F.
Allen. CSF 162
Prus, Boleslaw. FBK 147
Prussak, M. SIH 113
Pruyn, Leonard. BAA 134 HFI
81 SFE 478 SF1 428
Pryce, Devereux. CSF 162 SF1
428
Pryce-Jones, A. EXT 10/1 32,38
Prys, Joseph. BAA 189
Pryse, Spencer. FFC 21
Pseudoman, Akkad pseud. of
Edwin Fitch Northrup. AOW 109
CSF 162 MSM 209 PST 124-5,
193, 242, 274-5, 290 SFE 478
SF1 428

Ptolemy. EXT 5/1 22 MSF 6,
87 SFH 119, 157-8
Pubols, George. EXT 5/1 7
Puccetti, Roland Peter (1924-)
ES2 356 SFE 484 SF1 428 SF2
1040
Pudney, John (1909-) CSF 162
ES2 356
Pugner, (Wanda) Carol (1943-)
SF1 428 SF2 1040
Pukallus, Horst (1949-) LEX 522
Pukarich, Andrija (1918?-) ES2
356-7
Pulido, Shirley. FFC 130
Pullar, A. L. ES2 357 SF1 428
Pullen, Henry William (1836-
1903) CSF 162 SF1 428
Pulvermann, M. BAA 189
Pumilia, Joseph F. DTS 51 IAC
197
Punchatz, Don Ivan. SRB 51
Purcell, Charles. IMS 34
Purcell, (Dr.). VFS 262
Purchas, Samuel. WIF 183
Purdom, Thomas Edward (1936-)
ALW 212 DTS 29 EFP 17 ES2
357 HFI 121 IAC 197 SFE 486
SF1 428 SF2 1040-1
Purdy, Ken W. IAC 197 SFS 96
Purscell, Phyllis. FFC 136
Purtill, Richard L. (1931-) AAL
221 AOW 347 SF1 428 SF2
1042
Purviance, Harriet. LTN 267
Purviance, Jim. FLR 14, 41, 61
Pushkin, Alexander S. (1795-
1837) FBK 22, 41, 82 FFC 50
MSF 243, 245
Putnam, George Haven (1844-
1930) WGT 119 see also G. H. P.
Putnam, Israel. WTS 50
Putney, Susan K. HFI 121 SF1
428
Putz, Helmut. BAA 256
Pyburn, George. EXT 5/2 46
Pye, David. EXT 6/2 48
Pyeshkov, Alexei M. see Maxim
Gorky
Pygaster, Cal. I. SF1 429
Pyk, Jan. FFC 104
Pyle, Howard (1853-1911) AOW
304 CSF 162 CWD 51 ES2 357
FFC 22, 191 SF1 429 SRB 22-3
Pyles, Thomas. AAL 12, 16
Pym, Herbert. CSF 162 SF1 429

Pynchon, Thomas (1937-) ALW 31, 238 AOW 239 CAT 17, 27 CSC 101, 226 HFI 121 LEX 523-4 NWO 9, 36, 210-1, 261

SFE 486 SFH 97, 99 SL2 915-20
Pythagoras. LTN 157 WFS 219

Q

Q pseud. of Arthur T. Quiller-Couch. CSF 162
Quabbe, Georg. BAA 189
Quackenbos, John Duncan (1848-1926) CSF 162 SF1 429
Quackenbush, Robert. FFC 24
Quad, M. pseud. of Charles Bertrand Lewis. SF1 429
Qaudland, Olga Mae. WFS 132-3
Quandt, Jean B. BAA 256
Quarta, Cosima. BAA 189
Quattrocchi, Frank. IAC 197
Quattrocki, Ed. BAA 256
Queen, Ellery. ASF 318, 323 EXT 7/2 46 EXT 8/1 16 MSM 34-5 STH 133
Queffelec, Henri (1910-) SFE 488
Queneau, Raymond (1903-76) IAC 197 SFB 145 SFE 488
Quesnel, Pierre (1699-1774) WGT 120
Quest, Rodney (1897-) ES2 357 SF1 429 SF2 1042
Quick, Dorothy (1900-62) CSF 162 ES2 357 SF1 429
Quick, (John) Herbert (1861-1925) CSF 162 SF1 429 WGT 120
Quigley, Ray. WTS 76
Quiller-Couch, Arthur T. (1863-1944) CSF 162 ES2 357 EXT 4/2 20 IAC 197 SF1 429 WGT 120 see also Q
Quilp, Jocelyn. SF1 429
Quilty, Rafe. SF1 429
Quina, James H. EXT 6/1 15
Quincy, Josiah Phillips (1829-

1910) CSF 162 SF1 429
Quine, W. V. O. AAL 183
Quinn, Arthur Hobson. NWO 61
Quinn, Gerard A. (1927-) ES2 357 SFE 488 VES 150, 162, 168 207-8, 289
Quinn, James Louis. ES2 357-8 ETN 140 IAC 197 SFE 488 SF1 430 WFS 231, 242 WIF 117
Quinn, Seabury Grandin (1889-1969) BFP 413 CSF 162 CWD 33 ES2 358 FBK 69, 83 FL2 811-6 HFI 121 IAC 197 SFE 488 SF1 430 SOT 52, 73, 323, 340, 406 STH 152, 254 WIF 80, 117, 136, 248 WTS 5, 20-1, 23, 25-6, 28, 30-6, 38-9, 41-2, 44, 51-2, 54, 65, 67-8, 70, 80, 121, 123, 125-6, 128-31
Quinn, Simon (pseud) see Martin Smith
Quintero, Jorge. SF1 430
Quinton, John Purcell (1879-) WGT 120
Quinzio, Sergio. BAA 256
Quirk, James. WTS 50
Quiroga, Horacio. FBK 135
Quiros, Jorge Molina. BAA 185, 246
Quissell, Barbara Carolyn. BAA 286
Quoin. SF1 430
Quondam pseud. of Charles McClellan Stevens. SF1 430
Quong, Rose. CSF 162

R

R. S. pseud. of Robert Paltock.
CSF 162
Raabe, (Capt.) H. E. SF1 430
Rabelais, Francois (1494?-1553)
EXT 10/2 76, 80 FTF 18 IAC
197 IAH 23 MSF 10, 12, 57, 88,
96-8, 101-2, 106-7, 121, 127, 143,
153, 249, 259 MSM 159 SFB 94
SFE 489 SFN 51 SFS 96 SOI
43 WAA 31 WGT 121 WTS 9
Rabiega, William. SRB 67
Rabinowitz, Shalom (1859-1916)
WGT 121
Rabkin, Eric S. (1946-) AC2 76
BAA 189, 191 BRS 8 CAT 77
CYR 8 FBK 8 FHT 68 INT vii
KAU 139, 220, 237 RAH 258
RBY 110-26 SFE 489 SFW 313-
4 SHL 61 SRB 73-4, 78, 288
TSF 248
Racina, Thom. SFE 489
Racine, Jean. EXT 9/2 29 SFD
45
Rackham, Arthur. FBK 28, 38,
114-5 FFC 4, 7, 82, 119, 174, 180
Rackham, John (1916-76) BYS 296
FFR 145 IAC 197 LEX 525
SFS 96
Radcliffe, Ann (1764-1823) ALW
45 BYS 15, 17-9, 55 CSF 163
ES2 358-9 FBK 23, 27 FL2 787-
90 FL3 1075-80 KAU 6 SFH 192
SF1 430 SIH 16 TFC 41-2 TSP
7 WGT 121 WIF 41 WTS 17
Radcliffe, Henry Garnett (1899-)
CSF 163 ES2 359 SF1 430
Radcliffe, Mary-Anne. CSF 163
Radditz, Katie. LTN 238
Rader, Laura. FFC 72
Radford, John. IAC 197

Radin, Max (1880-1950) SF1 430
Radishchev, Alexander N. MSF
244
Rado, Jimmy. VFS 117
Rae, H. C. HFI 122
Raes, Hugo (1929-) FBK 146 LEX
525
Rafael, Richard. COT 242-3
Rafcam, Nal. ES2 359 SF1 430
Raffalovich, George (1880-) CSF
163 SF1 430
Raffel, Burton. EXT 10/1 31, 38,
41
Raffin, Alain. CSF 163 SF1 430
Raft, George. TSP 222
Ragged, Hyder pseud. of Sir Hen-
ry Chartres Biron. CSF 163
SF1 430
Raghavacharyulu, Dhupaty V. K.
BAA 189
Raginsky, Bernard B. ISW 216-7
Raglan, (Lord). BAA 102
Ragni, Jerry. VFS 117
Ragon, M. BAA 256
Rahner, Karl. BAA 256
Rahv, Phillip. BAA 256 ETN 118
Raible, Alton. FFC 34, 71
Raiden, Edward. SF1 430
Raife, Raimond. SF1 430
Raine, William MacLeod. SOT
170-1
Rainey, William B. pseud. of
Wyatt Blassingame. TSP 54
Rains, Claude. WFS 55
Raknem, Ingvald. BAA 189 EXT
8/2 55-6 FAN 182 WAA 242
Raleigh, Hilary Mason (1893-)
CSF 163 SF1 431
Ralli, Constantine. CSF 163 SF1
431

Ralph, Julian. IAC 197
Ralston, Gilbert Alexander (1912-) SF1 431 SF2 1042
Ralston, Henry. TSP 222
Ramakrishna, Rama. CWN 14, 30
Ramdagger, Geoffrey. SF1 431
Rame, David. CSF 163
Ramey, Ben see H. H. Hollis
Ramirez, Alice Louise. SF1 431
Ramirez, Medaro Figueroa (1887-) SF1 186
Ramos, Michael. FFC 151
Rampa, Tuesday Lobsang pseud. of C. H. Hoskin. SF1 583
Rampo, Edogawa pseud. of Taro Hirai (1894-1965) FBK 150 SFB 142 SF1 431
Rampton, Anthony. ES2 359 SF1 431
Ramsauer, Carl Wilhelm. MSM 218
Ramsay, Kathryn. IAC 197
Ramsden, Lewis pseud. of A. L. Dowding. SF1 431
Ramsey, Milton Worth (1848?- 1906) BAA 45, 163 CSF 163 SF1 431
Ramseyer, Edwin (1896-) SF1 431
Ramuz, Charles Ferdinand (1878- 1947) CSF 163 SF1 431
Ranald, Ralph A. BAA 256
Rand, Ayn (1905-) ALW 31, 99, 238 AOW 240 BAA 115, 132 CSF 163 ES2 359 EXT 6/2 51 FAN 146 NDA 94-5, 210 POE 236 RHN 114 RSG 53 SFE 490 SFH 56-7, 174 SFW 104 SF1 431 SF2 1042 SIH 86, 88 SRB 299 STH 101-2, 104 VES 165 WAA 135 WFS 163
Rand, Peter. HFI 122
Rand, Sally. RHN 9, 22
Randall, Florence Engle (1917-) HFI 122 SF1 431 SF2 1042
Randall, John Herman, Jr. BAA 256
Randall, Marta (1948-) BFP 414 HFI 122 IAC 197 RGS 144
Randall, Robert pseud. of Randall Garrett, Robert Silverberg. IAC 197 RFA 196, 207 RSG 10 SFE 490 VES 112
Randall-Stevens, Hugh C. CSF 163
Randers, Jorgen. IAC 197 INT 48
Randerson, W. CSF 183 SF1 431

Randi, (Amazing). WFS 260
Randlett, Samuel. SFN 76
Randolph, Georgiana Ann (1908- 57) WGT 121
Randolph, Paschal Beverly (1825- 74) CSF 164 SF1 431
Randolph, Vance (1892-) ES2 359 IAC 197
Random, Alex pseud. of Donald Sydney Rowland. SF1 431
Rang, Jack C. EXT 10/1 34, 38
Rank. CWN 54
Rank, Heiner (1931-) LEX 525-6
Rank, Otto. FLT 51-2
Rankin, H. D. BAA 256
Rankin, Hugh (1879-1957) ES2 359 WGT 121 WTS 65, 69, 80-2 see also Doak
Rankine, John pseud. of Douglas R. Mason. AOW 240 BAA 142- 3, 147, 149 IAC 197 RGS 145 SFS 96
Rankine, W. J. M. IAC 197
Rans, Geoffrey. NWO 61
Ransom, Arthur. BAA 189
Ransom, Ellene. BAA 286
Ransom, James. IAC 197 SFS 96
Ransome, Arthur Mitchell (1884- 1967) CSF 164 SF1 432
Ransome, James Stafford (1860- 1931) SF1 432
Ranzetta, Luan. SFE 490 SF1 432
Ranzetta, V. SF1 432
Raphael, John Nathan (1868-1917) CSF 164 SF1 432 STH 229-32
Raphael, Rick (1919-) ES2 359 ETN 32 FFR 145 HFI 122 IAC 197 LEX 526 RFA 211 SFE 490-1 SFS 96 SF1 432 SF2 1042-3 VES 207
Rappoport, Solomon (1863-1920) WGT 121 see also S. Ansky
Rapport, Samuel Berder. SF1 432
Rarey, John S. SFN 58
Rasch, Bodo. BAA 256
Rasch, Carlos (1932-) LEX 526-7 WAA 239
Rasch, Heinz. BAA 256
Rascoe, Burton. STH 240
Rascovich, Mark (1918-) ES2 359
Rash, Dora Eileen Agnew Wallace (1897-) see Doreen Wallace
Raskin, Ellen. FFC 150, 157
Raskolnikov. EXT 10/2 74

Raspail, Jean. HFI 185
Raspe, Rudolf Erich (1737-94)
BAA 14-5 FL1 78-80 IAC 198
SFS 96 SF1 432-3 WGT 121
Rasputin (1871?-1916) CWN 38-9,
56
Rath, E. J. STH 41
Rathbone, Basil (1892-1967) ES2
359 SF1 433
Rathbone, St. George. CSF 164
Rathenow, Lutz (1952-) LEX
527-8
Rathjen, Carl Henry (1909-) SF1
433 SF2 1043
Rathmann, August. BAA 256
Rationales. BAA 13
Raucher, Herman (1928-) SF1 433
SF2 1043
Raupach, Hans. BAA 256
Rauschenberg. JGB 6
Rauschenbusch, H. BAA 286
Ravel, Maurice. FLT 22
Raven, Anthony. SF1 433
Raven, Simon Arthur Noel (1927-)
ES2 359-60 SF1 434
Raven-Hart, (Maj.) R. VFS 5-6
Rawlings, Marjorie. FFC 70
Raworth, Tom. IAC 198
Rawson, Clayton. TSP 199
Rawson, Graham Stanhope. BAA
286
Ray, Frederick A. CSF 164
Ray, Gordon. FAN 7, 182
Ray, Howard William (1903-)
ES2 360
Ray, James. CSF 164 SF1 434
Ray, Jean pseud. of Raymond
Jean Marie De Kremer (1887-
1964) FBK 145-6 SF1 434
Ray, Rene. ES2 360 SFE 491
SF1 434
Ray, Robert. IAC 198 SFE 491
SFS 97 SF1 434
Ray, Satyajit. VFS 116
Rayer, Francis George (1921-)
BAA 120 ES2 360 HFI 122 IAC
198 SFE 491 SFS 97 SF1 434
SF2 1043 VES 182 see also
George Longdon
Rayjean, Max-Andre. ES2 360
Raymer, Anne Carolyn. SL4
1917-21 SL5 2283-6
Raymond, Alexander G. (1909-
56) COT 128 CSF 164 ES2 360
IMS 201 SFB 110 SFE 491

SFH 108 SF1 434 STH 175-6
WSF 305
Raymond, Ben. SF1 434
Raymond, Harold. EXT 6/1 8
Raymond, Henri. BAA 256-7
Raymond, Hugh pseud. of John
Michel. IAC 198 MIH 97
Raymond, James F. CSF 164
SF1 434
Raymond, John. SOT 183
Raymond, Rene Brabazon (1906-)
WGT 121 see also James
Hadley Chase
Rayner, Augustus Alfred (1894-)
CSF 164 SF1 434
Rayner, Claire (Berenice) (1931-)
SF1 434 SF2 1043
Rayner, Harold. WTS 93
Rayner, William. SF1 434
Raysor, Joan. FFC 108
Read, Elfrieda. FFC 57
Read, (Sir) Herbert Edward
(1893-1968) AOW 86, 93, 109
CSF 164 BAA 104 ES2 360
EXT 6/1 16, 20 EXT 9/2 41-4
FL2 654-7 POE 225 SFE 491
SF1 434 UKL 116-8
Read, Opie Percival (1852-1939)
SF1 434
Reade, Charles. EXT 7/2 29
Reade, Quinn. HFI 122 SF1 434
Reade, Willoughby. CSF 164
Reade, Winwood. FAN 59 POE
98-9, 290
Reader, Emily E. CSF 164 SF1
434
Ready, William Bernard (1914-)
AAL 148 ES2 360 EXT 10/1
29, 35, 38 IAC 198 SFS 97 SF1
434 SF2 1043-4 WAA 111
Reagan, Ronald. HEN 13 JGB
12, 27
Reage, Pauline. JGB 12 WAA 80
Reamy, Tom (1935-77) IAC 198
KWS 13-4, 91-2, 305 LEX 528
SFE 491 SRB 373
Reaves, J. Michael. IAC 198
Reckford, K. H. BAA 257
Redd, David. IAC 198
Reddin, Tom. HEN 13-4
Redgrove, Peter. EXT 8/1 17
IAC 198 SFS 97
Reding, Marcel. BAA 257
Redmond-Howard, L. G. CSF 164
Reed, Charlotte. LTN 270

Reed, Clifford Cecil (1911-) ES2
360 IAC 198 SFE 492 SF1 435
SF2 1044
Reed, David V. pseud. of David
Vern. HFI 122 IMS 45,186,213
SFE 492 SF1 435 STH 45
Reed, Herbert Langford (1889-
1954) SF1 435
Reed, Ishmael (1938-) FL5 2197-
9 MFW 25
Reed, Ivy Kellerman (1877-) ES2
361 SF1 435
Reed, James. RHN 12
Reed, Julia R. FL1 54-6 FL2
725-7 FL3 1268-70,1501-3
FL4 1657-61
Reed, Kit pseud. of Lillian Craig
Reed. ALW 212 AOW 240 BAA
150 BYS 305 FFR 145 HFI 122
IAC 198 NWO 125 SFE 492 SFS
97 SF1 435 VES 243
Reed, Langford. CSF 164
Reed, Lillian Craig (1932-) ES2
361 SF2 1044 WGT 122 see
also Kit Reed
Reed, Myrtle (1874-1911) SF1
435
Reed, Peter Fishe (1819-) CSF
164 SF1 435
Reed, Van (house name) SF1 435
see also Dennis Talbot Hughes
Reed, Zealia Bishop seeZealia
Brown Reed Bishop
Reed, F. Anton. COT 99 WGT
122 see also Anthony Riker
Rees, Abraham. NWO 71
Rees, Arthur John (1872-1942)
ES2 361 SF1 435
Rees, Helen Christina Easson
(1903-) SF2 see also Jane Oliver
Rees, Richard. BYS 255-6,282
Reese, John. IAC 198 ISW 119
SFS 97
Reeth, Allan. BAA 73 CSF 164
Reeve, Arthur Benjamin (1880-
1936) AOW 42-3,70 ES2 361
EXT 1/1 16 EXT 5/1 15 EXT
7/1 21 IAC 198 PST 117-8 RFA
2 SFE 492 SF1 435-6,584 SRB
8 STH 2,126-36,140-2,151-4
WTS 39
Reeve, Bryant. ES2 361
Reeve, Clara (1729-1807) CSF 164
ES2 361 FBK 23 SFD 42 SF1
436 SIH 16 TFC 41 WGT 122
Reeve, Helen S. BAA 257

Reeve, Lloyd Eric. MSM xvi
Reeves, Helen Buckingham Mathers
(1853-1920) WGT 122 see also
Helen Buckingham Mathers
Reeves, James. SF1 436
Reeves, James pseud. of John
Morris Reeves (1909-) ES2 361
FFC 27,57,183 SF1 436 SF2
1044
Reeves, Justin. WGT 122
Reeves, Rosser. IAC 198 SFS
97
Reeves, Ruth. FFC 175
Reeves, W. P. BAA 257
Reeves, William. CSF 165 FFC
182 SF1 436
Regberg, S. L. SF1 436
Reginald, Robert pseud. of Michael
Roy Burgess. AOW 362-3 FL1
4-6 FL2 695-7, 752-6,1004-6
FL3 1057-9,1099-104 FL4 1589-
91,1766-8,1901-3,1999-2001
FL5 2156-8, 2200-2 IAC 174
RSG 92 SFE 492 SF1 436 SL1
260-4 SL4 1660-4 SRB 65 VES
331
Regnas, C. BAA 70 CSF 165 SF1
436
Rehm, Warren S. BAA 59 WGT
122 see also Omen Nemo
Rehn, Jens (1918-) LEX 529
Reich, Ebbe Klovedal. BAA 182
Reich, Emil (1854-1910) CSF 165
SF1 436
Reich, Erna. BAA 286
Reich, Wilhelm. CWN 20, 55-6
FTF 106,137
Reichenbach, Hans. FTF 10
Reichert, John F. BAA 257
Reichert, Karl. BAA 257
Reid, Alastair. FFC 57
Reid, C. Lestock. CSF 165 SF1
436
Reid, Forrest (1876-1947) CSF
165 SF1 436-7
Reid, James. FFC 132
Reid, Julia. IAC 199
Reid, Leslie Hartley (1895-) SF1
437
Reid, Mayne (1818-83) see
Charles A. Beach
Reid, Vera W. SF1 437
Reid, Walter. SF1 437
Reida, Alvah. HFI 122 SFE 492
SF1 437
Reider, Florence. IMS 34,38

Reiff, Stephanie. SF1 437
Reifsnider, (Mrs.) Calvin K.
(1850-1932) SF1 437
Reigrotzki, Erich. BAA 257
Reik, Theodor. COT 105
Reilly, Joseph J. BAA 257
Reilly, Robert J. EXT 8/1 1
EXT 10/1 25, 31, 39 RBY 240
Rein, Harold. ES2 361 HFI 122
SFE 492 SF1 437
Reinders, Robert C. BAA 257
Reineke, L. Thomas. SFE 493
SF1 437
Reiner, Gertrude. FFC 11
Reiner, Julius. BAA 189
Reiner, Thomas A. BAA 189
Reiner, Walter. FFC 11
Reines, Donald F. IAC 199 SFS
97
Reines, Frederick. FTF 151
Reinhardt, Max. STH 252
Reinsberg, Diane. SFN 113
Reinsberg, Mark. HID 121 IMS
200, 205, 213, 222, 225, 237-42,
244-5 ISW 78 MIH 110-1 SFS
97 WSF 140
Reisen, M. X. SF1 437
Reiser, Oliver. MSM 271
Reiss, Edmund. NWO 227
Reiss, Malcolm. ES2 361 ISW
131 WFS 84 WIF 115 WSF 124
Reiss, Timothy J. BAA 257
Reissman, David. CWN 32 EXT
1/2 30
Reit, Seymour. FFC 89
Reitberger, Reinhold. SFH 240
Reitmeister, Louis Aaron (1903-
75) BAA 102 CSF 165 SF1 437
SF2 1045
Reizenstein, Elmer L. (1892-1967)
WGT 122
Remarque, Erich Maria. COT
124 KVT 46
Rembar, Cy. VFS 52
Rember, Winthrop Allen. ES2
361 SFE 496
Rembrandt (1609-69) [FUT]
Remenham, John pseud. of John
Alexander Vlasto. CSF 165
SF1 437
Remi-Maure. SL3 1497-500 SL4
1742-5 SL5 2362-5, 2534-7
Remington, Barbara. EXT 10/1
29 FFC 90, 127
Remington, Thomas J. FHT 67
UKL 153-77, 245

Renard, Christine. SFE 496
Renard, Georges. BAA 257
Renard, Joseph. HFI 122
Renard, Jules. IAC 199
Renard, Maurice (1875-1940) CSF
165 ES2 361-2 FBK 139-40
LEX 529 MSF 251-2, 263 PST
182-3, 202, 279 SFE 496 SF1
437 SL2 560-3 STH 228-9
Renault, Mary. CSC 31
Rencelaw, Brian pseud. of Ray
Russell. IAC 199
Rene, Joseph A. CSF 165
Renn, Thomas Edward (1939-)
SF2 1091-2 see also Jeremy
Strike
Rennie, James Alan (1899-1969)
CSF 165 SF1 437 SF2 1045
Renoir, Jean. WAA 90
Renouvier, Charles. MSF 138
Rensenbrink, John C. BAA 286
Renshaw, Robert. EXT 10/1 30,
39
Renton, Gertrude see G. Colmore
Renucci, Paul. BAA 257
Repnin, Saul. SIH 99
Repp, Ed(ward) Earl (1901-79)
CSF 165 ES2 362 HFI 122 IAC
199 IMS 8 LEX 529-30 MFW
19 SFD 23-4, 27 SFE 496 SFS
97 SF1 437 SF2 1046 SRB 15
STH 142, 154 WGT 122 WIF 89
WSF 50
Repton, Humphrey. IAC 199 SFS
97
Resnick, Michael Diamond (1942-)
ES2 362 HFI 123 SFE 496-7
SF1 437 SF2 1046 WGT 122
Resnier, Andre Guillaume (1729-
1811) WGT 122
Resnik, Henry. EXT 10/1 39
Ressich, John (1877-) SF1 437
WGT 122 see also Gregory
Baxter
Rettig, Helen. SF1 438
Revermort, John A. pseud. of
John Adam Cramb. CSF 165
SF1 438
Rey, Jean-Michel. FLT 152
Rey, Russell (house name) SF1
438 see also Dennis Talbot
Hughes
Rey, W. H. BAA 257
Reybaud, Louis. BAA 189, 257
Reymont, Wladislaw. FBK 46

Reynaert, (Rev.) John Hugh. BAA
82
Reynard, Elizabeth (1898?-1962)
SF1 438
Reynardson, Henry Birch. CSF
Reynolds, Bonnie Jones. SF1 438
Reynolds, Dallas McCord (1917-)
BFP 415-8 SF2 1046 WGT 122-
3 see also Mack Reynolds
Reynolds, Debbie. LTN 89
Reynolds, E. C. IMS 33
Reynolds, E. E. BAA 257
Reynolds, George William
MacArthur (1814-79) CSF 165
FBK 54 FL4 2049-53 SF1 438
Reynolds, James (1891-) ES2 362
Reynolds, John Murray (1901-)
CSF 166 SF1 438
Reynolds, Joseph. SF1 438
Reynolds, (Mrs.) Louis Baillie.
CSF 166
Reynolds, Mack pseud. of Dallas
McCord Reynolds. ALW 212
AOW 241 BAA 143,150,152,158,
160,162 BYS 303,308 COT 139,
180 CSC 55,132,180 ES2 362-3
ETN 65 EXT 8/1 7 FFR 147-8
HFI 123-4 IAC 66,199 IAH 29,
106 ISW 124,126,284 LEX 530-
1 MFW 201 MIH 113-6 RGS
145-6,221-2 SFE 497-8 SFH
176 SFS 22,39,97-8 SF1 438-9
STH 67-9,89-90,157-8 VES 183-
4 VF2 136-53,203-4 WAA 64,
67 WFS 292-4 WSF 187
Reynolds, Pamela (1923-) SF1 439
SF2 1047
Reynolds, Philip (1916-) ES2 363
HFI 124 SF1 439
Reynolds, Quentin. AOW 352
Reynolds, Stephen Sydney (1881-
1919) SF1 439
Reynolds, Thomas. BAA 189
Reynolds, Walter Doty (1860-)
BAA 59 WGT 123 see also
Lord Prime
Rheingold, Howard. HFI 124 SF1
439
Rhine, Joseph Banks (1895-) AAL
133-4 COT 153 ES2 363 EXT
10/1 15 MSM 202 RFA 187
SFH 156 TJB 11
Rhine, Louisa. SFH 156
Rhodes, Carolyn. BAA 258 MFW
15
Rhodes, Cecil. RHN 72 STH 206

Rhodes, H. Henry. BAA 75 CSF
166 SF1 439
Rhodes, Harold V. BAA 189,286
Rhodes, Henry Taylor Fowkes
(1898-) ES2 363
Rhodes, Hylda. CSF 166
Rhodes, William Henry (1822-76)
AOW 40,71 CSF 166 EXT 1/1
16 EXT 3/1 29 EXT 5/1 16
EXT 7/1 18,26 MSM 29 SFE
498 SF1 439 SRB 7,10 VES
208
Rhondda, Margaret Haig. BAA
104
Rhylick, Frank see Frank Riley
Rhys, Ernest (1859-1946) CSF 166
ES2 363-4 SF1 439
Rhys, (Rev.) T. Tudor. BAA 258
Riasnovsky, Alexander B. BAA
258
Ribbons, Ian. FFC 65
Ricci, Barbara Guignon. HFI 124
SF1 439
Ricci, Lewis A. see Bartlett
Riccioli, (Father). FTF 21
Rice, Allison pseud. of Ruth
Allison, Jane Rice. IAC 200
SFS 98
Rice, Anne (1941-) FBK 7,46,152
FL2 776-80
Rice, Charles D. IAC 200
Rice, Elmer Leopold (1892-1967)
CSF 166 ES2 364 EXT 10/1 12
IAC 200 SF1 439 SF2 1047
Rice, Harry E. BAA 73 CSF 166
SF1 439
Rice, James (1843-82) CSF 22
ES2 364 SF1 439
Rice, Jane. IAC 200 SFS 98 WGT
123 see also Allison Rice
Rice, Jeff. SF1 439
Richard, Francois. WGT 123 see
also F. Richard-Bessiere
Richard, Harold. STH 137
Richard-Bessiere, F. pseud. of
Francois Richard, Richard
Bessiere. ES2 364
Richards, Alfred Bate (1820-76)
SFE 498
Richards, Anna Matlock. SF1 439
Richards, Brian. ES2 364
Richards, Charles Napier. CSF
166 SF1 440 STH 13-4
Richards, D. BAA 258
Richards, Dick see Barry Wells
Richards, Frank. EXT 10/1 38

Richards, G. C. MSF 90
Richards, Guy (1905-) ES2 364
SFE 498 SF1 440 SF2 1047
Richards, H. Grahame. CSF 166
Richards, Harvey D. SF1 440
Richards, I. A. FLT 73
Richards, Laura Elizabeth (1850-
1943) ES2 364 SF1 440
Richards, Lysander Salmon (1835-
1926) SF1 440
Richards, Nelson. IAC 200
Richards, R. P. J. BAA 117 ES2
364 SF1 440
Richards, Strahan. CSF 166
Richards, Tad. SF1 440
Richardson, (Sir) Benjamin Ward
(1828-96) BAA 31,38-9 CSF 166
POE 174-6 SF1 440
Richardson, Dale. SF1 440
Richardson, Darrell C. (1918-)
ES2 364 EXT 3/1 24 VES 314
Richardson, E. BAA 91 CSF 166
SF1 440
Richardson, Frank Collins (1870-
1917) CSF 166 SF1 440
Richardson, Hal. ES2 364-5
Richardson, Lewis F. CSC 110-1
Richardson, Maurice Lane (1907-)
CSF 167 CWN 37 ES2 365 EXT
10/1 31,39 IAC 200 SF1 440
Richardson, Ralph. WFS 57
Richardson, Robert Shirley (1902-)
ASF 261 COT 193-4 ES2 365
IAC 200 IAH 85 RFA 139,167,
175-7,181,195,214 SFS 98 SF1
440 SF2 1047-8 WGT 123 WSF
114 see also Philip Latham
Richardson, Samuel. MSF 49
Richardson, Warren. CSF 167
SF1 440
Richer, Clement. SF1 440
Richet, Charles. EXT 2/1 9 POE
193-5
Richler, Mordecai. FFC 150
Richmond, Leigh Tucker. HFI
124 IAC 200 LEX 531-2 SFE
498 SFS 98 SF1 440-1 SF2
1048
Richmond, Mary. ES2 365 SFE
498 SF1 441
Richmond, Walter F. (1922-77)
ES2 365 HFI 124 IAC 200 SFE
498 SFS 98 SF1 441 SF2 1048
Richmond, (Sir) William Blake.
BAA 85

Richter, Conrad Michael (1890-
1968) BAA 123 ES2 365 IAC
200 SFS 98 SF1 441
Richter, Ernst H. (1901?-59?)
ES2 365 LEX 532-3 WGT 123
Richter, Eugene (1838-1906) CSF
167 SF1 441
Richter, Gerhard. BAA 179
Richter, Hans (1889-1941) LEX
533-4
Richter, Helene. BAA 287
Richter, Peyton E. BAA 176,189,
220,258
Rickard, Bob. TJB 54-5
Rickenbacker, Eddie. ASF 297
Rickett, Joseph Compton. BAA
45
Ricketts, Martin I. IAC 200
Rico, Don. SF1 441
Riddell, Charlotte Elizabeth (1832-
1906) FBK 60 WGT 123 CSF 167
ES2 365 SF1 441
Riddell, (Mrs.) Joseph H. see
Charlotte Elizabeth Riddell
Rideaux, Charles De Balzac
(1900-) WGT 123
Ridenour, (Dr.) Louis N. IAC
200 SFS 98
Rideout, Walter B. BAA 189,258
EXT 7/1 16
Ridge, Martin. EXT 7/1 16
Ridler, Anne Barbara (1912-)
CSF 167 ES2 365 SF1 441 SF2
1048
Ridley, Francis H. BAA 92 CSF
167 EXT 9/2 44 SF1 441
Ridley, James (1736-65) SF1 441
WGT 123 see also Charles
Morell
Ridley, Trevor. FFC 69
Riecken, H. W. AOW xxi
Riefe, Alan (1925-) ES2 365-6
SF1 441 SF2 1048
Riegal, Robert E. BAA 258
Riemann. EXT 7/2 33
Riemer, Neal. BAA 258
Rienow, Leona Train. HFI 124
SFE 489-9 SF1 441
Rienow, Robert (1909-) HFI 124
SF1 441 SF2 1048-9
Riesman, David. BAA 258
Rieti, Fabio. FFC 54
Rigaut, Jacques. SIH 53
Rigg, Robert B. SFE 499
Rihs, Charles. BAA 190,258

Riker, Anthony pseud. of F.
Anton Reeds. IAC 200
Riley, Dave. IAC 200
Riley, Dick. SRB 76 TSF 247-8
Riley, Frank pseud. of Frank
Rhylick. AOW 167 BAA 131
HID 103 IAC 200 MIH 121 RFA
202, 204, 214 SFE 499 SFS 98
SF1 441 SL5 2255-9 VES 182,
206
Riley, James Whitcomb (1849-
1916) CSF 167 WGT 123 WIF
54
Rilke, Rainer Maria (1875-1926)
CWN 24, 31 LTN 77 RZY 14,
25-6
Rimbaud, (Jean Nicholas) Arthur
(1854-91) CWN 24, 31 EXT 10/2
65 MFW 282 SFH 68, 95 TDI
5-6, 38 THM 45
Rimbeau. EXT 10/2 100
Rimel, Duane Weldon (1915-) FBK
74 IMS 30, 72, 94, 110-1 SF2
1120 see also Rex Weldon
Rimmer, Robert H. (1917-) AOW
31, 242 BAA 143, 162 SF1 441
SF2 1049
Ringer, Alexander L. BAA 258
Rinkoff, Barbara (-1975) FFC 91,
150 SF1 442
Rios, Marie Teresa pseud. of
Marie Teresa Rios Versace
(1917-) SF1 442
Rios, Tere pseud. of Marie Teresa
Rios Versace (1917-) ES2 366
FFC 157
Ripepe, Eugenio. BAA 258
Ripley, B. K. SF1 442
Risse, Heinz (1898-) SF1 442
Ritchie, Leitch. CSF 167
Ritchie, Lewis Anselm Da Costa.
WGT 124
Ritchie, Paul (1923-) SFE 499
Ritner, Peter. ES2 366
Ritt, William. CSF 167 WSF 305
Rittenberg, Max (1880-) CSF 167
SF1 442 STH 128
Ritter, Gerhard. BAA 190
Ritter, Hauptmann. POE 240
Ritter, Karl. FBK 82
Riurikov, Yury B. MSF 264
Riva, Valeria. SF1 442
Rival, Rico. VES 132
Rivere, Alec. HFI 124
Rivers, Elizabeth. FBK 67
Rivers, John. BAA 258

Riverside, John pseud. of Robert
A. Heinlein. HID 12, 22-3, 194
OWB 11 SFD 145, 166 SFH 54
Rives, Amelie (1863-1945) CSF
167 SF1 442
Rives, Hallie E. CSF 167
Rivkin, Jay. FFC 76
Rivoche, Paul. RHN 50 VES 226
Rivoli, Mario. FFC 58
Rizk, C. M. BAA 100
Roach, Robert W. A. (1933-)
WGT 124
Roach, (Rev.) Thomas E. BAA
121
Roan, Tom. ISW 37
Robb, John pseud. of Norman
Robson. SF1 442
Robb, Stewart. IAC 200
Robbe-Grillet, Alain (1922-)
MFW 113 SFH 72, 90 SF1 442
SF2 1049
Robbins, Clarence Aaron (1888-
1949) CSF 167 ES2 366 WGT
124 see also Tod Robbins
Robbins, Ruth. FFC 33
Robbins, Thomas E. SF1 442
Robbins, Tod pseud. of Clarence
Aaron Robbins. IAC 200 SF1
442 WTS 130
Robbins, W. Wayne pseud. of
Ormond Gregory. TSP 171-3,
187
Robbinson, Jerry. FFC 171
Robedonostev. VFS 45
Roberds, Sully. IMS 202, 214,
239, 241
Roberson, Rick. IAC 110, 200
Roberti, Maurice Chaudoir. BAA
172
Roberts, A. R. TSP 68
Roberts, Alaric J. CSF 167 SF1
442
Roberts, Anthony (1950-) SFE 499
Roberts, Arthur. SF1 442 see
also Berl Cameron, Rand Le
Page, Paul Lorraine
Roberts, Cecil Edric (1892-1976)
SF1 442 SF2 1049
Roberts, Charles Blanton (1874-)
SF1 442
Roberts, Charles George Douglas
(1860-1943) CSF 167 ES2 366
SF1 442 WIF 53
Roberts, Colin. SF1 442
Roberts, Eleanor. SF1 442

Roberts, Frank. EXT 7/2 47
IAC 200 SFS 98
Roberts, George Edward Theodore
(1877-1953) SF1 443
Roberts, H. Chalmers. CSF 168
Roberts, J.W. BAA xxii, 50 CSF
168 SF1 443
Roberts, James Hall pseud. of
Robert Lipscomb Duncan. SF1
443
Roberts, Jane pseud. of Jane
Roberts Butts (1929-) ES2 366
HFI 124 IAC 200 SFE 499 SF1
443
Roberts, Janet Louise (1925-)
SF1 443
Roberts, John Maddox. HFI 124
SFE 499
Roberts, Keith (1935-) ALW 212
AOW 242 BAA 147 BFP 419
BYS 301 ES2 366 EXT 6/1 20
FFR 148 [FJT] HFI 124-5 IAC
200-1 LEX 533-4 RGS 146-7
SFE 499-500 SFH 177 SFS 98-
9 SF1 443 SF2 1050-1 SL4
1660-4 SRB 15,346 VES 123,
171,180,207-8,235 WGT 124
WSF 255 see also Alistair
Bevan, John Kingston
Roberts, Kenneth. CWD 39
Roberts, Mark. EXT 10/1 25,39
Roberts, Michael. FAN 84 IAC
201 NDA 204
Roberts, Morley (1857-1942) ES2
366 EXT 7/1 9,16 IAC 201
SF1 443
Roberts, Paul K. SF1 443
Roberts, Richard Ellis (1879-
1953) CSF 168 ES2 366-7
Roberts, Terence pseud. of Ivan
Terence Sanderson. HFI 124
SFE 500 SF1 443
Roberts, Tony. [FUT]
Roberts, W.J. VES 289
Roberts, Walter Adolphe (1886-
1962) CSF 168 SF1 443
Roberts, Willo Davis. IAC 201
VES 198
Robertson, Alice Alberthe (1871-)
WGT 124 see also Berthe St.
Luz
Robertson, E. Arnot pseud. of
Eileen Arbuthnot Robertson.
SFE 500

Robertson, Eileen Arbuthnot
(1903-) AOW 95,109 see also
E. Arnot Robertson
Robertson, Frances Forbes. SF1
443
Robertson, Frank Chester (1890-)
WGT 124
Robertson, J.C. BAA 258
Robertson, John Mackinnon.
BAA 258
Robertson, Keith. FFC 124
Robertson, Mary. FFC 124
Robertson, Morgan Andrew (1861-
1915) CSF 168 ES2 367 EXT
1/1 16 IAC 201 SFS 99 SFW
60 SF1 443
Robertson, Olivia Melian (1917-)
ES2 367 SF1 584
Robertson, W.C. SF1 443
Robeson, Anna Weber. SF1 443
Robeson, Kenneth (house name)
AOW 83,110 CSF 168 FFR 149
FL1 401-3 SFE 500-1 SF1 443-
5 TSP 86,102,221 WSF 58 see
also Lester Dent, Paul Ernst,
Alan Hathaway
Robida, Albert (1848-1926) BYS
99 IAC 201 MSF 162,167 POE
105-6 SFB 43,93-5 SFE 501
SIH 74 SL2 932-5 VES 286
Robin, C. Ernest. CSF 168
Robin, Ralph. IAC 201 SFS 99
Robinet, Lee pseud. of Robert A.
Bennet. CSF 168
Robinett, Ralph F. ES2 367 SF1
445
Robinett, Stephen (1941-) HFI 125
IAC 201 LEX 534 SFE 501-2
VES 157 WGT 124 see also
Tak Hallus
Robinovitch, Sidney Paul. BAA
287
Robins, Jack pseud. of Jack
Rubinson. IMS 158
Robinson, A.T. MFW 256
Robinson, Charles. FFC 19,32,
103,162
Robinson, Charles Henry (1843-
1930) AOW 71 CSF 168 SF1
445
Robinson, Edith. CSF 168
Robinson, Edward A. CSF 168
NWO 63 SF1 445
Robinson, Edward Kay (1857-
1928) SF1 446

Robinson, Eleanor. HFI 125
SFE 502
Robinson, Frank M. (1926-) ALW
212 AOW 242 ASF 148 BFP
420 BYS 262 ES2 367 FFR 149
HFI 125 IAC 201 IAH 14 ISW
91, 278-83 KAU 43 RFA xxii,
81, 197 SFE 502 SFH 116 SFN
117 SFS 99 SF1 446 SF2 1051
SOT 404, 431 WFS 161
Robinson, Frank Steven (1947-)
HFI 125 SF2 1051-2
Robinson, Frederick. CSF 168
SF1 446
Robinson, George Platt (1893-)
SF1 446
Robinson, (Sir) Harry Perry
(1859-1930) SF1 446
Robinson, Henry Morton. TSP
214
Robinson, Jackie. WFS 222
Robinson, James. EXT 10/1 18
Robinson, Jeanne. SRB 377
Robinson, (Sir) John Charles
(1824-1913) ES2 367 SF1 446
Robinson, Kim S. IAC 201
Robinson, Lydia G. BAA 258
Robinson, Mabel. FFC 136
Robinson, Mary Darby (1758-1800)
CSF 168 WGT 124
Robinson, Paul (1948-) BFP 421
Robinson, Philip Bedford (1926-)
SFE 502 SF1 446 SF2 1052
Robinson, Philip Stewart (1847-
1902) ES2 367 SF1 446
Robinson, Ruth. FFC 112
Robinson, Spider (1948-) HFI 125
IAC 201 JHN 62 LEX 534-5
PJF 74 RGS 147-8 SFE 502
SFW 533 SRB 377
Robinson, William Henry (1867-
1938) SF1 446
Robison, Nancy L. IAC 201
Robles, Antonio pseud. of Antonio
Robles Soler (1897-) CSF 168
ES2 367
Robles, Edward G., Jr. IAC 201
SFS 99
Robson, James (1944?-) SF1 446
Robson, Morman see John Robb
Rocca, Guido. FFC 14
Rocha, Adolpho (1907-) WGT 124
see also Miguel Torge
Roche, Arthur Somers. BAA 86
Roche, James Jeffrey (1847-1908)
SF1 446

Roche, Regina M. CSF 168
Rochester, George Ernest (1905?-)
SF1 446
Rock, C. V. (1915-) LEX 535-6
Rock, James. BAA 75 CSF 168
EXT 1/1 16 SF1 446
Rock, James. SRB 64
Rock, Phillip (1927-) SF1 446
Rock, Wyndan. SF1 446
Rockefeller, John D. MSF 225, 229
Rockefeller, Nelson. ETN 105
Rockefeller (family). KVT 59
Rocken, Kurt Walter (1906-) WGT
124
Rocker, Rudolf (1873-1958) SF1
446
Rockey, J. BAA 228
Rocklin, Ross Louis (1913-) SF2
1052 see also Ross Rocklynne
Rocklynne, Ross pseud. of Ross
Louis Rocklin. ALW 234 AOW
293 BAA 155, 158 COT 19, 106,
248 ES2 367-8 FFR 149 HFI
125 IAC 201-2 IMS 213, 222
ISW 90, 129 RFA 43, 57, 69, 81,
92, 108, 114 SFD 210 SFE 506
SFS 99 SF1 446 SOT 385, 416
WGT 124 VES 82 WIF 146
Rockow, Karen (1949-) EXT 10/1
18 SF1 447
Rockwell, Carey. ES2 368 SF1
447 STH 178
Rockwell, Norman. [FUT] SFH
65
Rockwell, Thomas. FFC 70
Rockwood, Roy pseud. of Edward
Stratemeyer. AOW 303, 330
CSF 168-9 EXT 1/1 5 SFE 506
SF1 447-8 WFS 7
Rodda, Percival Charles (1891-)
SF1 448 SF2 1052
Roddenberry, (Eu)gene (1926-)
ALW 224 AOW 287 ASF 129,
328-9 FFR 149 IAC 202 SFB
119 SFE 506 SFH 105 SF1 448
SF2 1052 VES 68 WFS 114
WSF 313-4
Roddenberry, Majel Barrett. IAC
202
Rodenstein, Heinrich. BAA 190
Rodgers, Mary (1931-) FFC 150
SF1 448 SF2 1052-3
Rodgers, Searn Leonard. CSF
169 SF1 448
Rodin, Francois Auguste. ACC
121, 129 IAH 75

Rodman, Howard. IAC 202
Rodney, George Brydges (1872-) CSF 169 SF1 448
Rodnykh, Alexander A. MSF 251
Roe, Azel S. CSF 169
Roe, Ivan (1917-) ES2 368 WGT 125 see also Richard Savage
Roe, Richard L. SF1 448
Roe, William James (1843-1915) BAA 37-8 WGT 125 see also Hudor Genone
Roeg, Nicholas. KAU 203
Roelens, Maurice. BAA 258
Roemer, Kenneth M. BAA 190, 259, 287
Roentgen, Wilhelm. MFW 24
Roepke, Wilhelm. CSC 119
Roethke, Theodore. KVT 50
Roger, Noelle pseud. of Helene Pittard (1874-1953) CSF 169 SFE 506 SF1 448
Roger-Marx, Claude. ACC 121
Rogers, Alva (1923-) AOW 353 BYS 228 CYR 9 ES2 368 EXT 8/2 62 HID 14, 37, 192 IAC 202 MIH 17, 24 SFE 506 SF1 448 SF2 1053 SIH 169 SRB 75 VES 316 WAA 119, 215, 243-4, 246 WSF 53, 215, 383
Rogers, Angela. IAC 202
Rogers, B. B. MSF 94
Rogers, Bessie Story. BAA 69
Rogers, Carl R. NDA 54, 206
Rogers, Eva C. SF1 448
Rogers, Frederick Rand. BAA 114
Rogers, Ginger. WFS 55, 131
Rogers, Hubert. BYS 217 COT 184 ES2 368 JVN 76 RFA 60-1, 70-1, 73, 76-7, 79-81, 83, 86-9, 95-6, 98-100, 102-3, 106, 108-9, 112, 114, 118, 141, 143, 145, 148, 154-5, 157, 160, 163, 166, 173-4, 176, 181, 186, 188-9, 195-6, 198, 200, 205-6 RHN 25, 31, 35 SFE 506-7 SRB 45 VES 70, 91, 113, 118, 152, 155, 163, 167, 194, 206, 230, 288 WSF 94, 104, 110, 113
Rogers, Ivir. IAC 202
Rogers, Ivor A. AOW 79-116 EXT 9/2 25 EXT 10/1 2, 9-16, 19, 48 EXT 10/2 115 NWO 234 RAH 10, 222-39
Rogers, James M. IMS 69-70, 109, 161

Rogers, Joel Townsley. IAC 202 SFS 99 VES 153 WFS 105
Rogers, John Rankin. BAA 50
Rogers, Kay. IAC 202 SFS 99
Rogers, Lebbeus Harding (1847-1932) BAA 63 CSF 169 SF1 448
Rogers, Lew (1923-) SF1 448
Rogers, Mary. IMS 69-70, 109
Rogers, Melbourne A. SF1 448
Rogers, Michael Alan (1951-) SFE 507 SF1 448 SF2 1053 SRB 360
Rogers, Michale. HFI 125
Rogers, Monte. VES 156-7
Rogers, Norman L. IAC 202
Rogers, Robert. ACC 244 AC2 76
Rogers, Sidonie. RFA xxii
Rogers, Wayne. TSP 28, 36, 71, 104, 128, 144
Rogers, Will. OWB 75 SFN 90, 99 WFS 55
Rogers, William. VFS 105
Rogersohn, William. SF1 448
Rogow, Lee see Craig Ellis
Rogoz, Adrian. IAC 202 SFB 145 SIH 193, 196
Rohde, Erwin. BAA 259
Rohmer, Elizabeth Sax (1886-) AOW 356 ES2 368 SF1 448 see also Rose Elizabeth Knox Ward
Rohmer, Richard H. SF1 448
Rohmer, Sax pseud. of Arthur S. Ward (1883-1959) AOW 356, 403 BYS 169 CSF 169-70 ES2 368-71 EXT 5/1 4 EXT 9/2 62 FBK 104-6, 144 FFR 150 FL1 178-80 FL2 585-9 HFI 125-6 IAC 202 ISW 25 MIH 80, 83 SFE 507-8 SFW 69 SF1 448-9 SIH 110 STH 129 WIF 77 WTS 17, 32
Rohr, Wolf Detlef (1928-) ES2 371 LEX 536-8 WGT 125
Rohrer, Robert. IAC 202 SFS 99 VES 179
Rohrmoser, Gunter. BAA 259
Rojo, Salvador De Madariaga Y (1886-) BAA 91 CSF 131 SF1 338 SF2 986
Roland, Nicholas pseud. of Arnold Robert Walmsley (1912-) SF1 449
Rolfe, Felice. EXT 10/1 18
Rolfe, Frederick William (1860-1913) CSF 170 EXT 9/2 38

Rolfe, Frederick W. (cont.)
SF1 450 WGT 125 see also
Baron Corvo, Prospero and
Caliban
Rolland, Romain. CSF 170 SFB
11
Rollins, Clara S. CSF 170
Rollins, Frank W. CSF 170
Rollins, Peter C. AAL 160, 169-
70
Rolls, Brian. SF1 450
Rolo, Charles J. EXT 2/2 34
EXT 6/1 3, 19
Roloff, Ernst M. BAA 269
Rolt, Lionel Thomas Caswell
(1910-) ES2 371
Rolt-Wheeler, Francis W. (1876-
1960) CSF 170 SF1 450
Romains, Jules pseud. of Louis
Farigoule (1885-1972) ES2 371
SF1 584
Roman, Chet. SF1 450
Romano, Clare. FFC 18
Romano, Deane Louis (1927-)
HFI 126 SFE 508 SF1 450 SF2
1053
Romans, R. H. COT 30 ES2 371
IAC 202 STH 65
Rome, Alger pseud. of Jerome
Bixby, Algis Budrys. SFE 508
Rome, David. IAC 202 SFE 508
SFS 100
Romeo, Rosario. BAA 259
Romer, Isabella. CSF 170
Romilly, Eric (1886-1953) ES2
371 SF1 450
Romilus, Arn. SF1 450
Ronald, Bruce Walton (1931-)
ES2 371 HFI 126 SFE 508 SF1
450 SF2 1053-4
Ronan, Colin. IAC 202
Ronn, Yuval see Ionel
Roof, Katharine Metcalf. CSF
170 SF1 450 WTS 33
Rooks, Conrad. VFS 117
Rooney, Charles J. BAA 287
Rooney, Grace. IAC 202
Rooney, Lawrence. COT 271
Rooney, Mickey. STH 252
Roosevelt, Franklin D. ASF 108
COT 110, 126, 210 FAN 4 ISW
29 MSM 192 NWO 243, 246
OWB 72 RHN 51, 211 SFH 14
WFS 14, 29, 62-3, 67, 155, 202
WTS 22, 127

Roosevelt, Theodore. ACC 176
EXT 7/2 34 MSF 240 STH 38,
130-1
Root, Albert Waldo (1891-) ES2
371 SFE 508 SF1 450 SF2 1054
Roper, William. BAA 190
Ropes, Arthur Reed (1859-1933)
WGT 125 see also Adrian Ross
Roquemore, Austin. IMS 69
Rorschach. EXT 6/2 44-5, 48
Roscoe, Theodore. CSF 170 SF1
450
Roscoe, Thomas. CSF 170
Rose, Carl. FFC 187
Rose, Frederick Horace (1876-)
CSF 170 ES2 371 SFE 508 SF1
450
Rose, George see Arthur Sketchley
Rose, Gerald. FFC 48
Rose, Howard. SF1 450
Rose, Lisle A. BAA 259
Rose, Lois. AOW 353 BAA 190
NWO 15 RAH 258 SF1 450 SRB
507 VES 330
Rose, Mark. IAC 202 SFH 239
SFS 100 SRB 73
Rose, Maxine. SL2 712-6
Rose, Stephen C. AOW 353 BAA
190 NWO 15 RAH 258 SF1 450
SRB 507 VES 330
Rose, Steven. BAA 259
Rose, Walter. ALW 10 ES2 371
Roselle, Daniel (1920-) IAC 202
SF1 451 SF2 1054
Rosen, Harold. ISW 216
Rosenbaum, Jonathan. ETN 174
Rosenbaum, Sidonia. BAA 259
Rosenberg, Adam. BAA 259
Rosenberg, Aubrey. BAA 259-60
Rosenberg, Elinor Blaisdell
(1904-) WGT 125
Rosenberg, Ethel Clifford (1915-)
SF1 451 SF2 1054
Rosenberger, Joseph R. SF1 451
Rosenbergs, (The). ETN 48
Rosenblatt, Lee. VES 71, 85, 191
Rosenblum, J. Michael. IMS 97,
100, 116, 156, 199, 251
Rosendorfer, Herbert. FBK 142,
152
Rosenfield, Joe, Jr. SF1 451
Rosenquest, J. Wesley. WTS 39
Rosenthal, Munroe. SF1 451
Rosett, Joshua. IMS 216
Rosetto, Louis, Jr. SF1 453

Rosewater, Frank (1856-) BAA 52,
73, 85, 91 CSF 170 SF1 451
WGT 125 see also Marian Mayoe,
Franklin Mayoe

Roshwald, Mordecai (1921-) AOW
243 BAA 134, 138, 260 ES2 371
EXT 1/2 37 EXT 6/2 51 FFR
151 HFI 126 ISW 170-3 MFW
83-5, 199, 251 NDA xi, 149-51,
197, 214 NWO 134 SFE 508 SF1
451 SF2 1054 SL3 1204-8 SRB
332 STH 45 VES 107, 135, 303
WAA 69

Rositzke, Harry August (1911-)
BAA 158-9 SF1 451 SF2 1055

Roskolenko, Harry (1907-) SF1
451 SF2 1055

Rosmanith, Olga L. SF1 451

Rosmond, Babette. IAC 202

Rosner, Sara. IAC 202 SF1 451

Rosny-Aine, J. H. pseud. of
Joseph-Henri Boex (1856-1940)
CSC 27 CSF 171 ES2 371-2
EXT 5/1 14 EXT 8/1 1 FFR
151 HIF 126 IAC 202 LEX 538-
9 MSF 30, 207, 239 SFB 140
SFE 508-9 SFS 100 SF1 451
SIH 107-8, 110 SL2 513-8 SL3
1501-4 SL5 2516-9 TSO 9 VES
142 WIF 69

Rosokhovatsky, Igor. IAC 202
SFS 100

Ross, Adrian pseud. of Arthur
Reed Ropes. SF1 451

Ross, Albert pseud. of Linn Boyd
Porter. CSF 171

Ross, Albert Henry (1881-) WGT
125 see also Frank Morison

Ross, (Maj. Gen.) Charles (1864-
1930) BAA 86 ES2 372 SF1 451

Ross, Clinton (1861-1920) ES2 372
BAA 190

Ross, Harry. BAA 260

Ross, J. Elliot. BAA 260

Ross, Jean pseud. of Irene Dale
Hewson. ES2 372 SF1 452

Ross, John. FFC 18

Ross, Joseph pseud. of Joseph
Henry Wrzos (1929-) ES2 372
ETN 26 IAC 202 SFE 509 SFS
100 SF1 452

Ross, Malcolm Harrison (1895-
1965) ES2 372 SFE 509 SF1 452

Ross, Marilyn pseud. of William
Edward Daniel Ross. ES2 372
SF1 452

Ross, Olin. SF1 452

Ross, Olin Jones (1858-) BAA 67-
8 CSF 171 SF1 452

Ross, Raymond George. ES2 372
SFE 509 SF1 452

Ross, (Sir) Ronald (1857-1932)
CSF 171 SF1 453

Ross, Samuel Albert. CSF 171
SF1 453

Ross, Theodore John (1924-) SF1
453 SF2 1055

Ross, William Edward Daniel see
Marilyn Ross

Rossell, Ingrid. FFC 90

Rossen, Robert. CSC 264

Rossetti, Christopher. SRB 22

Rossetti, Dante Gabriel. OWB
25 WBW 5, 10, 16, 54

Rossi, Marcianus Filomeno (1869-)
CSF 171 SF1 453

Rossiter, Oscar pseud. of Vernon
H. Skeels. HFI 126 SFE 509
SF1 453

Rossmann, Hermann (1902-) CSF
171 SF1 453

Rossmann, John F. SF1 453

Rossochowatski, Igor (1929-)
LEX 539

Rostand, Edmond. ALW 44 CSC
122 FTF 21-2 IAH 25 MSF 107
MSF 107 SFB 41 SFS 37, 100
WAA 29 WSF 14

Rostand, Jean (1894-) ES2 372

Rosten, Leo. ALW 228

Rosteutscher, Joachim. BAA 190

Rostovtzeff, M. I. STF 13

Rostvig, Maren-Sofie. BAA 190

Roszac, Theodore. FSU 47 KAU
12, 86-7, 91

Roth, Arthur J. (1925-) SF1 453

Roth, Georges. EXT 2/1 15

Roth, Holly (1916-64) ES2 372

Roth, Paul. BAA 260

Roth, Philip (1933-) FLT 76, 79
FL1 169-72 SFE 509 SF1 453
SF2 1055-6 SIH 83 STH 45

Rothberg, Abraham (1922-) FBK
58 HFI 126 SF1 453 SF2 1056

Rothenberg, Alan Baer (1907-)
SF1 453

Rothery, Agnes Edwards (1888-
1954) CSF 171 SF1 453

Rothfork, John. FHT 67

Rothman, Milton A. (1919-) ASF
243 ES2 372 IAC 202 IMS 35,
70-1, 82, 84, 95, 117, 136, 141, 156,
161, 184, 186-7, 190, 200, 213,

Rothman, Milton A. (cont.)
232-4, 244, 249 SFS 100 SOT
199 SRB 99 TPS 175-96 WFS
58-9, 83, 89 WGT 125 WIF 131,
137, 167 WSF 72 see also Lee
Gregor
Rothman, Tony (1953-) LEX 539
Rothschild, Emma. ETN 179
Rotsler, William (1926-) AAL 40
DTS 51 FFR 151 LEX 540 HFI
126 IAC 202 RGS 148 SFE 509
SF1 453 SF2 1056 SRB 124
WGT 125 see also William
Arrow, John Ryder Hall
Rotstein, Abraham. BAA 260
Rottensteiner, Franz (1942-) AOW
297, 353 BAA 260 BYS 143
EXT 4/1 1 EXT 6/1 14 FFR
151 FL3 1121-3, 1511-5, 1527-
31 FL5 2235-46, 2391-414 FRN
22-3 IAC 202 KAU 23-4, 237
LTN 257 MFW 206 NWO 185
OSR 289-325, 356 PJF 12, 25, 28,
38, 40, 68, 74 RAH 173 SFD 93,
111 SFE 509 SF1 453 SF2 1056
SL1 163-7, 457-61 SL2 639-43,
865-8, 905-8, 960-4 SL3 1193-7,
1304-7, 1468-71 SL4 1627-31
SL5 2070-4, 2107-12, 2316-20,
2334-8, 2357-61, 2538-42 SRB
73 TSF 248
Rotter, Pat. LTN 248
Rotzer, Hans Gerd. BAA 260
Roueche, Berton (1911-) HFI 126
SF1 453 SF2 1057
Roughill, Frank. STH 153
Rounds, Emma. IAC 203
Rounds, Glen. FFC 150-1
Rourke, James. TSP 148
Rousseau, H. BYS 18, 120
Rousseau, Jean-Jacques. COT
242 MSF 114, 128, 249 SFH 193
SFN 58 STH 94 UKL 146 VES
265
Rousseau, Victor pseud. of
Victor Rousseau Emanuel. ALW
114, 129, 156 AOW 71 BAA xii
CSF 171 EXT 1/1 17 EXT 2/2
34, 39 EXT 7/1 25 EXT 7/2 29
[FUT] IAC 203 KVT 60 MSM
147 RFA 3-4 SFB 76 SFE 509
SF1 453 SOT 49, 70, 73 STH 41,
45, 259 TDI 43 TSO 49 VES
225, 312 WIF 38, 49, 57, 82 WSF
53

Roussel, Raymond (1877-1933)
SF1 453 SIH 79-80, 139
Rousselet, Louis. CSF 171
Rousset, Jean. TSO 36
Rovere, Richard. MIH 122
Rovin, Jeff. BRS 11
Row, Arthur. SF1 454
Rowan, Dan. INT 39
Rowcroft, Charles (-1856) BAA
25 SF1 454
Rowe, George. CSF 171
Rowe, John Gabriel (1874-) CSF
171 SF1 454 VES 322
Rowel, M. pseud. of Valdemar
Adolph Thisted. SF1 454
Rowell, Kenneth. FFC 102
Rowland, Donald Sydney (1928-)
SF1 454 SF2 1057 see also
Fenton Brockley, Alex Random
Rowland, Florence Wightman
(1900-) SF1 454 SF2 1057
Rowland, Henry Cottrell (1874-
1933) BAA 84 CSF 171 EXT
4/1 9, 13 SF1 454
Rowles, Daphne. FFC 130
Rowley, Ames Dorrance pseud.
of H. P. Lovecraft. EXT 3/1 16
Rowley, H. H. BAA 190 SOI 105
Rowley, Richard pseud. of Richard
Valentine Williams. CSF 171
SF1 454
Rowse, Alfred Leslie (1903-) ES2
372
Roxbury, Kyle. SF1 454
Roy, Katherine Morris (1907-)
SF1 454 SF2 1057
Roy, Lillian Elizabeth (1868-1932)
CSF 171 SF1 454 WIF 52
Royal, Matthew J. CSF 171 SF1
454
Royce, E. R. SF1 454
Royde-Smith, Naomi. CSF 171
Roys, Willis E. SF1 454
Ruark, Robert. SOT 268
Ruben, William S. HFI 126 WGT
125 see also Fred Shannon
Rubens, Peter Paul. ISW 115
Rubenstein, William C. BAA 287
SL1 418-22
Rubin, Rick. IAC 203
Rubinson, Jack. IMS 84, 140, 142,
158, 171, 183 WFS 71-2, 97 see
also Jack Robins
Rubinstein, Alvin Z. BAA 258
Ruby, B. F. IAC 203 SFS 95, 100

Ruck, (Amy Ro)berta (1878-) CSF
171 SF1 454 SF2 1057
Ruck-Pauquet, Gina. FFC 157
Rud, Anthony Melville, Jr. (1893-
1942) CSF 171 ES2 372 IAC
203 SFE 509-10 WTS 19, 56
Rude, Fernand. BAA 260
Rudhyar, Dane pseud. of Daniel
Chenneviere. SF1 454
Rudolf, (Mrs.) E. De M. CSF 171
Rudolf II, (Emperor). SFB 53
Rudolph, Marguerita (1908-) ES2
372
Rudorff, Raymond. SF1 455
Rudwin, Maximilian Josef (1885-)
CSF 171 ES2 373 SF1 455
Ruellan, Andre (1922-) LEX 540-
1 SFE 510
Ruffin, Edmund. CSF 172 POE
131-2
Ruh, A. K. POE 47
Ruhen, Olaf. IAC 203
Ruhle, Jurgen. BAA 260
Rumball, Charles. WGT 125-6
see also Charles Delorme
Rumi, Jalaludin. SFD 283
Rundberg, Arvid. WAA 234
Rundle, Anne. SF2 988 see also
Alexandra Manners
Runyon, Charles West (1928-)
AAL 112 HFI 126 IAC 203 SFE
510 SF1 455 SF2 1058
Rupert, M. F. SOT 396 STH 80
Ruppelt, Edward J. ES2 373 ISW
209-10
Ruppert, Conrad H. ES2 373 IMS
13-6, 18, 20-1, 25, 34-5, 74, 80-1,
84, 93, 197, 213, 223 ISW 161
SOT 105-7, 112 WTS 42
Ruse, Gary Alan. ASF 144
Rush, Norman. IAC 203
Rushdie, Ahmed Salman (1947-)
SFE 510 FL2 680-3
Rushdoony, Rousas John. BAA
190
Ruskin, John (1819-1900) AOW
356 BYS 86-7 EXT 5/2 28
EXT 9/2 46 FAN 89 FFC 8
FL2 852-4 JVN 188, 193 MSF
217 RBY 166, 184-5 SRB 22
WBW 5, 26, 55
Rusoff, Garry. HFI 127 SF1 455
Russ, J. J. IAC 203
Russ, Jacqueline. BAA 190

Russ, Joanna (1937-) AAL 124
ALW 212 AOW 243, 291 ASF
110-1, 128 BAA 152, 155, 162,
260 BFP 422 BYS 305 CAT 68
CEN 70-86 COT 173, 178, 196
CSC 93, 100, 172 ES2 373 ETN
65 EXT 10/2 100 FFR 151 FRN
19 HFI 127 IAC 203 INT 39, 41
KAU 18 LEX 541-2 LTN 12-3,
228 MFW 24, 152-4, 160, 290
MSF 67 RGS 149 SFD 4, 8, 12,
27, 58, 222, 226-9, 263, 279, 303,
322 SFE 510 SFH 64, 93, 96-7,
99, 186 SFS 100 SFW 483-90
SF1 455 SF2 1058 SL1 53-7
SL2 766-9 SL4 1678-81 SRB
346, 364 TPS 132-43 TSF 63-4,
240 UKL 69 WSF 186, 262
Russel, Margaret. BAA 287
Russell, Addison Peale. BAA 50
CSF 172
Russell, Arthur pseud. of Arthur
Russell Goode. SF1 455
Russell, Arthur James. SF1 455
Russell, Austin. SF1 455
Russell, Bertrand (Arthur) (1872-
1970) AOW 244 CSC 136 ES2
373 EXT 5/1 8 IAC 203 ISW
172 POE 230-1 SFD 49 SFE
510 SFS 100 SF1 455 SF2 1058
THM 52, 62 TSO 28 WAA 240
Russell, Eric Frank (1905-78)
AAL 25 ALW 136, 155, 160, 213,
234 AOW 244 BAA 120, 138
BFP 423-4 BYS 223, 234, 237,
287, 320 COT 151 CSF 172
ES2 373-4 ETN 68-9, 163 EXT
3/1 27 EXT 5/1 3 EXT 7/2 39,
41 FFR 151-2 HFI 127 IAC
203-4 IAH 22-3, 29, 43 IMS 96-
7, 195, 197 ISW 119, 178 KAU
31, 34 LEX 542-3 MIH 23-4, 36,
87 MSM 32, 186 RFA 42, 57, 64,
86, 91, 100, 106, 126, 141, 148, 158,
161-2, 164, 167-8, 184, 197, 200,
204, 206-7, 209-10, 214 RGS 150-
1 SFD 19, 28, 294, 310, 316, 318
SFE 510-1 SFS 100-1 SFW 197-
202 SF1 455 SF2 1058 SL5
2075-8 SOT 6, 45, 75, 133-50,
218, 377-8 SRB 301 STH 51,
243-5 TJB 4 TSF 57, 237 VES
71, 81, 88, 95-6, 108, 134, 148, 154,
156-7, 175, 199, 227, 233-4 WAA
117 WGT 126 WIF 145, 159, 164

Russell, Eric Frank (cont.)
WSF 388 see also Maurice G.
Hugi
Russell, Frances Theresa. BAA
190 EXT 5/1 7 FAN 184
Russell, George Warren (1854-
1937) CSF 172 SF1 455
Russell, George William (1867-
1935) SF1 455 WGT 126 see
also A. E.
Russell, (Mrs.) J. W. WGT 126
Russell, (Lord) John (1885-1956)
CSF 172 ES2 374
Russell, John Robert. HFI 127
SFE 511 SF1 456
Russell, John Russell (1792-1878)
SF1 456
Russell, Mariann Barbara. EXT
10/1 39
Russell, (Peewee). WFS 257
Russell, Ray (Robert) (1924-)
ES2 374-5 IAC 204-5 SFS 101
SF1 456 SF2 1058-9 STH 136-
7 see also Brian Rencelaw,
Roger Thorne
Russell, Samuel D. EXT 6/2 22
Russell, Solveig Paulson (1904-)
ES2 375
Russell, T. Baron. BAA 69
Russell, William Clark (1844-
1911) CSF 172 ES2 375 PST 71,
247-8 SFE 511 SF1 456
Russell, William Moy. IAC 205
SFS 101
Russell-Smith, Hugh F. BAA 190
Russen, David. ALW 43 CSF 172
PST 21 SFE 511 SF1 456
Russo, John. SF1 456
Russon, Mary. FFC 182
Ruth, Rod (1912-) SFE 512-3 VES
289
Rutherford, Ernest. OWB 35

Rutledge, Lyman V. SF1 456
Rutledge, Maryse pseud. of
Marice Louise Gibson? Marice
R. Hale? CSF 172 SF1 456
Rutley, Cecil Bernard. CSF 172
SF1 456
Rutter, Owen (1889-1944) CSF 172
SF1 456 WIF 50
Ruyer, Raymond. BAA 190-1, 260
MSF 42-4, 52, 55, 264 SFB 17
Ruzic, Neil P. (1932-) ES2 375
Ryan, Cornelius (1920-74) ES2 375
Ryan, J. B. COT 110 WIF 60
Ryan, J. S. EXT 10/1 18, 37, 39
Ryan, John K. BAA 260
Ryan, Loftus. CSF 172
Ryan, Marah Ellis (1866-1934)
ES2 375 SF1 457
Ryan, Marion. SOT 106
Ryan, Michael. STF 24
Ryan, R. H. SF1 457
Ryan, Rachel R. CSF 172 SF1
457
Ryan, Thomas. CSF 172 SF1 457
Ryan, Thomas J. HFI 127
Ryark, Felix. CSF 172 SF1 457
Rydberg, Abraham Viktor (1828-
95) SF1 457
Ryder, James. BAA 150 SF1 457
Ryken, Leland. NWO 43-4, 92-3
Ryley, C. L. CSF 172
Rylovich, Frank. ETN 127
Rymer, G. A. BAA 125 IAC 205
SFS 101
Rymer, James Malcolm (1814-84)
CSF 172 FBK 44 FL4 2017-22
SF1 457 WGT 126
Rynas, Stephen A. WGT 126
Rynin, Nikolai A. MSF 264
Ryves, Thomas Evans (1895-)
BAA 119 ES2 375 SF1 457

S

S. M. C. pseud. of Sister Mary
Catherine. CSF 173
Saadi (of Shiraz). SFD 127
Saari, Oliver E. IAC 205 IMS
93,112,136,141,169 SFS 101
Sabah, Victor. IAC 205
Saben, Gertrude Chetwynd Shall-
cross. WGT 127
Saben, Gregory pseud. of Frederick
Burkitt, Gertrude Saben. CSF 173
Saben, Gertrude see Gregory Saben
Saben, Lionel. HFI 185
Saberhagen, Fred (1930-) ALW
212 AOW 245 ASF 150 ATA 26
BAA 144,150,160 BFP 425 ES2
376 FL1 410-7,478-82 HFI
127-8 IAC 205 KAU 84 LEX
544 RGS 151 SFD 16-7 SFE
513 SFS 101 SF1 457 SF2 1059
SIH 141 SL1 168-72 SRB 275
VES 105,179 WFS 292-3 WSF
187
Sabin, (Dr.) Albert. VFS 37
Sabin, Edwin Legrand (1870-)
CSF 173 SF1 457
Sabine, Ted. HFI 128
Sacher, Hermann. BAA 260
Sackerman, Henry Claude (1940-)
SF1 457 SF2 1059
Sackett, S. J. BAA xxii,260 EXT
1/2 24,38 EXT 2/1 1,19
Sackett, Sam. IAC 205
Sackmary, Regina. CEN 132-43
Sacks, Janet. IAC 205
Sackville, Orme. SF1 458
Sackville-West, Edward Charles
(1901-65) SF1 458
Sackville-West, Victoria Mary
(1892-1962) BAA 111 CSF 173
SFE 513 SF1 458

Sadeur, Jacques pseud. of Gabriel
De Foigny. AOW 30 CSF 173
SFE 513
Sadler, Adam. SF1 458
Sadler, Elizabeth. BAA 260
Sadler, Glenn. EXT 9/2 25
Sadoul, Jacques (1937-) AOW 353-
4 BAA 191 FHT 67 SFD 213,
243 SFE 513
Safford, Mary J. EXT 2/2 32
Safroni-Middleton, Arnold. CSF
173 SF1 458
Safronov, Y. IAC 205 SFS 101
Sagan, Carl (1934-) AAL 90 ALW
232 ASF 43,128 COT 70 ES2
376 FLR 34,37 [FUT] IAC 205
OMN 18 SFE 513 SFH 241 TSF
1-8 VES 83 VFS 136,139,142,
161,171-2,197,211,262 WFS
222,300
Sagan, Francoise. SFN 42
Sagar, Keith M. BAA 260
Sage, Lorna. JGB 15
Sagerat, Jules. BAA 260
Saha, Arthur William (1923-) SF1
458 SF2 1059
Sahl, Mort. STF 17
Sahula-Dycke, Ignatz (1900-) SF1
458
Sail, Lawrence. IAC 205
Saine, Ute Miller. BAA 287
St. Amand, Arthur. WTS 29
St. Anthony. KVT 54,57 VMW
53
St. Armand, Barton Levi. NWO
69 SRB 81
St. Augustine. ATA 5,32 BAA x
CUA 45-6,48-9 EXT 8/1 23
MIH 106 SIH 104-5
St. Brendan. WIF 33

St. Cecilia. CUA 61
St. Christopher. WBW 49
St. Clair, Eric. IAC 223 SFS 101
St. Clair, Henry. CSF 173 SF1 584
St. Clair, Margaret (1911-) AAL 137 ALW 161 AOW 245 BAA 128 BFP 426 BYS 263 COT 194, 196 ES2 376 ETN 45 FFR 153 HFI 128 IAC 223-4 IAH 35 LEX 589 MSM 81 RGS 151-2 SFE 513-4 SFS 101-2 SFW 491-5 SF1 458 SF2 1059-60 WGT 127 WIF 221 see also Idris Seabright
St. Clair, Ray. COT 238-40
St. Cyr, Emil. BAA 95
St. Exupery, Antoine de (1900-44) ACC 127 CSF 173 ES2 376 FFC 8 FL2 891-3 LTN 125 SF1 458
St. Francis (of Assissi). SFH 221, 223
St. Germain, Marie. SF1 458
St. Jerome. SFH 211
St. John. CUA 15 NWO 4-6, 27, 101, 189, 208
St. John, Arthur. BAA 108 CSF 173
St. John, Christopher. BAA 74
St. John, David pseud. of Everette Howard Hunt Jr. SF1 458
St. John, J. Hector see Crevecoeur
St. John, John Allen (1872-1957) ES2 376 IAC 224 SFE 514 SFS 102 SF1 458 STH 254-5 VES 286 WTS 35-7, 65, 67-8, 71, 86, 122
St. John, Philip pseud. of Lester del Rey. IAC 224 IAH 42 VES 179 WIF 118
St. John (of Patmos). SFH 211
St. John-Loe, Gladys. SF1 458
Saint Leon, (Count) Reginald De pseud. of Edward Du Bois. CSF 173
St. Luz, Berthe pseud. of Alice Alberthe Robertson. CSF 173 SF1 458
St. Paul. EXT 2/1 19 EXT 7/1 10 FLT 48 PJF 23-4, 63 SFH 214
St. Peter. WBW 17
St. Reynard, Geoffrey (1919-) LEX 592
Saint Thomas Aquinas. IAH 59 KAU 23

St. Whitelock, Otto V. ISW 131-2
Saintsbury, George (1845-1933) CSF 173 SF1 458
Saki pseud. of Hector Hugh Munro. ALW 216 CSF 173 FBK 53, 65 FL4 1679-83 IAC 205 SFE 514 SFS 102 SOT 365, 368
Salcroft, Arthur. CSF 173
Sale, Kirkpatrick. SFH 97
Sale, Richard Bernard (1911-) ES2 376-7 SF1 459 SF2 1060 TSP 89, 163
Sale, Roger. EXT 8/1 1 EXT 10/1 31, 40
Saleeby, Dennis. BAA 261
Salgari, Emilio (1863-1911) MSF 162 SIH 39 SL3 1380-2
Salin, Edgar. BAA 191 EXT 8/1 23
Salinger, J. D. ETN 178 FHT 15-6 ISW 112 KVT 42, 59 STH 181
Salinger, Pierre Emil George (1925-) SF1 459
Salisbury, Henry Barnard. BAA 43 CSF 173 SF1 459
Salisbury, William (1875-) BAA 95 CSF 173 SF1 459
Sallaska, Georgia Myrle (1933-) SF1 459 SF2 1060-1
Sallis, James (1944-) ALW 212 AOW 285 BYS 298, 321 HFI 128 IAC 205-6 MIH 130 SFE 515 SF1 459 SF2 1061
Salmon, Arthur Leslie (1865-) CSF 174 SF1 459
Salomon, Louis B. IAC 206
Salten, Felix pseud. of Sigmund Salzmann. CSF 174 SF1 459
Salter, George (1897?-1967) ES2 377 VES 167
Saltoun, (Lady) Mary Helena (1863?-1940) CSF 174 SF1 459
Saltus, Edgar. ALW 41
Salvador, Tomas (1921-) SL3 1497-500
Salz, Arthur. BAA 261
Salzmann, Sigmund (1869-1945) see Felix Salten
Samaan, Angele Botros. BAA 261, 287
Samachson, Joseph (1906-) ES2 377 SFS 102 SF1 459 SF2 1061 WFS 200, 202 WGT 127 WIF 153 see also Brett Sterling, William Morrison

Samalman, Alexander (1904-56)
ES2 377 IAC 206
Samaris, Lucas. IAC 206
Sambourne, Linley. FFC 94
Sambrot, William Anthony (1920-)
ES2 377 HFI 128 IAC 206 SFE
515 SFS 102 SF1 459 SF2 1061-2
Samjatin, Jewgenij (1884-1937)
LEX 544-5
Sampliner, Louis H. WGT 127
see also Alexander Blade
Sampson, Ashley (1900-) CSF 174
SF1 459
Sampson, Charles. CSF 174
Samuel, Edwin Herbert (1898-)
ES2 377
Samuel, Fowler T. BAA 86
Samuel, (Viscount) Herbert Louis
(1870-1963) BAA 111 CSF 174
EXT 6/2 51 SF1 459
Samuel, Horace Barnett (1883-)
CSF 174 SF1 459
Samuel, Maurice (1895-1972) ES2
377 SF1 459
Samuels, Charles Thomas. SFB
147
Samuels, Philip Francis (1881-)
BAA 106 WGT 127
Samuelson, David N. (1939-) AAL
20-1 ACC 56-7, 196-210 AC2
76 BAA 261, 287 CEN 144-75
FL1 122-8, 222-7, 236-41 FL2
661-5, 781-6 FL4 1807-12, 1875-
9 JHN 38, 62 KAU 145 NWO 91-
2 RAH 32-63 RHN 197 SFE 515
SFW 313-20, 409-17, 475-82 SL1
207-12, 254-9, 337-42, 423-7 SL2
703-7, 858-64 SL3 1026-30, 1221-
5, 1328-32, 1453-8 SL4 1645-54,
1714-9, 1948-53 SL5 2140-5,
2173-8, 2195-200 SRB 508 TSF
194-6 TSO 3-4 VF1 104-52,
268-75, 282 VF2 56-81, 199-200,
208
San Blas, Caesario. BAA 21
San Miguel, Luis Garcia. BAA
177
Sanborn, Mary Farley. CSF 174
Sanborn, Robert Alden. CSF 174
SF1 459
Sanborn, Robin. AOW 245 HFI
128 SFE 515 SF1 459
Sanchez-Silva, Jose. FFC 14
Sancton, Thomas A. BAA 261

Sand, George pseud. of Amandine
Aurore Lucie Dudevant. CSF 174
MSF 153, 248 SF1 459
Sandburg, Carl (1878-1967) ES2
377 FFC 22 IAC 206
Sandeman, Mina. CSF 174
Sanders, Joe. FL1 184-6, 355-7,
396-400 FL2 959-60 FL3 1380-
3, 1436-40 FL4 1780-3, 1863-5,
1880-3 JHN 38, 62 PJF 74 RZY
89, 105-6 VF2 180-96, 205-8
Sanders, John see Ralph Comer
Sanders, Lawrence (1920-) HFI
128 INT 63 SFE 515 SFW 105
Sanders, Leonard M., Jr. (1929-)
ES2 377 SF2 1099 WGT 127 see
also Dan Thomas
Sanders, Scott. CAT 31, 58 FHT
67-8
Sanders, Thomas Edward (1926-)
IAC 206 SF1 460 SF2 1062-3
Sanders, Warren E. VES 211
Sanders, Winston P. pseud. of
Poul Anderson. AAL 92-3 IAC
206 RFA 210-1 SFS 102 TJB 25
Sanderson, Ivan Terence (1911-73)
ES2 377 IAC 206 SF2 1051 VES
339 WGT 127 see also Terence
Roberts
Sandin, Joan. FFC 112
Sandoe, James. EXT 3/1 25
Sandoz, Maurice Yves (1892-1958)
CSF 174 ES2 377 SF1 460
Sandrelli, Sandro. IAC 206 WAA
235
Sandrus, Mary Yost. SF1 460
Sands, Bernard. LTN 109
Sands, Dave see Bryce Walton
Sandys, Oliver pseud. of Florence
L. Barclay. CSF 174
Sanford, Charles L. BAA 191, 261
NWO 27
Sanford, Ezekial. BAA 20
Sanford, Hugh W. BAA 90
Sangster, Jimmy (1927-) HFI 95
SF1 460 SF2 1063
Sansom, William (1912-76) CSF
174 ES2 378 IAC 206 SF1 460
SF2 1063
Santayana, George. EXT 7/2 37
IAC 206
Sant'elia, Antonio. [FUT] SIH 53
Santesson, Hans Stefan (1914-75)
ES2 378 FFR 153 IAC 206-7
ISW vi JHN 42 RSG 10, 15 SFE

Santesson, Hans Stefan (cont.)
515 SFS 102 SF1 460 SF2 1063
SOT 262 SRB 289 STH 157, 267-
8 WFS 174 WSF 166, 224 see
also Vithaldas H. O'Quinn
Santos, Domingo pseud. of Pedro
Domingo. IAC 207
Santry. RFA 181
Santucci, Luigi. SF1 460
Sanz, Jose. SF1 460
Saparin, Victor (1905-) ASF 176
IAC 207 LEX 545 SFS 102
Sapir, Edward. AAL 14, 159
SFH 154
Sapir, Richard. AOW 246 SF1
460
Sapiro, Leland. AAL 218 BYS
179 EXT 6/2 22 EXT 8/1 1
EXT 9/1 1 EXT 10/1 48 MIH 3
NWO 46 VES 135
Sapper pseud. of Herman C.
McNeile. CSF 174
Sappho. CWD 37
Sapte, William, Jr. SF1 460
Sarabhai, (Dr.) Vikram. VFS
113, 116
Sarac, Roger pseud. of Roger
Andrew Caras (1928-) HFI 128
SFE 515 SF1 460
Sarban pseud. of John W. Wall.
AOW 246 COT 134-5 EXT 1/2
37 EXT 3/1 26 FL3 1320-4
FL4 1787-9 SFE 515 SF1 460-
1 VES 116, 123
Sarbrow, Cepre pseud. of P. S.
Barrows. SF1 461
Sargant, William Lucas. BAA 191
Sargent, Lyman Tower. BAA xxi,
261-2, 287 MFW 219
Sargent, Pamela (1948-) ALW 212
BAA 155, 162, 262 COT 196-7
ETN 66, 100 FFR 153 HFI 128
IAC 207 LEX 545 LTN 248, 251,
253 MFW 147, 161 RAH 111, 118
RGS 152 SFE 515 SF2 1064-5
SL1 402-5 WSF 262
Sargent, Samuel M. VES 205
Saroyan, William. EXT 7/2 37
IAC 207 WTS 57
Sarraute, Nathalie. CWN 49
Sarti, Ronald. RAH 107-36 RHN
100, 176, 196
Sarti, Sergio. BAA 191
Sarton, Eleanor May (1912-) SF1
461

Sartre, Jean-Paul (1905-) ALW
229 CWN 3, 8, 24, 30, 35-6, 41,
60 ETN 111 EXT 10/1 12 HEN
47 LTN 176 POE 275 RAH 228
SFN 42 SF1 461 SF2 1065 STF
17 UKL 220, 223-4
Sasoon, Siegfried. FLR 26 POE
225
Satan. ASF 67, 151, 160, 163, 188,
290 ATA 11-4, 18, 41 CWD 3
CYR 30-2, 46 INT 114 NWO 6,
39, 115, 124, 165, 177, 250, 272-
89, 292-5 RZY 34, 43, 67 SHL
22 WTS 11 see also Devil,
Lucifer, Mephistopheles
Satchell, William. CSF 174 SF1
461
Satterfield, Charles pseud. of
Frederik Pohl, Lester del Rey.
IAC 207 SFE 517 SFS 102
Satterlee, W. W. BAA 43
Satty, Harvey J. SL3 1140-3
Sauer, Gerda-Karla. BAA 191
Sauer, Julia Lina (1891-) FFC 168
SF1 461 SRB 24
Sauer, Robert C. IAC 207 SF1
461
Saul, George Brandon (1901-) ES2
378 SF1 461 SF2 1065
Saulnier, V. L. BAA 262
Saunders, Buddy. IAC 207
Saunders, Caleb pseud. of Robert
A. Heinlein. HID 22-3, 193 OWB
11 RFA 96 SFD 145, 150 SFH
54
Saunders, Charles. CWD 61
Saunders, Edith Alice. CSF 174
SF1 461
Saunders, Hilary Aiden (1898-
1951) SF1 461 WGT 127 see
also Francis Beeding
Saunders, Jake. HFI 128 IAC
207 SFE 517 SF1 461
Saunders, Mike. WFS 61
Saunders, Norman. TSP 71, 130,
135
Saunders, Phyllis. CSF 174
Saunders, W. J. BAA 77 CSF
174 SF1 461
Saurat, Denis. SF1 461
Saussur. TDI 3
Sauter, John. BAA 262
Sautto, Lidia. EXT 6/1 5
Sauvage. [FUT]
Sava, George (1903-) ES2 378
SFE 517

Savage, Arthur D. IAC 207
Savage, Hardley. SF1 461
Savage, Henry. CSF 161
Savage, Joseph Weber (1861-) CSF 174 SF1 461
Savage, Juanita. CSF 175 SF1 461
Savage, Mary pseud. of Mary Dresser. ES2 378 SF1 461
Savage, Mildred. MSM 303
Savage, Richard pseud. of Ivan Roe (1917-) SFE 517 SF1 462
Savage, Timothy. BAA 23 CSF 175 SF1 462 STH 72-3
Savarin, Julius May. SFE 517 SF1 462 VES 234
Savchenko, Vladimir I. (1933-) IAC 207 LEX 545 MSF 262 SFS 102
Savery, Thomas. FTF 34
Savidge, E. Van Pedroe. CSF 175
Savile, Frank Mackenzie. CSF 175 EXT 1/1 17 MFW 119 SF1 462
Savill, Mervyn. ES2 378 EXT 2/2 29 SF1 462
Saville, Leonard Malcolm (1901-) SF1 462
Savinkov, Boris Viktorovich (1879-1925) WGT 127
Savio, Mario. RHN 126, 147
Sawada, Paul Akio. BAA 262
Sawyer, Ruth. FFC 91, 96, 101
Sawyer, Walter I. CSF 175
Saxon, Peter (house name) ES2 378-9 FFR 153 SFE 517 SF1 462 see also W. Howard Baker, Wilfred McNeilly, Martin Thomas
Saxon, Richard pseud. of Joseph Laurence Morrissey. ES2 379 HFI 129 SFE 517
Saxton, Alexander. BAA 262
Saxton, Colin. IAC 207
Saxton, Josephine Mary (1935-) ALW 212 BYS 305 FFR 153 HFI 129 IAC 207 SFE 517-8 SFS 103 SF1 462 SF2 1065
Saxton, Mark. BAA 150 HFI 129 SF1 462
Say, Daniel. LTN 268
Saye, Lee. EFP 21 IAC 207
Sayers, Dorothy L. (1898-1957) AOW 84, 396 ASF 32 CSF 175 ES2 379-80 EXT 8/1 5 SF1 462-3 SOI 61

Sayers, Frances Clarke. EXT 10/1 32
Sayler, Harry Lincoln (1863-1913) SF1 463 WGT 127-8
Sayre, R. F. BAA 262
Scaevola, Peter. ES2 380 SF1 463
Scafford, Roger. LTN 269
Scanlon, C. K. M. (house name) TSP 25
Scannell, Vernon. EXT 6/1 19
Scarborough, Dorothy (1878-1935) AOW 354 CSF 175 ES2 380 SF1 463
Scarborough, Harold Ellicott (1897-) CSF 175 SF1 463
Scarborough, John. SFW 19-24, 219-24, 591-8
Schachner, Nat(han) (1895-1955) AAL 15, 111-2, 116 ALW 10 ASF 137 COT 23, 38, 117-8, 121, 124, 126-7, 138-9, 141-2, 144, 178, 210-1, 261-5, 269-70 ES2 380 ETN 15-6 HFI 129 IAC 207 ISW 36-7 LEX 545-6 MIH 95 RFA 6, 16-8, 20, 22, 28, 32, 36, 40-2, 57, 65, 67-8, 74, 76-7, 83, 92, 95, 98, 100, 146, 183 SFE 518 SF1 463 SOT 96, 254, 275-6, 357 STH 45 TSP 15, 33, 60, 71, 124, 155, 237 VES 71, 131, 140, 151, 198 WGT 128 WIF 60, 88 WSF 54, 59-61, 63, 66 see also Chan Corbett, Walter Glamis
Schachter, Stanley. AOW xxi
Schachterle, Lance. BAA 262
Schaeberle. EXT 5/2 42
Schaefer, Jack Warner (1907-) SF1 463
Schaeffer, Kurt. BAA 287
Schaeffer, Robin pseud. of Barry N. Malzberg. IAC 207
Schafer, Robert (1915-) ES2 380
Schafhauser, Charles. IAC 207 SFS 103
Schaftel, Oscar. BAA 265
Schaible, Walter. IMS 79
Schalansky. IMS 15
Schalimon, Alexander (1917-) LEX 546
Schaller, Jack. IMS 33
Schaper, Edzard Hellmuth (1908-) SF1 463
Schary, Jill (1936-) SF1 463
Schaub, Mary H. IAC 207

Schauffelein, Hans Leonhard.
SFB 30-1
Schealer, John Milton (1920-)
ES2 380 SF1 463 SF2 1065
Scheck, Frank Rainer. BAA 262
Schectman, Aaron Henry. BAA
287
Scheel, Lita. FFC 196
Scheele, Mitch. PJF 73
Scheepstra, D. ES2 380
Scheer, Karl H(erbert) (1928-)
ES2 380 FFR 154-5 FTF 78
LEX 546-50 SFB 146 SFE 518-
9 WGT 128
Scheerbart, Paul (1863-1915) FBK
142 LEX 550-1 MSF 207 SFE
519 SL3 1193-7
Schefner, Wadim (1915-) LEX 551
Schein, Herman. LTN 51
Schein, Ionel. BAA 262
Schellhous, E. J. BAA 34
Schempp, Hermann. BAA 191
Schenck, George. [FUT]
Schenck, Hilbert, Jr. IAC 207
SFS 103
Schepelmann, Wolfgang. BAA 287
Schere, Moses. IAC 207
Scherr, Karl Herbert (1928-)
WGT 128
Scherr, Marie see Marie Cher
Schiaparelli, Giovanni. EXT 1/1
3 EXT 1/2 31 EXT 5/1 16a
EXT 5/2 37-9, 41-2, 46-8 FAN
23 IAC 207 SFH 118, 161
Schick, Alice. FFC 151
Schick, Joel. FFC 151
Schick, Selma. BAA 287
Schiffman, Joseph. BAA 262-3,
288
Schiller. KVT 8
Schimmelbusch, Heinz. BAA 191
Schinagel, Geza. BAA 96
Schindelman, Joseph. FFC 63
Schindelman, Laurel. FFC 36,
147
Schindler, Solomon (1842-1915)
BAA 43, 52 CSF 175 SF1 463
Schioler, Carsten. SL2 845-9
SL3 1366-9
Schirra, Wally. VFS 73
Schisgall, Oscar. TSP 4, 218
Schjeldahl, Peter. AOW 2.00 IAC
207
Schlanger, Judith E. BAA 263
Schleicker, Klaus. BAA 263
Schlein, Miriam. FFC 57

Schlemihl, Peter. SFB 29
Schleppey, Blanche Bloor. CSF
175 SF1 463
Schlette, Heinz Robert. BAA 263
Schlobin, Roger C. BRS 3-4 FL3
1029-33 FL5 2139-49, 2259-66,
2532-8 SL2 969-71 SL5 2156-8
SRB 65, 68, 246-90, 453, 496-511,
516 TSF 253
Schloemp, Felix. FBK 141
Schlossel, J. SOT 10, 33 VES
174 WTS 23, 25, 120
Schlosser, Alfred. BAA 263
Schlosser, Anselm. BAA 263
Schmeltzer, Karl. SF1 463
Schmerl, Rudolph B. BAA 263
EXT 6/1 16 EXT 9/2 25, 53
OSR 105-15, 356
Schmid, Josef. BAA 288
Schmidlin, Dorothy Ruth. BAA
288
Schmidt, Annie. FFC 77
Schmidt, Arno (1914-) POE 259-
60 SL2 865-8
Schmidt, Burghard. BAA 263
Schmidt, Burghart. BAA 208
Schmidt, Dennis. HFI 185
Schmidt, Erich. BAA 263
Schmidt, James Norman (1912-)
ALW 161 see also James Norman
Schmidt, Sandra. EXT 10/1 40
Schmidt, Stanley (1944-) ASF 253
FHT 66 HFI 129 IAC 208 LEX
553 MFW 31, 44, 47 SFE 519
TSF 110-20
Schmidt, Werner. FFC 57
Schmidt, Willy (1896-) BAA 191
WGT 128
Schmied, Wieland. FBK 16
Schmiele, Walter. BAA 263
Schmitt, Carl. BAA 263
Schmitt, Edward E. IMS 106
Schmitt, Eugen Heinrich. BAA
191
Schmitz, H. H. FBK 82, 142
Schmitz, James H(enry) (1911-)
AOW 246 BFP 427-8 BYS 262
CSC 228 ES2 380-1 EXT 7/2
40 FFR 156 HFI 129 IAC 208
IAH 18, 119-20, 122 ISW 129
KAU 196 LEX 554-5 RFA 174,
191, 196, 198, 206 RGS 153, 222
SFD 299, 315, 322 SFE 519 SFS
103 SFW 212 SF1 464 SF2
1065-6 SL5 2482-7 TSF 61 VES
206-7 WSF 113

Schmitz, James R. AAL 55
Schmokel, Gerda. EXT 2/1 7
Schmuckle, Karl. BAA 288
Schnabel, Ernst Georg (1913-)
SF1 464
Schnabel, Johann Gottfried (1692?-
1750?) WGT 128
Schneeman, Charles. COT 75, 90,
215, 288 IMS 84, 213 RFA 38,
42, 50, 52-3, 55, 58, 62, 65, 67-70,
72-3, 75, 77, 81, 87, 93, 100, 105-
6, 108, 112-3, 118, 146-7, 149, 155,
167, 176-7, 195, 200 SFE 519
WSF 92, 104, 113 VES 288 BYS
217
Schneer, Cecil. TSO 10
Schneer, Charles. SRB 58
Schneider, Isidor (1896-) WGT
128 see also I. S.
Schneider, John G. (1908?-64)
BAA 130 ES2 381 SFE 519 SF1
464
Schneider, Vern. EXT 2/2 27
Schnirring, Alicemary. IAC 208
SFS 103
Schnittkind, Henry Thomas (1886-)
WGT 128
Schnitzler, Arthur. IAC 208
Schoeb, Erika. SF1 464
Schoeck, R. J. BAA 263
Schoenfeld, Howard. ALW 216
IAC 208 SFS 103
Schoenfeldt, Eberhard. BAA 288
Schoenherr, John (1935-) BYS
217 FFC 113, 135 SFE 519-20
SRB 49 VES 97, 147, 289, 291
Schoepflin, Harold Vincent (1893-
1968) ES2 381 ETN 15 IMS 8
SF2 1111 WGT 128 see also
Harl Vincent
Schoffer, Nicolas. [FUT]
Scholem, Gershom. FBK 57
Scholes, Robert (1919-) AAL 178,
180 AC2 76 AOW xix, 354 BAA
191 BRS 8 CAT 31 CYR 8 ES2
381 FHT 67-8 IAC 208 INT vii
KAU 139, 237 LTN 252 MFW
96, 184 RAH 258 SFE 520 SHL
61 SOI xiii SRB 74, 237, 508
TDI 3, 11-2 TSF 248 UKL 245
Scholl, Ralph. BAA 263 EXT
1/2 34
Schollgen, Werner. BAA 263
Scholtz, Harald. BAA 191
Scholz, Carter. ETN 142 IAC
208

Schomann, Emilie. BAA xvii, xxi,
191
Schomburg, Alex (1905-) ES2 381
SFE 520 SOT 112 SRB 37 TSP
30 VES 75, 79-80, 287-9, 291,
326
Schomerus, Hans. BAA 263-4
Schonauer, Franz. BAA 264
Schongauer. ATA 10
Schongut, Emanuel. SFS 103
Schoonover, Lawrence (1906-)
ES2 381 HFI 129 LEX 555 SFE
520 SF1 464 SF2 1066
Schopenhauer, Arthur (1788-1860)
CWN 43 KAU 157, 189-90 THM
17, 62
Schopfer, Jean (1868-1931) WGT
128 see also Claude Anet
Schorer, Mark R. (1908-77) ES2
381 EXT 9/2 39, 52 FAN 5
IAC 208 SF1 464 SF2 1066-7
Schotlaender, Rudolf. BAA 264
Schrader, Steven. IAC 208
Schram, Irene (1941-) HFI 129
SF1 464
Schramm, Wilbur Lang (1907-)
CSF 175 IAC 208 ES2 381 SFS
103 SF1 464
Schrank, Joseph. FFC 57
Schreiner, Olive (1855-1920) CSF
175 SF1 464
Schreiter, Rick. FFC 23, 26, 104
Schroder, Horst. BAA 225
Schrodinger, Erwin. EXT 7/2
30 [FUT] LTN 156, 163
Schroeder, Binette. FFC 123
Schroeder, Lynn. CSC 16
Schroth, R. A. EXT 10/1 40
Schubert, Franz. FLT 52
Schubert, G. FBK 60
Schuck, Frederick Hugh Paul
(1916-) ES2 381 SFE 520 SF1
464 SF2 1067
Schuck, Otto. IMS 34
Schuette, H. George (1850-) BAA
77, 97 CSF 175 SF1 464
Schuetz, Heinrich see Heinrich
Schutz
Schulman, Lester Martin (1934-)
SF1 464 SF2 1067
Schultz, Charles M. IAC 208
Schultz, Bruno. FBK 131-2, 148-9
Schultz, Robert. SRB 39, 49
Schuman, Samuel. RAH 258
Schumpp, Mechthild. BAA 288
Schuneman, Ann. RFA xxii

Schure, Edouard (1841-1929) CSF
175 SF1 464
Schuster, Gerry. WFS 203-4
Schuster, Joseph. WIF 134
Schuster, Melvin M. BAA 264
Schutz, Heinrich pseud. of Heinrich Schuetz.
CSF 175 SF1 464
Schutz, Joseph Willard (1912-)
SFE 521
Schuyler, George Samuel (1895-)
AOW 110 CSF 176 SFE 521
SF1 464
Schuyler, William M., Jr. FL1
380-2 FL2 827-30 FL3 1137-41
Schvan, Johan August. BAA 87
Schwab, Gunther (1904-) SF1 465
Schwahn, John George. BAA 48
Schwartz, Alan. ES2 381 HFI
129 SFE 521 SF1 465
Schwartz, Delmore. ETN 112
FLT 86-90, 99, 133
Schwartz, Jozua Marius Willen
Van Der Poorten (1858-1915)
WGT 128
Schwartz, Julius. IMS 10, 13-6,
20, 24, 34-6, 40, 45, 50, 71, 74-6,
80-1, 84, 93, 101, 115-7, 197-8,
213, 223 ISW 161 SFB 152 SOT
76, 80, 104-5, 107, 111, 114, 117,
139, 155, 305, 307, 324, 328, 358-
60, 362, 366 SRB 89 WIF 134,
136 WSF 75 WTS 53
Schwartz, Pedro. BAA 264
Schwartz, Sheila. IAC 208 SRB
464
Schwarz, Eugene S. FFC 8 RZY
73, 78
Schwarzchild, Karl. VES 77
Schwedtke, Kurt. BAA 264
Schweickart, Rusty. ALW 232
Schweitzer, Albert. IAH 71
VMW 31
Schweitzer, Britt. IAC 208
Schweitzer, Darrell. COT 284
FFR 156 JHN 33-4, 62 SRB 80
SV1 3
Schwerdtfeger, Erich. BAA 264
Schwerner, Michael. RHN 158
Schwitzgebel, Robert L. NDA 54
Schwob, Marcel. SIH 54
Schwonke, Martin (1923-) BAA
191, 264 EXT 3/2 48-50 EXT
5/1 7 EXT 9/2 31 SFB 17
SFE 521 SOT 432
Scithers, George (1929-) ASF 21,
41, 237, 247-8, 253-4, 256-7, 261,
264-6, 324-5 CWD 40 SFE 534
SF1 465 SF2 1067 SRB 117
WSF 287
Scoffern, David. CSF 176
Scoggins, Charles Elbert (1888-
1955) CSF 176 SF1 465 SOT 38
Scoles, A. B. SFN 30
Scortia, Thomas N. (1926-) AAL
129 AOW 298 BAA 264 BFP
429 DTS 52 ES2 381-2 FFR
158 FRN 44 HFI 130 HID 74
IAC 208-9 LEX 555-6 MFW 29
RGS 153-4 SFE 534 SFH 116
SFS 103 SF1 466 SF2 1067
SRB 508 VES 76, 136, 198, 201
WSF 176
Scot, Hew. CSF 176 SF1 466
Scotson-Clark, Ethel. CSF 176
SF1 466
Scotson-Clark, George Frederick
(1872-1927) CSF 176 SF1 466
Scott, Alan (1947-) HFI 130 SF1
466
Scott, Billy. SF1 466
Scott, Catherine Amy Dawson
(1868?-1934) CSF 166 SF1 466
Scott, David. ACC 52
Scott, Edward. CSF 176 SF1 466
Scott, Eleanor. CSF 176
Scott, Francis Reginald. BAA 114
Scott, Gabriel (1874-1958) CSF
176 SF1 466
Scott, George C. CSC 262
Scott, George Firth. CSF 176
SF1 466 WIF 50
Scott, James Maurice (1906-)
SF1 466
Scott, Jean M. BAA 150 HFI
144 SF1 466
Scott, Jeremy pseud. of Kay Dick.
CSF 176 ES2 382 SF1 466
Scott, Jody. HFI 130 IAC 209
SFS 104
Scott, John Reed (1869-) CSF 176
EXT 1/1 17 MFW 127 SF1 466
Scott, Peg O'Neill. SF1 466
WGT 129
Scott, Peter T. ES2 382 SF1 466
WGT 129 see also Barton Werper
Scott, Reginald Thomas Maitland
(1882-) SF1 467 TSP 58
Scott, Robert. WGT 129 see
also Blue Wolf
Scott, Robin pseud. of Robin Scott
Wilson. AAL 34-5 EXT 10/1 5
IAC 209 SFS 104

Scott, Samuel M. BAA 264
Scott, Sarah Robinson. BAA 12
Scott, T. T. TSP 17
Scott, Thomas Henry (1878-) SF1 467
Scott, (Sir) Walter (1771-1832) BYS 18, 82 CAT xiii, 5, 8, 91-3, 106-7 CSF 176 EXT 4/2 20 FBK 18 FL1 262-5 IAC 209 MSF 148, 193, 269 NWO 227 PST 72, 318 STH 96, 184 WGT 129
Scott, Winfield Townley. EXT 3/1 7, 21, 25 WTS 60
Scott-Elliot, W. EXT 7/1 16 WIF 66
Scotti, Giulio Clemente (1602-69) WGT 129
Scott-Moncrieff, David William Hardy (1907-) ES2 382 SF1 467
Scowcroft, Richard. MSM 275-6
Scram, Arthur N. pseud. of Leo Guild. SF1 467
Scriabin. CWN 39
Scrire O. T. O. 4-7 pseud. of Gerald Brosseau Gardner. SF1 467
Scriven, Gerard F. (1920-49) SF1 467
Scriven, R. C. EXT 10/1 40
Scrymsour, Ella M. BAA 87 CSF 176 SFE 535 SF1 467
Scudamore, Francis. SF1 467 STH 188
Scudder, Antoinette Quinby (1898-1958) CSF 176 SF1 467
Scudder, Edward S. STH 169
Scudder, Vida Dutton. BAA 191
Scully, Francis Joseph Xavier (1892-1964) ES2 382
Seaborn, (Capt.) Adam pseud? of John Cleves Symmes (1780-1829) ALW 57 AOW 30 CSF 176 EXT 3/1 30 PST 40, 42-4, 46, 128, 195, 217, 224, 227, 229, 239, 245, 250-1, 263, 271, 288, 299 SFE 535 SF1 467 SL5 2207-10 SRB 6
Seabright, Idris pseud. of Margaret St. Clair. ALW 216 IAC 209 ISW 221 SFS 104
Seabrook, William Buehler (1886-1945) ES2 382
Seabury, (Archbishop). WTS 21
Seabury, Florence Guy. COT 171

Seaforth pseud. of George C. Foster. CSF 176
Seaforth, A. Nelson pseud. of George S. Clarke. CSF 176
Seager, Allan. IAC 209
Sea-Lion pseud. of Geoffrey Martin Bennett (1909-) SF1 467
Seaman, Mary. FFC 86
Seamark pseud. of Austin Small. CSF 177 IAC 209
Search, Marion Pamela. ES2 382 SF1 467
Searight, R. F. COT 162
Searle, Arthur. EXT 5/2 46
Searle, Ronald William Fordham (1920-) ES2 382
Searles, A. Langley. FL2 612-5, 646-8 FL3 1044-6, 1428-35, 1532-5 IMS 213, 222 PST 122 SFW 40 SL1 89-92 SL3 1396-400
Searles, Baird. RAH 258 SRB 465
Searles, Paul J. IMS 191-2 see also Autolycus
Searls, Hank pseud. of Henry Hunt Searls, Jr. FFR 158 HFI 130 SFE 535 SF1 467
Searls, Henry Hunt, Jr. (1922-) ES2 382-3 SF2 1068 WGT 129 see also Hank Searls
Sears, Alfred Francis. BAA 40 see also Inca-Pablo-Ozollo
Sears, Edward S. STH 139
Sears, Paul B. BAA 264
Seary, Edgar R. EXT 8/2 63
Seaton, Dorothy. SFN 60
Seaton, Richard. ALW 132 SFN 60-2
Seavey, Ormond. RZY 106
Sebastien, Lee pseud. of Robert Silverberg. RSG 23
Sebesta, Sam Leaton. AOW 307
Sechrist, Elizabeth Hough (1903-) CSF 177 ES2 383 SF1 467-8 SF2 1068
Sedberry, James Hamilton (1863-) AOW 71 CSF 177 SFE 535 SF1 468
Sedgwick, Anne Douglas (1873-1935) CSF 177 SF1 468
Sedgwick, Henry Dwight. BAA 73
Sedgwick, Sidney Newman (1872-1941) BAA 75 CSF 177 SF1 468
Seeber, Edward D. BAA 264

Seeber, Hans Ulrich. BAA 191,
264
Seegar, Alan. EXT 3/1 17
Seeley, Charles Sumner pseud. of
John William Munday. CSF 177
EXT 1/1 17 SF1 468
Seely, (Sir) John Robert. POE
171-2
Seelye, John D. NWO 283
Seeman, Elizabeth. FFC 136
Seestern pseud. of Ferdinand H.
Grautoff. CSF 177
Sefton, Catherine. SF1 468
Segal, Howard P. BAA 265, 288
Segal, Lesley Keen. SF1 468
Segall, Don see Leo August
Segre, Cesare. CAT 57
Seguy, Jean. BAA 265
Seibel, George (1872-1958) SF1
468
Seibt, Ferdinand. BAA 192, 265
Seidel, Kathryn L. SL3 1161-4
SL4 1678-81 SL5 2488-91
Seiden, Melvin. BAA 265
Seidenfeld, Barbara Berman. SL2
729-34 SL3 1213-6
Seidler, Rosalie. FFC 136
Seidman, Mitzi. FFC 136
Seignolle, Claude (1917-) ES2
383 FBK 138, 140
Seims, Edith. TSP 89
Seitz, Franz. BAA 265
Seitz, (Sister) M. Agnes. BAA
288
Selby, Hubert, Jr. ETN 24 NWO
36
Selden, George pseud. of George
Selden Thompson. FFC 70, 124,
136 SF1 468, 584
Seldon, Hari. ALW 168
Selfridge, Oliver. FFC 61
Selikowitz, Arthur L. IMS 34-5
WFS 31
Selkirk, Alexander. EXT 7/2 33
Sell, Harry. STH 237
Sell, William. IAC 209 SFS 104
WSF 333
Sellers, Connie L. , Jr. (1922-)
HFI 130 SF1 468-9 SF2 1068
Sellings, Arthur pseud. of Arthur
Gordon Ley (1911-68) ALW 212
AOW 246 HFI 130 IAC 209-10
LEX 557 SFE 535-6 SFS 104
SF1 469 VES 180
Sellwood, A. V. ES2 383

Seltzer, Richard Warren, Jr.
(1946-) SF1 469 SF2 1068-9
Semenov, V. MSF 252
Sempe, Pierre. BAA 265
Sempers, C. T. BAA 265
Sen, Sri Chendra. BAA 265
Senanayake, Dudley. VFS 123
Senarens, Luis P(hillip) (1865-
1939) ALW 74, 87 ES2 383 EXT
1/1 5 EXT 5/1 15 EXT 7/1 26
IAC 210 MFW 143-4 RHN 11
SFB 39 SFE 536 SFS 104 SFW
53-8 SIH 40 SRB 26 STH 54,
163, 165 VES 173 WGT 129
WIF 69 WSF 18 YTS 9 see
also Noname
Sendak, Jack. FFC 191
Sendak, Maurice. FFC 6-7, 9, 18,
23, 53, 66, 91, 100, 112, 120, 124,
126
Senf, Curtis C. (1879-1948) WTS
30, 64-5, 84
Sengfelder, Carl. BAA 288
Sentry, Gordon John. MIH 60
Septimus. LTN 177
Sera, Manfred. BAA 192
Serao, Matilde. CSF 177
Seredy, Kate. FFC 14, 110, 129
Sergeant, John. FFC 75
Seriel, Jerome pseud. of Jacques
Vallee. SFE 536
Serjeant, Constancia. CSF 177
SF1 469
Serling, Rod (1924-75) AOW 207,
247 ES2 383-4 FFR 159 FL4
1684-5 IAC 210 KAU 152 SFE
536 SFH 103, 105-6 SFS 104-5
SF1 469 WAA 190 WSF 312
Serly, Ludovicus Textoris. BAA
107
Serner, Martin Gunnar (1886-
1947) WGT 129 see also Frank
Heller
Sernicoli, Davide. SF1 469
Serpell, Christopher. BAA 109
CSF 32 SF1 469
Serrano, Mary J. CSF 177
Serrano, Miguel (1917-) SF1 469
Servello, Joe. FFC 26
Serveson, Ed. ES2 384
Serveson, Marion. ES2 384
Service, Robert W. (1874-1958)
CSF 177 SFE 536 SF1 469
Servier, Jean. BAA 192, 265

Serviss, Garrett P. (1851-1929)
ALW 33, 85, 96, 106-7, 121 AOW
45, 71-2 BFP 430 BYS 144
CSF 177 ES2 384 EXT 1/1 2, 17
EXT 3/1 28 EXT 5/1 4 EXT
5/2 37, 39, 46, 48 EXT 7/1 20,
22, 24, 27 HFI 130 IAC 210 KAU
57-8, 60, 127 LEX 557 MFW 23
POE 113 PST 113, 274 RFA 1-2
SFB 54, 128 SFE 536 SFW 39-
44, 76 SF1 469 SL2 698-702
SOT 216 SRB 9, 11 STH 94 VES
69-70, 81, 92, 133, 161 WSF 23-
4, 44
Sessions, Archibald Lowry. ALW
110
Seton, Anya (1916?-) SF1 469
SF2 1069
Seton, Ernest Thompson. MIH 96
SOT 217
Settel, Irving (1916-) SF1 470
SF2 1069
Settles, James B. ES2 384
Seufert, Bernard A. IMS 161
Seuss, (Dr.). FFC 51
Seuss, John. EXT 9/2 25
Sevareid, Eric. COT 54 VFS 74
Severin, Jean (1911-) SF1 470
Severn, David pseud. of David
Storr Unwin (1918-) FFC 33, 172
SF1 470
Severs, Elisabeth. CSF 177
Severy, Melvin Linwood (1863-)
CSF 177 ES2 384 EXT 1/1 18
SF1 470
Sewall, Marcia. FFC 6
Sewell, Amos. TSP 22
Sewell, Brocard. CWN 24
Sewell, Elizabeth Missing. SF1
470
Sewell, Helen. FFC 95
Sewell, Margaret Elizabeth (1919-)
ES2 384 SF1 470 SF2 1069
WGT 129
Seymour, Alan (1927-) AOW 247
BAA 150 BYS 295 SFE 539
SF1 470 SF2 1069
Seymour, Cyril. CSF 177
Seymour, Frederick Henri (1850-
1913) WGT 129 see also Lord
Gilhooley
Seymour, Henry pseud. of Helmut
Henry Hartmann. SF1 470
Shaara, Michael. IAC 210 SFS
105 VES 113

Shackleton, C. C. BYS 214, 299
IAC 210 SFS 105
Shadegg, Stephen C. (1909-) SF1
470 SF2 1069
Shaefer, Jack. SFH 172
Shafer, Robert Jones (1915-) HFI
130 SF1 470
Shaffer, Eugene Carl. HFI 130
SF1 470
Shaftel, Oscar. COT 141 EXT
4/2 28
Shaftesbury, (Earl of). SOI 81
Shaginyan, Marietta. EXT 10/2
75 MSF 253
Shah, Idries. PJF 55 SFD 277
Shakespeare, William. ACE 16
AC2 14 ASF 35, 47, 67, 206 ATA
38-9 BAA 3 CAT 4, 39, 48, 52,
55-6, 132, 136 COT 174, 284
CSC 6, 8-10, 24, 74, 173 CUA 23,
26-9, 43, 56, 60 EXT 2/2 38
EXT 5/1 21 EXT 7/1 11, 16
EXT 9/2 26, 29, 48 FHT 70 FLT
2, 4, 23-4, 53, 128 [FUT] HID 174
IAH 16 INT 31-2, 79 ISW 213
JGB 59 KAU 20, 199 LTN 91-2,
231 MIH 78, 122 MSF 11, 18, 98-
9, 174 MSM 14 NWO 24, 281,
292 OWB 71, 73 PJF 21, 61 RBY
18, 186, 192 RZY 14, 18, 96 SFA
9, 136, 287-9, 292, 300 SFD 4, 39-
40, 45, 48-9, 225 SFH 33-4, 184-
5 SFN 92 STF 49 STH 252 TDI
38 TFC 34 VFS 173, 205 WBW
46-8 WFS 80 WTS 17, 121
Shalimov, Alexandr. SIH 142
Shallit, Joseph. IAC 211
Shamir, Moshe. IAC 211
Shango, J. R. IAC 211 SFS 105
Shanklin, Imelda Octavia. SF1
470
Shanks, Edward (1892-1953) BAA
85 CSF 177 ES2 384 IAC 211
POE 227-8 SFE 539 SF1 470
Shannon, Claude. VFS 241
Shannon, Doris (1924-) SF1 470
SF2 1069-70
Shannon, Frank pseud. of Dennis
Francis Joseph Shine. SF1 470
Shannon, Fred pseud. of William
S. Ruben. SF1 471
Shannon, John C. SF1 471
Shapiro, Arthur. ISW 216-7
Shapiro, Irwin. FFC 57
Shapiro, Neil. HFI 130 IAC 211
Shapiro, Karl. EXT 6/1 19

Shapley, Harlow (1885-1972) ES2 384 IAC 211 SFS 105
Shap-Shak, Rene. VFS 117
Sharapov, S. MSF 251
Sharkey, Jack pseud. of John Michael Sharkey. ES2 384 FFR 159 FRN 45 HFI 131 IAC 211 LEX 557-8 SFE 539 SFS 105 SF1 471
Sharkey, John Michael (1931-) SF2 1070 WGT 129 see also Jack Sharkey
Sharnik, John Seymour. IAC 211 ISW 129
Sharp, Dolph (1919-) SF1 471 SF2 1070
Sharp, D(rury) D. CSF 71 ES2 384 IAC 211 STH 98 VES 232
Sharp, Evelyn (1869-1955) BAA 84 CSF 177 SF1 471
Sharp, Henry. CSF 177
Sharp, Margery (1905-) CSF 178 FFC 124-5 FL3 1037-9 SF1 471 SF2 1070
Sharp, Robert George. SF1 471
Sharp, Roberta. FL4 1645-51 FL5 2112-4
Sharp, William (1855-1905) CSF 178 ES2 384-5 WGT 130 see also Fiona Macleod
Shatner, William. IAC 211 OMN 214, 260, 262-3
Shattuck, William (1864-1946) SF1 471
Shaver, Richard S. (1907-75) ASF 118 CSF 178 ES2 385 HFI 131 KAU 228 LEX 558-9 RFA 169, 191-2 RGS 154-5 SFE 540 SF1 471 SOT 28 STH 246, 261 VES 233, 336-40 WAA 109 WGT 130 WIF 92, 112 WSF 117 see also Alexander Blade, Edwin Benson, G. H. Irwin, Paul Lohrman, Frank Patton
Shaw, Arnold. SF1 471
Shaw, Artie. ISW 1
Shaw, Bob pseud. of Robert Shaw. ALW 212 AOW 247-9, 295, 300 BAA xvi BFP 431-2 BYS 286, 304 CSC 231 ES2 385 ETN 100 FFR 159 HFI 131 IAC 211 KAU 28-9 LEX 559-60 MFW 28, 33-4 NDA 181, 207-8 NWO 234 RGS 155-6 SFE 540 SFS 105 SF1 471 SIH 79 SL4 1617-26 VES 77, 96, 150, 232 WFS 231

Shaw, Brian (house name) SFE 541 SF1 471-2 see also John Russell Fearn, E. C. Tubb, David Griffiths, David O'Brien
Shaw, Cap. WFS 103
Shaw, Frank Hubert (1878-) SF1 472
Shaw, Frederick Lincoln, Jr. (1928-) ES2 385 HFI 131 SFE 541 SF1 472 SF2 1070-1
Shaw, Frederick Stanley (1870-) SF1 472
Shaw, George. SF1 472
Shaw, George Bernard (1856-1950) ACC 172-3, 177-92, 195 AOW 72 ASF 142 BAA 86 CSF 178 CWN 17-8, 27, 30-1, 36, 44-5, 47 ETN 63 FAN 4, 12, 64, 86, 96, 99, 118, 186 FL1 42-4, 74-7 FL2 955-8 FTF 93 IAC 211 IAH 26 MFW 281 MSF 193 MSM 244 MIH 20 NDA 55, 67-8, 74 POE 191-2 RBY 100, 106 RHN 23, 62 SFB 51 SFE 541 SFN 89 SF1 472 SL1 120-4 SOT 381 THM 6, 32, 34, 38, 51, 53-5, 58 VFS 75, 77
Shaw, Greg. EXT 10/1 18
Shaw, Irwin. IAC 211 MSM 113
Shaw, Joseph T. TSP 217
Shaw, Lao. IAC 211
Shaw, Larry pseud. of Lawrence Taylor Shaw. ALW 184 ES2 385-6 IAC 211 IAH 1, 3-4, 55, 60 ISW 47, 131 MIH 7, 20, 38 SFE 541 SFS 105 SF1 472 TJB 31 WIF 117
Shaw, Lawrence Taylor (1924-) SF2 1071 see also Larry Shaw
Shaw, Nonna Dolodarenko. BAA 288
Shaw, Noreen. IAH 1 MIH 7
Shaw, Robert (1931-) SF2 1070 see also Bob Shaw
Shaw, Robert Sanders pseud. of Sam Moskowitz. IMS 189
Shaw, William Jenkins. CSF 178 SF1 472
Shcherbakov, Vladimir. IAC 211
Shcherbatov, Mikhail M. MSF 244
Shchlebnikov, Velimir. SIH 53
She, Lao (1899-1966) SIH 75-6 SL3 1344-7 see also Shu She-Yu
Shea, J. Vernon. AOW 403 WTS 56

Shea, Michael. HFI 131 SFE 541
SF1 472
Shea, Robert. LEX 560 SFE 541
Sheahan, Henry see Henry Beston
Shear, David. HFI 131 SFE 541
SF1 472
Shearing, Joseph pseud. of Gabrielle V. C. Campbell. CSF 178
Sheckley, Robert (1928-) AAL 8-
9, 21-2, 33, 217 ALW 14, 99, 164,
212, 219, 234 AOW 248-50, 285,
295 BAA 121, 125, 128, 130, 132-
3, 135, 138, 143, 147 BFP 433-4
BYS 78, 247-9, 279, 289 CSC
107, 142-3, 228 DMK 19-26 DTS
43 ES2 386 ETN 1-2, 30, 33, 40,
65-6, 77, 119, 144 EXT 2/2 31
EXT 5/1 3 EXT 6/2 51 FAN
155 FBK 124 FFR 159-62 FHT
47 FTF 88, 90, 97, 99, 109-12,
125-6 HFI 131-2 IAC 211-3
IAH 35-6, 50-1, 104-5 INT 25-6,
38, 78 ISW 127, 129, 236-9 JGB
5 KAU 79, 184 LEX 560-2 LTN
262 MIH 34, 111 MSF 200 NDA
31, 103-4, 211 OMN 124-6 RGS
156 SFB 150-1 SFD 17, 254,
299, 322 SFE 541-2 SFH 84,
171, 181 SFS 105-6 SFW 149,
351, 497-503 SF1 472 SF2 1071-
2 SIH 44, 48, 53-4, 56-7, 79, 81,
94, 180 SL2 539-42 SL3 1413-
6 SL4 2046-50 SRB 330, 374
STH 45 TFC 172 TJB 5 TRB
54 TSF 61 VES 82, 151, 173,
177, 210, 215, 309 WAA 54, 65,
127, 138, 150, 229, 242, 244 WFS
161, 200, 202, 214, 227 WGT 130
WSF 175 see also Finn O'Donnevan
Shecter, Ben. FFC 33, 81, 139,
146 SF1 472
Shedd, Margaret. MSM 114
Sheean, James Vincent (1899-
1975) SF1 472 SF2 1072
Sheed, Rosemary. EXT 9/1 16
Sheedy, Alexandra. FFC 125
Sheehan, Bernard W. BAA 265
Sheehan, Carolyn. FFC 136 SF1
472
Sheehan, Edmund. FFC 136 SF1
473
Sheehan, Murray. CSF 178 SF1
473

Sheehan, Perley Poore (1875-1943)
ALW 106 CSF 178 ES2 386 HFI
132 SFE 542 SF1 473 WGT 130
Sheehan, Richard G. ES2 386
SF1 473
Sheeler, Charles. COT 207
Sheffield, Charles. SRB 377
Shefner, Vadim S. IAC 213 MSF
269
Shekerjian, Haig. FFC 63
Shekerjian, Regina. FFC 63
Sheldon, Alice Hastings (1916-)
BAA 159 BFP 435 ETN 101,
114, 138, 176 LTN 180-3 SF2
1100-2 SRB 372 WGT 130-1
WSF 236 see also Raccoona
Sheldon, James Tiptree, Jr.
Sheldon, Charles M. BAA 56
Sheldon, Lee pseud. of Wayne
Cyril Lee (1917-) HFI 132 SFE
542 SF1 473
Sheldon, Raccoona pseud. of
Alice Sheldon. IAC 213 LTN
181-2
Sheldon, Roy (house name) ES2
387 SFE 542 SF1 473 VES 75,
96 see also E. C. Tubb, H. J.
Campbell, George Hay
Sheldon, Walt. AAL 47 IAC 213
SFS 106 WGT 131
Sheldon, (Dr.) William. MSM
252
Sheldon, William D. SF1 473
Sheldon-Williams, Miles. SF1
473
Shelhamer, (Miss) M. T. BAA 36
Shellabarger, Samuel (1888-1954)
WGT 131 John Esteven
Shelley, Mary Wollstonecraft
(1797-1851) AAL 1 ACC 85, 136,
209 ALW 45, 87, 216 AOW 12,
14-5, 31, 90, 355 ASF 72-3, 105-
6, 142, 161, 181-4, 190 BYS 7, 15,
18, 20-40, 44, 83, 144, 199, 229,
253, 286, 313, 317 CAT xiii-xvi,
5-6, 19, 51, 56, 67, 106-8, 138
COT 93, 152, 203-5 CSC 26, 165-
6, 172 CSF 178 DTS 3 ES2 387
EXT 3/1 30 EXT 5/1 15-6 EXT
6/2 40 EXT 7/1 18 EXT 7/2
38 FAN 10, 37, 95, 168 FBK 7,
24-7, 44, 154 FFR 162 FL2
575-80 FTF 29-31 HFI 185
IAC 213-4 INT 7, 14, 63-4, 114
KAU 6-7, 153, 184 KWS 332 LEX

Shelley, Mary W. (cont.)
562-3 LTN 80-1, 156 MFW x-xi,
18, 117, 195-6, 247 MSF 12, 113,
115, 117, 124, 127-39, 141, 143,
166, 168-70, 198, 220, 246 NWO
133 OMN 5, 67, 71 OSR 171-80
POE 46-7 PST 27-9, 32, 34-5,
62, 100, 158, 183, 196, 216, 255,
271, 281 RFA 116 RGS 156-7
RHN 193 SFB 18-9, 32-3, 35, 51,
125 SFE 542-3 SFH 6-8, 15, 25,
91, 108, 114, 132, 136, 149, 165,
168, 180, 182-5, 189, 191-6, 198,
200, 207-8, 212, 220 SFS 106
SFW 3-9, 12 SF1 473 SIH 9, 17,
24, 127, 129, 132 SL2 832-9 SL3
1151-5 SOT 301, 305 SRB 7
VES 126, 132, 173, 225, 232, 255,
260, 262, 293 WAA 27, 83-5, 162,
243 WBW 32 WGT 131 WIF 41
WSF 15, 308
Shelley, Percy Bysshe (1792-
1822) ACC 209 ASF 182 BAA
18-9, 164 BYS 7, 18-21, 25- 6,
28, 31, 34, 98, 282 CSF 178 CUA
39 EXT 8/2 33 FBK 27, 44
INT 87 ISW 14, 219, 270 LTN
70, 111, 150-1 MFW 20, 195
MSF 113, 115, 117-8, 121-30, 132-
6, 138, 144, 153, 168, 171, 183, 229,
259 NWO 43 RZY 33-4 SFH
192 SFW 4-6 SF1 473 SIH 127
SOI 81, 83 THM 38-9, 45 TSO
34 UKL 77-8 VFS 145 WAA
86 WGT 131
Shelton, Frederick William (1814-
81) CSF 178 SF1 473
Shelton, Jerry. IAC 214 SFS 106
Shelton, William Roy (1919-)
AOW 330 IAC 214 SFS 106 SF1
473 SF2 1072
Shepard, E. R. FBK 114
Shepard, Jane. SF1 473
Shepard, Mary. FFC 56, 71
Shepard, Morgan (1865-1947) see
John-Martin
Shepard, Odell. BAA 265
Shepard, Ray. FFC 18
Shepard, Wilson. IMS 27-8, 30-1,
68, 79, 113 WIF 136 see also
Ivan Nepolis, Noname, N. E. P.
North, Willis W. Woe
Sheperd, Ernest. FFC 24-5, 54,
81, 88, 119, 178
Shepherd, Conrad (1937-) LEX
563

Shepherd, Jean. MIH 73 SOT
245-6
Shepley, Harlow. EXT 10/2 87
Shepley, John. IAC 214 SFS 106
Sheppard, Alfred Tresidder
(1871-1947) SF1 473
Sheppard, Ethel. CSF 178
Sheppard, H. R. L. BAA 104
Sherard, Robert Harborough.
EXT 2/1 16
Sherburne, Zoa L. (1912-) FFC
168 SF1 474 SF2 1072-3
Sheridan, (Mrs.) Frances (1724-
66) SF1 474
Sherman, Frank Dempster (1860-
1916) SF1 474 WGT 131 see
also Two Wags
Sherman, Harold Morrow (1898-)
ES2 387 HFI 132 SF1 474
Sherman, Jory (1932-) SF1 16
Sherman, Michael. IAH 65
Sherman, Roger. WTS 32
Sherman, Shirley. BAA 288
Sherman, Stuart. BAA 265
Sherred, T(homas) L. (1915-)
ALW 161 AOW 397 ES2 387
ETN 142 HFI 132 IAC 214
LEX 563-4 MSM 82 RFA 145
SFE 543 SFS 106 SF1 474 VES
144 WSF 111, 153
Sherrell, Carl (1929-) HFI 132
SFE 543 SRB 276
Sherriff, Robert Cedric (1896-
1975) AOW 250 BYS 292 CSF
178 ES2 387 EXT 8/1 5 HFI
132 LEX 564-5 POE 251 PST
175-6, 192, 212, 253, 311 SFB
128 SFE 543 SF1 474 SRB 299
THM 48
Sherring, Herbert. ES2 387
Sherry, Oliver pseud. of George
Oliver Lobo. CSF 178 SF1 474
Sherwin, Proctor Fenn. BAA 265
Sherwood, John. KAU 189
Sherwood, Martin (1942-) SFE
543
Sherwood, Mary Martha (1775-
1851) SF1 474
Sheton, Jerry. COT 51
She-Yu, Shu. SIH 75 see also
Lao She
Shibano, Takumi. SOT 432
Shideler, Mary McDermott. SOI
111
Shiel, M(atthew) P(hipps) (1865-
1947) ALW 82, 102 AOW 73 BYS

Shiel, M. P. (cont.)
143-4 CSF 178-9 ES2 387-8
EXT 3/1 28 EXT 4/2 24 EXT
5/1 3 EXT 7/1 14,17 FL5 2192-
6 HFI 132 IAC 214 IAH 57,60
KAU 93,127,186 NWO 139 PST
84-5,200,255,258,263 SFB 128
SFD 306 SFE 543-4 SFS 107
SFW 31-7 SF1 474 SL4 1735-8
SL5 2525-8 SRB 11 STH 31-2,
59,99-100,123,183,205-6,210-
1 TSF 230 VES 101,132,232,
251 WGT 131 WIF 169
Shields, Charles. FFC 19
Shields, Ralston. TSP 166-9
Shiflett, Ray C. SL2 1004-7
SL5 2179-83
Shine, Dennis Francis Joseph
(1908-) see Frank Shannon
Shinn, Roger L. BAA 265
Ship, Reuben. ES2 388
Shipley, Marie A. B. BAA 192
Shipley, Miriam Allen De Ford
(1888-1975) WGT 131-2 see
also Miriam Allen De Ford
Shipman, G. R. AAL 97,123
Shippey, T. A. CAT 43-4,115
FL1 17-21,232-5,248-55 FL2
822-6,948-50 FL3 1149-57,
1224-6 FL4 1586-8,1972-4
FL5 2069-73,2079-83 JHN 62
SL1 43-7,247-53 SL3 1312-6
SL4 1541-4,1583-7,1930-3 SL5
2051-5,2407-10 UKL 245
Shippey, Tom. IAC 214 FLR 61
Shipway, George (1908-) SF1 474
Shiras, Wilmar H(ouse) (1908-)
AOW 250 COT 195 ES2 388
HFI 132 IAC 214 IAH 81 LEX
565 MSM 83 RFA 158,164-5,
172,190,195 SFD 316 SFE 544
SFS 107 SFW 148 SF1 474 SL1
349-53 VES 195 WGT 132 WIF
204
Shir-Cliff, Bernard W. WFS 197
Shirer, William L. SOT 424 VES
123
Shirley, George Ernest (1898-)
BAA 144 ES2 388 SFE 544 SF1
475 SF2 1073
Shirley, John. AAL 114-5 IAC
214
Shirley, Robert. HFI 132 SF1
475 WAA 59
Shishko, Anatoly V. MSF 254,261

Shkarovsky-Raffe, Arthur. SF1
475
Shklar, Judith N. BAA xiii-xvi,
xx-xxi,192,265 FAN 174
Shklovskii, Iosef Shmuelovitch
(1916-) ALW 232 ES2 388 IAC
214
Shklovsky, Victor B. CAT 73
EXT 10/2 75 MSF 6,54,71,254
SFH 28 STF 46
Shober, Joyce Lee. EXT 6/1 2,12
Shodall, Reuben Sam. BAA 143
Shofner, Philip. IAC 214
Sholokhov. EXT 10/2 93
Shols, W. W. (1925-) LEX 565-6
Shore, Robert. FFC 21
Shore, Wilma. IAC 214 SFS 107
Shores, Louis (1904-) SF1 475
SF2 1072
Short, Dorothy D. CSF 179
Short, Gertrude. BAA 117
Short, Jackson pseud. of Peter
Hochstein (1939-) SF1 475 SF2
1073
Short, Richard (1841-1916) SF1
475
Shortall, Leonard. FFC 35,73,
136
Shorter, Elliot. SRB 124
Shorthouse, Joseph Henry. CSF
179
Shortt, Vere Dawson (1872-1915)
SF1 475
Shostakovich, Dimitri. IAH 38
Showalter, Dennis E. RAH 76,
155,258
Shreck, Max. SIH 27
Shriver, Gary G. BAA 141
Shroyer, Frederick. IMS 123,
138 SFW 161-7 SL3 1098-101,
1209-12 see also Erick Freyer
Shternfeld, Ari. COT 36
Shulevitz, Uri. FFC 9,107,151,
191
Shulman, Sandra Dawn (1944-)
SF1 475 SF2 1073
Shumaker, Wayne. EXT 8/1 1
SOI 161
Shumway, Harry Irving (1883-)
SF1 475
Shura, Mary. FFC 36,51,77,98,
136
Shurter, Robert L. BAA 265-6,
288

Shuster, Joseph (1914-) ES2 388 IMS 5,15 SFB 110 SFE 544 SFH 39,108 SOT 102,113-4 SRB 89 VES 325-6 WAA 219 WSF 306
Shute, Nevil pseud. of Nevil Shute Norway. ALW 31,228 AOW 251 BYS 256,271 EXT 5/1 4 EXT 8/1 5 FAN 168 FFR 162-3 HFI 132 IAC 214 KAU 93,126 MIH 16 NDA 147-9,151 NWO 76,134 SFB 18,128 SFE 544 SF1 475 SL4 1603-7 VES 135,296 WSF 334
Shuttleworth, H. C. BAA 266
Sibelius. WFS 56
Sibert, Richard. STH 202
Sibley, Donald. FFC 74,122
Sibley, Mulford Q. BAA 192,266
Sibley, Ruroy. IMS 222
Sibol, Frank. SF1 475
Sibson, Francis H. CSF 179 ES2 388 SFE 544 SF1 475 WIF 52
Sicard, Clara. SF1 475
Siciliano, Sam Joseph. UKL 245-6
Sickelmore, Richard. CSF 179
Sickels, Evelyn R. EXT 10/1 32
Siclari, Joe D. LTN 210 SRB 87-129,515
Siculus, Diodorus. AOW 11
Siddons, Anne Rivers (1936-) FL2 740-3
Siden, (Captain) pseud. of Denis Vairasse. CSF 179
Sidney, A. CSF 179
Sidney, Edward William pseud. of Nathaniel Beverley Tucker. CSF 179
Sidney, Kathleen M. IAC 214
Sidney, (Sir) Philip. BAA 2-3 CAT 48 STF 59
Sieg, Paul Eugen (1899-1950) LEX 566-7
Siegel, Jerome (1914-) ES2 388 IMS 5,15 SFB 110 SFE 544 SFH 39,108 SOT 69,76,102, 113-4,117 SRB 89 WAA 219 WIF 134 WSF 306 see also Bernard J. Kenton
Siegel, Mark. FL1 169-72 FL3 1071-4,1317-9,1520-6 FL4 1686-91,1979-82
Siegel, Martin (1941-72) HFI 132 SFE 544-5 SF1 475

Siegele, Herman Hugo (1883-) CSF 179 SF1 475
Siemon, Frederick. AOW 363 ES2 388 SF1 475-6
Sienkiewicz, Henry. SOT 94-5
Sieveking, Lancelot De Giberne (1896-1972) BAA 91,128 CSF 179 ES2 388-9 SFE 545 SF1 476
Sigerson, Dora Mary (-1918) SF1 476
Silberberg, Leslie Frances Stone (1905-) WGT 132
Silberberg, (Mrs.) William see Leslie Frances Stone Silberberg, Leslie F. Stone
Silberkleit, Louis H(orace) (1901-) ES2 389 STH 44 TSP 145,150, 207
Silberling, Edouard. BAA 192
Silberrad, Una L. CSF 179
Silbersack, John. FLR 27,61
Silberstang, Edwin (1930-) SF1 476 SF2 1073
Silent, William T. pseud. of John William Jackson, Jr. (1945-) HFI 132 SF1 476 SF2 1074
Sillitoe, Alan (1928-) BAA 153 SFE 545 SF1 476 SF2 1074
Sills, Yole G. BAA 266
Silvani, Anita. SF1 476 WGT 132 see also A. F. S.
Silver, Carole. WBW 36,58-9
Silver, R. Norman. CSF 179
Silverberg, Barbara. FFC 22 IAC 214 LTN 228 RSG 10 SF1 476
Silverberg, Robert (1935-) AAL 20,65,82-3 ACE 14,75 AC2 12,73 ALW 36,179,184-5,212, 222,239 AOW 251-4,285,290, 292,294,298-300,330 ATA 50 BAA 130,144,152-3,155 BFP 436-45 BYS 257,278,303,321 CAT 139 COT 72,112,269,284-5,291,297 CSC 25,224,150-1 DMK 261-8 DTS 7,39,41,44-5, 48 EFP 21 ES2 389-90 ETN 2,21-2,31-2,35,46,55-6,59,65-6,77-82,100,105-6,121,140-1, 146 EXT 10/2 94-113 FFC 45 FFR 163-4 [FJT] FRN 45 HFI 132-4 IAC 109,214-7 IAH 30 INT 22-3,34-6,57,65-6,76,79, 121 JGB 51 JVN 117-29,240

Silverberg, Robert (cont.)
KAU 31, 90-2, 98, 102, 116-21,
184, 210, 227 LEX 567-70 LTN
250-1, 253, 262 MFW 15, 19-20,
41, 61-3, 104, 172, 174-5, 178, 247
MIH 119 NDA 41-2, 104-5, 109-
10, 122-3, 126-9, 188-9 NWO vi,
183-5, 235 OMN 184-92 RAH
258 RFA 196, 207-9 RGS 157-8
SFA 16, 303, 305 SFB 117 SFD
17, 20, 27, 32, 54, 56, 63, 77, 131,
133, 247-8, 263, 265, 299, 311, 314,
322 SFE 545-6 SFH 98, 150, 243
SFS 50, 107 SFW 104, 505-11,
539 SF1 476-8 SF2 1074-5 SIH
181 SIN 158 SL2 591-4, 671-5
SL3 1526-30 SL5 2179-83, 2293-
7, 2303-6 SRB 12, 14, 17, 67, 124,
276, 332, 338, 348-51, 354, 360,
362, 364, 368 STH 45, 88-9 SV2
51-62 TJB 46 TSF 61, 233, 240
UFS 4 VES 82, 121, 123, 136, 147,
165, 173, 177, 179, 189, 206-7, 209,
215, 226, 245, 273, 319, 328 VF2
1-33, 197-8 WAA 126, 138, 164,
243 WFS 230, 292, 294-5 WGT
132-3 WSF 176, 222, 236, 241,
246, 275, 362, 385, 388-9 see
also Robert Arnette, Alexander
Blade, Ralph Burke, Walker
Chapman, Don Eliot, Don Elliott,
Richard Greer, E. K. Jarvis,
Ivar Jorgensen, Ivar Jorgenson,
Warren Kastel, Calvin M. Knox,
Clyde Mitchell, David Osborne,
Robert Randall, Lee Sebastien,
Leonard G. Spencer, S. M. Ten-
neshaw, Gerald Vance
Silverman, Burt. FFC 35
Silverman, Mel. FFC 129
Silverman, Michael. LTN 252
Silvers, Phil. VFS 195
Silverstein, Henry. BAA 266
Silverstein, Shel. IAC 217 SFS
107
Silvette, Henry (1906-) ES2 390
WGT 133-4 see also Barnaby
Dogbolt
Simak, Clifford D. (1904-) AAL
23-4, 53, 101-2, 104 ALW 10,
146, 155, 160-2, 213, 217, 230
AOW 110, 254-6, 288, 292, 294,
296 ASF 233, 252 BAA 144
BFP 446-9 BYS 234-5, 246, 249
CAT 102 COT 27, 63, 65, 76-7,
83, 154 EFP 17 ES2 390-2

ETN 33, 59 EXT 2/1 2 EXT
2/2 31 EXT 5/1 3 EXT 7/2 39,
42 FFR 164-5 FHT 58 FL2
549-52 FAN 155 FTF 138 HFI
134-5 IAC 217-9 IAH 140, 142
IMS 23, 205 INT 21-2, 35, 38, 52,
54, 62, 76 ISW 217 KAU 32-4,
61, 65-6, 78, 80-1, 84, 88, 124,
152, 174, 204, 214-5 LEX 570-3
MFW 9, 20, 23, 41, 103, 248 MIH
24, 36 MSF 9 MSM 32, 299
NDA 185-6, 194, 217 PST 147-
8, 194 RFA 6, 54, 57, 60, 62, 66,
79, 107, 115, 122, 132, 138, 140,
154-5, 184, 203, 209, 213, 215
RGS 158-9 RSG 53 SFB 62, 82-
3, 100 SFD 19, 289, 311 SFE
546-7 SFH 130-1, 147, 193, 243
SFS 107-9 SFW 91, 115, 513-8
SF1 478 SF2 1075 SIH 147 SL1
369-73 SL4 1794-8 SL5 2429-
32 SOT 6, 140, 174, 176, 186, 201,
218, 244, 254, 266-82, 332, 431
SRB 5, 7, 13-5, 124, 276, 313, 315
STH 11-2, 117 TJB 4 TSF 54,
233 UFS 4 VES 73, 80, 82, 87-8,
95-6, 113-4, 129, 142, 148, 150,
157, 176-7, 197, 210, 226, 235, 317
VF1 64-87, 265-7 WAA 89, 164,
167 WFS 35, 161, 200 WIF 145,
148, 160, 202 WSF 51, 92, 94, 107,
135, 148, 151, 154, 171, 174, 185,
234, 236, 242, 338, 340, 386, 388
Simak, Richard S. IAC 219
Sime, Sidney H. (1867-1942) ES2
392 FBK 89 IAC 219 SIH 47
Simeon, Fernand. FBK 36
Simmel, Georg. MSF 73
Simmonds, James D. BAA 266
Simmons, Henry Hugh. ES2 392
Simmons, Herbert A. IAC 219
Simms, Ruth L. EXT 9/1 16-7
Simms, William Gilmore. EXT
4/1 9
Simnett, John. IAC 219
Simon, Edith (1917-) SF1 478
SF2 1075
Simon, Erik (1950-) LEX 573
Simon, Frank. EXT 1/2 34
Simon, Heinrich. BAA 266
Simon, Joe. VES 326
Simon, Marie. BAA 266
Simon, Mayo. [FUT]
Simon, S. J. pseud. of Simon
Jasha Skidelsky, Caryl Brahms.
CSF 29 SF1 478

Simon, Walter M. BAA 266
Simon, Wolfgang. BAA 192
Simonds, Bruce. IAC 219 SFS
109
Simoneau, Arthur G. (-1955) SF1
478
Simons, Roger. ES2 392
Simons, Walton. IAC 219
Simonson, Lee. COT 203
Simont, Marc. FFC 10, 136, 157
Simpson, Alan. BAA 266 IAC
219
Simpson, Donald. IAC 219
Simpson, Helen De Guerry (1897-
1940) CSF 179 ES2 392 SF1 478
Simpson, Howard. ES2 392 SFE
547 SF1 478
Simpson, Robert. CSF 179
Simpson, William. BAA 45 WGT
134 see also Thomas Blot
Sims, Alan. BAA 96 CSF 180
SF1 479
Sims, Denise Natalie (1940-) SF1
479 SF2 1076
Sims, George Robert (1847-1922)
CSF 180 SF1 479
Simson, Eric Andrew (1895-) ES2
392 WGT 134 see also Laurence
Kirk
Sinbad pseud. of Aylward Edward
Dingle. CSF 180 SF1 479
Sinclair, Andrew Annandale (1935-)
ES2 392 HFI 135 SF1 479
Sinclair, Bertha Muzzy Bower
(1874-1940) WGT 134 see also
B. M. Bower
Sinclair, Clive. IAC 219
Sinclair, David. SF1 479
Sinclair, May (1863?-1946) CSF
180 ES2 392 IAC 219 SF1 479
SOT 305, 368
Sinclair, Upton (1878-1968) AOW
84 BAA 66, 71, 95, 100-1, 106
CSF 180 ES2 392 EXT 4/1 8
FFR 165 IAC 219 IMS 216 RAH
236 SFE 547 SFN 35, 50, 63, 99-
100 SF1 479 SF2 1076 UKL
137 WFS 16 WIF 22
Sinderby, Donald pseud. of Donald
Ryder Stepphens. SF1 479
Singer, Ignatius. BAA 56
Singer, Isaac Bashevis (1904-)
ES2 392-3 FFC 8, 23, 51, 70, 151
FL4 1686-91 IAC 219 SFS 109
SF1 479 SF2 1076
Singer, Judith. HFI 135

Singer, June. KAU 15
Singer, Kurt Deutsch (1911-) ES2
393 SF1 479-80 SF2 1076-7
Singer, Norman (1925-) SF1 480
Singleton, Esther (1865-1930)
SF1 480
Sinyavsky, Andrey Donatovich
(1925-) SFE 547 8 SIH 83 WGT
134 see also Abram Tertz
Sio, Enric. FBK 48
Siodmak, Curt (1902-) ALW 121
AOW 110, 256, 398 CSF 180 ES2
393-4 EXT 5/1 3 FFR 165
FRN 92, 206-7, 255 HFI 135
ISW 100-1 KWS 109, 132, 134,
184, 215, 257, 307 LEX 573-4
MSM 30, 298 RHN 178 SFE
548 SF1 480 SF2 1077 SL2
579-82 STH 45 VES 186, 203,
207
Sirisena. VFS 22
Sirius pseud. of Edward Martyn.
CSF 180 SF1 480
Sirota, Mike. HFI 135
Sisario, Peter. RBY 241
Sisk, John P. IAC 219
Sisson, Marjorie. ES2 394 SF1
480
Sisson, Rosemary. FFC 136
Sissons, Thomas Michael Bes-
wick. ES2 394 IAC 219 SF1
480
Sitwell, (Sir) Francis Osbert
(1892-1969) CSF 180 POE 205-
6 SFE 548 SF1 480 SF2 1077
Sizemore, Julius C. BAA 132
ES2 394 SF1 480
Sizemore, Wilkie G. BAA 132
SF1 480
Skaife, Sydney Harold (1889-)
CSF 180 SF1 481
Skal, Dave. BAA 155 IAC 219
Skeels, Vernon H. (1918-) see
Oscar Rossiter
Skelly, Joe. WFS 163
Skelly, Kathleen. WFS 163
Skelton, Gladys (1889-1975) see
John Presland
Skelton, Red (1913-) SF1 481
Skene, Anthony. PST 185
Sketchley, Arthur pseud. of
George Rose. SF1 481
Skidelsky, Simon Jasha see S. J.
Simon
Skidmore, Joseph William. ES2
394 IMS 138 WSF 62

Skilton, David. BAA 266
Skinkle, Dorothy E. HFI 135 SF1 481
Skinner, B(urrhus) F(rederic) (1904-) AAL 193-203 ACC 165 AOW 256,348 BAA xviii,117, 266 CAT 78,138 CSC 128-9 CWN 17 ES2 394 EXT 6/2 40, 48,51 EXT 9/1 18 FAN 46,118, 174 FFR 165 FTF 109 [FUT] IAC 219 INT 49 ISW 174-5 KAU 163 NDA 51-64,78,82,117, 207 SFE 548 VES 128 POE 286 SL5 2392-5 SRB 10 SFH 151-2 UKL 126,138,141
Skinner, Claude M. (1916-) SF1 481
Skinner, Conrad Arthur (1889-) WGT 134 see also Michael Maurice
Skinner, June O'Grady (1922-) ES2 394 WGT 134 see also Rohan O'Grady
Skinner, Martyn. ES2 394
Skinner, Quentin. BAA 266
Skipper, Mervyn. SF1 481
Sklar, Robert. EXT 10/1 40
Skripkin, Pierre. SIH 85
Skunks, (Major). SF1 481
Skura, Meredith Anne. FLT 156-7
Sky, Kathleen (1943-) HFI 135 IAC 219 LEX 574-5 SFE 548 SL2 539-42
Slade, Michael. ALW 164
Sladek, John T. (1937-) AOW 257 BAA 144,162-3 BFP 450 BYS 109,298-9 ES2 394 FFR 165 HFI 135 IAC 219-20 LEX 575 MFW 215,290 RGS 159-60 SFB 132 SFE 549 SFS 109 SF1 481 SF2 1077 VES 237,242 WGT 134 see also Thom Demijohn
Sladen, Douglas B. (1856-1947) CSF 180 SF1 481
Slaten, Jeff. IAC 220
Slater, Ernest (-1942) WGT 134 see also Paul Gwynne
Slater, Henry J. BAA 121 ES2 394 HFI 135 SFE 549 SF1 481
Slater, Joseph. BAA 266-7
Slater, Kenneth F. (1917-) ES2 394 EXT 3/1 25 WIF 133
Slater, W.H. CSF 180 SF1 481
Slatoff, Walter J. NWO 209
Slaughter, Charles E. SF1 481

Slaughter, Frank G(ill) (1908-) ES2 395 FFR 165 SFN 23 SF1 481 SF2 1077
Slaughter, John Willis. BAA 267
Slavitt, David Rytman (1935-) SF2 1094 see also Henry Sutton
Sleath, Eleanor. CSF 180
Sleath, Frederick. CSF 180
Sleator, William Warner, III (1945-) AOW 331 FFC 82 HFI 135 SF1 481 SF2 1077-8
Slee, Richard. AOW 73 CSF 180 SFE 549 SF1 482
Sleigh, Barbara (1906-) ES2 395 FFC 27,136,172 SF1 482 SF2 1078
Sleigh, Bernard (1872-) CSF 180 SF1 482
Slesar, Henry (1927-) ALW 212 DTS 22 ES2 395 FFR 165 HFI 135 IAC 220 LEX 576 SFE 549 SFS 109 VES 177 WGT 134
Slidell, (Lt.). NWO 54
Slipher, E.C. EXT 5/2 46
Slipher, Vesto Melvin. SOT 9
Slivnik, Charlene. ES2 395
Sloan, John. STH 41
Sloane, T(erence) O'Conor (1851-1940) ALW 126,180,219 ASF 117-8 COT 6-7,13,15,20,40-1, 163,251,260,296 ES2 395 ETN 26 IAH 46 IMS 8,48,221 ISW 284 MSM 304 RFA 2,129 SFD 24-5,27 SFE 549-50 SIH 189 SOT 15-6,32,39,106-7,270,307 WFS 45,47,49,112-3 WSF 47, 62,114
Sloane, William Milligan (1906-74) AOW 257 BFP 451-2 CSF 181 ES2 395 EXT 5/1 3,10 EXT 8/1 5 HFI 136 IAC 220 MIH 15 SFE 550 SFN 39 SFS 109 SF1 482 SL4 1784-8 SOT 297 SRB 298 STH 245 WIF 19
Slobodkin, Louis (1903-75) AOW 331 ES2 395 FFC 47,52,82, 153 SF1 482 SF2 1078
Slocombe, George E. (1894-1963) CSF 181 SF1 482
Slocum, Joshua. CSC 121-2
Slonim, Marc. FAN 104-5
Slonimski, Antoni. SFB 101
Slosson, Preston. BAA 267
Slote, Alfred. FFC 151

Slotkin, Joseph (-1929) WGT 134
Slotkin, Richard. INT 118-22
Slowacki, Juliusz (1809-49) SF1 482
Slusser, George Edgar (1939-) AC2 76 ATA 37 RAH 258 RBY 241 RHN 178,197 SFE 550 SFW 357-68 SF2 1078 SL2 513-8 SL3 1050-6,1488-96 SL4 1848-53 SL5 2343-9 SRB 77-80 UKL 246
Small, Austin J. (-1929) CSF 181 ES2 395-6 SFE 550 SF1 482 WGT 134 see also Seamark
Small, Christopher. AOW 355 BAA 192 BYS 28,38 SFW 6
Smart, Charles Allen. BAA 110
Smeaton, William Henry Oliphant (1856-1914) CSF 181 SF1 482
Smidley, Anne. IMS 44 RFA 45
Smiley, Marjorie B. SF1 482
Smilie, Elton R. CSF 181 SF1 482
Smith, Agnes (1906-) FFC 9 SF1 482
Smith, Artegall pseud. of Philip Norton. SF1 482
Smith, Arthur Douglas Howden (1887-1945) HFI 136 SF1 483
Smith, Brenda. FFC 79
Smith, Cara. WFS 122
Smith, Cecil. SOT 372
Smith, Clark Ashton (1893-1961) ALW 143,184 AOW 94,108,401 BFP 453-5 BYS 177 COT 216 CSF 181 CWD 37,50,56 DTS 18 ES2 396-7 EXT 3/1 5,7,9 EXT 5/1 3 EXT 7/2 38-9 FBK 78,81,83,95 FFR 166 FL4 1692-7 HFI 136 IAC 220-1 IMS 2,16,18-20,23,30,68,72, 83,107,110-1,134,178,189 ISW 129-30 JVN 87-102,192 KAU 191 LEX 576-7 MIH 79,81,84 MSM 128 RFA 64 RGS 161-2 SFA 85 SFB 58,113 SFE 550 SFH 37,168 SFS 110 SFW 139-44 SF1 483 SOT 3,52,73,304-5,309-10,340-1,347,384 SRB 300 STH 86,142,249,251 VES 134,140,142,199,313,317 WAA 97,106,108 WIF 78,113,136, 162,178,229,256 WSF 298 WTS 21,30-9,41-3,46,48-9,51,53, 56,58,65,76,85,123-4,126,128, 132

Smith, Cordelia Titcomb (1902-) ES2 397 IAC 221 SF1 483 SF2 1078
Smith, Cordwainer pseud. of Paul Linebarger (1913-66) AAL 110 ALW 212,227 AOW 258, 288,295 ASF 147 BYS 179,304 COT 82 CSC 14,31,55,68,182 ETN 114 EXT 8/1 15 FFR 166 FHT 10 [FJT] HFI 136 IAC 221 INT 52 KAU 20, 75-7, 80, 105,185,204,215 LEX 577-9 LTN 27,76,99,228 MFW 98, 286 MIH 5 RGS 160-1 SFB 150-1 SFD 222-4,227,229,251,300, 316,322-3 SFE 550-1 SFH 169, 172-3,181 SFS 110 SFW 519-24 SF1 483 SL1 186-90 SL4 1555-9 SL5 2122-6 TSF 61-2, 240-1 VES 74,113,161 WFS 240,244,292 WSF 172-3,177, 388
Smith, Curtis C. SFW 91-2,100 VF1 44-63,265,283
Smith, Curtis L. BAA 267
Smith, D.R. IMS 97-8
Smith, Dale R. ES2 397
Smith, David C. HFI 136
Smith, David E. BAA 267
Smith, David Eugene. BAA 107
Smith, David MacLeod (1920-) SF2 990 see also David Mariner
Smith, Dodie pseud. of Dorothy Gladys Smith (1896-) ES2 397 FFC 125 SF1 483
Smith, Dona. WFS 216 see also Dona Campbell
Smith, Dorothy Gladys. SF2 1079 see also Dodie Smith
Smith, E.A. Wyke. CSF 181
Smith, E(dward) E(lmer) (1890-1965) ACC 60 ALW 10,126,132, 135,146-7,154,169,184,213 AOW 85-6,91,111,258,296,394 ASF 24,107-8,137,151,196,203, 217-20 BFP 456-8 BYS 179, 217-20,235,265 COT 70,75,78-80,82,128-9,153,178,184,188-9,292 CSC 28-9,47,49,52,168-9,172,175,231 CSF 181 EFP 3 ES2 397-8 EXT 3/1 28 EXT 5/1 3 FTF 70,90,119,172 HFI 136-7 IAC 221-2 IMS 16,24, 68,83,199,205,241 INT 45,120 ISW vii,6,12,34,211 LEX 579-82 MFW 39 MIH 22,24,36,43,

Smith, E. E. (cont.)
45, 120 MSF 122 MSM 78, 80,
82, 86, 170, 173, 175, 187 NWO
332 OWB 77-87 PST 130-1, 194,
207, 210, 217, 220-1, 227, 236, 240,
243, 245, 265, 268, 289, 292 RAH
138, 235 RFA vi, xx, 2, 14, 19, 24,
26, 28-31, 42, 46-8, 54, 59, 62-3,
66, 71-3, 75-6, 99-100, 104, 149-
53, 155, 160, 168, 176, 187 RGS
162-5, 222-3 RHN 21, 206 SFB
54-5, 60, 137 SFD 22-3, 25, 27-
8, 73-4, 96, 236, 289, 306, 311
SFE 551-2 SFH 38-41, 52, 59-
60, 68, 114, 126 SFN 19-20, 28,
47, 59-62, 64, 83, 104 SFS 110
SFW 125-30, 151-3, 226 SF1 483-
4 SF2 1079 SIH 48, 113, 150, 152,
160-2, 165, 169 SL3 1183-7 SL5
2091-5 SOT 9-28, 31, 35, 38-9,
72, 94, 102, 107, 254, 260-1, 275,
387 SRB 5, 98, 303, 309 TJB 4
TSF 64, 230 VES 70, 74-5, 87,
97-9, 105, 108, 111, 134, 140, 155,
161, 179, 201, 206, 241, 287, 307,
312-4 WAA 16, 120, 240 WFS
69, 85-6, 89, 291-2 WIF 100, 145,
160 WSF 45-6, 48, 58, 63, 67, 84,
91, 94-6, 101, 111, 126, 132-4,
143, 146, 154, 235, 248, 322, 329,
386 WTS 32 YTS 9
Smith, (Lady) Eleanor Furneaux
(1902-45) CSF 181 ES2 398
IAC 222 SF1 484
Smith, Elizabeth Oakes (1806-93)
SF1 484
Smith, Elizabeth Thomasina Meade
(1854-1914) WGT 134-5 see
also L. T. Meade
Smith, Emma. FFC 125
Smith, Ernest Bramah (1868-1942)
BAA 71 ES2 398-9 SRB 276
WGT 135 see also Ernest Bramah
Smith, Evelyn E. (1927-) ALW 212,
219 BAA 138 COT 196 ES2 399
FFR 166 HFI 137 IAC 222 IAH
105 ISW 129 KAU 79 MIH 24
SFE 552 SFS 110-1 SF1 484
Smith, Frederick Edwin (1872-
1930) EXT 5/1 8 WGT 135
Smith, Garret (1876?-1954) ALW
114 CSF 181 ES2 399 SFE 552
SF1 484 SOT 48-9 SRB 9 STH
147
Smith, George Charles Moore.
BAA 267

Smith, George H(enry) (1922-)
CAT 115 ES2 399 HFI 137 IAC
222 SFE 552-3 SFS 111 SF1
484, 584 SF2 1079 WGT 135
Smith, George Hudson. IAC 222
Smith, George Lawson. SF1 484
Smith, George O(liver) (1911-)
ALW 160 AOW 258-9 BFP 459-
60 BYS 237, 242 CSF 182 DTS
7, 25 ES2 399-400 ETN 68
EXT 5/1 3 EXT 7/2 40 HFI
137 IAC 222 IAH 71, 85, 93, 146
ISW 84, 284 LEX 582-3 MIH 20,
24 MSM 77-9, 85-6, 187 PST
185-6, 277, 292 RFA 110, 120,
126-7, 129-30, 134, 139 RGS 165-
6 SFE 553 SFN 28, 110 SFS 111
SF1 484 SF2 1079-81 SOT 416
SRB 305 VES 105, 113-4, 158,
163 WFS 174, 204, 216 WGT
135 WIF 90, 145, 162 WSF 103-
4, 120-1, 134-5, 148, 154, 176, 386
see also Wesley Long
Smith, Godfrey. AC2 76
Smith, Goldwin. BAA 267
Smith, Guy Newman (1939-) SF1
484
Smith, (Mrs.) H. Scott. CSF 182
Smith, Harrison. SFN 31
Smith, Harry Allen (1907-76) BAA
128 ES2 400 HFI 137 IAC 222
SFE 553 SF1 484-5 SF2 1081
Smith, Henry Nash. NWO 216,
227 RBY 42, 53
Smith, Hoke. WFS 122
Smith, Irene. EXT 10/1 41
Smith, (Mrs.) J. Gregory (1818-
1905) CSF 182 SF1 485
Smith, James. CSF 182 SF1 485
Smith, Jeannie. WFS 291
Smith, Jeffrey D. [FJT]
Smith, John Maynard. BAA 267
Smith, Johnston. CSF 182
Smith, Joseph (1805-44) ISW 118
SFH 57
Smith, Joseph G. EXT 6/2 48
Smith, Joseph H. FLT 152, 157
Smith, Junius B. WTS 120
Smith, Keith. ES2 400 SF1 584
Smith, L. H. (1916-) ES2 400
WGT 135 see also Speedy
Williams
Smith, Langdon. ES2 400
Smith, Lawrence. FFC 17
Smith, Lewis Conrad, Jr. BAA
288

Smith, Louis C. IMS 67-8, 94, 107
Smith, Louisa A. FL2 765-7, 891-3 FL3 1037-9, 1230-3 FL5 2132-5
Smith, Lowell Kent. IAC 222
Smith, Maggie. FFC 64
Smith, Malcolm. ES2 400 SRB 37 VES 111, 291, 338-40 WSF 115
Smith, Marcus. BAA 267
Smith, Mark. VFS 29-30
Smith, Martin Cruz (1942-) HFI 138 SF1 485 SF2 1081
Smith, Mary J. Deer. WGT 135
Smith, Montague. SF1 485
Smith, Nancy. EXT 10/1 26
Smith, Ormond G. (1860-1933) WGT 135
Smith, Paul Jordan (1885-1971) CSF 182 SF1 485
Smith, Perry Michael (1937-) HFI 138 SF1 485
Smith, Philip E., II. RAH 137-71 RHN 58 UKL 77-96
Smith, Philip H. IAC 222 SFS 89, 111
Smith, R. A. ACE 13, 75 AC2 11, 73 [FUT] SOT 387
Smith, R. E. F. BAA 267
Smith, Reginald. SF1 485
Smith, Richard R. FFC 83 WGT 135
Smith, Ritchie. IAC 222
Smith, Robert Eugene (1920-) ISW 100-1 SF1 485
Smith, Ron(ald Loran) (1936-) ES2 400 IAC 222 SFS 111 WGT 135
Smith, Scott. EXT 10/1 18
Smith, Surrey. ES2 400 SF1 485
Smith, Susy (1911-) ES2 400
Smith, Sydney. EXT 9/2 48
Smith, Tevis Clyde. SF1 485
Smith, Thorne (1892-1934) CSF 182 ES2 400-1 EXT 8/1 5 FBK 119 FL3 1111-5 FL4 1848-50, 1958-62, 1983-5 ISW 140, 255 MSM 128 OWB 70-1, 74 SF1 485 WIF 81, 149, 162, 238 WSF 295 WTS 130
Smith, Titus Keiper (1859-) BAA 54 CSF 182 SF1 485
Smith, W. T. F. BAA 70
Smith, Walter A. BAA 288

Smith, Walter James (1917-) SF1 485 SF2 1081
Smith, Wayland. CSF 182 ES2 401 SFE 553 SF1 486
Smitter, Wessel H. IAC 222
Smith, Wilbur Addison (1933-) HFI 138 SF1 486 SF2 1081
Smith, William Augustus. SF1 486
Smithson, Annie Mary Patricia (1883-) SF1 486
Smollett, Tobias (1721-77) EXT 9/2 29 SF1 486 WTS 17
Smyer, Richard I. BAA 267
Smyth, Alfred. SF1 486
Smyth, Clifford (1866-1943) CSF 182 EXT 1/1 18 MFW 131 SF1 486
Smyth, H. D. MSM 225
Smyth, Henry D. RFA 138
Smyth, Robin. IAC 222
Smyth, W. H. RBY 98
Smythe, Alfred. CSF 182
Smythe, R. John. SF1 486
Snaith, John Collins (1876-1936) BAA 87 CSF 182 SF1 486
Snedden, David. BAA 89
Snell, Bruno. BAA 267
Snell, Edmund (1889-) AOW 111 CSF 182-3 ES2 401 SFE 553 SF1 486
Snell, George. NWO 4, 8, 168, 209
Snell, Roy Judson (1878-) SF1 486 STH 172-3, 176
Sneve, Virginia Driving Hawk (1933-) SF1 486 SF2 1081-2
Sniffen. RFA 143
Snilloc. CSF 183
Snow, C(harles) P(ercy) (1905-) ALW 52, 88 AOW xviii, 41, 345 BYS 256 CAT 132-3 COT 34 CSF 183 EXT 6/1 3, 7, 17 EXT 10/1 9 EXT 10/2 92 FAN 6 INT 13 MIH 10, 13, 118 MSM x RAH 236 SF1 486 SF2 1082 STF 22 WSF 155, 351
Snow, Edward Rowe (1902-) ES2 401
Snow, Helen Foster (1907-) see Nym Wales
Snow, Jack (1907-) CSF 183 ES2 401 SF1 486 WTS 131
Snow, Thomas Collins. BAA 267
Snyder, Cecil, III. AAL 47 HFI 138 SFE 553 SF1 486

Snyder, Eugene Vincent (1943-)
BAA 156 SFE 553 SF1 486
SF2 1082
Snyder, Gary. IAC 222
Snyder, Guy Eugene, Jr. (1951-)
HFI 138 SFE 553 SF1 486 SF2
1082
Snyder, John. BAA 66
Snyder, (Mrs.) R. J. ISW 223
Snyder, Zilpha Keatley (1927-)
FFC 34, 44, 71 SF1 486-7, 584
SF2 1082-3
Snyman, J. P. L. EXT 8/2 63
Soal, Samuel George. ES2 401
Soane, George. CSF 183
Sobel, Robert (1931-) SF1 487
SF2 1083 VES 121
Socrates. EXT 4/1 3 IAH 49
KAU 24 SFN 47 VFS 205 WIF
29, 97 WTS 12
Soddy, Frederick. FTF 59 IAC
222 POE 217-8
Soeffner, Hans-Georg. BAA 192
Sofsky, Wolfgang. BAA 192
Softly, Edgar pseud. of H. P.
Lovecraft. EXT 3/1 10
Sohl, Gerald Allan (1913-) BFP
461-2 SF2 1083 WGT 135-6
see also Jerry Sohl
Sohl, Jerry pseud. of Gerald
Allan Sohl. ALW 212 ES2 401-
2 HFI 138 IAC 222 ISW 96, 105-
7 KAU 33, 184 LEX 583 SFE
556 SF1 487
Sohn, David A. (1929-) SF1 487
SF2 1083
Soikin, P. P. SIH 194
Sokol, Bill. FFC 56, 159
Solataroff, Theodore. ETN 121
Solberg, Victor. BAA 288
Solbert, Ronni. FFC 11-2, 14, 51,
55, 122, 134, 148
Soler, Antonio Robles (1897-)
WGT 136 see also Antoniorrobles,
Antonio Robles
Soleri, Paolo. BAA 267 [FUT]
KAU 116
Solo, Gabriello. SF1 487
Sologub, Feodor (1863-1927) FBK
41-2
Solokov, Andrei. COT 57 SFB
123
Soloman, Maynard. BAA 267
Solonevich. VES 166
Soloviev, Mikhail (1908-) SF1 487
Solovyev, Vladimir A. MSF 251

Solt, Mary Ellen. IAC 222
Solzhenitsyn, Alexander. LTN
150, 214-7, 221, 232 SIH 89, 93
WFS 66
Sombart, Werner. MSF 73
Somer, John. AOW 348 SRB 83
Somerlott, Robert. ES2 402 SF1
584
Somerville, Mary. OWB 23
Sommer, Robert. BAA 268
Sommerfeld, Adolf (1870-) SF1
487
Sommerville, Frankfort pseud. of
A. M. Sommerville Story. CSF
183
Sonderlund, Nils O. TSP 191
Sonnemann, William K. AAL 59
ES2 402 IAC 222 VES 104
Sontag, Susan. BYS 136-7 CAT
54 IAC 222 JGB 4, 53 KAU 198
OMN 18, 37, 74 STF 8
Soper, Eileen. FFC 131
Sophocles. AOW 15 CAT 55 IAH
143 MSM 25 SFH 184
Sorel, Edward (1929-) ES2 402
FFC 27 SFE 557
Sorel, Georges. BAA 268 POE
153, 163
Sorensen, Theodore. RHN 117
Sorenson, Villy (1929-) ES2 402
SF1 487
Sorenson, M. Susan. BAA 268
Sorkin, Sophie. ES2 402 IAC
120
Sorley, Charles. POE 226
Sorokin, Pitirim. COT 223 POE
264
Soule, Gardner Bosworth (1913-)
ES2 402
Soule, George Henry (1887-1970)
ES2 402 POE 312
Soulie, George. CSF 183, 268
Soutar, Andrew (1879-1941) SF1
487
Southall, Ivan Francis (1921-)
ES2 402 SF1 487 SF2 1084
Southern, Terry. EXT 10/2 108
Southesk, James Carnegie (1827-
1905) CSF 183 SF1 487
Southey, Robert. POE 41-2, 58
SRB 22
Southwell, Samuel Beall (1922-)
ES2 402 HFI 138 SF1 487
Southwick, E. B. BAA 54
Southwold, Stephen (1887-1964)
BAA 96, 101 ES2 402-3 SFE

Southwold, Stephen (cont.)
557 WGT 136 see also Neil Bell, S. H. Lambert, Paul Martens, Miles
Southworth, (Mrs.) Eden. CSF 183
Southworth, Emma Dorothy Eliza Nevitt (1819-99) CSF 183 ES2 403 WGT 136
Souto, Marcial. IAC 222
Souvestre, Emile. MSF 138 POE 127-8
Souza, Steven Michael (1953-) HFI 138 SFE 557 SF1 488 SF2 1084
Sowden, Lewis (1903?-74) ES2 403 SFE 557 SF1 488 SF2 1084
Spacks, Patricia Meyer. EXT 10/1 31, 37, 41 SOI 150-9
Spalding, Helen. ES2 403 SF1 488
Spalten, Rona. IAC 222
Spanfeller, James. FFC 4
Spangenberg, Kurt. BAA 288
Spann, Sylvia. SRB 465
Spanner, Edward Frank (1888-) CSF 183 SFE 564 SF1 488
Spanuth, Jurgen. ES2 403
Spark, Muriel Sarah (1918-) ES2 403 FRN 23 IAC 222 SFS 111 SFW 7 SF1 488 SOI 158 VES 262
Sparks, David R. WIF 203
Sparks, Edwin E. BAA 268
Sparks, Eliza Kay. FL1 366-73 FL2 566-70 FL3 1280-5
Spassky, Boris. ETN 133
Spaulding, Wayland. BAA 72
Speaight, Robert William (1904-76) SF1 488 SF2 1084
Speaker, David M. VES 205
Spearing, Judith. FFC 34
Spearman, F. H. IAC 223
Spears, John Randolph (1850-1936?) ES2 403 SF1 488
Spears, Monroe K. EXT 9/2 48
Spector, Robert Donald (1922-) ES2 403 SF1 488 SF2 1084-5
Spectorsky, Auguste Comte (1910-72) CSF 183 ES2 403 SF1 488
Speed, Donald. ES2 403 SF1 488
Speer, Albert. COT 35, 137 FTF 127-8 [FUT]
Speer, Diane P. RAH 258
Speer, Jack. IAH 33-4 IMS 26, 69-70, 114, 122, 127-8, 131, 139, 149, 153, 155-7, 161-2, 168, 177, 179, 184, 186-8, 190-1, 200, 204, 209, 213-4, 227, 232-4, 249 RFA 133
Speer, Laura Belle (1883-) BAA 108 SF1 488
Speight, Ernest Edwin. CSF 183 SF1 488
Speight, Thomas Wilkinson (1830-1915) CSF 183 SF1 489
Speiss, Christian H. CSF 183
Speller, Jane. CSF 183 SF1 489
Speller, Robert. CSF 183 SF1 489
Speman, Hans. EXT 2/2 34
Spence. EXT 9/2 62
Spence, Geraldine. FFC 76
Spence, James Lewis (1874-1955) BAA 192 CSF 183 ES2 403 SF1 489
Spence, Thomas. BAA 13-7 MSF 122
Spencer, Charles. STH 151
Spencer, D. A. CSF 183 SF1 489
Spencer, G. F. ES2 403 SFE 564 SF1 489
Spencer, Herbert (1820-1903) MSF 223, 225, 229 POE 172 SFH 138 TJB 24
Spencer, John. BAA 163 SFE 564
Spencer, Kathleen L. FL1 275-81 FL2 966-9 SL1 468-73 SL2 802-6 SL5 2442-6, 246 9-73
Spencer, Leonard G. (house name) SFE 564 WGT 136 see also Randall Garrett, Robert Silverberg
Spencer, Paul. FL1 374-6 FL3 1060-4, 1262-7, 1496-500 FL4 1581-5 IAC 223 SFW 123
Spencer, Robin Edgerton (1896-1956) CSF 184 SF1 489
Spencer, Scott. SF1 489
Spencer, William. IAC 223 SFS 111 WGT 136
Spengler, Oswald (1880-1936) CAT 101 COT 87, 222-3, 225-6, 240 IAH 66 KAU 90, 129 MFW 170 MSF 29, 279 POE 221-2, 238-9, 248 SFB 137 SFD 273 SFH 54-5, 59-60 TJB 23, 26, 28, 59-60
Spenser, Edmund. FBK 123 SFD 309 SFH 44, 49 WIF 34 WSF 292
Sperlich, Hans G. BAA 173

Sperry, Henry Treat. TSP 23, 81,
134 see also Paul Howard
Sperry, Jane E. pseud. of Jane
Eisenstat (1920-) SF1 489
Spicer, Dorothy Gladys. ES2
403-4
Spicer, Paul R. SF1 489
Spickler, Charles Abraham (1880-)
WGT 136 see also Brogan the
Scribe
Spiegel, Charles A. SF1 489
Spiegelman, Joseph Marvin (1926-)
SF1 489
Spielberg, Steven. HFI 138 KAU
121, 152, 228 KWS 121, 172 OMN
12, 14, 49, 69, 94, 221 YTS 21
Spier, Laura B. CSF 144
Spiers, Hetty. CSF 164 SF1 489
Spike, Paul (1947-) SF1 489
Spilka, Arnold. FFC 7
Spillane, Frank Morrison (1918-)
WGT 136 see also Mickey
Spillane
Spillane, Mickey pseud. of Frank
Morrison Spillane. IAH 15, 21-
2 ISW 121, 213, 235, 258 MSM
98, 275 SFN 15, 115 THM 8
WAA 49, 184 WFS 200 WIF 151,
178, 241
Spiller, (Dr.). EXT 10/2 98
Spina, Giorgio. BAA 192
Spinoza, Baruch (1632-77) SFB
101
Spinrad, Norman (1940-) AAL 87,
176-7 ALW 212, 222, 235 AOW
259, 287, 299, 394 BAA 144, 150,
165 BFP 463-4 BYS 247, 298,
321 COT 99, 136-7, 274 CSC 19,
54-70, 94-5 DMK 49-56 DTS
37, 40, 48, 52 ES2 404 ETN 53,
72, 142 FFR 167 HFI 138-9
IAC 223 INT 15 JVN 13-22, 240
LEX 584 LTN 19, 86, 251, 262
MIH 146 NDA 215 OSR 181-5,
356 RGS 166 SFB 117 SFD 63,
263, 323 SFE 565 SFH 92-3
SFS 111 SFW 129 SF1 489 SF2
1085 SIH 54 SL1 265-71 SL3
1062-7 SRB 355, 508-9 STH 45
TSF 241 VES 116, 237, 242-3,
280 WAA 232 WSF 233, 235,
252
Spitteler, Carl (1845-1924) SF1
489
Spitz, David. BAA 268

Spitz, Jacques (1896-1963) CSF
184 SF1 490 SL4 1588-91
Spivak, Lawrence E. ALW 214-
5 SOT 364 STH 264 WIF 113
Spivey, Thomas Sawyer (1856-
1938) SF1 490
Spoerer, George. WFS 165-6,
171, 177, 180, 183, 205
Spofford, Harriet P. CSF 184
IAC 223
Spohr, Carl W. COT 116, 124
Sporn, Michael. FFC 20
Spotswood, Christopher. SF1 490
Spotswood, Claire Myers. CSF
184 SF1 490
Spotswood, Dillon Jordan. WGT
136 see also Nuverbis
Sprague, Carter. COT 49
Sprat, Thomas. CAT 106
Sprenger, William. WTS 4-7, 9,
52, 56, 63-6, 68, 80, 112
Spriel, Stephane. BAA 268
Sprigg, Christopher St. John
(1907-37) CSF 184 ES2 404 SF1
490 see also Christopher Caud-
well
Sprigg, T. Stanhope. IMS 252
SOT 125
Spring, Henry Powell. BAA 84
Spring, Summer. BAA 69
Springer, H. W. (1939-) LEX
584-5
Springer, Marilyn Harris (1931-)
SF2 931 see also Marilyn Harris
Springer, Nancy. HFI 139 SRB
277
Springer, Norman. CSF 184 SF1
490
Springer, Sherwood. IAC 223
LEX 585 SFS 111 SOT 394
Sprissler, Alfred. CSF 130 STH
148
Sprout, Monique. NWO 51
Spruill, Steven G. (1946-) HFI 139
SFE 565
Spunda, Franz. FBK 144
Spurrell, Herbert George Flaxman
(1877-1918) SF1 490
Square, A. pseud. of Edwin A.
Abbott. CSF 184 EXT 3/1 29
PST 70-1, 234, 239, 263 SFN 82
Squier, Emma Lindsay (1892-)
ES2 404
Squire, (Sir) John Collins (1884-
1958) CSF 14, 184 ES2 404 SF1

Squire, (Sir) John Collins (cont.)
490 SOT 152 VES 121-3 WGT
136
Squires, John D. FL1 26-8 FL5
2192-6
Squires, Patricia pseud of Patricia
Sylvia Ball. SF1 490
Squires, Roy A. IMS 67-8, 123,
138, 177, 182
Stableford, Brian M. (1948-) AOW
260 BAA 160 BFP 465-6 FL1
48-53, 69-70, 74-80, 84-6, 242-7,
287-8, 319-23, 328-30, 360-5, 377-
9, 425-7, 475-7 FL2 511-7, 535-
8, 575-80, 593-604, 658-60, 666-
74, 687-9, 718-9, 730-1, 760-4,
805-7, 844-7, 859-60, 887-90,
916-25, 945-7, 983-7 FL3 1047-
51, 1065-70, 1089-91, 1096-8,
1146-8, 1158-9, 1179-87, 1212-15,
1276-9, 1313-6, 1320-4, 1332-4,
1347-9, 1355-7, 1420-2 FL3
1452-6, 1465-7, 1544-6 FL4
1597-9, 1692-7, 1798-800, 1859-
62, 1884-90, 1898-900, 1918-21,
1930-2, 1986-8, 1992-4, 2005-12,
2033-5, 2046-8, 2059-62 FL5
2084-6, 2102-6, 2115-7, 2153-5,
2162-4, 2180-4, 2283-98, 2331-68,
2501-16 HFI 139 IAC 224 LEX
585-6 RGS 166-7, 223 RSG 47,
53-4, 92 SFE 565-6 SFW 119-
23, 139-49, 179-84, 203-8, 277-
82, 337-43, 351-6, 419-24, 525
SF1 490 SF2 1085 SL1 11-5, 67-
71, 149-52, 228-32, 238-41, 272-
6, 349-53, 358-62, 392-5, 433-42,
480-7 SL2 524-8, 629-33, 717-
20, 761-5, 869-72, 936-9, 945-9,
972-6, 1000-3 SL3 1045-9, 1126-
9, 1178-87, 1270-3, 1294-8, 1459-
62, 1526-30 SL4 1641-4, 1674-7,
1702-4, 1735-8, 1780-3, 1794-8,
1832-6, 1866-70, 1884-7, 1994-8,
2008-18 SL5 2065-9, 2075-8,
2091-5, 2207-10, 2218-22, 2255-
9, 2269-82, 2293-7, 2329-33, 2339-
42, 2474-81 SL5 2497-500, 2525-
8 SRB 77 VES 74-5, 200
Stableford, Vivien. FL1 164-5,
358-9, 423-4, 486-8 FL2 518-9,
684-6, 861-2 FL3 1188-90, 1378-
9 FL5 2087-9, 2217-9
Stables, William Gordon (1840-
1910) CSF 184 SFE 566 SF1 490

Stachurski, Marian. FBK 149
Stacpoole, Henry De Vere (1863? -
1951) CSF 184 SFE 566 SF1
491
Stacton, David Derek (1925-68)
SF1 491 SF2 1085
Stacy, Enid. POE 192-3
Stacy, Terry pseud. of Terrea
Lea. SF1 491
Stadler, John. IAC 224 SF1 491
Stadler, U. EFP 7
Stafford, B. M. BAA 268
Stafford, Terry. SF1 491
Stafford, Tom. ALW 232
Stafford, William. IAC 224
Stagg, John. SIH 28
Stahl, Benjamin (1910-) FFC 34
SF1 491 SF2 1085-6
Stahlmann, J. L. CSF 77
Stair, Bill. SF1 491
Stairs, Gordon. CSF 184
Stakhanov. EXT 7/2 36
Staley, M. L. RFA 5
Stalin, Joseph V. (1879-1953) ASF
277-9, 283, 286-7, 289 COT 123,
140 EXT 2/2 40 EXT 9/2 56
EXT 10/2 73, 77, 92-3 FAN 4,
147 FTF 72, 200 ISW 199 LTN
213-4, 219, 263 MSF 9, 119, 243,
253, 264-5, 267 SFB 90, 124
SFH 138-9 STH 48 VFS 254
WFS 68, 98-9, 120, 125
Stall, Michael. IAC 224
Stallard, (Mrs.) Arthur. CSF
184 SF1 491
Stallmach, Josef. BAA 268
Stamm, Russell. CSF 184 SF1
491
Stammhammer, Josef. BAA 192
Stammler, Heinrich A. BAA 268
Stammler, Rudolf. BAA 268
Stamp, Roger see R. Gresham
Mingston
Stamper, Joseph. CSF 184 SF1
491
Stanbury, C. M. HFI 139
Stancic, Miljenko. IAC 224
Standen, Anthony. ES2 404
Stander, Lionel. TSP 223
Standish, Burt L. STH 163 see
also Emerson Bell, Gilbert
Patten
Standish, Robert pseud. of Digby
George Gerahty. ES2 404 IAC
224 SFS 111

Stanford, John Keith (1892-1971) BAA 123 CSF 184 SFE 566 SF1 491 SF2 1086

Stangland, A. G. IAC 224

Staniland, Meaburn. BAA 115 ES2 404 SF1 491

Stanley, Alfred Mortimer (1888-) BAA 117-8 ES2 404 SFE 566 SF1 491

Stanley, Bennett see Stanley Bennett Hough

Stanley, Diana. FFC 93

Stanley, Dorothy (-1926) SF1 491

Stanley, George. IAC 224

Stanley, Henry Morton (1841-1904) TSO 40

Stanley, John. HFI 139

Stanley, Manfred. BAA 268

Stanley, Norman F. IMS 247

Stanley, Susan. LTN 269

Stanley, William Ford (1829-1909) BAA 66-7 CSF 185 POE 206-7 SFE 566 SF1 491

Stanton, Carol. WFS 213 see also Carol Pohl

Stanton, Edward pseud. of Edward Stanton Huntington. CSF 185 SF1 491

Stanton, Karen. WFS 213-4, 216, 278-82

Stanton, Ken. SF1 491

Stanton, L. Jerome. IAC 224 WFS 174, 203, 205, 213

Stanton, Lee. SIH 102

Stanton, Paul. ES2 404 HFI 139 SFE 566

Stanton, Will. IAC 224 SFE 566-7 SFS 111

Stanyukovich, Kirill. IAC 224

Stanzel, Frank K. BAA 268

Stapledon, (William) Olaf (1886-1950) ACC 36, 40-1, 62, 70, 161, 209 ACE 11-2, 15-8, 28-9, 37, 42, 46, 53, 61 AC2 9-10, 13-6, 26-7, 35, 40, 44, 51, 59 ALW 143-4, 169 AOW 85, 88, 96, 111-3, 354 ASF 308 ATA 51 BAA 96, 99, 107, 111, 113 BFP 467-8 BYS 91, 117, 200-8, 260, 313 CAT 83, 100-1, 138 COT 23, 149, 291 CSC 14, 27-8, 31, 67, 141, 224 CSF 185 CYR 8 ES2 404-5 EXT 1/2 24-5, 32, 34 EXT 3/1 28 EXT 4/2 25 EXT 5/1 3, 8, 15-6 EXT 6/2 42, 51 EXT 7/2 35, 41 EXT 8/1 5 EXT 9/1 18, 23 EXT 10/2 73, 100 FAN 12, 140-4 FFR 168 FHT 21 FTF 75, 138-40, 189-90 HFI 139-40 HID 187 IAC 224 IAH 123 IMS 99, 101 INT 52 ISW 151, 199, 245 JVN 88, 121, 188 KAU 88, 192-3, 204, 221-3 LEX 587-8 LTN 106, 205 MFW 5, 19, 23, 54, 94, 112, 167, 249, 253 MSF 23, 27-8, 60, 78, 121-2, 138, 201-2, 242 MSM 29, 58, 79, 86, 132, 178, 200-1, 233-4, 305 NDA 214 NWO 17, 44, 62, 102, 163 OWB 13 POE 236-7 PST 10, 120, 122, 138-46, 148, 168-72, 177, 187, 194, 197-8, 201, 209, 212-5, 217, 219, 221, 223, 225, 230, 232, 234, 237, 246, 249, 253, 255, 258-9, 265-6, 272, 275, 277-8, 280-2, 285-6, 288-9, 293, 296, 301, 305-6, 308, 311-2, 314-5, 317-8, 320 RFA 81, 165 RGS 167-70, 224 RHN 27, 42 RSG 9, 59 SFB 58, 64, 89, 148 SFD 57, 290, 306 SFE 567-8 SFH 32-3, 43-6, 51, 53, 55, 60, 62, 65, 70, 87, 104, 127, 142, 144-5, 156, 183, 189, 191, 212-6, 220 SFN 32, 40, 65-6 SFS 111-2 SFW 91-100, 251 SF1 491-2 SF2 1086 SIH 118-21, 183 SL3 1140-3 SL4 1583-7 SL5 2085-90, 2150-5 SOI 19 SOT 19, 131, 142-3, 150, 202, 214, 259, 275, 281, 297, 382, 384, 395-6, 423 SRB 12, 15, 295, 299 STF 19-21, 24, 62-7 TJB 22 TSF 54, 238 TSO 9, 29, 32-5 VES 83, 116, 120, 131, 144, 193, 195, 197, 199, 201-2, 208, 213, 220, 225, 236, 253-4, 259, 261, 270 VFS 208 VF1 44-63, 265 WAA 129, 168-9 WIF 87, 212, 217, 232 WSF 87, 129, 336, 386

Stapp, Arthur Donald (1906-72) ES2 405 SF1 492 SF2 1086

Stapp, Robert. BAA 165 SF1 492

Star, Maria. CSF 185

Stark, Ben. SF1 492

Stark, Delbert Raymond (1919-) SF1 492

Stark, Harriet. AOW 42, 73 SFE 568 SF1 492

Stark, J. Ben. RFA vii

Stark, Raymond. BAA 130 ES2 405 SFE 568

Starkey, Richard see Ringo Starr

Starr, Bill. HFI 140 RGS 170

Starr, Kevin. BAA 192

Starr, Nathan Comfort. ES2 405
Starr, Ringo pseud. of Richard
  Starkey. TDI 51
Starr, Roland. HFI 140 SFE 568
Starrett, (Charles) Vincent (1886-
  1974) CSF 185 ES2 405 EXT
  3/1 11 FBK 76 IAC 224 SFS
  112 SF1 492 TSP 145 WTS 20,
  36
Starzl, Raymond F. (1899-) ES2
  405 IAC 224 IMS 8 LEX 588-
  9 OWB 79, 84 SFE 571 SFS 112
  SOT 238 STH 141 VES 141
Stasheff, Christopher. AOW 260
  HFI 140 RGS 170-1 SFE 571
  SF1 492
Stasio, Enzo. BAA 192
Staton, Mary. HFI 140
Statten, Vargo pseud. of John
  Russell Fearn. ALW 141 VES
  179
Stauffer, Donald Alfred (1902-52)
  MSF 31 SF1 492
Stauffer, Mack (1857-1941) BAA
  81 CSF 185 SF1 492
Stauffer, Ruth Matilda (1885-)
  ES2 405
Staughton, Simon. ES2 405-6
  SF1 492
Stayton, Frank. CSF 185
Stead, Christina Ellen (1902-)
  CSF 185 ES2 406 SF1 492 SF2
  1086
Stead, Francis Herbert (1857-
  1928) CSF 185 SF1 492
Stead, Robert James Campbell
  (1880-1959) SF1 492
Stead, William Thomas. BAA 52
  EXT 7/1 14 FAN 12, 17, 66, 182
Stearns, Albert. CSF 185 SF1
  492
Stearns, Charles A. IAC 225
  SFS 112
Stearns, Edgar Franklin (1879-)
  EXT 1/1 10 WGT 136 see also
  Edgar Franklin
Stearns, Pamela. FFC 179
Stebbing, William. BAA 61 CSF
  185 SF1 492
Steber, A. R. (house name) SFE
  571 see also Ray Palmer, Rog
  Phillips
Steberl, Sharon. RZY 10-1, 15
Stecher, Lew J. , Jr. pseud. of
  Joseph Wesley. IAC 225 SFS
  112 VES 190 WFS 238-9

Steeger, Harry. TSP 3-5, 54, 58,
  226 WFS 104, 108-11, 113, 125-
  6, 133
Steegmuller, Francis (1906-) SF2
  1086 see also Byron Steel
Steel, Byron pseud. of Francis
  Steegmuller. SF1 493
Steel, Flora Annie (1847-1929)
  SF1 493
Steel, Mark. SF1 493
Steele, Alex. SF1 493
Steele, Curtis pseud. of Emile
  Tepperman. SF1 493
Steele, Mary Quintard Govan
  (1922-) ES2 406 FFC 9, 23, 44,
  71, 169 SF1 493 SF2 1087 WGT
  137 see also Wilson Gage
Steele, Morris J. (house name)
  VES 102 WGT 137 see also
  Berkeley Livingston, Raymond
  A. Palmer
Steele, Richard. STF 33
Steele, Robert D. SF1 493
Steele, Wilbur Daniel (1886-1970)
  CSF 185 ES2 406
Steele, William O. FFC 151-2
Steelnib, Jocundus. CSF 185
Steeman, T. MFW 250
Steen, Marguerite (1894-1975)
  ES2 406 SF1 493
Steere, C. A. BAA 73
Steeves, Harrison Ross (1881-)
  SF1 493
Stefanile, Felix. EXT 3/1 9
Steffanson, Con (house name)
  SF1 493 see also Ron Goulart,
  Carson Bingham
Stefula, Dorothea. FFC 83
Stegman, Carl. BAA 192
Stegmeyer, Frank. BAA 268
Steig, William. FFC 125 MSM 92
Steiger, Andrew Jacob (1900-)
  ES2 406 SFE 571 SF1 493 SF2
  1087
Steiger, Brad pseud. of Eugene
  E. Olson (1936-) ES2 406 IAC
  225 SF1 493
Stein, A. M. CSF 185
Stein, Gertrude. ETN 82 MSM
  92
Stein, Irwin. STH 44
Stein, Modest. RFA 111
Stein, R. BAA 260
Stein, Robert. BAA 268
Stein, Ruth M. EXT 10/1 24, 41

Steinbeck, John (1902-68) AOW 84
ES2 406 FFR 169 IAC 225 ISW
127 MFW 14 MSM 128, 281
SFN 20, 99 SFS 112 SF1 493
SF2 1087 TBC 6 WIF 151 WTS
57
Steinberg, Saul. IAC 225
Steinberg, Werner (1913-) LEX
590
Steinbrunner, Peter Christian
(1933-) SF1 493 SF2 1087
Steiner, George. AAL 183, 187-8
SFD 45
Steiner, Gerhard. BAA 192
Steiner, Gerolf (1908-) SF2 1092
WGT 137 see also Harold
Stumpke
Steiner, Manfred. LTN 177-8
Steiner, Rudolf. EXT 9/2 62
Steinhauer, H. BAA 268
Steinhoff, William R. BAA 192
Steininger, Alexander. BAA 268
Steinmuller, Karlheinz (1950-)
LEX 590
Steintrager, James. BAA 268
Stemo, L. Johanne. BAA 269
Stenbock, Stanislaus (1860-95)
CSF 186 SF1 494
Stendhal pseud. of Henri Beyle.
CAT 46 MSF 20
Stenhouse, David. ES2 406
Stent, Gunther Siegmund. BAA
192
Stephan, Peter. SF1 494
Stephen, (Sir) Leslie. POE 205
Stephens, Charles. VES 205
Stephens, Daniel Owen (1893-
1937) CSF 186 SF1 494
Stephens, Frances. IAC 225
Stephens, Henrietta Henkle. SF2
834-5 see also Henrietta Buck-
master
Stephens, James (1882-1950) CSF
186 ES2 407 FL1 324-7 IAC
225 MSM 97 SF1 494 WIF 81
Stephens, John. IAC 225
Stephens, Kevin. IAC 225
Stephens, Lawrence Sterne see
Stephen Lawrence
Stephens, Rosemary. IAC 225
Stephenson, Andrew M. (1946-)
IAC 225 LEX 590 SFE 571, 573
Stephenson, George. FTF 35
MSF 194
Steppenwolf. CWN 13

Stepphens, Donald Ryder (1898-)
see Donald Sinderby
Steranko, James (1938-) SFE 573
Sterba, Monica. IAC 225
Sterland, Carl pseud. of Roy
Newquist. SF1 494
Sterling, Barry pseud. of Robert
Lipton. SF1 494
Sterling, Brett (house name) IAH
12 SFE 573 SF1 494 WGT 137
WIF 153 see also Ray Bradbury,
Edmond Hamilton, Joseph
Samachson
Sterling, George. WTS 9
Sterling, John (1806-44) CSF 186
SF1 494
Sterling, Kenneth. EXT 3/1 3, 7
IMS 34, 213, 219, 244 NWO 262
WIF 203
Sterling, (Michael) Bruce (1954-)
HFI 140 IAC 225 LEX 590-1
Sterling, Steward. TSP 156
Sterling, Sybil Stewart. BAA 288
Stern, Daniel (1928-) SF1 494
SF2 1087
Stern, David, III (1909-) CSF 186
SF1 494
Stern, Donnel. IAC 225
Stern, Gladys Bronwyn (1890-
1973) SF1 494
Stern, (Rev.) Herman I. BAA 269
Stern, (Julius) David (1886?-1971)
ES2 407 SFE 573 SF1 494 STH
240
Stern, Paul F. pseud. of Paul
Ernst. WTS 39, 124
Stern, Philip Van Doren (1900-)
CSF 186 ES2 407 FBK 69-70
IAC 225 SF1 494 SF2 1087-8
Stern, Stuart. HFI 140
Sternbach, Rick (1951-) IAC 225
SFE 573 VES 71, 78, 163, 291
Sternberg, Jacques (1923-) AOW
260 EXT 5/1 7 HFI 140 IAC
225 SFB 139 SFE 573-4 SF1
495
Sternberg, Kurt. BAA 269
Sterne, Julian. CSF 186 SF1 495
Sterne, Laurence (1713-68) ASF
305 WTS 17
Sterne, Richard E. SF1 495
Sternig, Larry. IAC 225
Sterns, Justin. CSF 186 SF1 495
Steuert, Dom Hilary. BAA 269
Stevens, Carol D. SL4 1978-88

Stevens, Charles McClellan (1861-) see Quondam
Stevens, Clifford J. (1926-) SF1 495 SF2 1088
Stevens, David. FL4 1724-8 SL1 218-22 SL3 1204-8 SL4 1603-7 SL5 2264-8
Stevens, Francis pseud. of Gertrude Barrows Bennett (1884?-1939?) ALW 114 FL1 287-8 FL2 718-9 HFI 140 IAC 225 ISW 9-11 RFA 31 SFE 574 SF1 495 SOT 48-9 STH 259 TSP 68
Stevens, Irma Ned. BAA 269
Stevens, Isaac Newton (1858-1920) BAA 73 SF1 495
Stevens, James. IAC 225 SFS 112
Stevens, John. BAA 73 see also Frank Hatfield
Stevens, L. Clark. CSC 68
Stevens, Lawrence Sterne. ES2 407 ISW 284 STH 262-3 VES 140-1, 143, 196, 214-5 WGT 137 WSF 124
Stevens, Rowan. CSF 186 IAC 225
Stevens, Stella. EXT 8/2 30
Stevens, Wallace. KAU 184
Stevens, William Oliver (1898-1955) ES2 407-8
Stevenson, Adlai, II. ISW 173
Stevenson, Burton Egbert (1872-1962) CSF 186 SF1 495
Stevenson, Dorothy Emily (1892-1973) CSF 186 SF1 495 SF2 1088
Stevenson, E. M. WTS 63
Stevenson, Florence. ES2 408 SF 495
Stevenson, James. FFC 126
Stevenson, John (1853-) WGT 137 see also Stephen Jackson
Stevenson, Lionel. EXT 4/1 1 EXT 4/2 17-22 OSR 96-104, 356
Stevenson, Lynnda. IAC 225
Stevenson, Robert Louis (1850-94) ALW 97, 216 AOW 15, 34, 73 BYS 27, 103-4, 112, 117, 136-7 CAT 8-10, 52-3, 56, 63 CSF 186 CYR 14 DTS 3 ES2 408 EXT 1/1 15 EXT 3/1 29 EXT 4/2 20, 22 EXT 7/2 38 FAN 10 FBK 62-3, 100 FFC 9 FFR 169-70 FLT 48-66 FL4 1698-702, 1834-9 FTF 34, 41 IAC 225 ISW 168 MSF 69 PST 71, 198 RAH 166

SFB 35 SFE 574 SFH 169, 183 SFS 112 SF1 495-6, 584 SIH 32-3 SL5 2184-9 SRB 10 STH 109 THM 3 VES 210 WAA 89
Stevenson, Sylvia. CSF 186
Stevick, Philip. BAA 269
Stewart. EXT 8/1 5
Stewart, Alfred D. KAU 172 VF1 14-43, 263-4, 283
Stewart, Alfred Walter (1880-1947) ES2 408 WGT 137 see also J. J. Connington
Stewart, Arvis. FFC 68
Stewart, Bruce (1927-) SF1 496 SF2 1088
Stewart, Charles. FFC 22, 26
Stewart, Douglas J. EXT 10/1 41-2 IAC 225
Stewart, Douglass H. EXT 6/1 16
Stewart, Fred Mustard (1936-) HFI 140 SFH 186 SF1 496 SF2 1088
Stewart, George R. (1895-) AOW 260 BAA 118 BYS 79, 294 EFP 7 ES2 408 EXT 5/1 4 FAN 168 HFI 140 KAU 127 LEX 591 NWO 17, 139 POE 293-4, 297 SFB 18, 128 SFD 311 SFE 574 SFH 169, 243 SF1 496 SF2 1088-9 SL2 687-91 SOT 244 TSF 142-3, 233 VES 261 WIF 233
Stewart, Herbert L. BAA 269
Stewart, J. I. M. FAN 6
Stewart, James. SFN 116
Stewart, Kilton. LTN 152-4
Stewart, Mary (1916-) AOW 261 FFC 9, 191 FL2 1010-4 SF1 496 SF2 1089
Stewart, Ramona (1922-) SF1 496 SF2 1089
Stewart, Ritson. CSF 186 SF1 496
Stewart, Stanley. CSF 186 SF1 496
Stewart, Will pseud. of John Stewart Williamson. COT 250 IAC 225 MSM 85 RFA 107, 111-3, 170 VES 163, 314 WSF 306
Stickgold, Bob. IAC 225
Stickney, Corwin F. IMS 75-7, 93-5, 104-6, 109-10, 126, 133, 142 STH 252-3 see also Philip Sutter
Stiffoni, Giovanni. BAA 193
Stiles. IMS 105

Stilgebauer, Edward (1868-) SF1 496

Stillwell, Robert L. BAA 269

Stilson, Charles Billings. IAC 225 ALW 33, 111, 156 ES2 408 HFI 140-1 MFW 21 SFE 574 SF1 496 WSF 27

Stimpson, Catherine Roslyn (1936-) SF1 497 SF2 1089 WAA 112, 243

Stimson, Frederic Jessup. CSF 186 IAC 225 SF1 497

Stine, G(eorge) Harry (1928-) ES2 408-9 ETN 68 EXT 8/1 4 IAC 225 IAH 48, 71 RFA 198 SFN 31, 47 SFS 112 WGT 137 see also Lee Correy

Stine, Hank pseud. of Henry Eugene Stine. AOW 261 DMK 39-47 RHN 175 SF1 497 SFE 574-5

Stine, Henry Eugene (1945-) SF2 1089 WGT 137 see also Hank Stine

Stine, Wilbur Morris (1863-1934) SF1 497

Stirling, M. W. (1865-1965) ES2 409

Stirling, Yates, Jr. IAC 225

Stirrat, David. BAA 19

Stitzer, Daniel Ahrens (1869-) CSF 187 ES2 409 SF1 497

Stivens, Dallas George (1911-) ES2 409 SF1 497

Stivers, Mark see Kin I. Disrobeson

Stobbs, William. FFC 134

Stock, A. G. BAA 269

Stock, E. Elliot. SF1 497

Stock, Ralph (1882-1962) SF1 497

Stockbridge, Grant (house name) SFE 575 TSP 58 see also Norvell W. Page

Stockham, Richard. IAC 225 IAH 105

Stocking, Charles Francis (1873-) SF1 497

Stockl, Albert. BAA 269

Stockton, Frank R. (1834-1902) ALW 33, 82 AOW 37, 73 BAA 40 BYS 143 CSF 187 ES2 409 EXT 1/1 2, 4, 18 EXT 2/2 22 EXT 3/1 29 EXT 5/1 4, 16, 16a EXT 7/1 19, 27 EXT 10/2 99 FFC 9, 23, 100 HFI 141 IAC 225-6 MSF 203-4 MSM 144 PST 60, 101-2,

192, 263, 266, 269-70, 289, 304 SFE 575 SFS 112 SF1 497 SRB 10 VES 106 WSF 130 WTS 129

Stockwell, Lucius A. BAA 48

Stoddard, C. W. BAA 28

Stoddard, Charles pseud. of Charles Stanley Strong. SF1 497 WGT 137

Stoddard, Thomas A. SF1 497

Stoddard, William Osborn (1835-1925) SF1 497

Stoker, Bram pseud. of Abraham Stoker (1847-1912) BYS 48 CSF 187 ES2 410 EXT 5/1 4 FBK 7, 46-51, 141, 144 FL1 404-9 IAC 226 SFE 575 SF1 497-8 SIH 27, 29, 31 WAA 87, 89, 192 WGT 137 WIF 23, 72 WTS 17

Stokes, Ella Harrison. BAA 288

Stokes, H. A. C. SF1 498

Stokes, J. CSF 187

Stokes, Malcolm. IAC 226

Stokes, Manning Lee. WGT 137

Stokes, Peg. SF1 498 SF2 1089

Stokes, Simpson pseud. of Frank D. Fawcett. CSF 187

Stolpe, Dan. FFC 10

Stolz, Mary. FFC 92, 126, 137, 169

Stone, Alma. HFI 141 SF1 498

Stone, (Mrs.) C. H. BAA 43 CSF 187 NWO 97 SF1 498

Stone, Charles. VES 101

Stone, Christopher R. CSF 187

Stone, David. FFC 32, 65, 148

Stone, George. HFI 141

Stone, Graham Brice (1926-) ES2 410 EXT 8/2 30 SF1 498 SF2 1089-90

Stone, Helen. FFC 7, 185

Stone, Idella Purnell (1901-) IAC 226 SF1 498 SF2 1090

Stone, Isobel. CSF 187 SF1 498

Stone, Leon. EXT 3/1 25

Stone, Leslie Frances pseud. of Mrs. William Silberberg (1905-) ALW 10 COT 180 CSF 187 ES2 410 HFI 141 IAC 226 SFD 211 SFE 575 SF1 498 SF2 1090 SFS 112

Stone, Robert. ETN 141

Stone, Weldon. ES2 410 SF1 498

Stone, Wilfred. FAN 94

Stone, William Standish (1907-) SF1 498

Stoneham, Charles Thurley (1895-) CSF 188 ES2 410 SF1 498

Stones, Jonathan. IAC 226 SFS 112

Stoney, Leland. IAC 226

Stong, Phil(ip Duffield) (1899-1957) ALW 175 COT 21 CSF 188 ES2 410-1 EXT 3/1 20 EXT 7/2 46 FFC 137 FRN 48 IAC 226 ISW 4 SFE 575 SF1 498 SOT 179 SRB 300 WIF 19 WSF 129

Stonier, George Walter (1903-) ES2 411 SF1 498

Stonor, Oliver (1903-) SF2 818 see also Morchard Bishop

Stopa, Jon. IAC 226 WSF 215

Stopeck, Philip. SF1 498

Storey, Anthony (1928-) SFE 575

Storey, Margaret (1926-) SF1 499

Storke, Francis Eugene. CSF 188 SF1 499

Storm, Dennis. TSP 131

Storm, Harrison pseud. of Bruno Fischer. TSP 132

Storm, Jannick (1939-) BYS 304 SFE 575-6 SIH 59 WAA 234

Storr, Catherine (1913-) FFC 94, 157 SFE 576

Story, A.M. Sommerville. WGT 138 see also Frankfort Sommerville

Story, Jack Trevor (1917-) SFE 576 SF1 499 SF2 1090

Stout, Rex (1886-1975) AOW 113 CSF 188 ES2 411 RFA 108 SFE 576 SF1 499 SF2 1090 WIF 102

Stout, Tim. IAC 226

Stoutenberg, Adrien Pearl (1916-) AOW 306,331 SF1 499 SF2 1090-1

Stover, Leon Eugene (1929-)AOW 299,355,365 BYS 179, 242,319, 321 ES2 411 FHT 68 IAC 169, 226 KAU 48,50 SFE 576 SF1 499 SF2 1091 TSF 33-7,137-44

Stow, Julian Randolph (1935-) SF1 499 SF2 1091

Stowe, (Mrs.) H.M. WGT 138 see also Eleve

Stowe, Harriet Beecher (1811-96) CSF 188 ES2 411 EXT 4/1 6 SFH 10 SFN 50,98,108

Strachan, Geoffrey. MSF 103,106

Strachey, John St. Loe (1860-1927) BAA 36 SF1 499

Straight, Michael. EXT 10/1 42

Strand, K.Aa. ISW 178

Strang, Herbert pseud. of George Herbert Ely and C. James L'Estrange. CSF 188 SFE 576-7

Stranger, Joyce. FFC 9

Stratemeyer, Anna. STH 162

Stratemeyer, Edna C. STH 173, 179

Stratemeyer, Edward (1862-1930) STH 2, 56-7, 160-6, 168-70, 173-4 WGT 138 see also Henry Abbot, Victor Appleton, Roy Rockwood

Stratemeyer, George. STH 172

Stratemeyer, Harriet. STH 170, 173, 179

Stratemeyer, Henry Julius. STH 162

Strating, Jozeph Jacob. ES2 411 SF1 500

Stratton, Chris pseud. of Richard Hubbard. SF1 500

Straub, Peter (1943-) FL2 607-11

Straus, Ralph (1882-1950) BAA 72 CSF 188 IAC 226 SF1 500

Strauss, Erwin S. AOW 368 BRS 5 ES2 411 MIH 40 SFE 578 SF1 500 SRB 68

Strauss, Johann. ACC 124 TSO 57-8

Strauss, Johann, Jr. (1825-99) TSO 57-8

Strauss, L.F. CSF 188

Strauss, Oscar. STH 38

Strauss, Richard (1864-1949)ACC 124 ISW 157 TJB 31-2 VFS 52

Strauss, Sylvia. BAA 269

Stravinsky, Igor (1882-) CUA 8 WFS 65,129

Streblow, Lothar (1929-) LEX 591-2

Street, Arthur George (1892-1966) CSF 188 SF1 500 SF2 1091

Street, Cecil John Charles (1884-1964) WGT 138

Street, Claire Edwin. IAC 226

Streff, Michael. VES 85

Strehl, Rolf. ES2 411

Streichl, Karl. BAA 139

Strete, Craig (1950-) FFR 170 HFI 141 IAC 226 LEX 592 SFE 578

Stretzer, Thomas (-1738) SF1 500

Stribling, Thomas Sigismund (1881-1965) CSF 188 ES2 411-2

Stribling, Thomas S. (cont.)
IAC 226 MSM 30,298 PST 164-
5,205,225,232,237 SOT 87 VES
78
Strick, Philip (1939-) BRS 11 BYS
4,319 IAC 226 RBY 241 SFD
86 SFE 578
Strickgold, Bob. HFI 141
Strickland, (Sir) Walter William
(1851-1938) CSF 188 SF1 500
Strickland, William Peter (1809-
84) SF1 500
Strieber, Whitley (1945-) FL5
2150-2
Strike, Jeremy pseud. of Thomas
Edward Renn (1939-) HFI 141
SFE 578 SF1 500
Strindberg, August (1849-1912)
EXT 10/1 9 FL1 428-30
Stringer, Arthur John Arbuthnot
(1874-1956) CSF 188 ES2 412
SFE 578 SF1 500
Stringer, David. IAC 226 SFS 113
Strobl, Karl Hans (1877-1946) FBK
82,141,143-4 SIH 189
Strode, William. ES2 412 SF1 500
Strong, Charles Stanley (1906-62)
see Charles Stoddard
Strong, Leonard Alfred George
(1896-1958) CSF 188 EXT 10/1
42 SF1 500
Strong, Rod. SF1 500
Strong, Zachary. TSP 148
Stronghilos, Constantine. WFS 162
Strother, S. VES 104
Strugatski, Arkady (1925-) and
Boris (1931-) AOW 261,297 ASF
176 CAT 81,116 CSC 33 EXT
10/2 79-80 FBK 42 FFR 170
FLR 37 FTF 13 HFI 141 IAC
226 LEX 593-5 LTN 13,22,132,
257,261 MSF 199,230,269 OMN
288-9 RGS 171-2 SFB 122-4
SFE 578-9 SFH 85 SFS 113 SF1
501 SF2 1092 SIH 44,53,83,88,
95,99,109 SL2 756-60,776-81,
950-5 SL3 1488-96 SL4 1548-
54,1710-3,1817-20,1879-83
SOT 431 SRB 360 VES 170 WAA
71
Strughold, Hubertus (1898-) ES2
412
Strugnell, Ann. FFC 179
Strumilov, Andrzej. FBK 41
Strunksy, Simeon (1879-1948) SF1
501

Struther, Jan pseud. of Joyce
Maxtone Graham. IAC 226 SFS
113
Strutton, William Harold (1918-)
SF1 501
Stuart, Don A. pseud. of John W.
Campbell, Jr. ALW 126,147-8,
155,160 ASF 108 COT 106,291
EXT 7/2 40 IAC 226 ISW 8,34-
6 MFW 40 MIH 60 OWB 89,97,
99 RFA 28-33,36,38-9,42,56-
7,62,100,176,183 SFB 60-1
SFD 27,210,213,288 SFH 40
SFN 28 SFS 113 TSP 187 VES
170,181-2 WFS 86 WSF 68-70,
84,93-4,113,135
Stuart, Dona. RFA 29
Stuart, (Henry) Francis (Mont-
gomery) (1902-) CSF 188 SF1
501 SF2 1092
Stuart, (Mrs.) G. CSF 188 SF1
501
Stuart, Gerald Villiers. CSF 188
Stuart, Jeb. WTS 130
Stuart, Jesse. IAC 226
Stuart, Ruth McEnery (1849-1917)
ES2 412 SF1 501
Stuart, W.J. EFP 11 ES2 412
HFI 141 SFE 579 SF1 501
Stuart, William W. IAC 226-7
SFS 113
Stubbes, George. BAA 11
Stubbes, Phillip. BAA 2
Stubbs, Harry Clement (1922-)
ALW 160 BFP 469-70 ES2 412
EXT 3/1 26 SFD 292 SF2 856
SRB 320,341 TSF 56,235 WGT
138 WIF 167,276 see also Hal
Clement
Stubis, Talivaldis. FFC 54
Student of Occultism, (A) pseud.
of Franz Hartmann. CSF 188
Studer, Paul. CSF 189 SF1 501
Stump, D(avid) L(eroy). BAA 56,
80 CSF 189 SF1 501
Stumpke, Harold pseud. of Gerold
Steiner (1908-) ES2 413 SF1 501
Stupple, James A. AAL 143 BAA
269,289 RBY 24-32 SL3 1348-
52 SL4 2030-4 VF1 175-84,
276,283
Sturge, Ernest Adolphus (1856-
1934) SF1 501
Sturgeon, Theodore (1918-) AAL
8,14,26,85 ALW 7,31,50,60,
136,155,160,163,165-6,171,213-

Sturgeon, Theodore (cont.)
4, 218, 222, 233 AOW 261-4, 285,
287-92, 295-6, 298, 300 ASF 37,
123, 143-4, 215 BAA 135, 269
BFP 471-3 BYS 228, 237, 249,
281, 304 CAT 38 CEN 132-43
COT 24-5, 155, 167, 190, 219, 250-
1, 278, 291 CSC 14, 89-103, 197,
225 CSF 189 ES2 413-4 ETN
2, 16-7, 21, 33, 41, 45, 47, 56, 66,
69, 101, 137, 142-4, 159-60 EXT
3/1 27 EXT 5/1 3 EXT 7/2 40,
42 EXT 8/1 7, 16 EXT 10/2 59,
65 FBK 122, 124, 154 FFR 170-
2 [FJT] FL4 1703-11 FTF 2,
13, 131-2, 136-8, 140, 166 HFI
141-2 HID 3, 21, 100, 138, 142
IAC 227-9 IAH 9, 15, 22-4, 31-2,
42-3, 85-6, 104, 132, 146-7 INT
53, 85 ISW 8, 114-6, 121, 123, 125-
7, 147, 149, 199, 221-2, 224, 226
KAU 17, 31-2, 35, 38-44, 50, 79,
152, 169, 184, 190, 204, 216-22
KVT 49, 60 LEX 595-7 LTN 99,
230, 233 MFW 11, 20, 28, 41, 48,
97-9, 102, 107, 155-7, 160, 254,
281, 290 MIH 5, 12, 15, 24, 36, 60-
1, 67-78, 118, 120, 126, 135 MSM
32, 75-6, 126, 132, 172 NDO 210
NWO 38, 80, 118-22, 163, 253
OWB 98 PJF 12, 40, 74 RFA 64,
70, 83, 87-8, 90, 92, 95-6, 100, 104,
131, 138, 141, 143, 145, 153-5, 165,
176-7, 184, 206, 212-3 RGS 172-
4 RSG 15 RZY 39, 106 SFB 62,
116-7 SFD 20, 58, 64, 74, 256,
294, 317 SFE 579-80 SFH 33,
41, 51, 62-5, 69, 94, 106, 157, 167-
8, 175, 216, 243 SFN 15, 83, 90-1,
118 SFS 113-5 SFW 91, 203-8,
396, 398 SF1 501-2 SF2 1092-3
SIH 184 SL2 676-80 SL3 1453-
8 SL5 2056-8, 2215-7, 2370-2
SOT 62, 82, 159, 179, 182, 193,
218, 229-48, 257, 316, 330, 367,
395, 405, 409 SRB 11, 13, 15, 115,
317, 324, 334-5, 509 STF 51-3,
75, 78-9 STH 119-20 SV1 4-18
TPS 269-72 TSF 57-8, 237 VES
68, 96, 106, 135, 165, 190, 195,
201, 207, 210-1, 214-5, 245, 259,
263, 301, 307, 316-7 VF1 153-66,
275-6 WAA 25, 54, 157, 167, 175,
244 WFS 20, 173, 203, 216, 227
WGT 138 WIF 145, 162, 185, 194
WSF 95, 100, 107, 114, 129, 134,
148, 154, 174, 206, 222, 387-8
WTS 46, 48, 59 YTS 31
Sturgeon, William. FTF 35
Sturges, Preston. CSC 264
Sturgis, Melvin. WGT 138-9
Sturm, Dieter. FBK 51
Sturtzel, Howard Allison. WGT
139
Sturtzel, Jane Levington Comfort.
WGT 139
Stutfield, Hugh Edward Millington
(1858-1929) CSF 189 SF1 502
Styron, William. EXT 7/2 47
IAC 229 SFS 115
Suba, Susanne. FFC 129
Suchy, Viktor. BAA 269
Sudak, Eunice. ES2 414 HFI 142
SF1 502
Sudbery, Rodie (1943-) SF1 502
Sudbery, Tony. IAC 229
Suddaby, William Donald (1900-
64) AOW 331 ES2 414 SFE 580
SF1 502 WGT 139 see also
Alan Griff
Suddick, Louise F. CSF 189
Sue, (Marie Joseph) Eugene (1804-
57) CAT 46 CSF 189 FL4 2059-
62 SF1 502 SIH 25, 185 VES
232
Suero, J. B. Cobo. BAA 173
Suffling, Ernest Richard. CSF
189 SF1 502
Suffling, Mark. SFE 580
Sugar, Andrew. SF1 502
Sugarman, L. B. WTS 20, 23
Suggs, Robert C. IAC 229
Suits, Conrad. BAA 269
Sukenik, Ronald. SFH 97
Sullivan, Anita T. RBY 241
Sullivan, (Sir) Arthur Seymour.
ASF 313-4 SFA 89, 285-7
Sullivan, Charles William, III
(1944-) FL1 87-9 FL2 539-42,
798-800, 839-43, 932-7 FL3
1372-4 FL4 1851-3 IAC 229
LTN 251 MFW 229 SF1 503
SL1 38-42, 325-9 SL2 625-8
SL3 1439-43 SL4 1632-6
Sullivan, Ed. IAH 145
Sullivan, Edward Alan (1868-1947)
CSF 189 SF1 502
Sullivan, Eleanor. ASF 323
Sullivan, Frank. BAA 193
Sullivan, James Frank (-1936)
CSF 189 ES2 414 IAC 229
SF1 503

Sullivan, James William. BAA 59
Sullivan, Jean. IAC 229
Sullivan, John L. IAH 120
Sullivan, L. L. G. WSF 62
Sullivan, Philip Aloysius (1882-)
BAA 108 SF1 503
Sullivan, Richard E. NDA 4-6
Sullivan, Thomas Russell (1849-
1916) CSF 189 ES2 414 SF1
503
Sullivan, Walter (1918-) ES2 414
IMS 213 VFS 139 WFS 222
Sully, Kathleen M. (1910-) ES2
414 SF1 503 SF2 1093
Sulzberger, Cyrus Leo, II (1912-)
SF1 503 SF2 1093
Summers, Dorothy. CSF 189
Summers, Edward G. SF1 503
Summers, Leo. VES 217
Summers, Montague R. (1880-
1948) CSF 189 ES2 414-5 EXT
5/1 9 EXT 9/2 62 FBK 19 SF1
503 THM 39
Sumner, John S. FBK 118 WIF
76
Sumner, Park. BAA 102
Sumner, William Graham. BAA
34
Sun, Kim Il. VFS 124
Sundell, Abner J. TSP 147
Supek, Rudi. BAA 269
Supervielle, Jules (1884-1960)
SF1 503
Surrey, Lionel. CSF 189 SF1
503
Surtz, Edward L. BAA 193, 269-
70
Susann, Jacqueline. EXT 10/2
96 STF 21
Susman, Margarete. BAA 270
Sussman, Aaron. STH 240
Sussman, Herbert L. AOW 356
Sussmuth, Hans. BAA 193
Sutcliff, Rosemary (1920-) AOW
261 SF1 503 SF2 1093
Suter, Paul. WTS 20
Sutherland, George (1855-1905)
SF1 503
Sutherland, Herb. IAC 229 SFS
115
Sutherland, James Edward (1948-)
BAA 164 CSF 189 HFI 142 IAC
229 LEX 598 SF1 503 SF2 1093
Sutherland, James Runcieman
(1900-) SF1 503

Sutherland, Morris pseud. of
Gwendolen Sutherland Morris.
SF1 503
Sutphen, William Gilbert Van
Tassel (1861-1945) CSF 189
ES2 415 EXT 1/1 18 SFE 587
SF1 503
Sutter, A. Oliver. CSF 189 SF1
503
Sutter, Philip pseud. of Corwin F.
Stickney. IMS 93, 106
Sutton, David Ambrose (1947-)
SF1 504 SF2 1093
Sutton, (Eric) Graham (1892-)
CSF 190 SF1 504 WGT 139 see
also Antony Marsden
Sutton, Eugenia Geneva (1917-)
ES2 415 SF2 1094
Sutton, Henry pseud. of David
Rytman Slavitt. HFI 142 SF1
504
Sutton, Homer Lee (1916-) SF1
504 SF2 1094 IAC 229 SFS 115
Sutton, Jean pseud. of Eugenia
Geneva Sutton (1917-) AOW 332
SFE 587 SF1 504
Sutton, Jeff(erson Howard) (1913-)
AAL 142 AOW 332 ES2 415 HFI
142 IAC 229 LEX 598-9 SFE
587 SF1 504 SF2 1094
Sutton, John Wren. CSF 182 SF1
504
Sutton, Marilyn. AC2 76-7 FHT
68
Sutton, Paralee Sweeten. BAA
118 SF1 504
Sutton, Stephen P. ES2 415 SF1
504
Sutton, Thomas C. AC2 76-7
FHT 68
Suvin, Darko R. (1930-) AAL 19,
125, 204 ALW 7, 226 AOW 300,
363 BAA xv-xvi, xx-xxi, 193, 270
BYS 36 CAT 21, 69, 72-5, 77, 84,
88-9 COT 217, 298, 300 EXT
10/1 3 EXT 10/2 69-115 FFR
172 IAC 229 INT 18 JGB 51-2
LTN 204, 256, 262, 264 MFW 96,
188-9, 208 MIH 137 NWO xi-xii,
44-5, 48, 76, 186, 196, 201-2 SFE
587 SFH 9, 84, 239 SFW 126,
233, 552, 567-8 SF1 504 SF2
1094-5 SIH 54 SL1 58-62 SRB
66, 72, 83 STF 46 UKL 246
Svenson, Andrew E. STH 161, 179

Sviatlovskii, Vladimir V. BAA
193
Svilpis, J. E. FL2 894-6 FL4
1698-702
Swados, Harvey. BAA 134
Swaffer, Hannen (1879-1962) CSF
190 SF1 504
Swahn, Sven Christer (1933-) FFC
179 SFE 587
Swain, Dwight Vreeland (1915-)
BAA 123 ES2 416 HFI 142 LEX
599 SFE 587 SF1 504 SF2 1095
STH 85 WGT 139
Swain, Edmund Gill (1861-1938)
CSF 190 ES2 416 SF1 505
Swain, John. WTS 21
Swain, Virginia (1899-) CSF 190
SF1 505
Swan. EXT 10/1 9
Swan, Herbert E. BAA 56
Swan, Mark Elbert (1871-) SF1
584
Swan, Thor. SF1 505
Swan, Virginia. IAC 229
Swank, Paul. RSG 92-3
Swann, Donald. EXT 10/1 20
Swann, Ingo. HFI 142
Swann, Thomas Burnett (1928-76)
AOW 264 BFP 474-5 ES2 416
FL3 1029-33 HFI 143 IAC 229
LEX 599-600 SFD 60-1, 63, 75,
303 SFE 587-8 SF1 505 SF2
1095-6 SRB 277 TSF 64 VES
234-5
Swannell, J. N. WBW 48
Swanson. RFA 195
Swanson, H. N. ETN 110
Swanson, Logan pseud. of Richard
Matheson. IAC 229
Swanson, Robert. VES 106
Swartwout, R. Egerton. CSF 190
Swayne, Martin pseud. of Maurice
Nicoll (1884-1953) AOW 42, 74
CSF 190 SFE 588 SF1 505
Swayne, Samuel. FFC 152
Swayne, Zoa. FFC 152
Swedenborg, Emmanuel (1688-
1772) CWN 24, 31, 56 EXT 9/2
62 FBK 61 MSF 70 SFE 588
STH 4
Sweet, Darrell. VES 219, 227
Sweet, Paul R. BAA 270
Sweet, William Warren. BAA 270
Sweetland, James Harvey. BAA
289
Swem, Charles Lee. CSF 190

Swenson, May. IAC 229
Swet, Pearl Norton. STH 254
Sweven, Godfrey pseud. of John
Macmillan Brown (1846-1935)
BAA xxi CSF 190 SFE 588 SF1
505
Swiatek, Erik H. SL2 725-8 SL4
1844-7 SL5 2245-9
Swietochowski, Aleksander. BAA
193
Swift, Jonathan (1667-1745) AAL
55, 106, 198 ALW 32, 44, 101, 136
AOW 31-2, 343, 398 ASF 174, 191
BAA 10 BYS 10, 61, 65, 68, 71-5,
77-8, 122, 124, 189 CAT 7, 69,
73, 75, 106 CSC 207, 209 CSF
190 CUA 42 ES2 416 EXT 3/1
30 EXT 6/1 7 EXT 8/1 20, 22
EXT 8/2 33 EXT 10/2 65 FAN
9-10, 35, 54, 135, 185 FFC 180
FFR 172-3 FTF 24-6, 48 HEN
8 IAC 229 INT 49-50, 57 ISW
2, 5-6 JHN 55 KAU 121 LTN
124 MIH 47, 101-2 MSF 5-6, 10,
12, 25, 30, 59-60, 73-4, 88, 98-9,
103, 105, 107-14, 120, 123, 126,
130-1, 137-8, 148, 162, 164, 166,
174, 196, 201, 211, 213-5, 219,
236, 241-2, 275 MSM 12, 159-60,
169, 206, 258 NWO 101, 165, 252-
3 PJF 13, 60 PST 20, 22, 26, 40,
100-1, 129-30, 203, 206-8, 213,
226, 233, 239, 261, 265, 280, 311,
315 RAH 16, 93 SFB 94 SFE
588 SFH 6, 9, 13, 31, 103, 150,
161, 176, 214 SFN 56-8 SFS 115
SF1 505-6 SHL 7 SOT 2, 76
STF 30, 34, 39, 88, 96 TSO 21
UFS 5 VES 69, 80, 125, 164, 254
VF1 238-62, 280-1 WAA 31
WGT 139 WIF 36 WSF 14-5
Swift, Morrison Isaac. BAA 50,
67, 77
Swigart, Leslie Kay (1948-) AOW
363 LTN 238 SF1 506 SF2
1096 SRB 79
Swinburne, Algernon Charles.
EXT 2/1 11 IAH 15 MFW 135
Swirney, S. H. BAA 271
Swinton, Ernest Dunlop (1868-
1951) WGT 139 see also Ole
Luk-Oie
Swisher, Frances N. IMS 243
Swisher, Robert D. COT 16 IAC
229 IMS 73, 213, 243
Switzer, Robert. SF1 506

Swoboda, Helmut. BAA 193
Sydney, (Sir) Philip (1554-86)
    EXT 4/2 18
Sydow, Marianne (1944-) LEX
    600-1
Sykes, Arthur Alkin (-1939) ES2
    416
Sykes, Egerton. EXT 7/1 16
Sykes, Pamela. FFC 169 SF1
    506
Sykes, W. J. BAA 271
Sykes, William Stanley (1894-1961)
    CSF 190 SF1 506
Sykora, William S. ETN 98 IMS
    29, 35-9, 41-3, 48-52, 55-8, 64, 66,
    82-8, 94, 116-7, 119, 121, 125, 129,
    140-5, 147-51, 154, 167, 170-3, 175-
    80, 183, 186-8, 197-8, 200, 206, 209-
    11, 214, 216-9, 221, 225-8, 230, 234-
    7, 246, 250, 252 ISW 161 SRB 90
    WFS 52, 59, 74, 94-6 WIF 17, 135-
    40 WSF 142, 209
Sylva, Carmen (1843-1916) SF1 506
Sylvester, John. SF1 506
Sylvester, R. S. BAA 271
Symmes, John Cleves (1780-1829)
    ALW 57 ASF 188 BAA 18-9
    EXT 1/1 2, 6, 10 EXT 3/1 30
    EXT 3/2 44 MSF 132, 142 NWO
    70 POE 96-7 PST 41, 65, 241

SFB 20, 76 SFW 13, 62 SRB 6
    WGT 139 WIF 37, 44, 49, 67, 227
    see also Adam Seaborn
Symonds, John. FFC 84, 137
Symons, Geraldine. FFC 169
Symons, John Henry (1873-) BAA
    94 CSF 190 SF1 506
Synan, Arthur. CSF 190
Synge, (Dr.) John L. IAC 229
    MSM 257
Synton, Edward. CSF 190
Synton, Rosalie. CSF 190
Sypher, Willie. ACC 102
Syrett, Netta (-1943) CSF 190
    SF1 506
Szafran, Gene. SRB 47, 52 VES
    227, 235
Szafranski, Kurt. FBK 141-2
Szathmari, Sandor (1897-1974)
    SL3 1118-21
Szecsi, Maria. BAA 271
Szekeres, Cyndy. FFC 117-8,
    134
Szepes, Maria. LEX 601
Szerb, Antal (1901-45) SF1 506
Szilard, Leo (1898-1964) AAL 65
    ASF 198 BAA 117, 135 ES2 416
    EXT 8/1 2 HFI 143 IAC 229-30
    KAU 138 LEX 601-2 MIH 106
    SFE 591 SFS 115 SF1 506 UFS 5

T

T. E. pseud. of Thomas Erskine.
    CSF 190
Tabakow, Lou. IAH 29-30, 84
    MIH 119
Taber, Albert Ernest. BAA 80
Tabori, Paul (1908-74) ES2 416-7
    HFI 143 KAU 191-2 SFE 591
    SF1 507, 584 SF2 1096-7 WGT
    140

Tacitus. STF 13
Tadic, Ljubomir. BAA 271
Tafoya, Alfonso. IAC 230
Taft, Philip. BAA 271
Tafuri, Manfredo. BAA 193
Taieb, Heliane (1929-) see Julia
    Verlanger
Taine, John pseud. of Eric Temple
    Bell. ALW 141 AOW 114, 395

Taine, John (cont.)
BYS 208 CSF 190-1 EXT 3/1 28
EXT 5/1 3 EXT 7/2 35,38 HFI
143-4 IAC 230 IMS 138,159
ISW 192 LEX 603 MIH 22-3
MSM 34 OWB 98 PST 137-8,
161-2,198,249,257,278,280,312
RFA 32,63 RGS 174-5 RSG 9
SFB 135-6 SFE 592 SFN 23,28
SFS 115 SFW 75-82,145 SF1
507 SL1 149-52 SOT 108,214
SRB 9,295,304 VES 95,121,137,
149,330 WIF 86,89,223 WSF 51
Taine, Ted. STH 85
Tait, Douglas. FFC 81
Tait, George B. ES2 417 WGT
140 see also Alan Barclay
Tait, Stephen. BAA 106 SF1 507
Takei, George. IAC 230
Talbot, George E. (1901-) SF1 507
Tall, Stephen pseud. of Compton
N. Crook. AAL 89,105 HFI 144
IAC 230 KAU 194-5 RGS 175
SFE 593 VES 177
Tallant, Robert (1909-57) ES2 417
SF1 508
Talmon, Jacob L. BAA 193,271
Tamerlane. SFA 114-5
Tamisier, M. BAA 193
Tandrup, Harald (1874-) CSF 191
SF1 508
Tange, Kenzo. [FUT]
Tangent, Patrick Q. pseud. of
George H. Phelps. CSF 191
Tanguy, Yves. IAC 230 JGB 6
VES 289
Tanner, Charles R. (1896-1974)
ALW 10 ASF 137,150 ES2 417
IAC 230 SFD 211
Tanner, Leroy. MIH 137
Tanner, Tony. KVT 3 NWO 21,
212,227,261,298
Tanton, Ernest Coveney. CSF
191 SF1 508
Tanzy, Eugene. ACC 172-95
Tara, John. MIH 96-7
Tarascon, Louis Anastasius.
BAA 22
Tarbell, Ida M. BAA 271
Tarbouriech, Ernest. BAA 193
Targ, Harry R. BAA 169
Targ, Russell. WFS 261
Tarkington, Booth. CSF 191 IAC
230 STH 78,90,237-8,240
Tarkovsky, Andrei. CAT 122

Tarn, (Sir) William Woodthorpe
(1869-1957) CSF 191 FFC 77
SF1 508
Tarnacre, Robert pseud. of
Robert Cartmell. CSF 191 SF1
508
Taro, Hirai (1894-1965) FBK 150
Tarrant, Catherine. ETN 19,21,
23,72,75 EXT 10/2 105,107
IAH 94,98 RFA 181,194
Tart, Charles. LTN 152,154
Tarzan, Deloris Lehman. HFI 30
Tashlin, Frank. ES2 417
Tassone, G. L. IAC 230
Tate, Peter. AOW 264 HFI 144
IAC 230 SFE 593-4 SF1 508
VES 246
Tate, Sharon. FBK 44 RHN 127,
173 WFS 301
Tatham, Herbert Francis William
(-1909) SF1 508
Taubert, Hans (1928-) LEX 604
Taunton, Harold Roby. CSF 191
SF1 508
Taurasi, James Vincent (1917-)
ES2 417 IMS 24,29,104,106-7,
109,111,113-4,116,120-1,127,
135-7,140,143,145,154,156,169-
80,183-6,188,195,197-8,200,
202,205-6,209-11,214,216-8,
221-2,225-31,233,235-7,246-7,
252 MIH 7 RFA xxii WFS 59,
74,94 WIF 17,133,138,140
WSF 140-2
Taves, Ernest. IAC 230 VES
79-80
Tayler, John Lionel. BAA 90
CSF 191
Taylor, A. E. BAA 271
Taylor, Angus M. (1945-) BAA
271 SFE 594 SFH 242 UKL
246
Taylor, Ann. SF1 508
Taylor, Anna (1944-) SF1 508
Taylor, Bayard. CSF 191
Taylor, Bernard. IAC 230
Taylor, Bert Leston (1866-1921)
SF1 508
Taylor, C. Bryson (1880-) EXT
1/1 18 SF1 509
Taylor, Constance Lindsay (1907-)
see Guy Cullingford
Taylor, E. B. WBW 59
Taylor, Ean. [FUT]
Taylor, Elizabeth. JGB 27,48
VFS 17,121

Taylor, F. Sherwood. SFH 242
Taylor, Frank. SF1 509
Taylor, Frederick W. MSF 254,
256, 273
Taylor, Geoffrey. BAA 147 ES2
417 SF1 509
Taylor, J. Gibson. RFA 20
Taylor, John. IAC 230
Taylor, Malcolm. SF1 509
Taylor, Mark. AOW 307
Taylor, Merlin Moore. STH 138
Taylor, Phoebe Atwood. CSC 39,
51
Taylor, Ray Ward (1908-) SF1 509
Taylor, Richard. FBK 76
Taylor, Robert Lewis (1912-)
AOW 264 CSF 191 ES2 417 HFI
144 IAC 230 SFE 594 SF1 509
SF2 1097
Taylor, Rod. SFB 28
Taylor, Una Ashworth. CSF 191
Taylor, Walter Fuller. BAA 193,
271, 289
Taylor, Walter W. MFW 63
Taylor, William Alexander (1837-
1912) BAA 64 CSF 191 SF1 509
SRB 6
Taylor, William L. EXT 10/1
41-2
Tazewell, Charles. FFC 9
Teague, John Jessop (1856-1929)
see Morice Gerard
Teal, Mildred. FFC 157
Teasdale, Sara. MFW 282 RBY
122 TBC 59
Tebaldi, Renata. WFS 154
Tebbetts, Leon Harold. CSF 191
SF1 509
Teed, Cyrus Reed (1839-1908)
BAA 75 MSM 148-9 WGT 140
see also Lord Chester
Teerink, Herman. BAA 194
Teichner, Albert. IAC 230 SFS
115
Teilhet, Darwin Le Ora (1904-64)
SFE 595
Teitler, Stuart. BAA 194
Telemaque, Herve. IAC 230
Telfair, David. IAC 230
Teller, (Dr.) Edward. MIH 57
VFS 211
Teluccini, Mario (-1568) WGT 10
Tempest, William Dudley. SIH
181
Temple, Hugh O. CSF 191
Temple, M. H. SF1 509

Temple, Willard. IAC 230
Temple, William F(rederick)
(1914-) ALW 160 AOW 264 ES2
417-8 FFR 174 HFI 144 IAC
230-1 IMS 100 LEX 604 SFE
597 SFS 116 SF1 509 SF2 1097-
8 SOT 377, 379 VES 71
Templeton, Herminie pseud. of
Herminie Templeton Kavanagh.
CSF 191 SF1 509
Tench, C. V. RFA 5
Tench, Hubert. EXT 10/2 60-1
Teneti, Alberto. BAA 271
Tenn, William pseud. of Phillip
Klass. ALW 14, 161, 218 AOW
265, 292 BYS 279, 289 COT 141
CSC 140-1, 146-7 EFP 12, 17, 21
ETN 142 EXT 5/1 3 EXT 6/2
22 EXT 8/1 6-7 EXT 10/1 3
EXT 10/2 104 FFR 174 FTF 1,
93-4, 167-8 HFI 144 IAC 231-2
ISW 120 KAU 133 LEX 604-5
MSM 186 RFA 144, 200 RGS
175-6 SFD 8, 300 SFE 597-8
SFS 116-7 SFW 525-30 SF1
509 SL5 2065-9 SOT 241 STH
45 TSF 56 VES 108, 134, 144,
147, 151, 217, 238, 302 WAA 155,
177-8, 244 WFS 161, 173-4, 194,
200, 214, 227 WIF 91, 146, 226
WSF 110, 144, 206
Tennant, Emma (1937-) IAC 232
SFE 598 SF1 509
Tenneshaw, S. M. (house name)
SFE 598 WGT 140 see also
Randall Garrett, Edmond Hamil-
ton, Milton Lesser, Robert
Silverberg
Tenniel, John. FBK 89, 109 FFC
174
Tennyson, Alfred Lord. ALW 51
BYS 13, 86, 89 [FUT] IAH 16
MSF 145-6, 163, 169, 183, 193, 195
POE 69, 316 RZY 50, 52, 58 TSO
26-8, 34 UKL 210 VFS 145, 202-
3 WBW 37
Tepes, Vlad. FBK 49
Tepper, Matthew Bruce (1953-)
SFA 7, 9 SF1 510 SF2 1098
Tepperman, Emile C. TSP 79,
89 see also Curtis Steele
Teramond, Edmond Gautier see
Guy De Teramond
Tereshkova, Valentina. COT 51
Terhune, Albert Payson (1872?-
1942) HEN 34 WGT 140

Terhune, Everit Bogert (1877?- 1956) CSF 191 SF1 510
Terlouw, Jan. FFC 51
Terrall, Robert. ES2 418 HFI 144
Terrasson, Jean. CSF 191
Terrid, Peter (1949-) LEX 605-6
Terrill, G. Appleby. CSF 192 WTS 28,64
Terrill, Rogers. CSC 296 TSP 9,13,17-8,22-3,46, 81,200,211 WFS 101,104,209
Terris, Susan. FFC 195
Terrot, Charles Hugh (1917-) ES2 418 SF1 510
Tertz, Abram pseud. of Andrey Donatovich Sinyavsky. ES2 418 FBK 42 SF1 510 WAA 71
Teske, Gunter (1933-) LEX 606
Tesla, Nicola. EXT 1/1 3 EXT 5/2 38
Tesler, O. IAC 232
Tessier, Ernst-Maurice (1885-) SF2 875 see also Maurice Dekobra
Test, Roy. IMS 33,64
Teternikov, Fedor Kuz'mich (1863-1927) WGT 140-1
Tevis, Walter Stone, Jr. AOW 286,265 ES2 418 HFI 144 IAC 232 KAU 203 SFE 600 SFS 117 SF1 510 SRB 340
Thacker, Eric Lee (1923-) SFE 600 SF1 510 SF2 1098
Thackeray, William Makepeace (1811-63) BYS 73,75,82 ES2 418 EXT 4/2 19 FFC 51 FL3 1335-7 IAH 127 MSF 248 POE 69 SF1 584 SRB 22
Thales. Thal-Larsen, Margaret. BAA 289
Thames, C.H. pseud.? of Milton Lesser. ES2 418
Thane, Elswyth (1900-) CSF 192 SF1 510 SF2 1098
Tharp, Beebe. IAC 232
Thatcher, Arthur. WTS 23-4
Thayer, Frank D., Jr. IAC 232 SFS 117
Thayer, Tiffany Ellsworth (1902-59) CSF 192 ES2 418 IAH 23 SFN 118 SF1 510 SOT 143 STH 240,242,244-5,248
Thayer, Wade Warren. CSF 192 ES2 418

Theall, Donald F. AAL 104 BAA 271 IAC 232 UKL 246
Theim, Jon Edgar. BAA 289
Thelwell. IAC 232
Themerson, Stefan (1910-) SF1 510
Theobald pseud. of H.P. Lovecraft. EXT 3/1 11,13-5,17
Theobald, Lewis, Jr. pseud. of H.P. Lovecraft. EXT 3/1 2-4, 14-8 IMS 134
Theobald, Robert (1929-) AOW 241 BAA 147,150 HFI 144 SFE 600 SF1 510 SF2 1098 WFS 293
Theodamus pseud. of Theodore Glass. SF1 510
Theopompus. MSF 87 EXT 8/1 23
Theosopho pseud. of Gideon Jasper Richard Ouseley. SF1 510
Theroux, Paul. FFC 10
Theydon, John. SF1 511
Thibault, Jacques Anatole Francois (1844-1924) WGT 141 see also Anatole France
Thieben, Ludwig. BAA 271
Thier, Erich. BAA 271
Thiessen, J. Grant. WTS ix
Thimbleby, J. BAA 21
Thinkwell, (Senator). BAA 139
Thinnes, Roy. SFH 106
Thiry, Herman (1912-) see Johan Daisne
Thiry, Marcel. FBK 146
Thisted, Valdemar Adolph (1815-87) SF1 454 WGT 141 see also L.W.J.S.
Thiusen, Ismar pseud. of John Macnie. CSF 192 FTF 101 SFE 602 SF1 511 WAA 51
Thoby-Marcelin, Philippe and Pierre see Pierre Thoby Marcelin and Philippe Thoby Marcelin.
Thoenes, Piet. BAA 194
Thole, Karel. BYS 217 IAC 232 SFB 145 SFE 602 VES 115,125
Thom, Rene. MSF 75
Thom, Robert (1929-) BAA 147 NDA 135-8,141-2 SF1 511 SF2 1098-9
Thoma. SF1 511
Thomas, Allan. FFC 25
Thomas, Augustus (1857-1934) CSF 192 SF1 511
Thomas, Bertha. BAA 30

Thomas, Chauncey (1822-98) AOW 74 CSF 192 EXT 1/1 19 SFE 602 SF1 511
Thomas, Cogswell. BAA 159
Thomas, Craig (1942-) SFE 602
Thomas, D. M. (1935-) EXT 8/1 17 FL5 2122-5 IAC 232 INT 86
Thomas, Dan pseud. of Leonard M. Sanders, Jr. HFI 144 SFE 602 SF1 511
Thomas, Donald Serrell. SF1 511
Thomas, Dorothy Ada (1903-) CSF 192 SF1 511
Thomas, Dylan. ALW 229 EXT 9/2 47 MSM 103 VFS 117, 135 WAA 138
Thomas, Elizabeth (1805? -) WGT 141 see also Bridget Bluemantle
Thomas, Eugene. CSF 192
Thomas, Eugene E. (1893-) CSF 192 SF1 511
Thomas, Evan. SF1 511
Thomas, George Boyd. BAA 289
Thomas, Gilbert. IAC 232 SFS 117
Thomas, Jack. ES2 419 see also John Oram
Thomas, James Warren. EXT 3/1 21
Thomas, John B. IAC 232
Thomas, John L. BAA 271
Thomas, Martin pseud. of Thomas Hector Martin. HFI 145 SFE 602 SF1 511-2
Thomas, Myra Montfort. STH 173
Thomas, Norman. SFH 10
Thomas, Pascal. SFB 110
Thomas, Rowland. SF1 512
Thomas, Shirley. ES2 419
Thomas, Theodore L. (1920-) ALW 212 AOW 202, 266 ASF 143 ES2 419 HFI 145 IAC 232 IAH 115-8, 123 ISW 124-7, 267 LEX 606-7 SFE 602 SFS 117 SF1 512 SF2 1099 VES 161 WGT 141 WSF 175, 233 see also Leonard Lockhard
Thomas, W. E. BAA 271
Thomas, W. K. BAA 271
Thompson. RFA 58
Thompson, Alan Reynolds. FAN 118
Thompson, Ames. CSF 192 ES2 419

Thompson, Anthony Albert. BAA 147 WGT 141 see also Anthony Alban
Thompson, Arnold. SF1 512
Thompson, C. Hall. WTS 46
Thompson, Creswick J. (1862-1943) CSF 192 SF1 512
Thompson, Deane C. AOW 365 FHT 67 SF1 512 SRB 464
Thompson, Don. IAC 232
Thompson, Donald. EXT 10/1 19
Thompson, Dorothy. COT 121
Thompson, E. P. BAA 271 WBW 62
Thompson, Francis. VFS 73, 77-8
Thompson, G. R. NWO 68
Thompson, George Selden (1929-) SF2 1068 see also George Selden
Thompson, Harlan Howard (1894-) HFI 145 SF1 512 SF2 1099
Thompson, Harriet Alfarata Chapman. BAA 89
Thompson, Hunter S. SFH 92
Thompson, Irwin. ACC 84-6
Thompson, J. C. IAC 232
Thompson, Joyce. HFI 145
Thompson, Morton. ETN 2
Thompson, P. H. IMS 35
Thompson, R. E. MSM 99
Thompson, R. W. IAC 232
Thompson, Raymond H. FL5 2299-315
Thompson, Robert G. IMS 65, 79, 84, 111, 115-6, 135, 140, 145, 170, 174, 186-7, 213
Thompson, Stanbury Dugard (1905-) CSF 192 ES2 419
Thompson, Stith. EXT 1/2 38 MFW 94
Thompson, Vance (1863-1925) AOW 114 CSF 192 ES2 419 EXT 7/1 28 SFE 602 SF1 512
Thompson, Will. IAC 232 SFS 117
Thompson, William Mort. CSF 192
Thomson, Christine Campbell. CSF 192-3 ES2 419-21 EXT 3/1 20 SF1 512
Thomson, David. MSF 146
Thomson, George. MSF 25
Thomson, George H. EXT 10/1 19, 42

Thomson, (Sir) George Paget (1892-) ES2 421 POE 311-2 SFH 128
Thomson, Henry Douglas. CSF 193 ES2 421 SF1 512
Thomson, J. J. SFH 128 VFS 188
Thomson, James. ACC 85, 173
Thomson, Kenneth Graham. CSF 193 SF1 512
Thomson, Virgil. VFS 117
Thomson, W. see The Man of the People
Thomson, William. BAA 15
Thomson, William (1746-1817) BAA 52 WGT 141 SF1 512
Thomson, William (1824-1907) see Baron Kelvin
Thorburn, Septimus Smet (1844-1924) SF1 512
Thoreau, Henry David. COT 9, 252 FSU 47 FTF 107 HEN 26 ISW 95 MFW 80 MSF 173, 180 NDA 53, 69 NWO 21, 36, 44, 101, 280, 282-3 SFN 13 TBC 9, 35
Thorn, Joe. SF1 513
Thorndike, Arthur Russell (1885-1972) CSF 193 ES2 421 SF1 513
Thorndike, Lynn. EXT 9/2 62
Thorne, Diana. FFC 133
Thorne, Gerald. BAA 56
Thorne, Guy pseud. of Arthur Edward Ranger Gull. CSF 193 SFE 602
Thorne, Roger pseud. of Ray Russell. IAC 232 SFS 117
Thorner, William E. SF1 513
Thorp, Roderick. IAC 232
Thorpe. WBW 5, 9
Thorpe, Fred. CSF 193 SF1 513
Thouless, Robert H. WIF 21
Threlfall, T. R. CSF 193
Throckmorton, Peter. VFS 38-9
Thron, E. Michael. ACC 72-86 TSO 3-4, 6
Thrush, Arthur (1894-) SF1 513
Thucydides. MSM 125 STF 13
Thurber, Alwyn M. CSF 193 SF1 513
Thurber, James (1894-1961) CSF 193 ES2 421-2 FFC 10, 52 FFR 175 FL4 1712-7, 1904-7 FL5 2118-21, 2159-61 IAC 232 IAH 83, 126 MSM 98 SFS 117 SF1 513-4 SRB 22 TSP 81
Thurstan, Frederic. SF1 514

Thurston, Emily Temple. SF1 514
Thurston, Ernest Temple (1879-1933) CSF 193 SF1 514
Thurston, Robert. FLR 24, 62 IAC 232
Thylmann, Karl. FBK 41
Thynn, Alexander pseud. of Viscount Weymouth. SFE 604
Tibbles, T. H. BAA 48
Tiberius. ISW 62 WFS 221
Tidyman, Ernest (1928-) SFE 604
Tieck, Ludwig (1773-1853) FBK 32 FL4 1718-23 SFW 17 SIH 18 THM 15 WGT 141
Tiedman, Richard. JVN 127, 179-222, 240
Tiegreen, Alan. FFC 50
Tieje, Ralph E. BAA 289
Tiepolo, G. B. BYS 16, 37 CAT 26
Tierney, Richard. CWD 61 HFI 145
Tietjens, Christopher. EXT 9/2 39
Tiger, Hyman. IMS 198
Tigerman, Stanley. [FUT]
Tighe, Harry. CSF 193
Tighe, Virginia. ISW 216
Tigrina pseud. of Edythe Eide. IAC 232
Tihany, Leslie Charles. BAA 272, 289
Tikhonravov. VFS 45
Tikhov. ASF 169
Tilburne, A. R. STH 258 WTS 74, 76, 93
Tilden, Freeman. BAA 89
Tilden, Mike. TSP 226 WFS 104
Tilley, Arthur. BAA 272
Tilley, Patrick (1928-) HFI 145 SFE 604
Tilley, Robert J. IAC 232 SFS 117
Tillich, Paul. BAA xx, 194, 272 MSF 39
Tillotson, Geoffrey. BAA 272
Tillotson, Joe W. ES2 422 VES 145, 177 WGT 141
Tillyard, Aelfrida. BAA 96, 99 CSF 194 SF1 514
Tilman, Rick. BAA 272
Time, Mark pseud. of H. C. Irwin. CSF 194 SF1 514
Timins, Douglas. CSF 194
Timlett, Peter Valentine (1933-) HFI 145 SFE 607 SF1 514

Timlin, William M. CSF 194 ES2 422 SF1 514

Timmermans, Felix (1886-1947) SF1 514

Timmins, William. BYS 217 RFA 109, 111, 114, 118, 120-1, 126, 135-6, 141-3, 145, 157, 167, 190, 195 VES 152, 168 WSF 104

Timms, Edward Vivian (1895-1960) CSF 194 ES2 422 SF1 514

Timperley, Rosemary Kenyon (1920-) ES2 422 IAC 233 SF1 514 SF2 1099-100

Tincker, Mary Agnes (1831-1907) BAA 48 CSF 194 SF1 514

Tincrowdor, Leo Q. IAC 233

Tindall, Gillian (1938-) ES2 422

Tinkelman, Murray. FFC 76, 137 SRB 53 VES 241-3

Tinker, Chauncey Brewster. BAA 194 SRB 10

Tinkler, John. EXT 10/1 31, 42

Tinsley, Frank (1899-) ES2 422

Tipler, Frank J. COT 92

Tipple, H. CSF 194

Tiptree, James, Jr. pseud. of Alice Hastings Sheldon. AAL 120, 157 ALW 212 AOW 266, 298 BYS 304 CEN 70-86 ETN 2, 43, 66, 101, 106, 114, 138-9, 142, 176 FFR 175 HFI 145 IAC 233 LEX 607-8 LTN 131, 179-83, 258 MFW 24 RGS 176-7 SFD 57, 224 SFE 607-8 SFW 396, 398, 492, 531-41 SF1 515 SL4 1999-2002 SRB 372 VES 217, 219, 319 WSF 236

Titterton, William Richard. SF1 515

Titus, Eve. FFC 126

Tobier, Arthur. SF1 515

Todd, David. EXT 5/2 38, 40, 46

Todd, Lawrence. VES 179

Todd, Mabel Loomis. EXT 5/2 46

Todd, Richard. NWO 298

Todd, Ruthann. AOW 305

Todd, Ruthven (1914-) BAA 108 CSF 194 ES2 422 FFC 126 FL2 924-5 SFE 608 SF1 515 WGT 141

Todd, W. SF1 515

Todorov, Tzvetan (1939-) CAT xvii-xviii FBK 8-9, 11, 15 MFW 96 SFE 608 SF1 515 TBC 11, 23

Toffler, Alvin (1928-) ALW 13-4 CAT 31, 134, 137 CSC 306 JHN 31 NWO 24 SFE 608 SRB 509 VES 253 WFS 289 WSF 10, 353

Tofte, Arthur (1902-) HFI 145 IAC 233 LEX 609

Toksvig, Signe (1891-) CSF 194 SF1 515

Tokunaga, Laura. IAC 233

Toldo, Pietro. BAA 272

Tolkien, Christopher. EXT 10/1 39

Tolkien, J(ohn) R(onald) R(euel) (1892-1973) AAL 54, 148-50, 157 ACC 134 ALW 124 AOW 85, 88-9, 93, 95, 118, 346-8, 356, 396 ASF 193-4, 290-4 ATA 12, 15 BAA x BFP 476-80 BYS 162, 201, 265-9 CAT 17, 50 COT 84, 286 CSC 33, 74 CSF 194 CWD 10, 45, 47, 55 CWN 55 EFP 3 ES2 422-3 EXT 5/1 4 EXT 8/1 1 EXT 8/2 30 EXT 9/2 25, 61 EXT 10/1 14, 17-45 FBK 9, 11-2, 81, 96-8 FFC 40, 71, 89 FFR 176-7 FHT 15-6, 32 FLT 6 FL2 732-9, 897-915 FL4 1724-8, 1733-43 FSU 33 FTF 199-200 HFI 145-6 HWK 40 IAH 82 LEX 609-11 LTN 17, 26, 34, 40, 53, 68-9, 80, 88, 93, 95-6, 107, 125, 132, 172, 174, 204-5, 263 PJF 38 POE 275-6 RBY 112-3, 115-6, 120 SFB 112-3 SFD 71, 81, 306, 317 SFE 608-9 SFH 243 SFW 244 SF1 515 SF2 1102-3 SIH 33, 81 SOT 191, 244, 290 SRB 29, 277 STF 67, 78 THM 8, 18, 39 TSF 237 VFS 76 WAA 15, 22, 56, 76, 98, 110-1, 113, 122, 230 WBW 3, 23, 48-9, 57, 61 WSF 238, 247, 294, 301, 303, 387

Tolstoy, Alexander (1882-1945) AOW 358 CSF 194 ES2 423 EXT 1/1 7 EXT 9/2 33 EXT 10/2 73, 76-7 FFR 177 LEX 611-2 SFE 609 MSF 193, 252, 254, 260-1 SF1 516 SIH 39, 114 SL1 28-32 SOT 431 WFS 295

Tolstoy, Alexei K. (1817-75) FBK 41, 46 SF1 515

Tolstoy, Leo (1828-1910) CAT 73, 93 CSC 30 CWN 30, 37, 50 LTN 21, 27, 40, 172-3, 199, 215, 256 MSF 243, 245, 250, 269, 272 MSM 253 SFD 43 SFH 80 THM 7

Toman, Michael D. IAC 233

Toman, Nikolai V. IAC 233 MSF 262 SIH 114

Tomas, Andrew. HFI 146
Tomashevsky, B. CAT 73
Tombleson, James Bennett. SF1 516
Tomerlin, John. IAC 233
Tomes, Jacqueline. FFC 36
Tomkins, Calvin. IAC 233
Tomlinson, Dorothy. SF1 516
Tompkins, Harry G. EXT 2/1 16
Tompkins, J. M. S. BYS 37-8
Tompkins, Peter. IAC 233
Tompkins, Walker Allison (1909-) SF1 516 SF2 1103
Tonks, Angela. ES2 423 SFE 609 SF1 516
Tonnies, Ferdinand. POE 154-5
Tooker, Richard (1902-) CSF 194 ES2 423 IMS 22 SFE 609 SF1 516 TSP 8, 29, 71, 185 WGT 141
Toombs, Alfred Gerald (1912-) ES2 423 ISW 254-5 SFE 609 SF1 516
Toomey, Robert E(mmett), Jr. (1945-) HFI 146 IAC 233 SFE 609 SF1 516 SF2 1103
Topfer, Bernard. BAA 272
Topik, Fred S. BAA 289
Topitsch, Ernst. BAA 272
Toppe, Frank (1947-) LEX 609
Torday, Ursula see Charity Blackstock
Torell, Staffan. FFC 133
Torge, Miguel pseud. of Adolfo Rocha. SF1 516
Torkelson, Lucile. EXT 10/1 42
Torme, Mel. WFS 256
Torode, Brian. BAA 203
Torr, Dominic. ES2 423
Torrence, Lewis F. IMS 33
Torrens, James. EXT 10/1 43
Torricelli, Evangelista. SFH 117
Torro, Pel. SIH 102, 104
Tors, Ivan. ISW 101 KAU 152
Torsvan, Traven (1890? -1969) see B. Traven
Tourgee, Albion Winegar (1838-1905) WGT 142 see also Edgar Henry
Tourneur, Nigel. ES2 423 SF1 516
Tousey, Frank. ALW 74, 79 SFW 53-4, 57 SIH 132 STH 54
Tovey, Donald Francis. MIH 22
Tower, Harker. SF1 585
Tower, Washington L. SF1 516

Towers, Ivar (house name) SFE 610 WGT 142 see also Cyril Kornbluth, Richard Wilson
Towers, Tom H. BAA 272
Towle, (Mrs.) Arthur Edward. ES2 423-4 WGT 142
Towne, Anthony (1928-) SF1 516 SF2 1103
Towne, Mary. FFC 71
Towne, Stuart. TSP 199
Townes, Robert Sherman. IAC 233 SFS 117
Townroe, Bernard S. CSF 194
Townsend, Alan. EXT 9/2 63
Townsend, Alexander. CSF 194 SF1 516
Townsend, John Howard. ES2 424 SF1 516
Townsend, John Rowe. FFC 169
Townsend, Larry. SF1 516
Townsend, S. R. BAA 272
Toye, Nina. CSF 194
Toynbee, Arnold J. COT 56, 223-6, 247, 254, 274, 281 MSM 181, 238, 258, 305 POE 264-5 RBY 100 SFH 54 VFS 12
Toynbee, Philip. BYS 194, 320 CWN 3, 24
Toynbee, Polly Mary Louisa (1946-) SFE 610 SF1 516 SF2 1103
Toyota, Aritsune. SFB 142 WFS 305
Tozer, Basil. ES2 424
Tozer, D. C. IAC 233
Tracey, Robyn. IAC 233
Tracy, Donald Fiske (1905-) SF1 517 SF2 1103
Tracy, Louis (1863-1928) CSF 194-5 POE 107-8 SF1 517 STH 183, 202-6, 210, 212 WGT 142
Tracy, Roger Sherman (1841-1926) BAA 81 WGT 142 see also T. Shirby Hodge
Tracy, Spencer. SIH 28-9 WAA 90
Tracy, Thomas (1781-1872) SF1 517
Trafford-Taunton, Winefride. CSF 195
Traill, Henry Duff (1842-1900) CSF 195 SF1 517
Train, Arthur (Cheyney) (1875-1945) AOW 37, 74 CSF 195 ES2 424 EXT 1/1 4, 19 EXT 7/1 26 HFI 146 SFE 610 SF1 517

Train, Oswald. CSF 195 IMS 71-
2, 82, 95, 106, 116, 136, 186, 200,
213, 222, 226 SRB 495 WFS 58
WIF 124, 131 WSF 77
Tralins, Robert (1926-) BAA 160
ES2 424 HFI 146 SFE 610 SF1
517 SF2 1103-4 WGT 142
Transue, Jacob pseud. of Joan
Matheson. HFI 146 IAC 233
SF1 517
Trapnell, Coles. CSC 265, 289
Trask, John. TSP 134
Trask, Margaret. SF1 517
Traugott, John. BAA 272 MSF 11
Trautmann, Wolfgang. BAA 194
Traven, B. pseud. of Traven Tors-
van. IAC 233 SF1 517
Travers, Andrew. IAC 233
Travers, Pamela Lyndon (1906-)
FFC 71 SF1 518
Travers, Peter. SF1 518
Traversi, Derek A. EXT 10/1 43
Travis, James Richard. BAA 289
Tredyakovsky, Vassily K. MSF
244
Treece, Henry (1911?-66) ES2 424
FL2 666-9 HFI 146 SF1 518 SF2
1104-5 SRB 278 VES 233
Tregarron, Yate. CSF 195 SF1
518
Tregarthen, Enys. FFC 82
Tregaskis, Richard William (1916-
73) ES2 424
Trehune, Morgan. SF1 518
Treibich, Stephen John (1936-72)
ES2 424 SFE 612 SF1 518 SF2
1105
Trelawny, Edward. SFW 4
Trell, Max (1900-) SF1 518 SF2
1105
Tremaine. RFA 59
Tremaine, F(rederick) Orlin (1899-
1956) ALW 133, 147, 219 ASF 119,
137, 252, 260 COT v, 15-6, 18, 42,
109, 117-9, 155, 275 ES2 424-5
ETN 12 EXT 7/2 39 IAC 233
IMS 6, 30, 44, 48, 117, 194, 202
MSM 31 RFA xvi-xviii, xxii-
xxiii, 17-8, 24, 26, 29-30, 32, 38,
40, 44, 46-9, 57, 59-60, 65, 127-8,
153, 183-4 SFB 62 SFD 27, 213,
236 SFE 612 SFS 117 SFW 152
SOT 17-9, 21, 27, 39, 42-3, 45, 59,
93, 137, 139, 155, 218, 256, 310,
384 SRB 13, 44 STH 63, 150, 218,
244 VES 71, 135, 334 WFS 43-6,
68, 84, 86 WGT 142 WIF 87, 89
WSF 59-60, 66, 69-71, 80, 87, 91,
126, 157, 217, 298 see also
Warner Van Lorne
Tremaine, Nelson. WGT 142
Trench, Brinsley Le Poer. ES2
425
Trenery, Gladys Graves (1885-
1938) ES2 425 WGT 142 WTS
27, 128 see also G. G. Pendarves
Treni, Hugo. BAA 199
Trepoff, Ivan pseud. of Herman
Arthur Haubold. EXT 4/1 12
Tresilian, Stuart. FFC 132
Trevarthan, Harold P. BAA 104
CSF 195 SF1 518 VES 140
Trevelyan, G. M. VES 121
Trevelyan, Gertrude Eileen. CSF
195 SF1 518
Trevena, John pseud. of Ernest
G. Henham. CSF 195
Treves, Frederick. IAC 234
Trevisan, Bernard. THM 34
Trevithick, Richard. FTF 35
Trevor, Elleston pseud. of Trevor
Dudley-Smith (1920-) CSF 195
ES2 425 FFC 137 SFE 612 SF1
518 WGT 142-3 SF2 1105
Trevor, Lucy Meriol (1919-) SF1
518 SF2 1105
Trevor, M. CSF 195
Trew, Anthony Francis (1906-)
SF1 518 SF2 1105-6
Trier, Walter. FFC 13
Trilling, Lionel. FAN 86 FLT
157 STF 62
Trimble, Bjo. SF1 518
Trimble, Jacqueline (1927-) SF1
518 SF2 1106
Trimble, Louis Preston (1917-)
ES2 425 HFI 146 LEX 613 SFE
612 SF1 519 SF2 1106 UFS 5
Triplett, William Samuel (1899-)
WGT 143 see also Terry Bull
Triplett, Henry Franklin. BAA
90
Tripp, F. J. FFC 156
Tripp, Wallace. FFC 61, 131, 140
Trollope, Anthony (1815-82) BAA
33 BYS 82-3, 102, 165 CSF 195
EXT 4/2 19 EXT 7/1 7-8, 15
FLT 12, 31 FTF 42 MSF 166
SFE 612-3 SF1 519 THM 7
Trollope, Frances Eleanor (-1913)
CSF 195 SF1 519

Tronche, Philippe (1929-) see
Philippe Curval
Trotsky, Leon (1879-1940) ASF
279 EXT 9/2 56
Trott, Susan. FFC 180
Trotter, John. BAA 19
Troubetzkoy, (Princess) Paul.
CSF 195 SF1 519
Troubridge, (Lady) Laura. CSF
195
Trousson, Raymond. BAA 194,
272
Trout, Kilgore pseud. of Philip
Jose Farmer. SFE 613
Trout, Lawana. SF1 519
Trowbridge, Clinton. EXT 10/1
43
Trowbridge, John Townsend
(1843-1923) CSF 195 SF1 519
STH 164-5
Troy, Hugh. FFC 91, 101
Troyanovich, Steve. SRB 281
Trudeau, G. B. KVT 9
True, John Preston (1859-1933)
SF1 519
Trueman, Crysostom. STH 51-3
Truffaut, Francois. CSC 264
ETN 108, 111 RBY 19
Truman, Harry S. COT 140 RHN
12, 15, 94, 96, 211
Truman, O. H. BAA 35
Truman, Olivia M. CSF 195 SF1
519
Trumbo, Dalton (1905-76) CSF
195 SF1 519 SF2 1106
Trumbull, Douglas (1942-) KAU
121 SFE 613 WSF 310
Trygaeus. BAA 82
Tryon, Thomas (1926-) FFR 177
FL2 690-4 FL3 1169-72 SF1
519 SF2 1106
Trzynadlowski, Jan. MSF 67
Tschirgi, Robert D. IAC 234
SFS 117
Tschirky, L. Robert. ES2 425
Tse-Tung, Mao. ASF 283 COT
255 MSF 38
Tsiolkovsky, Konstantin (1857-
1935) COT 31, 33, 53, 91 ES2
425 EXT 10/2 76 IAC 234 LEX
680 MSF 251-2, 257, 259, 263
POE 202 SFB 44 SFE 613 SFS
117 SF1 519 SIH 39, 41 SOT
137, 430-1 VES 69 VFS 43-4,
220-1, 224 WAA 236
Tsutsui, Yasutaka. SFB 142

Tubb, E(dwin) C(harles) (1919-)
AAL 52 ALW 212 AOW 266
BAA 125, 155, 165 BFP 481-7
BYS 55, 262, 285, 296 DMK 227-
34 ES2 425-6 FFR 177 HFI
146-7 IAC 234 ISW 122 KAU
60-1, 67-9 LEX 613-6 RGS 177-
9, 224 SFB 100 SFE 613-4 SFS
117-8 SF1 519-20 SF2 1107
SIH 169 SRB 124 VES 73, 75, 77,
96, 108, 151, 163, 177, 180, 183,
187-9, 195, 209, 215, 314 WGT
143-4 WSF 245, 275, 282, 388
see also Charles Grey, Volsted
Gridban, Gill Hunt, Gregory
Kern, King Lang, Brian Shaw,
Roy Sheldon
Tuchman, Barbara. COT 272
Tuck, Donald H. (1922-) AOW 363
BAA 194 BRS 4 EXT 2/1 1
EXT 3/1 2, 7 EXT 5/1 7 SFD
208 SFE 614 SFH 239 SF1 520-
1 SF2 1107 SRB 66, 126 VES
316, 331 WAA 246 WSF 214,
284, 384
Tucker, Allan James (1929-)
BAA 147, 150, 152 SF1 123 SF2
868
Tucker, (Arthur) Wilson (1914-)
ALW 160 AOW 266-7 BAA 120
BFP 488-9 BYS 262-3, 295
COT 191 ES2 426 EXT 5/1 3
EXT 5/1 3 FFR 177 HFI 147
IAC 234 IMS 13, 19, 33, 40, 43-4,
83, 199, 202-5, 214, 226, 228, 232,
237, 239-41, 246-50 ISW 119,
179-81 KAU 93, 128 LEX 616-7
RFA 44-6, 133 RGS 179 SFB 43
SFE 614-5 SFN 62-5, 105, 117
SFS 118 SFW 125 SF1 521 SF2
1107-8 SIH 116, 169 SL3 1238-
41 SL5 2520-4 SOT 320 SRB
90, 94-5, 119, 362 STH 49 VES
135, 207, 215, 232, 259, 276 WAA
168 WGT 144 WIF 133 WSF
139, 141 see also Hoy Ping Pong
Tucker, Beverley R. CSF 196
Tucker, Frank H. FL2 942-4
RAH 172-93 SL3 1068-72, 1370-
4, 1521-5
Tucker, George (1775-1861) ALW
55, 95 BAA 20 EXT 5/1 4 MSF
142 MSM 210 NWO 71, 101 POE
97, 121 PST 45, 195-6, 207-8,
227, 239, 241, 243-6, 263-5, 274-
5, 279, 290 SOI 44 WGT 144 see

Tucker, George (cont.)
also Joseph Atterley
Tucker, Horace. BAA 52
Tucker, James Benjamin. SF1 521
Tucker, Louis. IAC 234
Tucker, Nathaniel Beverly (1784-1851) SF1 521 WGT 144 see also Edward William Sidney
Tucker, Prentiss. SF1 521
Tucker, Wilson see Arthur Wilson Tucker
Tuckwell, (Rev.) William (1829-1919) BAA 36 EXT 7/1 8, 16 SF1 521
Tudor, Tasha. FFC 83
Tuegel, Ludwig. CSF 196
Tuma, George. RSG 93
Tunbridge, Alan. VES 243
Tung, Lee. AOW 267 BYS 307 SFE 345 SF1 312
Tunstall, William Cuthbert Brian (1900-70) CSF 196 SFE 615 SF1 521
Tupper, Martin Farquhar. POE 68-9
Turek, Ludwig (1896-) LEX 617-8
Turenne, Raymond. CSF 196
Turgenev, Ivan (1818-83) FBK 41-2, 46 SF1 521
Turgot, Anne Robert Jacques. POE 24-6
Turing, A. MFW 210
Turkle, Brinton. FFC 34, 129
Turnbull, Ann. FFC 94, 192
Turnbull, Dora Amy Dillon. WGT 144
Turner, Alice K. ACC 244
Turner, Charles Cyril (1870-1952) CSF 196 SF1 521
Turner, David G. SF1 521 SRB 81
Turner, Edgar. CSF 196 SF1 522
Turner, Eileen Arbuthnot Robertson (1903-) WGT 144
Turner, Frederick. HFI 148
Turner, Frederick Jackson. HID 46 RAH 174 RBY 20, 30, 40-54
Turner, George (1916-) LTN 12 SFE 615 UKL 246
Turner, George Kibbe (1869-1952) CSF 196 SF1 522
Turner, Gerry. SF1 522 ES2 426-7
Turner, Harold R. SFN 29

Turner, J. M. W. MFW 21
Turner, James Ernest (1909-) ES2 427 SF1 522
Turner, Lana. WAA 90
Turner, Stephen C. IAC 234
Turner, Walter James (1889-1946) SF1 522
Turnerelli, Edward Tracy (-1891?) CSF 196 SF1 522 WGT 144
Turney, Catherine (1906-) ES2 427 SF1 522 SF2 1108
Turov, B. MSF 261
Turska, Krystyna. FFC 8, 108
Turton, Godfrey Edmund (1901-) CSF 196 SF1 522
Tuschel, Karl-Heinz (1928-) LEX 618
Tushnet, Leonard. IAC 234
Tusiani, Joseph (1924-) SF1 522 SF2 1108
Tuttle, Emma R. CSF 196
Tuttle, Hudson (1836-1910) CSF 196 SF1 522
Tuttle, Lisa (1952-) IAC 234 LEX 618-9
Tutuola, Amos (1920-) ES2 427 FL3 1071-4 SF1 522 SF2 1108
Tuveson, Ernest Lee. BAA 194 NWO 101
Tuwim, Julian. FBK 147, 149
Tuzinski, Konrad. BAA 194
Tuzinski, Ludwig. BAA 272
Twain, Mark pseud. of Samuel Clemens. ALW 33, 87 AOW 344 ASF 43, 57, 192, 301 CAT 6 COT 243 CSC 24-5, 95, 233 CSF 196 CWD 62 CWN 40 ETN 51 EXT 3/1 29 EXT 4/1 1 EXT 7/1 18 EXT 10/2 80, 99 FBK 72, 120 FFC 169 FL1 319-23 FL3 1081-5 HEN 3, 29 HID 112, 163 IAC 234 IMS 2 ISW 12, 80 KAU 28 MFW 24, 121, 281 MSF 30, 88, 171, 193-203, 220 NWO 20, 35, 94-5, 110-1, 204-5, 213-22, 236, 249-54 PJF 77 RAH 52 RHN 11, 31, 33, 44, 48 RSG 9 SFA 16 SFD 66-7 SFE 615-6 SFH 11, 98 SFN 98, 105 SFS 118 SF1 522 SIH 60 SL1 428-32 SOT 151-2, 156, 202, 350, 417 STH 60, 235 THM 11 VES 145 WFS 33, 310 WIF 59 WSF 19
Tweed, Thomas Frederick (1890-1940) CSF 196 ES2 427 SFE 616 SFN 16 SF1 522-3

Tweedale, Violet Chambers (-1936)
CSF 196 ES2 427 SF1 523
Tweet, Roald D. SFW 259-65, 369-
75, 513-8
Twiford, William Richard. BAA
110 CSF 196 SF1 523 STH
63-4
Twiggs, James (1933-) see Twiggs
Jameson
Twitchell, Paul (1908-71) SF1 585
Two Wags pseud. of John K. Bangs,
Frank D. Sherman. CSF 197
Two Women of the West pseud. of
Ella Marchant, Alice I. Jones.
CSF 197
Tybus, Peter. VES 186, 246
Tyler, Alice Felt. BAA 273
Tyler, J. E. A. SRB 82
Tyler, Steven. ES2 427

Tyler, Theodore pseud. of Edward
William Ziegler. HFI 148 NDA
20 SFE 618 SF1 523
Tyler, Wat. MSF 195, 197
Tymn, Marshall B. AOW 364
BRS 3-4, 10 JVN 227-34, 240-1
SF1 523 SRB ix, 63-83, 225-9,
453-79, 489-95, 513 UKL 241-6
Tynan, Katharine. CSF 197
Tynan, Kenneth. CWN 25
Tyner, Paul. CSF 197 SF1 523
Tyng, Dudley. BAA 273
Tyre, Richard H. IAC 234
Tyrrell, George Nugent Merle.
ES2 427
Tyrwhitt-Wilson, Gerald Hugh
(1883-1950) see Lord Berners
Tyson, John Aubrey (1870-) CSF
197 SF1 523
Tzu, Lao. UKL 78, 224

U

Udny, Ernest. POE 191
Ulam, Adam. BAA 273
Ulbrich, Bernd (1943-) LEX 620
Ulf, Carol Metcalf. WFS 213
see also Carol Pohl
Ulfeld, Leonora Christine. ATA
57
Ulidia. SF1 523
Ullman, James Ramsey (1907-71)
SF1 523 SF2 1108-9
Ullrich, Hermann. BAA 194
Ullrich, J. Rogers. COT 42
Ulrich, Hans. VES 239
Ulrici, Rolf (1922-) LEX 620
Umbstaetter, Herman Daniel
(1851-1913) ALW 85 ES2 427
Uminsky. MSF 252
Underhill, Evelyn (1875-1941)
CSF 197 EXT 9/2 62 SF1 523
Underwood, George. [FUT]

Underwood, John Curtis. BAA
273
Underwood, Leon (1890-) CSF
197 SF1 523
Underwood, Tim. JVN 7-12 SRB
82
Unger, Julius (1912?-63) ES2
427-8 IMS 10, 16, 34, 37, 213,
222-3, 245 SFD 171 SOT 320
WIF 134
Ungerer, Tomi. FFC 137, 140
Uniacke, T. I. CSF 197 SF1 524
Unitas. BAA 86 CSF 197
Unnerstad, Edith Totterman
(1900-) ES2 428
Unpatronized Female, (An). CSF
197
Untermeyer, Louis (1885-1977)
IAC 235 SF1 524 SF2 1109
Untruthful Thomas. SF1 524

Unwin, David Storr (1918-) ES2 428 SF2 1069 WGT 145 see also David Severn
Unwin, J. D. BAA 110
Unwin, Nora. FFC 74, 82, 134, 137, 173
Unwin, Reyner. EXT 10/1 21
Upchurch, Boyd Bradfield (1919-) BAA 147, 150, 152, 160-1 BFP 490 ES2 428 SF2 826 WGT 145 see also John Boyd
Updike, John (1932-) BAA 133 ES2 428 EXT 8/1 17 EXT 9/1 17 FFR 178 FL1 222-7 IAC 235 IAH 81 SF1 524 SF2 1109 SL4 1714-9
Upham, Edward (1776-1834) SF1 524
Upson, William H. IAC 235
Upton, Smyth. SF1 524
Upward, Allen (1863-1926) CSF 197 SF1 524
Urang, Gunnar. AOW 356 BAA 195 SF1 524 SOI 97-110
Urban, Helen M. IAC 235
Urbanek, Mae Bobb (1903-) SF1 524 SF2 1109
Urena, Pedro Henriquez. BAA 229

Urey, Harold. VFS 225
Uris, Auren (1913-) see Auren Paul
Urn, Althea pseud. of Consuelo Urisarri Ford. SF1 524
Urner, Nathan D. WGT 145
Urquhart, Elizabeth. FFC 91
Urquhart, M. CSF 197
Urwin, Iris. IAC 235
Usach, Pascual Enguidanos. SIH 141, 166, 169 see also George H. White
Uscatescu, George. BAA 195
Uscatescu, Giorgio. BAA 273
Usher, Wilfred. SF1 524
Uspensky, L. V. MSF 264
Utley, Brian R. HFI 148 SF1 524
Utley, Steven. FFR 178 FRN 45 IAC 197, 235
Utpatel, Frank. FBK 76, 78 IMS 23-4 WTS 84
Utterson, Sarah (1782?-1851) CSF 197 SF1 525
Uttley, Alison (1884-1976) CSF 197 SF1 525 FFC 197
Uyeda, Akinari (1734-1809) SF1 525

V

Vacca, Roberto. COT 274
Vachell, Horace Annesley (1861-1955) CSF 197 SF1 525
Vader, John. SF1 525
Vadim, Roger. FBK 44, 46 SFB 139

Vaihinger, Hans. MSF 52
Vail, Kay Boyle (1903-) WGT 146
Vairasse, Denis (1630-1700) WGT 146 see also Capt. Siden
Vaisberg, Maurice. VES 147
Valdez, Paul. CSF 197 SF1 525

345

Vale, Eugene. BAA 155
Vale, G. B. CSF 197
Vale, Rena Marie (1898-) ES2
428 HFI 148 SFE 623-4 SF1
525
Vale, Robert B. CSF 197 SF1
525
Valens, Evans G., Jr. (1920-)
ES2 428
Valentine, Richard. SF1 525
Valentine, Victor. ES2 428 SFE
624 SF1 525
Valentiner, Brigitta. SF1 525
Valentino, Rudolph. EXT 7/2 37
WAA 87
Valery. TDI 63
Valery, Paul. MSF 159 RZY 26
Valier, Max (1895-1930) COT 36,
38 ES2 428 IMS 17
Valigursky, Edward I. (1926-)
ES2 428 SFE 624 SRB 37 VES
81, 291
Valintcourt, Honore. FFC 182
Valkhoff, P. BAA 273
Valla, Riccardo. SL1 462-4 SL4
1896-7
Vallance, Karl. SF1 525
Vallee, Jacques (1939-) ES2 428
see also Jerome Seriel
Vallejo, Boris. FRN 409, 411-2
VES 151
Vallentin, Antonia. BAA 195
Valpy, Judith. FFC 170
Vamber, Arminius. FBK 49
Van Alm, Aidan. IAC 235
Van Arnam, David G. ES2 428
FFR 7 HFI 148 SFE 624 SF1
525-6
Van Ash, Cay. AOW 356 SF1
526
Van Beever, Robert F. SF1 526
Van Dalsem, Newton. BAA 111
Van De Bovenkamp, Valli. FFC
157
Van Der Elst, Violet (1882-1966)
ES2 428-9 SF1 526-7
Van Der Naillen, Albert (1830-
1928) CSF 198 SF1 527
Van Der Poel, W. I. ES2 429
Van Der Wolk, E. EXT 6/1 16
Van Deusen, Alonzo. BAA 36
SF1 527
Van Dine, S. S. MSM 27 STH 141
Van Dongen, Henry R. ES2 429
RFA 186, 198, 200, 202, 204-5,
208-9, 211 SFE 625 SRB 37

VES 83, 89, 91, 176, 232, 291 WSF
173, 224
Van Doren, Charles. SFN 78
Van Doren, Mark Albert (1894-
1972) CSF 198 IAC 235 SFS 118
SF1 527 SF2 1109-10
Van Dresser, Peter. COT 29, 35,
56 IAC 235 SFS 118
Van Dyke, Henry Jackson (1852-
1933) ES2 429 SF1 527
Van Eeden, Frederik Willem
(1860-1932) CSF 67 SF1 165
Van Gogh, Vincent (1853-90) CWN
10, 13-4, 30
Van Greenaway, Peter (1929-)
SFE 625 SF1 527
Van Herck, Paul (1938-) AOW 267
HFI 148 SFE 625 SF1 527 SL1
294-7
Van Herp, Jacques (1923-) BAA
180 SFE 625 SL1 109-12, 294-
7 SL2 932-5 SL4 1726-9 SL5
2389-91
Van Holk, Freder (1901-) ES2
429 LEX 374-6
Van Houten, Raymond (1919?-63)
ES2 429 IMS 64, 68, 73, 84, 116,
123-4, 177-81, 188, 214, 219, 230,
234 WIF 140
Van Ith, Lily pseud. of Emilie
Ida Friedli. SF1 527
Van Kampen, Karl pseud. of John
W. Campbell, Jr. ASF 197
ISW 247 RFA 30 WSF 69
Van Laerhoven, Bob (1953-) IAC
235 LEX 624
Van Laun, Henri (1820-96) BAA
67, 163 CSF 198 SF1 527
Van Leeuwen, Jean. FFC 126
Van Leeuwenhoek. VFS 195
Van Lihn, Erik pseud. of Lester
Del Rey. ALW 221 IAH 40-2,
67
Van Loden, Erle. SF1 527
Van Loggem, Manuel (1916-) BAA
273 IAC 235 LEX 436-7
Van Loon, Hendrik Willem (1882-
1944) CSF 198 SF1 527
Van Lorne, Warner pseud. of F.
Orlin Tremaine. ALW 10 IAC
235 RFA 59-60 SFE 625-6
SOT 40, 383-4 WFS 44-5
Van Lustbader, Eric. HFI 148
SFE 626
Van Marcus, Carl. SF1 528

Van Mierlo, H. A. ES2 429 SF1 528
Van Pedroe-Savidge, E. SF1 528
Van Petten, Albert Archer (1925-) BAA 134 SF1 528
Van Polen, Herman. BAA 106
Van Praag, Ganna Ottevaere. EXT 10/1 37
Van Rensselaer, Frederick. WGT 147
Van Ronkel, Alfred. SOT 206
Van Roosbroeck, Gustave Leopold (1888-1936) SF1 528
Van Rooyan, John. IMS 169
Van Scyoc, Sydney J(oyce) (1939-) AAL 100-1 FFR 158 HFI 149 IAC 235 LEX 556 RGS 181-2 SFD 17 SFE 626 SF1 528 SF2 1110
Van Slee, J. C. BAA 267
Van Thal, Herbert Maurice (1904-) ES2 429-30 SF1 528 SF2 1110
Van Troyer, Gene. LTN 270
Van Tuyl, Zaara Rosealthea (1901-) ES2 430 SFE 626 SF1 528 SF2 1110 WGT 147
Van Vogt, A(lfred) E(lton) (1912-) AAL 26, 40-1, 172-3, 177-8 ALW 8, 136, 144, 155, 160, 163-5, 171, 184-5, 213-4, 230 AOW 267-9, 288, 293, 394 ASF 123, 215, 218, 222 BAA 159 BFP 491-6 BYS 37, 205, 223, 227-8, 232, 242, 254, 265, 287, 304, 313 CAT 22, 67, 133 COT 20-1, 129, 152-3, 158, 215, 221-2, 292-3 CSC 29, 31, 61, 64-5, 67, 84, 149-52, 169-70, 172, 180, 210 CSF 198 CWD 61 CWN 48 DMK 133-44 ES2 430-2 ETN 16-7, 31, 33, 68-9, 114, 145, 159-60, 163 EXT 1/2 30 EXT 2/1 2 EXT 3/1 27 EXT 5/1 3 EXT 6/2 51 EXT 7/2 40 EXT 10/2 110 FBK 122 FFR 189-93 FL1 146-8 FTF 69, 117-8, 125, 130, 140, 193 HFI 149-50 HID 36-7, 53, 92, 103 IAC 235-7 IAH 18, 24-5, 38, 66, 85 INT 14 ISW 2, 47-62, 85, 121, 140, 151, 154, 186, 203, 217-8, 229, 236, 254 JVN 186-7, 205 KAU 14, 61, 129, 185-6, 216-7 LEX 632-6 MFW 8-10, 19, 22, 32, 41, 170, 173, 229, 253 MIH 22-4, 36, 114 MSF 22, 26, 79, 122, 279 MSM 32, 37, 75, 79, 85-6, 138, 172, 186-7 NWO 44, 163, 182 OWB 51-66, 79, 90, 97, 99 PJF 33 RFA 59, 68-70, 74, 78-9, 81-2, 84, 90, 94, 100-1, 104, 106-7, 110-2, 114, 116, 118, 123-6, 130, 134, 137-9, 144, 146-7, 155, 158, 162-3, 165-6, 168, 170, 176-7, 184, 187-9, 193, 195 RGS 182-4 SFA 244, 274 SFB 19, 62, 88-9, 140, 146 SFD 28, 64, 73-4, 97, 209, 232, 235-6, 239, 242, 244-6, 291, 294, 296, 311-2 SFE 626-8 SFH 41, 51-2, 63, 84, 152-3, 156, 159, 193 SFN 83, 90 SFS 118-9 SFW 148, 187, 209-17, 345, 394 SF1 528-9 SF2 1110-1 SIH 48, 54, 56, 184-5 SL5 2096-100, 2378-82, 2442-6, 2501-5 SOT 3, 6, 20, 45, 62, 72, 82, 96, 159, 182, 193, 201-2, 213-28, 231, 254-5, 259-60, 294, 315-6, 320, 333-4, 356, 361, 431 SRB 13, 15, 99, 278, 303, 305, 307, 328 SV2 30-40 SV3 3-7 TJB 4, 11-2, 21 TSF 58, 233 VES 72, 74, 77, 96, 105, 108, 113, 149-50, 154, 160, 174, 177, 179-80, 193, 195, 202, 205-6, 226, 230, 236, 261, 307, 342 WAA 131, 168 WFS 39, 111, 301 WIF 22, 95, 107, 145, 149, 160, 163, 202, 208, 214, 254 WSF 94-5, 97, 101-5, 109, 113, 135, 148, 154, 164, 167, 321, 336, 386
Van Vogt, Edna Mayne Hull (1905-75) ES2 432-3 WGT 147 see also E. Mayne Hull
Van Vorst, Marie. CSF 198
Van Wely, Babs. FFC 46
Van Wijngarden, Nicholas. BAA 277, 289
Van Winkle, Monica F. SF1 529
Van Zeller, Claude Hubert (1905-) BAA 116 SF2 1111 WGT 147 see also Hugh Venning
Van Zile, Edward Sims (1863-1931) CSF 198 ES2 433 SF1 530
Van-Anderson, Helen (1859-) SF1 525
Vance, Gerald (house name) SFE 624 WGT 146 WIF 120 see also Randall Garrett, Roger P. Graham, Robert Silverberg
Vance, Jack pseud. of John Holbrook Vance. AAL 5, 10, 116-7, 119, 122, 166-9, 212 ALW 161 AOW 269-70, 288 BAA 130, 132 BYS 263, 279 CSC 32-3, 121, 132 EFP 12 ES2 433-4 EXT 2/2 31

Vance, Jack (cont.)
EXT 5/1 3 EXT 8/1 6 FBK 94
FFR 179-81 [FJT] FL1 441-6
HFI 150-1 HID 19,106, 141-3
IAC 237-8 IAH 11-3, 20, 41-2,
50,103,119-23 ISW 139,158,
197-8, 219 LEX 621-4 LTN 92
RFA 191,199, 205, 209, 211-2,
214 RGS 180-1, 224-5 SFD 32,
75, 251, 260, 300, 312-4, 316 SFE
624-5 SFH 155 SFS 119-20
SFW 543-9 SF1 526 SIN 142
SL2 600-4, 665-70 SL3 1135-9,
1144-50 SRB 278, 328, 340 TJB
5 TSF 62, 233-4 VES 88, 92,
112-3, 208 WAA 108 WFS 240,
291-2 WIF 91, 146 WSF 121
Vance, John Holbrook (1916-)
BAA 150 BFP 497-501 SF2
1109 WGT 146 see also Jack
Vance
Vance, Louis Joseph (1879-1933)
CSF 197 SF1 526
Vance, Steve. HFI 151
Vancel, Doris. WGT 147
Vandel, Jean-Gaston. ES2 434
SF1 526
Vanden, Dirk. SF1 526
Vandenberg, Stephen G. BAA 273
Vanderbilt (family). KVT 59
Vandercook, John W. TSP 145
Vane, Sutton (1888-) CSF 198
SF1 527
Vanewords, John Pre. CSF 198
SF1 527
Vansittart, Peter (1920-) SFE 626
Vardeman, Robert E. IAC 238
Vare, Daniel (188-1956) ES2 434
SF1 530
Varley, John (Herbert) (1947-)
AAL 176 BFP 502 ETN 3,10,
36, 43, 99 FFR 182 HFI 151
IAC 238 LEX 624-6 RGS 184-5
SFE 628 SL4 1608-12 SRB 370,
375-6 WGT 147
Varma, Devendra P. (1923-) ES2
434 SF1 585
Varshavski, Ilya (1909-74) FFR
182 IAC 238 MSF 262, 269 SFB
122 SFS 120 SIH 44, 83, 94-5
SL3 1165-70 SL5 2113-6 VES
177
Varwig, Roland. BAA 273
Vas Dias, Robert. ALW 38
Vasbinder, Samuel H. FL1 22-5,
178-80 FL2 628-30 FL3 1221-3

Vasiliu, Mircea. FFC 26, 57, 86-7
Vasquez, Francisco. CSF 198
Vasseur, John. CSF 198 SF1 530
Vassilyev, Mikhail V. ES2 434
IAC 238 SFS 120
Vassilikos, Vassilius (1933-)
ES2 434 SF1 530
Vassos, John. BAA 96 CSF 198
SF1 530
Vassos, Ruth (1896-1965) BAA 96
CSF 198 SF1 530
Vattimo, Gianni. BAA 273
Vaughan, Anne. FFC 95
Vaughan, Auriel Rosemary Malet
(1923-) WGT 147 see also
Oriel Malet
Vaughan, Herbert Millingchamp
(1870-1948) BAA 82, 95 ES2
434 SF1 530
Vaughan, Hilda (1892-) ES2 434
SF1 585
Vaughan, Herbert M. CSF 198
Vaughan, Owen. WGT 147
Vaughan, Richard. COT 41, 43
ES2 434 WSF 64
Vaughan, Thomas Hunter. CSF
198 SF1 530
Vaughn, Frank E. SFS 120
Vaulet, Clement (1876-) WGT 147
Vautrin. CYR 6
Vaux, Patrick. CSF 198 SF1 530
WGT 147 see also Navarchus
Vax, Louis. FBK 8
Veblen, Thorstein. EXT 7/1 24
EXT 7/2 32 RHN 26 SFH 10
Vedel, Georges. BAA 273
Veiby, John. BAA 82, 89
Veidt, Conrad. STH 229
Veillot, Claude. AOW 295 IAC
238 SFS 120
Veiras. EXT 8/1 23
Veitch, Tom. IAC 238
Velasquez, Pedro. SF1 530
Veldhuis, Ruurd. BAA 195
Velikovsky, Immanuel (1895-)
ASF 188, 259-60 ES2 434 EXT
7/1 16 NWO 37 SFE 628 STH
247 VES 131, 342 VFS 203
WIF 51
Veloz, Nard. SF1 530
Venable, Clarke (1892-) WGT 147
see also Covington Clarke
Venezis, Elias. IAC 238
Vennerstrom, Ivar Teodor. BAA
195

Venning, Hugh pseud. of Hubert
Van Zeller. ES2 435 NWO 124
SF1 531
Ventris, Michael. AAL 38, 42
Venturo, Betty Lou Baker (1928-)
SF2 804 see also Betty Baker
Vepa, (Dr.) Prasad. VFS 112
Vercours pseud. of Jean Bruller.
ALW 31, 238 AOW 270 BYS
307 EXT 10/2 110 FBK 53
FFR 183 FL4 1872-4 HFI 185
HID 2, 45 MSF 239 SFE 630
SFN 117 SF1 531 SL5 2529-33
VES 95
Verhoeven, Cornelius. KAU 24
Verlanger, Julia pseud. of
Heliane Taieb. SFE 630
Verling, John. FFC 161
Vern, David (1924-) ES2 435 IMS
186 WFS 112-3 WGT 147 see
also David V. Reed, Craig Ellis,
Peter Horn
Vernadskii, V. I. COT 257, 273-4
Verne, Jean Jules. SRB 525
Verne, Jules (Gabriel) (1828-
1905) ACC 85, 159 ALW 11, 13,
33, 53, 55, 57, 62, 64-76, 79, 82,
87, 95, 97, 99-102, 104, 116-7,
120, 122, 125, 141, 191, 214, 216
AOW 6, 38-40, 75, 90, 338, 341,
347, 351, 394, 396, 404 ASF 23-
6, 35, 105-7, 123, 126, 165-7, 184-
9, 191, 194, 217 BYS 44, 62, 92,
94-9, 111, 120, 127, 145, 216, 239,
313 CAT xvi, 2-3, 7-8, 11, 13, 19,
27, 32, 41, 54, 88, 93, 138 COT 9,
23, 31-2, 53, 105, 119, 175 CSC
26, 38, 121-2, 166-8, 172-3 CSF
198-9 EFP 3 ES2 435-7 EXT
1/2 24, 26, 29-30 EXT 2/1 1, 5-
20 EXT 3/1 1, 29 EXT 3/2 31,
40 EXT 4/2 21, 24 EXT 5/1 4,
15-6, 16a EXT 5/2 2 EXT 6/2
32 EXT 7/2 34 EXT 9/2 29-30
EXT 10/2 80, 93, 107 FAN 10-1
FFR 185-7 FTF 37-41, 43-5,
54, 66-8, 70, 113, 120 HFI 151-2
HWK 6, 8 IAC 238-9 IMS 3 INT
6 KAU 55-6, 59 KWS 198-9,
201, 204-5 LEX 626-8 MFW ix-
x, 117, 122, 281-2 MIH 100-1, 103
MSF 5, 9-10, 12, 22-3, 35, 59, 65,
72-3, 87-8, 116-7, 120, 123, 132,
143, 147-65, 167-71, 198, 203, 209-
11, 217, 220, 236, 239, 244, 251-2,
254, 260-1, 263-4 MSM 29-30,

89, 101, 140-1, 200, 204, 207-8,
213, 222, 245, 297, 303-4 NWO x,
20, 50-2, 57, 71, 148 OMN 2, 67,
71, 81, 120-3, 130 OWB 9, 28
PJF 13, 37 POE 92-103, 133, 176,
179 PST 9-10, 29, 36-40, 44, 47-
8, 54-5, 58-62, 64, 67, 75, 79-80,
96, 98-9, 107, 116, 118, 120, 150,
161, 193-4, 196, 198, 200, 203-5,
208-9, 211, 213, 215, 228, 238,
240-5, 249-53, 256-8, 261-2, 264,
267-71, 273-6, 279, 282, 284, 286,
289-90, 294, 296, 315, 318, 320
RBY 19, 81, 83 RFA vi, 2 RGS
185-6 RHN 11, 21, 62 RSG 9
SFA 191 SFB 12, 21-3, 29, 31,
39, 42, 45, 54-5, 66-9, 72-4, 76,
94, 97, 136 SFD 9-10, 21, 23-4,
72, 235, 287 SFE 630-2 SFH 8-
11, 14, 37, 102, 107, 169-70, 191,
196-200 SFN 28-9, 32, 81, 103
SFS 120 SFW 7, 17, 28, 63, 126,
573-82 SF1 531-3 SIH 9, 11, 36-
41, 44, 53-4, 74, 170, 185, 202
SIN 12-3, 15-23 SL1 153-6, 386-
91 SL2 850-4 SL3 1102-5 SL5
2329-33 SOI 44-5 SOT 14, 105,
196, 234, 373, 399 SRB 7 STF
15 STH 25-7, 44, 55-6, 122, 184,
189, 195, 198-9, 209 TDI 6 TRB
54 TSF 28 VES 69, 103, 126,
130, 137, 155, 161, 173, 248, 250,
255, 257-60, 295, 305, 312, 322
VFS 239 WAA 7, 34-5, 92, 102,
242 WFS 7, 21 WIF 15, 20, 38,
45-9, 53, 59, 93, 149, 294 WSF
16-8, 35, 43-4, 128, 386 WTS 17
YTS 2-5, 9, 15, 110-2
Verne, Michel. EXT 3/2 47
MSF 162
Verne, Paul. EXT 3/2 36
Verne, Pierre. ALW 65
Verner, Gerald. ES2 437 SF1
533
Vernier, Jean-Pierre. KAU 94
Vernon, Charles see Captain
Anson
Vernon, George Shirra Gibb
(1885-) WGT 147 see also
Vernon George
Vernon, Roger Lee (1924-) ES2
437-8 HFI 152 IAC 239 ISW
206-8 SFE 632 SF1 533
Verrill, A(lpheus) Hyatt (1871-
1954) ALW 121 CSF 199 ES2
438 HFI 152 LEX 628 PST 127,

Verrill, A. Hyatt (cont.)
196, 205, 207, 218, 226, 231, 240,
264, 291 RFA 2 SFD 23-4 SFE
632 SF1 533 SOT 15, 354 STH
104, 110, 139, 145, 172 VES 93,
139, 232, 312, 340 WGT 147-8
WSF 44
Verron, Robert. ES2 438 SF1
533
Versace, Marie Teresa Rios
(1917-) SF2 1049 WGT 148 see
also Maria Teresa Rios, Tere
rios
Verschoyle, Catherine Mildred.
SF1 534
Versins, Pierre (1922?-) AOW
356 BAA 195 ES2 438 SFE
632 TPS 163-7
Vertlieb, Steve. WAA 244
Very, Pierre (1900-60) SF1 534
Vespucci, Amerigo. MSF 95
Vetch, Thomas. CSF 199 SF1
534
Vetsch, Jakob. WGT 148
Vetter, John. WTS 5, 92, 103
Vian, Boris (1920-59) BAA 268
IAC 239 SFB 89 SFE 633 SF1
534 SIH 53-4, 56, 79, 81 SL2
965-8 WAA 136, 229
Viard, Henri Louis Luc (1912-)
ES2 438 WGT 148 see also
Henry Ward
Vickers, Brian. IAC 239
Vickers, John. BAA 27 WGT
148
Vickers, Roy (1889-1965) WGT
148
Vico, Giovanni Battista. COT
225, 254 SFH 54, 60-1
Victor, Joan. FFC 117
Victoria, (Queen). SFH 14 WAA
33
Vidal, Eugene Luther, Jr. (1925-)
SF2 1111 see also Gore Vidal
Vidal, Gore pseud. of Eugene
Luther Vidal, Jr. ALW 99
AOW 271 BAA 125 ES2 438
EXT 2/2 27 EXT 3/1 26 EXT
5/1 4 FAN 148 HFI 152 IAC
239 ISW 175-6 NDA xi, 190-6,
218 SFE 633 SFN 105 SFS 120
SF1 534 SOT 332 VFS 126
WGT 148
Vidler, Anthony. BAA 274
Viele, Herman Knickerbocker
(1856-1908) CSF 199 ES2 438

Vielle, Eugene Emile (1913-)
SF1 534
Viereck, George Sylvester (1884-
1962) AOW 114 CSF 200 ES2
438-9 FL4 1918-21 HFI 152-3
SFE 633 SF1 534
Vieweg, Heinz (1920-) LEX 629
Vigers, Daphne. BAA 113 CSF
200 SF1 534
Viggiano, Michael. SF1 534
Vigures, R. H. EXT 10/1 43
Viking, Otto (1883-) SFE 633 SF1
534
Vildrac, Charles. FFC 137
Villa, Silvio. CSF 200 ES2 439
SF1 534
Villanueva, Luis Aguilar. BAA
198
Villard, Alexander. SF1 534
Villeneuve. WGT 148
Villgradter, Rudolf. BAA 195
Villon, Francois. MSF 97
Vinacua, Rodolfo. EXT 9/1 17
Vincent, Bernard. BAA 274
Vincent, Charles (1851-1920)
SF1 534
Vincent, Florence Smith. SF1
534
Vincent, George E. BAA 274
Vincent, Harl pseud. of Harold
Vincent Schoepflin (1893-1968)
ALW 10, 126 ASF 243 COT 39
HFI 153 IAC 239 IMS 24, 213
LEX 629 MIH 45, 62 RFA 6, 13,
15, 75 SFA 26 SFD 23-4 SFE
634 SFS 120 SF1 534 SOT 251
VES 104, 134, 173, 199 WIF 89
WSF 50, 54
Vincent, Joyce. CSF 200 SF1
534
Vindex. SF1 535
Vines, Walter Sherard (1890-)
CSF 200 SF1 535
Vinge, Joan D. (1948-) CSC 119
IAC 239 LEX 629-30 SFE 634
Vinge, Vernor (Steffen) (1944-)
HFI 153 IAC 239 LEX 630-1
RGS 186-7 SFE 634 SFS 120
SF1 535 SF2 1111 VES 208
Vinogradov, A. P. COT 257
Vinson, Rex Thomas (1935-) SF2
961 see also Vincent King
Vinter, Mary. CSF 200
Vinton, Arthur Dudley (1852-1906)
BAA xxii, 43 CSF 200 SF1 535
Viot, H. G. DTS 26

Virg, Leo. ES2 439 SF1 585
Virgil. CUA 5-6, 26 FTF 16
LTN 63 MSF 87, 118 PJF 57
WIF 27, 33
Virilio, Paul. BAA 274
Virnisch, M. BAA 274
Visiak, E. H. pseud. of Edward
Harold Physick (1878-1972) BYS
213 CSF 200 ES2 439 FL2 993-
7 SFE 634 SF1 535 THM 4-5,
11-4, 33, 38-40, 45-7 TSP 121
Visick, Jacquelyn. SF1 535
Visser, A. J. BAA 274
Vitarelli, Robert Francis (1940-)
SF1 535 SF2 111-2
Viteles, Morris S. BAA 274
Vittorini, Elio. WFS 147
Vittorini, Maria. WFS 147
Vittorini, Ugo. WFS 147
Vitu, Auguste. CSF 200
Vivenair. CSF 200 FTF 26-7
Vivian, Evelyn Charles (1882-
1947) CSF 200 ES2 439 HFI
153 SFE 635 SF1 535 STH 81
WGT 148 see also Jack Mann
Vivian, Francis pseud. of Arthur
Ernest Ashley (1906-) CSF 200
SF1 535
Vivian, Thomas J. IAC 239
Vlachos, Evan. BAA 274
Vlad (the Impaler). FBK 48 see
also Voivod Tepesch Drakula
Vlasto, John Alexander (1877-
1958) ES2 439 WGT 148-9 see
also John Remenham
Vlcek, Ernst (1941-) LEX 631-2
Voegeli, Max. FFC 57
Vogel, (Sir) Julius (1835-99) BAA
40 CSF 200 POE 110 SF1 535
Vogel, Klaus. SF1 536
Vogelin, S. BAA 274
Vogt, Karl. BAA 274 POE 86
Voight, Andreas. BAA xii, xx,
195 MSF 41
Voise, Waldemar. BAA 274
Voiskunsky, Yevgeny (1922-)
IAC 239 SFS 77, 120 SF1 536
SF2 1112
Volk, Gordon. CSF 200
Volk, Winfried. BAA 289
Volkmann-Schluck, K. H. BAA
274
Volkov, A. SIH 113
Volokhov, V. MSF 252
Volta, (Count) Alesandro. ASF
182 SFH 113

Volta, Ornella. ES2 439 SF1
536
Voltaire pseud. of F. M. Arouet.
AOW 32 ASF 149 BYS 76-9
CAT 69-70 COT 56 CSC 170
CSF 200 EXT 2/1 4 EXT 3/1
30 EXT 7/1 13 EXT 10/2 80
FBK 82 FTF 26, 48, 97, 183 IAC
239 MIH 26 MSF 30, 114, 139,
244, 275 NWO 253 PST 21-3,
170, 221, 301 SFE 635 SFH 31,
67 SF1 536 SHL 21-2 WAA 27,
31 WFS 21, 33 WIF 38, 232
WTS 11
Voltz, William (1938-) LEX 636-7
Von Arnim, Ludwig Achim. FBK
32 SIH 6, 124 SOI 31
Von Beethoven, Ludwig (1770-
1827) CUA 41 CWN 39 LTN
62, 116 THM 26, 36 WFS 65
Von Bernhardi, Julius. POE 240
Von Bertanalaff, Ludwig. BAA
204
Von Bondy, M. BAA 205
Von Borries, Achim. BAA 170
Von Braun, Wernher (1912-77)
COT 33-5, 46 ES2 439-40 EXT
8/1 3 HFI 153 MSM 199 NWO
29 RHN 67 SFN 31 SF1 536
SF2 1112 SOT 206 VFS 9, 131,
211, 225 WFS 262 YTS 30, 58
Von Bruck, Max. BAA 208
Von Camp, Magdalene Baker.
STH 162
Von Chamisso, Adelbert (1781-
1838) CSF 41 FBK 32 FL3
1234-7 SF1 99 SIH 6, 18, 24
Von Clausewitz, Karl. MSM 250
Von Czibulka, Alf. FBK 82
Von Daniken, Erich (1935-) ACE
51 AC2 49 AOW 166 FTF 134
MSF 83 NWO 262 PJF 74 SFE
635 SFH 159 VES 273, 336, 339-
40 WSF 8, 167
Von Degen pseud. of Baroness
Ann Von Rabe. CSF 201 SF1
536
Von Der Gabelentz, Georg. FBK
142
Von Der Muhll, Emmanuel. BAA
195
Von Eichendorff, Joseph (1788-
1857) FBK 32 FL2 970-2
Von Franz, Marie Louise. LTN
66-7
Von Frisch, Karl. AAL 59

Von Geldern, Egmont Colerus (1888-1939) see Egmont Colerus
Von Glahn, George A. CEN 109-31
Von Goethe, Johann Wolfgang (1749-1832) ACC 136 CSC 10, 129,170 CWN 13 CYR 50 FBK 44 FFR 85 FL2 973-5 IAC 119 KVT 26 MIH 76 MSF 117,130, 135,139,171 NWO 259 POE 56-7 RAH 74 RZY 59 SF1 213 TFC 34 WAA 86
Von Grosse, Karl Marquis. CSF 88
Von Guenther, Johannes (1886-) SF1 227
Von Guericke, Otto. FTF 23, 25
Von Hanstein, Otfrid (1869-) ES2 440 LEX 355 PST 150,196,223, 227,264,268,270,279,285,290-1,302 STH 64-5 VES 103,128
Von Harbou, Thea (1888-1953) AOW 92,103 CSF 93 ES2 440 FFR 89 HFI 153 KAU 87,105 LEX 356-7 MSF 218 OMN 87-9 SFE 635 SFW 104 SF1 537 SIH 21,135,138 SL3 1383-6 SOT 176 VES 71,175 WAA 36
Von Hardenberg, Friedrich (1772-1801) see Novalis
Von Helders, (Major) pseud. of Robert Knauss. CSF 98
Von Helmholtz-Phelan, Anna A. BAA 195
Von Herbert, Frederick William. SF1 251
Von Herzmanovsky-Orlando, Fritz (1877-1954) FBK 131,144
Von Heyse, Paul Johann Ludwig (1830-1914) CSF 99 SF1 253
Von Himmel, Ernst pseud. of Carlyle Petersilea. CSF 100
Von Hippel, Olga. BAA 180
Von Hoerschelmann, Rolf. FBK 82
Von Hofe, Harold. BAA 230
Von Hofmannsthal, Hugo (1847-1929) THM 45
Von Karman, Theodore. VFS 225
Von Kartoffel, (Baron). SF1 537
Von Khuon, Ernst (1915-) LEX 397
Von Kirchenheim, Arthur. BAA 182
Von Kleist, Heinrich. SIH 24

Von Kuhnelt-Leddihn, Christiane. BAA 109 CSF 116 SF1 301
Von Kuhnelt-Leddihn, Erik (1909-) BAA 109 CSF 116 SF1 301 SF2 965
Von Laffert, Karl-August (1872-) LEX 414
Von Leibnitz, Gottfried Wilhelm. MFW 194 SFN 57
Von Linne, Carl. WAA 33
Von Linnaeus, Carl. MSF 227
Von Manndorf, Rudolf Freih. BAA 243
Von Mohl, Robert. BAA 246
Von Munchausen, A. RFA 110, 118
Von Neumann, John. MFW 209
Von Opel, Fritz. COT 36
Von Oppolzer, Theodor Ritter. NWO 218
Von Puttkamer, Jesco (1933-) LEX 522-3
Von Rabe, (Baroness) Ann Crawford. WGT 121 see also Von Degen
Von Rachen, Kurt pseud. of L. Ron Hubbard. RFA 80-1, 86, 104 WIF 94
Von Ravn, Clara Iza (1870-) CSF 201 SF1 537
Von Rudhart, Georg Thomas. BAA 190
Von Sacher-Masoch, Leopold. WAA 159
Von Scheidt, Jurgen (1940-) IAC 239 LEX 552-3
Von Schelling, Friedrich Wilhelm. MSF 245 SFW 13
Von Schiller, Johann. NDA 130
Von Schmidt, Eric. FFC 143-4, 190
Von Schutz, Philipp Balthasar Sinhold (1657-1742) WGT 134
Von Sternberg, Josef. CSC 264
Von Suttner, Bertha (1843-1914) CSF 189 SF1 504
Von Swartwout, William H. BAA 38,43,48,50,52-3
Von Tramin, Peter (1932-) LEX 612-3
Von Voss, Julius. POE 47-8
Von Wald, E. G. IAC 239 SFD 17
Von Wilbrandt, Adolf (1837-1911) SF1 558
Von Wrede, Friedrich. BAA 279

Vonnegut, Kurt, Jr. (1922-) ALW
31, 99, 212, 238-9 AOW 271-2,
348, 351 BAA 121, 123, 136, 139,
148, 155-6 BFP 503-5 BYS 258,
278-9, 313-6 CAT 18, 72, 104,
106-19, 121 CSC 122, 125, 191
DMK 27-37 DTS v, 41 EFP 17
ETN 119-20 ES2 440 EXT 1/2
26-7 EXT 2/2 25, 31 EXT 3/1
27 EXT 4/2 29, 32 EXT 5/1 3
EXT 6/2 51 EXT 8/1 6, 17 EXT
9/1 23 EXT 10/1 5 FAN 13, 155
FFR 195 FHT 39, 51 FRN 46,
193 FTF 84, 86, 93, 106-7, 116-
8, 145-8, 158, 164 HFI 153 IAC
239-40 IAH 141-6 ISW 119, 166-
7, 236-7 JGB 3-5, 7 LEX 637-9
MFW 10-1, 23, 67-73, 90, 173,
202, 227, 229, 246, 254, 290 MIH
34, 122 MSF 200, 242 NDA ix,
9, 17-20, 22, 25, 37, 65, 69, 77,
123-4, 215 NWO ix, 19, 36, 39, 125,
206, 242, 263, 270, 272, 296-333
OMN 31 OSR 193-8 PJF 16, 59,
61-2 POE 261, 275-6 SFB 147,
151 SFD 4, 17, 300-1, 317 SFE
635-6 SFH 28-9, 31, 67, 93, 97-9,
104, 109, 129, 132, 182 SFS 120-
1 SFW 101, 105, 372, 551-61 SF1
537 SF2 1112 SIH 43 SL1 313-
7 SL5 1697-701 SL5 2079-84,
2101-6, 2447-50 SOT 423-4
SRB 14, 82, 316, 331, 339, 347
TJB 4 TSF 62, 91, 129, 237 VES
83, 116, 128-9, 153, 168, 179, 188,
211, 214, 229-30, 253-4, 256, 270
VF1 238-62, 280-1 WAA 156
WBW 23 WGT 149 WSF 175-6,
243, 346 YTS 23
Voorhis, Stephen. FFC 137
Vorhies, John Royal Harris
(1920-) ES2 440 SFE 636 SF1
537 SF2 1112-3
Vorzimer, Peter. SRB 110
Vose, Reuben. WGT 149
Voss, Richard (1851-1918) CSF
201 SF1 537
Voss-Bark, Conrad Lyddon. SF1
537
Voute, Kathleen. FFC 74
Voyager, Krystofalus. SF1 537
Voznesensky, Andrei. ALW 238
Vuarnet, Jean-Noel. BAA 274

W

W. S. L. S. pseud. of Wladislas
S. Lach-Szyrma. CSF 201
Wackwitz, Friedrich. BAA 289
Waddington, Conrad Hall. POE
304-6
Wade, James. FLR 62 ISW 223
Wade, Robert Allison (1920-)
WGT 149
Wade, Tom. SFE 638 SF1 538
Wadelton, Maggie-Owen (1896-)
CSF 201 SF1 538
Wadey, Victor. ES2 440 HFI 153
SFE 638 SF1 538
Wadsworth, Phyllis Marie. ES2
440 IAC 240 SFE 638 SF1 538
Waechter, Friedrich. FFC 44

Waelder, Robert. RAH 97
Wagar, W. Warren. AOW 357
BAA 153, 196, 274 EXT 8/2 59
FAN 19, 84, 188
Wagener, Hans. BAA 274
Wagenknecht, Edward Charles
(1900-) BAA xxii, 196 CSF 201
ES2 440-1 EXT 10/1 43 SF1
538 SF2 1113
Waggoner, Diana. FLR 38, 41
SRB 66 TSF 253 WSF 382
Waghorne, Arthur. CSF 201
Wagner, Belle M. CSF 201 SF1
538
Wagner, Friedrich. BAA 275
Wagner, Geoffrey Atheling (1927-)
EXT 5/1 7 SF1 538
Wagner, George. FBK 54
Wagner, Karl Edward (1945-)
CWD 8, 10, 46, 61-2 EXT 10/1
24 FLR 62 HFI 153-4 LEX
640 LTN 136 SFE 638 SF1
538 SF2 1113 SRB 279 TSP 212
Wagner, Richard. COT 35, 126,
134 EXT 9/2 33 FLT 42 IAH
26 ISW 249 WAA 98
Wagner, Sharon Blythe (1936-)
SF1 538 SF2 1113
Wahl, Jan. FFC 10, 34, 126-7,
152
Wahlke, John. BAA 289
Wahloo, Per (1926-75) AOW 272
ES2 441 HFI 154 NDA 98-100
SFE 638
Wain, John. CWN 25
Wait, Frona Eunice pseud. of
Frona Eunice Wait Colburn.
CSF 201 EXT 1/1 19
Wait, Robert A. IMS 8, 23, 83
Waite, Arthur Edward (1857-
1942) CSF 201 EXT 9/2 62
RZY 83 SF1 538
Wajda, Andrzej. SFB 120
Wakefield, Herbert Russell
(1888-1964) BFP 506 CSF 201
ES2 441 FBK 63, 78 IAC 240
SFS 121 SF1 538 SF2 1114
WTS 47
Wakefield, S. A. ES2 441
Wakeman, Frederic. SFN 20
WFS 193
Wakowski. EXT 10/2 54
Walbridge, Earle F. EXT 2/1
16 EXT 10/1 43
Walch, Jean. BAA 196
Walcutt, Charles C. EXT 10/2 70

Wald, George. SFH 141
Walde, A. A. IAC 240 SFS 121
Walden, Daniel. BAA 275
Walderick, Frederick. CSF 201
Waldman, Milton. VES 121
Waldo, Bud. WSF 134
Waldo, Cedric Dane pseud. of
Cecil Drummond Wolff. SF1
538
Waldrop, F. N. ATA 43 COT
230, 251 IAC 240 RFA 144
WSF 110
Waldrop, Howard. FFR 196 FRN
45 HFI 185 IAC 240 SFE 638
SF1 539
Wales, Hubert pseud. of William
Piggott. CSF 201 SF1 539
Wales, Nym pseud. of Helen
Foster Snow. SF1 539
Waley, Arthur. CSF 201
Walford, Astrid. FFC 136
Walford, Frank (1882-) CSF 201
SF1 539
Walker, Clifton Reginald see
Richard Dixon
Walker, D. P. EXT 9/2 62
Walker, Dale Lee (1935-) IAC
240 SF1 539 SF2 1114
Walker, Danton MacIntyre (1899-
1960) ES2 441-2
Walker, David Harry (1911-)
HFI 154 SFE 638 SF1 539 SF2
1114
Walker, Earl. CSF 201 SF1 539
Walker, Frances A. BAA 275
Walker, Gwen. FFC 183 SF1 539
Walker, Hugh (1941-) LEX 641-2
Walker, Jerry (1888) ES2 442
HFI 154 SF1 539
Walker, John Bernard (1858-)
CSF 201 SF1 539
Walker, Kenneth Macfarlane
(1882-1966) FFC 157 SF1 539
Walker, Norman (1897-) CSF 201
SF1 539
Walker, Paul. FLR 37, 62 JHN
62 LTN 269
Walker, Richard (1791-1870) BAA
22-3 WGT 149
Walker, Rowland (1876-) SF1 539
Walker, Roy. BAA 196
Walker, Samuel. BAA 45-6
Walker, Stuart. FBK 54
Walker, Victoria (1947-) SF1 539
Walker, W. H. SF1 539
Walkey, Samuel. SF1 539

Walkover, Andrew. BAA 196
Wall, Alfred H. CSF 4 SF1 539
Wall, George A. CSF 168 SF1
539
Wall, John W. BAA 121 ES2 442
POE 279 VES 116,123 WGT 149
see also Sarban
Wall, Mervyn (1908-) CSF 202
ES2 442 SF1 540
Wallace, Alfred Russel. FTF 36
Wallace, Barbara. FFC 127
Wallace, Bryan Edgar (1904-)
SF1 540
Wallace, C. H. ES2 442
Wallace, Doreen pseud. of Dora
Eileen Agnew Wallace Rash
(1897-) ES2 442 SFE 638 SF1
540 SF2 1114
Wallace, E. G. FTF 180-1
Wallace, Edgar (1875-1932) BAA
81 BYS 152-5,159 CSF 48,202
ES2 442-3 FFR 196 SFE 638
SF1 540 SOT 128 THM 41 VES
122,137 WGT 149-50
Wallace, F(loyd) L. ALW 212,
219 BYS 37 ES2 443 ETN 36,
40 HFI 154 IAC 240 SFE 638
SFS 121 SF1 540 VES 173,197
Wallace, George. ETN 74
Wallace, Henry Marriage see
Ashton Hilliers
Wallace, Ian pseud. of John Wal-
lace Pritchard (1912-) AOW 272
ES2 443 HFI 154 LEX 642
RGS 187,225-6 SFE 638-9
SF1 540
Wallace, Irving (1916-) AOW 207
BAA 139 ES2 443 ETN 144
Wallace, John. COT 185
Wallace, King. AOW 76 CSF
202 EXT 1/1 19 SFE 639 SF1
540
Wallace, Lew. SFH 10
Wallace, May Nickerson. SF1
540
Wallace, Richard Race. TSP 11,
71
Wallace, Robert. BAA 12 IAC
240 SFS 121
Wallace, Robin E. IAC 240
Wallas, Graham. POE 167
Waller, Leslie (1923-) ES2 443
SF1 585 WGT 150 see also
C. S. Cody
Waller, Louise. SF1 585

Waller, Robert Ferns (1913-)
BAA 130 ES2 443 SF1 540
Wallerstein, James S. (1910-)
ES2 443 HFI 154 SF1 540
Walling, William Herbert (1926-)
HFI 154 SFE 639 SFW 8 SF1
540 SF2 1115 VES 81
Wallis, David (1917-) BAA 140
ES2 443 HFI 154 SFE 639 SF1
540
Wallis, George C. CSF 202 ES2
444 IAC 240 SFE 639 SF1 540
STH 202 VES 95,104,322 WGT
150
Wallis, Geraldine McDonald
pseud. of Hope Campbell (1925-)
ES2 443-4 HFI 154 SFE 639
SF1 540 SF2 1115 WGT 150
Wallmann, Jeffrey. IAC 240
Wallop, John Douglas, III (1920-)
ES2 444 SF1 540
Walmsley, Arnold Robert (1912-)
SF2 1053 see also Nicholas
Roland
Walpole, Horace (1717-97) ALW
45 ASF 190 BYS 16,24,36-7,
79 CSF 202 ES2 444 FBK 12,
18-9,23 FL1 211-6 FTF 29
IAC 240 RBY 166-8,170-2,176,
178,181 SFH 192 SFS 121 SF1
541 SIH 16 TFC 41 TSP 7
VFS 7 WAA 82,77,145 WGT
150 WIF 40
Walpole, (Sir) Hugh (1884-1941)
CSF 202 ES2 444 EXT 7/1 15
SF1 541
Walsen, Fred J. IMS 52
Walsh, Brian. BAA 203
Walsh, Buthram. IAC 240 SFS
121
Walsh, Chad (1914-) AOW 357
BAA 118,196,275 ES2 444 EXT
1/2 27 EXT 2/2 23-6 EXT 4/2
23-4,28 EXT 6/1 19 EXT 8/2
32,59 FAN 33,184 MFW 269-
70 NDA x,54,102,209 NWO
100 SF1 541 SF2 1115 SOI 1-
14 SRB 69 STH 105
Walsh, George E. IAC 240
Walsh, Goodwin. CSF 202 SF1
541
Walsh, J. EXT 6/1 16
Walsh, James. BAA 275
Walsh, James J. BAA 275

Walsh, James Morgan (1897-1952) CSF 202 ES2 444-5 SFE 639 SF1 541 SOT 124 VES 71, 93 WGT 150 see also H. Haverstock Hill
Walsh, Jill Paton. FFC 169
Walsh, M.C. CSF 202
Walsh, Maurice (1879-1964) SF1 541
Walsh, Rupert. SF1 541
Walsh, William. BAA 164, 275
Walsh, William Emmet (1868-) SF1 541
Waltari, Mika Toimi (1908-) SF1 541
Walter, Arnold. SFS 121
Walter, Dorothy Charlotte. EXT 3/1 9, 21, 25
Walter, Elizabeth. ES2 445 SF1 541 SF2 1115
Walter, H. SL3 1165-70 SL4 1710-3 SL5 2113-6
Walter, Helmut. BAA 289
Walter, L.G. BAA 196
Walter, Lorraine. SFS 121
Walter, Nicolas. BAA 275
Walter, W(illiam) Grey (1910-77) BAA 130 ES2 445 EXT 6/2 51 FTF 118 HFI 155 IAC 240 SFE 639 SFS 121 SF1 541 SF2 1115-6
Waltermire, Beecher Wesley (1858-1932) CSF 202 SF1 541
Walters, David H. IAC 240
Walters, Eugene. SF1 541
Walters, Francis E. ETN 34, 48
Walters, Hellmut. BAA 275
Walters, Hugh pseud. of Walter Llewellyn Hughes. AOW 332 SFE 639 SF1 541-2
Walters, John Cuming (-1933) ES2 445
Walters, Margaret Curtis. PST 259
Walters, Raube. CSF 202
Walters, Tom. ES2 445
Walther, Daniel (1940-) LEX 642-3 SFB 139 SFE 639-40
Walther, Klaus. BAA 196
Walton, Bryce (1918-) ALW 161 COT 45 ES2 445 HFI 155 IAC 240 IAH 40 SFE 640 SF1 542 SF2 1116 WGT 150 see also Kenneth O'Hara
Walton, Evangeline pseud. of Evangeline Ensley (1907-) BFP

507 CSF 202 ES2 445 FFR 197 FL2 932-7 HFI 155 LTN 92 SF1 542 WSF 302
Walton, Harry. ALW 10 IAC 240 RFA 86, 90 SFS 121 SOT 200 WFS 168 WGT 150
Walton, Luke pseud. of Bill Henderson. SF1 542
Walton, Nathan. BAA 110
Walton, Stephen (1945-) SF1 542
Walton, Su (1944-) SF1 542 SF2 1116
Waltz, George H., Jr. EXT 2/1 5, 7-8, 16
Walworth, Jane. FFC 182
Wambaugh, Joseph. CSC 25-6
Wanderer pseud. of Elim Henry D'Avigdor. SF1 542
Wandrei, Donald (1908-) ALW 141, 143, 184 BFP 508 BYS 48, 178 COT 118, 146, 292 CSF 202 ES2 445-6 EXT 3/1 7, 9 EXT 5/1 3 IAC 240-1 IMS 16, 24, 93, 112, 134, 169, 219 ISW 224 MSM 37 PST 147 RFA xv, 20, 30 SFE 640 SFS 121 SFW 141 SF1 542 SOT 73, 310, 343, 347 STH 253 VES 130, 135, 142, 148 WIF 18 WSF 66, 296 WTS ix, 12, 27, 29-30, 35-6, 42, 48-9, 52, 123, 128-9
Wandrei, Howard Elmer (1909-56) ALW 10 ES2 446 IAC 241 SOT 310 WGT 150 WTS 39, 48-9 see also Howard W. Graham, H.W. Guernsey
Wangerin, Walter (1944-) FFC 10 FL1 149-53
Warburg, Sandol Stoddard (1927-) FFC 10 SF1 542 SF2 1116
Warburton, Robert. FL3 1363-8 FL4 1640-4
Ward. RFA 195
Ward, Artemus. CSC 233
Ward, Arthur Henry Sarsfield (1883-1959) WGT 150-1 see also Sax Rohmer
Ward, Beatrice see Paul Beaujon
Ward, Charles W. IAC 241
Ward, Christopher (1868-1943) CSF 202 SF1 542
Ward, Colin. BAA 196
Ward, Donald G. (1911-) ES2 446 SF1 542-3
Ward, E.D. CSF 202 SF1 543
Ward, Edward. BAA 9

Ward, Elizabeth Stuart Phelps (1844-1911) BAA x ES2 446 EXT 4/1 9 WGT 151
Ward, George Whiteley. CSF 203 SF1 543
Ward, Harold. TSP 148 see also Zorro
Ward, Henry pseud. of Henri Louis Luc Viard (1913-) SFE 642 SF1 543
Ward, (Mrs.) Herbert see Elizabeth Stuart Phelps, Elizabeth Stuart Phelps Ward
Ward, Herbert Dickinson (1861-1932) CSF 203 ES2 446 SF1 543
Ward, Jonathan. FSU 47 LTN 15, 267, 269
Ward, Julian. BAA 121
Ward, Lauriston. EXT 5/1 7 EXT 5/2 2
Ward, Lynd Kendall (1905-) FFC 3, 171 SF1 543 SF2 1116-7
Ward, Margarete. SF1 543
Ward, Patricia. FFC 77
Ward, Richard Heron. BAA 104 CSF 203 SF1 543
Ward, Robert A. IMS 33
Ward, Rose Elizabeth Knox (1886-) WGT 151 see also Elizabeth Sax Rohmer
Ward, Taylor pseud. of Alan Hyde. TSP 134
Ward, (Capt.) Will(iam) J. BAA 77 CSF 203 SF1 543
Warde, Beatrice Lamberton Becker (1900-69) BAA 107 WGT 151 see also Paul Beaujohn
Warde, Reginald (1878-) SF1 543
Warden, Anthon. IAC 241
Warfel, Harry R. NWO 171
Warhol, Andy. JGB 6 VFS 117
Warland, Alan. IAC 241
Warman, William Eric (1904-) SF1 543 SF2 1117
Warner, Anne (1869-1913) SF1 543
Warner, Douglas. SF1 543
Warner, Edwin. BAA 275
Warner, Harry (Backer), Jr. (1922-) ALW 8, 182-3 AOW 83, 357 ETN 82, 85 IMS 182, 199-200, 205, 210 RFA 133, 142 SFB 152 SFE 642 SF1 543 SF2 1117 SRB 74, 95, 123-4 VES

316 WAA 246 WSF 140, 215, 278, 383
Warner, Kenneth Lewis (1918-) ES2 446 SF2 1005 WGT 151 see also Dighton Morel
Warner, Rex (1905-) CAT 26 CSF 203 ES2 446 EXT 2/2 31 EXT 8/1 5 EXT 9/2 48-9 SFE 642 SF1 543
Warner, Sylvia Townsend (1893-1978) CSF 203 ES2 446 FBK 120 FL2 855-8 HFI 155 SF1 543 SF2 1117 SRB 279
Warner, William Henry. CSF 203 SF1 544
Warner-Crozetti, R. pseud. of Ruth G. Warner Crozetti (1913-) SF1 544
Warnes, Herbert. IMS 99-100
Warnke, Frank Joseph. EXT 6/1 16, 20
Warr, (Sir) Charles L(aing) (1892-1969) CSF 203 SF1 544
Warren. SFA 8
Warren, Austin. MSF 33 SOI 43
Warren, Benjamin Clark (1859?-1952) CSF 203 SF1 544
Warren, Bill. SF1 544
Warren, C. Delves. SF1 544
Warren, Charles Marquis. TSP 106
Warren, James. ES2 446 SOT 3
Warren, John Russell (1886-) SF1 544 VES 205
Warren, William F. EXT 1/1 2
Warrick, Patricia Scott (1925-) ASF 153 BAA 275 FHT 66 IAC 82, 123, 142, 172, 187, 241 LTN 251, 263 MFW 15 SF1 544 SF2 1117 TSF 121-36 VF2 136-53, 203-4, 208
Warschawski, Ilja (1909-) LEX 643
Wartofsky, William Victor (1931-) SF1 544
Washburn, Abbott. VFS 105
Washington, George. MSM 11 RFA xvii SFN 37 VFS 199
Washington, S. H. CSF 203
Wason, Sandys. CSF 203 SF1 544
Wasserburg, Joseph. WGT 151
Wasserburg, Philipp (1827-97) WGT 152
Wasson, Richard. EXT 9/2 44
Waterhouse, Elizabeth. BAA 163

Waterloo, Stanley (1846-1913)
ALW 88 AOW 37, 76 BAA 59
BYS 152 CSF 203 EXT 1/1 19-
20 EXT 3/1 29 EXT 7/1 22, 27
IAC 241 MFW 129 PST 88-9,
114, 197, 238, 257 SFE 643 SF1
544
Waters, Thomas Allen. HFI 155
SFE 643 SF1 544
Wates, Cyril G. IMS 22
Watkin, Lawrence Edward (1901-)
CSF 203 SF1 544
Watkins, Joan N. IAC 241
Watkins, Peter (1935-) KAU 126
POE 282-3 SFE 643 SF1 544
WAA 67
Watkins, William Jon (1942-)
BAA 156 HFI 155 IAC 241
LEX 644 SFE 643 SF1 545
SF2 1117-8
Watkins-Pitchford, Denys James
(1905-) FFC 99 SF2 803 see
also B. B.
Watlock, W. A. BAA 37 MSF
203 SF1 545
Watson. EXT 2/2 34-5 EXT
7/2 36
Watson, Aaron (1850-1926) SF1
545
Watson, Aldren. FFC 101
Watson, Christine. FL1 90-4,
350-4, 418-22, 441-6 FL2 808-
10, 870-2, 988-92 FL3 1111-5,
1350-4, 1516-9 FL4 1563-7,
1866-8 FL5 2097-101
Watson, Frederick (1885-1935)
SF1 545
Watson, Gene. WFS 168
Watson, Gilbert (1864-1941) SF1
545
Watson, Goodwin. BAA 275
Watson, Henry Brereton Marriott
(1863-1921) CSF 203 SF1 545
Watson, H(enry) C(rocker) M(ar-
riott). BAA 32, 43 EXT 7/1 13
MSF 177 SF1 545 WGT 152
see also H. C. M. W.
Watson, Ian (1943-) AAL 11, 185-
91 AC2 77 AOW 272 BFP 509
DMK 235-41 FL2 593-5 HFI
155 IAC 241 KAU 29 LEX 644-
5 RGS 188 SFB 133 SFE 643-
4 SFH 155 SF1 545 SF2 1118
SL2 712-6 UKL 65, 73, 170, 246
Watson, James. SFH 141
Watson, Lyall. CSC 10

Watson, Raymond. IAC 241
Watson, Sally. FFC 57
Watson, Simon. SFE 644
Watson, Sydney. CSF 203-4 SF1
545
Watson, Wendy. FFC 73
Watson, William Henry. CSF 204
Watt, Donald. RBY 195-213
Watt, James. FTF 34 MSF 194
POE 21, 34, 59
Watteau, Monique (1929-) ES2 446
Watts, Alan. VFS 117
Watts, Marjorie-Ann. FFC 157
Watts, Newman (1895-) BAA 108
CSF 204 SF1 545
Watts-Dunton, Walter Theodore
(1832-1914) SF1 545
Waugh, Arthur. ES2 446
Waugh, Charles G. ASF 30
Waugh, Evelyn Arthur St. John
(1903-66) ACC 32 ALW 99
AOW 273 BAA 123 ES2 446
EXT 2/2 24, 31 FAN 148 FTF
106 ISW 136 LEX 645-6 NDA
186-7 OWB 73 POE 279 SFE
644 SFH 90 SFN 63 SF1 545
Waugh, Michael. SF1 545
Way, Peter. SF1 545
Wayman, Tony Russell (1929-)
ES2 446 HFI 155 SFE 644 SF1
545 SF2 1118-9
Wayne, Charles M. SF1 585
Wayne, Charles Stokes (1858-)
CSF 204 ES2 446 WGT 152
Wayne, John. ISW 102
Wayne, Raymond pseud. of
Harold R.W. Benjamin. CSF
155
Weales, Gerald. FFC 196
Weatherhead, John. BAA 150
Weaver, Gertrude Renton. WGT
152 see also Gertrude Dunn
Weaver, Henrietta. CSF 204
SF1 545
Weaver, Jack. FFC 157
Weaver, Wertie Clarice. BAA
114
Webb, Augustus Caesar (1894-)
ES2 446 SFE 646 SF1 546 SF2
1119
Webb, Beatrice. FAN 64 POE
190
Webb, Blanche A. see Blanche
A. Draper
Webb, Charles Thomas. BAA
102, 196

Webb, Jane. FTF 31 BAA 20 POE 47, 56-7
Webb, Jean Francis, III (1910-) SF1 546 SF2 1119
Webb, Kaye. LTN 253
Webb, Leland. IAC 241 SFS 122
Webb, Michael. [FUT]
Webb, Richard Wilson. WGT 152
Webb, Ron. IAC 241 SFS 122
Webb, Sidney. FAN 64
Webb, T. W. EXT 5/2 47
Webb, Vic. IAC 241
Webb, W. T. IAC 241
Webb, Walter Prescott. RBY 41
Webbert, James. IAC 241 SFS 52
Webbling, Peggy. SFB 35
Weber, Eugen. BAA 275
Weber, Henry William (1783-1816) CSF 204 ES2 447 SF1 546
Weber, Jean-Paul. BYS 54
Weber, Katherina. BAA 275
Webster, Charles. BAA 196, 275
Webster, Elizabeth Charlotte SF1 546
Webster, Frederick Annesley Michael (1886-) CSF 204 ES2 447 SF1 546
Webster, Henry Kitchell (1875-1932) CSF 204 SF1 546
Webster, J. Provand. CSF 204 SF1 546
Webster, R. M. BAA 16
Wechter, Nell Wise (1913-) SF1 546 SF2 1119
Wedeck, Harry Ezekiel (1899-) ES2 447
Wedlake, George E. C. CSF 204 SF1 546
Wedmore, F. CSF 204
Weedman, Jane B. SL2 614-7
Weekes, Agnes. CSF 204
Weekley, Ian George (1933-) SFE 646 SF1 546
Weekley, Maurice Arden. WGT 152
Weekley, Richard. BAA 163
Weeks, Edward Olin. ALW 85 SFE 646
Weems, R. Monroe. SFD 202
Wegener, Manfred (1935-) LEX 646-7
Wegener, Paul. FBK 57-8 SFH 183 SIH 138 WAA 192
Wegner, Fritz. FFC 117, 150
Wehrle, Joe, Jr. IAC 241

Wei, Tan Tai. BAA 275
Weigel, John. CWN 3, 30, 47, 49
Weihs, Erika. FFC 95
Weil, Lisl. FFC 190
Weil, Simone. POE 254-5 SOI 83, 85, 89 THM 28
Weinbaum, Helen. RFA 33
Weinbaum, Margaret. IMS 80
Weinbaum, Stanley G(rauman) (1900?-35) AAL 87, 138-9 ACC 61 ALW 143, 157 AOW 83, 107, 114-5, 299 ASF 217-22, 308 BFP 510-1 CAT 76 COT 57, 72-9, 81, 150-1, 266, 290-1 CSC 28-9, 146, 172 CSF 204 ES2 447 ETN 137 EXT 4/2 25 EXT 5/1 3, 15 FFR 197 HFI 155 IAC 241-2 IAH 30 IMS 16, 24, 26, 29, 45, 74-5, 80-1, 106, 148, 186, 189, 195, 213, 221 INT 28 ISW 217 KAU 193, 205 KWS 386 LEX 647-9 LTN 99 MFW 38, 51, 54, 138, 255 MIH 25 MSM 173, 305 OWB 79-80 PJF 13 RFA 32-8, 40, 63, 81, 100, 167, 183, 201 RGS 188-91 SFB 114 SFD 21-2, 28, 117, 210-3, 236, 242, 290, 294 SFE 646 SFH 40-1, 140-1 SFS 122 SFW 145-9 SF1 546 SIH 112 SL1 238-41 SL3 1353-6 SOT 2, 44, 108, 110-1, 136-8, 174, 192, 294, 325, 334, 342, 365, 394, 400 SRB 16, 299, 307 STH 45, 86, 261 TSF 54, 230 VES 80-1, 83-4, 92-3, 95, 122, 147, 170, 193, 197, 211, 258, 313 VFS 54, 140 WAA 174 WFS 40, 45-6, 89 WGT 152 WIF 89, 108, 137 WSF 64-5, 69, 78, 84, 119, 121, 129, 133, 283, 336, 389 see also John Jessel
Weinberg, Arthur. BAA 196
Weinberg, Lila. BAA 196
Weinberg, Margarete. BAA 196
Weinberg, Robert (1946-) FL1 300-7 FL2 811-6 FL5 2447-63 SFE 646 SF1 546-7 SF2 1119 SRB 67, 75, 495
Weinberg, Steven. CAT 86
Weinberg, Sydny. LTN 238
Weinberger, J. BAA 276
Weiner, Andrew. IAC 242
Weiner, Anthony J. ES2 447
Weiner, Guy. IAC 242
Weiner, William. IMS 34

Weiner, William M. pseud. of
Sam Moskowitz. IMS 125-6, 189
Weininger. EXT 8/2 54
Weinkauf, Mary S. BAA 276
Weinstein, Aaron (1898-1967)
WGT 152
Weinstein, Elliot. VES 273
Weinstein, Nathan Wallenstein
(1903-40) see Nathanael West
Weinstein, Richard S. IAC 242
Weinstein, Sol (1928-) SF1 547
SF2 1120
Weintraub, Stanley. BAA 276
EXT 9/1 23 FAN 164, 189
Weir, John J. IMS 84-5, 106, 110
Weir, Rosemary. FFC 91, 137
Weise, Lothar (1931-66) LEX
649-50
Weiser, Samuel. EXT 9/2 62
Weisgard, Leonard. FFC 70
Weisinger, Mort(imer) (1915-78)
ALW 8, 184 ASF 118, 243 ES2
447-8 IMS 10, 13-6, 18, 20, 45,
53, 74, 76, 80, 84, 93, 147-8, 185-
7, 197, 209, 213, 219, 221 ISW 161
SFB 152 SFE 648 SOT 4, 43, 80,
102-17, 155, 305, 307-8, 325, 328
SRB 89 STH 45, 64, 258 TSP 30,
89 WFS 112 WGT 152 WIF 87,
134, 136, 138, 294 WSF 65, 74-5,
119, 138 WTS 53
Weiss, Alan. IAC 242
Weiss, Ehrich (1874-1926) WGT
152 see also Harry Houdini
Weiss, George Henry (1898-1946)
ES2 448 WGT 152 see also
Francis Flagg
Weiss, Harvey. FFC 57
Weiss, Jan (1892-1973) SL2 644-6
Weiss, Jiri (1913-) BAA 114 CSF
204 SF1 547
Weiss, Joseph G. BAA 276
Weiss, Miriam Strauss. BAA
196
Weiss, Renee K. FFC 15
Weiss, Sara. CSF 204
Weisskopf, Walter A. BAA 196,
276
Weissman, Barry. IAC 242
Weissner, Carl. SF1 548
Welbore, Mina Walker. CSF 204
SF1 548
Welch, D. R. IMS 33, 43
Welch, Edgar Luderne (1855-)
BAA 33-5 SF1 548 WGT 152-3
see also Grip

Welch, Raquel. VFS 53
Welch, Ronald. FFC 172
Welcher, Jeanne K. BAA 262
SF1 548
Welcome, S. Byron. BAA 54
CSF 205 EXT 5/1 4 SF1 548
Weldon, Rex pseud. of Duane
Weldon Rimel. SF1 548
Weldrik, Valerie. FFC 170
Weldt, Bernard. IMS 52
Welker. RFA 200
Wellard, James Howard (1909-)
SF1 548 SF2 1120
Wellbank, Joseph H. BAA 276
Wellek, Rene. MSF 33 SFA 8
SOI 43
Wellen, Edward Paul (1919-) ES2
448 FFR 197 HFI 156 IAC 242
LEX 650 SFS 122 SF1 548 SF2
1120
Weller, Anthony. IAC 242
Welles, (George) Orson (1915-)
ALW 96, 156 ASF 195 CAT 107
COT 34-5, 115 CSC 41, 264 ES2
448 EXT 8/1 4 IAC 242 IMS
195 MSF 214 MSM 61, 236, 239
PST 9, 12, 36, 319 SFB 36 SFH
104-5 SFS 122 SF1 548 SOI 51
SOT 252 WAA 21 WFS 92
WIF 15 WSF 20, 311 YTS 2, 23
Wellman, Bert J. BAA 59-60
SF1 548 WGT 153 see also A
Law-Abiding Revolutionist
Wellman, Manly Wade (1903-)
AAL 56 ALW 141 ASF 243 BFP
512-5 COT 44, 291 CSF 205
CWD 61 DTS 7, 20 ES2 448-9
FFR 197 FL4 1744-8 HFI 156
IAC 242-3 IMS 45, 110, 147, 213
LEX 650-1 RFA 51, 60, 70, 91,
207 RGS 191 SFE 648 SFN 80
SFS 122 SF1 548 SF2 1120-1
SOT 111, 174 SRB 332 STH 65
VES 234 WFS 112, 118 WGT
153 WIF 80, 136, 153 WTS 42-
3, 45-6, 49, 54, 59, 123, 128-9,
132 see also Gabriel Barclay
Wellman, Paul Iselin (1898-1966)
ES2 449 SFN 40
Wellman, Wade. IAC 243
Wells, Angus. IAC 243
Wells, Barry pseud. of Dick
Richards. HFI 156 SF1 549
Wells, Basil (1912-) ES2 449
HFI 156 IAC 243 SFE 648 SF1
549 SF2 1121 SRB 509 WGT

Wells, Basil (cont.)
153
Wells, Braxton pseud. of Donald
A. Wollheim. IMS 191
Wells, Carolyn (1872?-1942) CSF
205 SF1 549 ES2 449
Wells, Catherine Robins. ALW 91
Wells, Celia Townsend. EXT
6/1 10
Wells, David Ames. BAA 31
Wells, (Frank Charles) Robert
(1929-) HFI 157 IAC 246 SFE
648 SFS 125 SF1 551 SF2 1121
Wells, Geoffrey. EXT 8/2 58
Wells, George. SF1 549
Wells, H(erbert) G(eorge) (1886-
1946) AAL 18-9, 127, 131-2 ACC
48, 55, 70, 85-6, 158, 175-7, 185,
188, 191, 209, 211 ACE 11, 15-8,
33, 35, 52, 58, 68-9, 71 AC2 9, 13-
6, 31, 33, 50, 56, 66-7, 69 ALW 8,
11, 33, 39-40, 44, 53-5, 59-61, 75-
6, 83-105, 116, 120, 122, 125-6,
136, 141, 144-5, 156, 168, 170, 172-
3, 191, 194, 213-4, 216 AOW 9, 12-
5, 36, 42, 47-8, 76-7, 115, 288, 298,
339-40, 346-9, 351, 353-4, 356-8,
395-6, 401 ASF 83, 106-7, 123,
126, 129, 142-3, 148-50, 166, 190-
5, 217 ATA 61 BAA xv, xxi, 54,
61, 65, 68-70, 80, 87, 90, 94, 96, 101,
108, 276 BFP 516-30 BYS 8, 26,
36, 38, 61, 81-2, 85-6, 96, 102-3,
108-9, 113-33, 136, 138, 140, 142,
144-5, 156-9, 171, 190, 200-1, 213,
225, 282, 313 CAT xiv, xvi, 2, 7,
10-4, 16, 19-20, 32-3, 36, 41, 43,
53, 56, 58, 68, 72-3, 75, 79-81, 83-
4, 88, 91, 93-9, 103, 106-8, 115-6,
119, 122, 131-2, 138-9 COT 7-9,
23, 31-2, 53, 67, 91-6, 100, 112,
119-20, 145, 175, 178, 214, 233-7,
240, 247, 253, 259-60, 282, 291,
297-8 CSC 26-7, 30-1, 41, 121,
164, 167-9, 173, 195, 200 CSF
205 CWN 36 DTS 3 EFP 3 ES2
449-52 ETN 12, 54 EXT 1/1 17
EXT 1/2 24, 29-31 EXT 2/1 11,
13, 15, 17-20 EXT 2/2 22-3, 27
EXT 3/1 28-9 EXT 3/2 47 EXT
4/2 21-4, 30, 32 EXT 5/1 4, 16,
16a, 19-20 EXT 5/2 38-9, 47
EXT 6/2 32-40, 51 EXT 7/2 38
EXT 8/2 31-63 EXT 9/1 18, 22-
3 EXT 9/2 34, 38-9, 44, 55, 60,
63 EXT 10/1 47-8 EXT 10/2

72-3, 75-7, 86-7, 90 FBK 16, 82,
134, 139 FFR 197-9 FHT 54
FL3 1369-71 FL4 1729-32 FL5
2162-4 FTF 10-1, 19, 38, 40-1,
43, 45, 47-63, 66-70, 73, 75, 78,
88, 95, 101-2, 107-9, 120, 133-4,
136, 139-40, 142, 149, 155, 158,
163, 165-6, 187-9, 192-3, 199-
200 HFI 156-7 HID 189 HWK
6, 22 IAC 243-6 IAH 32, 58, 128
IMS 2-3, 55, 75, 99, 195 INT 13,
15, 45, 104 ISW 8, 35, 72, 91, 178-
9, 207, 252-3, 276 JVN 118, 121
KAU 10, 27, 56-7, 59-60, 63, 93-
104, 117-8, 156, 184, 189, 191, 200,
202, 206, 219 KWS 151-3, 157-8,
260, 311 LEX 651-3 LTN 104,
111, 135, 205 MFW ix-x, 15, 23,
54, 99, 117, 166-7, 169, 188, 221,
224-5, 230, 249, 281-3, 285, 287
MIH 14, 25-6, 30-1, 35, 45, 47-8,
50, 58, 76, 98-105, 144 MSF 5, 9-
10, 12, 23, 25, 27-8, 30, 36, 45, 49,
54, 70-2, 76, 79, 87, 92, 95, 103,
106, 116, 120, 130, 134-7, 139, 143,
162-3, 165-7, 171, 177-8, 185, 193,
199-204, 206-42, 245, 247, 251-7,
259-61, 263-4, 266, 272, 279-80,
282 MSM 25, 29, 51, 58, 61-2, 76,
89-90, 140, 145-6, 148, 166, 169,
201, 209, 211, 222, 233-4, 236, 239,
244, 297, 301-2, 304 NDA 17, 25-
6, 55, 108, 199-200, 204 NWO x,
16, 18, 21, 32, 50, 67, 76-7, 95, 124,
126, 131, 134, 147-8, 162, 213, 233-
4, 253 OMN 2, 5, 24, 32, 39, 45, 52,
54, 56, 90, 93-4, 96, 189, 227, 229-
31 OSR 204-15 OWB 9, 13, 29,
35-6, 39 POE 112-4, 117, 119, 144-
6, 168, 180-1, 196-201, 205, 209-15,
235, 253 PST 9-11, 17, 33, 49, 53,
63, 69, 71, 78, 80-3, 86, 88-96, 98-
108, 110-20, 122, 128-9, 133, 137,
148-50, 153, 155, 163, 166-8, 182,
184-5, 192-5, 197-9, 202, 204-6,
208-18, 220, 222, 224-5, 227-31,
235-8, 240-9, 252-8, 261, 264-70,
272-5, 277-82, 284-8, 290-1, 293-
4, 296-300, 302-15, 318, 320, 322
RAH 18, 25, 62, 94, 137, 141, 167
RBY 36-7, 84, 98, 100, 109 RFA
vi, xvii, 2, 96 RGS 191-4 RHN
11, 18, 21, 62, 67, 93 RSG 9, 78
SFA 16, 22, 226, 303 SFB 10, 12,
20, 22-3, 26-9, 34-6, 42, 65, 71,
74, 90, 128, 148-9 SFD 10, 21,

Wells, H. G. (cont.)
23-4, 57, 72, 83, 189-91, 235, 272-
4, 276, 287, 305-7, 314 SFE 648-
50 SFH 14-27, 32-4, 37-8, 43,
49, 51, 54, 59, 62, 70, 98, 103-4,
118, 121, 138-9, 148, 155-6, 159,
167-8, 170, 176, 185, 200-4, 207-
8, 212, 214, 220 SFN 12, 28, 32,
39, 81, 102-3 SFS 122-4 SFW
7, 25-30, 61, 91, 101, 103, 126,
233-4 SF1 549-51 SIH 29, 33,
37, 41, 43-4, 47, 53, 60, 77, 79, 109,
111, 121, 152, 170, 181, 194 SIN
12-3, 19, 23-31 SL2 782-6, 807-
12 SL3 1057-61, 1079-83, 1375-
9, 1429-34 SL4 1902-7, 1967-72
SL5 2287-92, 2407-10, 2416-23,
2459-62 SOI xiv, 19, 42, 44-5, 51,
55, 58 SOT 14, 40, 100, 120, 129,
139, 203, 206, 234, 252, 271, 373
SRB 5, 7-8, 59, 297 STF 6, 24,
62, 79 STH 7, 29-31, 52, 93, 107,
182-3, 204, 206-10, 216, 229 TDI
6, 8 THM 55 TJB 21 TRB 54
TSF 28-9, 50, 230 TSO 9, 11, 13,
24, 27-30, 34-5, 56 VES 69, 80,
92, 100-3, 106, 124-5, 127-8, 130-
3, 135, 137, 140-2, 144-5, 148, 152,
154, 156, 158, 160, 173, 191, 193,
198, 205, 208-9, 219, 225, 236, 238,
246, 248, 251, 255, 257-61, 270,
286, 294-5, 300, 305, 312, 317, 334-
5, 341 VFS 49, 70-1, 141, 146, 180,
193-4, 197, 202, 217, 239, 253 WAA
16-7, 21, 24, 36-7, 39-40, 52-3, 59,
89, 171, 242 WBW 32-3, 55 WFS
7, 57, 68, 99, 113, 305 WIF 15, 20,
40, 58-63, 67, 71, 82-6, 89, 102,
149, 151, 187, 201, 232 WSF 19-
20, 23, 30, 35, 43-4, 129-30, 152,
254, 263, 309, 337, 343, 345, 385
WTS 17, 54-5 YTS 3, 5, 9, 15, 17,
46, 110-1, 115, 133
Wells, Hal K. MIH 32 TSP 29
Wells, Isabel. ALW 91
Wells, James W. CSF 206
Wells, Joel Freeman (1930-)
SF1 551 SF2 1121
Wells, Joseph. ALW 89-90
Wells, Keith. IAC 246
Wells, O. R. SF1 551
Wells, Sarah. ALW 90
Wells, Stuart W., III. SRB 66
Welsh, Charles Whitefield. BAA
289

Welskopf, Elisabeth Charlotte.
BAA 276
Welty, Eudora. ETN 176
Wendell, Carolyn. MFW 146
TSF 102-9
Wendt, Frederick. CSF 206
Wenger, Laurel. EXT 10/1 26
Wenning, Elizabeth. FFC 127
Wenskes, Helmut. FBK 38, 57, 77
IAC 246
Wentworth, Patricia pseud. of
Dora A. Dillon. CSF 206
Wentworth, Richard. STH 82-3
Wentworth, Robert pseud. of
Edmond Hamilton. TSP 189
Wentworth-James, Gertie De S.
CSF 206 SF1 551
Wentz, Elma. HID 24, 193 IAC
246 SOT 201
Wentz, Walter James. SF1 551
Werfel, Franz V. (1890-1945)
ALW 99 AOW 273 CSF 206
EXT 2/2 26, 32 FAN 148 FL4
1807-12 HFI 157 IAH 142, 144-
5 ISW 182 MIH 138 POE 256,
258-9 SFE 651 SF1 551
Werner, Alice. CSF 206
Werner, Edward Theodore Chal-
mers (1864-1954) ES2 452
Werper, Barton (house name)
ES2 452 HFI 157 SFE 651 SF1
551 see also Peter T. Scott,
Peg O'Neill Scott
Wersba, Barbara. FFC 11, 58
Wershofen, Christian. BAA 196
Wertenbaker, G. Peyton (1907-)
COT 7 ES2 452 IAC 246 MSM
297-8 VES 232 WGT 153 see
also Green Peyton
Werth, Kurt. FFC 21, 130, 144
Wertham, Fredric (1895-) AAL
103 ALW 187 AOW 82, 357
BRS 9 SFB 152 SFD 84-5 SF1
551 SF2 1121 SRB 75
Wertheim, Alexander. CSF 206
Wertheim, Frederic. SFB 110
Wertmuller, Lina. CSC 264
Wescott, Roger W. BAA 276
Wesley, John (1703-91) CUA 23
Wesley, Joseph. IAC 246 see
also Lew J. Stecher, Jr.
Wesley, Mary pseud. of Mary
Aline Eady (1912-) HFI 157 SF1
552 SF2 1122
Wessex, Martyn. SF1 552

Wesso(lowski), H(ans) W(aldemar) (1882-) BYS 216-7 COT 17, 144, 176, 184, 207 ES2 452 ISW 284 RFA 3, 6-7, 9-11, 13-4, 16, 38, 42-3, 47, 51, 57-8, 60, 62-3, 72, 141, 186 SFE 651 SRB 35 VES 110, 149, 287-8 WGT 153 WIF 276 WSF 53, 70 WTS 132

West, Alroy. CSF 206 SF1 552

West, Anthony Panther (1914-) ES2 452 FAN 17 SFE 651 SFN 71 SF1 552 SF2 1122

West, D. IAC 246

West, Douglas. VES 189

West, Edward Sackville. CSF 206

West, Geoffrey. FAN 17, 34, 64, 182-3

West, John Anthony. EXT 8/1 17 IAC 246 SFS 125

West, Julian pseud. of Ernst Muller. CSF 206 SF1 552

West, (Mary) Jessamyn (1907-) ES2 452 HFI 157 IAC 246 ISW 121-2, 176 SFS 125 SF1 552 SF2 1122

West, Michael. IAC 246

West, Nathanael pseud. of Nathan Wallenstein Weinstein. NWO 4, 9, 35, 208 SF1 552

West, Paul (1930-) EXT 6/1 19 EXT 10/1 43 HFI 157 SF1 552 SF2 1122

West, R. H. BAA 276 EXT 4/2 26

West, Rebecca pseud. of Cecily Isobel Andrews (1892-) CSF 206 SF1 552

West, Richard C. EXT 9/2 25 EXT 10/1 2, 17-45 SF1 552 SRB 82

West, Robert. EXT 4/2 27

West, Wallace George (1900-) BAA 164 COT 122, 172, 178-9, 186 ES2 452-3 HFI 157 IAC 246 LEX 653-4 RFA 74 SFE 651 SFS 125 SF1 552 SF2 1122-3 SOT 394 WGT 153 WTS 29, 34-5, 53-4 see also Loup Garou

Westall, Robert. FFC 170

Westall, William Bury (1835-1903) CSF 206 SFE 651 SF1 552

Westerfield, Jerry K. COT 22, 75, 173

Westerman, John Francis Cyril. CSF 206 SF1 552

Westerman, Percy Francis. CSF 206 SF1 552-3, 585

Westermayer, Arthur Joseph (1864-) CSF 206 SF1 553

Western, Ernest. SF1 553

Westheimer, David (1917-) SF1 553 SF2 1123

Westlake, Donald E(dwin) (1933-) BAA 145 ES2 453 IAC 246 SFE 651 SF1 553 WGT 153-4

Westlake, J. H. J. BAA 276

Westmeyer, Russell E. BAA 277

Weston, George (1880-1965) BAA 102 CSF 206 ES2 453 HFI 158 SFE 651 SF1 553

Weston, Jessie L. PJF 57 RZY 33, 35-7, 81-2, 84-5 SOI 160

Weston, John. FFC 11

Weston, Kim. SF1 553

Weston, Peter (1944-) IAC 246 MIH 7 SFE 651

Weston, Sam. COT 234

Westreich, Alice. SF1 553

Westreich, Budd. SF1 553

Westropp, J. J. CSF 206

Westward, Elton. SF1 553

Westwood, Alvin. SF1 553

Wetherell, June (1909-) HFI 158 SF1 553

Wetjen, Albert Richard (1900-48) SF1 553

Wetmore, Claude Hazeltine (1863-) CSF 206 SF1 553

Wetzel, George T. EXT 3/1 2, 6, 9, 21, 25 SF1 553

Weverka, Robert (1926-) SF1 553 SF2 1123

Weyl, Hermann. ISW 76

Weyman, Stanley J. BYS 137 CAT 8 EXT 4/2 20

Weymouth, (Viscount) (1932-) see Alexander Thynn

Whale, James. FTF 30 SFB 35 SFH 101 SIH 138

Whaley, Stephen V. LTN 251 SF1 553

Wharton, Edith (Newbold Jones) (1862-1937) AOW 77-8 CSF 206-7 ES2 453 EXT 1/1 20 EXT 4/1 9 FBK 73 FL2 612-5 IAC 246 SFE 652 SF1 553 SOT 305

Wharton, Thom Lee. IAC 246

Whateley, Richard. CSF 76 VES 116

Wheat, Linda. SL2 735-8
Wheat, Susanne Chambers. SF1 554
Wheatley, Dennis (Yeats) (1897-1977) CSF 207 ES2 453-4 EXT 8/1 5 EXT 9/2 61 FBK 78,105-6 FFR 199 FL1 383-6 FL2 715-7 FL3 1358-62 FL4 1954-7 FRN 9 HFI 158 SFE 652 SF1 554 SF2 1123 VES 140
Wheatley, Richard. BAA 277
Wheatstone, (Sir) Charles. EXT 6/2 30
Wheeler, David Hilton. BAA 54
Wheeler, Edward L. TSP 85
Wheeler, Ethel Rolt. CSF 207
Wheeler, Hugh Collinson. WGT 154
Wheeler, Ida Worden. CSF 207 SF1 554
Wheeler, (John) Harvey (1918-) AOW 158 BYS 55 ES2 454 FFR 199 MFW 199-200 SFE 652 SF1 554 SF2 1123
Wheeler, Paul (1934-) ES2 455 SF1 554 SF2 1124
Wheeler, Post (1869-1956) SF1 554
Wheeler, Thomas Gerald. ES2 455 FFC 180 SFE 652 SF1 554
Wheeler, William Wallace (1853-1916) CSF 207 SF1 555
Wheeler-Bennett, (Sir) John. VES 121
Wheeler-Nicholson, Malcolm (1890-) SF1 555
Wheelock, Warren H. SF1 555
Wheelwright, John Tyler (1856-1925) CSF 85 SF1 555
Wheelwright, Philip. MSF 32 MSM 144
Wheen, Natalie. EXT 10/1 43
Whelpley, J.D. IAC 246
Wherry, Edith. CSF 207
Whetstone, Raymond (house name) TSP 132
Whewell, (Dr.) William. IAC 246
Whipple, Chandler H. TSP 108-11
Whitaker, David (1930-) SF1 555 SF2 1124
White. JGB 33
White, Anne. FFC 127,137
White, (General) Ared. CSF 207 POE 251 SFE 653 SF1 555
White, Arnold Henry (1848-1925) SF1 555

White, Cecil B. pseud. of William H. Christie. AAL 41-2 IAC 246
White, Charles E. EXT 3/1 7
White, David. FFC 176
White, Don. IAC 246 SFS 125
White, Edward Lucas (1866-1934) CSF 207 ES2 455 FBK 73 IAC 246 SF1 555 WTS 26
White, E(lwyn) B(rooks). AOW 288 EXT 8/1 6 FFC 127 IAC 246 ISW 129 SFS 125
White, Ethel Lina. CSF 207
White, F.V. STH 205,216
White, Frank. ES2 455
White, Fred(erick) M(errick) (1859-) CSF 207 ALW 85 IAC 246 SFE 653 SF1 555
White, George H. pseud. of Pascual Enguidanos Usach. SIH 141,166
White, H. Ray. SF1 555
White, Hester. CSF 207
White, Howard B. BAA 277
White, James. CSF 207 WGT 154
White, James (1928-) ALW 212 AOW 273-4 BFP 531-2 ES2 455 FFR 199 FTF 166-7 HFI 158 IAC 246-7 KAU 61,78 LEX 654-6 RGS 194-5,226 SFE 653 SFS 125 SF1 555 SF2 1124 SL2 614-7 SRB 340,343 VES 87,97,99,162,180 WAA 176,178 WSF 175
White, Jane. HFI 158
White, Jay C. (1925-) SFE 653 SF1 555
White, John Blake. BAA 50 BYS 263 CSF 207 MFW 50,63 SF1 555
White, Kenneth. SOT 400 WFS 103,105
White, M.E. IAC 247 SFS 125
White, Matthew, Jr. ALW 105 SOT 47
White, Michael. STH 128-9
White, Milton. IMS 52
White, Percy (1852-1938) CSF 207 SF1 555
White, Stewart Edward (1873-1946) AOW 78 CSF 207 EXT 1/1 2,20 EXT 3/1 28 EXT 7/1 19-20,26-7 SFE 653 SF1 555-6
White, T.H. CSF 208
White, Ted (1938-) ALW 128 AOW 274 BYS 304 COT 274-5,

White, Ted (cont.)
279-80, 282-3, 294 DTS 7, 30
ETN 27 FFR 199 [FJT] HFI
158-9 IAC 247 KAU 9 LEX
656-7 LTN 247, 252 MIH 130
PJF 74 SFE 653 SF1 556 WSF
230, 274, 280 see also Theodore
Edward White, Norman Edwards
White, T(erence) H(anbury) (1906-
64) AOW 93, 261, 265 BFP 533-
4 CSF 208 ES2 455-6 EXT 5/1
4 FBK 120 FFC 52, 106 FL3
1052-6, 1149-57 HFI 159 SFE
654 SFN 40 SF1 556 SOI 82
SRB 279
White, Theodore Edward (1938-)
BFP 535-7 ES2 456 SF2 1124
WGT 154 see also Ted White,
Norman Edwards
White, Thomas I. BAA 277
White, Tim. [FUT]
White, William Allen. SFH 10
White, W(illiam) A(nthony)
P(arker) (1911-68) ALW 215
BAA 135 COT 301 EXT 10/1 4
RFA 109-10, 116, 122 SFN 47
SF2 823-5 WGT 154 see also
Anthony Boucher, H. H. Holmes,
Herman W. Mudgett
White, William Chapman (1903-
55) CSF 208 SF1 556
Whiteford, Wynne N. ES2 456
Whitehead. [FUT]
Whitehead, Alfred North (1861-
1947) CWN 8, 10, 31, 41 THM 32
Whitehead, Frank. EXT 6/1 8
Whitehead, Henry St. Clair (1882-
1932) BFP 537 CSF 208 ES2
456 FBK 78, 83 IMS 134 RFA
64 SF1 556 SOT 52, 73, 347
VES 142, 211 WTS 22-5, 27, 29,
32-4, 43, 49, 51, 86, 125-7, 132
Whitehead, Robert John (1928-)
SF1 556 SF2 1125
Whitehill, Joseph. IAC 247 SFS
125
Whitehorne, Chester. ES2 457
Whitehouse, Arch. TSP 89
Whitehouse, John Howard. BAA
108-9
Whiteing, Richard. CSF 208
Whiteley, Elizabeth. CSF 208
SF1 556
Whiteley, John. SF1 556
Whitell, Evelyn. CSF 208 SF1
556

Whitelock, Louise Clarkson
(1865-) WGT 154
Whitenight, Cynthia S. SF1 557
SRB 465
Whiteside, Edward. BAA 117
SF1 557
Whiteside, Thomas. ES2 457
IMS 115, 186
Whitfield, Christopher. CSF 208
Whitfield, Stephen Edward. SFE
654 SF1 557
Whitham, Ed. WTS 80
Whitham, John W. BAA 99 CSF
208 SF1 557
Whiting, Adeline D. T. CSF 208
Whiting, John. EXT 6/1 11
Whiting, Sydney (-1875) BAA 26
CSF 208 EXT 5/1 4, 14 SF1
557 WGT 154
Whitley, George pseud. of A.
Bertram Chandler. IAC 247
SFS 125
Whitman, John Pratt. BAA 102,
196
Whitman, Walt (1819-92) ACE 58
AC2 56 ALW 64 CYR 48 EXT
4/1 8 EXT 8/1 12 IAC 247
MIH 125 NWO 44, 46-7 RBY 86
RZY 14, 48-50 SFN 119 SHL 7,
47 TBC 7
Whitmore, H. WGT 154
Whitmore, James. SFH 101
Whitmore, Tom. LTN 238
Whitnall, Harold Orville (1877-
1945) SF1 557
Whitney, Eli. MSF 194
Whitney, Verner Meurice. SF1
557
Whittemore, Reed. IAC 247
Whitten, Leslie Hunter (1928-)
SF1 557 SF2 1125
Whittier, John Greenleaf. BAA
277
Whittington, Harry. SF1 557
Whorf, Benjamin Lee. AAL 159-
69, 180-1, 204-5 COT 157 SFH
153
Whybrow, Geoffrey. IAC 247
SFS 125
Whyte, Andrew Adams. SF1 557
Whyte, Ewen. WTS 47
Whyte, H. Walter. HFI 159
Whyte, William. CWN 32
Whyte-Melville, George John
(1821-78) CSF 208 SF1 557

Wibberley, Leonard (Francis)
(1915-) AOW 332 ES2 457 EXT
6/2 48 EXT 8/2 66 FFC 101,
152-3 FFR 199 FL3 1301-3
HFI 159 SFE 654 SF1 557 SF2
1125 WGT 154-5
Wickenden, Dan. EXT 10/1 43
FFC 183
Wicker, Thomas Grey (1926-)
ES2 457 WGT 155
Wickersham, James Alexander
(1851-) SF1 558
Wickert, Max. WBW 33, 42
Wickes, George. EXT 6/1 10,
13, 16
Wickham, Harvey (1872-1930)
CSF 208 SF1 558
Wickramasinghe, W. C. SFW 89
Wicks, Mark. AOW 78 BAA 78
CSF 208 EXT 1/1 3, 20 EXT
5/2 37 EXT 7/1 27 PST 114,
193, 203, 223, 234, 238, 241, 243
SFE 654 SF1 558 VES 70
Widener, Donald (1930-) SF1 558
SF2 1125
Widmer, Harry. TSP 81, 89
Widmer, Kingsley. BAA 277
CWN 27-8
Widnall, Samuel Page. SF1 558
Widner, Arthur L. IMS 33, 35,
213 SOT 320 STH 266 WGT 155
Widney, Stanley A. ES2 457 SF1
558
Wiebling, Peggy. SIH 129
Wiek, Bruno S. (1897-) LEX 657
Wieland, Christopher Martin.
POE 31
Wiemer, Rudolf O. FFC 157
Wiene, Robert. STH 229 WAA
192
Wiener, Anthony. CSC 133
Wiener, Norbert (1894-1964) ASF
320 ES2 457 EXT 8/1 4 FAN
160 IAC 242 ISW 165 KAU 22,
152 MFW 184, 190-2 SFE 654
SFH 134 SFS 125 SOT 34 STF
35 TRB 60 VES 188 VFS 207
WGT 155 see also W. Norbert
Wiener, Philip P. NWO 61
Wiese, Kurt. FFC 114, 129, 132-
3, 137
Wieser, Wolfgang. BAA 277
Wiesner, (Dr.) Jerome. VFS 241
Wiesner, William. FFC 74, 98
Wiggin, Kate. FFC 11

Wiggins, Olon F. IMS 33, 52, 70,
72-3, 103, 109, 115, 122-3, 127-8,
131, 135-6, 141, 145, 154, 184,
189-92, 208-9, 211, 229, 233, 236,
243 ISW 162
Wiggins, Walter, Jr. SF1 558
Wigglesworth, Katherine. FFC
125
Wignall, Trevor C. (1883-) CSF
208 SF1 558
Wikland, Ilon. FFC 182
Wilbrandt, Conrad. CSF 208
EXT 2/2 32 FAN 34 SF1 558
Wilbur, Richard. IAC 247 NWO
61, 63
Wilcox, Collin (1924-) SF1 558
Wilcox, Don (1908-) COT 164 ES2
457 IAC 247 RFA 91 SFE 654
SFS 126 SF1 558 SOT 201 VES
73, 160 WGT 155 WIF 120 WSF
116, 329 see also Alexander
Blade
Wilcox, Jayem. TSP 30 WTS 85
Wilcox, Marrion (1858-1926)
CSF 209 WGT 155
Wilcoxin, Fred. KAU 199
Wild, P. H. BAA 277
Wilde, Niall. IAC 247 SFS 126
Wilde, Oscar (1854-1900) BYS
17, 116 CSF 209 CWN 17 ES2
457-8 EXT 6/2 32 FBK 112, 117
FFC 11, 23 FFR 200 FLT 49
FL1 190-2 FL2 687-9 FL3
1257-61 FTF 101 IAC 247 MFW
280 MSM 259 NDA 201 RBY
164, 168 SFH 167 SFN 29 SF1
558 SIH 33 SRB 22 VFS 208
WBW 21, 38
Wilder, Billy. CSC 264
Wilder, Cherry (1930-) HFI 159
IAC 247 SFE 654
Wilder, Thornton. CSF 209 FL4
1760-2
Wilderhope, John. CSF 209
Wilding, Eric. VES 187
Wilding, Michael. IAC 247
Wilding, Philip. ES2 458 SFE
654 SF1 558 WGT 155
Wildsmith, Brian. FFC 171
Wiley, Carl A. WGT 155
Wiley, John P. AAL 92
Wiley, Ray H. BAA 119 SF1 558
Wilhelm, Clarence J. IMS 33
Wilhelm, Kate (1928-) ALW 212
AOW 202, 266, 274-5, 290-1, 294

Wilhelm, Kate (cont.)
BAA 156 BFP 538-9 BYS 305
CSC 146 DMK 193-204 ES2 458
ETN 65 EXT 9/1 21 EXT 10/1
6, 8 FFR 200 HFI 159 IAC 247-
8 LEX 657-8 LTN 228, 238
RFA 208 RGS 195 SFA 38 SFE
655 SFS 126 SF1 559 SF2
1125-6 SL3 1122-5 SL5 2469-
73 SRB 366-7, 370, 375 TSF 184-
9 VES 180, 232 WSF 183-4, 262,
268
Wilhelm, Lambert. SF1 559
Wilhelm II, (Kaiser of Germany).
SFB 67
Wilis. SF1 559
Wilkes, A. B. BAA 55
Wilkie, G. ES2 458
Wilkie, J. BAA 65 CSF 209
Wilkins, Harold Tom (1891-) ES2
458
Wilkins, Hilliard. BAA 97-8
Wilkins, Hugh Percival (1896-
1960) ES2 458
Wilkins, (Bishop) John (1614-72)
ALW 32, 42 BYS 63 FTF 20
PST 13, 18, 272, 275-6, 284 SFB
30 SFE 655 WAA 13-4, 31, 132
Wilkins, Lura M. CSF 209
Wilkins, Mary Eleanor Freeman
(1852-1930) ES2 458 FBK 73
SF1 559
Wilkins, Percy H. IAC 248
Wilkins, Ralph. STH 141
Wilkins, (William) Vaughan (1890-
1959) ES2 458-9 HFI 159 ISW
213-5 SFE 655 SF1 559
Wilkinson, Louis Umfreville (1881-
1966) WGT 155 see also Louis
Marlow
Wilkinson, Percy T. IMS 137
Wilkinson, Sarah Scudgell. CSF
209 SF1 559
Will, John N. ES2 459 SFE 655
SF1 559
Willard, Charles Dwight (1860-
1914) SF1 559
Willard, Mark. JVN 103-16, 241
Willard, Mildred Wilds (1911-)
SF1 559 SF2 1126
Willard, Nancy. FFC 180
Willard, Theodore Arthur (1862-
1943) MFW 129 SF1 559
Willeford, Charles Ray, III (1919-)
ES2 459 IAC 248 SFE 655 SF1
559 SF2 1126

Willer, Jim. SF1 559
Willetts, R. F. EXT 9/1 6-7, 16
Willey, Robert pseud. of Willy
Ley. IAC 248 RFA 42, 84 VFS
134
William, (Sir). SF1 559
William (of Occam). CAT 12
William (the Conqueror). STH 206
Williams, Alfred Rowberry (1888-)
SF1 559
Williams, Anne. FFC 109
Williams, Arthur. BAA 91
Williams, Basil. MSF 209
Williams, Ben A. IAC 248
Williams, Beryl (1910-) ES2 459
Williams, C. H. BAA 277
Williams, Cecil B. EXT 4/1 11
Williams, Charles (Walter Stans-
by) (1886-1945) AOW 89, 93, 115,
347, 356, 396 BFP 540-1 BYS
201 CSC 34 CSF 209 ES2 459
EXT 8/2 30 EXT 9/2 47-8 EXT
10/1 18-20, 31, 39-40, 45 FAN
138 FBK 97, 126-7 FL1 17-21,
366-73 FL2 649-53, 966-9 FL3
1262-7, 1384-6 FL5 2063-6
IMS 20 WIF 81 SFE 655-6 SF1
559-60 SRB 280 STH 7, 13
Williams, Cora Lenore. CSF 209
Williams, David. EXT 6/1 18
Williams, David N. IAC 248
Williams, David Rhys. WGT 155
Williams, Donald C. BAA 277
NDA 54, 206
Williams, Earl Willoughby (1885-)
SF1 560
Williams, (Edward) Francis (1903-
70) ES2 459 HFI 160 SFE 656
SF1 560
Williams, Eric Cyril (1918-) IAC
248 IMS 100, 159 SFE 656 SFS
126 SF1 560 SF2 1126
Williams, Frances Fenwick. SF1
560
Williams, Francis Howard (1844-
1922) CSF 209 SF1 560
Williams, Frank Chenhalls (1880-)
CSF 209 SF1 560
Williams, Frank P. CSF 209
Williams, Frank Purdy. BAA 63
Williams, Frederic Conde. BAA
55
Williams, Garth. FFC 124, 127-8
Williams, Geoffrey. CSF 209
SF1 560
Williams, Gerald. SF1 560

Williams, Gordon. HFI 160
Williams, Harold (1853-) WGT 155
Williams, Harper. CSF 209
SF1 560
Williams, Herbert (1914-) ES2
459 EXT 3/1 20 SF1 560
Williams, Idabel. CSF 209
Williams, Islwyn. ES2 459 SF1
560
Williams, J. X. (house name)
SFE 656 SF1 560 see also
Andrew J. Offutt
Williams, James A. SF1 560
WIF 124 WSF 134
Williams, Jay (1914-78) AOW 333
ES2 459-60 FFC 23, 27, 52, 58,
71, 180 IAC 248 SFS 126 SF1
561 SF2 1126-7
Williams, Jim. WFS 205
Williams, John. ALW 238 IAC
248
Williams, John Alfred (1925-)
AOW 275 NDA 170, 172 SFE
656 SF1 561 SF2 1127
Williams, Jonathan. IAC 248
Williams, Kathleen M. BAA 277
Williams, Lloyd. CSF 209
Williams, Margery see Margery
Williams Bianco
Williams, Miles Sheldon. CSF
210
Williams, Neil Wynn. CSF 210
SF1 561
Williams, Nick Boddie (1906-)
ES2 460 HFI 160 SFE 656 SF1
561 SF2 1127
Williams, (Mrs.) Pat. ES2 460
Williams, Pat. EXT 7/2 40-1,
45
Williams, Paul. SFD 8
Williams, Preston N. BAA 277
Williams, R. F. BAA 22 WGT
155
Williams, Ralph. IAC 249 SFS
126
Williams, Raymond. ACC 85-6
CAT 32 EXT 6/1 19 KAU 95
MSF 77, 186, 206
Williams, Richard Valentine see
Richard Rowley
Williams, Robert Folkestone
(1805-72) POE 147 SF1 561
Williams, Robert Moore (1907-
78) AOW 394 BAA 108 COT 47
DTS 24 ES2 460 HFI 160 IAC
249 ISW 133 KAU 177-8 MIH

24 LEX 658-9 OWB 98 RFA
52 SFE 656 SFS 126 SF1 561-
2 SF2 1127-8 SOT 181 VES
177, 179, 335 WGT 155-6 WIF
120, 145, 163, 190 WSF 93, 115
see also John S. Browning
Williams, Roswell (1893-1968)
ES2 460-1 see also Frank Owen
Williams, Speedy pseud. of L. H.
Smith. SF1 562
Williams, T. Owen. HFI 160
SF1 562
Williams, Tennessee pseud. of
Thomas Lanier Williams. FLT
43 FL1 187-9 HID 135 IAC
249 SF1 562 WTS ix, 30, 48
Williams, Thaddeus Warsaw. SF1
562
Williams, Thomas. HFI 160
Williams, Thomas Lanier (1914-
83) SF2 1128 WGT 156 WTS 30
see also Tennessee Williams
Williams, Ursula Moray (1911-)
ES2 461 FFC 34, 77, 84, 128,
137, 153, 158 SF1 562, 585 SF2
1128-9
Williams, William Carlos. IAC
249 NWO 44
Williams, William Frederic. CSF
210
Williams-Ellis, (Lady Mary)
Amabel (1894-) ES2 461 IAC
248 SFS 126 SF1 562 SF2 1129
WGT 156
Williams-Ellis, Mably Owen.
IAC 248
Williamson, Al (1931-) ES2 461
VES 326
Williamson, Blanche. WFS 299
Williamson, Ethel. WGT 156
see also Jane Cardinal
Williamson, George Hunt (1926-)
ES2 461-2
Williamson, Henry. CSF 210
THM 12
Williamson, Ian. IAC 249 SFS
126
Williamson, Jack pseud. of John
Stewart Williamson (1908-) AAL
46-50, 56-7, 79, 213 ALW 7, 10,
36, 89, 91, 94-5, 97, 123, 125-6,
129, 136-40, 154, 185, 213, 234
AOW 83, 115, 275-6, 296, 357,
366, 399 ASF 119, 137, 146, 232-
3, 243, 252 BAA 110, 116, 118,
139, 141, 196 BFP 542-5 BYS

Williamson, Jack (cont.)
210, 217, 220-4, 227, 229, 231-2,
238 CAT xvii, 14, 72, 139-40
COT 20, 27, 111-2, 178, 223-7,
247-8, 250, 281, 283, 286, 292,
298, 301 CSC 29, 48-9, 52, 195-
215, 311 CSF 210 ES2 462-3
ETN 59 EXT 3/1 27 EXT 5/1
3 EXT 7/2 39 EXT 10/1 48
FAN 155 FBK 55 FFR 200 FL1
336-40 HFI 161 HID x, 13 IAC
249-50 IMS 5, 8, 72, 75-6, 83,
197, 199, 205, 213, 218, 243 ISW
45-6, 58, 207, 258 KAU 20, 27,
129, 157, 159, 164-74, 177 LEX
659-61 MFW 209, 219 MIH 22,
24, 27, 36, 38, 102 MSM 32, 74,
80, 83, 132, 138, 169, 172, 202,
299, 302, 304-5 NDA xi, 28-30,
34-6 OWB 33, 37-49, 79, 84, 93-
5, 100 POE 277 RAH 15-31
RFA 2, 6, 13, 20, 22, 24, 28, 32, 36,
39, 50, 53, 57, 60-5, 79, 95, 102-3,
107, 113, 118, 143, 146, 155, 158,
160-1, 166, 168, 170, 183, 187, 214
RGS 195-7, 226 SFB 55, 62 SFD
8, 22, 27-8, 73, 83, 213, 236, 242,
290, 294, 307, 312, 318 SFE 656-
7 SFH 62-3, 66 SFS 126-7 SFW
115, 225-31, 476 SF1 562-3 SIH
32 SL1 374-7 SL2 782-6, 981-
5 SL3 1057-61, 1178-82 SL5
2459-62 SOT 42, 76-8, 80, 84-
100, 174, 293, 309, 331, 406, 416
SRB 5, 126, 280, 305, 309, 510
STH 104, 244 TJB 4, 8 TSF 8-
18, 54, 223, 230, 234 TSP 29, 190
UFS 4 VES 71, 75, 77, 87, 93, 105,
108, 114, 122, 140, 142, 147-8,
159, 163-4, 177-8, 198, 218, 235,
314, 328, 335 VF1 1-43, 263-4
WAA 119 WFS 96, 140, 161, 178-
80, 266, 299 WIF 134, 145, 151,
153, 164 WSF 29, 45, 59, 66-7,
92, 94, 104, 112, 122, 133, 135, 241,
246, 265, 306, 386, 389 WTS 15,
36-8, 41, 52-3, 67, 69
Williamson, John Stewart (1908-)
EXT 8/2 56, 58 SF2 1129-30
WGT 156 see also Will Stewart,
Jack Williamson
Williamson, Phyllis E. CSF 210
Williamson, Thames Ross (1894-)
CSF 210 SF1 563
Willie, Albert Frederic pseud. of
H. P. Lovecraft. EXT 3/1 16

Willink, Margaret D. R. BAA 197
Willis, Donald Chalmers (1947-)
AOW 362 SF1 563 SF2 1130
Willis, (George) Anthony Arm-
strong (1897-76) ES2 463 WGT
156-7
Willis, Katherine Tappert. EXT
10/1 44
Willis, Walter A. (1919-) ES2
463 SRB 105-6 WSF 145, 212
Willmer, John H. CSF 210
Willms, Bernard. BAA 197
Willoughby, Frank. BAA 91 CSF
210
Wills, Bernard. BAA 277
Willy (the Wisp) pseud. of Donald
A. Wollheim. IMS 53-4, 127
Wilmot, Eileen. SF1 563
Wilson, Angus (Frank Johnstone)
(1913-) ACC 17 BYS 257, 298
CWN 3 ES2 463 IAC 250 ISW
242 LTN 102, 109-10, 112-3
POE 280 SFE 657 SFS 127 SF1
563 SF2 1130
Wilson, Bryan A. BAA 277
Wilson, Carter. IAC 250
Wilson, Clarence True. BAA 104
Wilson, Colin (Henry) (1931-)
ALW 238 AOW 276, 358 BAA
197 BYS 177 DTS 37 ES2 463
EXT 10/1 23, 44 FBK 74, 77, 81
FFR 200 HFI 161 MIH 101, 121
NDA 111-5 NWO 263 SFE 657
SFW 131-7, 209-17 SF1 563-4
SF2 1130 SL3 1401-6 SL4 1674-
7 SOI xiv SOT 2
Wilson, Dagmar. FFC 118
Wilson, David Alec (1864-1933)
BAA 90 CSF 210 SF1 564
Wilson, Doris Marie Claire Baum-
gardt Pohl. WGT 157
Wilson, Earl. TSP 25
Wilson, Edmund (1895-1972) CSF
210 EXT 3/1 25 EXT 10/1 44
FBK 74, 76, 98 KAU 198-9 LTN
204 SF1 564 SF2 1130 SOI 110
Wilson, Elizabeth. VFS 13, 23-5
Wilson, Ellsworth. SF1 564
Wilson, F. Paul (1946-) HFI 161
SFE 657-8
Wilson, G. F. EXT 7/1 16
Wilson, Gabriel pseud. of Ray
Cummings. TSP 180
Wilson, Gahan. ES2 463 FFC
128, 155 FRN 29, 46 IAC 250
SFS 127 SRB 2, 289 WSF 297

Wilson, Hardy. BAA 125
Wilson, Harris. EXT 8/2 55
Wilson, Hazel Emma Hutchins
(1898-) ES2 463 SF1 564 SF2
1130-1
Wilson, Henry Leon. STH 239-40
Wilson, Henry Lovejoy (1908-58)
BAA 104 SF1 564
Wilson, Herbert Wrigley (1866-
1940) SF1 564
Wilson, Jesse. BAA 75 CSF 210
SF1 564
Wilson, Jessica. WFS 79,128
see also Jessica Gould
Wilson, John Anthony Burgess
(1917-) BAA 138 SF2 836 SRB
337 WGT 157 see also Anthony
Burgess
Wilson, John Fleming (1877-1922)
ES2 463 IAC 250
Wilson, John Grosvenor (1866-)
BAA 63-4 SF1 564
Wilson, John Rowan (1919-) ES2
463 SF1 564
Wilson, John T. BAA 277
Wilson, Mary Badger. SF1 564
Wilson, Mike. ACE 11,13-4,22,
75-6 AC2 9,11-2,20,73-4 SOT
389 VFS 13-4,21-3,27-31,33
Wilson, Miles. SF1 564
Wilson, Mitchell. MSM 303
Wilson, Philip Whitewell. BAA
110
Wilson, R. IAC 45,250
Wilson, R., Jr. EFP 7
Wilson, Rathmell. SF1 564
Wilson, Raymond. ES2 463 SF1
564
Wilson, Richard (1920-) AAL 15
ALW 8,156,160 AOW 294 BAA
128 ES2 463-4 ETN 162-3 FFR
200 HFI 161-2 IAC 250 IMS 79,
104,106,111,115-6,121-2,125,
135-8,140-2,145,148,151,153,
156,158,170-2,174,178-9,181-
2,188,210-1,213-4,217,227,
244-7 LEX 662 MIH 95-6,135
NDA 159-60 SFD 16 SFE 658
SFS 127 SFW 394,401-2 SF1
564 SF2 1131 UFS 5 VES 211,
319 WFS 71-2,79,117,128 WGT
157 see also Ivar Towers
Wilson, Robert Anton (1932-)
SFE 658 SF1 565
Wilson, Robert H. EXT 2/1 2-4
IAC 250
Wilson, Robin Scott (1928-) AOW
300,366 COT 165 EXT 1/2 24
EXT 9/1 21 EXT 10/1 5-8 EXT
10/2 115 IAC 250-1 LTN 32,
186,192,251,257,262,265 SFB
7 SFE 658 SF1 565 SF2 1131
SRB 239 TSF 38-43 WGT 157
WSF 268 see also Robin Scott
Wilson, Robley, Jr. IAC 251
Wilson, Sandy (1924-) SF1 565
Wilson, Sloan. ETN 130
Wilson, Steve (1943-) HFI 162
SFE 658
Wilson, Theodora (-1941) CSF
210 SF1 565
Wilson, Thomas. IAH 13-6 RFA
200
Wilson, Wilfred (1869-) CSF 25
SF1 565
Wilson, William. CAT 2-3 SFE
658 SF1 565 SIH 9
Wilson, William Huntington (1870-)
CSF 210 EXT 1/1 20 MFW 127
SF1 565
Wilson, Woodrow. COT 123 FBK
109 MSM 26 RHN 211
Wilson, Yates. SF1 565
Wilstach, John. EXT 3/1 25
Wimsatt, W. K., Jr. BAA 277-8
NWO 69
Winch, Edgar. CSF 210 SF1 565
Winchell, Paul. SFN 79-80
Winchell, Walter. ISW 277
Windsor, William (1857-) BAA
58 CSF 210 SF1 565
Winfield, Arthur M. STH 162,164
Winfield, Dick pseud. of Dick
Perry. ES2 464 SF1 565
Winger, Frank Stover. CSF 210
Wingrave, A. pseud. of S. Fow-
ler Wright. CSF 210 STH 100
Winiki, Ephriam. VES 159
Winn, (Mr.). VFS 230-2
Winn, Pip. IAC 251
Winn, Rowland Denis Guy (1916-)
ES2 464 SF1 585
Winner, Langdon. KAU 13
Winnicott, D.W. FLT 140-1
Winning, Charles Del Norte.
BAA 289-90
Winship, George P., Jr. SOI
111-24,142
Winship, Glen Brian (1887?-1966)
BAA 91 SF1 565
Winslow, Dorian pseud. of Daoma
Winston. SF1 565

Winsor, Frederick (1900-58) ES2
464 EXT 5/1 9 IAC 251
Winsor, George McLeod. CSF
210-1 ES2 464 SFE 658 SF1
565
Winsor, Kathleen. MSM 253
Winstanley, Gerrard. BAA 4
Winston, Daoma (1922-) see
Dorian Winslow
Winston, David. BAA 278, 290
Winter, H. G. pseud. of Harry
Bates, Desmond Hall. RFA 10
Winter, Joseph A. IAC 251 IAH
85 RFA 167, 193 SFS 127 WIF
95
Winterbotham, Russ(ell Robert)
(1904-71) ALW 141 ES2 464
HFI 162 IAC 251 LEX 662-3
MIH 93-5 SFE 658 SFS 127
SF1 565 SF2 1131-2 WGT 157
Winterburn, Katherine. BAA 137
Winterfeld, Henry. AOW 333 ES2
464 HFI 162 SF1 565
Winters, Dorothy. WFS 140
Winters, Joseph S. WFS 139-40
Winters, Rae pseud. of Raymond
A. Palmer. IMS 16
Winthrop, Henry. BAA 278
Winthrop, John. NWO 35
Winthrop, Theodore. CSF 211
Winthrop, William Y. CSF 211
Wintle, Alfred Daniel see Michael
Cobb
Wintle, Elizabeth Rhoda (1943-)
SF2 971 see also Louise Law-
rence
Wintle, Harold. CSF 211 SF1 566
Wintle, Hector. CSF 211 SF1 566
Wintle, William James. CSF 211
IAC 251 SF1 566
Winwar, Frances pseud. of Fran-
ces V. Grebanier. CSF 211
Wise, Arthur (1923-) ES2 464
SFE 658 SF1 566 SF2 1132
WGT 157
Wise, David. IAC 251
Wise, Herbert Alvin (1893?-1961)
CSF 211 ES2 464-5 EXT 3/1 20
EXT 5/1 9 SF1 566
Wise, P. C. MSF 177
Wise, Robert (1914-) SFE 658-9
Wise, Robert A. pseud. of Fred
J. Gebhart. SF1 566 SFE 659
Wismer, Helen. TSP 81
Wisniewski-Snerg, Adam (1937-)
LEX 663-4

Wissel, Rudolf. BAA 278
Wissner, Robert. IAC 251
Wister, Owen (1860-1938) COT
60 SFH 172-3 SF1 566
Withers, Julia. SF1 566
Witt, Currie B. SF1 566
Witt, Lavinia Lee. SF1 566
Witt, Otto (1875-1923) ES2 465
FTF 68 SIH 187, 191
Wittels, Franz. BAA 197
Wittgenstein, Ludwig. CAT 130
CWN 24, 31 EXT 10/2 52 MFW
184 STF 35
Wittig, Monique (1935-) SFE 659
SF1 566
Wittke, Carl. BAA 197
Witwer, Benjamin. SOT 71
Wobig, Ellen (1911-) ES2 465
HFI 162 SFE 659 SF1 566 SF2
1132
Wodehouse, P(elham) G(renville)
(1881-1975) ACC 32 ALW 216
ASF 43, 57, 308 CSF 211 ES2
465 EXT 8/2 66 EXT 10/2 106-
8 HID 20 ISW 191, 214 MSM
128 OWB 71 SFE 659 SF1 566
SF2 1132
Wodhams, Jack (1931-) ALW 212
ETN 27-8 HFI 162 IAC 251
SFE 659 SF1 566 VES 157, 211
Woe, Willis W. pseud. of Wilson
Shepard. IMS 27
Wohl, Burton see Baldwin Hills
Wohl, Louis D. CSF 211
Wojcik, Jan S. J. EXT 10/1 45
Wolf, Barbara Herrman (1932-)
SF1 566 SF2 1132
Wolf, Frederick Ellsworth. BAA
115
Wolf, Hans. BAA 290
Wolf, Howard. BAA 106
Wolf, Jack Clifford (1922-) SF1
567 SF2 1132
Wolf, Leonard. FBK 49 IAC 251
SFW 6
Wolf, M. SFS 127
Wolf, Mari (1927-) ES2 465
Wolf, Victoria Trude (1903-) SF1
567
Wolfe, Aaron. HFI 162
Wolfe, Bernard (1915-) ALW 31
AOW 276, 291 BAA 121 BYS 263
ES2 465 EXT 2/2 32 EXT 5/1
4 EXT 6/2 51 FAN 186 HFI
162 IAC 251 IAH 141-2, 144-5
ISW 164-5 JGB 6 KAU 155

Wolfe, Bernard (cont.)
MFW 1-2, 10, 83, 203-5 NDA 65-7, 69, 181-2, 185 POE 275-7 SFE 659 SFH 180-1 SFS 127-8 SFW 104 SF1 567 SF2 1133 SL3 1221-5 VES 188
Wolfe, Charles S. STH 137
Wolfe, Don M. BAA 278
Wolfe, Gary K. BAA 278 FL1 282-6, 391-5 FL2 744-8, 993-7 FL3 1173-5, 1457-64 FL4 1547-53, 1684-5, 1760-2, 1769-73, 2039-45 FL5 2220-34, 2267-82 HFI 162 IAC 251 MFW 2, 9-10 RBY 33-54 SFE 659 SL1 186-90 SL2 676-80 SL3 1242-5, 1391-5 SL4 1751-8, 1859-62, 1888-91, 1898-901, 1926-9 SL5 2378-82, 2492-6 SRB 74, 510
Wolfe, Gene (Rodman) (1931-) AAL 157 ALW 212 BFP 546 ETN 146 FFR 200 [FJT] FL1 154-60 HFI 162 IAC 251-2 INT 26-8, 58-9, 122 LEX 664-5 MFW 24 RGS 197-8 RSG 49 SFE 659-60 SFS 128 SF1 567 SF2 1133 SL2 770-5 VES 87, 319
Wolfe, Jack C. IAC 252
Wolfe, Louis (1905-) ES2 465 HFI 162 SF1 567 SF2 1133
Wolfe, Mari. IAC 252
Wolfe, Nero. PJF 15
Wolfe, Peter. BAA 278
Wolfe, Thomas (1900-38) IAC 252 IAH 87-8 MIH 69, 125 SFA 143 SOT 217, 220 TBC 50 THM 13 TJB 31
Wolfe, Tom. HEN 10 NWO 206 SFH 92 STF 9-10
Wolff, Cecil Drummond. WGT 157 see also Cedric Dane Waldo
Wolff, Emil. BAA 290
Wolff, Max J. BAA 278
Wolff, Peter. SFH 242
Wolfkind, Peter Daniel. FBK 144
Wolgin, W. P. BAA 278
Wolk, Anthony. LTN 192, 267
Wolk, George see Heinrich Graat
Wolk, Susan Stanley. LTN 267
Wolkow, Konstantin (1907-) LEX 665
Wolle, Francis. STH 25
Wollheim, Donald A. (1914-) AAL 124-5, 133-4 ACC 244 ALW 7-8, 18, 30, 136, 156-61, 175-6, 180, 184-5, 225-7, 237 AOW 83, 282-3, 300-1, 333, 400, 403 ASF 120, 242 BAA 197 BFP 547-54 BYS 226, 232, 235, 241, 285-6 COT v, 22, 94-5, 119, 121, 238, 277, 282, 291, 293 CSF 211 ES2 465-7 ETN 33, 38, 43, 118 EXT 3/1 20, 27 EXT 5/1 10 EXT 7/2 46 FBK 85 FFR 201 [FJT] HFI 162-3 IAC 252-3 IMS 23, 28-31, 34-6, 39-44, 46-58, 64, 66-8, 72, 78-9, 82-8, 94-5, 103-5, 113-6, 118-20, 122-3, 125, 127-32, 135, 137, 140, 142-4, 148-9, 153-62, 167, 170, 172-3, 175-6, 180-1, 183-5, 187-8, 190-3, 200, 208-11, 214, 216-7, 225-7, 233-7, 241, 243-7, 250-2 ISW 161-2, 220 KAU 12-3 LEX 665-7 LTN 250, 263 MFW 7-9, 24 MSM 35 NWO 102 PJF 74 RAH 258 RBY 36-7 RFA 44, 157 RSG 9, 11 SFA 7, 139 SFB 152 SFD 16, 64, 84, 323 SFE 660-1 SFH 240 SFS 128 SFW 293, 393, 401 SF1 567-8 SF2 1133 SIH 114, 190-1, 201 SOT 164, 252, 256, 418 SRB 74, 90, 234, 289-90, 510 STH 45 TJB 4, 24 TSP 77 VES 83, 115, 275, 318, 330 WAA 8-9, 11, 128, 206, 217, 246 WFS 34-5, 37-8, 42-3, 45, 51-4, 59, 63, 69, 71, 73, 79, 93, 95, 97, 116-7 WGT 157-8 WIF 111, 136-9 WSF 74, 78, 126, 129, 138, 146, 204-5, 243, 245, 248, 282, 300 WTS 54, 124 see also Arthur Cooke, David Grinnell, Martin Pearson, Braxton Wells, Willy the Wisp, Lawrence Woods
Wollheim, Elsie. WFS 79
Wollheim, Richard. EXT 6/1 18
Wollonover, Fred pseud. of Sam Moskowitz. IMS 127
Wollstonecraft, Mary. BYS 15 MSF 126-7
Wolseley, Robert E. TSP 41
Woltor, Robert. CSF 211
Wonder, William pseud. of Thomas Kirwan. CSF 211
Wood, Charles Erskine Scott (1852-1944) ES2 467 SF1 568
Wood, Edward D., Jr. SF1 568
Wood, Edward W. AOW 360 BAA 171 EXT 2/1 1 HID x IAC 253 MSM 306 RFA vii, xxiii SFH

Wood, Edward W. (cont.)
238 SF1 568 SFS 128 SRB 63
WSF 215, 284
Wood, Ellen Price (1814-87)WGT
158
Wood, Forrest G. AAL 66
Wood, Frederick T. EXT 6/1 18
Wood, George (1799-1870) BAA
25-6 CSF 211 SF1 569
Wood, (Mrs.) Henry. CSF 211
Wood, (Mrs.) J. BAA 34 CSF
211
Wood, (Mrs.) J.G. CSF 212
Wood, James Playsted (1905-)
SF1 569
Wood, Joseph. BAA 278
Wood, Margaret. IAC 253 SFS
128
Wood, Michael. BAA 278 SF1 569
Wood, Ramsey. IAC 253
Wood, Robert William (1868-1955)
AOW 37, 74 CSF 195 ES2 467
EXT 1/1 19 EXT 7/1 26 HFI 146
SFE 663 SF1 569 SF2 1133
Wood, Samuel Andrew (1890-)
CSF 211 SFE 663 SF1 569
Wood, Susan. FLR 35 LTN 11-
8, 21-3, 33-7, 129-32, 187-9, 209-
10, 239, 246, 267-8 TSF 65-72
SFW 531-41 SRB 126 UKL 246
VF2 154-79, 204-5, 208 see also
Susan Glicksohn
Wood, Wallace (1927-) ES2 467
SF1 569 VES 170, 201, 326
Wood, Walter (1866-1961) CSF
211 IAC 253 SF1 569
Wood, William Parker, Jr.
(1931-) SF1 569
Woodard, George C. SF1 569
Woodard, Wayne (1914-64) BFP
555-6
Woodbridge, (Dr.) Richard. VFS
205-6
Woodbridge, William Witherspoon
(1883-) SF1 569
Woodbury, David Oakes (1896-)
HFI 163 SFE 663 SF1 569
Woodcock, George. BAA 278
EXT 9/2 53 FAN 83
Wooden, Warren Walter. BAA
290
Woodford, Jack (1894-1971) ES2
467
Woodforde, Christopher (1907-62)
ES2 467-8 SF1 569
Woodhouse, A.S.P. EXT 8/1 23

Woodhouse, Martin (1932-) HFI
163 SF1 569 SF2 1134
Woodington, Charles. CSF 212
Woodiwiss, John Cecil. CSF 212
ES2 468 SF1 569
Woodman, George David. BAA
139 SF1 569
Woodman, T.E. SF1 569
Woodroffe, Patrick (1940-) SFE
663-4
Woodrow, William. IAC 253
Woods, James. WGT 158
Woods, Katharine Pearson. BAA
278
Woods, Lawrence pseud. of Don-
ald A. Wollheim. SFE 664
Woods, Margaret Louisa (1856-
1945) SF1 569
Woods, Margaret Murray. SF1
569
Woods, P.F. pseud. of Barring-
ton J. Bayley. IAC 253
Woodward. VFS 73
Woodward, Wayne (1911?-64)
WGT 158
Woody, Thomas. BAA 278
Wooldridge, Charles William
(1847-1908) BAA 60, 65 CSF
212 SF1 569
Woolf, Virginia (1882-1941) CSF
212 ES2 468 FL3 1164-8 LTN
101-5, 110, 115, 118, 141, 161,
177, 183 SFE 664 SF1 570 STF
6
Woolfolk, Josiah Pitts (1894-1971)
WGT 158
Woolhiser, Harvey. VES 161
Woollcott, Alexander. FBK 108
STH 240
Woolrich, Claire. ETN 109
Woolrich, Cornell pseud. of Cor-
nell George Hopley-Woolrich
(1906-68) ES2 468 ETN 15, 38,
108-12 SF1 570, 585 SF2 1134
WGT 158
Woolsey, Janette (1904-) SF1 570
SF2 1134
Wootton, Barbara Frances (1897-)
BAA 197 CSF 212 SFE 664 SF1
570
Wordsworth, William (1770-1850)
CAT 3-4 CWN 60 EXT 1/2 38
EXT 9/2 26 EXT 10/2 114 IAC
253 MFW 20 MIH 144 MSF 123,
144 NWO 43 POE 49-50 SOI
88, 95-6 THM 32-3, 35, 39, 45, 56

Wordsworth, William (cont.)
UKL 64, 66-7, 69-70, 72
Worfel, W.G. SF1 570
Workman, James. ES2 468 see
also James Dark
Works, Austin M. BAA 279
Worley, Frederick U. BAA 43
WGT 158
Wormser, Gwendolyn Ranger
(1893-) CSF 212 ES2 468 SF1
570
Wormser, Richard Edward (1908-)
ES2 468 HFI 163 SF1 570
Worrell, Everil (1893-1969) ES2
468 WGT 158 WTS 28
Worth, Margaret pseud. of Helen
Arvonen. SF1 570
Worth, Nigel pseud. of Noel
Wright. CSF 212 SF1 570
Worth, Peter (house name) SFE
665 WGT 158 see also Chester
S. Geier, Roger P. Graham
Worthington, Will. IAC 253 SFS
128
Worts, George Frank (1892-) CSF
212 ES2 468 SFW 153 SF1 570
TSP 218 WGT 158-9 see also
Brent Loring
Wouk, Herman (1915-) ALW 31,
238 AOW 276 BAA 130 ES2
468-9 HFI 163 IAH 142 NDA
177-81 SFE 665 SFN 40 SF1
570 STH 45
Wratislaw, Albert C. (1862-)
CSF 212 SFE 665
Wray, Reginald pseud. of W.B.
Home-Gall. SF1 570
Wren, (Sir) Percival Christopher
(1885-1941) CSF 212 ES2 469
EXT 6/1 7 FTF 23 LTN 14-5
SF1 571
Wright, Albert Jay (1858-1940)
CSF 212 SF1 571
Wright, Allen Kendrick. BAA 75-
6, 87-8 CSF 212 SF1 571
Wright, Austin Tappan (1883-1931)
AOW 277 BAA xxi, 111 BFP
557 COT 259 CSF 212 ES2 469
EXT 6/2 51 FL2 781-6 HFI 163
LTN 104-6, 125 MFW 21, 271
SFE 665 SF1 571 SL3 1084-8
SRB 10, 301
Wright, Farnsworth (1888-1940)
ALW 121 COT 7, 17, 67, 176, 280
CWD 5, 15, 17-20, 32-3, 38, 40,
42, 45, 47, 50-1, 55 ES2 469 FBK

76, 82-3 IAC 253 IMS 6, 25, 213
SFE 665 SFW 161, 419 SOT 52,
67, 71, 76, 303, 305, 308-9, 322,
340, 358 STH 142, 152, 249, 251-
4, 257, 260 WGT 159 WIF 76, 81,
117 WSF 296 WTS ix, 3-15, 19,
22-3, 25-33, 35, 37-44, 49-50, 52-
8, 60, 63, 65-6, 68-9, 71-2, 74, 80-
2, 86, 92-3, 96, 112, 118-26, 128-
9, 132 see also Francis Hard
Wright, Frank Lloyd. EXT 9/2
46-7 [FUT] KAU 116
Wright, Frank Stover. CSF 212
Wright, Fred. WTS 13
Wright, Freire. FFC 11
Wright, Gary. IAC 253 SFS 128
Wright, George Francis. WTS 12
Wright, Gilbert Munger (1901-)
see John Lebar
Wright, Grahame (1947-) SF1 571
Wright, Hamilton (1912-) ES2 469
SF1 571
Wright, Harold Bell (1872-1944)
CSF 212 SF1 571 see also
John Lebar
Wright, Henry. BAA 32, 61-2
Wright, John K. BAA 279
Wright, Kenneth. ES2 469
Wright, Lan pseud. of Lionel Per-
cy Wright (1923-) HFI 163 IAC
253 LEX 667-8 SFE 665 SFS
128 SF1 571 VES 157
Wright, Laura Jane (1954-) SF1
571
Wright, Lee. ES2 469-70 SF1
571
Wright, Lionel Percy (1923-) ES2
469 SF2 1134-5 WGT 159 see
also Lan Wright
Wright, Mabel Osgood (1859-1934)
SF1 585 WGT 159 see also
Barbara
Wright, Majorie Evelyn. EXT
10/1 45
Wright, Marjorie Zenk. SOI 76
WTS 4-5, 9, 12-5
Wright, (Mary) Helen (1914-) SF1
571 SF2 1134
Wright, Mary M. Dunn (1894-)
WGT 159 see also Lilith Lor-
raine
Wright, Noel (1890-1975) WGT
159 see also Nigel Worth
Wright, Orville (1871-1948) and
Wilbur (1867-1912) FTF 23 SFH
35 SFN 93 TBC 44 VFS 87

Wright, R. Glenn. IAC 253
Wright, R. H. CSF 212
Wright, Raymond. WTS 13
Wright, Robert (1930-) WTS 4
Wright, Roscoe E. RFA 133
Wright, Sewell Peaslee (1897-
1970) ES2 470 IAC 253 SFS 128
WGT 159 WSF 54
Wright, S(ydney) Fowler (1874-
1965) ALW 141 AOW 116, 394
BAA 90, 95, 99, 108 BFP 558-61
BYS 116, 208 CSF 212-3 ES2
470 EXT 3/1 28 EXT 5/1 3
EXT 6/2 51 FL1 425-7 HFI 164
IAC 253 KAU 127, 156, 160, 162,
169, 174 LEX 668 MFW 195
MSM 86, 132 OWB 13 PST 134-
6, 173, 222, 248, 266, 289, 312, 314
SFB 128 SFD 307 SFE 665-6
SFN 40 SFS 128 SFW 83-9 SF1
571-2 SL5 2497-500 SOT 73, 89,
301, 395 SRB 10, 294 STH 2, 92-
106 TSF 230 VES 133, 139, 177
WGT 159 WIF 38, 67, 86, 94, 245
see also Sidney Fowler, A.
Wingrave
Wright, Thomas (1859-1936) CSF
213 SF1 572
Wright, Vincent. SF1 572
Wright, Willard Huntington (1888-
1939) WGT 159-60
Wright, William Henry. BAA 64
SF1 572
Wrightson, Patricia (1921-) AOW
334 ES2 470 FFC 40, 72 HFI
185 SF1 572 SF2 1135
Wrinch, Dorothy Maud. BAA 279
Wrzos, Joseph Henry (1929-)
SF2 1055 SL2 883-7 WGT 160
see also Joseph Ross
Wul, Stefan pseud. of Pierre
Pairault (1922-) AOW 277 ES2
470 HFI 164 LEX 668-9 SFE
666 SF1 572 SL4 1537-40 SL5
2241-4
Wulff, Eve. IAC 197 SF1 572
Wuorio, Eva-Lis. FFC 77
Wurlitzer, Rudolf (1937-) SFE 666
SF1 572
Wyal, Pg. IAC 253
Wyatt, Horace Matthew (1876-
1954) SF1 572
Wyatt, Lee. SF1 572
Wyatt, Patrick. BAA 163 SFE
666

Wybraniec, Peter Frank (1882-)
BAA 104 WGT 160 see also
Raphael W. Leonhart
Wyckoff, Nicholas Elston (1906-)
ES2 470 SF1 573
Wydmuch, Marek. FBK 77
Wye, Alan. SF1 573
Wylie, Dirk pseud. of Joseph Har-
old Dockweiler. IAC 253 IMS
84, 245 ISW 193 SFE 666 SFW
401 WFS 24-31, 38, 47, 71-3, 79,
97, 117, 124, 151, 175-7, 205, 234
WSF 221
Wylie, Elinor Hoyt (1885-1928)
CSF 213 FL4 2029-32 SF1 573
Wylie, Philip (Gordon) (1902-71)
ALW 143-6, 173 AOW 98-9, 116,
277-8 BAA 120, 153 BFP 562-
4 BYS 208 COT 253 CSF 14,
213 EFP 7 ES2 470-1 EXT 1/2
26 EXT 3/1 28 EXT 4/2 25
EXT 5/1 4, 15 EXT 7/2 37 EXT
8/1 2, 5-6 HFI 164 IAC 253
KAU 93, 125-7, 146-7 KWS 4, 59
LEX 669-70 MFW 19, 151-2
MSM xiv, 29, 51, 55-7, 62, 221-41,
305 NDA 42-3, 148, 151 NWO
33-4, 137-9, 163, 165 OMN 226
OWB 13-4 PST 125-7, 166-7, 192,
196, 210, 213-5, 229, 241, 246, 253
258-9, 264, 275, 280 RFA 81, 158
RGS 198-9 SFB 19, 89, 128 SFE
666-7 SFH 63 SFN 23, 28, 32,
101 SFS 128 SF1 573 SF2 1135
SL2 543-7, 888-93 SL5 2463-8
SOT 40, 115, 123, 206, 214 SRB
11, 295, 297, 510 STH 90-1, 98,
108, 123 VES 82, 107, 131, 227,
236, 330 WIF 22, 91, 285 WSF
87, 309, 385
Wylie, Rosalind. WFS 79, 177
Wyllarde, Dolf (-1950) CSF 213
ES2 471
Wylwynne, Kythe pseud. of M. E.
F. Hyland. CSF 213 SF1 573
Wymer, Thomas L. FHT 66
KAU 213 MFW 16 PJF 17, 73-
5 VF1 238-62, 280-1, 283 VF2
34-55, 198-9, 208
Wyn, A(aron) A. (1898-1967) ES2
471 TSP 76-8, 129, 212
Wyn, Rose. TSP 77
Wyndham, Eric. SF1 573
Wyndham, John pseud. of John
Wyndham Parkes Lucas Beynon
Harris (1903-69) AAL 109-10

Wyndham, John (cont.)
ACC 61 ALW 141 AOW 278-9,
288 BYS 116,148,279,290-1,
293-4,299,317 CAT xiv, 116
CSC 230,233 EFP 8,17 EXT
3/1 26-7 EXT 4/2 29 EXT 5/1
3 EXT 7/2 39,47 EXT 8/1 6
EXT 10/2 50 FAN 169,171-2,
188 FBK 124 FFR 201-3 FTF
75,78,85-6,89,132-3,168-9,193
HFI 164-5 IAC 253-5 IAH 134
ISW 119,147,169,178-9,245-6,
252-4,264 JGB 18 KAU 19,62,
75,128,131-5,137,188,191-7
LEX 670-2 MFW 19,23,149-50,
253 MIH 36 NDA 68-9,181,184-
5,196-8,210 NWO 135,139,165
POE 294 RGS 199-200 SFB 128
SFD 252,317 SFE 667-8 SFH
83,99 SFS 92,128-9 SFW 219-
24 SF1 573 SL1 502-7 SL3
1391-5 SL4 1755-8 SOT 118-
32,300,427 SRB 11,15,327 STH
10,88 TSF 237 VES 71,92,95,
129,132,139,148-51,160,173,
178,195,207,214,218,230,302
WAA 151,168,244 WFS 161,182,
200 WSF 202,254,387
Wyndham, Lee. FFC 137 see
also Jane Hyndman
Wynne, May pseud. of Mabel W.
Knowles. CSF 213
Wynne-Tyson, Esme (1898-) BAA
112,279 CSF 21 EXT 9/2 44
SF1 574 SF2 1135 SL4 1780-3
Wyss. EXT 3/2 44

X

X. BAA 68 SF1 574
X pseud. of Frank A. Fawkes.
CSF 213
X, (Mr.). CSF 141
X, Malcolm. RHN 158
X, Molly. SF1 574
X. Y. Z. BAA 46

Xenophon. MSF 153
Xerxes, B. T. H. IAC 255
X. L. pseud. of Julian Osgood
Field. CSF 213 ES2 471
Xlebnikov, A. IAC 255
Xongo-Tee-Foh-Tchi. CSF 213
SF1 574

Y

Yaches, E. Bruce. STH 85-6
Yaco, Murray P. IAC 255 WSF 165
Yamin, Michael. RFA 155
Yanikian, Gourgen (1895-) SF1 574
Yano, Ryukei. SIH 40
Yano, Tetsu. WFS 305-6
Yarbro, Chelsea Quinn (1942-) ALW 212 BAA 156 FL3 1343-6 HFI 165 IAC 208, 255 LEX 673 SFE 668 SF1 574 SF2 1136 SRB 375
Yarmolinsky, Avrahm. FFC 13
Yaroslavski, Alexander B. MSF 262
Yarov, Romain. IAC 255 SFS 129
Yasugi, Issho. BAA 139
Yates, Allan. HFI 165
Yates, Donald. EXT 9/1 3, 17
Yates, Dornford pseud. of Cecil William Mercer. CSF 213 SF1 574
Yates, Elizabeth. FFC 82
Yates, Frances A. BAA 197 EXT 9/2 62
Yates, R. F. IAC 255
Yat-Sen, Sun. WFS 292
Yazvitsky, Valery I. MSF 261
Ycas, Martynas (1917-) ES2 471 SF1 574
Yeats, W(illiam) B(utler) (1865-1939) ACC 123, 143 CWN 35-6 EXT 10/2 67-8 FBK 69 FTF 112 MFW 282 NDA 58 PJF 38 RBY 18-9, 162 SFD 49 STF 40 THM 35, 38-9, 58 UKL 77
Yefremov, Ivan A. (1907-73) AOW 279 ASF 175 BYS 307 CSC 33 CSF 67 ES2 471-2 EXT 10/2 77-9, 92-3 EXT 5/1 14 EXT 5/2 2 FAN 174-8 FTF 109, 121 IAC 255 KAU 207 LEX 386-7 MSF 9, 27, 35, 78, 252, 261, 265-9 SFB 114, 122 SFE 668-9 SFS 129 SF1 165 SF2 887-8 SIH 114, 117, 195 SL1 58-62 SOT 62, 430-1 VES 128 WAA 236
Yelnick, Claude. ES2 472 SFE 669 SF1 574
Yelverton, Christopher. BAA 40 SF1 574
Yenter, Charles E. SF1 574
Yep, Lawrence (Michael) (1948-) AAL 60 EXT 9/2 25 FFR 204 HFI 165 IAC 255 SFE 669 SF1 574 SF2 1136
Yerby, Frank. VES 233 WFS 164-5
Yerex, Cuthbert pseud. of Estella Y. Cuthbert. BAA 102 CSF 213 SF1 574
Yerke, T(heodore) Bruce. IMS 122, 138, 161-2, 228 SOT 356-7 WGT 160
Yershov, Peter (1895-) BAA 197 SF1 574
Yerxa, Leroy (1915-46) ES2 472 SFE 669 VES 102 WGT 160 WIF 120 see also Alexander Blade, Richard Casey
Yexley, Lionel (1861-1933) CSF 198 SF1 574 see also Navarchus
Yin, Leslie Charles Bowyer see Leslie Charteris
Yoke, Carl B. FL1 29-35, 166-8, 181-3 FL2 980-2 FL3 1407-11 FL4 1763-5 RZY 9, 106 SL1

Yoke, Carl B. (cont.)
157-62, 474-9 SL2 608-13 SL3
1251-6 SRB 83
Yolen, Jane Hyatt (1939-) FFC 11-
2, 15, 23-4, 52, 72, 128, 196 IAC
255 SFE 669 SF1 574 SF2
1136-7
Yolton, John. EXT 10/1 45
Yorburg, Betty. BAA 197
Yore, Mary Jane. IAC 255
York, Carol Beach (1928-) ES2
472 FFC 78
York, Simon pseud. of Robert A.
Heinlein. HID 22-3 OWB 11
SFH 54
York, Susannah. FFC 192
Yorke, Curtis. CSF 213
Yorke, Henry Vincent (1905-) see
Henry Green
Yorke, Jacqueline. SF1 575
Yorke, Preston. BAA 123 SF1
575
Yost, Daniel. LTN 270
Youd, Christopher Samuel (1922-)
ALW 184, 212 BAA 128, 152
BFP 565-8 ES2 472-3 IAC 255
IMS 200, 251 RFA 174 SFS 130
SF2 853 SRB 324 WGT 160 see
also John Christopher
Young, Alfred Michael. SF1 575
Young, Arthur Nichols. BAA 197
Young, Bertram Alfred (1912-)
ES2 473 SF1 575
Young, Charles A. EXT 5/2 38, 47
Young, Charles Van Patten (1876-
1960) CSF 214 SF1 575
Young, David. ACC 61 MFW 22
Young, Ed. FFC 12, 15
Young, Ella (1867-1956) FFC 58
SF1 585
Young, Florence Ethel Mills (1875-
1945) CSF 214 SF1 575
Young, Francis Brett (1884-1954)
CSF 214 SF1 575

Young, Frank Herman. BAA 148
Young, Henry B. CSF 214
Young, Laurence Ditto. CSF 214
SF1 575
Young, Marguerite (1909-) ES2 473
Young, Mary Julia. CSF 214
Young, Michael Dunlop (1915-)
BAA 133 EXT 6/2 51 NDA 78,
82-4 NWO 125 POE 280-2, 314
SFE 669 SF1 575
Young, Miriam (1913-74) FFC 192
SF1 575 SF2 1137
Young, Noela. FFC 72
Young, Peter. IAC 255 SFS 130
Young, Peter William (1920-) SF1
575
Young, Phyllis Brett. SF1 575
Young, Red. SF1 575
Young, R. V., Jr. SL3 1278-83,
1375-9 SL4 1692-6
Young, Robert. CSF 214
Young, Robert F(ranklin) (1915-)
ALW 212 BFP 569 COT 27, 252
ES2 473 FFR 204 HFI 165 IAC
255-6 IMS 137, 213 LEX 674
SFE 669 SFS 130 SF1 575 SF2
1137 VES 179, 230, 234
Young, Roger Flint. SFS 130
Young, Wayland. SFS 130
Young Lady, (A). CSF 214
Youngblood, Gene. BAA 279
Younghusband, (Sir) Francis.
BAA 94 CSF 214
Youngman, William Godfrey. TSP
197
Yourell, Agnes Bond. CSF 214
Yoxall, (Sir) James Henry (1857-
1925) SF1 575
Yulee, Charles Wickliffe (1849-)
SF1 575
Yuma, Gary. SF1 575
Yutang, Lin (1895-1976) BAA 127
ES1 276 EXT 6/2 51 SFE 359
SF1 322 SF2 978

Z

Zabelin, Igor. IAC 256
Zacharaslewicz, Waldemar. BAA 197
Zachary, Hugh (1928-) BAA 163 SF2 944 WGT 161 see also Zach Hughes
Zacherle(y), John C. (1919-) ES2 473 FRN 449, 453 IAC 256 SF1 576 WGT 161
Zaehner, R. C. BAA 279
Zagat, Arthur Leo (1895-1949) ES2 473 ETN 16 HFI 165 IAC 256 IMS 68 RFA 140 SFE 670 SF1 576 STH 45 TSP 15, 33, 41, 44-7, 89, 104, 127, 158, 189, 218 WGT 161
Zahn, Oswald Francis. BAA 112
Zahorski, Kenneth J. LTN 248, 252 SRB 66, 281
Zajdel, Janusz A. (1938-) LEX 675
Zakharchenko, Vassily. BYS 281 WFS 305-6 WIF 19
Zamagna, Bernard. SFB 31
Zamecznik, Stanislaw. FBK 149
Zamiatin, Evgeny (1884-1937) ACC 214 ALW 99 AOW 49, 78, 346 BYS 67, 252 CAT 53, 80, 106, 110-1, 138 CSF 214 ES2 473-4 EXT 2/2 25, 32, 41 EXT 3/1 28 EXT 4/2 24 EXT 5/1 4 EXT 5/2 2 EXT 6/2 51 EXT 9/1 18, 22-3 EXT 9/2 53 EXT 10/2 75-7 FAN 3, 5, 12, 20, 34, 38, 82, 85, 97, 99-109, 129-30, 133, 146-7, 150, 175, 185-6 FFR 204 FHT 50 FTF 103-4, 200 HFI 165 ISW 17-9, 171-2 KAU 101 KVT 9 LTN 13, 104-6, 118,
205, 212-3, 215, 217, 219-21 MFW 23, 202-3 MSF 10, 13, 25-7, 54, 74, 185, 202, 218, 230, 254-61, 264, 280 NDA xi, 17, 89, 96-8, 100-2, 210 NWO 125-6 POE 231-3, 259, 261, 269 SFB 90-2 SFD 274, 307 SFE 670 SFH 15, 25, 28, 32, 34-6, 70, 144, 176, 191, 204-8, 212 SFW 104, 233-4 SF1 576 SIH 85-6, 98, 114 SL5 2433-41 SOI xiii STF 71 STH 105 TSF 126-7, 230 VES 128, 213, 261 WAA 71, 236
Zamorra, Lonnie. WFS 266-8
Zanger, Jules. FL2 557-60, 625-7 FL3 1335-7 FL4 1926-9
Zangwill, Israel. ALW 82 CSF 214
Zaniello, Thomas. BAA 279 EXT 9/1 3-17
Zarem, Lewis. ES2 474 HFI 165 SFE 670 SF1 576
Zarovitch, (Princess) Vera pseud. of Mary E. Lane. CSF 214 SF1 576
Zaschik, Almos. SFB 26-7
Zavala, Iris M. BAA 279
Zavala, Silvio. BAA 197, 279
Zebrowski, George (1945-) ALW 212 AOW 298 BAA 159, 162 BYS 304 COT 137 ETN 65 FFR 204 HFI 165-6 IAC 89, 208, 256 LEX 675-6 RGS 200-1 SFE 670-1 SFW 91 SF1 576 VES 217, 219, 301
Zecchi, Stefano. BAA 197
Zegalski, Witold (1928-74) LEX 676

Zeigfried, Karl (house name) ES2 474 SFE 671 SF1 576 see also R. L. Fanthorpe
Zeisel, Hans. EXT 6/1 19
Zeitlin, Ida. SF1 576
Zelazny, Devin. RZY 11, 15
Zelazny, Jonathan Trent. RZY 12, 15
Zelazny, Joseph. RZY 10, 14
Zelazny, Roger (1937-) AAL 117, 139, 160 ALW 212, 234, 239 AOW 279-81, 294, 299 BAA 145 BFP 570-1 BYS 52, 299, 303-5 CAT 18, 34, 122 COT 159, 169 CSC 31, 155 ES2 474 ETN 66 EXT 8/1 16 EXT 10/2 59, 65 FFR 204-5 FHT 32 FL1 29-35, 228-31, 396-400 FL2 794-7 FTF 149-50, 192 [FUT] HFI 166 IAC 256-7 INT 53, 77-8, 80 KAU 92, 155, 178-83 LEX 676-8 LTN 29, 91-2 MFW 52-6, 86, 149, 214-5, 227, 232, 290 MIH 134-7 MSF 26 NWO 44, 77 OMN 40 PJF 12, 33, 38, 40, 75 RGS 201-2, 226 SFA 85, 194 SFD 3-4, 22, 53, 63, 75-6, 212, 228-30, 239-40, 248, 252-3, 262, 264-5, 277-8, 303, 305, 308, 314, 319-21, 323 SFE 671-2 SFH 93-4, 168, 183-4, 243 SFS 130-1 SFW 351, 563-70 SF1 576 SF2 1137 SIN 8, 126-7 SL2 583-6, 608-13 SL3 1251-6 SL5 2260-3 SRB 12, 83, 125, 280, 343, 345, 347-8, 368 STF 79 TSF 64, 241 VES 92, 136, 143, 148, 160, 177, 210, 227, 280 VF2 180-96, 205-7 WAA 138, 230 WGT 161 WSF 205, 233-4, 243, 388-9 see also Harrison Denmark
Zelikovich, Emmanuil S. EXT 10/2 75 IAC 257 MSF 253 SFS 131
Zelinsky, Paul. FFC 139
Zemach, Harve. FFC 58
Zemach, Margot. FFC 17, 23, 51, 58
Zemke, Kurt. BAA 279
Zenghelis, Elia. [FUT]
Zenk, Marjorie see Marjorie Zenk Wright
Zenkovsky, V. V. BAA 279
Zeno. EXT 8/1 23 JGB 6
Zeno (of Cyprus). UKL 116
Zeno (of Elea). UKL 119, 122

Zerwick, Chloe (1923-) ES2 474 FFR 205 HFI 166 SFE 672 SF1 576 SF2 1138
Zettersten, Arne. EXT 10/1 45
Zhdanov, G. ES2 474
Zhilin, Ivan. SIH 88
Zhuravleva, Valentina. IAC 257 SFS 131
Zicree, Marc Scott. IAC 257
Ziegler, Edward William (1932-) ES2 474 SF2 1108 WGT 161 see also Theodore Tyler
Ziegler, Rudolf. BAA 290
Ziegler, Theobald. BAA 279
Ziegler, Thomas (1956-) LEX 679
Ziergiebel, Herbert (1922-) LEX 679-80
Zierold, Norman J. (1927-) HFI 166 SFE 672 SF1 576
Ziff, William Bernard (1898-1953) ES2 474 STH 44
Ziff, Larzer. NWO 168, 170-1, 173, 179
Zilberfarb, Johanson. BAA 279
Zilboorg, Gregory. EXT 2/2 32
Zimbardo, Rose Abdelnour (1932-) EXT 10/1 31, 45 SF1 577 SF2 1138
Zimmer, Heinrich. ACC 106
Zimmermann, Werner see Drake Douglas
Zimnik, Reiner. FFC 12, 15
Zimpel, Lloyd (1929-) SF1 577 SF2 1138
Zindel, Paul. IAC 257
Zinn, Howard. CWN 21
Zipes, Jack. BAA 279
Zirul, Arthur. IAC 257 IAH 93-8, 125 ISW 127 SFS 131
Zissman, Merril. WFS 206
Zola, Emile (1840-1902) CAT 9 CSC 163 CWN 35 EXT 1/1 7 EXT 2/2 35 EXT 9/2 33 EXT 10/1 9 IAH 41 MFW 279 POE 202-4 STF 14, 72-3
Zoline, Pamela A. (1941-) BYS 298-9, 305, 312 IAC 257 MFW 24 NWO 187 SFE 672
Zolotow, Charlotte. FFC 78
Zoof, Ben. ALW 73
Zori, Henri. BAA 112
Zorin, Leo. IAC 257
Zorn, Jacqueline. SL5 2362-5
Zorn, Ray G. EXT 3/1 25

Zorro pseud. of Harold Ward.
SF1 577
Zoss, Joel. IAC 257
Zschokke, Heinrich. CSF 214
ES2 474
Zuber, Stanley. BAA 128 ES2
474 SF1 577
Zubkov, Boris. SIH 94
Zubkov, E. IAC 257

Zuccolo. EXT 8/1 23
Zuckerkandel, Victor. BAA 279
Zugsmith, Albert. SF1 577
Zulawski, Jerzy (1874-1915) SFB
101 SFE 672
Zuyev-Ordynets, M. E. MSF 261
Zweig, Allen pseud. of Frederik
Pohl. IMS 169

WORKS INDEXED
(Listing by author/editor)

See page 9 for listing by code

Aldiss, Brian W.
Billion Year Spree
Allen, L. David
Science Fiction--An Introduction
Alpers, Hans-Joachim
Lexikon Der Science Fiction Literatur 1
Apter, T. E.
Fantasy Literature: An Approach to Reality
Ash, Brian
Faces of the Future
The Visual Encyclopedia of Science Fiction
Atheling, William, Jr. (James Blish)
The Issue at Hand
More Issues at Hand
Asimov, Isaac
Asimov on Science Fiction
Bailey, J. O.
Pilgrims Through Space and Time
Barron, Neil
Anatomy of Wonder
Bendau, Clifford P.
Colin Wilson: The Outsider and Beyond
Berger, Harold L.
Science Fiction and the New Dark Age
Bleiler, E. F.
The Checklist of Science Fiction and Supernatural
Fiction
Science Fiction Writers: Critical Studies of the
Major Authors
Bretnor, Reginald
The Craft of Science Fiction
Modern Science Fiction--Its Meaning and its Future
Brizzi, Mary T.
Philip Jose Farmer
Carter, Paul A.
The Creation of Tomorrow: Fifty Years of Magazine
Science Fiction

Clareson, Thomas D.
   Extrapolation
   Many Futures, Many Worlds
   Robert Silverberg
   Science Fiction: The Other Side of Realism
   Voices for the Future
   Voices for the Future, Vol. 2
Clarke, Arthur C.
   The View from Serendip
Clarke, I. F.
   The Pattern of Expectation 1644-2001
Contento, William
   Index to Science Fiction Anthologies and Collections
Corn, Joseph C.
   Yesterday's Tomorrows: Past Visions of the
      American Future
Currey, L. W.
   Science Fiction and Fantasy Authors: A Bibliography
      of First Printings of Their Fiction
Davenport, Basil
   The Science Fiction Novel: Imagination and Social
      Criticism
De Camp, L. Sprague
   The Science Fiction Handbook--The Writing of
      Imaginative Fiction
Del Rey, Lester
   The World of Science Fiction: The History of a
      Subculture
Dozois, Gardner R.
   The Fiction of James Tiptree, Jr.
Elliot, Jeffrey M.
   Science Fiction Voices 2
   Science Fiction Voices 3
Eshbach, Lloyd Arthur
   Of Worlds Beyond
Frane, Jeff
   Fritz Leiber
Franklin, H. Bruce
   Robert A. Heinlein: America as Science Fiction
Franklin, Michael
   A Reader's Guide to Science Fiction
Fuchs, Werner
   Lexikon Der Science Fiction Literatur 1
Gaasbeek, R.
   Fantasfeer: Bibliografie Van Science Fiction En
      Fantasy in het Nederlands
Glut, Donald F.
   The Frankenstein Catalog

Gordon, Joan
  Joe Haldeman
Gorremans, G.
  Fantasfeer: Bibliografie Van Science Fiction en
    Fantasy in het Nederlands
Greenberg, Martin Harry
  Arthur C. Clarke
  Ray Bradbury
  Robert Heinlein
  Ursula K. Le Guin
Gunn, James
  Alternate Worlds: The Illustrated History of
    Science Fiction
Hahn, Ronald M.
  Lexikon Der Science Fiction Literatur 1
Hillegas, Mark R.
  The Future as Nightmare
  Shadows of the Imagination: The Fantasies of C. S.
    Lewis, J. R. R. Tolkien and Charles Williams
Holland, Thomas R.
  Vonnegut's Major Works
Horrigan, Brian
  Yesterday's Tomorrows: Past Visions of the
    American Future
Jeschke, Wolfgang
  Lexikon Der Science Fiction Literatur 1
Jones, Robert Kenneth
  The Shudder Pulps
Ketterer, David
  New Worlds for Old: The Apocalyptic Imagination,
    Science Fiction and American Literature
Knight, Damon
  In Search of Wonder
  Turning Points: Essays on the Art of Science Fiction
Last, Martin
  A Reader's Guide to Science Fiction
Le Guin, Ursula K.
  The Language of the Night
Lundwall, Sam J.
  Science Fiction--An Illustrated History
  Science Fiction: What It's All About
Lynn, Ruth Nadelman
  Fantasy for Children--An Annotated Checklist
Magill, Frank N.
  Survey of Modern Fantasy Literature
  Survey of Science Fiction Literature

Malone, Robert
  The Robot Book
Malzberg, Barry N.
  Engines of the Night: Science Fiction in the Eighties
Mathews, Richard
  The Clockwork Universe of Anthony Burgess
Mayo, Clark
  Kurt Vonnegut: The Gospel from Outer Space
Meacham, Beth
  A Reader's Guide to Science Fiction
Meyers, Walter E.
  Aliens and Linguists: Language Study and Science Fiction
Miesel, Sandra
  Against Time's Arrow: The High Crusade of Poul
    Anderson
Miller, Chuck
  Jack Vance
Miller, David M.
  Frank Herbert
Moskowitz, Sam
  The Immortal Storm: A History of Science Fiction
    Fandom
  Seekers of Tomorrow: Masters of Modern Science
    Fiction
  Strange Horizons: The Spectrum of Science Fiction
Nicholls, Peter
  The Science Fiction Encyclopedia
Olander, Joseph D.
  Arthur C. Clarke
  Ray Bradbury
  Robert Heinlein
  Ursula K. Le Guin
Panshin, Alexei
  Heinlein in Dimension
  Science Fiction in Dimension
Parrinder, Patrick
  Science Fiction: Its Criticism and Teaching
Patrouch, Joseph F., Jr.
  The Science Fiction of Isaac Asimov
Peary, Danny
  Omni's Screen Flights/Screen Fantasies: The Future
    According to Science Fiction Cinema
Platt, Charles
  Dream Makers
Pohl, Frederik
  The Way the Future Was: A Memoir
Pringle, David
  Earth is the Alien Planet: J. G. Ballard's Four-
    Dimensional Nightmare

Rabiega, William A.
    Environmental Fiction for Pedagogic Purposes
Rabkin, Eric S.
    Arthur C. Clarke
    Arthur C. Clarke, 2nd ed.
    Science Fiction: History, Science, Vision
Reginald, R.
    Science Fiction and Fantasy Literature, Vol. 1:
        Indexes to the Literature
    Science Fiction and Fantasy Literature, Vol. 2:
        Contemporary Science Fiction Authors II
Riley, Dick
    Critical Encounters: Writers and Themes in Science
        Fiction
Rock, James A.
    Who Goes There: A Bibliographic Dictionary of
        Pseudononymous Literature in the Fields of
        Fantasy and Science Fiction
Rogers, Alva
    A Requiem for Astounding
Rottensteiner, Franz
    The Fantasy Book
    The Science Fiction Book: An Illustrated History
Sargent, Lyman Tower
    British and American Utopian Literature 1516-1975:
        An Annotated Bibliography
Scholes, Robert
    Science Fiction: History, Science, Vision
Schweitzer, Darrell
    Conan's World and Robert E. Howard
    Science Fiction Voices 1
Searles, Baird
    Heinlein's Works Including Stranger in a Strange Land
    A Reader's Guide to Science Fiction
Sheckley, Robert
    Futuropolis: Impossible Cities of Science Fiction and
        Fantasy
Siemon, Frederick
    Science Fiction Story Index 1950-1968
Silverberg, Robert
    Drug Themes in Science Fiction
Slusser, George Edgar
    The Classic Years of Robert A. Heinlein
    The Farthest Shores of Ursula K. Le Guin
    Harlan Ellison: Unrepentant Harlequin
    Robert A. Heinlein: Stranger in His Own Land
    The Bradbury Chronicles

Slusser, George Edgar (cont.)
    The Delany Intersection
    The Space Odysseys of Arthur C. Clarke
Spaink, A.
    Fantasfeer: Bibliografie van Science Fiction en Fantasy
        in het Nederlands
Stableford, Brian M.
    A Clash of Cymbals: The Triumph of James Blish
Suvin, Darko
    Metamorphoses of Science Fiction
Todorov, Tzvetan
    The Fantastic: A Structural Approach to a Literary
        Genre
Tuck, Donald H.
    Encyclopedia of Science Fiction and Fantasy (2 vols.)
Tymn, Marshall B.
    A Basic Reference Shelf for Science Fiction Teachers
    The Science Fiction Reference Book
Underwood, Tim
    Jack Vance
Warren, Bill
    Keep Watching the Skies! American Science Fiction
        Movies of the Fifties 1950-1957 Vol. 1
Weinberg, Robert
    The Weird Tales Story
Wells, Stuart W. , III
    The Science Fiction and Heroic Fantasy Author Index
White, Anthony G.
    Urban Futures: Science Fiction and the City
Williamson, Jack
    Teaching Science Fiction: Education for Tomorrow
Wilson, Colin
    The Haunted Man: The Strange Genius of David Lindsay
Wolfe, Gary K.
    The Known and the Unknown: The Iconography of
        Science Fiction
Wood, Susan
    The Language of the Night
Wymer, Thomas L.
    Intersections: The Elements of Fiction in Science Fiction
Yoke, Carl B.
    Roger Zelazny

WORKS INDEXED
(Listing by title)

Against Time's Arrow: The High Crusade of Poul Anderson
    Sandra Miesel (San Bernardino, California: Borgo Press,
    1978)
Aliens and Linguists: Language Study and Science Fiction
    Walter E. Meyers (Athens, Georgia: University of Georgia
    Press, 1980)
Alternate Worlds: The Illustrated History of Science Fiction
    James Gunn (Englewood Cliffs, New Jersey: A&W Visual
    Library, 1975)
Anatomy of Wonder: Science Fiction
    Neil Barron, ed. (New York: R. R. Bowker Co., 1976)
Arthur C. Clarke
    Joseph D. Olander and Martin Harry Greenberg, eds.
    (New York: Taplinger, 1977)
Arthur C. Clarke
    Eric S. Rabkin (West Lin, Oregon: Starmont House, 1979)
Arthur C. Clarke (2nd ed., revised and expanded)
    Eric S. Rabkin (Mercer Island, Washington: Starmont
    House, 1980)
Asimov on Science Fiction
    Isaac Asimov (Garden City, New York: Doubleday, 1981)
Basic Reference Shelf for Science Fiction Teachers, A
    Marshall B. Tymn (Monticello, Illinois: Council of Planning
    Librarians, Exchange Bibliography No. 1523, 1978)
Billion Year Spree
    Brian W. Aldiss (New York: Doubleday, 1973)
Bradbury Chronicles, The
    George Edgar Slusser (San Bernardino, California: Borgo
    Press, 1977)
British and American Utopian Literature 1516-1975: An
    Annotated Bibliography
    Lyman Tower Sargent (Boston: G. K. Hall, 1979)
Checklist of Science Fiction and Supernatural Fiction, The
    E. F. Bleiler (Glen Rock, New Jersey: Firebell Books, 1978)
Clash of Cymbals, A: The Triumph of James Blish
    Brian M. Stableford (San Bernardino, California: Borgo
    Press, 1979)
Classic Years of Robert A. Heinlein, The
    George Edgar Slusser (San Bernardino, California: Borgo
    Press, 1977)

Clockwork Universe of Anthony Burgess, The
  Richard Mathews (San Bernardino, California: Borgo Press,
  1978)
Colin Wilson: The Outsider and Beyond
  Clifford P. Bendau (San Bernardino, California; Borgo
  Press, 1979)
Conan's World and Robert E. Howard
  Darrell Schweitzer (San Bernardino, California: Borgo
  Press, 1978)
Craft of Science Fiction, The
  Reginald Bretnor (New York: Barnes & Noble, 1976)
Creation of Tomorrow, The: Fifty Years of Magazine Science
  Fiction
  Paul A. Carter (New York: Columbia University Press, 1977)
Critical Encounters: Writers and Themes in Science Fiction
  Dick Riley, ed. (New York: Frederick Ungar, 1978)
Delany Intersection, The: Samuel R. Delany Considered As A
  Writer of Semi-Precious Words
  George Edgar Slusser (San Bernardino, California: Borgo
  Press, 1977)
Dream Makers
  Charles Platt (New York: Berkley, 1980)
Drug Themes in Science Fiction
  Robert Silverberg (Rockville, Maryland: National Institute
  on Drug Abuse, 1974)
Earth is the Alien Planet: J. G. Ballard's Four-Dimensional
  Nightmare
  David Pringle (San Bernardino, California: Borgo Press,
  1979)
Encyclopedia of Science Fiction and Fantasy, Vol. 1
  Donald H. Tuck (Chicago: Advent, 1974)
Encyclopedia of Science Fiction and Fantasy, Vol. 2
  Donald H. Tuck (Chicago: Advent, 1978)
Engines of the Night: Science Fiction in the Eighties
  Barry N. Malzberg (Garden City, New York: Doubleday,
  1982)
Environmental Fiction for Pedagogic Purposes
  William A. Rabiega (Monticello, Illinois: Council of Plan-
  ning Librarians, Exchange Bibliography No. 590, 1974)
Extrapolation: A Science Fiction Newsletter, Vols. 1-10
  Thomas D. Clareson, ed. (Boston: Gregg Press, 1978)
Faces of the Future
  Brian Ash (New York: Taplinger, 1975)
Fantasfeer: Bibliografie Van Science Fiction en Fantasy in het
  Nederlands
  A. Spaink, G. Gorremans, R. Gaasbeek (Amsterdam:
  Meulenhoff, 1979)

Fantastic, The: A Structural Approach to a Literary Genre
  Tzvetan Todorov, translated by Richard Howard
  (Cleveland, Ohio: The Press of Case Western Reserve
  University, 1973)
Fantasy Book, The
  Franz Rottensteiner (New York: Collier, 1978)
Fantasy for Children--An Annotated Checklist
  Ruth Nadelman Lynn (New York: R. R. Bowker, 1979)
Fantasy Literature: An Approach to Reality
  T. E. Apter (Bloomington, Indiana: Indiana University
  Press, 1982)
Farthest Shores of Ursula K. Le Guin, The
  George Edgar Slusser (San Bernardino, California: Borgo
  Press, 1976)
Fiction of James Tiptree, Jr., The
  Gardner R. Dozois (New York: Algol Press, 1977)
Frank Herbert
  David M. Miller (Mercer Island, Washington: Starmont
  House, 1980)
Frankenstein Catalog, The
  Donald F. Glut (Jefferson, North Carolina: McFarland and
  Co., 1984)
Fritz Leiber
  Jeff Frane (Mercer Island, Washington: Starmont House,
  1980)
Future As Nightmare, The
  Mark R. Hillegas (Carbondale, Illinois: Southern Illinois
  University Press, 1974)
Futuropolis: Impossible Cities of Science Fiction and Fantasy
  Robert Sheckley (New York: A&W Visual Library, 1978)
Harlan Ellison: Unrepentant Harlequin
  George Edgar Slusser (San Bernardino, California: Borgo
  Press, 1977)
Haunted Man, The: The Strange Genius of David Lindsay
  Colin Wilson (San Bernardino, California: Borgo Press,
  1979)
Heinlein in Dimension
  Alexei Panshin (Chicago: Advent, 1968)
Heinlein's Works, Including Stranger in a Strange Land
  Baird Searles (Lincoln, Nebraska: Cliff's Notes Inc., 1975)
Immortal Storm, The: A History of Science Fiction Fandom
  Sam Moskowitz (Atlanta: The Atlanta Science Fiction
  Organization Press, 1954)
In Search of Wonder (2nd ed., revised and enlarged)
  Damon Knight (Chicago: Advent, 1967)
Index to Science Fiction Anthologies and Collections
  William Contento (Boston: G. K. Hall, 1978)

Intersections: The Elements of Fiction in Science Fiction
  Thomas L. Wymer, Alice Calderonello, Lowell P. Leland,
  Sara Jayne Steen, R. Michael Evers (Bowling Green, Ohio:
  Popular Press, 1978)
Issue At Hand, The
  William Atheling, Jr. (James Blish)
  (Chicago: Advent, 1973)
Jack Vance
  Tim Underwood and Chuck Miller, eds. (New York:
  Taplinger, 1980)
Joe Haldeman
  Joan Gordon (Mercer Island, Washington: Starmont House,
  1980)
Keep Watching the Skies! American Science Fiction Movies of
  the Fifties 1950-1957 Vol. 1
  Bill Warren (Jefferson, North Carolina: McFarland and
  Co., 1982)
Known and the Unknown, The: The Iconography of Science Fiction
  Gary K. Wolfe (Kent, Ohio: Kent State University Press,
  1979)
Kurt Vonnegut: The Gospel From Outer Space
  Clark Mayo (San Bernardino, California: Borgo Press, 1977)
Language of the Night, The
  Ursula K. Le Guin, ed. by Susan Wood (New York: G. P.
  Putnam's Sons, 1979)
Lexikon der Science Fiction Literatur 1
  Hans-Joachim Alpers, Werner Fuchs, Ronald M. Hahn,
  Wolfgang Jeschke (Munich: Wilhelm Heyne Verlag, 1980)
Many Futures, Many Worlds
  Thomas D. Clareson (Kent, Ohio: Kent State University
  Press, 1977)
Metamorphoses of Science Fiction
  Darko Suvin (New Haven, Connecticut: Yale University
  Press, 1979)
Modern Science Fiction--Its Meaning and its Future
  Reginald Bretnor (Chicago: Advent, 1979)
More Issues at Hand
  William Atheling, Jr. (James Blish)
  (Chicago: Advent, 1970)
New Worlds for Old: The Apocalyptic Imagination, Science
  Fiction and American Literature
  David Ketterer (Bloomington, Indiana: Indiana University
  Press, 1974)
Of Worlds Beyond
  Lloyd Arthur Eshbach, ed. (Chicago: Advent, 1964)
Omni's Screen Flights/Screen Fantasies: The Future According
  to Science Fiction Cinema

Danny Peary, ed. (Garden City, New York: Doubleday, 1984)
Pattern of Expectation 1644-2001, The
   I. F. Clarke (London: Jonathan Cape, 1979)
Philip Jose Farmer
   Mary T. Brizzi (Mercer Island, Washington: Starmont House, 1980)
Pilgrims Through Space and Time: Trends and Patterns in Scientific and Utopian Fiction
   J. O. Bailey (Westport, Connecticut: Greenwood Press, 1972)
Ray Bradbury
   Joseph D. Olander and Martin Harry Greenberg, eds. (New York: Taplinger, 1980)
Reader's Guide to Science Fiction, A
   Baird Searles, Martin Last, Beth Meacham and Michael Franklin (New York: Avon, 1979)
Requiem for Astounding, A
   Alva Rogers (Chicago: Advent, 1964)
Robert A. Heinlein
   Joseph D. Olander and Martin Harry Greenberg, eds. (New York: Taplinger, 1978)
Robert A. Heinlein: America as Science Fiction
   H. Bruce Franklin (New York: Oxford University Press, 1980)
Robert A. Heinlein: Stranger in His Own Land
   George Edgar Slusser (San Bernardino, California: Borgo Press, 1977)
Robert Silverberg
   Thomas D. Clareson (Mercer Island, Washington: Starmont House, 1983)
Robot Book, The
   Robert Malone (New York: Push Pin Press, 1978)
Roger Zelazny
   Carl B. Yoke (West Linn, Oregon: Starmont House, 1979)
Science Fiction--An Illustrated History
   Sam J. Lundwall (New York: Grosset & Dunlap, 1977)
Science Fiction: An Introduction
   L. David Allen (Lincoln, Nebraska: Cliff's Notes, 1973)
Science Fiction and Fantasy Authors: A Bibliography of First Printings of Their Fiction
   L. W. Currey (Boston: G. K. Hall, 1979)
Science Fiction and Fantasy Literature, Vol. 1: Indexes to the Literature
   R. Reginald (Detroit, Michigan: Gale Research, 1979)
Science Fiction and Fantasy Literature, Vol. 2: Contemporary Science Fiction Authors II

R. Reginald (Detroit, Michigan: Gale Research, 1979)
Science Fiction and Heroic Fantasy Author Index, The
  Stuart W. Wells, III (Duluth, Minnesota: Purple Unicorn
  Books, 1978)
Science Fiction and the New Dark Age
  Harold L. Berger (Bowling Green, Ohio: Bowling Green
  University Popular Press, 1976)
Science Fiction Book, The: An Illustrated History
  Franz Rottensteiner (New York: Seabury Press, 1975)
Science Fiction Encyclopedia, The
  Peter Nicholls, Ed. (New York: Doubleday, 1979)
Science Fiction Handbook, The--The Writing of Imaginative
  Fiction
  L. Sprague de Camp (New York: Hermitage Press, 1953)
Science Fiction: History, Science, Vision
  Robert Scholes and Eric S. Rabkin (New York: Oxford
  University Press, 1977)
Science Fiction: Its Criticism and Teaching
  Patrick Parrinder (New York: Methuen, 1980)
Science Fiction Novel, The: Imagination and Social Criticism
  Basil Davenport, ed. (Chicago: Advent, 1969)
Science Fiction of Isaac Asimov, The
  Joseph F. Patrouch, Jr. (London: Panther Books, 1976)
Science Fiction Reference Book, The
  Marshall B. Tymn, ed. (Mercer Island, Washington:
  Starmont House, 1981)
Science Fiction Story Index 1950-1968
  Frederick Siemon (Chicago: American Library Associates,
  1971)
Science Fiction Voices 1
  Darrell Schweitzer (San Bernardino, California: Borgo
  Press, 1979)
Science Fiction Voices 2
  Jeffrey M. Elliot (San Bernardino, California: Borgo Press,
  1979)
Science Fiction Voices 3
  Jeffrey M. Elliot (San Bernardino, California: Borgo Press,
  1980)
Science Fiction: What It's All About
  Sam J. Lundwall (New York: Ace, 1971)
Science Fiction Writers: Critical Studies of the Major Authors
  From the Early Nineteenth Century to the Present Day
  E. F. Bleiler, ed. (New York: Charles Scribner's Sons, 1982)
Seekers of Tomorrow: Masters of Modern Science Fiction
  Sam Moskowitz (Cleveland, Ohio and New York: World
  Publishing Co., 1966)
SF in Dimension

Alexei Panshin (Chicago: Advent, 1976)
SF: The Other Side of Realism
    Thomas D. Clareson (Bowling Green, Ohio: Bowling Green
    University Popular Press, 1971)
Shadows of Imagination: The Fantasies of C. S. Lewis, J. R. R.
    Tolkien and Charles Williams
    Mark R. Hillegas, ed. (Carbondale, Illinois: Southern
    Illinois University Press, 1979)
Shudder Pulps, The
    Robert Kenneth Jones (West Linn, Oregon: Fax Collector's
    Editions, 1975)
Space Odysseys of Arthur C. Clarke, The
    George Edgar Slusser (San Bernardino, California: Borgo
    Press, 1978)
Strange Horizons: The Spectrum of Science Fiction
    Sam Moskowitz (New York: Charles Scribner's Sons, 1976)
Structural Fabulation: An Essay on Fiction of the Future
    Robert Scholes (Notre Dame, Indiana: University of Notre
    Dame Press, 1975)
Survey of Modern Fantasy Literature, 5 vols.
    Frank N. Magill, ed. (Englewood Cliffs, New Jersey:
    Salem Press, 1983)
Survey of Science Fiction Literature, 5 vols.
    Frank N. Magill, ed. (Englewood Cliffs, New Jersey:
    Salem Press, 1979)
Teaching Science Fiction: Education for Tomorrow
    Jack Williamson, ed. (Philadelphia: Owlswick Press, 1980)
Turning Points: Essays on the Art of Science Fiction
    Damon Knight, ed. (New York: Harper & Row, 1977)
Urban Futures: Science Fiction and the City
    Anthony G. White (Monticello, Illinois: Council of Planning
    Librarians, 1973)
Ursula K. Le Guin
    Joseph D. Olander and Martin Harry Greenbers, eds. (New
    York: Taplinger, 1979)
View From Serendip, The
    Arthur C. Clarke (New York: Random House, 1977)
Visual Encyclopedia of Science Fiction, The
    Brian Ash, ed. (New York: Harmony Books, 1977)
Voices for the Future
    Thomas D. Clareson, ed. (Bowling Green, Ohio: Bowling
    Green University Popular Press, 1976)
Voices for the Future, Vol. 2
    Thomas D. Clareson, ed. (Bowling Green, Ohio: Bowling
    Green University Popular Press, 1979)
Vonnegut's Major Works
    Thomas R. Holland (Lincoln, Nebraska: Cliff's Notes, 1973)

Way the Future Was, The: A Memoir
   Frederik Pohl (New York: Ballantine Books, 1978)
Weird Tales Story, The
   Robert Weinberg (West Linn, Oregon: Fax Collector's
   Editions, 1977)
Who Goes There: A Bibliographic Dictionary of Pseudononymous
   Literature in the Fields of Fantasy and Science Fiction
   James A. Rock (Bloomington, Indiana: James A. Rock & Co.,
   1979)
World of Science Fiction, The: The History of a Subculture
   Lester del Rey (New York: Ballantine, 1979)
Worlds Beyond the World: The Fantastic Vision of William Morris
   Richard Mathews (San Bernardino, California: Borgo Press,
   1978)
Yesterday's Tomorrows: Past Visions of the American Future
   Joseph C. Corn and Brian Horrigan, eds. (New York:
   Summit Books, 1984)